W9-ATX-716

EFFECTIVE MANAGERIAL ACTION

Cases in Organizational Behavior

EFFECTIVE MANAGERIAL ACTION

Cases in Organizational Behavior

James C. Rush
Joseph J. DiStefano
Jeffrey Gandz
Henry W. Lane

In collaboration with
Eileen D. Watson
The University of Western Ontario

Prentice-Hall Canada Inc.
Scarborough, Ontario

Canadian Cataloguing in Publication Data

Main entry under title:
Effective managerial action

Includes bibliographical references.
ISBN 0-13-244260-4

1. Personnel management – Case studies.   I. Rush,
James C. (James Cameron), 1946–

HF5549.E37 1988   658.3   C87-095010-X

Copyright to the cases in this book is held by The University of Western
Ontario, except for the following cases: St. Joseph's Health Centre of
London, copyright © 1985 by The Banff Centre; Northridge Psychiatric
Hospital, copyright © 1986 by The Banff Centre and The University of
Western Ontario; Neiman Marcus, copyright © 1975 by the President
and Fellows of Harvard College, reprinted by permission of the Harvard
Business School.

© 1988 by Prentice-Hall Canada Inc., Scarborough, Ontario

ALL RIGHTS RESERVED

No part of this book may be reproduced in any form
without permission in writing from the publisher.

Prentice-Hall, Inc., Englewood Cliffs, New Jersey
Prentice-Hall International, Inc., London
Prentice-Hall of Australia, Pty., Ltd., Sydney
Prentice-Hall of India Pvt., Ltd., New Delhi
Prentice-Hall of Japan, Inc., Tokyo
Prentice-Hall of Southeast Asia (Pte.) Ltd., Singapore
Editora Prentice-Hall do Brasil Ltda., Rio de Janeiro
Prentice-Hall Hispanoamericana, S.A., Mexico

ISBN 0-13-244260-4

Copy Editor: Heather Strongitharm
Production Editor: Kateri Lanthier
Production Coordinator: Matt Lumsdon
Typesetting by Attic Typesetting Inc.

Printed and bound in Canada by T.H. Best Printing Company Limited

1 2 3 4 5 THB 92 91 90 89 88

To the original teachers of Organizational Behavior at
The University of Western Ontario's
School of Business Administration:

WALTER A. THOMPSON

JACK J. WETTLAUFER

CONTENTS

PART TWO/**The Effective Manager** / *245*

PART THREE/**The Management of Change** / *485*

PREFACE

Effective Managerial Action is designed from the manager's perspective. It contains what every manager ought to know about the management of people. It is not designed to make the reader aware of the history of the field or technically expert in it; the reader will not become an expert in the design of a performance appraisal system, but will understand why one might be necessary in a given circumstance, and how it can best be used.

The text has a problem-solving/decision-making orientation. Through the cases, in particular, the reader will experience a variety of situations faced by managers. The reader's role is to understand these situations and the problems faced by the managers, and to make decisions on a course of action. These cases are actual (although sometimes disguised) situations faced by real managers.

A case is a factual description of a situation faced by someone in an organization. It provides the reader with the information that the individual in the organization had when he or she faced that situation. In addition, the cases in *Effective Managerial Action* provide some background information on the company. Although some names of companies and their people are disguised, all the cases describe real events. As case-writers, we take painstaking efforts to ensure that we represent the situation accurately. Cases are not released until they are approved by someone in a position of responsibility in the organization. These cases are not meant to be examples of effective or ineffective managerial behavior, or instruments of social policy. They are intended as vehicles by which students can develop analytic, problem-solving, decision-making and implementation skills.

The letter references that follow the case titles, such as (A) or (B), indicate the sequence of cases in their original copyright form. In our selection of cases, we have sometimes included only an (A) or a (B) case.

The Modules: An Overview

The three parts, or modules, presented in this book are the result of considerable work on the part of the Organizational Behavior Area Group at the School of Business Administration at The University of Western Ontario, and have been tested at both the graduate and undergraduate levels. The three modules are:

• Part One   The Effective Organization (Macro Module)

• Part Two   The Effective Manager (Micro Module)

• Part Three   The Management of Change

The Effective Organization

Part One focuses on the organization as the unit of analysis. We are interested in the effective or successful organization. Effectiveness results when a congruence has been achieved between organizations, the environments in which they operate, the tasks they must perform and their people.

Managers have certain tools at their disposal to bring about fit between these various elements. First, management formulates and implements its strategy to tie it to its environment. That outward looking perspective helps define the organization's mission and set its objectives to enhance its competitive position. Second, managers can also structure an organization such that its critical tasks get done. For example, if managers determine that the organization must be a marketing organization to be successful, they can organize it along marketing lines, segmenting it on either a product basis or a geographical basis. Third, managers can integrate the people and the organization by means of administrative systems and management styles. Managers have at their disposal a variety of administrative mechanisms to help establish fit among people, jobs, and the organization. These systems include selection and development, reward and punishment, information, control, and measurement systems. A manager's style also has a significant role in relating people both to their jobs and to their organization. By utilizing this framework as a diagnostic tool, many organizational problems can be better understood. Strategy, structure and systems must also be congruent.

The primary emphasis in the macro section of this book is on structure and systems. Our assumption is that strategy is a given. Although most of the cases do not give enough information to make changes to strategy, the reader must be aware of the firm's strategy in order to assess the appropriateness of its structure and systems. The reader must also realize that a firm's strategy can be changed implicitly by making structural or systems changes.

We are also conscious of not reifying structure, systems or strategy; we frequently point out that these are tools designed to get people to behave in more effective ways. Every time we make a structural change to an organization, or a change in one of its systems, it is to facilitate some type of behavior that is deemed appropriate for that particular organization at that time.

The Effective Manager

Part Two deals with the concepts necessary for understanding and managing individuals and groups. The emphasis is on using these concepts to maximize productivity, satisfaction, and development for both the organization and its people.

This section of the book focuses on the manager and human resources as the unit of analysis. We are interested in effective behavior in the organization. Given an organization, a set of tasks, systems, people, and a strategy for operating in a specific environment, how can managers best behave to contribute both to the firm's and to their own success?

Again, the notion of *fit* is important. Effective behavior requires a manager whose style and skills serve the needs of others, match the requirements of his or her specific job (organizational role) and implement the systems that are in place. To achieve congruence between the manager and these elements of the context in which the manager operates, change in either the manager, the other people, systems, or jobs (or all of the above) is frequently required. Explicit focus on the management of change occurs in the final course module described below.

In determining the optimum of fit between the manager and these elements, a number of *tools* are available for analysis. First, concepts and theories about individual behavior such as needs, motivation and personality are used, as well as an integrated framework around the notion of self-concept. At another level of analysis, interpersonal work relationships will be considered, and a social systems schema involving background and required factors, and emergent processes and outcomes will be employed. This same schema will be used to develop the managing of effectiveness in work groups. At this third level of analysis, the concepts of integration and differentiation introduced in the macro-module will be adapted to understand and manage cohesiveness and social structure as a basis for work group effectiveness. Finally, the notion of leadership is discussed, with all levels of analysis in mind.

The Management of Change

Parts One and Two emphasize congruence, or fit between various elements. Effectiveness results from achieving such congruence.

Part Three emphasizes a process for achieving such congruence when one or more of the elements change. If a sound change process is followed, effectiveness is more likely to result than if change is mismanaged.

One premise of this module is that people tend to resist change for many reasons. To be successful, changes must be carefully selected and analyzed, an appropriate change strategy must be developed, and the change must be carefully planned, implemented, monitored, and adjusted.

This module considers managing change both at the individual (or individuals within groups) level and at the organizational level. Each draws heavily on the respective earlier module. A model for the management of change is then presented.

ACKNOWLEDGMENTS

As with any project of this scope, many people have been involved and contributed willingly and helpfully along the way. We offer our sincere thanks to those named below.

First, to the Organizational Behaviour Area Group at The University of Western Ontario's Business School. The design of this book mirrors the design of our core course in Organizational Behaviour. The design is the result of this group's effort to create, develop, deliver and modify a course that has been well received by students. Special thanks to: Dick Hodgson, Al Mikalachki and Dave Peach, who have shaped the development of the course by their involvement; John Howard, Dave Burgoyne and Dave Whitehead for their case contribution; Eileen D. (Jackie) Watson, whose superb case-writing skills have brought so many of these cases to their present state.

Second, to all the participating organizations and their people who allowed us to expose them to the scrutiny of students. In so doing, they have helped create more knowledgeable and skilled managers to run our country's organizations.

Third, to our individual secretaries who have typed, re-typed and edited our work. From this group, we wish to single out Margaret Reffle, who has done as much to keep this project organized and on time as anyone. From coordinating the work of four professors (who probably resisted coordination) to interacting with the publisher, she has gone well beyond what we had reason to expect and she did it all with a smile.

Fourth, to the School. Our Dean, Bud Johnston, and our Research Director, Jim Hatch, as well as his predecessors, gave us the opportunity and encouragement to keep going.

Fifth, to Richard H.G. Field of the University of Alberta, who reviewed the manuscript for Prentice-Hall.

Sixth, to the folks at Prentice-Hall Canada, many of whom are only voices on the other end of the phone, who provided useful and timely feedback. Thanks particularly to Yolanda de Rooy who encouraged us from the start.

Finally, to our families. Writing cases took us away from them. Interacting with each other took us home cranky. And we could not tell them it was for the money. Thanks for your support.

The Effective Organization

INTRODUCTION

In this section, we emphasize the organization as our unit of analysis. We are interested in how managers design the structures and administrative systems of organizations to achieve the firm's strategic goals. Both structures and systems send signals to managers and employees about what is important — what they should do and should not do. We are also interested in the culture, or set of values, shared by members of the organization. Like structures and systems, culture is a way of sending messages to employees to help them focus their activities.

We provide a framework for analyzing complex organizations that should help you organize and interpret data in the case studies and ultimately in the situations you will face as a manager. We recommend that, if necessary, you try to modify the framework so that you feel comfortable using it.

Although we will discuss different types of structures and systems, we will not specify the best one or provide general rules. What we do suggest is that your choice of structure, systems or cultures is dependent on the particular circumstance in which you find yourself. The analytic framework will help you reduce a long list of alternatives to a few choices.

CHAPTER 1

Managing the Effective Organization

Today's complex organizations need well-qualified managers. Good management is perhaps the most important element in the long term growth and success of an organization. To know how to develop good managers we must understand both the demands that are placed upon them and the characteristics of modern organizations.

When we think of present-day organizations, four characteristics immediately come to mind: complexity, systems, resources, and change. *Complexity* can result from the technology used by the company. Complicated, state-of-the-art communication and computer systems, for example, require sophisticated organizations and managers to plan, install, and support the technology. These organizations also require many different types of people with different educational backgrounds and job specialties.

Just as there is a dimension of technological complexity in modern organizations, there is also a social complexity dimension related to the size of a company. As a successful organization grows, the number of people and departments expands. Managers have to deal with more people with different viewpoints and responsibilities within the organization. And external complexity affects managers, too. Environmental complexity is a function of the activities of governments, customers, suppliers, and domestic and international competitors.

Organizations are *systems*. They comprise connected, interdependent parts. In practical terms this means that what happens in one part of the organization has implications for and probably affects other parts of the organization. Managers may not be free to make and implement decisions without reference to, or consideration for, other parts of the organization.

Organizations must acquire and manage *resources*. Most obvious of these are the financial and technical resources of the organization. However, managers must be aware of the people in their organization—their human resources. Managers devote considerable time and effort to budgeting and

3

controlling the organization's limited funds; to expanding physical facilities and technological capacities; to the introduction of new equipment and technology and to the maintenance of the existing equipment. They also devote a great deal of attention to accomplishing the many varied operating tasks of the organization. Often the least attention is given to the most important asset — the people. Management must focus on the acquisition and development of their human resources, which are the future of the organization.

Finally, as one wise man noted, "there is nothing as constant as change." We live in a world of technological and social *change*. Technology has decreased the distance between companies and countries, so that they are more interdependent than ever before. What is done in one part of the world has an impact elsewhere. Neither companies nor countries can any longer afford to ignore developments in other parts of the world. It is a truism that we have become a "global village." We live in a world of change also because resources alternately become more or less abundant.

Managers are responsible for the functioning of these complex systems made up of human, technical and financial resources. Obviously, the complexity and amount of resources vary by job and by level within the organization. While people at the highest levels generally are more concerned with forces outside of the organization, linking the organization to its external environment, those people at lower levels are more concerned with internal operations, with linking people to their jobs and with linking groups inside the organization. Our primary focus will be on the internal operations and the development of people for assuming increased responsibility.

Managing is an active occupation, involving more than simply the solving of problems as they appear. It also involves defining problems. It is said that a problem well-defined is at least 50 percent solved. Many people possess techniques and skills for solving well-defined problems. A critical, and usually less emphasized, managerial skill is the ability to define or anticipate problems. This is particularly important when dealing with social and organizational systems. These skills also become important as managers advance in their careers. As managers assume increased responsibility within the organization, they must manage a greater number of increasingly complex and varied systems. They are also responsible for more resources and for adapting their organization to the changing world around it.

If management were a science, we would simply have to learn the laws regarding management. Unfortunately, laws regarding management have not yet been discovered — and may never be. If management were an art, we could rely on the intuition and insight of the individual, and there would probably be little that could be done to create managers in the numbers our organizations require. We would have to rely on a few naturally gifted people. We prefer to think of management as a craft, an undertaking that requires some knowledge of facts and principles and an ability to interpret what these mean for the organization. It is also an undertaking that requires the development of judgment and decision-making in relation to the interpretation of facts. The idea that management is a craft implies that we can learn about and practice management to improve upon our craft.

Organizations — An Overview

In this chapter we emphasize the organizational level of analysis. Our intent is to help managers develop effective and successful organizations: those that set the right goals and achieve them. Effectiveness results from a congruence or "fit" between organizations, the environments in which they operate, the tasks that must be performed, and the people who perform those tasks. This means understanding your market demands and other external constraints, and organizing your human, physical and financial resources to respond to those demands and constraints. Although this is simple to say, in reality it is difficult to do. Our objective is to help you develop a set of analytical and action skills to use in your roles as managers in order to achieve congruence in your organization.

Managers use certain "tools" to create the fit between people, tasks and external demands. These tools create the form and feel of the organization and channel the activities of employees; they are *relational tools*. Structure, for example, creates relationships between people at various levels of responsibility, while budgets and performance appraisals direct behavior toward specific tasks and goals.

First, management formulates and implements a strategy to link the organization to its environment — the market place, technological changes and political issues, for example. It is this outward looking perspective that defines the organization's mission and sets the objectives to enhance its competitive position. In the cases in this book we will accept the organization's espoused or implicit strategy as a given. Most of these cases do not provide enough detailed data to permit students to recommend changes in strategy. However, you must be aware of the firm's strategy in order to assess the appropriateness of its structure and systems. You must also realize that you may, implicitly, change a firm's strategy by making what seem to be only isolated structural or systems changes. These seemingly simple changes may encourage employees to act differently, possibly to the detriment of organizational objectives.

Second, managers structure organizations to facilitate the completion of critical tasks. For example, if the company's success depends upon it being primarily a marketing organization, it can be organized along market lines, segmenting itself on either a product basis or geographical basis. We will also examine structures that help us to relate to the external environment and to achieve our tasks and goals internally. Specifically, we will focus on the differentiation and integration of functions, and organizational structures such as functional, product, divisional and matrix forms.

Third, managers can align people to the organizations by means of administrative mechanisms. Managers have a variety of administrative mechanisms that help align people and jobs. These include selection criteria and processes, development programs, allocation of rewards and sanctions, information and control systems, and performance evaluation methods. These administrative mechanisms or tools can be designed to support effective behavior in organizations. Every time you make a structural change, or a change in one of the administrative mechanisms, it should be to facilitate some type of behavior that is appropriate for both that particular person or group and for the organization at that particular time.

A simple example can take this discussion from the conceptual to the practical level. Consider contractors who build homes, specializing in medium-priced, wooden frame houses with brick exteriors. They have to employ, or sub-contract to, the appropriate tradespeople. They need carpenters to build the structure or frame, and they must use the right tools — saws, hammers, and so on. They also need bricklayers with, among other things, cement mixers and trawls. If one contractor decided to change his or her strategy to build expensive homes, he or she might need cabinet-makers and carpenters to build frames or install customized kitchens, for example. Or, alternatively, if he or she decided to build stone homes, an entirely different set of craftspeople, such as stone cutters and masons, using a unique set of tools would be needed.

Although this example may seem obvious, its parallel in modern organizations is not so simple to see. The homebuilder metaphor may help you to identify the appropriate people for certain jobs and to ensure that the proper signals are being sent, through reward or evaluation systems, for example. Just as you don't want carpenters doubling as bricklayers, you don't want to pretend that a custom, job-shop production system and the people that work in it can be easily or quickly transformed into a mass production system. Similarly, a sales force that sells discrete, high technology products on an individual commission basis may not be effective selling systems of integrated technology that require years of sales effort before the deal is signed. Managers must pay close attention to each task and ensure that they have the right people with the right skills and tools to achieve success.

Finally, management is responsible for creating the culture and climate of the organization. With the advent of major competitive challenges by large Japanese companies and the accompanying research into the reasons for their success, a significant finding is the existence of strong organizational cultures, or explicit statements of values to guide the organization and its members. These shared values, like other administrative mechanisms, direct employee behavior in appropriate directions and also resolve conflict. An example of such explicit values comes from Matsushita Electric Company[1]:

[1]R.T. Pascale and A.G. Athos, *The Art of Japanese Management*. Warner Books, New York, 1982, p. 75.

Basic Business Principles
To recognize our responsibilities as industrialists, to foster progress, to promote the general welfare of society, and to devote ourselves to the further development of world culture.

Employees' Creed
Progress and development can be realized only through combined efforts and cooperation of each member of our Company. Each of us, therefore, shall keep this idea consistently in mind as we devote ourselves to the continuous improvement of our Company.

> *The Seven Precepts*
> 1. National Service Through Industry
> 2. Fairness
> 3. Harmony and Cooperation
> 4. Struggle and Betterment
> 5. Courtesy and Humility
> 6. Adjustment and Assimilation
> 7. Gratitude

Similarly, a company like YKK Zipper has a philosophy of the "cycle of goodness." In a company publication, *The World of YKK*, Mr. Tadao Yoshida explained this philosophy:

> I firmly believe in the spirit of social service.
>
> Wages alone are not sufficient to assure our employees of a stable life and a rising standard of living. For this reason, we return to them a large share of the fruits of their labor, so that they may also participate in capital accumulation and share in the profits of the firm. Each employee, depending upon his means, deposits with the company at least ten percent of his wages and monthly allowances, and fifty percent of his bonus; the company, in turn, pays interest on these savings. Moreover, as this increases capital, the employees benefit further as stockholders in the firm. It is said that "the accumulation" of savings distinguishes man from animals. Yet, if the receipts of a day are spent within that day, there can be no such cycle of saving.
>
> The savings of all YKK employees are used to improve production facilities, and contribute directly to the prosperity of the firm. Superior production facilities improve the quality of the good produced. Lower prices increase demand. And both factors contribute to the prosperity of other industries that use our products.
>
> As society prospers, the need for raw materials and machinery of all sorts increases, and the benefits of this cycle spread not just to this firm, but to all related industries. Thus the savings of our employees, by enhancing the prosperity of the firm, are returned to them as dividends that enrich their lives. This results in increased savings which further advance the firm. Higher income means higher tax payments, and higher tax payments enrich the lives of every citizen.
>
> In this manner, business income directly affects the prosperity of society; for businesses are not mere seekers after profit, but vital instruments for the improvement of society.
>
> This cycle enriches our free society and contributes to the happiness of those

who work within it. The perpetual working of this cycle produces perpetual prosperity for all.

This is the cycle of goodness.

The concept of culture or shared values is not new, nor is it a product of Japan. The inspiration for the "cycle of goodness" came from the American, Andrew Carnegie, who said, "Unless you render profit or goodness to others you cannot prosper."[2] Peters and Waterman, in their book, *In Search of Excellence*,[3] also showed that America's best-run companies at the time had explicit statements of important values that helped to bind people to the organization. AT&T and IBM have always had strong organizational cultures. What is at least more obvious now is how important these sets of shared values can be in achieving organizational effectiveness. A set of values and philosophy will develop in every organization, whether it is created explicitly with careful forethought and contributes a positive, constructive viewpoint, or whether it happens implicitly without specific guidance and is perhaps more negative. Excellent management specifically shapes and guides the development of corporate culture.

If values provide the content of the culture, managers' styles shape the climate and feeling for how managers and subordinates relate — the day-to-day process of taking action and solving problems. Management style can create an atmosphere of openness, trust, sharing and problem solving, or one of insecurity, fear and unquestioning obedience. The challenges facing today's organizations would seem to call for flexible, innovative organizations and for managers whose personal styles can create or contribute to those characteristics.

Figure 1.1 is an analytic model or framework that we use to assess organizations and their effectiveness and to understand organizational problems and opportunities. The remainder of this chapter will develop a more detailed appreciation of this framework.

Perspective: organizations are systems

Organizations are open systems, both affected by and influencing the larger social, political and economic environments within which they function. In this regard an effective general manager must scan the environment, read the signals and establish appropriate goals. He or she must then interpret this information and translate its implications into organizational action by de-

---

[2]Hideo Ishida, *Y.K.K. (Yoshida Kogyo K.K.)*, Keio Business School case, ICCH 9–377-880, Keio University, Japan.

[3]Thomas J. Peters and Robert H. Waterman, Jr., *In Search of Excellence: Lessons from America's Best Run Companies*. Harper and Row Publishers Inc., New York, 1982.

Figure 1.1

Organization Design Framework

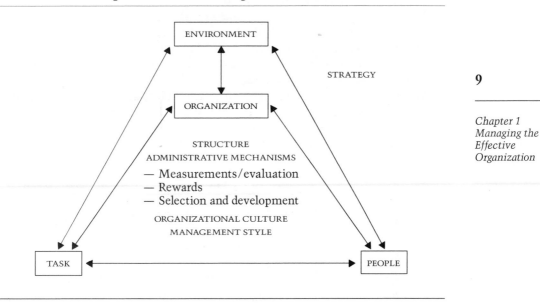

signing appropriate structures and administrative mechanisms to achieve these goals and finally, to motivate the people in the organization.

Organizations are dynamic and adaptive. Managers are constantly interacting with the environment, reading signals, interpreting these signals and taking action; they must be responsive. Conditions can change and no longer be stable. This affects the organization. Changes in the environment get translated into changes in the organization and in the tasks that the organization is doing. It is not sufficient to have adapted to your environment once; rather, you must be re-adaptive, able to change when conditions change. When "misfits" occur you must be able to re-establish a new fit between the people, tasks and organizational objectives.

Internally, organizations are systems, or sets of interrelated parts. The parts are not connected randomly, but in a coherent fashion to achieve a specific purpose. Conceptually, the two major components of an organizational system are the *technical* and *social* sub-systems. The technical sub-system is the collection of numerous technical and/or functional tasks of the organization. They encompass the acquisition of inputs (capital, labor, raw material), as well as the technology and work processes used in the various functional areas in the output of the finished products or services. Each of the major functional areas of an organization such as production, marketing, finance and research and development (R & D), for example, are technical systems within the larger organizational system. Each has a set of tasks and operations necessary to the functioning of the whole organization.

The social sub-system is the human component — the people in the organization. Individuals and groups, with their skills, needs, expectations, orientations and experience, make up both the functional areas and the total organization. It is as important to have the right people for a job as to have the proper tools, raw materials and technology.

Managers need to be concerned with the efficient and effective functioning of each of the sub-systems, and with linking the two effectively. Good management works to achieve positive results within both sub-systems, and for the ultimate result of their interaction — the performance of the overall

Figure 1.2

Organizations Are Socio-Technical Systems

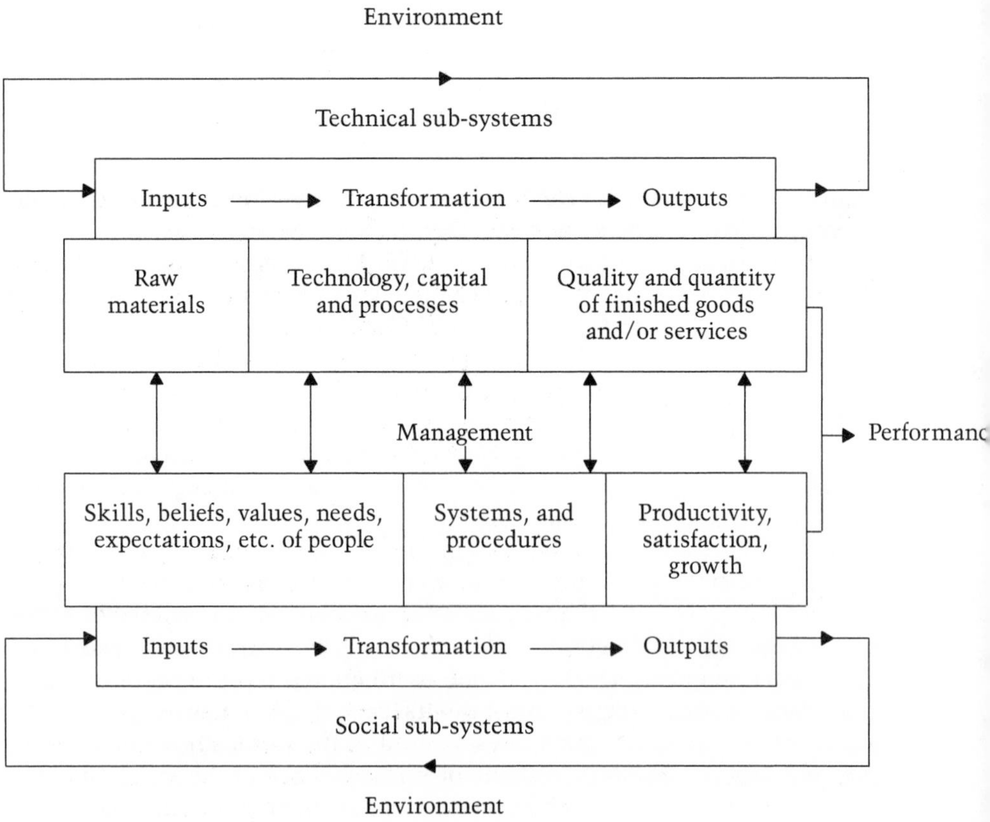

Environment

organization. The manager's role is the active coordination of the two sub-systems and the solving of problems that arise, not only from the interaction of the technical and social systems, but also within each of the sub-systems. People and their behavior cannot be studied independently of the business of the firm and the demands placed on the people by technology, financial constraints and the systems used to administer the business. This socio-technical perspective is depicted in Figure 1.2.

What are the implications of this perspective for managers? Managers must understand that if they make a change in either sub-system, this action may have ramifications in the other sub-system and implications for overall results — and not always the ones intended. This is one of the properties of a system; a change in one part affects the other parts. This is why a systemic and integrated perspective of organizations is essential in diagnosing problems before taking action.

The Organization Design Framework

Earlier we referred to tools that managers could use to construct and direct their organizations. We will now discuss each in more detail, beginning with strategy.

Strategy

A *strategy* is the direction chosen for a firm. It defines the way an organization chooses to relate itself to its external environment. It encompasses such things as the firm's chosen niche in its industry and the control of critical factors for competing successfully in that niche, the way in which the firm develops resources and the mode in which the political and social environments are scanned and interpreted.

Companies develop knowledge, skills and expertise in specific industries. This expertise is often referred to as a firm's *distinctive competence*. Company executives continually search for new opportunities for the firm to apply its expertise and resources. One element of the strategic process is the matching of a firm's distinctive competence with potential opportunities. Another is the expansion of the range of knowledge and expertise beyond current products, markets or even industries — diversification.

To be successful in a business or industry there are certain activities that an organization must do well. These *key success factors* vary from industry to industry and from one industry segment to another. For example, if you are producing a commodity product it might be critical to have a secure source of supply and efficient production or processing operations so you can be the low cost producer. If you are producing highly differentiated products, advertising, marketing and product development are likely the critical activities. If you are in the aerospace industry, your R&D capability, and the ability to manage contracts to produce on time and within budgets may be key success factors.

The important point is that you have to know what you must do well in a business to succeed, and you must recognize that these factors may vary from industry to industry. Although we could say "you have to do everything well," that truism would not reflect the specific competitive situation within an industry. Any firm may need finance, production, marketing, sales and human resource capabilities, but the relative emphasis or importance of each of these may vary according to the nature of the business.

Once you understand how you have to compete in your business, you can translate this into the tasks that must be performed within the organization. Once you know what tasks need to be done and how they should be done, a structure and set of administrative mechanisms can be implemented to get the jobs done properly.

It is our belief that you cannot understand an individual's behavior, or the behavior of groups in an organization, or conflict between individuals or groups unless you understand the jobs they are trying to do, and where the organization is trying to go. You must understand the constraints and pressures on people. As a manager you must understand the behavior of people in the context in which that behavior occurs. To implement a strategy you have to rely on your employees and minimize the organizational barriers.

In a management behavior course such as this, we generally accept statements of strategy (or proposed changes in strategy) and environmental conditions made by managers in a case. You may, however, have to evaluate these statements in relation to potential fit with the internal structure, administrative mechanisms, and the skills and abilities of your human resources.

Structure

Structure is the set of relationships between people in an organization and the mechanisms that communicate to organization members what behavior is expected of them, what tasks to work on, what not to do, what goals to work towards, with whom to work, whom to obey, and whom to direct. This includes such things as division of labor, special integrating roles, teams and task forces, the hierarchy, and rules and procedures.

Specialization and Coordination

Organizations must have internal specializations. They require people with different orientations and skills for the specialized tasks. There usually are patterns of differences, or systematic variances, between people in various functional departments. The notion that segments of a company are organized for specific tasks and that some people by education, experience, and attitude seem more appropriate to some jobs rather than others is essentially the concept of *differentiation*. Lawrence and Lorsch[4] defined differentiation as the "difference in cognitive and emotional orientation among managers in different functional departments." The concept of differentiation encompasses the organizational segmentation of jobs, the specialized knowledge required for the jobs, and the differences in attitude and behavior of the people in the jobs. In their research, Lawrence and Lorsch found systematic variances in employees' orientation towards goals, time, and interpersonal relations, and in the formality of structure in various functional departments.

As the competitive demands of an industry require specialized knowledge and skills, this is reflected in an increase in the differentiation of various specialties in an organization. As this happens, the potential for departments to pursue their own particular goals increases, as does the likelihood for potential conflict. Therefore, it is important to coordinate these departments or functional areas. Integrating mechanisms are required to coordinate the activities of different groups in an organization to achieve desired goals. This is not always easy in large corporations, since people may be separated physically and psychologically by their personal predispositions and orientations.

The concept of integration also includes the notion of conflict resolution, as well as the coordination of activities and inter-relationships. A problem-solving approach to resolving conflict is generally regarded as the most appropriate way to contribute to organizational effectiveness. This means that managers confront problems rather than avoiding them or smoothing them over. As they confront them, they recognize that the conflicts may be rooted in legitimate task differences and different viewpoints held by different specialists. Managers should avoid letting situations develop where departments attempt to prevail and win-out over other departments. Win-lose situations can be very destructive for organizations. Managers should attempt to resolve conflicts so that the organization as a whole wins. In fact, developing an integrated, overall organizational orientation and a superordinate set of goals and values can contribute substantially to the resolution of conflict.

The other aspect of integration is coordination. To ensure the proper coordination of departments, you must be aware of how each department is dependent on the others to get its jobs done.

Thompson[5] identified three types of internal interdependence in organizations, and most complex organizations exhibit all three types. The simplest level is *pooled* interdependence. This means that each part of an organization can pursue the achievement of its goals independently without input from other parts of the organization, and still contribute to the overall objectives of

---

[4]Paul R. Lawrence and J.W. Lorsch, *Organization and Environment*. Richard D. Irwin, Homewood, Ill., 1969.

[5]James D. Thompson, *Organizations in Action*. McGraw Hill, Inc., New York, 1967.

the organization. For example, in a department store, personnel from the furniture department probably do not have to interact with people from sporting goods for each to fulfill its objectives. Each can contribute, independently, to the goals of the store.

Higher up on the complexity scale is *sequential* interdependence. As the name implies, one group must accomplish its task before the next one can begin. There is an ordered progression by which some tasks must proceed. In manufacturing a relatively standard product, you could see a progression from the design department to engineering to purchasing to production scheduling and then to manufacturing. In each case, a specific task must be accomplished before the next is begun.

An even more complex form of interdependence Thompson labelled *reciprocal*, which means "the output of each becomes the input for the others." Rather than having discrete linear relationships between groups, the relationships are continuous and almost circular in nature. For example, in creating sophisticated technology systems, production must understand what the researchers have developed, but the development engineers must also understand the constraints on manufacturing. Similarly, both the researchers and the engineers must understand the customers' needs in order to accurately forecast delivery dates. As can be inferred from this simple example, the level of intergroup communication and potential conflict escalates dramatically in situations of reciprocal interdependence.

The managerial issue is how to coordinate the various types of interdependence. At the simplest level standardization of rules can be used. A department is given a budget, a set of operating procedures, hours of operation and a set of well defined tasks to do, and measured on its results against set objectives. With sequential interdependence, coordination is usually accomplished with plans and schedules. However, at the level of reciprocal interdependence, direct, face-to-face communication is usually required. Thompson called this "coordination through mutual adjustment." In these situations you usually have meetings between departments or representatives of departments. A lot of face-to-face communication is required.

Finally, technology and computer systems permit a rapid and comprehensive exchange of information and increase our ability to coordinate. Although the literal requirement for face-to-face communication may diminish, the underlying spirit of mutual adjustment and the need to share information on an ongoing basis will remain a necessity even when computers talk directly to each other.

Rules, plans, schedules and budgets, although important, are not in themselves sufficient to coordinate the complex activities required in an organization. Other integrating mechanisms must be used. Galbraith[6] identified a

---

[6] Jay R. Galbraith, *Organization Design*. Addison-Wesley, Reading, Mass., 1977.

hierarchy of integrating mechanisms: rules and procedures, planning processes, hierarchical referral, direct contact, and liaison departments. The last two, direct contact and liaison departments, are mechanisms fostering mutual adjustment between departments or groups. Examples include task forces, teams, liaison people, product or project managers, product management departments and matrix organization designs. These are structural responses to the increasing coordination needs of an organization.

Administrative Mechanisms

Structure is one vehicle that managers use to implement strategy, and there is a need for consistency between strategy and structure. So too is the manager responsible for designing and/or interpreting a series of administrative mechanisms. The ultimate purpose of such mechanisms is to help employees understand what it is that they are expected to do, and to encourage them to do it. It is critical that these messages of what is expected be consistent with both strategy and structure.

There are a number of mechanisms available to a manager to achieve these ends. In the section that follows we will describe these mechanisms and show how they can influence the effectiveness of the organization.

Our intention is not to deal with any particular mechanisms, such as a reward system, in depth, but to show how the system, used effectively or ineffectively, can create fits or misfits between people and their jobs, or between people and the organizations in which they work. We show in many cases how critical the fit between different types of systems is to the effective running of the organization. Each system gives an employee some type of message about what is expected of him or her. These systems send *signals* and these signals are important. Quite often different systems give people different messages or signals. Ineffectiveness results when individuals try to reconcile those differences. Often they pay attention to one system to the exclusion of messages coming from another.

These administrative mechanisms are relational tools. Managers use them to create a relationship, or link, between the organization and its environment, the employees and the organization, and the employees and their tasks. Other appropriate metaphors include "levers" or "dials" used to set and reinforce the course of an organization.

Organizations should be designed so that the behavior elicited by the administrative mechanisms matches the needs of the organization. All too often, procedures are imposed without due consideration of the job at hand, simply because, *de facto*, they just "have become company policy." In such situations, the administrative mechanisms may become the controlling factors, and the jobs and the people forced into fitting the systems, when it should be the other way around. Administrative mechanisms are tools, not ends in themselves. Judgment is required in assessing the likely impact of administrative mechanisms on people in jobs, and in adjusting these mechanisms accordingly to support job achievement and organizational results. Systems and procedures should aid managerial judgment; they can never replace it.

Recruitment and Selection

The way people are brought into the organization can have very dramatic effects on the fit among the elements of our model, as we saw in Figure 2.1. The most obvious effect is on the pool of knowledge, skills and attitudes that a manager can call upon. A less obvious but equally powerful effect is the impression left on the new employee by the process — recruits learn something about the key values of the organization (its culture), not the least of which is the way it treats its people.

Recruitment takes a variety of forms — newspaper advertising, campus visits, search firms and networking are among the most popular. Each has a way of attracting elements of the labor force. Often costs associated with recruiting prevent exhaustive searches for new employees. Firms therefore make assumptions about the performance potential of groups of people in the way that they recruit.

We will take as an example a firm that is looking for people with management ability. They decide to recruit from the three best MBA programs and ask graduating students to sign up for interviews. They prescreen, from that list, those students with the best performance in their business programs. The assumption made here is that the best students from the best schools will make the best managers, or that the probability is higher with this group than with any other. Questioning this assumption, one must ask who is most likely to apply to those top schools and who among them is most likely to get the best grades. Might they be the best at analyzing; might they be the best at conducting and writing about research? Does the job call for those skills? Might the job call for more interpersonal and leadership skills? What kinds of needs do these recruits have for salary and advancement? Can the firm fulfill these needs?

These questions are not raised to suggest that recruiting, especially campus recruiting, is not well done, but to suggest the importance of understanding the nature of the job and the organization in defining the person specifications before deciding on a recruitment plan. In the previous example, if the organization had determined that they were deficient in decision-making skills, and that the top students at the top schools were most likely to be the best decision makers, then the recruiting plan makes sense. The example also shows the importance of understanding the unexamined assumptions involved in recruiting.

Recruiting is not only a mechanism for bringing potential employees to the organization, it is a process by which the organization sells itself to potential employees. As mentioned above, recruits get a lasting impression about the firm, its culture, and the way it manages people from the behavior of the recruiters. Expectations are set about what life will be like inside. Potentially effective employees can either be attracted to or repulsed by the organization as a result of the recruiting experience. A significant amount of research suggests that satisfaction and ultimate tenure is affected by the degree to which both the job and the organization were realistically described to the applicant.

Selection is the mechanism by which the pool of candidates is narrowed to the number of job vacancies. This is often done by having a number of people in the firm interview the short-listed candidates, by checking their references, and in some cases by having an assessment done by professionals. Final decisions are often made by committees and reflect either a consensus or majority view.

Several sources of assessment error can enter these decisions. The one most frequently described is the "just like me" error in which the successful candidate is the one who is closest in skills and personality to those making the decision. Although it might augur well for the fit between person and organization, this type of decision might not provide the required congruence between person and job.

Selection, like recruitment, involves a careful analysis of both the job(s) and the organization to determine the right type of person. Candidates can then be assessed against these criteria.

Finally, managers must be aware of employment equity legislation that pertains to their jurisdiction. These laws or guidelines require that certain steps be followed to protect the rights of many segments of the population. Managers following sound selection practice will not find themselves in violation of these requirements.

Training and Development

Rarely does a selection decision leave us with a perfect person-job or person-organization fit. If it is only to find out how things are done in the company, most employees need some form of training or development to make them effective performers. Even if the fit is perfect it is not likely that that condition will last for long. Continual development is needed as conditions change — one need think no further than recent technological changes to recognize the need for development.

Training and development is big business. The Carnegie Commission in the United States estimated the training and development budget of American corporations to be in the area of $80 billion. The value of that expenditure has recently been the subject of much debate.

Effective training and development programs are those based on needs established for the organization and for the individual, designed with principles from learning theory in mind, and evaluated against a set of objectives. Training can be done to develop a skill set currently missing from the organization, to bring inadequate performers up to standard, to ready an individual for a future position, or for a variety of other reasons. The reasons must be consistent with the goals of the organization. Learning theory helps the training designer determine for a given set of objectives what the appropriate techniques, milieu, and timing are. Skill training often requires the learner actively to practice the new skill with feedback provided frequently in the early phases and with spaced refreshers later. Finally, some form of program evaluation is critical. Such information is critical to decisions such as whether to continue the program, revise it in content or format, or scrap it altogether.

Training ought not to be thought of as a panacea for organizational problems. But it ought to deserve the kind of attention that other managerial decisions of the same order of magnitude warrant and get.

Appraisal and Rewards

Two of the most talked about and studied mechanisms are the ways in which we appraise and reward performance. Most organizations have recently changed, are in the process of changing, or are thinking about changing their performance appraisal system. Debates still rage about the feasibility and effectiveness of pay for performance systems.

Appraisal Appraisal processes are seen in so many forms and administered in so many ways, that it would be an impossible task to catalog. However, at the core there are several common purposes:

- to communicate expectations or standards of performance,
- to provide feedback on how well one is doing against expectations or standards,
- to identify areas of developmental need and develop a plan of remedy,
- to provide information and documentation for decisions about salary, promotion, or discipline.

Performance appraisal is one area where a substantial gap exists between state-of-the-art and state-of-the-practice. The number one pet peeve for many managers is filling out performance appraisal forms and sitting down with employees and telling them how well or poorly they have done. Beyond the logistical problem of finding the time to do it, managers are not often trained in how to observe, how to document, how to provide negative feedback in ways that will be heard, and how to listen. Managers are uncomfortable articulating the judgments which they undoubtedly make every day. It is one thing to have a rank order of your direct reports in your head; it is quite another thing to tell someone face-to-face that he or she is in the third quartile and be able to justify it.

Research on appraisal mechanisms seems oriented more to the development of performance criteria than to the process in which that measurement is just a component. In trying to improve the accuracy of the appraisal (its reliability and validity), much research has been done on various approaches. Current thinking suggests that a behavioral approach is preferable. For instance, managers actually rate performance by noting some behavior having taken place. Even within this approach there are three or four ways to proceed. We feel that more attention is warranted to the entire process than to just the development of the criteria. Effort directed toward improving managerial skills in observation, documentation, and the set of interpersonal skills critical to effectively communicating expectations and providing feedback may have greater payoff than that directed toward better criteria.

Rewards   Rewards come in different forms and in different ways for different people. One person's reasons for working are different from another's. Basically, we can assign rewards to one of two categories — *intrinsic*, those that come from doing the job itself or being directly part of the work situation, and *extrinsic*, those more tangible aspects mediated by others. Assuming more autonomy is an example of the former, while getting a raise is an example of the latter.

Rewards have different meanings for different people. Some rewards (particularly the financial reward) have instrumental value, helping us get other things of importance such as food and shelter. It often serves as a signal that one's contribution or presence is valued — a form of recognition. It can serve as a signal to others of one's value, thereby enhancing self esteem. Individual needs determine which of these meanings are most important at any one time, and which type of rewards have an effect. (More will be said about this in the chapter on The Effective Manager.)

In designing and administering reward mechanisms from the individual's point of view, several issues are important. First, are they sufficient? Is the sum of both the intrinsic and extrinsic rewards enough to attract, motivate and retain employees? Do they get enough to satisfy their needs? Second, are they equitable? Are the rewards commensurate with what the employee brings to the job in terms of skill, knowledge, aptitude, attitude and effort? Are they more, less or the same as others bringing the same amount to the job? Third, are they competitive? Can you attract the people you want to your organization?

In designing these same systems from the organization's point of view, such issues arise as how much it can afford and where it wants to be, competitively, with other organizations in the industry or in the same geographical area. The organization must decide whether it wants to provide rewards before performance is exhibited or afterwards.

Appraisal and Reward Mechanisms   With the range of options, how does any manager decide which mechanisms are most appropriate, and how should they be administered and communicated to employees? The answer to these questions should come from the analysis of the organization and the environment in which it operates. Once the strategy is developed, goals have been established, and the key tasks have been laid out, the type of people required are definable. The parameters for both the appraisal and reward mechanisms are those which attract, motivate, and retain these people and get them to do the required task in an effective manner. But too often reward decisions are made because of unexamined assumptions about motivation, rather than careful analysis.

To be more explicit, let's take the case of a sales organization. Their strategy includes maintaining the existing share of market in their mature product lines. Selling these products involves the development of a high trust relationship with the buyer. The task is really one of creating demand. An appraisal and/or a reward system that focuses sales representatives on volume or new accounts exclusively sends conflicting messages to them. They are told the task involves relationships which indicates "soft" selling. However, the appraisal/reward system says sell, sell, sell—which indicates more "hard selling." Yet faulty notions of "sales-type people" responding to sales volume incentives frequently lead to less than effective reward systems. We strongly advise you to do your analysis and beware of projecting your own values or experience onto your reward system.

Information and Control
The final category of administrative mechanism to be discussed includes accounting, auditing and management information systems. These mechanisms coordinate different interests and potentially different behavior of people in the organization. Formal mechanisms replace personal observation as the size of the organization increases. As the complexity of organizations increases, the need to coordinate and control the activities of diverse groups of individuals also increases.

Many types of control mechanisms exist. Most organizations systematically collect, analyze and disseminate information on production, finances and personnel. Budgets are developed, refined and monitored. Like other mechanisms, these give messages about what is required or valued. Making production concentrate on costs and sales on volume could in some circumstances produce high levels of dysfunctional conflict. Production wants long runs to minimize down time and re-tooling costs, while sales wants runs stopped to meet a valued customer's urgent need for another product. Making them both responsible for profit prevents production from concentrating just on costs, and sales from concentrating just on volume. Both need to understand the other and act in a coordinated fashion if either is to satisfy their needs.

Again, careful analysis is needed, rather than design based on a manager's personal preferences or assumptions.

Conclusion

Christopher Alexander, in writing about the process of design of physical things like buildings, transportation systems or vacuum cleaners states that:

> "...every design problem begins with an effort to achieve fitness between two entities: the form in question and its context. The form is the solution to the problem; the context defines the problem. In other words, when we speak of design, the real object of discussion is not the form alone, but the ensemble comprising the form and its context.[7]
>
> The form is a part of the world over which we have control, and which we decide to shape while leaving the rest of the world as it is. The context is that part of the world which puts demands on this form; anything in the world that makes demands of the form is context. Fitness is a relation of mutual acceptability between these two."[8]

Managers are also designers. They are engaged in an ongoing design process to create and maintain effective organizations.

---

[7]Christopher Alexander, *Notes on the Synthesis of Form*. Harvard University Press, Cambridge, Mass., 1964, pp. 15–16.

[8]*Ibid.*, pp. 18–19.

C · A · S · E · S

BANK OF MONTREAL: DOMESTIC DEVELOPMENT PROGRAM (A)

James C. Rush and Cheryl Harvey

Gord MacAskill was at work early Monday morning. As he rode the elevator to his eighteenth floor office, he thought about the week that lay ahead of him. By the end of this next week he, with a dozen other people, would have totally redesigned the domestic banking operations of the Bank of Montreal. The bank had undertaken many changes, but this was the most massive restructuring ever. It would involve all 20 000 branch employees across Canada.

Banking in Canada

The five major Canadian banks were among the top 40 banks internationally. In 1982 the asset size of these five banks ranged from 45 billion to 88 billion dollars. These assets comprised almost 90 percent of all chartered bank assets in Canada. The Bank of Montreal, founded in 1817 as the Montreal Bank, was the oldest bank in Canada and the third largest.

The number of banks in Canada remained fairly stable until the 1980 revision to the Bank Act. This revision allowed the chartering of "closely held" banks controlled by one or a small number of shareholders. These Schedule B banks operated under restrictions on branching and size which did not apply to the 11 "widely held," Schedule A banks. By the end of 1981, there were 57 Schedule B banks, including all foreign banks operating in Canada as well as a few Canadian-owned banks. The Schedule B banks aggressively recruited experienced commercial account managers from the A banks and quickly established themselves as a competitive force in the mid-market business segment.

Banks also competed with "near banks" (trust companies, mortgage companies, credit unions, savings banks), savings and insurance intermediaries (life insurance companies, trusted pension plans and registered retirement savings plans, investment companies) and lending intermediaries (finance companies, term lenders, venture capital firms, merchant bankers, real estate investment trusts, mortgage investment companies). Trust and mortgage companies had become particularly adept at marketing their products to customers. Some recent campaigns to attract deposits featured lotteries for cars while mortgage lenders offered a variety of interest rates, payment schedules, and renewal options.

The banking environment had changed in several other ways over the preceding years. Increasing computerization of processing functions reduced the amount of time required to complete transactions. This advance shrunk float,[1] reduced operating expenses, and helped reduce foreign exchange losses. Computerization had also led to the introduction of automated teller machines (ATMS) which placed the responsibility for some transactions on customers and reduced customer line-ups for teller service. Computerization facilitated the expansion of the number of products and services available to customers. Daily interest accounts, for example, were not feasible prior to computerization.

Customers had become increasingly sophisticated. Computers had taught them to expect speed and accuracy. They, like the banks themselves, had learned to manage float. They shopped for products and services that promised the most for their money, and they became impatient with long noon-hour and Friday afternoon line-ups. A common complaint referred to the large number of people "just sitting at desks" behind the tellers while the lines grew longer and longer.

Banks earned profits from the "spread" — the difference between the average rate of interest on money loaned and the amount paid to acquire it. Exhibit 1 summarizes sources and uses of funds for the Canadian banking industry as a whole.

William D. Mulholland

William D. Mulholland was recruited from Brinco Ltd. to be president of the Bank of Montreal in 1975. Mulholland had been president of Brinco while the company was building the Churchill Falls, Labrador, hydroelectric power

---

[1]float: The amount of funds tied up in cheques that have been written but are still in process and have not yet been collected.

plant. Churchill was the largest hydro plant ever constructed in North America and the project experienced several problems. A railway strike delayed the construction schedule and, subsequently, contractors sued for more money. Mulholland's handling of the project and his participation on the bank's board since 1970 impressed the bank's officers and resulted in the presidency offer.

Mulholland also had worked at Morgan Stanley, a New York investment bank, where he had helped to arrange the financing for Churchill Falls. However, neither his finance background, nor his board experience diminished his astonishment at the number and scope of the problems the bank was facing.

Profitability was low. Liability management was non-existent and there were money market and foreign exchange problems. The bank had undertaken a major expansion in computerizing its network of 1300 branches and this had proven extremely costly. The bank's stock price was depressed, and its market share of personal deposits was lower than it had been for years. The bank could not identify which branches or services were profitable. Turnover among clerical personnel exceeded 50 percent, management trainee turnover was in the 40 to 50 percent range, and management turnover was 15 to 17 percent. The picture was totally changed by 1982, and Mulholland, by then the Chairman, was credited with the turnaround (See Exhibit 2).

In 1975 there were two major banking functions within the Bank of Montreal. One, termed Domestic, served all Canadian customers, including individuals, small and medium-sized companies and large corporate businesses. The International function served corporate and government customers outside Canada as well as the international needs of Canadian customers. The personnel and policies of the bank were oriented towards serving the dominant, domestic function. The divisional structure of the bank was geographically oriented. Specialized markets were not identified and a relatively small number of homogenous products and services were offered.

Mulholland felt that this type of structure had negatively affected the bank's efficiency, its service to its customers and the professional development of its staff. Mulholland moved to adopt a structure which would reflect a market focus and which would create an environment that would facilitate the professional development of commercial banking officers while improving service to the bank's customers.

Reorganizing the Bank

At the end of 1976, Mulholland took the first step by establishing the Corporate Banking Group. This group served large national and international companies in Canada. The credit requirements of these companies ranged from $10 million to over $100 million. This particular market was large enough to justify internal specialization. Specialized groups focused on oil, gas, mining, real estate, financial institutions, and governments, among other industries. The establishment of Corporate Banking enabled the bank to develop expertise in world-scale project loans and in the management of large internationally syndicated loans. Sophisticated cash management services for customers were also developed. This group's success in boosting market share, arranging syndicated loans, and acquiring a reputation for excellence was attributed to the increased professionalism of its staff members.

Mulholland's next initiative was the creation of a globally-integrated treasury function. The treasury managed assets and liabilities for the bank as a whole. This function included managing cash, liquidity, and float; funding and controlling risk; dealing in financial markets; and providing financial support to the bank's account management organization. By 1982, the Treasury Division had developed to the point where the bank reconciled global positions daily, maintained a 22-hour-a-day active dealing capability, and monitored open positions on a 24-hour basis. The treasury's personnel resources, operational support and information systems had been strengthened significantly.

Mulholland next moved to establish a world-wide, integrated, electronic data processing organization that increased the speed of transaction processing and the opportunity for managerial control. The Domestic Operations and Systems Division incorporated the systems group from International Banking and assumed responsibility for the world-wide system. By 1982, the entire domestic network was "on line," linking eight regional data centers, over 5000 branch terminals, automated teller machines (ATMs), and customer terminals with two central computing centers. More than three million transactions were processed each day.

With the EDP organization in place, Mulholland and other bank officers began to study ways of reorganizing the bank by developing key markets and understanding existing and predicted client needs. In 1981 the World Corporate Banking Group was created to serve markets with international or transnational characteristics which lent themselves to centralized account management. Multinational corporations were served by a world-wide network of account management districts whose executive officers were located in strategic financial centers. Also served were specific international industries such as the petroleum industry. Also included in this group were foreign governments and foreign banks.

At the same time, the Canadian Corporate Banking Group's mandate was broadened to include the United States and it became responsible for large, North American-based corporations. This group was designated as the North American Corporate Banking Group. Later, World and North American Corporate were combined into a single group, Corporate and Government Banking. The International Banking Group was reorganized to provide indigenous commercial and international banking services in selected markets and to provide specialized international banking support, and operational and administrative support, to global account management and treasury units located outside Canada. The bank was no longer a Canadian bank with some international operations. It was an international bank with a Canadian base.

In 1981, the bank had 30 488 employees scattered through corporate headquarters, international branches, and 1300 domestic branches. By the beginning of 1982, Mulholland was ready to turn his attention to reorganizing the Domestic Banking Group.

Domestic Banking Group

The Domestic Banking Group contained eight geographically oriented divisions. The divisions were divided into several districts, each with 17 to 50 branches. Exhibit 3 illustrates, generically, the 1982 structure of the Domestic Banking Group.

The cornerstone of the Domestic Banking operation was the branch. A branch had two groups of customers. Retail customers wanted their money in an account that would earn a high rate of interest while permitting access to their funds. They wanted to make deposits quickly and needed assurance that the bank accurately recorded their transactions. Retail customers also often wanted to borrow money at the lowest interest rate and with minimal notice. Loans were usually under $25 000 and secured by personal assets. Retail products included monthly and daily interest savings accounts and chequing accounts, term deposits, and safety deposit boxes.

Commercial customers were more interested in the credit the bank would extend to them. Mid-market businesses had sales of $1–100 million and credit requirements ranging from $200 000 to $10 000 000. Credit was given on the strength of the company's balance sheet. Small businesses' credit needs were in the $25 000 to $200 000 range. These companies usually had sales of $300 000 to $1 000 000. Credit was extended as much on an assessment of the customer's entrepreneurial spirit as cash flow projections. Current accounts, payroll services, and cash management services were among the non-credit products and services available to commercial customers.

Branch managers were responsible for serving both commercial and retail customers, for granting credit and making personal loans, for selling non-credit services and for securing deposits. They had to sell and assess risk, to be trustworthy and suspicious, to be reassuring and demanding, to be rigid and flexible.

A branch manager's job grade and salary was based primarily on the size of the loan portfolio, which was heavily influenced by the commercial activity level of the branch. This system naturally directed the manager's attention to the commercial credit responsibilities. Most branch managers spent 80 percent of their time in credit-related activities. The much lower credit approval limits of loans officers and account officers meant that branch managers frequently had to re-assess credit applications. If the amount requested exceeded the branch manager's limit, a referral to the divisional credit manager was necessary.

The branch manager was expected to motivate, train, and develop a staff of clerks, tellers, account officers, administration managers, loans officers and trainees. They were responsible for the marketing of all the bank's products to customers as well as for the selling of those products. They had to develop business plans, targeting the branch's performance in areas of productivity, efficiency, and market penetration.

Branch managers also had to maintain the branch premises, ensuring that the branch was clean and physically well-organized and that equipment was in good working order. They were also expected to manage the maintenance of on-line records, manual ledgers and records, the audit and internal control procedures, the filing, and the processing of paper transactions. Branches provided all support services at cost to all other bank groups. All of this was to be done while circular after circular hit their desks. Exhibit 4 illustrates a typical branch manager's day.

Changing the Domestic Group

The bank had been aware for several years that the branch manager's job was a very difficult one. In 1976 a task force had been struck to look at the different ways that banks organized their domestic operations in the United Kingdom and in the United States. That task force concluded that the bank should reorganize its domestic operations based on market focus. But Mulholland felt that the bank was not prepared for such a large-scale change at that time and shelved the recommendations. However, several people in the bank knew of those recommendations and had been thinking about their applicability.

In 1975, the Central Commercial Branch Concept was developed in the Central Ontario Division, which essentially comprised Metropolitan Toronto. Three branches were designated commercial branches and commercial business was assigned to them. The other branches took care of retail business. In 1977 this same region was divided into three Retail districts of 36 to 52 branches each and one Commercial district of 23 branches. Each retail branch was associated with a commercial branch. The segmentation of different types of business was developing. In November 1979, two divisions were created. These were separate divisions for retail and commercial business in Central Ontario. In 1980 the Ontario Retail and the Ontario Commercial Divisions were expanded to include all of that province except southwestern Ontario. In 1982 this reorientation was further extended through the creation of two separate headquarter organizations for retail and commercial business in Ontario. The Ontario segmentation was the most highly developed one, but the retail/commercial separation was also becoming a reality in the provinces of Alberta and British Columbia. The rest of the Canadian Domestic operations remained essentially as they had been.

Another development was the segregation of the branch's processing function from its customer service functions. By 1982, 55 ADCON (Administrative Consolidation) centers were processing transactions for several branches from a screened-off location in one branch or from a separate location. Some branches, which processed only their own transactions, had also separated and screened this function from the customer service area.

As previously mentioned, by 1982 the Chairman of the bank was ready to move to the restructuring of the Domestic Banking Group. He appointed a steering committee to examine how this might be done. The steering committee resurrected the 1976 task force study and recommendations. They examined the recommendations to see if they would apply to the bank in 1982 and also to see how well they fit with the strategic thrusts that the bank had been following over the past several years. The committee recommended that the Domestic Banking Group be restructured to achieve three objectives: to bring a sharper organizational focus to the principal domestic market segments, the personal and commercial sectors; to improve the opportunities for professional development of officers and staff within each of these principal market groupings; and to reverse the decline in the quality of credit and customer service.

Mulholland quickly accepted the recommendations. The committee then struck a task force and set about designing a hypothetical organization that would meet the objectives established for the disaggregation, or separation, of retail and commercial business in the Domestic Banking Group.

Designing the New Structure

As the vice president of the Ontario Retail Division, Gord MacAskill was asked to chair the mini-task force which would redesign the retail structure. On this task force were a half-dozen people from across Canada. A similar group would design the commercial organization. They had a week to accomplish their tasks. The whole group would meet together on Monday morning before splitting up into the two mini-task forces. On Friday afternoon they would regroup to combine their efforts. Gord knew, as everyone else did, that the task was not to design a hypothetical organization, but to design an organization that would make the disaggregation work.

In spite of this, Gord wondered if this was the time to disaggregate domestic banking. It was a year during which the banking industry and the country as a whole was in a major recession. Loan losses were high. During the 1970s the Bank of Montreal had been very aggressive in providing loans to all markets, and now was experiencing many defaults. Throughout the bank there was a great emphasis on increasing productivity and many programs had been undertaken at branch levels and at the district and divisional levels to develop ways of increasing efficiency. Automated teller machines (ATMs) were being placed in several locations across the country. The bank was also engaged in closing unprofitable branches. Turnover was reduced but there was an increased probability that some people might have to be laid off. All of these activities and the economy itself created an atmosphere of tension, pressure, and reduced morale within the bank. Job security was a major concern for many of the staff.

Still, Gord felt excited as he walked toward the conference room. The task was there: design a retail and commercial structure to align with a dual-market focus and yet fit together to serve the Canadian customer, describe the jobs in this new organization, do it all by Friday, and do it using existing resources.

EXHIBIT 1
BANK OF MONTREAL
DOMESTIC DEVELOPMENT PROGRAM (A)

Selected sources and uses of funds
Canadian Banking Industry

Selected sources	
Canadian dollar deposits	*$ Million*
Personal savings	90 037
Personal chequing accounts	3 943
Other demand	12 921
Other notice	43 033
Government of Canada	3 677
Provincial governments	821
Other banks	2 695
Total	157 127
Selected uses	
Loans in Canadian currency	
Business	73 562
Personal	32 864
Mortgages	16 400
Farm	7 472
Government	2 578
Other	6 391
Total	139 267

SOURCE: CBA Bank Facts, 1982.

EXHIBIT 2
BANK OF MONTREAL
DOMESTIC DEVELOPMENT PROGRAM (A)

Selected Financial Data
1974–1981

	1974	1975	Year 1976	1977	1978	1979	1980	1981
Total assets at Oct. 31 ($ billion)	17.65	18.24	20.49	25.17	32.09	38.18	48.84	63.78
Return on average	.32%	.56%	.49%	.54%	.69%	.65%	.60%	.64%
Book value per share	14.88	16.79	18.12	19.18	22.02	24.72	27.29	30.86
Return on equity	14.02%	22.64%	17.73%	18.33%	22.30%	23.06%	20.97%	22.15%
Per share profit	$1.65	$2.99	$2.71	$3.18	$4.32	$4.58	$4.75	$6.16
Loan loss provision ($ million)	—	32.3	37.7	44.2	62.4	94.1	123.7	196.3
Loan loss experience ($ million)	—	48.6	35.2	39.3	70.0	127.5	154.2	268.1
Stock price (high)	20.8	17.8	17.5	18.125	26.125	27.50	34.75	33.50
(low)	11.25	11.25	13.25	13.625	17.375	21.375	22.50	23.50

SOURCE: Annual Reports: 1981, 1982, 1979.

EXHIBIT 3
BANK OF MONTREAL
DOMESTIC DEVELOPMENT PROGRAM (A)

Domestic Banking Group

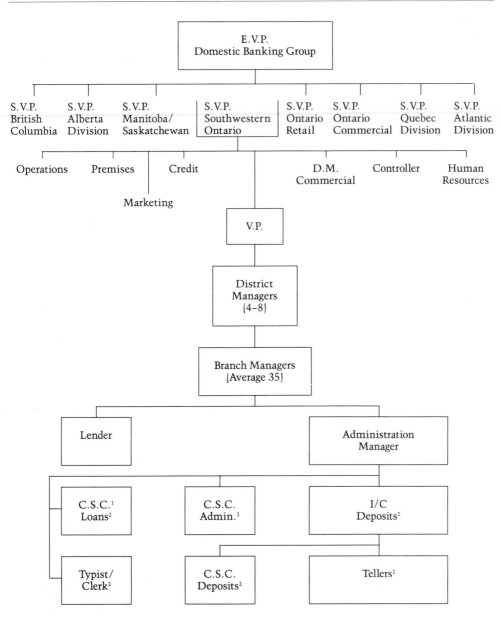

¹ C.S.C.: Customer Service Clerk
² Non-management position

EXHIBIT 4
BANK OF MONTREAL
DOMESTIC DEVELOPMENT PROGRAM (A)

From Richard Andrews' Diary

Tuesday, Nov. 10

8:30   Started work on performance appraisal forms. Eight to do.

8:45   Peter Morgan, account officer, asking about the Wesley Plumbing Co. loan. Discussed the security increases required. Approved, pending security arrangements.

9:00   Back to performance appraisals.

9:30   Mary Picelli came in to vent her frustrations with training Joan Harris. Says Joan keeps fouling up posting transactions and customers won't go to her station. Mary's made the same complaint about at least a dozen other trainees. She always gets them on the right track eventually.

10:05   Mr. Cheshire was waiting for the doors to open. His annuity was bothering him again. Discussed that, the weather (rain) and his plans to march in the Remembrance Day parade tomorrow.

10:25   Peter Morgan. Wesley says the Bank of Nova Scotia will give him a better deal. It is too good to be true. No change to our offer.

10:35   Interview with the Esposito's re: mortgage. He is earning $20 000 a year as a carpenter. She is pregnant and they want a house to bring the baby to. Explained the bank can't give them a 90% mortgage on the $59 000 house they want. Not with these interest rates, his type of seasonal job, in this economy. Suggested they lower their sights or hold on at her parents'. Too bad.

11:15   Caroline Burcyk, account trainee. Question about procedure for a credit check for a car loan. Japanese car. Suggest lien.

11:25   Paul Johnson calls. Loud complaint re: messing up clearing of personal Master Card payment through his business account. I'll buy him a drink at the curling club tonight.

11:45   To the Holiday Inn. On Chamber of Commerce panel "Attracting New Business to Cook's Mills". Lunch meeting.

2:15   Peter Morgan. Finalizing Wesley Plumbing.

2:30   Meeting with controller, Al Bates, and two staff, from the mill. Topic: cash management and payroll services. Went well. They will get back in three weeks.

3:45   Check on daily audit. Joan and Mary aren't balancing anything. Other tellers comment that line-ups were long today—customers thinking that tomorrow is a bank holiday. Mention the mess in the staff room.

4:05   District manager calls. Here next week to look us over. Dinner with Shirley and I.

4:15   Peter and Caroline. Review new credit procedures. Run through the forms.

4:40   Peter re: appraisal. Set interview for next week. Ask him to think about aspirations, competencies.

4:50   Call from Shirley. Should we have dinner at the curling club? Meet her at 6. An hour for performance appraisals.

DMR GROUP, INC. (A)*

James C. Rush and Eileen D. Watson

On the 14th anniversary of the founding of DMR Group, Inc. (DMR), a multinational information systems consulting firm, President Pierre Ducros was discussing the firm's management practices with Executive Vice President Alain Roy. Ducros remarked to Roy,

> We're already more than halfway through the year in which we were going to find some way of dealing more effectively with the "people results" of our crazy, rapid expansion. So far, nothing has changed, despite clear signals that we need to improve our management practices. Our people are our only asset; and with our profitability currently decreasing, we've got to do something about the way we manage people.
>
> Yet we seem to be in a Catch 22 situation — every hour spent managing our people is an hour not billed. I'm concerned about the future of our company...do you have any ideas about how we should change our management mode?

Background: The Information Systems (IS) Industry

DMR's operations had been profoundly influenced by the dramatic technological changes which had occurred in the information systems industry over its short 30-year history. Old timers in the industry talked about three distinct eras in the growth of information services and products:

- *Batch era*, from 1955 to 1971 (approximately). Separate computerized files were kept for every function — marketing, accounting, personnel, purchasing, etc.

- *On-line data base* era, from 1972 to 1982 (approximately). Centralized data storage and retrieval became available, and a beginning was made at placing terminals in user sites for activities like order entry and inventory control.

---

*All names in this case have been disguised, except the names of DMR founding partners.

• *End-user era*, from 1983 onward. End users gained access to data for personal use in developing various types of business plans. More information processing power was on the desk of the individual user.

By the mid-1980s management of information systems was becoming a strategic issue. Data processing managers and their equipment formerly were situated in one location and had limited functions. Now, they were becoming involved in broadly based strategic decision making. New uses of the technology were constantly being developed. For example, in the banking industry, customers had begun interfacing directly, through auto-tellers, with a data base which formerly had been closely guarded and inaccessible.

The changing focus of IS functions, together with constantly expanding technological horizons, placed new and different demands on client firms. This, in turn, impacted on the breadth of skills and knowledge required of the consulting professionals who were servicing the industry.

Background: The Company

A specialized information systems consulting firm, DMR was wholly owned by its partners. With a staff of 850 worldwide, DMR offered a variety of services including management consulting, systems development, and technical services, as well as educational seminars and courses. The company prided itself on its versatility. A DMR consultant stated, "We are qualified to handle the full spectrum of information management consulting assignments; management or technical, complex or bread-and-butter, large or small, micro or mainframe... and even artificial intelligence."

The company's head office was situated in Montreal. Local offices were located in four regions — Eastern Canada (including Ontario), Western Canada, U.S.A., and International. Each local office operated independently and autonomously, responding to the specific needs of its markets. (See Exhibit 1 for partial organizational charts for the company and a typical local office.)

As a result, each office developed its own areas of specialization. In Quebec City, for instance, long-term development contracts for large government departments provided a significant portion of the firm's business. In contrast, the Toronto office dealt mainly with management consulting-related activities including educational services and smaller short-term projects.

Company revenues had risen rapidly to $55 million the previous year, and further increases were expected this year. However, profitability as a percent of revenues was declining (see Table 1) — a fact which concerned many senior managers.

The demand for consulting services in the computer field was growing by leaps and bounds, as was the competition. Toronto was home base for approximately 50 such consulting firms, although DMR was one of the largest and most versatile.

TABLE 1
Distribution of Revenues, Last 6 Years
(in percent)

Revenues apportioned to:	Year 1	Year 2	Year 3	Year 4	Year 5	Year 6
Professional staff	57.4	50.8	54.7	58.9	60.0	61.0
Administration	8.9	8.0	6.6	9.8	7.5	10.5
Profitability	33.7	41.2	38.7	31.3	32.5	28.5

The number of requests for proposals (RFPs) from potential clients was rising steadily each year. For example, one office responded to 171 of the 250 it received last year; and of these, DMR won 95 contracts (56 percent) — a satisfactory achievement.

Company Origins

DMR Inc. was founded by Pierre Ducros, Serge Meilleur and Alain Roy, former IBM employees. Ducros recalled,

> It was completely illogical for me to leave a senior management position with IBM, to go off on my own. I was successful, secure, enjoyed my work...but something in my gut, a force of some kind, meant I *had* to do it. And so with two other maverick risk-takers, I opened a little office in the basement of a dingy old office building, hired a terrific secretary, and DMR was in business! Well, *almost* in business — our survival phase lasted almost a year, as we worked desperately hard to get a few clients.
>
> By the end of the first year, we could afford to move out of that basement...and the company has been on the move ever since! Four years later we hired two more consultants, also from IBM. In another six years, we had 110 employees. Today, our staff numbers nearly 900 in 23 office locations in four countries, and we're still growing.
>
> It was so much fun in the beginning! I could stay close to the customers and to my staff. I personally knew all the details of the products and services we offered. No one thought about formal controls or procedures — none were needed! And I knew all my people so well — their marriages, their kids — not like today...

Company Operations

Information systems consulting consisted of two basic activities — development work and consulting. Development included such activities as systems delivery for clients, end-user computing at executive work stations, and office automation. It usually necessitated the long-term deployment of programmers and programmer analysts to work closely and cooperatively with client personnel. DMR people worked on-site, hopefully with their clients' full cooperation and assistance, to produce the systems needed by client firms.

Consulting activities often were more *ad hoc*, and might include client education, strategic planning, technical consulting, and advising on systems development and applications. These activities tended to be of relatively short duration, and required adaptability and versatility on the part of confident, experienced, highly-skilled consultants.

Because each DMR office operated independently from the others and the head office, there was no "universal" DMR organizational structure. The organization and administration of each office tended to reflect the special interests and capabilities of the partner in charge (the general manager or director). However, responsibilities for varying degrees of the following functions were shared among the senior managers at every location:

- Personnel recruitment, selection, job assignment, orientation, training and development, formulation and implementation of personnel policies, assignment of personnel to management "mentors," etc. (Often, a small core group would be responsible for the ongoing recruitment of "star performers," as well as overseeing the various personnel programs mentioned above. However, no full-time human resources management professionals were employed anywhere in the system.)
- Projects, accounts: marketing and management of work projects, as well as the supervision of various accounts ranging from huge corporations to small one-owner companies.
- Products, services: services and technical consulting, personal computer products, client education, DMR product development.
- Administration: support services for DMR staff, including reception, files, secretarial services, word processing.

Generally, local managers tried to keep their departments as small as possible, but at the same time provide high quality service to their clients.

People Management at DMR

DMR people were predominantly young. The majority were in their mid-to-late twenties, some middle managers were in their thirties, and the president and vice president were in their early forties. In most offices, the percentage of male to female staff was approximately 60/40. One manager remarked, "DMR is clearly in favor of equality; and I would imagine there will be an equal male-female balance in another couple of years."

DMR had no job titles, as such, that were visible to outsiders. However, certain personnel classifications existed within the organization: programmer analyst; senior programmer; senior analyst; consultant; senior consultant; manager consultant; principal consultant; partner; and administrator.

DMR's recruitment policy was to look for talented individuals with proven track records. At one time, IBM had been a main supplier of talent — three-quarters of DMR's partners were former IBM employees. Now fewer than one in five new recruits came from that source. The president stated, "We look for entrepreneurial, self-motivated people with integrity, and 'the spark in the eye' — visible enthusiasm, interest, intelligence. And, of course, outstanding competence in the field."

One senior manager characterized the company's management style as "adhocratic": "It's flexible and adaptable — at any given time, each person has a number of different responsibilities which may be shifted quickly, in response to changing situational requirements."

In fact, it was common for one individual to be working on three or four projects simultaneously. For example, a manager might be both a personnel manager (coaching, championing, and mentoring a group of junior staff persons) and a project manager (working with a client to develop the new program needed by the user). In addition, he/she might have some product or service responsibility — ideas from a successful project might be incorporated into the development of a universally acceptable program or service.

The company's managers were directly responsible for the success of their own current projects, and consultations. Some managers supervised project groups of from two to twenty DMR people. Others essentially worked alone, while supervising a client's staff; and others frequently managed DMR programmers/analysts and staff of the client company. Talking about his management responsibilities, one senior consultant said:

> The people I manage are constantly changing. Many different DMR people pass through the 10 or 12 major projects I manage in a given year. There's a manager-level person on every site — the project manager — who can catch on-site problems when they're still small, and solve minor problems right away. I hold project control meetings every month or six weeks, and my accounts are reviewed by our very senior people every three or four months...unless there is a blow-up in the meantime.
>
> I deal with problems with the client, the user, as soon as I hear about them. Difficulties with our own personnel are resolved whenever there is time. I usually address these one to one, mostly over lunch. I use a different style depending on the person — I listen, we talk together, make a connection.
>
> I'm also a "mentor manager" to a half dozen junior people. I represent them for assignments and promotions. I can be the ear of the company for that person if he wants to express an idea, if he wants to change work assignments, wants to complain about a project manager's attitude, etc....a counsellor, if you will.
>
> We have to react fast when a new person is needed for a project. Everybody plays the game. The person best suited is selected, and his/her manager speaks for him/

her as to competence and career wishes. Sometimes when a mandate (project assignment) is offered, our employee says "no." Most of the time we respect that "no," although sometimes we have no other alternative.

Another manager stated,

We hire programmers, and as quickly as possible make them analysts. We like to know how motivated a potential employee is. One way to find out is to ask how much overtime he or she did to get past projects completed on time! And it pays to find out how much this person really *wants* the job . . . perhaps it is simply an escape from an intolerable working situation elsewhere.

Even the most junior people must be self-motivated, have a desire to learn, not be afraid to try new things. And they must be flexible. They have to adapt for the client's sake. We can't have an employee who is rigid and needs firm parameters for the job.

Promotions to management and to partnership were guided by the principle, "We give responsibility to those who have earned it." Throughout the DMR organization, 52 senior employees had been made partners in the business. The focus of the partners' work tended to be external, though many were also involved in overseeing the work of managers reporting to them. (Some of these managers were extremely independent. One said, "I'm not actually managed by a partner, because I don't really need it.")

Hiring additional staff was a constant concern. One office was attempting to recruit an additional 100 staff, immediately! The problem was where to recruit the necessary number of well-trained, experienced people?

Compensation

Keeping trained junior staff was another issue. Other consulting firms offered higher salaries and benefits — DMR people were tempted to leave. One senior manager said, "I tell our people that they will benefit financially over the long term by remaining with DMR. If they leave us, their income may jump at first; but over a period of time, DMR salaries catch up to our competition, and surpass them by far."

Partners received a basic minimum salary, and the balance of their income (50 percent or more) depended on a division of the year's net earnings. At a senior level, people were hired by DMR for approximately 10 percent less than their previous salaries; and junior people entered the firm at approximately their previous salaries.

After six months, non-partners became eligible for a profit-sharing plan. A percentage of the quarterly profits was divided among approximately one-third of the non-partners. Those selected to share in the pool were chosen "according to what they contribute, and by how good they are."

The company covered the full cost of all benefits, including provincial health insurance premiums. A pension plan was being considered. Vacation time was based on each employee's total years of experience, not just on the length of their employment with DMR.

Training and Development

The common wisdom in the business (and the industry) was expressed by President Pierre Ducros:

> Our assets are *people*, not buildings or things. We have to attract and develop managerial professional people by providing intellectually challenging mandates for them, and giving them entrepreneurial opportunities within DMR.

Three and a half days of formal education were provided each year for junior and middle-management people. However, providing training opportunities seemed only part of the answer to the problem of developing effective consultants and managers:

> We can train people in technical areas, but we have run into difficulty training them in business and human relations. Also, it's much easier to train a generalist to become a specialist, than the reverse.

The "DMR Way"

Pierre Ducros often talked about his original vision for the company, and his perception of the main reasons for the success of DMR Group, Inc.:

> In starting DMR, I envisioned an autonomous new organization founded on a policy of maintaining close contact with the customer, with no internal politics getting in the way. All of our people would be flexible and adaptable, supremely competent and responsible, and able to work independently for the good of the company — effective entrepreneurs.
>
> And in fact, it is this entrepreneurial spirit which has made us so successful, in spite of the difficulties we're now having coordinating and controlling the people side of the business.

Ducros himself was a dynamic example of the type of managerial leadership he espoused. He used every opportunity to encourage his people to be constantly aware of the key success factors to which he attributed the company's phenomenal growth, and which were critical to the organization's future success. He described four major factors which he considered should guide all DMR operations:

- *Quality* — sell the correct services to the client, be sure of their needs, and ensure quality of the product and excellent project management;

- *Client* — find and keep customers, and keep them happy;
- *Profitability* — aim for the highest profitability potential;
- *People* — provide effective personnel management, to produce high-quality, well-motivated, satisfied employees.

Pierre Ducros said, "For each of these four elements, there has to be a set of values. What is missing at DMR is the mechanism to transmit these values throughout the organization. I want everyone at DMR to share in the task of seeking to obtain a balance among these four areas!"

The managing partner in charge of the Quebec City office, Marc Girault, agreed wholeheartedly with these principles. When asked to describe his philosophy of management, Marc said:

> First and foremost is respect for the individual — that is, our customers are our main concern, and deserve to receive our thoughtful consideration. Give them credit where due; manage through deliverables; satisfy the customer's real needs, not what they at first think they want; and be responsive to all their needs. And, of course, the quality of our work must be impressive. Eighty-five percent of our business comes from previous mandates, so high quality of all our work is a must.
>
> In other words, we need to know the market — customers, potential consultants, competitors — and select the right market opportunity at the right time. We must look for innovative opportunities with clients, recruit talented people and help them to progress to high standards of excellence, produce work of a better quality than the competition. We have to constantly strive to be known as the most productive firm in our province.
>
> It goes without saying that we must also closely manage growth and profitability of the office. And more: I want every member of this organization to be aware that the basic values of this company are rooted in close attention being paid to four areas — quality, the client, profitability, and our people.

The Utilization Issue

It was the norm at DMR Group, Inc. to work long hours in order to provide a quality product. It was not unusual for consultants to work 60 or 70 hours a week, yet bill only 35. Most DMR managers achieved an 80 percent utilization rate — ie. they could bill 80 percent of their 35 weekly basic hours to a client at a chargeable rate. However, utilization standards varied widely from office to office, and from manager to manager. Differences ranged from 10 percent to 95 percent; and one partner even expressed the opinion that consultants should be billing 100 percent (200 days per year), while managers should bill within a 70 to 90 percent range.

One manager asked, "Do you really improve quality if instead of accomplishing three projects in two weeks, you finish only two projects in the same time?" Opinion on the issue was divided.

Although a high utilization rate would bring increased financial returns for the company, it would leave little time to manage people. On the other hand, a low utilization rate would give more time to manage people (thus improving quality, supposedly) but fewer dollars. A project manager talked about the "balancing act" involving Pierre Ducros' four criteria:

> Any time you forget any one of these four, you're in trouble. If you're too concerned with the client and the mandate, you have trouble with your personnel and dollars. If your employee wants to develop the nicest possible "thing" in the world for his own intellectual stimulation and satisfaction, you're going to have trouble with your dollars. You'll also have trouble with the client because you won't be able to deliver on time! And if you work on the dollars and the client, then what's to become of your personnel and the mandate? It's a balancing act all the time!

Changes and Challenges

The rapid growth of DMR Group, Inc. had brought many problems affecting the working lives of employees. Some of the difficulties expressed by various employees are summarized below:

> We're growing too fast. The more people we get, the more rules we need, and the more security that is required. And with so many of us demanding fast word processing services, it's sometimes impossible to get rush jobs done.

> We start some projects before we're ready. Maybe we should be better organized before setting up certain projects. We're getting lots of client demand, but we're not fully prepared in some areas.

> Some people dread new responsibility. They wonder how much harder they're going to have to work...they are working 50 hours a week already! They're tired, and their families and social lives are suffering.

> A limiting factor for DMR in the future will be its management personnel. It's a very demanding business, and we need the very best people; and with all the competition, the supply is drying up.

> There's the ever-present danger of becoming a bureaucracy. Even the number of partners we have now makes our organization somewhat top-heavy.

> Whatever way we expand our services, there's always the possibility of misjudging the market. We don't want to produce another Apple or micro-computer mistake....

> We need to communicate more with each other. We don't take the time to make each other aware of good work experiences we've just had, so we're continually re-inventing the wheel.

> I need to more fully understand the overall goals of the business, the context in which I operate. I'm sometimes in the dark about our ultimate goals, in spite of all my questioning.

Because we recruit senior people with successful track records, we get leaders, not followers. Molding a team of these leader types is difficult.

We're away from the office so much, we sometimes don't feel part of DMR. In my first year, I was in the central office only twice. And I'm noticing how some other new people are left adrift for as long as a year...left alone with their assignments, and little or no orientation.

Performance appraisals are never done for us consultants. With no written objectives, what constitutes success for a consultant? It's easy to see if a development manager has achieved a goal — the product works! It does what the client wants it to do. And in technical services, there are similar tangible, visible results to be achieved. But it seems impossible to set standards or criteria for consultants.

I'd like to have more manuals for information — literature about mainframes, software, hardware, etc. And there should be a standard way of approaching tasks like doing an evaluation of existing software — a micro-based tool. Also, I don't have enough time to go to manufacturers' information sessions, so I need complete in-house information about the latest technological developments.

Seeking an Answer

As he talked with Alain Roy about improving DMR's management of its human resources, Pierre Ducros reaffirmed his belief in the effectiveness of the DMR Way:

I still believe that the DMR Way is best. It's so important that the four values become part of every facet of our operations. The trouble is, we have achieved so much growth, so rapidly, that we haven't been able to adequately diffuse the values throughout the total organization yet.

What do you think, Alain? Do you agree that disseminating the four values is the way to go? Or do we need something else — more structure and controls, for example? I'd like to hear your opinion.

EXHIBIT 1
D M R G R O U P I N C . (A)

Partial Organizational Chart for DMR Group, Inc.
May, 1986

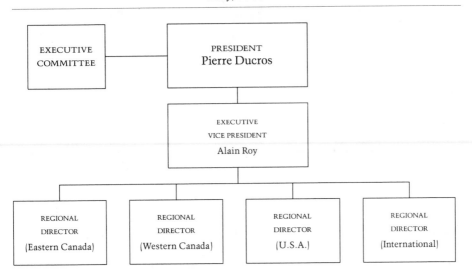

Organizational Structure of One Local Office,
Eastern Canada Region

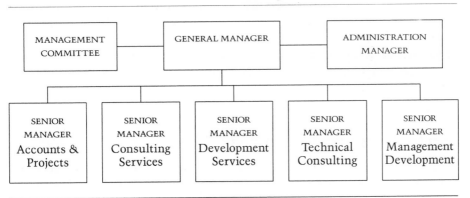

ST. JOSEPH'S HEALTH CENTRE OF LONDON

Joseph J. DiStefano, James C. Rush and James McNee

Sister Mary Doyle smiled as the banner unfurled across the front of St. Joseph's Hospital. The banner read:

SHARE IN OUR TRADITION OF CARE

Sister Mary thought the phrase was appropriate, not only as a fundraising slogan, but also as a message from the newly-formed St. Joseph's Health Centre.

Over a period of years, three Catholic health care facilities owned and operated by the Sisters of St. Joseph — St. Joseph's Hospital, St. Mary's and Marian Villa — had inched toward merging their efforts and organizations to better serve the community in which they operated. The objective was to develop a total health care facility providing a continuum of care from conception to old age. In 1984 the boards of the institutions were merged and Sister Mary Doyle was named chief executive officer. She was asked to propose to the board an organization structure and the sequence and timing of the activities and functions to be merged. After years of talking, it was time for action. The board wished to announce the new structure by the spring of 1985.

London's Sisters of St. Joseph

With a population of 275 000, London was the largest city, and unofficial "capital" of southwestern Ontario. London's hospitals served the needs of the city and surrounding area. The Sisters of St. Joseph had been active in London since the 1860s. The sisters operated three health care facilities located on two diagonally adjacent blocks in the city's "old north" section (see Exhibit 1). St. Joseph's Hospital was one of London's three acute care teaching hospitals; St. Mary's Hospital was one of two chronic care institutions in the city; and Marian Villa was one of the city's largest homes for the aged.

The organizations were owned and operated by the Corporation of the Sisters of St. Joseph in the Diocese of London under the authority of the Bishop of London. Catholic health care facilities were ecclesiastical communities participating in the mission of the Church through the ministry of healing. The facilities were committed to providing quality care for the whole person in order to heal as Jesus did. Sister Katherine McKeough, General Superior of the Sisters of St. Joseph, London, believed that St. Joseph's Health Centre had to be "prophetic" in the sense of promoting and upholding the sacredness of human life from conception to natural death. Qualities of caring, serenity and steadfastness were necessary in the prophetic pursuit of trying to be an inspiring force in the effort to create a peaceful society.

It had been said that Catholic hospitals were not necessarily better than their secular counterparts, but that they were different. The difference was due mainly to the philosophy of the sisters and to the active participation by the sisters in the organizations. Many sisters were of the opinion that if a Catholic hospital was not different, it should let the secular community take it over.

Sister Mary knew that changes were necessary and that there was some urgency. Elsewhere in the country, people had been shocked by the closing of Catholic hospitals because of the declining number of sisters available to run them. It had been taken for granted that sisters would always be available to run the hospitals. However, that would not necessarily be the case in the future. The number of women joining the order had declined and not all sisters were interested in hospital management careers.

In London, the Catholic Church was interested in and committed to maintaining a Catholic health care presence. The merger was, in part, an attempt to increase the ability of the sisters to manage the hospitals more efficiently, given the sisters' scarce time and limited energies. The challenge was to find a structure which would provide excellent patient care in the tradition of the order and which could function with less operational involvement of the sisters, should their number available to the London hospitals diminish.

London Hospitals

There were three major teaching hospitals in London. In addition to St. Joseph's 534 beds, the city was served by the University Hospital with 421 beds and the 850-bed Victoria Hospital.

One measure of a hospital's areas of expertise was the tertiary services (the expensive, intensive, major services) it provided. The University Hospital, located on the campus of The University of Western Ontario, had nine areas of tertiary service, including neurosciences, cath lab, nephrology, intensive care, infertility and four surgical tertiary services: neuro, cardio-vascular, transplant and arrhythmia surgery. It had an international reputation in neurosurgery and transplants (including the testing of a new anti-rejection drug). A major unit specializing in the study of strokes was in the development stages.

Victoria Hospital had tertiary services in all of the major areas of surgery (burn unit, neuro and cardio-vascular), pediatrics, cancer, obstetrics and gynecology, intensive care and medicine (cath lab and nephrology). Victoria was also relocating to a new site and brand new facilities. Phase One of the new Victoria Hospital, with approximately one-third of Victoria's treatment beds, was slated to open in mid-1985. The hospital would operate from two locations until the later building phases were completed late in the decade.

St. Joseph's Hospital

St. Joseph's was an active treatment, acute care hospital where patients stayed for relatively short periods of time while receiving treatment such as having surgery, undergoing tests or delivering a baby.

With 534 active treatment beds and a staff of over 2100, St. Joseph's Hospital was, by far, the largest of the three Catholic facilities. As a teaching hospital associated with The University of Western Ontario, St. Joseph's was required to balance the three areas of education, patient care and research. In the past, St. Joseph's had not been noted for its research prowess but had taken steps to strengthen that component.

Through the 1970s and into the 1980s, St. Joseph's confidently developed as a teaching and research institution and gained an international reputation. Specific areas of expertise included prenatal and neonatal care, diabetes, orthopedic surgery, and the training of family physicians. Although other institutions might focus on narrow, highly specialized projects, it was St. Joseph's strategy to focus on the future needs of the population. St. Joseph's planned to continue as a modern, sophisticated teaching hospital with the "needs of the community" as its strategic focus for research, education and care in the years to come.

Examples of St. Joseph's strategy in action included:

- the opening of a $1.3 million family medical center to provide an improved teaching and training facility for family medicine residents, as well as to serve a varied cross-section of patients. The new center was located a few blocks from the main complex. It was the second relocation for the centre, which was one of the first in Canada when it was founded in 1968
- the Research Institute's first "Scientific Day in May" which dealt with the effects of maternal lifestyle on fetal development
- the ongoing efforts to recruit a researcher with an international reputation to establish a major research program in diabetes and metabolism

• tertiary services such as Neonatal Intensive Care, High Risk Pregnancy, Orthopedic Reconstructive Surgery, Diabetes and Nephrology.

In 1984, the $12.9 million St. Joseph's Hospital Research Institute had completed its first year of operation. Many of the researchers had previously worked at the hospital, but now the Research Institute was expanding and recruiting the best people available for research positions. A director of the institute had been recruited from outside the hospital. The annual budget for medical research at St. Joseph's was almost $2 million in 1985. The total operating budget for St. Joseph's in 1985 was $77 million.

Sister Mary Doyle was the executive director of St. Joseph's Hospital (see Exhibit 2). Traditionally, the executive director was a Sister of the Order. Sister Mary was a graduate of the Hospital's School of Nursing, and for over 30 years she had been a member of the Sisters of St. Joseph of London. Prior to being named executive director in 1969, Sister Mary had served in a variety of administrative positions in the Order.

The associate director of the hospital was Mr. Chet Singh. Before joining St. Joseph's in 1982, Mr. Singh had been a senior official with the provincial Ministry of Health, which was responsible for overseeing the province's hospitals. Trained as a professional health administrator, Mr. Singh had a long history of health care management in Canada and abroad. Both Sister Mary and Mr. Singh had attended the Banff School's Senior Health Administrators' Course (SHAC).

St. Mary's Hospital and Marian Villa

St. Mary's Hospital was a chronic care facility which catered to patients who would require long-term hospitalization. A chronic hospital did not offer as intensive or as expensive treatment as an acute care facility offered. For example, although St. Mary's had 183 beds (153 chronic care and 30 rehabilitation beds) — approximately one-third the number at St. Joseph's — the hospital had an operating budget one-eighth the size of the active treatment hospital. The 1985 operating budgets of the two institutions were: St. Mary's — $9 million and Marian Villa — $3 million.

Located side by side, and physically linked through a connecting wing, St. Mary's and Marian Villa historically had a close relationship. As a home for the aged, Marian Villa came under the jurisdiction of the Ministry of Community and Social Services, while hospitals like St. Mary's and St. Joseph's were under the Ministry of Health. However, the two had always shared physical plant and services such as dietary and laundry facilities.

In 1980, a consultant studying the two organizations saw immediate potential for more sharing of services. Over the following few years, whenever there was the opportunity, changes were made to bring the organizations together.

By September 1983, the two institutions, although still separate entities, had common membership on their boards. The positions of executive director, assistant executive director-administrative services and the directors of finance and personnel were staffed by the same people in the two organizations.

Sister Cecilia Dronzek joined the staff of St. Joseph's Hospital in 1961 as a technologist in the Department of Radiology. In 1978, she was appointed chief executive officer of St. Mary's. In 1983, Sister Cecilia also took responsibility for Marian Villa and its 247 residents (97 residential and 150 extended care beds). In 1984, Marian Villa and St. Mary's were united with Sister Cecilia as the executive director (see Exhibit 3). Sister Cecilia, too, had attended the Banff SHAC, as had St. Mary's assistant executive director-administrative services and St. Joseph's assistant executive director-medical and special services.

Key Tasks at the Hospitals

Providing health services in the 1980s was a challenge. A key task in every health care facility was to provide the best patient care possible. At the same time, with government involvement and financial constraints, it was essential that hospitals stayed within budgets and acted as efficiently as possible. The challenge was to maximize both care and efficiency.

In a chronic care hospital like St. Mary's, usage was relatively easy to forecast. The patient load was fairly constant and the patients tended to require the same level of care. In contrast, in an active treatment hospital like St. Joseph's, patient load and the types of treatment required could vary greatly. However, even with this uncertainty it was important that an active treatment facility be able to show that the most efficient use had been made of its resources.

At Marian Villa and other homes for the aged it was also important to have good management and to provide efficient care. It was very difficult to define what services were really needed in a home for the aged or nursing home. Beyond very basic physical comforts, one could argue either that extra services were needed or that they were not really necessary. However, it seemed that both the public and government had confidence in organizations like the Sisters of St. Joseph. Their competency and experience provided the basis for addressing current management issues and for making the care/efficiency decisions and trade-offs.

Even with budget constraints, changing technology and increasing ethical issues, patient care was always the most important task. As Sister Mary explained, "It is our constant endeavor amidst this challenge in our healing ministry to ensure a constant respect for the primacy of people over things, ethics over technology, and the spiritual over the material."

Fundraising Concerns

London hospitals were making great demands on the city's philanthropic financial resources. Parkwood Hospital, London's other chronic care hospital, had just relocated to a completely new facility. Both St. Mary's and St. Joseph's were about to undertake projects to replace old facilities. The other active treatment teaching hospitals in the city were also involved in building (and, therefore, fundraising) projects — Victoria was building a brand new facility and the University Hospital was adding a major wing. Most of St. Mary's would be rebuilt for $26 million, and a $34 million wing was planned for St. Joseph's. Of the total cost, approximately $10 million would have to be raised from the community. Fundraising consultants had studied the situation and found that St. Mary's and St. Joseph's were perceived to be one entity. The community would support the building fund, but would be unlikely to accept two separate fundraising campaigns. In addition to fundraising campaigns by the health service organizations, there were numerous other fund drives in the city competing for donations. These included social services (United Way and the YMCA, for example) and virtually all of the cultural institutions such as the Grand Theatre, London Symphony Orchestra and the London Regional Art Gallery.

Given the fundraising realities, the boards saw that they had to present a united front to the community. Although the logic of combining the facilities had long been recognized, years of unsuccessful attempts to bring the organizations together led people to believe that there had been resistance at the top of the organizations. The building projects proved to be the catalyst that the merger needed, and the boards decided that they should merge their organizations. With the sisters and boards committed to the merger, it was hoped that the pieces could be fit together.

Other Reasons for the Merger

Improved patient care was often cited as an advantage of the merger. A combined organization, with an acute care, a chronic care and a residential facility, could offer more flexible services and a broader continuum of care. Patients could move between the three facilities without being discharged and readmitted with new medical histories and documentation being taken at each stage. The interaction of the medical staffs could improve patient care through the exchange of ideas. Chronic care professionals could learn acute care techniques, and acute care practitioners would be more likely to consider the broader problems of care for the aged.

The potential for financial savings also made a merger attractive. Operating economies from combining operations and reducing duplication could be dramatic, as could capital savings from sharing expensive equipment and from combined building services. For most of the staff, a merger would provide better promotional opportunities. A larger organization would have more jobs, more job openings and greater potential for advancement. Increased bargaining strength could be another advantage of an amalgamation. In dealing with the government, larger organizations might receive more and better attention. The increase in power and prestige would be of value when undertaking fundraising activities. Also, in the climate of restraint, the government had been pushing for greater efficiency through mergers and the sharing of services. A St. Joseph's – St. Mary's merger likely would be viewed with favor by the government, particularly in London where the three major teaching hospitals were all undertaking extensive building projects.

Resistance to the Merger

Over the years, staff had developed strong loyalties to their institutions and were concerned about the results of a merger. At St. Joseph's, there were fears that merging with St. Mary's could lessen their status — that the hospital would be "downgraded to chronic." People feared that St. Joseph's would give their expertise and receive little in return. A feeling of "What's in it for us?" was voiced by some.

At St. Mary's, there was a fear that St. Mary's would be "swallowed up" by the much larger St. Joseph's. People at St. Mary's took great pride in the excellent care given in the smaller, older hospital. They wondered if the quality of care would be compromised by a merger. The concern was that the larger, acute care teaching hospital could have costly technical programs that would siphon funds from St. Mary's "bread and butter" patient concerns. People also wondered if the St. Mary's medical staff of general practitioners would be "lost" — both in terms of status and in sensitivity to longer term care — among the highly-trained, active-treatment specialists at St. Joseph's.

There were other concerns as well. Administrative staff saw that there would be fewer opportunities if the institutions were completely integrated. The St. Mary's staff feared for their status under the merger. St. Mary's was a much smaller organization and, if forced into direct competition with their St. Joseph's counterparts, people assumed that those with experience in the larger hospital would have a decided advantage. Other staff knew that, in the long run, there could be greater promotion opportunities in the combined organization. But in the short run, people were concerned that some jobs might be lost.

When people voiced concerns they were careful not to couch them in personal terms. Rather than say, "I'm afraid for my job or my status," one would say, "Patient care might suffer." Since patient care was of paramount importance, these concerns were taken seriously. Resistance had been voiced at the board level, too. Although board members' concerns likely reflected their own personal opinions, board members often had loyalties to their administration and staff, so resistance from elsewhere in the organization could also manifest itself at the board level.

Past Experience

St. Mary's — Marian Villa

Marian Villa and St. Mary's Hospital had taken a long time to come together. The 1980 consultant's report had called for change in the organizational structures but change had been gradual. Little was done following the consultant's report until the executive director of the villa decided to retire in 1982. Simultaneously, St. Mary's was searching for a new director of finance, and so it seemed the proper time to begin the process of consolidation. The administrative and finance functions were the first to come together. Gradually other operations were combined when there was an opportunity and the potential for savings. Still, with Marian Villa providing residential care and St. Mary's giving chronic hospital care, it was not possible to integrate all activities. Even though the two organizations had been united, people still spoke of and had loyalties to "the villa" or "the hospital."

Previous attempts to merge St. Mary's and St. Joseph's

In the late 1970s, there had been talk of amalgamation which had resulted in some negative feelings. Since the rumbles had not been validated, Sister Mary was not sure whether they represented real grass roots concerns or claims of such by people interested in self protection. There continued to be talk of sharing of services, but limited progress had been made.

In 1982, an attempt had been made to combine the St. Mary's and St. Joseph's Rehabilitation Departments. There had been a supervisor of occupational therapy, speech therapy and physiotherapy reporting to a manager of rehabilitation at each hospital. When both positions of manager came open, it was decided to combine the Rehabilitation Departments under the one manager, and an individual had been hired from outside of London.

People were very upset. There were feelings that the hiring competition had been biased in favor of the outside candidate. The staffs involved were also extremely territorial and loyal to their respective institutions. People were concerned for their jobs. The feeling seemed to be, "If they can get by with one manager, won't one supervisor be next?" The staffs requested, and were granted, a meeting with the administration to voice their concerns. Judging the attempt to merge Rehabilitation a failure, top management backed off. The manager was reassigned and the departments were separated.

St. Joseph's Health Centre, Toronto

A similar situation had occurred in Toronto with the integration of St. Joseph's Hospital (an acute care hospital) and Our Lady of Mercy Hospital (a chronic care facility). The Toronto approach had been to set a date for the merger and work toward it. It was decided that as of March 31, 1980, the combined unit would be the St. Joseph's Health Centre. A single new board of directors had met on May 1, 1979, and the new organization was in place 11 months later. Even though the titles of the two major components were retained, the integration of the two hospitals was complete. Each functional hierarchy was structured as a part of the new health centre and did not distinguish between the two physical units except where there were overriding reasons to do so.

The Toronto situation was not as complex as the London one. There were not the concerns of being a major research and teaching hospital, the buildings were on the same property, and a home for the aged was not involved. Although Sister Mary had studied the Toronto merger, she was uncertain as to how relevant the Toronto model was for the London integration. As well, she wondered what lessons had been learned from the previous attempts to merge in London and how relevant those experiences were.

Amalgamation

The St. Joseph's, St. Mary's and Marian Villa boards were amalgamated in September 1984. An amalgamation committee had been struck and Sister Mary was named to head the combined organization. As she studied the situation, Sister Mary wondered about the degree to which the new organization should be integrated.

It would be possible to leave the current structures the same under the new, united board. At the other end of the spectrum, the organizations could be fully integrated under a strict time constraint as Toronto had done. Sister Mary wondered whether either of these options was appropriate, or if she should take a middle-ground approach with the partial integration of selected departments. Or perhaps this was an opportunity to reorganize along some completely new lines, rather than being limited to the existing organizational logic and structures.

St. Joseph's, St. Mary's and Marian Villa had a strong tradition of care. Sister Mary explained that organization and care were obviously linked. "We believe that culture equals care. If you disrupt the culture, you disrupt care." What organizational structure would maximize the use of resources without compromising patient care? Each institution had had a separate and unique pace, identity and culture. The challenge was to think in strategic terms of the whole health care organization, to realize the benefits of amalgamation, and to keep the distinctive character of each unit.

EXHIBIT 1
ST. JOSEPH'S HEALTH CENTRE OF LONDON

Location of the Three Health Care Facilities

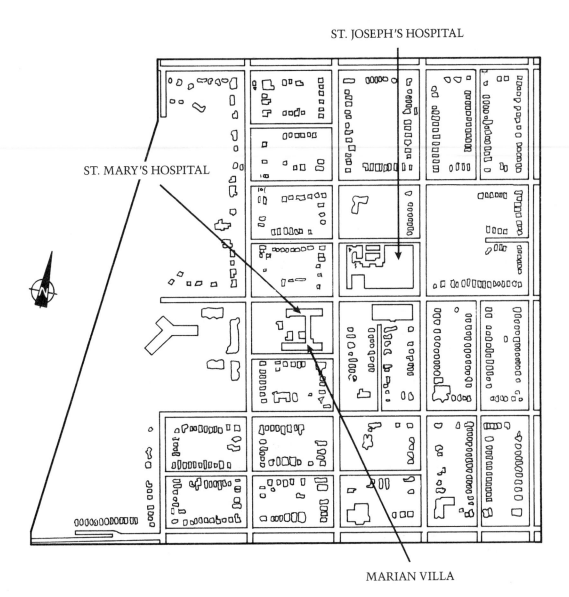

ST. JOSEPH'S HOSPITAL

ST. MARY'S HOSPITAL

MARIAN VILLA

EXHIBIT 2
ST. JOSEPH'S HEALTH CENTRE OF LONDON

Organizational Chart

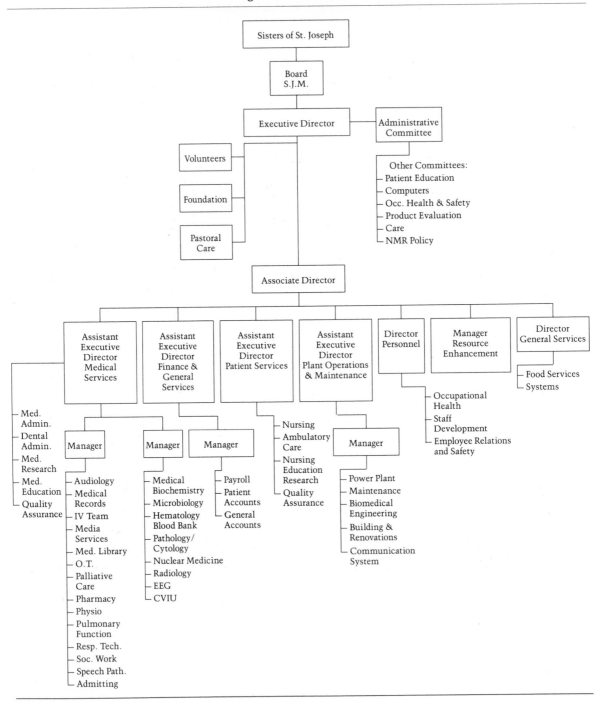

EXHIBIT 3
ST. JOSEPH'S HEALTH CENTRE OF LONDON

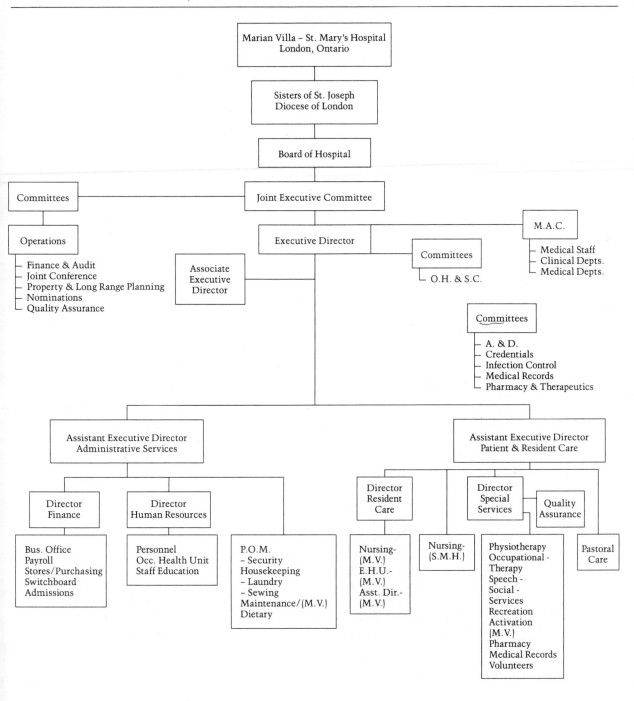

NORTHRIDGE PSYCHIATRIC HOSPITAL*

Henry W. Lane and Shawna O'Grady

In August, Dr. Monique Simpson, executive director of the Northridge Psychiatric Hospital, was wondering how she should respond to the recent annual audit of Northridge. The Correctional Service's audit team recommended that she consider the use of permanent program directors to head Northridge's multidisciplinary teams. Team members would report formally to a program director, in addition to the head of their functional department. Although program directors might solve some of the current problems with the program coordinator role, she felt they would also create others.

The Northridge Psychiatric Hospital

Northridge was an accredited, 135-bed, mental health facility operated by the Correctional Service of Canada. Its mission was to provide clinical assessment and treatment services for mentally ill patients of the criminal justice system at the high standards of hospital and psychiatric care required by the Canadian Council on Hospital Accreditation. The hospital was responsible for inmates who had been sentenced to two or more years for federal crimes. All inmates/patients were male.

Northridge was classified as a multi-level security penitentiary. Patients had security classifications from S1 to S7 (lowest to highest), and, therefore, Northridge functioned at a maximum security level. The hospital had a fence around its perimeter, and control centers were staffed by security personnel on each ward. Overall, however, it had an open atmosphere. Patients were allowed freedom of the wards and grounds, and their living units more closely resembled hospital rooms than prison cells. To stay in the hospital, inmates had to be certified or to consent to treatment, and to agree to obey the rules.

---

*Names in this case have been disguised.

This understanding, plus a well-trained staff, meant that there had been no major problems with escapes or other inappropriate behavior.

In addition to Northridge, the Correctional Service had 11 penitentiaries in the region which serviced 1700 inmates, plus another 500 people who, because of good behavior, were released to the community and were under mandatory supervision or on parole.

Organizational Structure

Northridge had four functional divisions (departments) and five programs (wards) of treatment. The three functional departments involved in treatment were Clinical Services, Psycho-Social Services and Nursing Services.

Clinical Services   The clinical division was responsible for the medical (drug treatment), psychiatric and program functions of the hospital. Patients were assessed and placed in one of the hospital's treatment programs. Psychiatrists in the division primarily were responsible for the medical aspects of patient treatment and for placement into one of the treatment programs. Once assigned to a program, patients were then under the care of a treatment team, coordinated by a program coordinator.

Nursing Services   Nursing staff were available on a 24-hour basis. They provided individual and group counselling, administered medications, and performed therapy as planned by the treatment team. The head nurse on each ward belonged to the treatment team for that ward.

Psycho-Social Services   The Psycho-Social Division coordinated the social workers, psychologists, and auxiliary services. Their major role was to prepare patients to return to the community or to another institution. Social workers were responsible for social/cultural programs, volunteer programs, case management documentation, transfer coordination, and parole liaison. Social workers assisted patients with family problems and concerns, and also coordinated patient interviews. Group and individual counselling was also provided. Psychologists administered initial tests to determine a patient's psychological status, which formed the basis for the patient's treatment. Group and individual therapy was also provided. Auxiliary services included occupational therapy and educational, recreational and religious services. Attendance at these programs was usually voluntary.

In addition to the functional departments, Northridge had five wards offering programs designed for specific problems.

Ward 1   This was the admission/assessment ward, which provided general assessments of inmates for parole hearings or, more frequently, determined suitability for treatment at the hospital. This ward also accepted emergency and crisis intervention cases. The assessment process usually took from three to five weeks to complete.

Ward 2   This ward handled acute and chronic psychotic patients. Psychotic offenders were individuals with major psychiatric illnesses. They could not function effectively on their own because they were not in touch with reality. Chemotherapy, art therapy, and individual and group counselling were some of the techniques employed in the treatment of these people. The programs continued until the patient was able to adequately care for himself and to participate in the activities of daily living.

Ward 3   This ward accepted patients whose abilities to cope with everyday life were impaired or deficient in some way. These marginal patients were offered a variety of life skills training in a supportive, structured environment. Training included behavior modification, assertiveness training, temper control, communication modules, education, recreation, and work programs.

Ward 4   This ward ran the violent offenders program. The prime emphasis was to reduce violent behavior by developing a sense of responsibility toward self and others. The primary mode of treatment was group therapy, in which personal interaction, communication skills, and general coping mechanisms were stressed. This was a two year program.

Ward 5   This ward treated sex offenders. The treatment was divided into eight steps over a period of two years, and it was more intensive than the violent offender program. Sexual offenders required assertiveness training, whereas violent offenders had to be taught how to control their aggression. The patients started by acknowledging responsibility for their offenses, and progressed through an understanding of the origin and operation of their crime cycles, controlling deviant fantasies, learning about thinking errors, and incorporating self-directed behavior into their day-to-day activities. Group therapy was the central feature of this program.

Professionals at Northridge did not necessarily have specialized training to work in a prison setting, and were not hired specifically for a given program. Some of the professionals were assigned permanently to particular programs. For example, a head nurse and 10 to 12 staff nurses were permanently assigned to each ward, and each of the five social workers was assigned to a program. Other professionals had multiple assignments and responsibilities because there was not enough staff to dedicate one to each program. In addition, there was an occupational therapist and an educational worker who offered programs which patients from all wards could attend. These personnel assignments, and an organizational chart are shown in Exhibits 1 and 2.

The hospital utilized a multidisciplinary approach to patient care. On each ward there was a treatment team comprised of staff from each of the various disciplines. The purpose of the team was to coordinate the disciplines to provide holistic care to patients. It was believed that patients' problems had many dimensions in addition to medical considerations. Regular team meetings were required to ensure that all aspects of a patient's problem were addressed, and to make efficient use of professionals' time. Patient care was enhanced because of an integrated treatment program for each patient.

The average length of time a patient remained at Northridge was one and a half years or, if they were being assessed, one to three months. However, one individual had been at the hospital for approximately eight years. The length of stay was largely dependent on the nature of a patient's problem and, therefore, the program to which he was assigned.

Committees

The organizational structure at Northridge was complemented by two committees: the Professional Advisory Committee (PAC), and the Hospital Executive Committee (HEC). The PAC was a forum for discussing issues from a professional perspective. The committee discussed developmental approaches to care, as well as the developmental needs and requirements of the programs. Members included the coordinators of the hospital's five wards/programs, and the directors of Nursing Services, Psycho-Social Services, and Clinical Services. The committee was chaired by Dr. Gardiner, the clinical director. Recommendations of the PAC for program development issues had to be ratified by the HEC. Issues relating to the treatment of patients were dealt with by the PAC.

The Hospital Executive Committee was made up of the executive director, who acted as chairperson, and the directors of Clinical Services, Psycho-Social Services, Operational Services and Nursing Services. The committee discussed issues such as hospital policy, the budget, and human resource management. Both the HEC and the PAC met every two weeks.

The Executive Director

Dr. Simpson had a PhD in Psychology and had taught at a university for a number of years. Wanting a more "real world" focus, she worked as a chief psychologist in the Correctional Service. She later decided that she would like a managerial position within Correctional Services. Realizing that she had no managerial experience, she spent one year rotating from institution to institution to gain as much experience as possible. For an additional year she worked as assistant warden at one of the institutions.

The Early Situation

When Dr. Simpson arrived at Northridge three years earlier, it had been without a director for two and a half years. The clinical director had been acting as director during this time. Dr. Simpson was the first non-medical person to fill the position which had always been occupied by a psychiatrist. However, the deputy commissioner of the region, Simpson's direct supervisor, felt that to correct the lack of structure and accompanying problems at Northridge, a person with management skills was required. Cost effectiveness was also an important concern, and psychiatrists were very expensive.

Martin Smith, the deputy commissioner, was very concerned about the lack of direction at Northridge, and felt that there was not enough feedback to the Correctional Service. In addition, he had just received the audit report for that year. The audit team had recommended that the hospital investigate applying a matrix type structure, like the one being considered for the penitentiaries. This would mean developing a team for each unit/ward that would be managed by a unit manager. Team members would report to the unit manager as well as to their functional department head. Smith asked Simpson to look into this issue as well as the other problems and to develop a plan to resolve them.

Dr. Simpson spent her first four months as executive director talking with the staff to determine what the problems and issues were. She commented on the overall situation:

> When I arrived, a structure existed on paper, but not in reality. Because people were left on their own, they had no formal process of communication. Everybody was attending all of the meetings — there were no representatives — which was inefficient. Then they complained they had no time for any of their own work.

Dr. Simpson explained that, although there was supposed to be a treatment team for each patient, there was no coordination between the various disciplines (i.e., among psychologists, social workers, etc.). Instead of an integrated, holistic approach, each professional really was responsible only for one aspect of a patient's problem. There was no way of developing accountability for a single patient because no one team member was in charge of a particular patient's program. This affected the quality of patient care, created difficulties when decisions regarding patients arose (such as release decisions) and also led to confusion and duplication of efforts among professionals.

Prior to Dr. Simpson's arrival, the hospital had attempted to change from a "medical staff model" to a "professional staff model." In the medical staff model psychiatrists, supported by nursing staff, were totally responsible for treatment programs. Other disciplines such as psychology, social work, and occupational therapy served only as adjuncts to the medical treatment plan. The professional model meant developing a multidisciplinary approach to patient care on each ward. Professionals from each of the various disciplines were assigned to work on one or more specific programs. Patients would be seen by each of the professionals separately, and then these professionals would meet as a team to discuss each patient's overall treatment program.

However, Dr. Simpson found that neither the structure nor the staffing of the hospital reflected this change.

Another problem centered around Correctional Services' requirement for consolidated summary reports of each patient's treatment and progress. Each discipline was filling out a separate report, with no unified report on a patient resulting. The multiple reports that were received often contained contradictions and, of course, duplication.

Dr. Simpson began to make some changes. She created the position of Director of Psycho-Social Services. Psychologists and social workers would report to the person in this position. Previously these two groups reported to Dr. Gardiner, the director of Clinical Services.

Dr. Simpson also presented a proposal for structural changes in the programs. The details of the proposal were presented to the Professional Advisory Committee (PAC) and the Hospital Executive Committee (HEC). The proposed plan was based on the premise that mental health services would be provided by a multi-disciplinary team wherein professional staff were equal partners in the delivery of services. To foster such a multi-disciplinary approach, each program would be headed by a program director with psychiatry, psychology, social work, and occupational therapy as integral disciplines within the treatment team, supported by a head nurse for that program, and a group of staff nurses.

The program director could be a psychiatrist, psychologist, social worker, occupational therapist, or head nurse, and was to be chosen on the basis of training, experience, and personal suitability. Each program director would have full responsibility for the coordination of the development and provision of a treatment plan, and would report to the clinical director with regard to any program issues. The program director would be responsible for ensuring the development and maintenance of current program objectives, and their regular evaluation. Although the staff within the programs would still be responsible to their respective divisional heads, they would also be responsible to the program director for those issues dealing with the delivery of service to their particular program. Dr. Simpson explained that by creating a program director, professionals could be coordinated on a patient's case. Moreover, it would resolve the issues of duplication.

The reaction to the proposal was mixed. It met the approval of the hospital executive, but not all of the treatment staff. Particularly upset was the nursing staff. According to Dr. Simpson, the director of nursing (now retired) was afraid that nurses would lose their control as primary therapists, and passed this notion on to her staff. The nurses also felt that it was unlikely that a nurse would be chosen to fill the program director's role, and nurses did not want to report to a non-nursing person.

Psychiatrists were concerned about their legal responsibility for the treatment of a patient. Psychiatrists, as medical doctors, were the only ones who could prescribe drugs and decide when patients could be released. They were unable to see how they could give up some of that responsibility to a psychologist, for example, if one was chosen as a program director.

Not knowing what to do, Dr. Simpson decided to ask the Professional Advisory Committee for suggestions. Through the PAC, the position of program coordinator evolved. A program coordinator, it was suggested, would organize team meetings and ensure a multidisciplinary approach to patient care. Unlike the proposed program director, however, a program coordinator would not have any authority over team members. They would continue to report to their functional heads.

The program coordinator idea also met with resistance, and there was a struggle to define what the program coordinator would do. There was concern that this new position would be unattractive because it demanded extra time and responsibilities without any authority. However, the program coordinator role was more acceptable than the program director position to most people on the committee, including the director of nursing.

This left Dr. Simpson with a difficult decision. She was particularly concerned with the threat that her proposal had presented to the nursing staff since nursing was the largest group. She also was worried about some of the problems the role of Program Director would create. For example, with a limited number of psychologists and psychiatrists available, it would mean that they would each be responsible to two Program Directors, plus their own functional boss. In addition, Dr. Simpson commented on the climate in the hospital at the time:

> When I arrived, many changes had been taking place. Nurses were very concerned with the multidisciplinary model. They saw my coming as a total banishing of the medical model. There seemed to be a negative view toward psychologists in the hospital. People seemed to feel that they were taking over the world. Being a psychologist, I knew I had a problem with credibility. Also, there were worries about the institution becoming a penitentiary instead of a hospital. The overall climate was one of real fear and worry.

After much consideration, Dr. Simpson decided to accept the program coordinator role, instead of a program director. She explained:

> You have to wait until the climate is right with these issues. I believe that it is much easier to get things done if the people who have to work with it think it is their idea. Then they'll push it downward. A program coordinator was one area where we could bend, and compensate for the other changes taking place.

Over the next few months, the program coordinator role was implemented. Members of each team chose from among themselves a program coordinator. The difficulty in making this choice led to a decision to rotate program coordinators every six months. The reactions to the program coordinator role, its implementation, and its functioning, were subjects of discussion by the Professional Advisory Committee for months.

The Current Situation at
Northridge Psychiatric Hospital

The casewriter interviewed a number of key personnel at the hospital. They provided their perspectives and opinions about the changes that had taken place, the functioning of the program coordinators and the multidisciplinary teams' program directors; and they gave their recommendations for improving the situation.

Director of Nursing (Acting)

Suzanne Grey began only recently in her position. However, she had worked in the Correctional Service for some time, and therefore was familiar with the issues at the hospital. She commented:

> When Monique arrived the nurses felt they were doing everything. Nurses did the complete patient assessment, and then the social workers would extract the information they needed for their reports and sign their name to it, so there was a degree of animosity there. There was a problem with getting involvement in patient care among professionals. There was no team approach. A psychiatrist was in charge of a unit and he ruled the roost. This wasn't necessarily official — it was just the way it was.
>
> When I arrived there was a lot of negativity about the changes in the organization. The person years (P/Ys) have dropped from 79 to 67 in nursing. Nurses actually have fewer duties, but they feel that there aren't enough nurses left to do the work. Everyone always wants more P/Ys. Overall, things are a little better now, but there are still some problems. Program coordinators have become frustrated because they have no authority to get people to the meetings. The problem is that no one takes the program coordinator seriously. It was felt that it was just another thing someone had to do, and there was resentment that you, the psychologist, are telling me, the nurse, how to nurse.
>
> I think program directors are a good idea, but it wouldn't work here. Old ideas and old politics would prevent it from working.

Suzanne Grey also explained that there were a lot of professional conflicts:

> There's a real negativism toward psychologists because they have no medical training. A lot of nurses were really upset that Monique was not a doctor. There's a lot of fear of change, because the nurses fear losing their jobs. This fear is the biggest threat to meeting our changing needs. And, nurses have always been suspicious of psychologists and social workers because they don't seem to do anything.
>
> The positive side of a program director would be that there would finally be some organization, and the work would be more evenly split. We need a functional emphasis and a program emphasis, but there has to be a functional emphasis. We need a modified unit manager — having a unit manager, but retaining functional managers too. But then there's the problem that nurses don't want to report to someone other than a nurse. Certain professional boundaries exist. It might work

if there was a functional nurse manager — a new role of nursing consultant — who nurses could go to with nursing problems.

Head Nurse A

The problems we have come from trying to run a hospital from within a penitentiary. It's the same medical care whether patients are criminals or not, but there are other demands, such as consolidated reports.

No nurse should report to anyone other than a nurse. Who can legitimately tell a nurse what to do? Only a nurse.

I am diametrically opposed to matrix type organizations. There needs to be some hierarchy for people to work well. I truly believe it's the only way it can work.

Head Nurse B

You can guess who does all the work around here. We do. The nurses do a comprehensive patient history and assessment with everything in it. I saw one social worker the other day copying the social section of a nurse's report for his own report to Correctional Services.

Staff Nurse

It's my feeling that the nurses carry the load. None of the professionals is focused on any one program. We are, and therefore do not think it is fair that they be over us when we are the ones in touch with patients. We'd like to see the other professionals around more, but they're just not committed to any one program.

Dr. Gardiner, Psychiatrist and Clinical Director

A multidisciplinary team cannot work unless people want it to work. A multidisciplinary team must sharpen its roles, responsibilities, and direction. A good program director could produce that. He must be able to see the views of each of the other disciplines — the strengths and what they can bring to the team — as well as being sensitive to the feelings of others.

The problem with program coordinators is that they don't feel they have the authority to do these things. They have to be careful not to be critical of their colleagues, and they have their other work to do. I don't think coordinators feel strongly enough that they can do what a program director could.

Dr. Gardiner discussed the disadvantages of changing to a program director:

There could be a problem with the nurses, who are limited by their traditional medical approaches. Also, could all the professionals function as equals? That is a key question. Psychiatrists, particularly, feel they are first among equals. To work, people have got to become more flexible.

Also, we've had too many changes. There needs to be a settling period. What has been changed needs time to grow. There's a lot of rigidity in the organization. The hierarchy needs to be flattened.

Then, more optimistically, he said:

> Personally, I think "let's try it." But don't put it in as a *fait accompli*. We would have to talk about it on the PAC and on the wards. Let people see it coming and have some say. Otherwise it wouldn't work. With the program coordinators we were not involved in the discussions.
>
> It all comes down to whether you can get good people as program directors. Putting professionals' skills together requires a certain *finesse*. That person would have to be a good manager, and that means good human relations skills.

Head Nurse and Program Coordinator (Ward 3/Marginals)

> Before the program coordinators, each discipline worked mostly independently and saw each other during conferences. But, each person's role and functions were relatively well defined. People were somewhat removed.
>
> My feeling is that the program coordinator role was imposed on us. There was no need for it. We were told that this is the way it has to be. It was very much top down.
>
> Before, the psychiatrist made the decisions. When nursing has to report to a team for a decision they're pressured into doing a lot of things they otherwise wouldn't do. Under majority rule you could sign a patient release when you knew the patient shouldn't be released. If three of five people on the team thought he should be released, it was a majority and the two were out of luck. And, some of the program coordinators were psychologists. Suddenly, they started saying "Here's the way we should be doing things," and began trying to run the show.
>
> Also, they told us that the program coordinator role would take up five percent of our time when, in fact, it takes 60 percent of my time. There was no written job description for the program coordinator at the time, and they gave us no direction on the new role.
>
> As a coordinator, I have difficulty getting people together. People have multiple tasks and they're not there when you need them. One team member who is a program coordinator of another program has assignments from his boss, and works on the sex offender program. So, there's no real team.
>
> I see no advantage to giving authority to the coordinator. Well, it might cut through the bickering and fighting. But, I have certain professional ethics I must meet. No one other than a nurse could understand a nursing role and, therefore, wouldn't always give my view proper consideration. To have a specialist telling a different specialist how to do their specialty — well — you can't do that.
>
> I'd like to see us get back to a treatment team where every discipline has certain responsibilities and there are functional parameters. Rather than giving authority to the coordinator, what we need is a restructuring of our facilities. We need to be physically close as a team with our offices next door to each other. Then you'd have a hands on approach to patient care. Now, psychologists are in a different part of the organization, so they come in, do their assessment, and leave. They're not around for communication.
>
> Duplication is not a problem. A disproportionate work load is. The nurses record everything. You definitely need communication and a treatment *team* concept, but we can't do their jobs for them. I don't feel it's my responsibility to talk to

problem team members, or to act as a heavy on another discipline to get them to attend team meetings.

It never would work, even if the coordinator had authority. There are a lot of personality conflicts. We're used to working on a medical model. I prefer to work on a medical model. The coordinator role shifted power from psychiatry and nursing to social work and psychology.

Overall, I would recommend a team concept, but emphasize that we work on the unit together—and that we go back to a medical model, where a psychiatrist directs the treatment.

Psychologist and Program Coordinator (Ward 2/Acute and Sub-Acute Patients)

As program coordinator, my main purpose is to ensure that there is participation of all team members. I have the problem of multiple loyalties. I act as program coordinator for the team, and I have my duties as a psychologist for two programs. With many meetings on all sides, it's inevitable that I cannot attend them all. The only way it would work is if there was one psychologist per program. Before the program coordinator, there was a team process, but the teams met more informally, on an as needed basis. I thought we had program directors before the program coordinator role, when the psychiatrists were known as unit managers. The psychiatrist accepted input from team members.

Going to a program director structure now would provide the opportunity for other team members to take the head role. People of various disciplines would be equally effective provided they were team players. It must be someone who acts with the consent of the team and who listens to the views of each of the team members. But, as a psychologist, it's better to report to a psychologist for professional issues.

Since the appointment of the program coordinators, things are the same or better. We are getting team involvement—no one person is dominating. Initially, we had personality/professional conflicts with the psychiatrists. Psychiatrists would not act as team members. And, nurses tried to get more than one vote because they represented more staff. But, we were given no guidelines about the program coordinator role. Each team was to define the role of coordinator for the team itself. There was a lot of debate about the role of coordinator with no clear definition. It could work better if there was a more clearly defined role. For the role of program coordinator to function effectively, he or she needs the goodwill of the team.

A program director who had authority would work better in the sense that there would be more control. Right now, the program coordinator is in a weak position. It's unclear what the coordinator does. It would be better if people reported to him. A potential disadvantage is that there may be cases where program directors may not fully listen to the team members.

Psychologist and Program Coordinator (Admissions/Ward 1)

Before the program coordinator role was created, psychiatry had all the power. There was a lack of direction in the various programs. Psychology and social work weren't seen as part of the team. Rather, they were seen as consultants — not having much to do with clinical management.

We have made progress. We definitely work together now. Two to three times a week we meet as a team. There's very democratic decision making.

I think the coordinator role was a compromise. A director would have been a challenge to medical authority. I think there was a conspiracy not to define the role of coordinator. There was a debate over whether it should be a coach, captain, trainer, or manager.

As a coordinator I'm always frustrated because we have no clean mechanism for decision making. There are problems with accountability and responsibility. The program coordinator role lacks teeth. We live according to the goodwill of the team. It's a bit loose.

I think almost any model would work on the admissions ward. Any model which would clarify the roles would be better.

But a formal model may not be as good as what we have now. If you try to define roles and reporting relationships too clearly there's trouble. Some people may have to go outside of their role's bounds to deal with a patient. If there is too rigid a model, people would start passing the buck, saying, "That's not my job." You need flexibility in any structure.

If program directors had line responsibility it could work if it was counterbalanced by a committee structure. We'd need one committee for program development and program management issues, and another for clinical issues. We need a better mechanism for resolving problems as they arise. The problem is that no one here has the power on behalf of a program to speak about program problems. We need someone who is responsible for program issues, rather than hope that everyone's going to forget about their disciplines and be concerned about the program. So it's not an issue whether it is a coordinator or a director, as long as the position has authority and responsibility for a program.

Then, of course, there are personalities. I don't think I could have gotten along with two of the three psychiatrists, but I get along fine with the one I have to work with. We need an organizational structure that minimizes conflicts.

Social Worker (Temporary Program Coordinator Ward 4/Violent Offenders)

One advantage of the coordinator role is that it does away with hierarchical relationships. It allows every discipline to take an equal role. The problem is not so much with the coordinator role, but with the team itself. There is a lack of resources — staff people. We don't have enough psychiatrists in the hospital in my opinion. They have too many tasks and they can't focus. They get stretched. People are not going to the meetings ... and their absence often means cancelling the meetings.

If the role had line authority and if the person was internally chosen there would be problems with discipline bias. I mean, how can nursing have line authority over social work? But, these are not insurmountable problems. If chosen externally, people would see it as a more fair and legitimate process. Nurses still tend to feel they should be running the program.

I'd recommend strengthening the role. I think it would work. Previously, it couldn't have worked, because they had social workers reporting to the clinical director, Dr. Gardiner, who's a psychiatrist. They felt they had no one on their side. Now, we have a functional reporting mechanism. (This was referring to the new position of Director of Psycho-Social Services.) We now have vehicles for working out most of those difficulties. Before, my frustration was, "Who do I go to with professional problems." It's a better system now.

Monique Simpson, Executive Director

My objective is to solidify the roles of the other disciplines. Their roles are not as extensive as they should be. Overall, the program coordinators have worked well, but it's still not perfect. There is still no single person in charge of a patient's case and there are no consolidated reports — just pieces. We have internal problems of duplication and also external pressures from Correctional Services. There is no formal procedure for making a decision about when a patient leaves. If there was a program director he/she would have foreseen this and done something about it.

The Annual Audit

In the fall of the current year, the annual audit of Northridge was conducted by a team from Correctional Services. Exhibit 3 outlines some of the findings and suggestions of the audit team. The team verified Dr. Simpson's concern about duplication and the hospital was still not meeting the need of Correctional Services for a unified report on a patient. Basically, the team recommended that Dr. Simpson review her original proposal to use program directors to head the multidisciplinary teams.

Over the last three years, Dr. Simpson felt that the program coordinators had functioned fairly well. However, there were still a number of problems that had not been resolved. Dr. Simpson had one final concern. Downsizing (reducing staff) had become a major issue in the Correctional Service. Dr. Simpson knew that this would directly affect the number of nursing supervisory staff employed at the hospital, because nursing had a much larger percentage of staff in supervisory roles than any other area. (16.5 percent of nursing staff were supervisory, whereas, it was 10 percent in other areas)

Dr. Simpson wondered what action she should now take. Should she leave the program coordinator role intact; change the role to a program director; or take some alternative action? She knew she would have to present her proposed plan of action to the deputy commissioner very soon.

EXHIBIT 1
NORTHRIDGE PSYCHIATRIC HOSPITAL

Organizational Chart (Northridge)

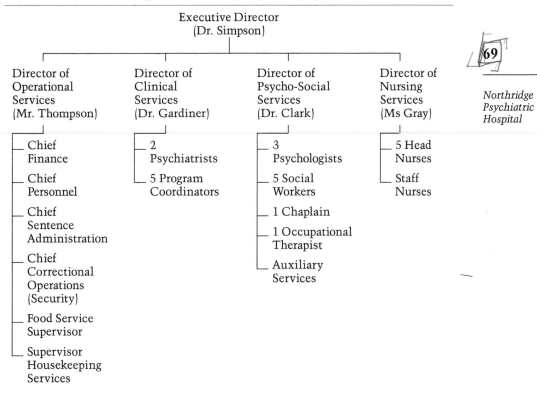

Executive Director
(Dr. Simpson)

Director of Operational Services (Mr. Thompson)	Director of Clinical Services (Dr. Gardiner)	Director of Psycho-Social Services (Dr. Clark)	Director of Nursing Services (Ms Gray)
Chief Finance	2 Psychiatrists	3 Psychologists	5 Head Nurses
Chief Personnel	5 Program Coordinators	5 Social Workers	Staff Nurses
Chief Sentence Administration		1 Chaplain	
Chief Correctional Operations (Security)		1 Occupational Therapist	
Food Service Supervisor		Auxiliary Services	
Supervisor Housekeeping Services			

Northridge Psychiatric Hospital

EXHIBIT 2
NORTHRIDGE PSYCHIATRIC HOSPITAL

Personnel Assignments

	Ward 1	Ward 2	Ward 3	Ward 4	Ward 5	Total
Head Nurse	1	1	1*	1	1	5
Staff Nurse	10–12	10–12	10–12	10–12	10–12	50–72
Social Workers	1	1	1	1*	1	5
Psychiatrists	2/5	2/5	2/5	2/5	2/5	2
Psychologists	1*	1/2*	1/2	1/2	1/2	3
Occupational Therapists	1/5	1/5	1/5	1/5	1/5	1
Educational Workers	1/5	1/5	1/5	1/5	1/5*	1

*Program Coordinator for the ward.

EXHIBIT 3
NORTHRIDGE PSYCHIATRIC HOSPITAL

Executive Summary

(From the most recent operational audit)

Although the audit team observed continued improvement in management and administrative practices, there are still some problems:

1.   There appears to be some inefficiency and overlap in the committee structure in the hospital. Although there appears to be an excessive number of meetings, interdepartmental communications have improved significantly. Staff appear satisfied with the overall direction provided by management and indicated support for many measures taken to improve administrative practices.

2.   The team feels that it is appropriate to now initiate further planning with respect to program structure and management. It is felt that the more systematic organization of

EXHIBIT 3 (continued)

major programs would greatly enhance the effectiveness of the hospital. Although the hospital has adequate person year resources, consideration should be given to reallocation of some of the resources in order to improve effectiveness.

2a. *Social Work/Occupational Therapy*

The challenge for the division lies in the continuing need to integrate case management practices into the multi-disciplinary approach. Nursing staff are slowly taking a more active role, with social work completing the majority of the documentation. Duplication of case recording and record keeping remains a problem. However, the integration of case management documentation into all phases of the treatment program will install a unified recording system.

2b. *Psychological Services*

In part, the problem is related to the present organization of the treatment teams using program coordinators rather than permanent program directors. Some psychologists are required to fill dual roles on the team (e.g. program coordinator and psychologist), and too few positions necessitate some individuals representing their discipline on two teams (e.g. psychology).

2c. *Nursing Services*

Coordination of nursing services with other health care providers i.e. medical, psychiatric, psychology, dental, radiology, etc. is well established. The multi-disciplinary approach is part of the treatment team concept in all program areas and has experienced some difficulties. It has been addressed by senior management and warrants monitoring in the months ahead.

Summary

The present organization and structure of the multi-disciplinary treatment team requires further review and development. The audit team notes that there has been continuing development of multi-disciplinary teams in delivering major programs.

The team feels, however, that there should be a much more formal structure of the treatment programs organized under a permanent program director. Although the present use of program coordinators facilitates program operations, it does not adequately provide for the most efficient use of resources. It is felt that permanent program managers would provide the following:

- Professional direction in specific program design
- Consistent direction and supervision of programs
- Integrated quality control process
- Professional evaluation of program effectiveness

Recommendation

It is recommended that a review be made of present program structure with the view of establishing permanent program directors within existing resources.

NEIMAN-MARCUS*

Henry W. Lane and Eileen Morley

Background

In late 1974, Richard Marcus, president of Neiman-Marcus, and Neal J. Fox, general merchandise manager, were listening to details of a marketing study of the Chicago area, where Neiman-Marcus planned to open a new store. Chicago was the second largest retail market in the country, offering both a strong demand for high-priced quality goods and intense competition for Neiman-Marcus. After the presentation Neal turned to Richard and commented:

> Much as I believe that centralized merchandising can work for us as we expand, Dick, I wonder if we shouldn't start thinking about some alternatives for organizing our merchandising activity — not in popular priced goods, but maybe in furs and couture and gifts. After all these represent about 25 percent of our sales, and they project our image and personality.
>
> I'm not totally happy with the way our present stores are selling these items now. I wonder what will happen when we get to eighteen or twenty stores. Can we continue to buy for them all on a centralized basis, or should we give the stores more autonomy?

History of Neiman-Marcus

Neal's words were an indication of the way the Neiman-Marcus organization had grown since it was first established by Al Neiman, his wife Carrie Marcus-Neiman, and her brother Herbert Marcus, in Dallas, Texas in 1907. At that time wealthy Dallas women had their clothing custom-made in Paris or New York; other women went to a local dressmaker. The three young entrepreneurs

---

*Copyright © 1975 by the President and Fellows of Harvard College.
This case was prepared by Henry W. Lane, Research Assistant, under the supervision of Eileen Morley, Lecturer, as a basis for class discussion rather than to illustrate either effective or ineffective handling of an administrative situation.

were convinced of the potential of the Dallas market for fine quality ready-to-wear women's apparel, even though such a thought was a daring innovation at that time. Their ideas quickly proved right. Neiman-Marcus grew with the Texas economy. Initially based on cotton and cattle, the source of wealth changed when oil was discovered and Neiman-Marcus found itself located in the heart of the Texas oil fields. Dallas prospered as a banking and trade center. Population grew from 84 000 in 1907 to 260 000 in 1930. The store prospered with the city as Herbert Marcus added other lines — men's and children's wear; giftware; jewelry and furs. Through the expansion however, he maintained the Neiman-Marcus image as a specialty store.[1] During this period Herbert Marcus bought out Al Neiman's share of the business and became president.

In the late 1930s and early 1940s Herbert Marcus wanted to expand and build other stores, but his plans were hampered by temporary financial problems and he never managed to do so. During World War II and the period which followed, industrial activity boomed in Dallas, which by 1950 had grown to 538 000.

In 1950 Herbert Marcus died, and his son Stanley[2] was elected president. Mr. Stanley, as he was known in the company, immediately began the expansion program his father had wanted. In 1951 he opened his first suburban store in the Preston Center Mall, north of downtown Dallas. The following year he built a central service center for both Dallas stores. In 1955 he opened a store in Houston and in 1963 another in Fort Worth. In the same period he added two hotel boutiques. In 1965 he replaced Preston Center with a new store in the North Park Shopping Mall. Other stores in Bal Harbor, Florida (1971), Atlanta (1972), and St. Louis (1974) followed quickly, and plans were under way to build in Chicago, Chevy Chase, Maryland and in two California locations. These were the stores which increased Neal Fox's concern.

Philosophies and Policies

Herbert Marcus had defined the Neiman-Marcus policies very early. The store was to concentrate on quality, exclusivity, good value at all price levels, and customer satisfaction.

As far as quality was concerned, he wanted to sell the finest and most fashionable merchandise in the world. He also wanted its selection to be unique. Stanley Marcus referred to this selection as editing:

> The quality that makes one paper like the New York Times really stand out lies in the editing. One paper features its foreign news on the front page, another buries

---

[1] A specialty store sold quality merchandise with highly personalized service and did not carry a range of hard goods such as furniture and appliances which could be found in department stores.

[2] Known throughout the store as Mr. Stanley to avoid confusion with Mr. Herbert Marcus. In the same way his son was known as Mr. Richard.

it . . . inside; one plays up violence . . . the other relegates [it] to its local news section. So it goes with stores. Essentially all of us buy in the same market but we select differently.[3]

At Neiman-Marcus exclusiveness meant more than sole representation and reliance on manufacturers' workmanship. It included the improvements in style and fabrication which Neiman-Marcus buyers insisted on and paid extra for—such as silk instead of rayon linings, and handmade buttonholes. The principle was always to improve the merchandise, never to reduce its quality in order to lower cost.

Herbert Marcus held actual price to be a poor indicator of value. Whether merchandise cost $5 or $50 000 he expected it to represent a true value to his customer. Despite its image of catering only to the very wealthy, the store always carried popular price merchandise. Stanley Marcus called it "a store with a split personality" selling fur coats or jewelry items at $50 000 but also doing a large business in $50 dresses.

Customer satisfaction was Herbert Marcus' final maxim. He believed there was a right customer for every piece of merchandise and that a merchant should match customers and goods, even if this meant losing a sale rather than selling an inappropriate garment or product. Stanley Marcus quoted his father: "There is never a good sale for Neiman-Marcus unless it is a good buy for the customer." His comment became the Neiman-Marcus "Golden Rule."

Beautiful, spacious, uncluttered store interiors and attentive personal service were also considered by Stanley Marcus to be highly important contributions to shopping pleasure and satisfaction—at a cost which the founders judged worthwhile.

> We want to sell satisfaction, not just merchandise . . . This may prove expensive to us and a few may take advantage of this policy unfairly but we are convinced that adherence to this idea will cement our customers' loyalty to Neiman-Marcus.

The Second Generation: Promotional Activities

The values and policies of Herbert Marcus established a strong foundation for the initial store operation. It was Stanley Marcus, however, who turned it into a world-renowned institution through his promotional genius.

> My contributions to the business took shape in my ability to translate the store's ideals into ideas that a larger number of potential customers could find credible. Somewhere in my education I had picked up a sense of promotion, an understanding of how to do things that would get a maximum amount of desired publicity, a flair for communicating with people by doing things that commanded attention.

In 1924 Stanley Marcus chose to leave the Harvard Business School after one year to help his father expand the Dallas store. He had worked in many

---

[3]All of Mr. Stanley's comments are taken from his book, *Minding the Store*. Little Brown and Co., Boston, 1974.

different departments and knew the organization inside out. His first promotional event was a weekly fashion show and luncheon which gave women a reason to shop in downtown Dallas during hot summer months. The shows ran for 28 years. In 1934 Mr. Stanley started a national advertising campaign in *Vogue* and *Harper's Bazaar*—then unknown media for a Texas store. This move enhanced the store's emerging national reputation but was also defensive. Mr. Stanley wanted to get the Neiman-Marcus name under the eyes of his Texan customers, who would otherwise assume that the exclusive merchandise advertised could only be purchased in New York. In 1936 he invited the fashion editor of *Vogue* to visit the store's Texas Centennial Fashion Show, and word of Neiman-Marcus spread even more rapidly. By the end of the 1930s the store had been featured in *Fortune, Colliers* and *Life* magazines. In 1938 Mr. Stanley established the Neiman-Marcus Award for Distinguished Service in the Field of Fashion—presented each year in Dallas at a fashion gala with an invited audience of thousands from the fashion world. All of these promotional activities immensely increased the sense of pride which the Dallas community felt in Neiman-Marcus.

The promotional feature for which Neiman-Marcus was best known originated with "Men's Night"—a pre-Christmas gift show at which men shopped for wives, daughters, lovers and friends. This event provided the original stories of extravagant purchases—such as the entire window display replicated in a customer's playroom on Christmas Eve. Mr. Stanley soon realized that newscasters had picked up these stories, so in order to ensure that he had something for them to publicize each Christmas, he invented unique and extravagant catalog gift offerings. The first such gift was "His and Hers" Beechcraft airplanes. Many others followed, ranging from Chinese junks to camels. Stanley Marcus commented:

> We usually sell from one to a dozen of these bizarre catalog offerings, but the important thing is that they help sell millions of dollars of gifts from our under $10 and under $20 pages...dresses, sweaters, neckties...and toys, of good quality and taste, which are sent all over the world.

The most spectacular promotional event was the annual "Fortnight" which Mr. Stanley started in 1957. In each, a particular country was featured both in the store and by the city. Art, music and entertainers were brought in, and cultural and social events were planned for the Fortnight. This was one of the ways in which Stanley Marcus tied the store closely into Dallas community life.

Merger with Carter, Hawley, Hale

In the mid-1960s, with four stores and an international reputation, Stanley Marcus wanted to expand beyond Texas. As with all expansion programs, financing was an important issue. Would internally generated funds be sufficient to support an ambitious program? Furthermore, while sale of stock would reduce family control of the business, how should the problems of management succession typical of family businesses be dealt with? As a result of these considerations, Stanley Marcus decided that the best course of action was to seek a merger.

The decision was not easy to implement because he insisted on finding a partner who would want Neiman-Marcus to continue doing business in its traditional high style. In 1969, after turning down other offers, Neiman-Marcus sold to Carter, Hawley, Hale, who promised Stanley Marcus the autonomy he sought. In the period 1969–1974, Carter, Hawley, Hale exhibited a "hands off" policy, demonstrating faith in Neiman-Marcus management ability.

Carter, Hawley, Hale's business consisted of specialty stores, department stores, bookstores, and a national catalog sales operation (Exhibit 1).

For the fiscal year ending February 2, 1974, Carter, Hawley, Hale sales were over $1 billion, with pre-tax income of $80.1 million. Neiman-Marcus contributed approximately 15 percent of the total corporate sales and Neiman-Marcus pre-tax profit in 1972 and 1973 exceeded the national average for specialty or department stores, which ranged respectively from 4.9 to 6.4 percent of sales in 1973.[4]

Expansion Outside Texas

Once the merger was accomplished, Neiman-Marcus went ahead with plans to expand. By late 1974 seven stores were in operation; six more on the way or planned, two of which would open in 1975–6; two more in Chicago and one in California were planned but deferred due to economic conditions; three additional California store sites had been located. [See Exhibit 2.]

The new stores were designed with the same high architectural and interior standards consistent with Neiman-Marcus's image — one of the world's finest specialty stores.

During this period, the downtown Dallas, North Park and Houston stores continued to provide the major share of sales volume, representing approximately 60 percent of total sales, with the remainder divided equally between branches and catalog sales.

Competition

Competition for Neiman-Marcus came primarily from small specialty store operators. The small store owner had more flexibility than a large chain store in responding to local environment. Store owners knew their customers, selected merchandise for their particular environment and market sector, and gave personal service. Collectively Neiman-Marcus was trying to do on a

---

[4]Financial Executives Division, National Retail Merchants Association, *Financial Operating Results of Department and Specialty Stores for 1973.*

grand scale what small stores were doing individually. Neiman-Marcus had proved that it could be done with a small number of large stores. The question now was whether it could continue to be done nationally, in widely dispersed and differing communities.

A different kind of competition came from other major specialty stores such as Saks Fifth Avenue, Lord & Taylor and I. Magnin. Neal Fox pointed out that he had watched some of these chains grow and could detect variations of quality among stores. In some cities the store had a price point emphasis, merchandise mix, and overall milieu that was inconsistent with their favorable pre-expansion image. He commented that this might well be related to location, and emphasized that it was crucial to choose only those areas where the Neiman-Marcus point of view and standard of quality could be established and maintained.

Reorganization

In 1972, Stanley Marcus reorganized the company in order to orient it towards future demands (Exhibit 3). He became chairman of the board—a move designed to allow time to work with a new president before he retired. Richard Marcus, his son, was elected president. He was 35 years old, and had moved successfully through positions in buying, merchandise management and store management.

Merchandising responsibility was divided between two senior vice president-general merchandise manager positions, instead of a single traditional role. Stanley Marcus explained that this move was intended to give each manager more time to concentrate on particular merchandise, establish more intimate contact with their departments, and find new market opportunities. In 1974 these two posts were held by Neal J. Fox, who had worked eight years with Neiman-Marcus after nine years' experience with Brooks Brothers; and by Murray Friedman, who brought 12 years' experience from Saks Fifth Avenue.

A new position of director of stores was also created at the senior vice president level. Richard Marcus commented that store managers had to seek help from many different corporate groups, and it was decided that these efforts should be coordinated as the number of stores increased, and that store management should have a voice at the top. The new Neiman-Marcus organization is shown in Exhibit 3.

How the Neiman-Marcus Organization Functioned

Store Management

The senior vice president and director of stores coordinated activities between the various Neiman-Marcus stores and the merchandising groups in Dallas. The occupant of this role was Max Brown, who had spent eleven years with a multi-store chain in Florida.

P   In Max Brown's opinion tension inevitably existed between buyers and store management personnel.

> Buyers may often feel they purchase great merchandise but that the store people don't know what to do with it. Store executives may wonder why buyers don't buy things that sell. It's my job to help synthesize the "buy" and "sell" aspects of the business.

Max Brown and the store managers reporting to him were accountable for the stores' sales, expenses and profits. Towards these ends store management was responsible for presenting merchandise, for directing the sales effort, and for control of store expenses. Max Brown referred to this process as a "four walls" responsibility.

P   The separation between merchandising and store management responsibilities was not always clear. Grey areas included initial inventory levels, price changes, and responsibility for taking markdowns. Max commented that:

> If store personnel are good communicators, they will provide judgmental input into the buying organization to change faulty distribution mixes. We need this input because customer patterns do change by store over time, so the distribution should change. But some buyers continue to write a standard mix.

The internal organization of a typical store is shown in Exhibit 4.

Two important characteristics of the store organization structure were (a) separation of operations and merchandising responsibilities, and (b) the informal yet expected and critical communications between central merchandise managers and buyers on the one hand, and store merchandise managers and department heads on the other. The store merchandise managers had direct responsibility for the selling departments. They assisted department managers with promoting and presenting merchandise, and coordinated merchandising interactions with the central buying group.

The first store outside Texas was opened in Bal Harbor, Florida. The store manager who opened the Bal Harbor store then moved on to manage the opening of the Atlanta store. He described his job as being the exporter of Neiman-Marcus standards into new areas.

> It's a challenging experience [not least because] customers expect to find 300 Stanley Marcuses behind the counters and every single piece of merchandise in the building to be different from anything they have ever seen before.

In his store, the manager and the two assistant managers worked as a team, meeting daily to discuss problems. He described changes he had seen during his seventeen years with the Neiman-Marcus organization.

> In the old days buyers also had more of a managerial role. While the buyer was involved in the department manager's role, the department manager had no say in buying. It was an overwhelmingly one-sided relationship. Now buyers concentrate on buying and managers on managing.

In addition to maintaining communication with the buyers in Dallas, a department manager's prime responsibility was sales leadership. This meant motivating a sales staff of up to 35 people while ensuring they lived up to the "Golden Rule" laid down by Herbert Marcus. One department manager commented that to accomplish this she had to keep herself motivated, which took a lot of time and maturity. She also stressed the importance of her sales people:

> They're not just clerks; they're important members of the team. Many customers have commented that they shop at Neiman-Marcus because the sales people make them feel special. It's important for the buyers to understand that customers shop here for more than just the merchandise.

On the store operations side, types of expertise were needed which contrasted sharply with the talents of merchandising and sales people. Management and motivation skills were needed in operations as well, but in more diverse areas. Operations managers were responsible for all support functions such as receiving and marking merchandise, accounting, packaging and mailing, maintenance, alterations, and fur storage. An assistant store manager for operations typically controlled an expense budget of around $250 000 per month.

One assistant store manager for operations found himself involved in improving the design of work areas in the Atlanta store.

> In the downtown Dallas store, goods sold on the sixth floor were manually transported to the basement for packing and shipping. Atlanta's system of belt conveyors and chainveyors on which sales people hang garments to be transported three floors to the basement are all great improvements.
>
> The receiving and ticketing area was designed by people who were not totally knowledgeable about work functions. By changing locations and redesigning work flow I was able to reduce the number of employees in that operation from twenty to twelve.
>
> There were no work standards when the store opened. I believed a person could make a certain number of tickets and hang a certain number of garments in a day, and I set out to find a standard. We started with 1200 garments a day and increased it to 2500.

The St. Louis store manager also commented on the critical future role of operations.

> My assistant store manager for operations came from the systems and planning area of Neiman-Marcus. He has a real love for the detail of the business — for seeing that standards of productivity are met and improved. He's done a great job staying on top of expenses and the operations part of the store. Thirty to forty percent of store personnel are in operations and it's a really important area. It can well determine profitability.
>
> Merchandising is the area of the store that's going to keep the doors open, but over the years I think it's been romanticized. I see a great upgrading of the

operations end of the business. It used to be almost a stigma. Now it's gained great respectability. However, there's still a lot of room for improvement. The non-selling department managers are usually not college graduates and there aren't adequate training mechanisms for operations people.

Merchandising

Reporting to the two senior vice president-general merchandise managers were various vice president-division merchandise managers. Buyers in turn reported to division managers. (Exhibit 5)

Due to differing volumes of business, and different gross margins, different departments commanded different levels of attention and concern, as well as resources.

Richard Marcus spoke of the effect of an economic downturn on problems facing merchandisers in 1974:

> Inventive buying has become even more important as quality manufacturers go out of business and resources in the marketplace dry up. Many young buyers grew up in an era of declining quality, which inevitably affects their standards. At the same time a large segment of manufacturers can no longer produce to old standards at reasonable prices. Everyone is buying from the same source, and consequently all the stores look alike. The traditional Neiman-Marcus emphasis on improving merchandise is more critical than ever now.
>
> Buyers still really need to know what a manufacturer can do to improve the product, rather than how to take something out to reduce the price. We will go to market with buyers, and also counsel manufacturers. One of our challenges is not to be tempted to lower our sights, but if anything, to raise them. I'm not convinced that when the economy is down people who have experienced better quality merchandise will step down to something of lower quality — they may well buy fewer pieces instead.
>
> At one time differences in labor costs in Europe made buying there advantageous, but inflation has changed that too. The newer markets are in the Far East and in South America where manufacturers can produce quality. But they haven't developed the fashion flair of Europe. This means that fashion buyers and merchandisers have to spend a lot of time in the market developing design ideas, and not simply buying goods already made. They sit down with manufacturers and create their own styles, and fashion excitement is often created by the items which result.

The division merchandise manager for gifts talked about his job.[5]

> The prime job of a merchandise manager is drawing up the sales operating plan for his departments and following up by working with buyers in individual areas. It's important to be able to make decisions about where to put the money. Am I going to put it into food service or the bath shop? Within food service does it go into

---

[5]His division included decorative home and hard goods such as china, silver, antiques, bedroom and bath shops, fine linen, and the epicure shop.

conventional things, or into the greatest new line of ashtrays I've seen in years? These are value judgments. Each buyer has to be gutsy and take a chance.

A division merchandise manager is also responsible for setting the taste and quality level in his division and for developing creative merchandising themes.

We start much of it here in-house. A buyer came to me with a great picture of ripe juicy tomatoes. Another buyer suggested we should do a glass with luscious tomatoes on it — maybe a new type of Bloody Mary glass. That was great but we had to use the design in other ways too . . . a new line of tomato red cookware. The bath shop buyer is going to do a beach towel with a big red tomato. The dish buyer remembered dishes in the market that would fit nicely. We also had some tomato-red Haitian coasters. Before you knew it, we had the whole theme for spring — Tomato Red.

In addition to imagination and creativity, the division merchandise manager said that buyers need to be knowledgeable in the field as a whole and about Neiman-Marcus customers.

Buyers have to have knowledge to back up their creativity. I'm looking for an antique buyer, a person who has a knowledge of Chinese, Japanese and European antiquity. That buyer would have to go to market and come back with the decorative accessory antiques of the type Neiman-Marcus wants. Something priced within means of, not necessarily a modest customer, but not a museum either.

They have to have an inventory in proportion to their clientele and really know them. They have to remember that it's easier to buy than sell. I have customers call me directly on specific merchandise. If I have it in inventory and it's a fine piece, I even place it in their home. It's service like this that makes Neiman-Marcus different.

Neal Fox commented that customer knowledge of this kind was equally vital in couture:

It's difficult for a buyer to go to market — even with a great deal of knowledge and preparation, without knowing the customers. It creates confidence to know that the blue dress with sequins coming down the runway is perfect for Mrs. Smith. It might be a $750 dress and there is always a moment of truth when you have to make a decision.

Division of Responsibility Between Merchandising and Store Management

Unlike many retail organizations, the Neiman-Marcus central buying group was not responsible for displaying or selling merchandise in the stores. The merchants planned inventory levels in different kinds of merchandise, procured and priced it, planned advertising campaigns, and determined initial distribution. They also planned sales promotions and provided selling departments with salient information about fabrics or fashion news. Store department managers were responsible for actual display and sales.

Two-way communication was important in a multi-store operation of this kind: information from store branches to buyers about what was selling and being asked for; information from buyers to store sales personnel about what merchandise was coming, and how to treat merchandise at point of sale. One way Neiman-Marcus achieved this was by video-taping fashion shows put on by designers at the downtown Dallas store and sending the tapes to other stores, simultaneously presenting the message firsthand in all locations. Other buyers made training video-tapes on such special topics as varieties of jade, latest men's fashions, or the treatment of damaged merchandise, which were circulated in the same way.

Elements of Profitability

Richard Marcus indicated that two basic elements of profitability which concerned him most were gross margin and expenses. A number of factors contributed to achieving gross margin, particularly properly determined markups and inventory levels. Buyers for each department had different individual markup goals depending on merchandise. The buying group also had a collective markup objective. For domestic goods under the retail method of inventory, the markup was approximately 40 percent – 50 percent, standard in the industry. Because of this, buyers needed to find unique merchandise so they weren't tied as strongly to competitive pricing. Richard Marcus also said that the Neiman-Marcus philosophy of value at all prices also meant that buyers were not constrained by a fixed price-line concept covering either a few selected price points or an entire range of prices. Price ranges were determined by the quality of available merchandise, but buyers had to be conscious of the fact that too many inexpensive items would lower the store's average "sale per square foot." Murray Friedman, a senior vice president-general merchandise manager, commented:

> It's a constant struggle. Do you need the extra volume at the expense of sacrificing a standard that you need to survive? We shouldn't sacrifice standards for the sake of getting other customers.

If inventories got out of line, unplanned markdowns were taken and gross margin diminished. Richard Marcus explained that markdowns were charged against a buyer's performance, because in most cases markdowns exceeding plan resulted from over-buying, not from failure to sell an inventory that was on plan.

> Inventory management is absolutely essential, and both buyers and store personnel have to be concerned about it. When a buyer goes into a store and sees merchandise that came in three days earlier still in the stockroom and not on the floor, and it is marked down and sold six weeks later, whose fault is it?

In a similar vein one merchandise manager commented that:

> You often hear stores complain when inventories are below plan, but never when they are above plan, even though excess inventory later gets marked down.

In 1974 the stores were experimenting with a new markdown system. Under the traditional system, initial markdowns (usually 33–40 percent) and second markdowns (50 percent) had been dictated by the buyers and implemented in all stores simultaneously. With the new system, judgment on timing of the second markdown was given to store management because it was difficult for buyers in Dallas to feel the rhythm of sales in different areas, or to know which stores should go to 50 percent immediately. Making this a local procedure also saved buyers' administrative time.

The second determinant of profit was expenses, according to Richard Marcus. These included direct store expenses and a pro-rated share of non-assigned multi-store expenses such as executive salaries, credit and advertising costs. These were charged as a percentage of sales. Richard Marcus saw a real irony in these interactions.

> If the stores went haywire and really exceeded their expense plan substantially we would rarely respond by making cutbacks in the merchandising procedures. But the opposite does occur. If we get over-inventoried and take higher markdowns and lose our gross margin, then we have to make up for it some place fast and the fastest place is in store expenses. The stores say, "Thanks for coming back again. How much blood do you want this time?"

Other Interactions Between Merchandisers and Store Management

Richard Marcus commented that perhaps the most common confrontation between merchants and store management occurred when a buyer went into a store, didn't like the way the department looked, and started rearranging merchandise.

> A wise store manager will find a way to straighten out the buyer and explain that, though he wants constructive ideas, "Don't come blowing in here and changing everything." Store managers have to be able to mediate situations like that. It's easy to tell which buyers have had past store management experience — their perspective is different. Those who lack this are apt to get on their high horse too frequently.

He explained that one important aspect of the store manager's role was credibility with buyers so he or she could intervene without a fight.

> Managing those relationships is a day-to-day challenge that everyone has to work on. I think it would be impossible to try and clear the air forever by mandating these relationships, and anyway, such an action would probably be stifling.

One store manager commented on the interaction of buyer and store department manager on inventory:

> I see a need for more store autonomy, not in buying but in reordering. I think the ideal would be for the buyer to be a selector and make the initial buy, but have department managers reorder merchandise that is selling. Our reorders now

depend on the buyers' funds. Many multi-store companies do this by store. We don't.

At the same time he recognized the skills of Neiman-Marcus buyers:

> I feel that our buyers are the best in their specialties in the world. I want that knowledge in my stocks.

Another department manager in *couture* described the way in which buyers made efforts to keep communications with department managers open.

> I make two market trips a year with buyers. Even though markets are thinning and many manufacturers are shutting down, I feel our four buyers are exceptionally selective and this is a primary reason I can build up my business. It helps me a great deal to know how they make their decisions and what to expect.

Several other department managers reported making similar trips with buyers.

Planning and Measurement Systems

Sales plans were established by the divisional vice presidents (merchandise managers) and their buyers for two separate seasons, or six month cycles — February/July and August/January. The planning was done department by department within each division for each store location; and collectively for all stores. For example, Atlanta might have its sales planned at 105 percent of the previous year, while St. Louis was planned at 108 percent, both within an overall corporate sales objective of, say, 106 percent. The merchandise managers and buyers determined the levels of inventory, including receipt of new merchandise required to achieve their sales plan. They planned the dollar value and mix of inventory, and the dollar value of markdowns for each store. They monitored their performance month to month using stock-to-sales ratios set by the general merchandise managers.

The plans for each season were a result of a process which Neal Fox called "plan as you go." At the end of each month, when statistical data was available, the buyers and merchandise managers re-evaluated that month in light of their plan and made projections for that same month for the next year. They looked at their performance on sales, inventory levels, and markdowns by location, and decided where improvements could be made. They committed these projections to paper and sent them to Neal for review. Neal reviewed performance monthly with his merchandise managers and buyers, and at the end of a six-month season reviewed their cumulative plans for the following year.

At the end-of-season review Neal told merchandising managers and buyers the overall corporate sales goal as well as the goals for each location so that they could adjust their planning documents accordingly. The corporate goals were established jointly by the general merchandising managers, director of stores, and treasurer, under the overall direction of the chief executive officer.

Neal Fox did not give his people these goals earlier because he did not want their planning hindered. He said:

> I try to encourage my people to think of the business as if it were their own, and make continual efforts to improve, but without undue pressure.

Sales goals were also established by store management as the basis for setting expense goals. Neal commented that the merchandising people tended to set more optimistic goals than did store management:

> For instance, I might plan sales at 105 percent of the previous year's sales, while the stores plan expenses at 102 percent of the previous year's sales.

This was an advantage when sales goals were reached, because the differential between the two figures was all profit, but when sales goals were not reached, inventory backed up, creating unplanned markdowns and gross margin erosion. Neal Fox indicated, however, that with the economic slowdown these sales goals were tending to be closer, and that eventually both groups would probably use one mutually reconciled sales objective.

Information Processing

Richard Marcus, Neal Fox and Murray Friedman all agreed that they would like their merchandise system to be more refined. Store expansion was beginning to strain the present manual unit control system. Under this system a merchandise position report (MERPO) was produced twice a month by the MIS group at the Dallas Service Center showing basic inventory and sales information for each store location. It was prepared from reports of cash sales, sales audits, accounts receivable and markdowns sent to Dallas by the stores and it usually lagged one week behind actual merchandise sales. The buyers used this report, along with a form showing their consolidated, monthly merchandise orders, to compute their "open to buy" — the amount of money they had left to spend that month. This MIS group also produced a weekly Markdown Analysis Report, listing markdowns by store and department from worksheets prepared in each store. The report compared the actual dollar amount of markdowns against the sales plan and against the previous year's markdowns. It was used primarily by the buyers during high markdown periods such as the end of a season.

Each merchandising division had a unit control office. In these offices data from ticket stubs were entered in unit control books as merchandise was sold or transferred between stores. While the Unit Sales Analysis Report was an ongoing process, it was recapped and analyzed monthly. The report provided a breakdown of sales by store, department, classification (i.e., cotton dresses, pantsuits, etc.) and gave rate-of-sale information. It facilitated analysis of sales by classification and price points and allowed buyers to reorder in proper volume. This report, like the others, went to the general merchandise managers, merchandise managers, appropriate buyers, and store managers.

The executives at Neiman-Marcus realized that buyers needed almost daily information on how their merchandise was performing; how much stock they had in-house; and how much stock on order. The executives also realized that their system was old and that some of their competitors reported this information on a more timely basis while it was still highly actionable. Neal Fox explained that:

> by "actionable" I mean that a buyer has time to reorder or to move goods from one store to another. If a $250 dress isn't moving in St. Louis where there are four pieces, but three of the four in Dallas have already sold, then she could move them from St. Louis to Dallas.

Richard Marcus commented that improving the information system should allow their basic stock programs to be improved. One way of decentralizing the buying functions would be by delegating maintenance of inventory levels of certain basic items back out to the stores.

> With expansion we can't expect the buyers' offices to process all the routine flow. We need standards and systems to handle that. One possibility might be a separate basic stock unit in Dallas, but outside the buying offices. A buyer would set minimum stock levels and quality criteria for merchandise, but the paperwork traffic would be done outside his office.

For Murray Friedman the need for a new system seemed relatively urgent.

> From a merchandise point of view we are behind the times with the control system. We need a more automated system and we need it fast for merchandise information — date of receipt — rate of sales — on-hand by style and store. You can't operate a multi-store operation without it. We're on manual unit control right now. It's going to be difficult to expand properly without a proper system. We can do it but it makes the buyers' job tougher — increases reliance on stock counts and escalates communication between buyers and stores, because they have to spend more time getting information about what's happened in the stores.

Rewards and Compensation

At Neiman-Marcus everyone except sales people were on straight salary. Until 1971 the merchandise group had a bonus system, but this was discontinued because it was considered unfair to offer it only to the merchants. At the time of the change the company added a percentage figure to merchandisers' salaries, based on each person's historical bonus earnings. No changes in the incentive systems were being contemplated. If any improvements in rewards were made, Richard Marcus said that these would probably be in terms of increased benefits.

> Some incentive systems lead people into short-term thinking — maximize today and let tomorrow take care of itself. We would like to develop the kind of philosophy whereby people realize they have strong opportunities to earn, based on meeting longer-term objectives.

Plans are there to be met — that's basic. But we also look at other subjective areas as well, such as the level of housekeeping for a store manager. On the more subjective items we try to get concurrence on standards.

One store manager mentioned his own performance evaluation:

> I'm evaluated more and more on profit, and that lost gross margin can really hurt. I'm also evaluated on maintaining a good merchandise image and good morale in the store. It's an appropriate procedure. I don't like the thought of someone telling me my whole career is based on profit and loss because in that case I'd have a whole store full of items that delivered the best gross margin, and not a quality store, and that would be an image change that Neiman-Marcus wouldn't like.

Career Development

Two separate career paths had previously existed at Neiman-Marcus for merchants and store management. In the past two years a new training program had been introduced in which everyone followed a course alternating between the two. A typical sequence of assignments would be:

Assistant Buyer → Store Department Manager

Buyer → Assistant Store Manager for Merchandise

At the assistant store manager level a crossroads was reached and people had to choose either merchandising or management. The senior executives all said they felt this flexible interchange was essential, at least through the buyer rank. Richard Marcus said:

> It's important for buyers to have experience in the stores so they understand the problems of running departments offering merchandise which five or more buyers are shipping into, and trying to motivate a sales force at the same time. It's also beneficial for store department managers to understand that manufacturers aren't just sitting around with goods waiting to be shipped; that buying involves a lot more than placing orders.
>
> I see a great deal of progress in the previous five years in raising the stature and responsibility of store management as a career. There was a time when buyers and merchandising managers were in all the positions of authority and store management wouldn't consider standing up to them. Now store managers and divisional merchandise managers are at the same level of responsibility — vice presidents — and are paid accordingly.

Max Brown commented that the Executive Progression Program was capable of producing senior store managers for the new stores at the present rate of expansion.

> It is easier to take Neiman-Marcus people and train them to qualify for a job than to take someone already qualified and teach them Neiman-Marcus.

This resulted in transferring 28 people from Dallas to St. Louis at considerable cost. The policy, which offered many career opportunities, had resulted from experience in opening new stores. Richard Marcus commented:

> In all new stores the top management are Neiman-Marcus people. In Bal Harbor many of the department managers were hired from the local area, but they had difficulty "unlearning" their way of operating and learning our way. The result was a complete turnover of department managers within eighteen months. In Atlanta 60 percent of the supervisory force came from within Neiman-Marcus, but there another problem showed up. We probably hadn't set our sights high enough in some instances. People were eager to go to the new stores because they were losing ground in their existing position. As a result we took care to staff St. Louis initially with 80 percent strongly performing Neiman-Marcus people.

Training for New Store Openings

The St. Louis store manager said he was convinced of the importance of training sales and service personnel by experienced Neiman-Marcus managers.

> I had 6000 applications for 393 sales and operations jobs. By the time I finished hiring I had the cream of the crop. I brought every sales and service person into the store thirty days before opening for business and spent that time explaining what Neiman-Marcus was all about and its philosophy for dealing with people. Department managers discussed merchandise, selling points, quality factors, and why the store did or did not carry certain merchandise. I believe a great rapport and ability to communicate developed during this period.

Expansion Issues

Neiman-Marcus' store expansion program presented challenges at many levels. A key issue was choice of communities in which Neiman-Marcus standards could be established and maintained and where the store could also stand alone and grow as part of that community. While each store would have a different merchandise mix, all had to project a consistent Neiman-Marcus image to customers.

Once a store was designed and constructed another challenge consisted of identifying and responding to local needs and preferences. In Atlanta, the assistant store manager for merchandise commented that since a different merchandise mix is generally required in each store, communication about local lifestyles to Dallas was essential: "This is one of my jobs." Sometimes educating the local market was also necessary. The St. Louis store manager remarked that:

> This city is probably more traditional and less fashion-minded than Bal Harbor or Dallas. I see an educational process ahead of me. We've proved we can sell some higher priced merchandise but giftware is behind expectations and so is *couture*.

In Atlanta the store manager commented:

> I feel this market perhaps isn't ready for our really total concept of *couture*. Many customers are probably still convinced they could buy *couture* at a lower price. The women here have been largely educated by another store in the city, which presented an image of *couture* which isn't ours.

The store responded to this situation, not by downgrading its *couture* range but by getting a change in the percentage commitment to a designer whose apparel had been well received, from 10% to 25%. Local tastes had to be explained very carefully to buyers the first year.

> I felt our managers might be guilty of wanting to stock the items the Atlanta customers wanted to buy — even if they weren't altogether our standard — and not trying to educate them. If the buyers bought only lower priced *couture*, that would lower our standards.

Another problem involved the need to increase the number of central merchandising personnel in order to provide buying support as each new store was added. In 1974 Neiman-Marcus therefore had many new young buyers with departments having a $3 or $4 million sales volume. Richard Marcus commented:

> These new young people don't thoroughly know our philosophies. They say they know them but they haven't lived with them long enough to have internalized them. Unless they do, we shall end up looking like everyone else.

The problem was complicated by a shift in economic conditions which Murray Friedman noted:

> Buyers in the last ten years have bought to the market and over-bought because they could sell everything they bought. It was a glamor era. Young buyers have never had to face problems. It's a tremendous teaching job, making a buyer a buyer again instead of a market selector. You work one-to-one and train them to Neiman-Marcus. It's basic.

John Mashek, vice president in charge of the mail order operation, uncovered yet another problem.

> In talking to buyers about getting a better markup on some exclusive items submitted for mail order, I found they thought the kind of markup which is necessary and normal at Neiman-Marcus to be almost immoral. These young buyers had grown up in the retail business during a period of heavy regulation and price control and had been subjected to more stringent pricing and categorizing of merchandise in the previous four years than perhaps ever before. We now have to educate them in our standards and operations so they will understand our principle of good value at all price levels and that we're not out to gouge the customer.

One store manager described a different shift in orientation — of people promoted from assistant buyer to department managerships in new stores.

> A department manager's prime responsibility, in addition to communication, is

sales leadership. This means motivating a staff of up to 35 people. For people who were in buying offices without anyone reporting to them, this is initially a huge change. They have been primarily technicians. Now they have to be aware that everything they say has an effect on other people. Also that they're much more independent and able to structure their way of doing business.

Opening new stores also changed people's perceptions of the merchandising-store management relationship. An assistant store manager commented:

> Before we felt that everybody should get along and be very nice — don't make a controversial decision without a lot of memo writing, which stifled any change. It certainly made it difficult to react quickly, which is the key to high performance in retailing.
>
> With the opening of this store, buyers have listened and been responsive to what we said. In cases where we asked for merchandise they didn't think was right for this store, we were able to go to the merchandise manager. He usually indicated that we should do what was right for the store and each side might have to adjust. This is the real change — recognizing that confronting differences of opinion is good and constructive.
>
> When my department managers come to me I try to convince them that confronting the buyers is constructive. They don't have to tell them that the merchandise is fabulous if they don't believe it. There used to be a great tendency to do that. This change really started when we began to expand outside Texas. We built so many stores in other places that buyers needed this information, since we had gone beyond the point where they could watch each store carefully. Now they recognize the value of getting it from us since they can no longer generate it themselves.

As Neiman-Marcus expanded, the size of individual stores remained approximately the same. The merchandising organization was under great pressure however, to expand to meet the greatly enlarged merchandise needs of the whole organization. The fur merchandise manager had already conjectured how he might recommend restructuring his fur department if expansion made it necessary.

> If we were to have regional divisions, Washington, Atlanta and Florida would be one; Chicago, St. Louis would be a midwestern division; the Texas complex another; and California the west coast division.
>
> Buyers could basically become technicians concerned with purchasing quality skins, arranging contracts with workrooms to have coats made; finding new markets and being fashion innovators. The decision as to what merchandise went into each area would be up to regional merchandising management.
>
> In a multi-store operation, coordinating transfer of expensive merchandise is a headache. It's easy to have a large inventory in transit or even lost or stolen. With a regional structure, buyers could be involved if really big ticket items were transferred between regions — perhaps even get on a plane to make the deal and come back with the merchandise; much better than having a $30 000 fur coat sitting in the mail for a week.

We could also have regional sales. For example, all "fun" furs in the southeast region could be sent to Florida for a week; then moved on to Atlanta.

A china and crystal buyer had already experienced some adverse effects of expansion.

> The stores have to find competent people who know the quality of merchandise, and have the expertise necessary to sell it. Just receiving it and getting it onto the selling floor is a problem which will increase with each new store opening. And with expansion, each new store will be more difficult to visit. This is already happening. My merchandise manager comes back from a store and asks when I was last there. I tell him the last time was when I was budgeted to go. I have budgets to live with and so do the other buyers. We would like to get out to the stores more often.

Other problems which he reported had to do with the balance between work and personal life. He commented that he had a wife and children at home who liked to see him once in a while, and he wasn't at all certain how he could handle twenty stores. He saw the buying job:

> ...getting so bloody big that it will probably have to be redefined. I have all I can handle now. The phone never stops ringing. I try to keep in daily contact with the people in the stores but pretty soon it will be humanly impossible.

His biggest problem, however, was inventory. Giftware had a slow turnover compared to apparel, and the maintenance of a basic stock was difficult on two counts.

> First I have to convince management, whose experience tends to be in high turnover fashion and apparel items, to invest money in this low-turning inventory. The second problem is the mechanics of getting and maintaining a good basic stock in each of the stores. I operate a large central reserve stock in Dallas for the four Texas stores. They each have their personalities — they're not just extensions of the downtown store. But other locations are so remote that centralized stocks are impossible. This means higher stock-to-sales ratios in the other stores, which management naturally doesn't like. The same thing is happening in our competitors' stores. Many of them just don't maintain good crystal and china departments anymore.

He had discussed these problems with his division merchandising manager. The two of them had agreed that he could probably establish guidelines within which the stores themselves could choose merchandise to fit their regional differences.

> For instance, I have bought from Wedgwood and other traditional companies over the years. I could give department managers leeway to choose from a range of items that I selected — put an asterisk next to some basic items that all stores must carry, then allow some latitude on the fringes. Maybe even let some stores buy a fine quality Swedish crystal with exceptionally clean lines that just doesn't sell in Dallas. But some guidelines are essential to define the look and ambiance.

Murray Friedman summarized some of the problems connected with expansion:

> We expect buyers to be wizards now that we have stores all over. Any number of problems can come up that we cannot anticipate.
>
> Remember that the same coat buyer who's trying to find lightweight raincoats for the early warm spring season in Texas and Florida, will at the very same time be looking for heavy coats for promotion in Chicago when the snow's coming down. Multiply that by every ready-to-wear operation in the organization and you certainly have a problem.

EXHIBIT 1
NEIMAN-MARCUS

Carter, Hawley, Hale Stores, Inc. Subsidiaries

The Broadway; Los Angeles, California   Thirty-seven department stores in South California, Arizona, Nevada and Utah.

The Emporium; San Francisco, California   Eleven department stores in North California.

Capwell's; Oakland, California   Five department stores in North California. Capwell's along with The Emporium were the dominant general department stores in the Bay area. Five additional stores were planned for that area.

Weinstock's; Sacramento, California   Nine department stores in California and Nevada.

Neiman-Marcus; Dallas, Texas   Seven specialty stores in Texas, Florida, Georgia, and Missouri.

Bergdorf Goodman; New York, New York   A specialty store on Fifth Avenue and one in White Plains.

Holt, Renfrew; Montreal, Quebec   Twenty specialty stores coast-to-coast in Canada.

Sunset House; Los Angeles, California   Nationally distributed catalog and thirty-four gift shops in Arizona, California, Texas and Utah.

Walden Book Company; Stamford, Connecticut   Three hundred thirty-eight book shops in forty states.

In addition to the subsidiaries listed here, Carter, Hawley, Hale owned 20% of the voting stock in the House of Fraser, a department store business in the United Kingdom.

EXHIBIT 2
NEIMAN-MARCUS

Neiman-Marcus Stores in 1974

Chicago
(Northbrook) ⊙
○
Downtown
Chicago

Chevy Chase
(1976)

San Francisco ○

St. Louis ●

Atlanta
●

Beverly Hills ○
Newport Beach ○

North Park ●
Dallas ●

Bal Harbor ●

Fort Worth ●
Houston ●

Stores in 1974
● Existing
⊙ Under construction
○ Planned

EXHIBIT 3

NEIMAN-MARCUS

Neiman-Marcus Organization, December 1974

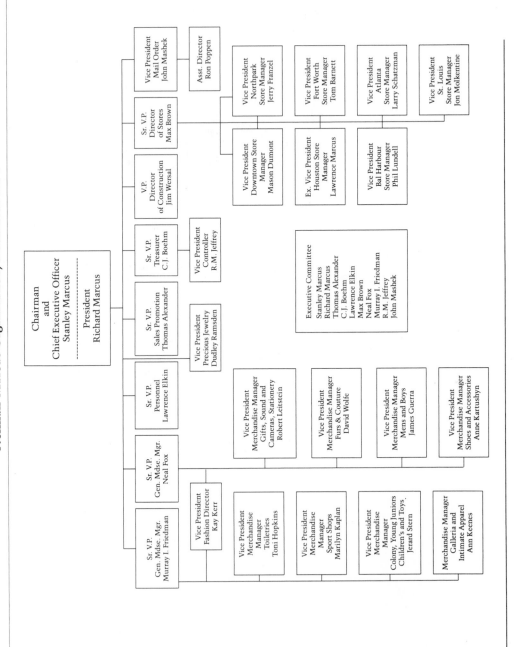

EXHIBIT 4

NEIMAN-MARCUS

Typical Store Organization, 1974

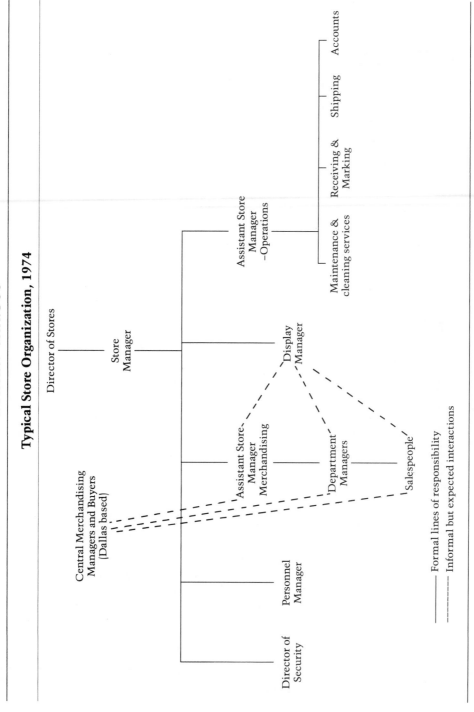

EXHIBIT 5
N E I M A N – M A R C U S

Merchandising Organization, December 1974

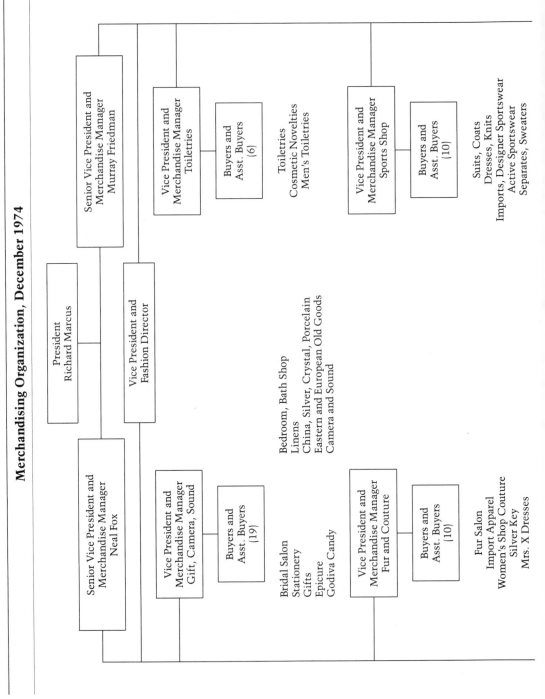

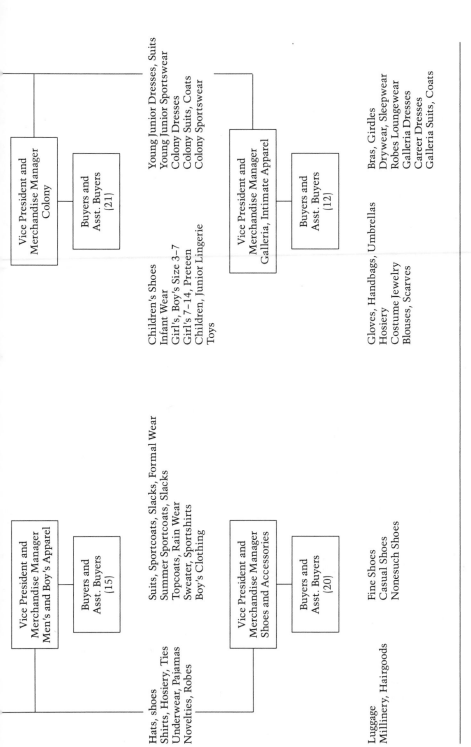

BANK OF MONTREAL: DOMESTIC DEVELOPMENT PROGRAM (B)

James C. Rush and Cheryl Harvey

Jack Phillips, district manager of Western Ontario Division, looked at the stack of personnel files on his desk. He was meeting with Ken Law, Human Resources planning and recruitment manager, later in the week to begin the process of reviewing the current staff in his district to make recommendations for placement when conversion to the new Commercial and Domestic structure took place. He wanted to be sure his people were assigned to the most suitable jobs, which would take into account both their skills and their career aspirations. Some assignments would be particularly easy, since the employee's aspirations would be consistent with where the bank would want them to go. Others would be particularly difficult because aspirations and assignments would not match; others would be even more difficult because there would be no place for them in the new bank. So he had set himself the task of reading each file and noting his suggestions before his meeting with Ken.

The Domestic Banking Organization Study

At the beginning of 1982, William D. Mulholland, chairman of the Bank of Montreal, appointed a steering committee to examine the feasibility of restructuring the Domestic Banking Group. This group, operating through a network of some 1300 branches across Canada, provided deposit gathering services and lending services to individuals, and to small and medium sized businesses. As well, the branches provided transaction processing and other services to the other bank groups; the Treasury Group, Corporate and Government Banking, and International Banking. These three groups were the result of an extensive reorganization orchestrated by Mulholland since his arrival at the bank as President in 1975. The emphasis in all these changes was on increased efficiency and professionalization within a particular market segment (see Bank of Montreal (A)).

The objectives of the Domestic Banking Study reflected the emphases of the previous changes. These were to explore ways of bringing a sharper organizational focus to the principal domestic market segments (the personal and commercial sectors), to improve the opportunities for professional development of officers and staff within each of these market groupings, and to reverse the decline in the quality of credit and customer service. The steering committee Mulholland had established set a task force to design the hypothetical organization that would accomplish these objectives.

The task force, headed on the personal side by Gord MacAskill, vice president of the Ontario Retail Division, and on the commercial side by Ron Call, senior vice president of Corporate Planning, devoted a week in March to its efforts. The task force members developed four organizational hypotheses as guidelines.

- The domestic market can be differentiated according to whether the customers' banking needs are primarily of a personal or commercial nature.
- The personal banking and commercial banking sectors lend themselves to differentiation on the basis of human resources skills requirements.
- The branches are best administered by those who manage the personal banking marketing and administrative structures.
- The commercial banking function can be housed in, or contiguous to, the branch facility, but does not necessarily have to be part of the management structure of the branch, nor report through the same channels.

By the end of the week, the task force had designed the new structure and defined the new jobs associated with it. Exhibit 1 illustrates the existing structure. Exhibits 2 and 3 show the proposed structures for Commercial and Domestic Banking respectively.

The task force defined the mandates for the two new groups as:

(1) *Commercial*. To provide, at a profit, a full range of commercial products and services that meet the financial needs of independent and mid-market businesses that are generally local or regional in nature, including such specialized industries as real estate/construction, agri-business, etc.;

(2) *Domestic*. To provide, at a profit, a wide range of products and services which meet the personal financial management needs of customers; and to provide the processing facilities and administrative support needed to deliver products and services to all customers in Canada. This latter mandate of Domestic Banking was congruent with its existing responsibility for the provision of all operational and administrative support in Canada to all other groups in the bank. Within each new group an explicit structural distinction was made between the credit and service functions. The task force's recommendations for mandate, structure, and jobs were approved by Mulholland, the board, and senior bank executives.

Effects of Restructuring

The restructuring necessitated numerous changes in the bank's control, reporting, and physical systems. Many processing forms had to be revised. A new 450-page procedures manual was written. This manual was a temporary one and would become much more detailed and closer in size to the 10 volumes it replaced. New financial reporting demands, based on products rather than branches, required changes to the on-line system and the general ledger system, as well as some hardware enhancements to the mechanized system. The within-branch separation of the processing function from the customer-oriented functions led to other modifications to support the concept of processing as a cost center. Many branch premises needed physical alterations. Some CBUs were located in new facilities which had to be found and altered.

Changes to the human resource systems were massive. Job descriptions had to be re-written. The old jobs were organized around the concept of the branch manager as a "total banker." This person was a jack-of-all-trades expected to have the skills and abilities to carry out all the responsibilities associated with commercial and small business lending, personal lending, deposit gathering, branch administration, and processing. His or her job grade, however, was determined by the size of his or her loan portfolio, which was greatly influenced by the particular branch's volume of commercial activity. Promotions were to larger and larger branches, which meant doing more of everything already being done. The new jobs, however, reflected a commercial-retail and a credit-service dimension of professionalism (See Exhibits 4 and 5). A new job grading system was developed based on the move to specialization.

Training programs had to be redesigned. The training courses offered and conducted by the training department had been developed to assist in the growth of "total bankers." Broadly organized in five categories, administration, management, credit, finance and marketing, the 14 courses focused on developing basic skills and knowledge. For example, conducting daily audits, appraising performance, conducting a credit interview, financial analysis, product knowledge and selling were all topics covered in these courses. Courses were usually held at divisional headquarters and lasted from one day to two weeks. Specific courses were required for promotion to some positions.

The new training programs were developed around each position. While some modules were drawn from the old courses, some 30 new modules were designed. These programs were designed to be completed on the job and lasted from two to 18 months. Exhibits 6–9 are examples of the training programs.

Career Planning

Just two years prior to this reorganization the Western Ontario Division, headquartered in London, had developed and implemented a career planning program. A 1978 employee survey had revealed major dissatisfactions with the amount of information available to help employees deal with their career concerns and with the lack of opportunity to talk about their careers with their bosses.

The bank hired Joy Bollen, who had done extensive work in this area with a bank in California. Trained in organizational development, she was most concerned with the way the program was developed and implemented. After researching the organization and career programs being used within the bank, she began by involving both the Human Resource Department and all senior management in the division. Four members of the Human Resource Department developed career paths, skills inventories and job catalogues — the tools of career development. Senior managers were brought together for several full day sessions to review these tools as they were being developed and to discuss the implications of their use. Both groups were assisted by Bollen and two external consultants.

This process produced the tools which would provide the kind of information that would be useful to both the employees and their bosses. It also secured a commitment on the part of the district managers to spend time counselling their branch managers on career issues. This was a significant commitment considering that district managers had from 25 to 40 branch managers reporting to them, and each counselling session could last up to three hours.

The old organization had offered six career paths. Each showed the progression to different senior positions and showed points of crossover from one path to another. All district managers had been through a two and one half day counselling skills training program. Following this each district manager conducted a career counselling session with all his or her branch managers.

New career paths were developed within the Commercial and Domestic Groups by focusing on the top positions in each group and then working down through the structures to define prerequisite skills and positions. Transition paths from the old to the new positions were also mapped out and were distributed throughout the bank to explain the new positions to the staff. Exhibits 10–13 illustrate the new career and the transition sourcing for the new positions in each group.

Staffing the New Positions

There were 20 000 management and clerical positions in what had been called the Domestic Banking Group. Each employee had to be assigned a position within the new structure as the conversion took place over the next two years. Jack was thankful that he was involved with only a fraction of that number. Still, the 100 or so management people in his district meant 100 decisions. He hoped some would be obvious ones, but he felt each could be difficult. He was only too aware that the organization on which people had built their careers (their lives for some) no longer existed. The three he had to deal with first were Susan Gerrard, Richard Andrews and Martin Chin. Besides his personal knowledge of these candidates, Jack also had the employee's latest performance appraisal, career aspiration sheet and career history.

Susan Gerrard

Jack did not know Susan very well. He had met her only once, about six months ago when he visited the Grand Rivers branch. He remembered her as a talkative and intense person. She seemed intelligent and knowledgeable about her job. Mark Edwards, the branch manager, had commented on her above-average competence as an account manager, although a few customers had complained that they had felt pushed into purchasing some products or services. She got along well with her co-workers. Susan was single and willing to relocate to advance her career in the bank. The information in Mark's appraisal of her performance (Exhibit 14) was really all Jack knew about Susan.

Richard Andrews

Andy was another story. Jack had known him since his own first days with the bank, 18 years ago. They had been on a course together, Andy as a branch manager, himself as a trainee. They had hit it off well and developed a friendship that had continued despite long gaps in contact when their jobs were located far apart.

Andy was a branch manager in Cook's Mills and had been for ten years now. He did an excellent job there. The town itself was small — about 36 000 people, a couple of major industries and dozens of smaller ones. It had the usual collection of professional people who served the town folk and the surrounding farm and fishing families. Andy had captured the majority of the town's credit business over the years. There was only one other bank left in town, and the two banks and the mill's credit union shared the deposit business.

Andy and his wife, Shirley, loved the town. Andy was the Rotary Club president, curling club member, and a Chamber of Commerce member, while Shirley was chairman of the school board, president of the curling club, and a consistent prize winner in the horticultural society.

Jack was going to Cook's Mills next week and Andy would be asking him about how the new structure would be implemented in this district. Jack cringed. The town's branch would be a retail one associated with a CBU in London. This staffing decision was definitely one of the hard ones. (See Exhibit 15)

Martin Chin

Martin was 43, and had been with the bank for seven years. He had worked in a variety of jobs before joining the bank and Jack was surprised he had stayed. But he had, and he was doing very well indeed. The last time Jack had talked with him, Martin had told him of his growing interest in the commercial side of banking. That hospital account experience had really whetted his appetite, and Jack knew Martin was now working on another potentially larger account. (See Exhibit 16)

EXHIBIT 1

BANK OF MONTREAL — DOMESTIC DEVELOPMENT PROGRAM (B)

Domestic Banking Group
January, 1982

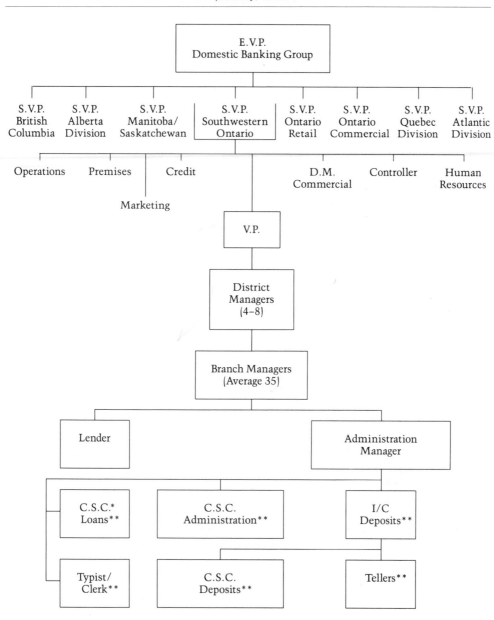

* C.S.C.: Customer Service Clerk
** Non-management position

EXHIBIT 2

BANK OF MONTREAL

DOMESTIC DEVELOPMENT PROGRAM (B)

Canadian Commercial Banking Group

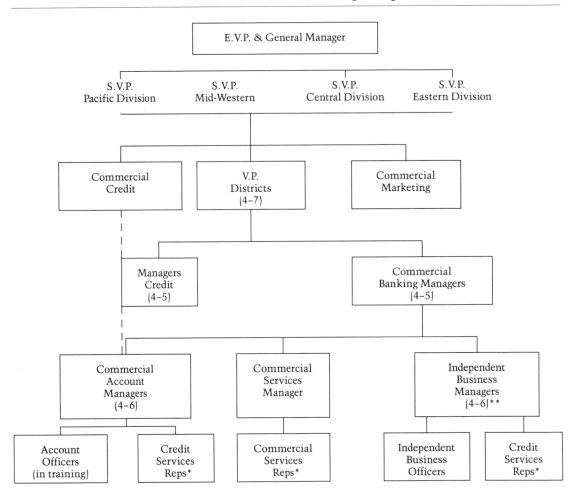

* Non-management position
** A senior independent business manager would exist where numbers warranted.

New Struct

EXHIBIT 3
BANK OF MONTREAL
DOMESTIC DEVELOPMENT PROGRAM (B)

Domestic Banking Group

```
                    ┌─────────────────────────┐
                    │ E.V.P. & General Manager│
                    └─────────────────────────┘
        ┌────────────────┬────────────┬─────────────────┐
┌──────────┐  ┌───────────────┐  ┌──────────┐  ┌──────────────┐
│  S.V.P.  │  │    S.V.P.     │  │  S.V.P.  │  │ Staff Support│
│Operations│  │Consumer Credit│  │ Consumer │  │              │
│          │  │               │  │Marketing │  │              │
└──────────┘  └───────────────┘  └──────────┘  └──────────────┘

        ┌────────────────────┼────────────────────┐
┌───────────────┐   ┌───────────────┐   ┌───────────────┐
│    S.V.P.     │   │    S.V.P.     │   │    S.V.P.     │
│Western Region │   │Central Region │   │Eastern Region │
└───────────────┘   └───────────────┘   └───────────────┘

   ┌──────────┬──────────────────┬──────────────┐
┌─────────┐ ┌──────────────┐ ┌──────────┐ ┌──────────┐
│Consumer │ │V.P. Executive│ │ Consumer │ │Operations│
│ Credit  │ │   Manager    │ │Marketing │ │          │
│         │ │    (4–5)     │ │          │ │          │
└─────────┘ └──────────────┘ └──────────┘ └──────────┘

                ┌──────────────┐
                │ Area Manager │
                │     (9)      │
                └──────────────┘

   ┌────────────────────────────────────┐
┌───────────────┐                  ┌──────────┐
│Personal Loans │                  │ ADCON**  │
└───────────────┘                  └──────────┘

┌───────────┐     ┌──────────────┐
│ Personal  │     │    Branch    │
│   Loans   │     │   Manager    │
│  Officer  │     │   (10–15)    │
└───────────┘     └──────────────┘

   ┌────────────────┼────────────────┐
┌──────────┐ ┌──────────────┐ ┌──────────────┐
│ Tellers* │ │   Customer   │ │  Processing  │
│          │ │   Service    │ │  Personnel*  │
│          │ │   Clerks*    │ │              │
└──────────┘ └──────────────┘ └──────────────┘
```

* Non-management position

** Administrative consolidation unit. Exists as off-site processing facility servicing several branches. Only 55 existed. More planned.

EXHIBIT 4
BANK OF MONTREAL
DOMESTIC DEVELOPMENT PROGRAM (B)

The Canadian Commercial Banking Group Jobs

The Canadian Commercial Banking Group was divided into four divisions, each of those subdivided into four to seven districts, which contained from 18 to 33 Commercial Banking Units. The principal jobs in this group were:

Commercial Banking Manager
Responsible for the development of new business, both credit and non-credit, and for the supervision of the loan portfolio through the Commercial Account manager and Independent Business managers. No direct account responsibility but might participate in more complex negotiations/transactions. Not normally involved in the credit approval process and reviews applications on an exception basis only.

Manager Credit/Assistant Manager Credit (where volume warrants)
Responsible for providing on-site training and credit support for the account managers and for concurring in loan applications within an assigned discretionary limit.

Commercial Account Manager
Responsible for recommending and implementing plans for the development of assigned accounts and prospects, toward meeting growth and profit goals set for the unit and for effectively managing accounts.

Senior Independent Business Manager
Responsible for supervising and providing direction to a group of Independent Business managers in units where there were multiple I.B.M.s and the Commercial Banking manager's span of control was prohibitive. Senior I.B.M. were particularly beneficial if several of the I.B.M.s travelled or were domiciled in locations outside of the Commercial Centre.

Independent Business Manager
Responsible for the Independent Business manager's requirements (both credit and non-credit). Lending was frequently on the basis of personal as well as company assets and, to be successful, the manager has to be street-wise and have an inherent ability to accurately size up the type of entrepreneurial spirit which was generally found in this market. Major job was to manage a portfolio, rather than a group of individual accounts.

Commercial Service Manager
Responsible for providing the account managers and Independent Business managers with sales training and sales support for a variety of non-credit products and services, and/or for bringing in specialists (Trade Finance, Cash Management, etc.) to assist with the packaging of these products. Also acted as the Commercial Centre's formal interface with the processing area(s), ensuring that its needs were promptly and efficiently satisfied.

EXHIBIT 5

BANK OF MONTREAL

DOMESTIC DEVELOPMENT PROGRAM (B)

The Domestic Banking Group Jobs

The Domestic Banking Group was divided into three regions, each of those subdivided into four to five districts. Each district was further divided into nine areas containing from 10 to 15 branches. The principal jobs were:

Area Manager
Principal role was one of "hands-on" general management of assigned Domestic Banking Branches. Emphasis was placed on the training, development and motivation of Branch Managers. Skilled in professional merchandising techniques and co-ordinated and directed promotional development campaigns focused on deposits markets. Alert to the detection and correction of quality of customer service deficiencies in the Branches. Generally established the tactics and directed the actions necessary to achieve penetration of the area's personal marketplace. Also expected to establish a strong presence in the committees in the area, by speaking at local functions, running displays at consumer trade shows, etc. In addition, had overall responsibility for the area's personal loans portfolio growth, yield and quality performance.

Area Personal Loans Manager
Directly supervised activities of the Personal Loans Officers in the area, numbering 10–15 people. Responsible for market development, lending officer training and development, and control of portfolio yields and quality of business. Assumed a direct line responsibility for results and was measured against them.

Branch Manager
Responsible for the "hands-on" management and development of personal deposit business through the provision of quality service. Had a retail, merchandising orientation, and was concerned with such things as Branch appearance and service levels, promotion, participation in community affairs, and other aspects of the Branch's community image. Also responsible for all routine processing and administrative activities carried out in support of the day-to-day banking transactions of the Domestic, Commercial, Corporate, and Government, Treasury, and International Banking customers dealing with the branch. Performance measured by volume growth, non-interest expense trends, customer service standards, personnel productivity, and non-interest expense containment.

Personal Loans Officer
Responsible for growth and profit for personal loans branch and for attainment of established objectives through effective programs for development of accounts and prospects.

ADCON Centre Manager
Responsible for organizing and supervising the processing of non-customer routine transactions. This was provided in a screened-off area of a branch or in an off-site Adcon Centre which serviced the processing needs of a number of branches in a designated area.

EXHIBIT 6

BANK OF MONTREAL

DOMESTIC DEVELOPMENT PROGRAM (B)

Commercial Services Manager Program

Objective	To provide qualified individuals with structured on-the-job-training

Content

— Operations — Depositor services
Cash management services
Investment services
Domestic exchange
Foreign exchange
Securities

— Marketing — Product knowledge
Profitability and pricing

Methodology   Self-directed completion of work and learning objectives while on-the-job

Evaluation   Self-assessment and performance evaluation and discussion with the Commercial Banking Manager.

Course Linkage   Attendance on Practical Selling Skills Seminar and Commercial Services Seminar.

EXHIBIT 7
BANK OF MONTREAL
DOMESTIC DEVELOPMENT PROGRAM (B)

Independent Business Manager Program

Objective	To provide qualified individuals with structured on-the-job-training to assume the role of an independent business manager within a maximum of 12 months.
Content	Phase I — *Retail Banking* Retail operations Product knowledge Personal lending Phase II — *Commercial Banking* Support operations Commercial lending Commercial marketing
Methodology	To complete a series of on-the-job performance activities in each area.
Evaluation	Performance reviews at two months, five months, eight months and eleven months.
Course Linkage	Personal lending skills Commercial lending skills Practical selling skills IBM seminar

tran prog.

EXHIBIT 8

BANK OF MONTREAL

DOMESTIC DEVELOPMENT PROGRAM (B)

Branch Manager Program

Objective	To enable a qualified candidate to assume the duties of a Retail Branch Manager within a maximum nine-month time period.
Content	Customer Services & Operations — Deposit Services Special Services Branch Support
	Retailing & Management Control — Human Resources Physical Resources Planning
Methodology	Perform on-the-job and managerial objectives with supervision from a Current Branch Manager.
Evaluation	Two performance appraisals @ two month and eight month time periods.
Course Linkage	Orientation Banking Skills (123) Retailing Supervisory Skills/DPE

EXHIBIT 9

BANK OF MONTREAL

DOMESTIC DEVELOPMENT PROGRAM (B)

Customer Services Representative—Administration

Objective	To enable selected individuals to fulfill the duties of a customer service representative (Administration).
Content	Customer Services Foreign Exchange Securities Reports and Returns
Methodology	To complete a series of routine/or supervisory activities (performance objectives) through on-the-job training.
Evaluation	Testing at program completion Evaluation certificates at successful completion of objectives and testing to Area Training Manager.

EXHIBIT 10

BANK OF MONTREAL

DOMESTIC DEVELOPMENT PROGRAM (B)

Commercial Banking Career Paths

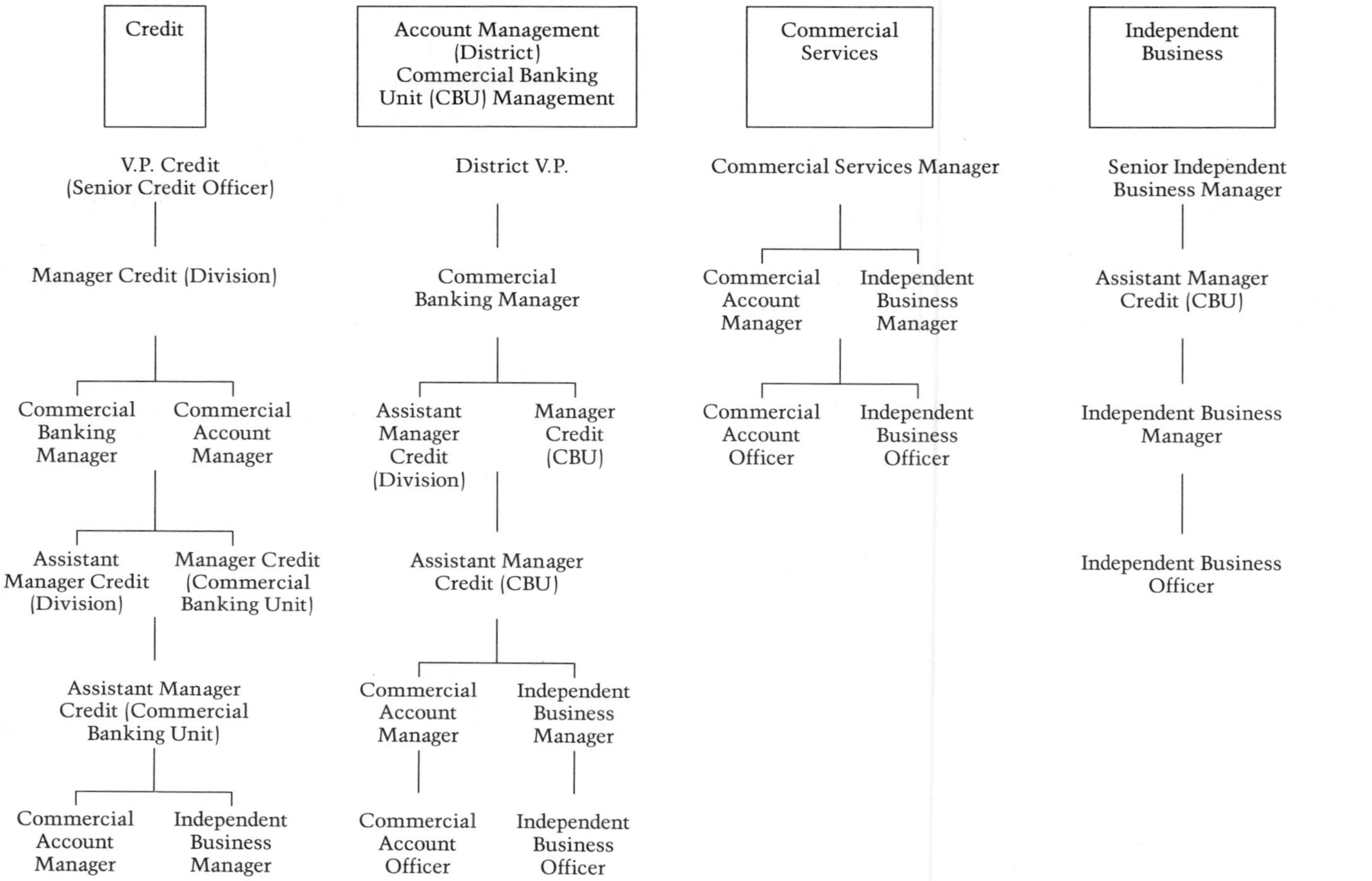

New careers & positions

Credit

V.P. Credit (Senior Credit Officer)

Manager Credit (Division)

Commercial Banking Manager — Commercial Account Manager

Assistant Manager Credit (Division) — Manager Credit (Commercial Banking Unit)

Commercial Account Manager — Assistant Manager Credit (Commercial Banking Unit) — Independent Business Manager

Account Management (District) Commercial Banking Unit (CBU) Management

District V.P.

Commercial Banking Manager — Assistant Manager Credit (Division) / Manager Credit (CBU)

Assistant Manager Credit (CBU) — Commercial Account Manager / Independent Business Manager

Commercial Account Officer / Independent Business Officer

Commercial Services

Commercial Services Manager

Commercial Account Manager / Independent Business Manager

Commercial Account Officer / Independent Business Officer

Independent Business

Senior Independent Business Manager

Assistant Manager Credit (CBU)

Independent Business Manager

Independent Business Officer

111

EXHIBIT 11
BANK OF MONTREAL
DOMESTIC DEVELOPMENT PROGRAM (B)

Domestic Banking Career Paths

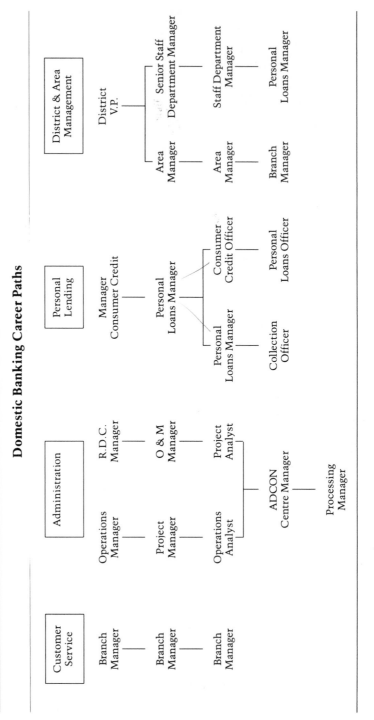

Customer Service	Administration	Personal Lending	District & Area Management

Customer Service
- Branch Manager
- Branch Manager
- Branch Manager

Administration
- Operations Manager — R.D.C. Manager
- Project Manager — O & M Manager
- Operations Analyst — Project Analyst
- ADCON Centre Manager
- Processing Manager

Personal Lending
- Manager Consumer Credit
- Personal Loans Manager
- Personal Loans Manager — Consumer Credit Officer
- Collection Officer — Personal Loans Officer

District & Area Management
- District V.P.
- Senior Staff Department Manager
- Staff Department Manager
- Personal Loans Manager
- Area Manager
- Area Manager
- Branch Manager

EXHIBIT 12

BANK OF MONTREAL

DOMESTIC DEVELOPMENT PROGRAM (B)

Sourcing for new Commercial Banking positions

New Inventory Requirements Commercial Banking Positions	Current Inventory and Initial Sources
Commercial Banking Manager	— Branch Manager ✓— Account Manager
Manager Credit	—— Assistant Credit Manager ⊣ Credit Officer
Commercial Services Manager	— Branch Manager — Administration Manager
Independent Business Manager/ Officer ✓	— Branch Manager — Account Manager — Personal/Consumer Loans Manager/Officer — Small Business Manager/Officer — Credit Department
Commercial Account Manager ✓	— Branch Manager — Account Manager✓ — M.D.P. Program — Credit Department

Bank of
Montreal:
Domestic
Development
Program (B)

EXHIBIT 13

BANK OF MONTREAL
DOMESTIC DEVELOPMENT PROGRAM (B)

Sourcing for new Domestic Banking positions

New Inventory Requirements Personal Banking Positions	Current Inventory and Initial Sources
Area Manager	— District Manager — Senior Branch Manager
Branch Manager	— District Manager — Branch Manager — Administration Manager — Staff Development Officer
Personal Loans Manager/Officer	— Branch Manager — Personal/Consumer Loans Manager/Officer — Jr. Account Manager
ADCON Centre Manager	— Administration Manager — Organization and Methods Officer

EXHIBIT 14

BANK OF MONTREAL
DOMESTIC DEVELOPMENT PROGRAM (B)

Performance Appraisal of Susan Gerrard

Personal History
Fiche de renseignements personnels

Bank of Montreal ⛰ Banque de Montréal

Photograph
Photo

Name/*Nom*   GERRARD, SUSAN A.   Soc. Ins. No./*N° d'ass. sociale* 793-849-271

Date of Birth/*Date de naissance*   OCTOBER 25/51

Date of Hire (or re-hire)/*Date d'engagement ou de rengagement*   NOVEMBER 1/76

Marital Status/*État civil*   SINGLE

Dependent Children (Show Y.O.B.)/*Nombre d'enfants à charge (indiquer leur date de naissance)*

LANGUAGES SPOKEN — Specify degree of fluency as "good" or "fair". Include "English" only if NOT mother tongue.
LANGUES PARLÉES — *Indiquer le niveau de maîtrise pour chacune des langues mentionnées : Ex.: excellente, bonne ou moyenne.*

French (conversation 70% fluency, reading and comprehension 60% fluency)

EXPERIENCE OTHER THAN BANK OF MONTREAL/EMPLOIS ANTÉRIEURS

Year to Year/*De – à*	Job Title/*Titre du poste*	Organization/*Nom de l'entreprise*
January /74 to January /75	Internal Auditor	Bell Canada
January /75 to November /76	Internal Auditor	Royal Trust

BANK OF MONTREAL EXPERIENCE - Summarize junior experience
EXPÉRIENCE À LA BANQUE DE MONTRÉAL — *Ne donner qu'une description sommaire de ses fonctions antérieures.*

Month	Year/*Mois*	*Année*	JobGrade/*Niveau du poste*	Job Title/*Titre du poste*	Component, e.g., Branch, Department, Division *Succursale, service ou division*
11	76			Credit Analyst	Corp. Credit, Head Office
09	77			Credit Officer	Market & University, Ottawa
02	79			Account Manager	Kitchener, Ontario
03	80			Credit Officer	Divisional Office, Ontario
10	81		M7	Account Manager	Grand Rivers, Ontario

EXHIBIT 14 (continued)

EDUCATION — Show highest formal education level attained. If university degree is held, show "Major". Indicate university, night-school or other work-related courses, including In-Bank Seminars, with appropriate detail, such as whether employee has passed Part I, II or III or I.C.B. or the 1st, 2nd, etc., year of R.I.A.

ÉTUDES — Préciser le niveau d'instruction ainsi que la spécialisation si celui-ci est représenté par un diplôme universitaire. Inscrire les titres de cours suivis par le soir, à l'université ou dans tout autre cadre, y compris les séminaires donnés par la Banque. Indiquer à cet égard les certificats decernés (I, II ou III dans le cas du programme de l'I.B.C.) ou les années complétées, ex.: 1re, 2e année du programme de comptabilité en gestion industrielle (R.I.A.).

Year/*Année*	Academic Achievement Completed/*Certificat ou diplôme obtenus*
1969	Junior Matriculation - Province of Quebec
1974	Bachelor of Commerce - McGill University - Quebec Major in Management

OTHER DATA — Major association memberships, committee and community activities held during last 5 years.

RENSEIGNEMENTS GÉNÉRAUX — Associations professionnelles, comités et activités communautaires dont vous avez fait partie au cours des cinq dernières années.

Year/*Année*	Office Held/*Titre ou fonction*
1974	McGill Alumni Association - no office held

December 10th, 1982
Date revised/*Date de révision*

EXHIBIT 14 (continued)

Skills Identification Chart

Fiche d'aptitudes

Name/Nom	Job/Poste	Grade/Niveau du poste
GERRARD, SUSAN	ACCOUNT MANAGER	M7

1 - Has particularly strong skill at this grade level.
2 - Has normal skill expected at this grade level.
3 - Would require improvement before skill level would be considered satisfactory.

1	2	3	Not Rated Sans objet

1 - Compétence exceptionnelle à ce niveau.
2 - Compétence satisfaisante à ce niveau.
3 - Amélioration souhaitable.

Planning & Organizing

Select realistic, yet challenging objectives
Develop programs and activities to achieve objectives
Establish priorities
Schedule and coordinate, using time, personnel and facilities to advantage

Rating: 2

Sens de la planification et de l'organisation

Choisit des objectifs à la fois réalistes et stimulants
Se fixe un programme en vue d'atteindre ces objectifs
Établit une liste de priorités
Coordonne les activités de ses subordonnés en fonction des délais, des priorités et des ressources humaines et matérielles.

Communication Skills-Written

Logic, clarity, conciseness
Empathy, tact, style
Persuasiveness

Rating: 2

Facilité d'expression écrite

S'exprime avec clarté et concision
Fait preuve d'empathie, de tact
Expose ses arguments d'une manière logique et convaincante.

Communication Skills-Verbal

Listens, comprehends and identifies needs
Speaks clearly, concisely, and confidently
Tactful, persuasive and inspirational
Persistent when appropriate

Rating: 2

Facilité d'expression verbale

Écoute, comprend et reconnaît les besoins
S'exprime clairement, avec concision et sans hésitation
Use de tact, de persuasion, de force de conviction
Se montre tenace, s'il le faut.

Supervisory Skills

Selection of people for tasks
Control of task execution
Production of results through subordinates
Employees treated fairly and with understanding
Group operates as a "Team"

Rating: 2

Aptitude à superviser

Répartit les tâches en fonction de la compétence des employés
Contrôle l'exécution des tâches
Produit des résultats par l'intermédiaire des subordonnés
Motive les employés, les traite avec équité, fermeté et compréhension
Est capable de travailler en équipe

Personnel

Writing and dealing with performance appraisals
Training, improving and developing subordinates
Administration of personnel policies, e.g. Compensation, Benefits, Hours of work, etc.
Recruitment

Rating: 3

Aptitude à diriger le personnel

Suit les progrès et prépare les fiches d'appréciation du personnel
Voit à la formation, à l'amélioration, au perfectionnement des employés.
Applique les directives touchant le personnel (rémunération, avantages sociaux, heures de travail, etc.)
Participe au recrutement des employés.

Analytical Skills

Identification and organization of data
Analysis of data
Quality of conclusions and recommendations

Rating: 1

Esprit d'analyse

Rassemble et organise les données
Analyse les données
Émet des conclusions et des recommandations logiques.

Administration

Accuracy of forecasts
Preparation of budgets
Control of expenses
Up-keep of premises and equipment
Systems and Methods

Rating: Not Rated

Aptitude à administrer

Fait des prévisions exactes
Établit les prévisions budgétaires
Surveille les dépenses
Voit à l'entretien des locaux et du matériel
Établit les systèmes de gestion et les méthodes de travail.

Credit Skills

Financial Statement Analysis
Negotiation
Collection and follow-up
Realistic loan pricing
Interpretation of policy
Appropriate security

Rating: 2

Jugement en matière de crédit

Analyse les états financiers
Négocie les prêts
Voit au recouvrement et au rappel
Suit une politique de prix réaliste
Interprète les directives
Obtient les garanties nécessaires

Marketing

Service to the Public
Public relations
Selling the Bank's services
Retail
Commercial
Investments & Securities
Master Charge
Computer
Foreign

Rating: 2

Marketing

Offre un service de qualité
Entretien de bonnes relations avec les clients
Fait la promotion des divers services bancaires
Services aux consommateurs
Services à l'entreprise
Service de titres
Master.Charge
Traitement informatique
Change

117

EXHIBIT 14 (continued)

Bank of Montreal 🔚 Banque de Montréal

CONFIDENTIAL

Management Performance Appraisal

CONFIDENTIEL

Fiche d'appréciation du personnel cadre

Name/Nom et prénom	Soc. Ins. No./N° d'ass. sociale	PREVIOUS three ratings most recent at right
		Cotes des trois dernières années - inscrire la plus récente dans la case de droite
GERRARD, SUSAN A.	793-849-271	

Position Title/Titre du poste	Branch/Dept./Succursale ou service	Job Grade	Time on present Job / Ancienneté à ce poste
			Year(s)/Année(s)	Months/Mois
ACCOUNT MANAGER	GRAND RIVERS	M7 *Niveau du poste*	1	3

Evaluation of Performance & Rating/Appréciation du rendement — Cote   HIGH COMPETENT

An energetic, self-motivated officer who displays an intense desire to succeed. Has a good understanding of the Bank's credit policies and communicates these well to customers and prospects.

Enthusiastically participated in commercial account calling during the summer with an excess of 20 calls made and viable proposals developed for four accounts. Has been successful in developing professional accounts (Dr.'s Copper, Smith, Rodrows) with loan and deposit business of $150M+. Upsells existing accounts well, responsible for $3,393M in SVP authorizations in 1982. Co-ordinated deposit campaign in branch for November 1982 with 16 new deposit accounts gained with deposits totalling $421M.

Keeps informed of key and prime accounts of branch, successfully relieved Manager for total of eight weeks during 1982 and met client needs, including $1,030M in commercial mortgages to Voddor Group.

Improvement made during year in administrative function of loan department but, because of limited exposure and CAP background, requires more than normal support at this grade level.

Collection of doubtful accounts considered above average, as evident by below District average arrears and write-offs.

Personal lending skills are adequate but indicates through activities a distinct preference for commercial lending.

In dealings with personnel and customers has a tendency to press towards her desired objectives and is not always cognizant of other party's desires or views. Further party's improvement in this area is warranted, although improvement since last discussion is noticeable Ms. Gerrard has shown good improvement in the last six months, concentration on people skills, coupled with existing strong credit skills could result in improved rating.

Description of Potential

Promotability - Q - Account Manager M8

Normal Potential - Short Term - Account Manager, Sr. Account Manager M8
              Medium/Long Term - Senior Account Manager M9, Account Officer
                              Corporate Banking M9/10

Aspirations - Preferred Progression/Aspirations de l'employé - Filière d'avancement souhaitée

Plans - Continue to develop people skills
      - Continue commercial account calls

Interim Review Dates/Dates de révisions intérimaires

Date Prepared/Date	Prepared by/Rempli par	Concurred in by/Approuvé par	Discussed with/Discuté avec
December 1982	Manager	District Manager	
	Title & Signature - Titre et signature	Title & Signature - Titre et signature	Employee s Signature/Sign. de l'employé

EXHIBIT 15
BANK OF MONTREAL
DOMESTIC DEVELOPMENT PROGRAM (B)

Performance Appraisal of Richard Andrews

Personal History   Bank of Montreal ▲ Banque de Montréal
Fiche dè renseignements personnels

Name/*Nom* Richard Andrews (Andy)   Soc. Ins. No./*N° d'ass. sociale*

Date of Birth/*Date de naissance*   November 6th, 1929

Date of Hire (or re-hire)/*Date d'engagement ou de rengagement* April 1952

Marital Status/*État civil* Married
Dependent Children (Show Y.O.B.)/*Nombre d'enfants à charge (indiquer leur date de naissance)*

Photograph
Photo

LANGUAGES SPOKEN — Specify degree of fluency as "good" or "fair". Include "English" only if NOT mother tongue.
LANGUES PARLÉES — *Indiquer le niveau de maîtrise pour chacune des langues mentionnées: Ex.: excellente, bonne ou moyenne.*

EXPERIENCE OTHER THAN BANK OF MONTREAL/EMPLOIS ANTÉRIEURS

Year to Year/*De – à*	Job Title/*Titre du poste*	Organization/*Nom de l'entreprise*
1948-1952	Clerk & Purchasing Agent	Retail Hardware Store

BANK OF MONTREAL EXPERIENCE -- Summarize junior experience
EXPÉRIENCE À LA BANQUE DE MONTRÉAL — *Ne donner qu'une description sommaire de ses fonctions antérieures.*

Month	Year/*Mois*	*Année*	JobGrade/*Niveau du poste*	Job Title/*Titre du poste*	Component, e.g., Branch, Department, Division *Succursale, service ou division*
April	1952	- 57	Various Junior Posts		Ontario Division
April	1957	- 59	Accountant		Kincardine
Feb.	1959	- 60	Accountant		Kingsville
Feb.	1960	- 61	Accountant		Sudbury
Aug.	1961	- 64	Manager		Cooksville
Jan.	1962	- 66	Manager		Chapleau
June	1966	- 68	Assistant Manager		Ottawa
Nov.	1968	- 71	Manager		Timmiskiming
Nov.	1971	- 73	Assistant Credit Manager		Credit Dept., Ontario Div.
Nov.	1973	- 77	Manager		Cook's Mills, Ontario
Nov.	1977	- 82	Manager		Cook's Mills, Ontario

EXHIBIT 15 (continued)

EDUCATION — Show highest formal education level attained. If university degree is held, show "Major". Indicate university, night-school or other work-related courses, including In-Bank Seminars, with appropriate detail, such as whether employee has passed Part I, II or III or I.C.B. or the 1st, 2nd, etc , year of R.I.A.

ÉTUDES — *Préciser le niveau d'instruction ainsi que la spécialisation si celui-ci est représenté par un diplôme universitaire. Inscrire les titres de cours suivis par le soir, à l'université ou dans tout autre cadre, y compris les séminaires donnés par la Banque. Indiquer à cet égard les certificats decernés (I, II ou III dans le cas du programme de l'I.B.C.) ou les années complétées, ex.: 1ʳᵉ, 2ᵉ année du programme de comptabilité en gestion industrielle (R.I.A.).*

Year/*Année*	Academic Achievement Completed/*Certificat ou diplôme obtenus*
1970	Management Institute I
1975	Commercial Call Seminar

OTHER DATA — Major association memberships, committee and community activities held during last 5 years.

RENSEIGNEMENTS GÉNÉRAUX — *Associations professionnelles, comités et activités communautaires dont vous avez fait partie au cours des cinq dernières années.*

Year/*Année*	Office Held/*Titre ou fonction*
1973 - 1982	Member - Cook's Mills Rotary Club; Cook's Mills Curling Club Cook's Mills Gold & Country Club
1976 - 1982	Director - Cook's Mills Chamber of Commerce

Date revised/*Date de révision*

EXHIBIT 15 (continued)

The First Canadian Bank   La Première Banque Canadienne
Bank of Montreal ▰ Banque de Montréal

CONFIDENTIAL   CONFIDENTIEL

Management Performance Appraisal   *Fiche d'appréciation du personnel cadre*

Name/*Nom et prénom* ANDREWS, Richard (Andy)	Soc. Ins. No./*N° d'ass. sociale* 417-893-617	PREVIOUS three ratings most recent at right *Cotes des trois dernières années - inscrire la plus recente dans la case de droite.*		
Position Title/*Titre du poste* Branch Manager	Branch/Dept./*Succursale ou service* Cook's Mills, Ontario	Job Grade M11 *Niveau du poste*	Time on present job *Ancienneté a ce poste* Year(s)/*Annees)* 10	Months/*Mois* 1

Evaluation of Performance & Rating/*Appréciation du rendement* — *Cote*   COMPETENT

PERSONNEL: Provides strong overall direction to his management staff of three and experienced clerical staff of 15. Morale is generally high and operating efficiency gradually increasing in this stable market. Establishes clearly defined objectives for his officers and has capably developed an Account Manager, Peter Morgan, in the past 12 months. Maintains a sound program of staff social activities, in-branch training, job rotation, and product knowledge.

CREDIT: Discretionary Limit $60,000. D/L's $14MM, Small Business $5MM, F.F.P.'s $4MM. A well-experienced lender, maintains a top quality portfolio and consistently applies sound lending practices. Credit proposals are well prepared with a good working knowledge of, and adherence to, lending policy. Credit control is excellent with a small number of overdrafts and minor number of accounts (6) reported on Form 549. Problem situations are identified early and corrective action plans firmly implemented. Portfolio growth in D/L's of 13.5% over 1981. F.F.P's increased .8%, below the Divisional level of 18%, with delinquency exceptionally well controlled at .75%.

CUSTOMER SERVICE: Provides a good level of service to customer base. While the base is receding in recent years due to population decline, basic deposits increased 11.3%, District average, and TDR and TSA increased 20%. Branch displays are attractive and in-branch team promotions maintain a good interest in increasing customer business.

(continued)

Description of Potential - Improvement and Development Plans/*Définition du potentiel et perspectives de carrière - programme de perfectionnement*

PROMOTABILITY: Q - Commercial Branch Manager, 12
                 Q - Manager, Credit - Divisional Commercial, 12

NORMAL POTENTIAL: Short Term - As Above
                    Medium Term - Senior Commercial Branch Manager, 13/14

PLANS: Expand market share and continue program to increase branch
                    operating efficiency.

Aspirations - Preferred Progression/*Aspirations de l'employé - Filière d'avancement souhaitée*

Preferred progression.

Interim Review Dates/*Dates de révisions intérimaires*

Date Prepared/*Date* Nov.26/82	Prepared by/*Rempli par* District Manager Title & Signature - *Titre et signature*	Concurred in by/*Approuve par* Vice-President Title & Signature - *Titre et signature*	Discussed with/*Discuté avec* Employee's Signature/*Sign. de l'employe*

EXHIBIT 15 (continued)

Skills Identification Chart / *Fiche d'aptitudes*

Name/*Nom*	Job/*Poste*	Grade/*Niveau du poste*
ANDREWS, Richard	Branch Manager	M11

1 - Has particularly strong skill at this grade level.	1 - *Compétence exceptionnelle à ce niveau.*
2 - Has normal skill expected at this grade level.	2 - *Compétence satisfaisante à ce niveau.*
3 - Would require improvement before skill level would be considered satisfactory.	3 - *Amélioration souhaitable.*

Rating columns: 1 | 2 | 3 | Not Rated / Sans objet

Planning & Organizing / *Sens de la planification et de l'organisation*

	1	2	3	Not Rated
		X		

Select realistic, yet challenging objectives
Develop programs and activities to achieve objectives
Establish priorities
Schedule and coordinate, using time, personnel and facilities to advantage

Choisit des objectifs à la fois réalistes et stimulants
Se fixe un programme en vue d'atteindre ces objectifs
Établit une liste de priorités
Coordonne les activités de ses subordonnés en fonction des délais, des priorités et des ressources humaines et matérielles.

Communication Skills-Written / *Facilité d'expression écrite*

	1	2	3	Not Rated
		X		

Logic, clarity, conciseness
Empathy, tact, style
Persuasiveness

S'exprime avec clarté et concision
Fait preuve d'empathie, de tact
Expose ses arguments d'une manière logique et convaincante.

Communication Skills-Verbal / *Facilité d'expression verbale*

	1	2	3	Not Rated
		X		

Listens, comprehends and identifies needs
Speaks clearly, concisely, and confidently
Tactful, persuasive and inspirational
Persistent when appropriate

Écoute, comprend et reconnaît les besoins
S'exprime clairement, avec concision et sans hésitation
Use de tact, de persuasion, de force de conviction
Se montre tenace, s'il le faut.

Supervisory Skills / *Aptitude à superviser*

	1	2	3	Not Rated
		X		

Selection of people for tasks
Control of task execution
Production of results through subordinates
Employees treated fairly and with understanding
Group operates as a "Team"

Répartit les tâches en fonction de la compétence des employés
Contrôle l'exécution des tâches
Produit des résultats par l'intermédiaire des subordonnés
Motive les employés, les traite avec équité, fermeté et compréhension
Est capable de travailler en équipe

Personnel / *Aptitude à diriger le personnel*

	1	2	3	Not Rated
		X		

Writing and dealing with performance appraisals
Training, improving and developing subordinates
Administration of personnel policies, e.g. Compensation, Benefits, Hours of work, etc.
Recruitment

Suit les progrès et prépare les fiches d'appréciation du personnel
Voit à la formation, à l'amélioration, au perfectionnement des employés.
Applique les directives touchant le personnel (rémunération, avantages sociaux, heures de travail, etc.)
Participe au recrutement des employés.

Analytical Skills / *Esprit d'analyse*

	1	2	3	Not Rated
		X		

Identification and organization of data
Analysis of data
Quality of conclusions and recommendations

Rassemble et organise les données
Analyse les données
Émet des conclusions et des recommandations logiques.

Administration / *Aptitude à administrer*

	1	2	3	Not Rated
	X			

Accuracy of forecasts
Preparation of budgets
Control of expenses
Up-keep of premises and equipment
Systems and Methods

Fait des prévisions exactes
Établit les prévisions budgétaires
Surveille les dépenses
Voit à l'entretien des locaux et du matériel
Établit les systèmes de gestion et les méthodes de travail.

Credit Skills / *Jugement en matière de crédit*

	1	2	3	Not Rated
	X			

Financial Statement Analysis
Negotiation
Collection and follow-up
Realistic loan pricing
Interpretation of policy
Appropriate security

Analyse les états financiers
Négocie les prêts
Voit au recouvrement et au rappel
Suit une politique de prix réaliste
Interprète les directives
Obtient les garanties nécessaires

Marketing / *Marketing*

	1	2	3	Not Rated
		X		

Service to the Public
Public relations
Selling the Bank's services
Retail
Commercial
Investments & Securities
Master Charge
Computer
Foreign

Offre un service de qualité
Entretien de bonnes relations avec les clients
Fait la promotion des divers services bancaires
Services aux consommateurs
Services à l'entreprise
Service de titres
Master.Charge
Traitement informatique
Change

EXHIBIT 15 (continued)

Andrews, Richard   Branch Manager   M11

Evaluation of Performance & Rating (cont'd)

ADMINISTRATION: Inspection ratings improved to 17; well above the District norm
of 11. Expenses are carefully controlled increasing only 4.1%, and part-time help
effectively utilized in place of full-time personnel to service peak customer flows.
Business plans are thoroughly prepared and well supported by action plans.
MARKETING: Well known through community affairs. Because of his long tenure at
this branch, motivation to aggressively promote business has waned somewhat. Branch
completed 22 non-customer calls; well below the District average. 1983 plans call
for a drive to expand agri-business which should bring good results. Commercial
customers are well serviced and competitive threats capably fended.
THE PERSON: A well experienced, capable lender with seasoned credit skills. Works
independently, is well organized, and provides firm control to operations.

EXHIBIT 16

EXHIBIT 16
BANK OF MONTREAL
DOMESTIC DEVELOPMENT PROGRAM (B)

Performance Appraisal of Martin L. Chin

Personal History   Bank of Montreal 🏛 Banque de Montréal
Fiche de renseignements personnels

Photograph
Photo

Name/*Nom* CHIN, Martin L   Soc. Ins. No./*N° d'ass. sociale*

Date of Birth/*Date de naissance*   March 18th, 1940

Date of Hire (or re-hire)/*Date d'engagement ou de rengagement*   December 15, 1974
(Re-hire) April 19th, 1976
Marital Status/*État civil*   Married - Child   (1964)
Dependent Children (Show Y.O.B.)/*Nombre d'enfants à charge (indiquer leur date de naissance)*

LANGUAGES SPOKEN – Specify degree of fluency as "good" or "fair". Include "English" only if NOT mother tongue.
LANGUES PARLÉES – *Indiquer le niveau de maîtrise pour chacune des langues mentionnées: Ex.: excellente, bonne ou moyenne.*

French - fair
German - fair

EXPERIENCE OTHER THAN BANK OF MONTREAL/EMPLOIS ANTÉRIEURS

Year to Year/*De – à*	Job Title/*Titre du poste*	Organization/*Nom de l'entreprise*

BANK OF MONTREAL EXPERIENCE – Summarize junior experience
EXPÉRIENCE À LA BANQUE DE MONTRÉAL – *Ne donner qu'une description sommaire de ses fonctions antérieures.*

Month Year/*Mois Année*	JobGrade/*Niveau du poste*	Job Title/*Titre du poste*	Component, e.g., Branch, Department, Division *Succursale, service ou division*
Dec. 1974 (re-entered)		Management Trainee	Clayton, Ontario
Apr. 1976		Management Trainee	1st & Clayton
Oct. 1976		Management Trainee	Main Office, Parkdale
Sept. 1977	M5	Manager	King & Queen, London
Oct. 1980	M6	Manager	King & Queen, London
Apr. 1982	M7	Manager	King & Queen, London

EXHIBIT 16 (continued)

EDUCATION — Show highest formal education level attained. If university degree is held, show "Major". Indicate university, night-school or other work-related courses, including In-Bank Seminars, with appropriate detail, such as whether employee has passed Part I, II or III or I.C.B. or the 1st, 2nd, etc , year of R.I.A.

ÉTUDES — *Préciser le niveau d'instruction ainsi que la spécialisation si celui-ci est représenté par un diplôme universitaire. Inscrire les titres de cours suivis par le soir, à l'université ou dans tout autre cadre, y compris les séminaires donnés par la Banque. Indiquer à cet égard les certificats decernés (I, II ou III dans le cas du programme de l'I.B.C.) ou les années complétées, ex.: 1re, 2e année du programme de comptabilité en gestion industrielle (R.I.A.).*

Year/*Année*	Academic Achievement Completed/*Certificat ou diplôme obtenus*
	Grade XIII - G.C.E. U.K.
1974	St. Mary's University - B.A. Economics & Pol. Science
1976	Personal Loans Workshop and Management Education Institute I.

OTHER DATA — Major association memberships, committee and community activities held during last 5 years.

RENSEIGNEMENTS GÉNÉRAUX — *Associations professionnelles, comités et activités communautaires dont vous avez fait partie au cours des cinq dernières années.*

Year/*Année*	Office Held/*Titre ou fonction*
1982	United Appeal - Chamber of Commerce
1980	Member - London Chamber of Commerce

_____

Date revised/*Date de révision*

EXHIBIT 16 (continued)

Bank of Montreal Banque de Montréal

CONFIDENTIAL

CONFIDENTIEL

Management Performance Appraisal

Fiche d'appréciation du personnel cadre

Name/*Nom et prénom* CHIN, Martin L	Soc. Ins. No./*N° d'ass. sociale*	PREVIOUS three ratings most recent at right *Cotes des trois dernières années - inscrire la plus récente dans la case de droite*		
Position Title/*Titre du poste* Manager	Branch/Dept./*Succursale ou service* LONDON, ONTARIO	Job Grade M07 *Niveau du poste*	Time on present Job *Ancienneté a ce poste*	
			Year(s)/*Année(s)* 2	Months/*Mois* 2

Evaluation of Performance & Rating/*Appréciation du rendement — Cote*   HIGH COMPETENT

PERSONNEL - Is enthusiastic in his approach to banking, which reflects favorably in strong personnel morale evidenced by team spirit and dedication to "selling the Bank". Inspectors commented on his good leadership qualities. Allows subordinates maximum degree of self-development with good results. (previous Acct. Mgr. received 3 grade promotion, previous Admin. Mgr. now Acct. Mgr, Smyth Main and doing well) although more critical assessment of Acct. Mgr. specific work performance (particularly credit submissions) is required. CREDIT - Discretionary limit $15M. Good mix of personal and small to medium commercial accounts. Recent lapse in previously good basis credit judgement; tends to be overly sympathetic to customers' needs (Strong Con. - unauth. $31M - potential loss $15M; Dr. Miller $66M NCL with occasional O/D's permitted). FFP del. ratio increased to over 2% vs. 1.1% L/Y. Is capable of better and contributing factor has been his strong emphasis on marketing. Recent counselling session expected to effect required improvement.
MARKETING - Strongly customer and service oriented. Selected as District Co-ordinator of Gold Medal Programme and worked very hard to achieve highly satisfactory results. Branch FFP loans increased 30% (now $2.3MM net) and strong growth continues. Active in commercial calls; arranged for formal bid for St. Catherines Hospital Acct. - unsuccessful so far, but continues his efforts. ADMINISTRATION - Inspection March '82 confirms good overall branch control - scored 14 pts vs. 10 L/Y. Personnel losses minimal. No O/T last six months. Profits increased 30% year over year.

Description of Potential - Improvement and Development Plans/*Définition du potentiel et perspectives de carrière - programme de perfectionnement*

CHARACTERISTICS - Is intelligent, enthusiastic and strongly inclined towards retail banking. Commercial credit development required before he can progress further.

DESCRIPTION OF POTENTIAL - IMPROVEMENT AND DEVELOPMENT PLANS
PROMOTABILITY - Q. Account Manager Gr. M07 (Developmental)
NORMAL POTENTIAL - Short Term: Account Manager Gr. M07
                   Long Term: Branch Manager Gr. M10

PLANS: 1) Closely follow improvement in credit assessment and observance
            of limits.
        2) Encourage continued self-development through University courses
            (studying towards his M.A.).

Aspirations - Preferred Progression/*Aspirations de l'employé - Filière d'avancement souhaitée*

Medium term aspirations: Branch Management Gr. M08 - 11; prefers to remain in same area for a further 18 months for child's education and his own studies.

Interim Review Dates/*Dates de révisions intérimaires*

Date Prepared/*Date* Dec. 6/82	Prepared by/*Rempli par*	Concurred in by/*Approuvé par*	Discussed with/*Discuté avec*
	Title & Signature - *Titre et signature*	Title & Signature - *Titre et signature*	Employee's Signature/*Sign. de l'employé*

EXHIBIT 16 (continued)

Skills Identification Chart   *Fiche d'aptitudes*

Name/*Nom*	Job/*Poste*	Grade/*Niveau du poste*
CHIN, Martin L	Manager	M07

	1	2	3	Not Rated Sans objet

1 - Has particularly strong skill at this grade level.
2 - Has normal skill expected at this grade level.
3 - Would require improvement before skill level would be considered satisfactory.

1 - *Compétence exceptionnelle à ce niveau.*
2 - *Compétence satisfaisante à ce niveau.*
3 - *Amélioration souhaitable.*

Planning & Organizing
Select realistic, yet challenging objectives
Develop programs and activities to achieve objectives
Establish priorities
Schedule and coordinate, using time, personnel and facilities to advantage

Sens de la planification et de l'organisation
Choisit des objectifs à la fois réalistes et stimulants
Se fixe un programme en vue d'atteindre ces objectifs
Établit une liste de priorités
Coordonne les activités de ses subordonnés en fonction des délais, des priorités et des ressources humaines et matérielles.

[X in column 2]

Communication Skills-Written
Logic, clarity, conciseness
Empathy, tact, style
Persuasiveness

Facilité d'expression écrite
S'exprime avec clarté et concision
Fait preuve d'empathie, de tact
Expose ses arguments d'une manière logique et convaincante.

[X in column 2]

Communication Skills-Verbal
Listens, comprehends and identifies needs
Speaks clearly, concisely, and confidently
Tactful, persuasive and inspirational
Persistent when appropriate

Facilité d'expression verbale
Écoute, comprend et reconnaît les besoins
S'exprime clairement, avec concision et sans hésitation
Use de tact, de persuasion, de force de conviction
Se montre tenace, s'il le faut.

[X in column 2]

Supervisory Skills
Selection of people for tasks
Control of task execution
Production of results through subordinates
Employees treated fairly and with understanding
Group operates as a "Team"

Aptitude à superviser
Répartit les tâches en fonction de la compétence des employés
Contrôle l'exécution des tâches
Produit des résultats par l'intermédiaire des subordonnés
Motive les employés, les traite avec équité, fermeté et compréhension
Est capable de travailler en équipe

[X in column 2]

Personnel
Writing and dealing with performance appraisals
Training, improving and developing subordinates
Administration of personnel policies, e.g. Compensation, Benefits, Hours of work, etc.
Recruitment

Aptitude à diriger le personnel
Suit les progrès et prépare les fiches d'appréciation du personnel
Voit à la formation, à l'amélioration, au perfectionnement des employés.
Applique les directives touchant le personnel (rémunération, avantages sociaux, heures de travail, etc.)
Participe au recrutement des employés.

[X in column 1]

Analytical Skills
Identification and organization of data
Analysis of data
Quality of conclusions and recommendations

Esprit d'analyse
Rassemble et organise les données
Analyse les données
Émet des conclusions et des recommandations logiques.

[X in column 2]

Administration
Accuracy of forecasts
Preparation of budgets
Control of expenses
Up-keep of premises and equipment
Systems and Methods

Aptitude à administrer
Fait des prévisions exactes
Établit les prévisions budgétaires
Surveille les dépenses
Voit à l'entretien des locaux et du matériel
Établit les systèmes de gestion et les méthodes de travail.

[X in column 2]

Credit Skills
Financial Statement Analysis
Negotiation
Collection and follow-up
Realistic loan pricing
Interpretation of policy
Appropriate security

Jugement en matière de crédit
Analyse les états financiers
Négocie les prêts
Voit au recouvrement et au rappel
Suit une politique de prix réaliste
Interprète les directives
Obtient les garanties nécessaires

[X in column 3]

Marketing
Service to the Public
Public relations
Selling the Bank's services
Retail
Commercial
Investments & Securities
Master Charge
Computer
Foreign

Marketing
Offre un service de qualité
Entretien de bonnes relations avec les clients
Fait la promotion des divers services bancaires
Services aux consommateurs
Services à l'entreprise
Service de titres
Master.Charge
Traitement informatique
Change

[X in column 1]

SENTINEL PETROLEUM (A)

James C. Rush and Eileen D. Watson

On July 26, 1985, a special meeting was in progress in the Toronto head office of Sentinel Petroleum Inc. (SPI). Seated around the boardroom table with President Alec Henderson were several senior managers and executives. The group was engrossed in an urgent discussion concerning the future of Sentinel Petroleum, with a particular focus on future management needs.

Alec Henderson stated:

> We've weathered some stormy conditions in the past few years, but the situation facing us today is the most disturbing ever. As SPI's profitability decreases, pressures to improve our performance are becoming stronger. It's too late for 'band-aid' solutions. I'm appointing a special task force to embark immediately on a six-month study of the best ways to meet present challenges, and at the same time, prepare the company to be a successful competitor into the twenty-first century.
>
> We are already in the transition phase that Naisbitt writes about in *Megatrends* [see Appendix A]. Vast fundamental changes and restructuring are already under way in North American society which certainly are affecting our company...and the entire petroleum industry, for that matter! But what exactly does that mean, in terms of how we organize and manage ourselves today and prepare our people for the future? Let's tentatively identify some possible scenarios for Sentinel Petroleum in the year 2000. What kinds of people will we need in senior management positions 10 or 15 years from now? What kind of leadership is going to be needed to run this organization in the future?

Background: The Petroleum Industry and SPI

During the late 1970s and early 1980s the entire Canadian oil industry was jolted out of its steady growth mode by a sharply declining demand for petroleum products. Several factors caused this decrease — higher prices (primarily due to worldwide increases in the price of crude oil), a new focus on energy efficiency, government off-oil programs, and the economic recession of 1982.

The drastically reduced demand resulted in surplus capacity, forcing the closure of nine Canadian refineries, one of Sentinel's included. Keen competition for share in the declining market brought extensive price wars at the retail level, a downward pressure on margins, a shifting product mix, and generally low return on investments.

Sentinel Petroleum Inc. was established as a separate division under the umbrella of Sentinel Oil Canada Limited (SOC) in the early 1980s. One of the oldest integrated oil companies in Canada, SOC conducted its operations in three main segments — natural resources, chemicals, and petroleum products (SPI — the "downstream" operation). SOC had moved to a more functional organization, to provide greater focus and effectiveness within the major segments of its overall business. The diversity of opportunities available to it were retained through its wide-ranging involvement in all aspects of the oil business and its sound financial health.

Sentinel Petroleum's stated purpose was "to be the leading integrated petroleum products operation in Canada, achieving profit for shareholders and benefits for the community." (See Exhibit 1 for a complete mission statement.) In 1985, SPI operated several refineries and sold its products through an extensive network of retail outlets, agencies, and distribution facilities, and was responsible for extensive research in fuel and specialty products. The company employed approximately 6000 people in its refineries, numerous sales offices, and other facilities (see Exhibit 2 for a partial organization chart).

Earnings in 1984 amounted to $124.1 million, an increase from $51.9 million in 1983. (1982 earnings were $124 million, down from $280.5 million in 1981.) Although Sentinel was one of the largest single suppliers of petroleum products in Canada, total sales volumes were clearly declining (see Exhibit 3).

The generally accepted prognosis for the balance of the decade was that the demand for petroleum products would continue to decline slightly, which would result in a continuation of the highly competitive environment already in existence. Competition for retail gasoline customers was expected to be particularly intense.

Human Resources Management at SPI

SPI's complex and complete human resources (HR) management systems were based on the "Sentinel Petroleum Philosophy of Management" (see Exhibit 4). An extensive system of personnel committees guided all aspects of the function — committees for job openings, appraisals, ranking of performance, compensation, actual replacement of jobs, and development of and review of replacement plans. One HR manager commented,

> Our personnel management system is a very thorough system — time-consuming, but it works. Some people think we may be spending an inordinate amount of time

developing people, but I don't believe we are. It's one of the most important things we do. If you pay the appropriate attention to it — and good managers should — you identify people who have potential, and put them in developmental areas and positions. You'll give them the kind of exposure in terms of jobs, training, and assignments that hopefully will bring them along — will help them expand their capacities, and stretch them to the utmost. And as long as they continue to deliver, the real serious planning for their future continues, and the development opportunities continue to be provided.

Although the career paths of individual managers might appear to the outside observer somewhat erratic and random, they were actually very thoughtfully and carefully conceived (see Exhibit 5, Criteria for Advancement). Examples of management career paths developed for one high-potential individual may be seen in Exhibit 6. As one area manager remarked,

I don't believe that the specifics of the plan are nearly as important as actually putting a plan together. What I mean by that is if you've got someone you want to develop, it doesn't really matter whether he gets this job today or that job today; the point is that you want him to get those kinds of exposure at some point. So you work along a zigzag course to get to where you're heading.

A succession plan for every management position was developed annually. SPI's plans were integrated into SOC's personnel development and succession planning process. A five-year plan existed for every individual; and for every job, incumbents were identified covering the next five years. Every employee was appraised annually, and rated on his or her level of performance — outstanding (10 percent of the population), excellent (25 percent), very good (25 percent), and good (30 percent). Poor performers constituted the remaining 10 percent of the employee population. Concerning these ratings, one manager commented, "One's performance rating can change more frequently than one's potential — the potential level to which a person can aspire tends not to go up and down, but one's performance can change from year to year."

Future Considerations

In July, 1985, twenty-four Sentinel Petroleum managers and executives representing a cross-section of managerial levels and functions throughout the company were interviewed about their concerns regarding the future of the organization. Certain potentially significant issues were mentioned frequently:

- Changing customer demands (e.g. reduced sales of heating fuels, increased sales of diesel and aircraft fuels).
- Technological innovation (e.g. development of ceramic engines requiring little or no lubrication).

- Changes in information-handling technology (e.g. automated processing of cross-functional information).
- Governmental legislation (e.g. deregulation of the petroleum industry, institution of vehicle emission control standards).
- Changing employee attitudes (e.g. new work ethic, pressures for equal opportunity).
- Decreasing mobility of professional employees (e.g. two-career families, life-style considerations).
- Age distribution changing (e.g. 1985 population "blips" in two age groups — 20 to 29, and 50 to 55 years of age).
- Changes in the retailing business
  (e.g. 1950s — Many two-bay gas stations
  1960s — Fewer multi-bay gas stations
  1970s — Addition of car washes, self-serve mode
  1980s — Addition of "Service Plus," restaurants, sales outlets for convenience items.)
- Increasing importance of social and political issues (e.g. the Retail Trade Practices Inquiry, the Berger Commission re Arctic gas pipeline applications, unemployment, budget deficits, world conflicts, public attitudes toward free enterprise).

Future Management Needs at SPI

When asked for opinions about SPI's future management needs, the representative group of managers and executives made frequent mention of the difficulties inherent in accurately forecasting the future. One manager said, "The biggest single factor driving our business is the world price of crude oil, which is something over which we have absolutely no control. I've seen forecasts made in 1970 that the price of oil would only go from $2 to $2.50 a barrel by 1980. Hindsight makes me wonder how we could have been so naive!"

Responses to questions about future management requirements were many and varied. In order to simplify the resulting vast and complex mass of data, frequently expressed opinions were sorted into groups related to common themes. The resulting "individual" statements which follow actually represent a composite picture of one "group" of responses.

Response #1: More of the Same, or Different Only By Degree

Nothing's going to be very different in terms of necessary management skills. A good manager today is somebody who already has managed to adapt to massive changes, and I think that requirement is going to be the same in the year 2000. Our people today are obviously willing to accept changes — look at their positive response to accepting personal computers and other new technology — so I don't know what's going to be different from people today versus in the future. We already have the people and the skills to continue to be an effective and profitable organization.

Sure, we might get more efficient car engines and unleaded gasoline or whatever, but I think we'll still have our refineries and our petroleum products. The thing is, when companies get out of their own sector, they get into trouble. So that's why SPI is perhaps a little conservative, in that it takes plenty of time to research and make progress slowly — but that's okay.

We must ask the question, what business do we want to be in, 10, 15, 20 years from now? My prediction is, more of the same — only better! We'll get more efficient, we'll develop new products, come up with new technologies, but they'll all still be derived from the same basic roots. The business will be significantly rationalized and sized down, and the strong will inherit the earth . . . but if anybody thinks that plants like our big refineries will not be around in the next century, they're crazy. I don't know what's going to flow into them, but it'll be some sort of hydrocarbon. So once we accept that, then the pathway is very clear — it's only a matter of asking how big or small will we be, and who else is out there?

Response #2: Rationalization and Restructuring

We've got to make some hard decisions about the deployment of our resources. For instance, in order to be profitable in Eastern Canada, a gasoline service station should serve a minimum of 25 000 people; but the average service station in Eastern Canada serves an average of only 10 000! The implication of that is, two out of three have to shut down. How long are we going to stay in that game? Some would be quite content to run the manufacturing site as a no-name refinery, and simply supply products . . . Who knows what the outcome will be by the year 2000!

We have already taken steps to rationalize our human resources. Significant downsizing initiatives have already taken place — more than 1000 employees went out in a short period of time — and there's more to come. I look at our demographics, which are very different from four or five years ago. More than 50 percent of our population is now less than 35 years old, and over 50 percent of our people have less than 10 years' service. Of the present senior executive group, only one person is over 60. So you've got a very different population in terms of values. Younger people today challenge things a lot more . . . they ask why, they don't just accept blindly. They don't want an authority figure in charge; they want to get in there and feel they're part of the action.

I think the company will begin a gradually accelerated movement towards a more diverse portfolio of activities, becoming more of a conglomeration of loosely connected initiatives under the SOC umbrella, in areas that will be growing on their own. You see some of it already — there is far less clarity of relationship between SPI and the other two SOC companies than there used to be; and there are far fewer uniformities and blanket policies about people development and budgeting and forecasting and planning. Management styles in SOC's three main offshoot companies will become even more diverse. Decentralization is already underway, and will still be with us in the next few decades.

There'll be an increasing and continuing need to change the organizational structure for more efficient operations, as in the recent transfer of a large section of the accounting department from SOC to Sentinel Petroleum. Senior personnel, such as division managers, will be changing every year or so...I wonder, will they be churning around too much?

We've got to minimize the bureaucracy typical of a big company, or we'll stifle innovation. I think what we'll eventually wind up doing is just removing layer after layer of bureaucracy, while keeping sufficient control — you cannot allow one individual to make half-billion dollar decisions and be wrong two times in a row! And a flatter organization will come, along with new information technology, to provide the keys to management productivity — not just computer components on our desks, but fewer layers through which to pass the word.

Response #3: New Management Skills and Systems

In the past, the oil business has been inward-looking and technical. The future lies in our reading of the *outside* world — societal trends, political trends, market shifts. In order of importance, you'll have to be able to read the outside world, energize people, and manage or understand the technology.

Entrepreneurial skills will be valued more. Today, the question is whether we want creative entrepreneurs or very pushy process-oriented administrative people? You look around the organization at the kinds of people we have...my contention is that we vastly underestimate and undervalue people's creative capability — or possibly we may be misinterpreting creativity. Like most other organizations, we traditionally have not evaluated people on the right kinds of characteristics, so that we've got people with some very entrepreneurial qualities who are perhaps innovating like crazy, but we just don't realize and appreciate it.

And to some extent we'll need a better mix than we may have had. I am not of the school that says you have to junk the old management style, get rid of the present administrators and bring in a bunch of free thinkers. I think the problem is that we have not, perhaps due to lack of experience, learned how to mix management styles — to have the entrepreneurial creative types able to work comfortably with the thorough, process-minded, reliable, technically proficient types. Both types are valuable assets in any kind of a total management system, and you certainly have to understand the leading edge of technology in your core business. However, for people whose interests are primarily technical, supervising people and all that sort of 'soft' stuff simply does not interest them. We clearly need to identify those people earlier on, because the really valuable technical people, to be honest with you, are probably too valuable to waste as managers.

We need managers with very good communications skills, able to relate to people at all levels in the organization. Some can do that very easily; some have a lot of trouble with it. But managers should be people who feel comfortable interacting with technical people, managers, marketers, supply people, and presidents, and who are able to get their points across and change their message to match their audience. And we'll probably have more interactions with government institutes and universities in the future — a lot more interactions outside of the parent group than in the past.

But in my opinion, there's a dramatic difference between the communications skills needed at the president and vice-president level versus the skills needed by, say, a distribution terminal manager in Regina. Top executives must have superb communications skills — the ability to articulate their thoughts fluently, transferring their thoughts to others effectively. And their communications skills must be very effective in the public forum. It isn't good enough simply to be able to talk internally with those who are experts in the business along with yourself; you've got to have an equal ability to talk to others who know nothing of your business.

They must have an ability to function with the government linkages, the ability to appreciate government motivation (which is often very different from free enterprise motivation), and they need to understand how that great big government machine works. And an ability to manage a continuously changing group of employees, whose needs for supervision are constantly changing. There's no guarantee that today's style of people management will work tomorrow.

In the future we should act a little faster. By the time we've studied things to death, somebody has beaten us to it. Quickness and swiftness of decision making should be encouraged within our working environment. In this ambiguous world, in a shrinking business you need to be a little faster on your feet, or accept that you're going to have to look at different ways of doing things. And you're going to have to give up some of those nice rigid controls — in other words, you'll have to take a little more risk. And to do that, the manager has to be able to motivate people, and be more willing to take risks himself, as well as encourage risk-taking in others; and he's got to be able to look past some mistakes. The company culture had better say it's OK to make mistakes — we've got to grow fewer people who can say "no" and more people who can say "yes."

"Although there's never going to be any substitute for talking to somebody face to face, the technology to transfer information is changing and will continue to change very rapidly. What we're seeing now is electronic mail where people just type a message onto a computer terminal and zap it instantaneously half-way across the world to some guy sitting in a room in Europe somewhere...so there's no question that people coming into the industry now need to be computer-literate. Computer technology is going to be part of their everyday life in the future, when every manager will have a terminal in his office. He'll work differently than today — he's going to have to know what information he wants, rather than relying on analysts to provide him with the information *they* think he should have. And in a more computer-driven environment, I suspect that the *qualities* that you'll need to manage people will shift somewhat as well. There may be a little less interaction with people, and more interaction with information or keys. Your management skills will be geared to getting people to work more independently, seeing objectives more clearly and earlier in the process. It will be essential that people be self-starters with a high degree of initiative.

Other changes...the ability to work with minorities. We're only dealing with the tip of the iceberg today. A very small percentage of our professional staff here is female, and an even smaller percentage is a physical minority, physically disabled; and I'm sure that the future will include a much greater percentage of both. Some of our senior managers have difficulty working with some of those groups — it's a new experience for them, especially when you consider they're a group of engineers mostly. Surprisingly, I see some *young* chaps in our organization who are first-class chauvinists — how can that be, chauvinist 23-year-olds in today's world? I know that type of person is going to have problems in the future — if they're having problems today, I can guarantee it's going to get worse and worse.

The primary motivation of the young people coming into the organization today is to get more responsibility and take on more risk and have more authority delegated to them to do that. Young professionals moving in at the supervisory and lower management rungs are very outspoken about the fact that they think that we older guys are basically incompetent. I don't remember being like that — they're a different breed of cat than I went to school with, far more interested in their careers and the practical side of their education. They are coming into these companies and are saying to people like me, "Get out of the way. Give us a piece of the action!" So we are going to be driven as a management team to delegate more responsibility, or these people are not going to stick around.

"I think there'll be an even greater demand for financial skills. If you look at 1985 versus ten years ago, our awareness of the world of finance has grown dramatically. Interest rates going from the traditional six or seven percent to 22 percent in 1982 — that kind of thing has heightened the awareness of financial markets, of the world of finance and cash flow. And it's not just the treasurer or the controller and the president who are interested in finance, today; that interest is much more acute throughout the organization. I suspect it will increase even more in the next ten or fifteen years.

With all of that heightened awareness and new, sophisticated technology, I still think it will be very important for the manager to have both feet on the ground from a practical standpoint. People are still going to be people and a manager's success will be, to a great extent, determined by how practical and realistic the manager is, how he perceives his staff and what they're doing on a day-to-day basis, and how his markets are behaving."

EXHIBIT 1
SENTINEL PETROLEUM (A)

Mission Statement

Sentinel Petroleum is committed to creating an organization that stimulates innovative thinking and business risk-taking. It is a place in which people have the opportunity to develop their full potential and sustain a high quality of life.

Sentinel Petroleum's mission is to be the leading integrated Petroleum Products operation in Canada, achieving profit for shareholders and benefits for the community. This leadership role will be achieved by marketing refined petroleum products, providing value to customers and effectively utilizing Canada's resources. Future profitability will be enhanced by developing growth opportunities for new products and services that build on fundamental strengths and are related to existing businesses.

EXHIBIT 2
SENTINEL PETROLEUM (A)

Partial Organizational Chart, June 1985

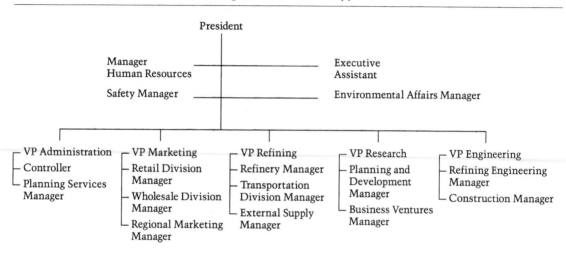

EXHIBIT 3

SPI PETROLEUM PRODUCTS SALES VOLUMES 1980–1984

	1980	1981	1982	1983	1984
Petroleum products sales volumes of $m^3/d*$)					
Gasolines	21.6	20.6	19.0	18.6	17.6
Jet fuels	3.4	3.8	3.7	3.1	3.8
Heating fuels	8.2	6.6	6.3	5.6	4.8
Diesel fuels	10.3	10.9	9.8	9.6	10.2
Heavy fuel oils	5.4	5.6	4.5	3.5	3.1
Liquid petroleum gas	3.8	3.6	3.6	2.9	2.6
Other products	3.2	3.1	2.7	2.9	2.8
Total Petroleum Products	55.9	54.2	49.6	46.2	45.0
Total Domestic Sales of Petroleum Products (percent)	82.1	81.6	81.2	79.7	78.5
Refinery capacity utilization at Dec. 31 (percent)	79	76	64	66	75

*One cubic metre (m^3) is equal to approximately 6.3 barrels or 35.3 cubic feet.

EXHIBIT 4

SENTINEL PETROLEUM (A)

The Sentinel Petroleum Philosophy of Management

We are part of Sentinel Oil Canada Limited. We are respectful of the latitudes given us by Sentinel management and seek their counsel and assistance to help us improve.

Long-term success means we have to be the best, because our business is mature, capital intensive and very competitive. The highest practical levels of efficiency and productivity are fundamental. Being more responsive to customers' needs will result in sustaining our customer franchise base and high market shares.

Our people are our prime resource. We are organized so that individual initiatives are highly valued, but team efforts are also promoted. We strive to be entrepreneurial, and seek to provide an environment and processes which are not burdensome, with an appropriate balance of sound business controls.

Our management group is a team. We believe no one member has all the right answers. Minority views and new ideas are sought and respected. We try hard to reach decisions by consensus, not compromise.

Final decisions are made by those responsible for the actions to be taken. Within agreed guidelines, managers are expected to accept personal responsibility for their function, and they are similarly held accountable. Where initiatives may have an impact beyond a manager's area of responsibility, decisions are appropriately shared.

We must keep each other informed of significant and potential business activities and external situations, so we can benefit from the synergy of collective innovation. Informality and personal contact work best for us. We try to be each other's friend. Empire-building is frowned upon. If effective services are available from others, they are utilized.

We deal with customers, associates and each other in a highly ethical manner. Not only do we adhere to the letter of the law but also to its intent. If mistakes are made, we take immediate corrective action. We keep SOC's interests in mind at all times.

EXHIBIT 5

SENTINEL PETROLEUM (A)

Criteria for Advancement—Management Career Paths

A career path for an employee considered to have the potential to assume general management positions (Potential Rating 13) will typically include job assignments in as many different departments of Sentinel Petroleum as is practical. Generally, this will mean from 4 to 6 different assignments, from attainment of the fully qualified professional level (Salary Group 33/34) to attainment of the executive job levels (Code 35).

Assignments within the two core operating departments of Sentinel Petroleum (Marketing and Refining) are, of course, regarded as the primary targets of these inter-departmental moves. Frequently, the plan will include a loan assignment to another operating division (Sentinel Resources or Sentinel Chemical), or to another department of SOC. Time interval per assignment would generally be one to two years.

Career plans for employees with potential ratings at the 13 level should also involve a number of inter-departmental assignments during their management potential training and development careers. However, assignments within *both* core operating departments would be less characteristic, and the time interval between assignments would tend to be six months to a year longer.

Career plans for employees whose potential does not extend beyond the management potential training and development category will generally consist of a series of vertical and lateral assignments, often within the same department. Assignments will tend to lengthen with time but, on average, would be about five years in duration, following attainment of the professional level (Salary Group 33/34).

Once again, keep in mind that the above criteria are generalizations and, to some extent, over-simplifications of actual career paths. In actuality, for example, the potential of individual employees is subject to continuing re-assessment and revision, particularly during the early stages of their careers. Accordingly, the actual career path of any one individual is very likely to switch from one path to another and this, in turn, will affect such factors as the nature, location, and duration of specific assignments.

EXHIBIT 6

SENTINEL PETROLEUM (A)

A Typical Career Path Leading to Management Level Positions

SKILL AND EXPERIENCE AREAS

GROUNDING	ANALYTICAL	SUPERVISORY	PLANNING/MANAGERIAL
• Technical competence, implementing • Understanding the business/organization	• Planning • Decision-making • Problem-solving	• Leading/directing developing staff • Int. interfacing • Organizing	• Strong business/organization understanding • Co-ordinating • Strategic planning

External Supply Manager
Refining Manager

REFINING

External Environmental Coordinator

EXTERNAL AFFAIRS

Supply Coordinator
Planning Assoc.

REFINING

Area Sales Manager
Strategic Plng. Mgr.
Distribution Opns.
Manager

MARKETING

Financial Analyst
Economic Analyst
Sr. Coord.-Plng.

ADMINISTRATION

Project Engineer
Product Advisor
Asst. Terminal Mgr.
Merchandising Asst.
Sr. Sales Rep.

MARKETING

Project Eng.
Contact Eng.

REFINING

Age	Experience (Years)
34	3-4
35-36	4-5
	5-6
36-37	6-7
37-38	7-8
	8-9
38-39	9-10
	10-11
40-41	11-12
	12-13

EXPERIENCE (YEARS)

141

APPENDIX
SENTINEL PETROLEUM (A)

Selected Excerpts from Megatrends[1]

We are living in the time of the parenthesis, the time between eras. It is as though we have bracketed off the present from both the past and the future, for we are neither here nor there. We have not quite left behind the either/or America of the past — centralized, industrialized, and economically self-contained. With one foot in the old world where we lived mostly in the Northeast, relied on institutional help, built hierarchies, and elected representatives, we approached problems with an eye toward the high-tech, short-term solutions.

But we have not embraced the future either. We have done the human thing: We are clinging to the known past in fear of the unknown future.... Those who are willing to handle the ambiguity of this in-between period and to anticipate the new era will be a quantum leap ahead of those who hold on to the past. The time of the parenthesis is a time of change and questioning.

As we move from an industrial to an information society we will use our brainpower to create instead of our physical power, and the technology of the day will extend and enhance our mental ability. As we take advantage of the opportunity for job growth and investment in all the sunrise industries, we must not lose sight of the need to balance the human element in the face of all that technology.

Yet, the most formidable challenge will be to train people to work in the information society. Jobs will become available, but who will possess the high-tech skills to fill them? Not today's graduates, who cannot manage simple arithmetic or write basic English. And certainly not the unskilled, unemployed dropouts who cannot even find work in the old sunset industries.

Farmer, laborer, clerk. The next transition may well be to technician. But that is a major jump in skill level....As we tread water, unwilling to choose the winning businesses of the future and unable to let go of the losers, Japan and the "new Japans" of the Third World are free to eclipse our lead in electronics, biotechnology, and other sunrise sectors. But do we have the courage to abandon our traditional industries, industries that other countries can now do better? Do we have the innovative ability to venture forward into the future?

·   ·   ·   ·

This newly evolving world will require its own structures. We are beginning to abandon the hierarchies that worked well in the centralized, industrial era. In their place we are substituting the network model of organization and communication, which has its roots in the natural egalitarian, and spontaneous formation of groups among like-minded people. Networks restructure the power and communication flow within an organization from vertical to horizontal. One network form, the quality control circle, will help revitalize worker participation and productivity in American

_____

[1] John Naisbitt, *Megatrends: Ten New Directions Transforming Our Lives*. Warner Books, New York, N.Y., 1982, pp. 249–.

business. A network management style is already in place in several young, successful computer firms. And the computer itself will be what actually smashes the hierarchical pyramid: With the computer to keep track of people and business information, it is no longer necessary for organizations to be organized into hierarchies. No one knows this better than the new-age computer companies.

The computer will smash the pyramid. We created the hierarchical, pyramidal, managerial system because we needed it to keep track of people and things people did; with the computer to keep track, we can restructure our institutions horizontally.

. . . .

. . . .We have diversified into a society where almost anything is possible. The wide range of choices in work arrangements, the new definitions of family, the enormous diversity in the arts, the dazzling array of newly promoted specialty foods are only some of the reflections of a society that is exploding with diversity. One measure is the way we have responded to the new wave of immigrants in recent years: We have . . . learned to celebrate ethnic diversity. The new languages, ethnic food and restaurants, and the additional layer of foreign cultures all around us seem to fit the multiple-option mood. This new openness enriches us all.

Such is the time of the parenthesis, its challenges, its possibilities, and its questions.

Although the time between eras is uncertain, it is a great and yeasty time, filled with opportunity. If we can learn to make uncertainty our friend, we can achieve much more than in stable eras.

In stable eras, everything has a name and everything knows its place, and we can leverage very little.

But in the time of the parenthesis we have extraordinary leverage and influence — individually, professionally and institutionally — if we can only get a clear sense, a clear conception, a clear vision, of the road ahead.

My God, what a fantastic time to be alive!

SENTINEL PETROLEUM (B)

James C. Rush and Eileen D. Watson

The special meeting on July 26, 1985, involving the president of Sentinel Petroleum Inc., Alec Henderson, and several of the company's senior managers and executives, was drawing to a close. Various recommendations regarding the company's future management needs were being discussed. Henderson declared,

> Within six months, I expect that the task force I mentioned earlier will bring in recommendations which will profoundly change this organization. And I'm convinced that by the year 2000 SPI will look a lot different than it looks today. I know it is absolutely fundamental that it be organized differently, the business mix will be different, the management style will be different, the information that's processed through the company will be different. And I accept that. But I'm not rigid in trying to think of precisely what that might look like.
>
> However, we need to set our goals, realizing that many intervening influences may necessitate modifications. We've been concentrating on issues affecting human resource management, and I'd like to hear your individual recommendations for future changes and adjustments in that area. Who will lead off?"

Future Management Needs: Suggestions for Change

Response #1: Better Communication Skills

> We have to be prepared to get up in front of our people and talk about our goals. We must take advantage of every opportunity — communications meetings with our people, informal discussions, all sorts of chances to get right up in front. And whether we like it or not, the fact is that when the boss gets up and models a certain kind of behavior, it sinks in.
>
> The basic job of all our senior management is the leadership of people, particularly in a strategic sense. I feel very strongly that all 7015 people in Sentinel Petroleum deserve to have some understanding of where we're going as a company.

They have a tremendous stake in this company — of all our stakeholders, they are the ones who are most personally affected by what we do. So we need to spend a lot of time communicating with them, both telling them what we think, and having them tell us what they think.

In my opinion, a two-way appraisal is really important. People say it sounds good, but you don't get nearly enough of it. And you've got to keep encouraging it; you've got to really listen and say "thank you" and be willing to change your behavior. I continue to tell the people reporting to me, "You know, I'm going to feel a lot better about you as a person if you help me to make myself better as a person. The only way you can do that, is to tell it like it is!" . . . but I acknowledge that we're quite a ways from that as a society and as a business community, today.

Response #2: Improved Management Skills and Abilities

SPI will not be a growth business in the future, but it may not shrink fast either. So senior managers of the future need to be capable of managing in a mature, very competitive, low-margin kind of business. They must be people who understand technology very well, and who can use that technology to give them a competitive edge; and they must possess really good skills related to their functional area.

Obviously we are going to need intelligent, bright people — people who can get their minds around a big chunk of our business. In addition, our people must be able to exist in the social milieu of a very large company. It is true that being a small fish in a rather large pond is a different kind of challenge for a person than is being one of a very few people running a small business — the difference between an entrepreneur and an intrapreneur, I guess. So you're looking for people who can exist in this big-company environment . . . but you're also looking for people who can appreciate the scope, the support, and the latitude available in a large company which, after all, is greater because a large company has many flexibilities, vast opportunities.

Future managers will have to be able to deal with complexity and ambiguity; and they need to have that vital interpersonal dynamics capacity to access the people required to get the job done effectively. They must be able to generate the kind of relationships that will allow a junior upstart who's obviously well-regarded in the eyes of all the people he has to deal with (by virtue of the short track he's had to date) to effectively get the job done.

People who'll be in our positions in a couple of decades will need a different perspective, different skills, in the sense of being less technical, and a somewhat broader perspective. And although I've never had direct hands-on responsibility for the delivery of results at the customer level, I don't think anybody will get to be in my job in the future who hasn't had some of that in his background. We'll continue to require lots of good technical people, as we do now; but we'll probably be focusing a little harder than we have in the past on developing a broader range of skills — marketing skills, for example. I think we'll probably find ourselves looking outward more for training, and for help in getting the right mix of marketing skills very solidly in place with all our people.

I think we'll have to build in a willingness to accept failure constructively. Not every initiative is going to be successful. When we clearly must make a decision to stop a program, we should post a bulletin board announcement saying, 'Look, we ran down seven paths on this one, they're all dead ends. Our group did a fantastic job, but we're quitting; and John's going here, Mary's going there, and Tim's going there'... so it becomes a win-win instead of a win-lose situation. And that's what managerial leadership is all about.

We'd better have future managers who are not only prepared to be entrepreneurial, risk-taking, and innovative, but who have a great ability to change with the times. They've got to be managers who aren't set in their ways. And above all, we're looking for *leadership* qualities. The senior people have got to be able to lead — not push, but lead by example; and they'll be able to show, not tell, how to get technological innovation underway. They've got to like to coach people. They've got to like to listen to people. They've got to exhibit all of these qualities that make good leaders — the natural leaders. And they have to work all those facets *consciously* — team building, developing innovative qualities, etc. It's a people-management game.

Response #3: Focus on Recruitment and Selection

I believe that in 1995 the selection process for big companies like ours will be, "Put your hand on their foreheads and if they're warm, they've got a job!" You think there's unemployment now and it's going to stay? The demographics of this country indicate that by the year 2000 we will have the direct opposite of unemployment. But being in a declining business, a dying business, which is ultimately going to be replaced by nuclear energy or natural gas or whatever, the real challenge for us is to recruit the kind of people who will be concerned about rejuvenating the company — therefore, innovative free thinkers. The natural tendency of a manager today is to replenish in his own image and likeness, which isn't necessarily good.

We need to sell ourselves better, and try to turn people on. Our recruitment procedures must continually improve and evolve, to attract the exceptional young men and women we need. I think we should accumulate a very large pool of talented young people — they're the life blood of our company. I've always felt that we should start with as large a group to develop as we can, because when we're through, we're left with a relatively small group to choose from for senior positions. And you want those people not only to learn, but to contribute, as they go along; because if they don't contribute, they don't get the support of the organization, and can get into trouble very quickly in the future.

The way the company workload is changing, and the way demands on people are evolving, we can no longer afford to have many people in the organization who have a very finite limit around the kind of job they can do. I get pretty fidgety today with a young employee who doesn't look like he can do anything except his present job; because although he may do his present job acceptably, you worry about what to do with him if that job disappears. We should be selecting people with more flexibility and a broader range of skills, in fairness to everybody.

At the senior level in our organization, leadership is the key component; so what I look for in young applicants is that mystical quality called leadership. It's the willingness of a person to say, "Hey, this is where I think I'm going; and as I look around the edges of my job, here are some things that I don't think are right — maybe I should try to work with my neighbor on those interfaces to correct them." That's leadership in a young sense. It's an awareness, too, of the need to establish a network.... You've got to look sideways, as well as up and down.

We have the prosperity to try and produce all our business managers out of a technical mold. But I think you can't be sensitive enough to some of the social, political, economic, and other aspects of modern society if you've come straight out of an engineering or business school type of environment. If we really want to develop some well-rounded management teams in the future, maybe we should be putting some honors history grads on the road as sales reps, or some political science students in our refineries. And when you say that, some people think you're a little crazy — but those are the young people with the brains who'll bring the new dimensions we'll need for future success.... Besides, if we're prepared to spend millions of dollars on a new electronics venture, then why shouldn't we risk putting a few non-business and non-engineering grads in our company here and there, and see whether or not they develop as good managers?

And when I go out and interview someone who can't communicate well, I wouldn't say that person isn't going to be a good employee, but I can say with certainty, that candidate isn't presidential material. You can be smart as can be, but if you can't communicate, forget it; and you've got to be able to communicate on *all* stages — internally, externally, everywhere. So we might as well select new employees who have already developed some good presentation skills.

Response #4: Changes in Compensation Policies

I don't think we should pay people by the hour anymore — it's demeaning, and the practise surely is going to disappear, maybe by 2000 or sooner. Also, we need to have a culture that allows progression and growth and development of wage people. We have a system with a cap on the top, which says, "If you don't have a university degree, you can't rise beyond this level — you can't be a professional." When employees want to expand and grow, the company should allow them growth opportunities in their function. And a lot of them want cross-functional development, too — that's coming. It's only a matter of time. Industries that don't provide such opportunities are going to die.

I myself am motivated primarily by tangible rewards....I like money! And I like the perks that accrue as you go up the ladder. Another significant motivator for me is that I like to learn — I've learned 10 jobs in 10 years! And the first year in a job, you're just struggling to survive. By the second year in a job, you say, "I'm starting to get the hang of this...I know what's going on now." In the third year in a job, you're comfortable, you're in the driver's seat. Well, 10 jobs in 10 years...I never made it to third! But the rewards are there, nevertheless.

We'll need to have policies and systems which are much more attuned to different needs of different people. The culture will become one of accepting differences, so we're going to need different compensation systems. Then some people could be on fixed salaries, others could be on salaries and bonuses — all sorts of different incentive methods, varying from area group to area group. Also, we'll have to provide different compensation systems for people involved in the long-term development of new products, and maybe give them the benefit of sharing the proceeds of patents, too."

Response #5: Emphasis on Management Training and Development

Twenty years from now, top SPI managers should be equipped with much broader background experience. They may have gone to the resources side, or may have been in marketing, refining, and supply for a number of years, and maybe even touched over on SOC. I think the best senior managers are ones who understand the full scope of the company, and don't favor any one particular part. However, going through a multitude of jobs in a relatively short time in order to get broad exposure to the company, I worry whether or not our fast trackers have really been in any one job long enough to contribute anything; and secondly, have they been there long enough so that one could see how many mistakes they've made? It's very easy to make mistakes, then leave the job before they catch up with you!

A dilemma in a stabilized or downsizing organization is how to develop future presidents by providing a variety of job experiences when many positions are blocked by an incumbent who is doing a good job, but who is not going to move out or move ahead. I expect we'll have solved that problem by the year 2000 — but I'm not sure *how*!

People need help, sometimes, in learning different management skills as they advance through the company. When I was a young designer I relied on my own hands-on experience, my technology, and the reference resource material that told me how to design a good thing. It was pretty easy to manage! I didn't have to worry too much about reinforcing other people; but when I moved into supervision, and had to worry about counselling people . . . well, when we downsized our division, there was a whole batch of people we had to relocate. That's a pretty frightening experience for people. So you get heavily involved in dealing one-on-one with a lot of people, and you learn in a hurry what are the right things and wrong things to do. You also have to deal with a far greater variety of situations — you've got to handle your day-to-day, managing-your-mail style in a totally different way. A different work style has evolved in almost every job I've been in. Perhaps we should help managers of the future to anticipate and deal with new ways of managing, as they progress through the levels.

I think it's very important for our future human resource (HR) managers to move closer to the line part of business — to understand the problems and the opportunities that the line is experiencing, so that appropriate skills can be developed and nurtured. We'll want the staff and the line to work more closely together, to better understand one another's problems — I think there is a danger, in this world of specialization, that the two can diverge. It's vitally important that HR managers move the right people with the right skills at the right time into jobs that need certain talents. And those responsible for management development should continue doing what we do well in this company — shining a small spotlight on some very key young people. Recognizing that our success rate will be low — most of these people will leave, because they aren't motivated toward long-term commitment — still, we've got to manage them almost separately from the whole population. We've got to cross-loan them — this zigzagging is very, very critical.

But realistically speaking, some aspects of providing cross-functional development opportunities to our young people may hit some snags in the next couple of decades. People today are, in my opinion, getting their life objectives in order better than ever before; and life objectives today are broader than just work or career objectives. Giving geographically distant developmental experiences to young people, there are definitely going to be some who dig their heels in and don't want to go — often, those in two-career families. On the opposite side of the coin is a friend of mine who has been moved 13 or 14 times in the last 15 years. He loves it — uses it as an opportunity to see Canada at company expense! So I guess there'll still be two camps in the year 2000 — one that wants to stay stationary, and one that loves to move. I suspect that career-wise, more advantages will accrue to the mobile person.

Of course, we are a company which produces superb managers, and we do it by taking people with intrinsic talent and then developing them. But we are inbred by definition, almost, and that tends to produce managers who are less sensitive to the environment. They haven't seen the environment for a long time! You join the company when you are 25 or so, and 18 years later you get your senior position, and 10 years after that you become part of the most senior management, so it's been a long time since you immersed yourself in something else. Now, we have lots of courses and outside training, but that's not work experience with responsibilities and accountabilities outside the company. But I don't know how we can do that, especially when you have someone with a career which is burgeoning, and the last thing he or she wants is to stop for a diversion and come back — to what?

But the need for immersion in another environment for a short period of time is going to increase as years go by, because by the time you become a senior manager, you're one generation older than the people coming in, one generation older than the majority of the population. And if you believe like I do that the change process is accelerating so swiftly, just getting almost out of hand, the instinct for the environment won't be there. That would really impact on what goes on in technology and engineering areas. There's no point in following a certain line of research, if there's going to be no payoff out there in the environment — you can't do pure research anymore. So an absolute necessity for the one being groomed for the top (and desirable for others), would be a system put in place to accommodate that idea — give senior managers one or two hiatuses in order to work outside the company. Government jobs might be an option. Academia is the other obvious one.

And we've got to develop and change our culture to accommodate the part-timer — the person who's only going to be here for a while, and not forever. We have to tolerate those exceedingly proficient people who do their thing and leave, not having that lifelong allegiance to the company. There's still a distaste for people who don't have a sense of mission "forever" — we've got to break that long-term mission down into smaller, short-term missions. We've really got to work hard to make that cultural change.

Maybe we need to take more risks in assigning developmental opportunities. I personally have been involved in championing a "maverick." We ultimately picked someone for a job which no one ever thought that person could do; and that "maverick" person just shocked the living daylights out of everybody — did it very proficiently! We'll need to do more of that, instead of closing our minds to such possibilities. Some of the people that you'd think don't have the goods, really *do* have the goods. Looking at your bank of people, you often find someone who is potentially a five thousand dollar bill, even though most people think he's only a hundred dollar bill. Why not develop him to his full potential?.... There are implications here for appraising our people. I think good managers should always give the individual the benefit of the doubt in terms of their potential for future development; and it's only after particular failings or limitations start to appear and get proven, that they fall down the potential list.

TRENDCO RESEARCH INC. (A)* 151

James C. Rush and Eileen D. Watson

Leaving the June Management Update training session, Adam Blackburn was deep in thought. The information he and other Trendco managers had just received ("Bill C-62 and Employment Equity") seemed directly related to a promotion recommendation he would be making the following day. He had been somewhat undecided before attending the seminar—now he was in a quandary. Given the company's new focus on equal opportunity for its female employees, which of his first-level managers (five male, two female) should receive his support?

Walking briskly back to his office, Adam mentally reviewed the facts he had just been given about Bill C-62. He understood that the Employment Equity Bill, which was the sequel to past voluntary Equal Opportunity and Affirmative Action programs, differed from the concept of "equal pay for work of equal value," which was primarily concerned with eliminating gender bias from compensation and job evaluation systems. As well, Adam knew that both types of legislation related to and were governed by the Charter of Human Rights and Freedoms. What had been unfamiliar to him (and to most of the other managers who had attended the training session) were actual details of the act, and requirements for its enforcement.

Bill C-62

The Employment Equity Bill was proposed as law a year ago "in order to achieve equality of employment." The formally stated purpose of the legislation, passed a few months later, was:

> To achieve equality in the work place so that no person shall be denied employment opportunities or benefits for reasons unrelated to ability and, in the fulfillment of that goal, to ameliorate the condition of disadvantage in employment

---

*All names in this case have been disguised.

experienced by women, aboriginal peoples, persons with disabilities and persons who are, because of their race or color, in a visible minority, by giving effect to the principle that employment equity means more than treating persons in the same way but also requires special measures and the accommodation of differences.

The act required all federally regulated companies with over 100 employees (banks, airlines, telecommunication companies, interprovincial railway, trucking, and other industries governed by the Canada Labour Code) to implement employment equity, and report their results to the government. As well, federal government contractors with contracts worth over $200 000 would be required to adhere to employment equity guidelines under a contract compliance agreement.

While no requirements were stipulated for establishing numerical targets, employers would have to develop specific affirmative action plans, and provide statistical evidence of a change in the distribution of employees to include more members of designated groups. (An example of a proposed statistical summary sheet may be found in Exhibit 1.)

The implementation of employment equity would require employers to integrate equal employment concerns into their normal business practices. This would include the identification and removal of elements in existing employment systems, practices, and attitudes that might limit opportunities for women, native people, the disabled, and visible minorities. As well, special measures to facilitate the integration of previously under-represented groups into the organization's workforce would be introduced.

Adam glanced at the printed information he had picked up at the training session — a list of requirements under the Employment Equity Bill:

1. Employer's Duty:

   1. To identify and eliminate any employment practice which has the effect of excluding members of designated groups.
   2. To implement new policies and practices with the objective of positively encouraging and facilitating the participation of the excluded groups.
   3. To make appropriate accommodation for members of designated groups to enable their entry into areas from which they have previously been excluded.
   4. To set up a program to ensure that the composition of the employer's personnel reflects the composition of the relevant pool of available workers, that is, the workforce.

2. Reports:

   Reports must be submitted annually by industrial sector and location, providing data on:

— hires		— women
— promotions	for	— aboriginal people
— terminations		— disabled persons
— salary		— visible minorities

On a voluntary basis, an additional narrative segment (no more than five pages) may be submitted, describing any activity in support of employment equity.

Once submitted and reviewed, *all reports will be available for public inspection.*

Trendco Research Inc.

The origins of the company for which Adam worked stretched back nearly 20 years, when Trendco Technology Corporation (TTC), a high-profile employer in Midway City, established Trendco Research Inc. (TRI) in the same municipality. TRI was a research and development organization which specialized in designing advanced telecommunications and information management system products, primarily for the parent company. Later, TRI performed systems engineering, long-range network planning, and research and development for a variety of other clients as well, when the work complemented the overall direction of TRI's laboratories.

TRI's major client, however, continued to be its parent company, Trendco Technology Corporation. TTC represented the marketing, manufacturing, and service operations for products designed and developed at TRI. TRI's new product innovations and technologies contributed to TTC's placement at the leading edge of the telecommunications equipment industry.

TRI was organized into two major areas — Network Products (60 percent of the company's human resources) and Office Products (the remaining 40 percent). (See Exhibit 2 for a partial organizational chart.) The Network Products area, organized into four divisions, was concerned with a great variety of activities related to the design of public and private telecommunication networks — for example, the development of new transmission, switching, and outside plant network products. The four divisions of the Office Products area were concerned with the design and development of such products as terminal sets, private switching systems, and data products.

Currently more than 1100 men and women were employed at TRI's Midway City location. Close to 60 percent held university degrees (see Exhibit 3), the majority in electrical engineering. Computer scientists comprised the second-largest employee segment. One senior manager observed,

> Although the stereotypes are not as clear today as they once were, there seems to be a typical systems engineer — very methodical and systematic, someone who takes time to do processes such as performance evaluation, giving feedback, looking after people's training needs. That's because systems, even human systems, are this person's stock in trade.
>
> Electrical engineers are typically quite different — their motto is, if it works, don't fix it! They only pay attention to their people when they break down, just as they only pay attention to a system when it is not working.
>
> Employees were broadly defined by two groupings — "technical" (computer scientists, engineers, and others responsible for designing and operating products and equipment) or "non-technical" (professionals, administrators, support staff, and others). New technical recruits were designated "MSS" (Member of Scientific

Staff[1]) or "MTS" (Member of Technical Staff[2]). Technical employees outnumbered non-technical roughly three to one.

TRI's organizational structure, like that of other research and development companies, displayed a high degree of flexibility in response to constantly changing demands. One employee remarked, "In spite of its size, Trendco Research is more dynamic than most." Massive reorganizations could be expected two or three times a year in response to revectoring of projects, changes in divisional responsibilities, etc. For example, the recent promotion of an assistant vice-president triggered many shifts, promotions, and other changes, "for the purpose of consolidation and trying to get projects and people working together."

Individual employees found that their career mobility was affected not only by internal shifts but also by the transfers and promotions which were exchanged regularly between TRI and its parent. Career opportunities were available for most TRI employees in TTC, and vice versa.

Recruiting

TRI prided itself on its non-discriminatory hiring practices, and on providing equal opportunities to all its employees. As explained by a trainer at the seminar attended by Adam Blackburn,

> We are committed to attracting and retaining exceptionally talented people, regardless of race, sex, or physical disability. TRI employs several disabled people, as well as people from a wide variety of different cultures — a fact which is underlined by the approximately 40 languages spoken by our employees!
>
> But few women have chosen to pursue careers in technical areas such as electrical engineering and computer science; so women form a relatively small proportion of the technical employees at TRI. This is changing as more qualified women become available.

As Adam thought about what the seminar leader had said, he recalled seeing some hiring statistics from the previous year in the company's recruiting office:

Female Graduate Recruiting

	Electrical Engineering	Computer Science
Graduating Class	1277	1276
Females Graduating	94	372
Females applied to TRI	41	105
Females hired by TRI	4	25

[1]MSS, or Member of Scientific Staff, was the designation given to a graduate of a four-year honors technical degree program.

[2]MTS, or Member of Technical Staff, was the designation given to a graduate of a three-year university degree or community college diploma program.

Comparative figures for male applicants to TRI were 315 (electrical engineering) and 328 (computer science). Actually hired by TRI were 100 male electrical engineers and 83 male computer science grads.

Junior Management

Different management tasks were performed at each of the two lowest management levels. First-level managers had to be able to organize and delegate work to others; but they also were expected to pitch in and help their people with their day-to-day assignments, whenever necessary. The essential ingredients of a second-level manager's job were mature, effective interpersonal skills, and superior integrative ability. A "second level" should be capable of assuming the role of integrator, going beyond established boundaries, making outside contacts, relating to work going on in other areas, and having a broad view of the organization.

Trendco Research Inc. (A)

Discrimination at TRI?

As he considered his upcoming promotion decision, Adam looked at some statistical tables which had been distributed at the seminar. It was clear that women were not proportionally represented in management positions at TRI, as indicated in the following chart:

TRI Female Employees
(as a percent of same-level male/female population)

	Year Before Last	Last Year	Current Year
Technical			
1st Level Managers	4.0%	3.3%	5.4%
2nd Level Managers	2.6%	3.0%	3.6%
Non-Management	14.8%	15.9%	17.0%
Non-technical			
1st Level Managers	22.5%	22.0%	21.1%
2nd Level Managers	11.4%	10.8%	10.0%
Non-Management	54.8%	54.1%	53.4%

Adam noted that, although there had been an increase in the percentage of women in technical positions over the past three years, this was offset somewhat by reductions in female participation in non-technical positions. He thought about remarks made by a colleague regarding promotions within TRI:

Our typical male promotee (for first-level management, at any rate) is the hot-shot, technical whiz-kid. But we sometimes recognize technical expertise by giving the title, "manager," simply as recognition of outstanding performance — a title bearing no actual management responsibilities along with it.

And we tend to create jobs that fit the people we have, not appoint someone for a specific position — the mandate changes with the person in the position. A second-level manager here, who has a dozen or so first-level managers working for him or her, is doing one kind of project . . . but when people change, so does the mandate."

Compensation statistics had been prepared, comparing salary distributions between male and female employees (see Exhibits 4 and 5). Possible explanations for discrepancies were implicit in another statistical table which indicated male-female differences in salary, length of service, and chronological age (see Exhibit 6).

One second-level manager described his practical approach to salary raises, indicating that he gave no thought to the gender of the recipients:

> Giving raises in my department is no problem for me. I allocate my "pot" of money after ranking my people, picking out the best producers and making adjustments for effort and merit. I also sort them according to year of graduation, ranking, age — after juggling the data for a while, names become meaningless!

Performance Appraisal

A company-wide audit confirmed that performance reviews were being done regularly, manager with employee, twice a year, for 98 percent of TRI employees. The format was a personal, one- to two-hour discussion mainly devoted to the subordinate's objectives, and the level of achievement of them. The audit discovered some individual expressions of dissatisfaction, written as comments on questionnaire forms:

- It is hard to know what you are being rated on.
- I'm given objectives, but there is no one-to-one correspondence of the objectives to my salary increases.
- I'm not sure how my set of responsibilities stacks up against other people's.
- You should rate us on an absolute scale — or if it is a relative scale, then tell us what the relative rating is.
- The question is, are we being scored against stated objectives or unstated expectations?

A human resources manager explained:

> Individual objectives are unequal due to individual differences in experience, skills, expertise, etc. For instance, managers will assign more difficult and far-reaching objectives to people they know have the capability of reaching those objectives. So, under "Critical Responsibilities" in the individual's performance review, the rating 'Fully Satisfied' is really a judgment call on the managers' part regarding what they have assigned to their various people.

And goals are constantly set and revised. Any group can review what has changed in the project, what else needs to be done, what additional goals need to be set.

But there are various checks and balances so that no one is unjustly overlooked or over-criticized. There are very few operations in this company where you work one-to-one, only yourself with one manager—mostly you deal with other management people, other groups. There is a great deal of cross-checking among managers—frank discussions, typically fair. Employees never see that, and are cynical. They commonly complain "My manager never stands up for me, never takes my part."

As a formal process, there is the regular managers review, where a number of managers get together and talk about their ratings for their people, and their reasons for giving those ratings. A manager can be, and sometimes is, challenged to give reasons for his or her assessment of a particular person.

Discussions about placement also occur in this management group review—should this employee be retained on this particular assignment, or is he or she looking for a developmental move? Also, promotions are discussed...but some groups are different in the way they make promotions possible. There is no typical way with which promotions are dealt.

Training and Development

In the complex technological environment of TRI, new hires were required to spend thirteen weeks in an intensive training program to learn the systems with which they would be working. Many other training opportunities were offered on an ongoing basis. One manager stated,

> We're provided with endless technical and management programs, both internal and external—courses galore! Millions of dollars are spent each year on training and development. However, there is no required number of days for any individual laid down or prescribed. Each manager lays out what he or she feels necessary for the development of his or her employee, during the performance evaluation process. The follow-through by management can be spotty, unfortunately.

Adam's Choice

Adam Blackburn had worked at Trendco Research for six years. He had joined TRI as a Member of Scientific Staff (MSS) following his graduation with an M.Sc. (Electrical Engineering) degree. His career had followed a typical path—promotion to first-level manager after three years, where he supervised from five to ten people in developing a new major product. When that particular project wound down two years later, Adam was promoted to a second-level manager's position reporting to the Divisional Manager, Digital Switching Systems.

The seven first-level managers and 38 MSS and MTS personnel of Adam's department were recognized as an effective, productive unit. When Adam was approached in June this year regarding the transfer (and promotion) of one of his first-level managers, he agreed somewhat regretfully to consider the request — any such change would cause a ripple effect throughout the department.

The "open" second-level position was located in the Software Development department, and required the supervision and coordination of seven or more project groups working toward the development of a complex new software product. Three of these projects groups were already in existence, having been recently formed through the efforts of three capable first-level managers. The remaining four (or five or six) groups were still to be established — no first-level managers had yet been designated, although the software to be developed was needed urgently in another TRI division.

Adam wondered which of his seven first-level managers should receive his strong recommendation for the promotion. He thought about the overall ratings he had given his subordinates (out of a possible 5 points) during their most recent performance evaluations: Gilles, Jozef and Natalie, 4; Ashok and Laura, 3; Todd, 2.5; and Barry, 2. His criteria for high performance ratings were clear:

> I evaluate people carefully, using TRI's rating range of one to five (five is the highest) for each task or category. If you give someone a job and they do it really well, that rates a three. For four or five, you must do *more* than just your immediate job. You must find things that need to be done, and do them — nobody ever gets promotions for just doing their job.
>
> My biggest problem is forecasting how long a job will take. One person does a certain job in a week, while another person might take two months to do the same work. After a job is done, I have to assess how difficult the job *really* was, and how innovative were the solutions that this particular person provided.
>
> One way of judging effort is overtime slips...which seem to be turned in by more male than female employees, generally. But is that overtime necessary because the person's done a crummy job? Or is it because he or she is very dedicated to the work?
>
> Above all, I appreciate, and look for, a positive attitude. I look for people who say, "Here's the deficiency — now here's how to go about fixing it."
>
> I tell my first-level managers that my success hinges on their success. Anything I can do to help make them successful, I'll do.

Seeking an objective outside opinion about which manager to recommend for promotion, Adam arranged to meet with his divisional manager, Brent Norton. In response to Brent's suggestion, "Why not give me a brief summary of your perception of each manager?," Adam replied:

> Technically, Gilles is probably my best manager. He is brilliant, and has bailed TRI out of deep trouble, many times; but he's deficient in people management skills. Gilles expects others to be as brilliant as he is, and doesn't realize they need coaching. When his people ask for help, he tells them, "This is how to do it!" He gives solutions, but doesn't describe the process. I've had to move some people

who couldn't tolerate his style, out of his department. I don't consider Gilles promotable to second-level...unless, of course, he works on changing his management style.

Todd is my newest promotion; but the function of his department hasn't developed as fast as we had hoped, so he still has no staff. Todd tends to be very short, almost confrontational, with people in "outside" departments. My gut feeling is that he'll be OK with managing his own department. He's technically outstanding. Put him on a problem, and he'll work night and day to fix it. A bit demanding, no patience with small talk, Todd won't butter people up when asking them to do something.

Jozef is a man with a good mix of abilities. Technically, he's above average; but his real *forte* is management skills. Jozef's very good at organizing his department so everybody's working as a team, producing what's needed. All the jobs in his department are clearly defined — so when he's away, the department carries on as usual. When Gilles is away for a couple of weeks, everything's in disarray! But an AVP I used to work for favors promoting Gilles. He was surprised when I championed Jozef recently. However, he has been watching Jozef in operation, and I think he's changing his mind.

Laura's technical ability is above average. She is well organized and has her department perfectly coordinated, doing all the right things. However, I see her as personally not dedicated enough for the job she has to do. It's a particularly high-pressure job — requires 18 hours a day commitment — she doesn't want to spend the time required. And Laura's not forceful enough. Her department has many demands placed on it, and she hasn't learned how to say "no." Also, a second-level manager has to be involved in a lot more than his or her immediate job — getting people to do things for you, doing things for them. Laura doesn't seem to be interested. If you give her a job, she does that job very well; but she doesn't look outside her immediate area of responsibility.

Barry is another man who is very strong technically, but who has some communication and management deficiencies. His work is usually successful, but he has a problem with slipped schedules. When a deadline is going to be missed, Barry doesn't recognize this soon enough; and he doesn't effectively drive the bad news up the line, to make sure everybody who needs this information, gets it!

Ashok is a good mix of managerial and technical abilities. He does a capable job of managing his own department. His deficiencies are his inability to work with people *outside* his department. Ashok's focus is too narrow. He forgets he's just one piece of a bigger picture, and he fights doing any extra thing which would benefit the total program but might cause problems for his group. But he works almost 24 hours a day — he has doubled the amount of legal overtime he's allowed to do.

Natalie's technical abilities are quite a bit above average — not at the same level as Gilles and Ashok, but high up there. Her best asset is probably in the effective way she interfaces with other people — not only inside the company, but outside, with our customers. She combines technical ability plus the ability to get her point across to others, and to get things coordinated. I'm not sure she's promotable right now — she's been with TRI only two years. But ultimately, yes...and in 10 years, she'll be higher on the ladder than I'll be!

My people are such a high-spirited team — I have to hold them back from all the things they'd like to do. But I don't want to discourage them, because they may come up with some great innovative things which will advance TRI tremendously.

I'm going to regret losing any one of them, though I don't want to stand in their way of advancement.

As his conversation with Brent continued, Adam was remembering the information he had received in the "Bill C-62 and Employment Equity" seminar. He told Brent,

I assume Employment Equity is a problem, although most TRI people really believe that they get ahead on their skills and merit alone. Maybe the company wants better statistics to show the government that it's serious about emphasizing equal opportunity for female employees. I think TRI is extremely fair, already — but there is definitely a smaller percentage of women managers than men, and certainly a small percentage of women managers who are promotable. Typically, there are not many aggressive women in this organization — Natalie is an exception. Guys who do what she does get ahead.

I recollect promoting Laura and Natalie to first-level management. Prior to promoting Laura, we gave her the informal position of team leader, still reporting to a manager. Because she hadn't previously been identified as promotable, we watched carefully to see how competent she really was, and if she liked the new position. We noticed that people started to look to her as a leader. She was seen as competent, bright — not super-bright, but she still did good, if not particularly innovative, work.

Compared with other managers, Laura was not as sociable. She was a lot older than the rest of her people, by 10 or 12 years. And she was not single — no beer after work, or long lunches. I am disappointed with my own performance managing her. When I took over this department, it was in a crisis mode and needed hours and hours of intensive managing. I didn't spend much time with Laura when she was a new manager. It's a credit to her that she didn't screw up...and so, I had no immediate concerns about her performance.

It was different with Natalie. I had reservations about her promotion, too, but mostly because she was so young. And she had only been here a couple of years — typically, the average first-level manager has been an MSS for four years or more. But I needn't have worried. When a promotion announcement is made, someone usually walks out in a huff from the meeting. It's to Natalie's credit that nobody walked out in a huff following her promotion! People acknowledged she was a good candidate for first-level — when Natalie sees a problem, she goes and fixes it herself, whether it is in her area or not. She's outgoing, and does what needs to be done.

Decision Time

Adam left Brent's office mentally comparing two possible choices for promotion to the second-level position. The fact that one was male and the other female caused him to think about a promotional issue more carefully than ever before — given the company's new focus on equal opportunity for its female employees, which person should receive his support?

EXHIBIT 1

TRENDCO RESEARCH INC. (A)

Example Statistical Summary Sheet

PROPOSED CONTENTS OF REGULATIONS

NUMBER AND PERCENTAGE OF DESIGNATED GROUP EMPLOYEES LOCATED OR BASED AT EMPLOYER'S LOCATIONS: METROPOLITAN LEVEL

Name of Business Establishment:	Employer's Industrial Sector:	Metropolitan location(s) in the Province of: (use a separate form for each province)	Report for 19_____, December 31

NUMBERS AND PERCENTAGES OF EMPLOYEES LOCATED OR BASED AT LOCATION(S) INDICATED

METROPOLITAN LOCATIONS (indicate addresses of metropolitan area headquarters)	NUMBER OF BUSINESS UNITS IN EACH METRO AREA	ALL EMPLOYEES			PERSONS WITH DISABILITIES			ABORIGINAL PEOPLES			VISIBLE MINORITIES		
		TOTAL	M	F	TOTAL	M	F	TOTAL	M	F	TOTAL	M	F
		#	#	#	#	#	#	#	#	#	#	#	#
		%	%	%	%	%	%	%	%	%	%	%	%
TOTAL NUMBERS IN PROVINCE													

EXHIBIT 2

TRENDCO RESEARCH INC. (A)

Partial Organizational Chart (Current)

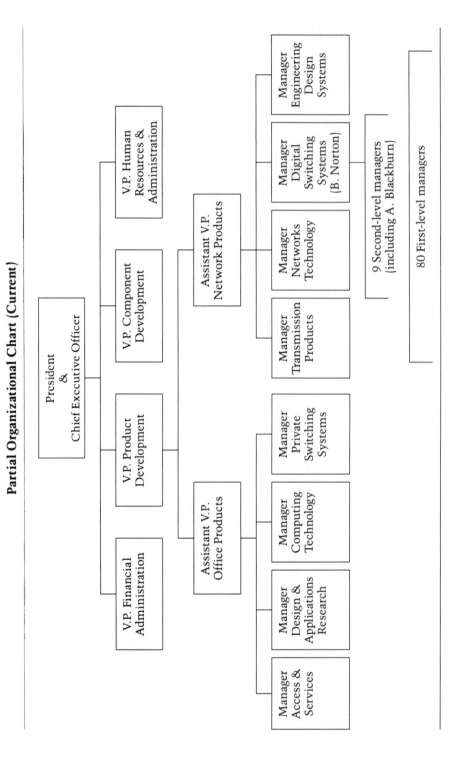

EXHIBIT 3

T R E N D C O R E S E A R C H I N C . (A)

TRI Employees—Education by Degree

Major	Bachelor	Master	PhD
		(number of employees)	
Physics, Physical Chemistry, Applied Science	25	7	10
Chemistry, Chemical Engineering	4	1	1
Electrical Engineering, Communications	177	125	31
Mechanical Engineering	10	3	0
Metallurgy, Metal Engineering	2	0	1
Engineering—Civil, Systems, Industrial, Structural, etc.	6	4	3
Math, Statistics, Information Theory	23	11	4
Computer Science	98	59	9
Business Administration, Law, P.R., Engineering Administration	8	18	1
Economics, Finance, Accounting	7	4	0
Psychology, General Arts, Library Arts, Human Factors	16	15	6
% of total population with degrees	32.6%	21.4%	5.7%

Current # of Employees: 1155   Total Degrees: 689

EXHIBIT 4
TRENDCO RESEARCH INC. (A)

Technical Employees' Salary Distribution (Previous Year)

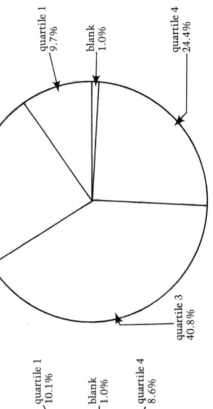

*Distribution Across Salary Quartiles
for Technical Employees*

MALES

quartile 2
24.2%

quartile 1
9.7%

blank
1.0%

quartile 4
24.4%

quartile 3
40.8%

*Distribution Across Salary Quartiles
for Technical Employees*

FEMALES

quartile 1
10.1%

blank
1.0%

quartile 4
8.6%

quartile 2
41.9%

quartile 3
38.4%

QUARTILE 4 = Highest Salaries
QUARTILE 1 = Lowest Salaries

EXHIBIT 5

TRENDCO RESEARCH INC. (A)

Non-Technical Employees' Salary Distribution (Previous Year)

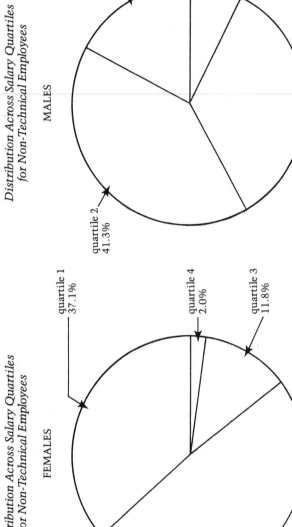

*Distribution Across Salary Quartiles
for Non-Technical Employees*

FEMALES

quartile 1
37.1%

quartile 4
2.0%

quartile 3
11.8%

quartile 2
49.1%

*Distribution Across Salary Quartiles
for Non-Technical Employees*

MALES

quartile 1
17.4%

quartile 4
7.0%

quartile 2
41.3%

QUARTILE 4 = Highest Salaries
QUARTILE 1 = Lowest Salaries

165

*Trendco
Research Inc.
(A)*

EXHIBIT 6

TRENDCO RESEARCH INC. (A)

Male/Female Differences By Level,
(Current Year)

Level	Number of Employees Male	Number of Employees Female	MEDIAN Salary ($K) (M-F)	MEDIAN TRI Service (Yrs.) (M-F)	MEDIAN Age (Yrs.) (M-F)
AVP	8	0	n/a	n/a	n/a
Division Manager	28	1	8.3	1.3	1.5
2nd Level Manager					
—Non-Technical	9	1	4.75	3.6	.5
—Technical	53	2	1.2	2.8	5.8
1st Level manager					
—Non-Technical	30	8	1.95	1.3	1.5
—Technical	122	7	3.45	.8	3.3
MSS	411	54	5.7	.5	3.1
MTS	89	5	5.5	1.8	6.6
Specialist	63	60	6.5	(.8)	1.3
Support	76	128	3.16	.5	(.9)
Total	889	266			
	1155				

Richard C. Hodgson and Eileen D. Watson

Peter Boyd, national personnel and training director of Clark, Steele & Carson, a Toronto-based firm of chartered accountants, was facing a difficult decision. He was thinking about the training needs of various groups within the firm's professional and support staff population. While satisfied with his training initiatives in some areas, Peter wanted to develop some new, relevant training programs for certain groups which he perceived as having unmet needs — the partners and managers, in particular.

The semi-annual meeting of Clark, Steele & Carson's national education committee was scheduled to be held in six weeks, and Peter was expected to present his recommendations for new Canada-wide management training programs at this time. Peter was attempting to decide on the specific nature of the partners' and managers' training and development needs, in order to recommend relevant programs for next year.

Chartered Accountancy: A Changing Profession

A directory published in the late 1970s by the Canadian Institute of Chartered Accountants (CICA) gave the following information about the profession:

> Chartered accountants belong to Canada's fastest-growing profession ... CAs hold a wide variety of responsible positions in public accounting — acting as auditors, accountants, tax advisers and management consultants — in industry and commerce, in government and education.
>
> Only those who have met the rigorous entrance standards and who maintain the

---

*All names in this case have been disguised.

professional standards demanded by their provincial Institute of Chartered Accountants are entitled to use the CA designation. Members of the provincial Institutes are automatically members of the Canadian Institute.

The education of accounting students remained primarily a provincial responsibility, from the recruitment of university graduates by individual CA firms to the students' final examination two years later. During their "apprenticeship," CA students received on-the-job training and attended courses taught by proficient graduates. Coast-to-coast uniformity of standards was maintained by the Canada-wide Uniform Final Examination. The graduate CA was required by the institute to continue the learning process through an individual program of professional development, involving a minimum of 35 hours study time per year. To this end, both the CICA and the various provincial institutes offered extensive selections of professional development courses, which were available to all members.

The image of the chartered accountant had undergone vast changes over the years. Gone was the bookkeeper with his green eye-shade and black sleeve-bands, bent over long columns of figures in a dimly-lit back room. Increasingly, the professional self-concept of the modern CA was that of a business advisor—an "executive hand-holder," as described by one partner—a well-presented university graduate, highly visible in the community, assisting the client with a multitude of transactions and decisions.

Since the improved status of the chartered accountant required better-qualified students—the acknowledged "backbone" of every CA organization—firms were forced to pay higher wages to attract suitable people. Increasing costs prompted individual firms to seek greater efficiency and sophistication. For example, research and development got more attention. One partner noted, "More R & D has been done in the last 20 years than in all the previous 200." A dramatic expansion in technical expertise supported a constant increase in the variety and quality of special services for the client.

Other trends were appearing. The Canadian Institute of Chartered Accountants continued to set more onerous standards, requiring accounting services at steadily higher levels. In addition, government requirements frequently changed, constantly challenging the conscientious CA to keep abreast of continuing legislation. Moreover, there was concern that the trend toward increased litigation involving CA firms in the United States might soon affect the Canadian scene.

Clark, Steele & Carson

Clark, Steele & Carson (CS & C) was a medium-sized national firm of chartered accountants, formed 85 years ago through several mergers of small firms and sole practitioners. A total of 75 partners and 63 managers supervised

28 offices from Victoria, British Columbia, to St. John's, Newfoundland. The professional services provided by CS & C were described in its recruitment handbook:

> In addition to a significant *audit practice*, CS & C offers *specialized services* in taxation, liquidation and bankruptcy, business valuation, insurance claims investigations, and management consulting, which includes consulting services in the hospitality and recreation industry, executive recruiting, computer systems and general business consulting.

The Toronto office provided some services within the company on a national basis — research and development, quality control, personnel and training. The head office personnel in Toronto consisted of 147 members — partners, managers, staff CAs, undergraduates and support staff as outlined below.

CS & C HEAD OFFICE PERSONNEL

29   Partners — direct owners of the firm, personally responsible for every aspect of its operation. Admission to partnership is achieved through election by existing partners.

17   Managers and Supervisors — experienced CAs with the responsibility and authority to conduct complex audit assignments. They supervise the work of senior accountants, and consult frequently with partners and clients.

72   Staff CAs — Assistant Seniors (university graduates in their first or second years with CS & C) and Staff Accountants (graduate CAs, or accountants who are writing the Uniform Final Examination).

29   Support Staff — secretaries, bookkeepers, filing clerks, printing operators and receptionists.

An office managing partner, assisted by a management committee, supervised the operation of the Toronto office. There, four groups, each comprised of approximately 25 professionals, provided audit services (see Exhibit 1). Partners and managers not affiliated with an audit group provided specialized services whenever and wherever needed. CAs from smaller CS & C offices often telephoned to avail themselves of this special expertise.

Clark, Steele & Carson's clients were generally medium-sized businesses, many owner-managed. Partners' closeness to their clients reflected the firm's desire to provide outstanding personalized service. This service, it was thought, gave CS & C a competitive edge over the "big eight" — the eight CA firms acknowledged as leaders in Canada because of their enormous size and influence.

Partners from the east and west met annually in two separate groups, usually in Montreal and Calgary. Each group had a management committee, comprised of five or six provincial representatives, and met quarterly. The firm's national executive committee met annually, and was responsible for the planning and organization of the plenary meeting of all CS & C partners held every other year. At the latest biennial meeting, the partners expressed their satisfaction with CS & C's rate of growth in size and revenue, and with all indications of an excellent growth potential for the future.

CS & C's Student Training Program

Clark, Steele & Carson provided a professional development program for their students, as part of a comprehensive program directed at three levels of development. Information about the program was included in the recruitment handbook, along with a description of personnel policies regarding professional development and working conditions (see Exhibit 2).

Peter Boyd's Thoughts and Concerns

Peter Boyd began his accounting career with one of the "big eight," and received his CA designation in two years. Ten years later, he decided to join a small firm — Clark, Steele & Carson — and quickly advanced to the position of manager in the Toronto office. In his first five years with CS & C, Peter became a member of the national education committee,[1] and was then appointed CS & C's national personnel and training director. Two years later, he became a partner in the firm. He did not, however, become a member of the Toronto office management committee.

About his route to the national personnel and training position, Peter said: "I grew into the personnel and training job through teaching accounting courses part-time at York University. I really enjoyed teaching, and did more and more of it, gradually becoming the teacher! I was given increasing responsibility for organizing the courses, and finally took complete charge of student education at CS & C. The personnel function followed — we said the same person should do both.

In addition to his personnel and training responsibilities, Peter maintained a client base. He explained, "I have removed some of my clients to free time for my other activities; but I like the clients, and feel I need them. I've been accounting seven hours per day for 20 years, and people expect me to have chargeable hours. In fact, I would feel somewhat uncomfortable without them."

---

[1]CS & C's national education committee, chaired by a member of the Toronto office management committee, was composed of Peter Boyd and five regional representatives from across Canada. The committee's function was to approve and formalize education programs, six to eight months in advance.

Although no formal job description existed for Peter Boyd's position, Peter considered that his job required him to set CS & C's personnel and education policies on a national basis. He described the personnel aspects of his position:

> Most public accountants believe that the personnel function in an accounting firm is not a major area in the total operation. We recruit, bring the students in, put them out on the job, and we train them. Two or three years later they're CAs, and 80 percent of them leave us. We recruit them, and train them for somebody else! An on-going dilemma is how to retain the people we've trained.
>
> In our 28 offices coast-to-coast, each has an individual local group to look after personnel matters. There are a lot of feelings throughout the firm that personnel only involves hiring people and explaining salary and benefits. That's the traditional viewpoint, not mine!

Currently, the training portion of Peter Boyd's job was uppermost in his mind. The semi-annual meeting of his national education committee was scheduled for six weeks hence, and Peter was expected to present his assessment of training needs, suggest new training ideas, and recommend the means of implementing his programs.

Peter was satisfied with his past training initiatives for students. He felt that the quality of Level I and Level II programs at CS & C was second to none, and that the method of instruction — case studies, simulations, role plays, discussion, workshops — gave the courses a practical, work-related orientation. Peter planned to turn his attention to the non-professional staff at a later date, remarking, "There are areas I want to train the non-professional staff in, and I think I know what they need."

In conversation with a friend, Peter Boyd talked about his concerns:

> I want to initiate a good national training program for professional staff — the partners and managers, specifically — and I want to get going with something that is systematic, job-related, of a continuing nature. There are substantial advantages to providing in-house courses for our people — costs are less than for CICA & ICAO courses, and our course material is much more relevant, because we use specific CS & C client situations and our own methods.
>
> It's difficult to know what sort of training opportunities to provide, and there's really no one who can help me formulate strategy. I see the need for both technical and interpersonal skills training. It seems to me that each partner and manager has uniquely different training needs — one needs help in communicating with the clients, another needs information updates, and so on. Where do I start to plan a program? What should I do?
>
> I also have the problem of trying to define exactly what type of training experiences constitute the 35 hours of professional development required of each CA annually. Some say they read books and articles three hours per week, so that constitutes three times their quota! Some go to conferences, and claim 15 to 20 hours of professional development — and I know they only attended one or two sessions.
>
> I'm convinced of the need for professional development for our partners and

managers, and there is head office support and recognition for the training function. The fall—September to December—is the best and probably the *only* time during the year to offer courses to top management, since they're too busy to attend at any other time. I want to begin this September, and I'll need to have my recommendations ready for the national education committee meeting on June 30—but I'm uncertain about what these recommendations should be!

The Attitude Survey

To assist with his assessment of training needs, Peter Boyd sent a "staff attitudes feedback questionnaire" to every employee across Canada. One month later, he had received and tabulated the results from 76 members of the Toronto office professional staff—an 85 percent response from that particular group of managers, supervisors, and staff. (See Exhibit 3 for the questionnaire form and the Toronto office results). Peter had anticipated some of the findings, but was puzzled by certain results, such as the response to the salary/responsibility question in #12). Peter had made it his business to research the salary policies of other CA firms, and he knew that CS & C personnel were earning the equivalent of other Toronto firms, including the "big eight."

Interviews with Partners and Managers

Feeling that additional input from an objective outside source would be helpful, Peter Boyd engaged a management consultant in organizational development to interview selected members of CS & C's professional staff. Peter hoped to gain a new perspective to aid his decision making, and some ideas for possible action steps.

The management consultant proposed a series of 10 interviews, half with partners and half with managerial staff. The interviewees selected by Peter Boyd would include four partners and four managers from the Toronto office, as well as one partner and one manager from a representative small office (Parry Sound, Ontario). This approach would provide the opportunity to compare opinions among the partners and managers in large and small offices.

Peter and the consultant discussed the interview methodology. They decided that each interview should last an hour or less. The consultant would ask a limited number of primary questions, probing further in as non-directive and supportive a manner as possible. At the close of the interview, the partner or manager would be asked to think about training for him or herself and others, and asked to choose, from a list of 20 topics developed in advance by Peter and the management consultant, the training topics most appropriate for partners. The process would then be repeated, this time choosing the most appropriate topics for managers. The choices were to be rank ordered each time. (See Exhibit 4 for the list of 20 training topics and for the interview responses to those topics.)

The interviews took place two weeks prior to the national education committee's scheduled meeting. Six primary questions were asked of each interviewee. The most remarkable finding was the diversity and complexity of answers to each question, the resultant interviews averaging one hour and a half in duration. Exhibit 5 summarizes the most frequent responses to each question.

The Next Step

One week before his deadline, Peter sat at his desk reviewing the data that he and the consultant had collected. He wondered how he could use it to decide on the training needs of CS & C partners and managers. His goal was to design a relevant and interesting Level III training program which he could offer across Canada during the next five years. Peter hoped that he would be able to make some appropriate recommendations to the national education committee at its June 30 meeting.

EXHIBIT 1

CLARK, STEELE & CARSON (A)

CS&C Partners and Professional Staff, Toronto Office, June 1979

	Audit Group A	Audit Group B	Audit Group C	Audit Group D	Tax	Consulting	Admin.	R.&D.	P.&E.	Computer Audit
Partners	Ackerman Elgie Lyon* Maynard Oswald	Bishop Duncan Rogers Taylor Thomas*	McCann Meyer Van Eck* Wilson Young	Clements* Fairley Harman Pepper Reaney	Lindsay Ross	Butts Simpson	Nugent Percy	Dawson	Boyd	Martyn
Managers	Bancroft	McLure	Bulani*	Hahn*	Cullen	Willis, N.		Reesor	Eddie	
Supervisors	Templeton Wiersma*	Cheng Norris*	Brownlee	Little Quigley	Norton					Downs
Staff	Espey Grasby Hall, D. Laaskso Lewis Logan Morris Newman Owen Payne Sprague Willis, P. Wright Wyatt Yates	Dyson Elliott Feasby Fife Gauci Kelly Marshall Miko Mitchell Noble Olson Osborne Proctor Regnier Rice	Adams Clarke Giron Hall, A. Lamb Lanci Pattison Phelp Pearce Rand Rosati Savage Sexton Shaw Towers Weston	Britten Eaton Gowdey Griffith Jackson Kushnir Lobb Lupa Manyari Marsh O'Neil Owens Robbins Whelan Zurkan	Bray Dolan Nisbet	Geddes Metcalf Miko Nursey Rose	Fonti Hill Pfaff Skaith			

*Interviewed by management consultant

EXHIBIT 2
CLARK, STEELE & CARSON (A)

Excerpts from the Recruitment Handbook

CS & C'S STUDENT TRAINING PROGRAM

Formal training programs are directed at various levels of your own self development. Your salary and expenses are paid by the firm during all professional development courses.

Level I is conducted in September (one week) and is attended by all new professional staff members. It is designed to assist you through your first audits by providing practical instruction in basic audit concepts and techniques and in the documentation required by the firm in the statutory audit examination.

Level II is attended by all staff members who have completed approximately one year of practical audit experience. This course is designed to provide the necessary training to carry out the professional assignments that you are most likely to encounter in your second year, such as the complete field work of small and medium-sized clients, as well as complete sections of large clients.

Level III is available to all professional staff members. Specific topics, such as income taxes, analytical auditing, computer auditing, CICA requirements, etc., are presented by specialists in order to round out the practical and theoretical knowledge to ensure that the staff member is capable of managing the complete field of most statutory audit engagements.

CS & C'S PERSONNEL POLICIES

Staff Allocation
Our staff is organized in groups comprising approximately 30 professional individuals. This will result in your working with clients involved in many different industries during any given year. The audit assignments are scheduled in such a manner that you will *not* spend endless months on any one assignment.

In addition, a sincere effort will be made to ensure that you receive a varied experience prior to attempting the uniform final examinations.

Performance Evaluations
Staff evaluation reports will be completed by your immediate senior or supervisor and reviewed with you after each significant assignment. The reports will then be summarized and your personal development reviewed with a partner of the firm at least twice a year.

Through this system you have the very important advantage of immediate on-the-job feedback, together with the more formalized semi-annual review.

Bulletins
Information releases are issued on a regular basis within the firm, in order to keep you informed of current events as they affect our professional development and our profession.

On-The-Job Training
At Clark, Steele & Carson we consider on-the-job training combined with regular performance evaluations to be an integral part of your professional training. This ensures that, when you have attained your CA designation, you will be competent not only from a technical standpoint but from a practical standpoint. This will prepare you for assignments and responsibilities not only in the profession but also in industry.

EXHIBIT 3

C L A R K , S T E E L E & C A R S O N (A)

Professional Staff Attitudes Questionnaire

(Results Indicated in Percentages)

Responses from Toronto Office Managers, Supervisors and Staff

176

CS & C STAFF ATTITUDES FEEDBACK QUESTIONNAIRE

Office _____   Position _____

1. Are you proud when you tell people what Firm you work for?

   86.20 Yes   3.45 No   10.34 Not Sure

2. Do you feel that the appearance of the office enhances the image of the Firm?

   86.20 Yes   3.45 No   10.34 Not Sure

3. Is Clark, Steele and Carson readily identifiable as a National CA firm?

   20.69 Yes   75.86 No   3.45 Not Sure

4. Do you feel that you are a part of the Firm of Clark, Steele and Carson?

   72.41 Yes   17.24 No   10.34 Not Sure

5. **X** Do you think the Firm offers you the chance to have the kind of position that you want five years from now?

   24.14 Yes   31.03 No   41.38 Not Sure
   (3.45 no answer)

6. If you were to start again, would you work with our Firm?

   82.76 Yes   10.34 No   6.90 Not Sure

7. How would you rate the growth potential of the Clark, Steele and Carson office in your city?

   31.08 High   44.83 Average   20.69 Low
   (3.45 no answer)

8. **X** Do you feel there are more opportunities available to you in public accounting as opposed to private industry?

   17.24 Yes   44.83 No   37.93 Not Sure

9. Do you think that promotions are based on merit as opposed to seniority?

   72.41 Yes   13.79 No   13.79 Not Sure

10. Are you given an opportunity for growth in the areas of staff supervision and training?

    62.0 Yes   27.59 No   6.90 Not Sure
    (3.45 no answer)

11. Do you believe you are being compensated fairly in comparison to other professionals in your area of expertise?

    37.93 Yes   34.48 No   27.59 Not Sure

12. Are you being compensated fairly in relation to your responsibilities?

    31.03 Yes   65.52 No
    (3.45 no answer)

13. Are you satisfied with the annual salary review procedures?

    34.48 Yes   48.28 No
    (17.24 no answer, don't know)

14. Are the Firm's Policies on group insurance and other similar benefits satisfactory?

    82.76 Yes   17.24 No

15. Are you adequately and fairly reimbursed for the following costs and expenses?

    a. Mileage allowance 20.69 Yes 79.31 No
    b. Meals   37.93 Yes 62.07 No
    c. Other   89.66 Yes 10.34 No

    If c. is No, what expense?

    _____

EXHIBIT 3 (continued)

16. Have you made satisfactory progress with the Firm?

    _100_ Yes ___ No

17. Do you feel free to discuss your problems, personal or otherwise, with the partners in your office?

    _27.59_ Always _44.83_ Sometimes _27.59_ Rarely

18. Although you must spend so much time at clients' offices, to what extent are you made to feel that you are really a part of this organization?

    _24.14_ To a small degree
    _51.72_ To a large degree
    _20.69_ In every way possible
    (_3.45 no answer_)

19. If an employee is doing unsatisfactory work, will he be warned and given a chance to improve before being released?

    _51.72_ Usually _13.79_ Seldom _34.48_ Not Sure

20. How would you evaluate your performance with and/or contributions to the Firm to date?

    _41.38_ Above average _55.17_ Average
    _3.45_ Below average

21. Are your reviews adequate and helpful?

    _41.38_ Yes _48.28_ No
    (_10.34 no answer_)

22. Are you reviewed on a regular basis?

    _27.59_ Yes _68.96_ No
    (_3.45 no answer_)

23. In general do your supervisors and managers set a good example in their own work habits?

    _79.31_ Yes _10.34_ No
    (_10.34 no answer_)

24. When you want information or help on a difficult problem, do you get the kind of help you need?

    _93.10_ Yes _3.45_ No
    (_3.45 sometimes_)

25. Are the following Firm policies satisfactory?

a. Vacations	_100_ Yes		___ No
(3.45) b. Holidays	_89.66_ Yes	_6.90_ No
(10.34) c. Sick leave	_86.21_ Yes	_3.45_ No
(3.45) d. Absence	_86.21_ Yes	_10.34_ No
(3.45) e. Overtime	_51.72_ Yes	_44.83_ No
    (_no answer_)

26. In general, how do you feel about the amount of work expected of you?

    _6.90_ I feel I could do more work.
    _48.28_ The amount of work expected is reasonable.
    _10.34_ The amount of work expected is excessive.

27. Here are some comments about your hours of work. Check ANY of them (one or several) that are true in your case.

    _2.70_ I have to work too many hours per day.
    _2.70_ I have to work too many hours per week.
    _8.11_ I have too much weekend work.
    _2.70_ I have too much overtime.
    _16.22_ I do not like busy seasons.
    _64.86_ I have no objections to the hours.
    (_2.70 no answer_)

28. Does the support staff in your office (statement typing, secretarial, reproduction) meet the requirements of the professional staff and clients in terms of the finished product?

    _89.66_ Yes ___ No _6.90_ Sometimes
    (_3.45 no answer_)

29. How often are you criticized in front of other employees by your superiors?

    ___ Often _17.24_ Sometimes _82.76_ Never

30. When you first started to work here, did you get the training and help needed on the job to learn the work properly and quickly?

    _6.90_ I got very little help.
    _17.24_ I got less than I needed.
    _68.97_ I got all I needed.
    (_6.90 no answer_)

31. How do you feel about the closeness of the supervision of your work?

    ___ Too close _89.66_ About right
    _10.34_ Not close enough

32. Is the Firm's staff training program beneficial?

    _37.93_ Yes _13.79_ No _48.28_ Not Sure

33. Are you adequately informed by the Firm of the latest technical developments within the profession?

    _58.62_ Yes _13.79_ No _27.59_ Sometimes

EXHIBIT 3 (continued)

34. When you started with the Firm, did you feel that you were given a proper orientation and break-in period?

79.31 Yes *17.24* No
(3.45 no answer)

35. How do you feel about the authority delegated to you?

The authority that I have is too *3.45* much for the work that I perform.
The authority is adequate to get *89.66* the job done.
I do not have enough authority to *6.90* perform my duties.

36. When you were being interviewed for employment, did the people who talked with you about the Firm, and the opportunities within it, describe it fairly and honestly?

88.66 Yes *6.90* No
(3.45 no answer)

37. Does your office keep you informed about its activities and plans?

58.62 Yes *41.38* No

38. When you are given new duties and responsibilities, are they adequately explained?

69.96 Yes *24.14* No
(6.90 no answer)

39. When you began with the Firm were the Firm's professional and personnel policies adequately explained to you?

69.96 Yes *31.04* No

40. Are you told promptly are regularly whether your work is satisfactory?

41.38 Usually *31.04* Sometimes *27.58* Rarely

41. When you are given instructions on a new job, are they clear enough so that you know what you are expected to do?

72.41 Usually *27.58* Sometimes ___ Rarely

42. Did you read the Firm's brochure before accepting your position?

51.72 Yes *41.38* No
(6.90 no answer)

43. Are you aware that there is an organizational structure in your office?

79.31 Yes *20.69* No

44. Are you familiar with the organizational structure of the Firm on a national basis?

27.58 Yes *72.41* No

45. Are you familiar with the Firm's goals and objectives?

37.03 Yes *62.07* No

46. Do you feel that you receive constructive criticism?

65.52 Yes *34.48* No

47. In general, do you find the work assigned to you challenging and interesting?

75.86 Yes *24.14* No

48. Are you encouraged to offer ideas and suggestions?

79.31 Yes *17.24* No
(3.45 no answer)

49. Do you think the Firm will make changes based on this questionnaire?

75.86 Yes *24.14* No

50. How well do the partners in your office know which staff members are best qualified for promotion to higher jobs?

10.34 They know very little about it.
37.93 They have only a fair idea.
48.27 They know very well.
(3.45 have no idea)

51. Do you believe your office should hold an annual party for all personnel?

100 Yes ___ No

52. Should spouses be included in the annual party?

89.66 Yes *10.34* No

53. Since you have been employed by Clark, Steele and Carson, how would you say your attitude toward the Firm has changed?

My respect for the Firm grows *41.38* the longer I am with it.
It is about the same as it was *48.28* when I started.
I think less and less of the *10.34* Firm the longer I work for it.

EXHIBIT 4
CLARK, STEELE & CARSON (A)

Number of Times Each Training Topic Was Listed Among
Five Top Priority Items By Sampled Partners and Managers

Training Topics Listed By P. Boyd and Consultant	Training Topics Chosen By Interviewees			
	Partners for		Managers for	
	Partners	Managers	Partners	Managers
1. Principals of auditing, planning, administration and performance	3	3	2	1
2. Audit problems of manager-dominance	3	3	0	2
3. Accounting and auditing update of Handbook pronouncements	2	2	1	1
4. Tax planning for corporations	2	2	1	2
5. Audit findings to audit reports	2	1	2	2
6. Accounting principles and disclosure	1	2	2	1
7. Management letters	1	2	0	0
8. Legal and professional responsibilities	2	0	2	1
9. Estate planning	1	0	1	1
10. Computer controls and computer auditing	0	0	0	0
11. Federal sales tax	0	0	0	1
12. Interpersonal relations	0	1	3	3
13. Team building	2	0	3	3
14. Goal-setting and performance review	2	3	2	3
15. Market penetration	2	0	2	2
16. Conflict resolution	1	1	1	1
17. Managing stress	0	1	1	1
18. Motivation to work	1	1	1	0
19. Supervisory leadership	0	1	0	1
20. Quality of life, self-renewal, life planning	0	1	1	0

EXHIBIT 5
CLARK, STEELE & CARSON (A)

Summary of Partners' and Managers' Most Frequent Responses to Interview Questions

QUESTION 1

What is your concept, understanding, or definition of an outstanding public accountant?

1. One who can communicate well with people, listens, understands people's needs, can find out what clients really want.
2. Enjoys working with people, outside social and community activities and contacts.
3. Leads a professional life, identifies with the professional, has professional self-concept and image.
4. Has high degree of technical knowledge, and is always learning more.
5. Has personal qualities such as intelligence, organization, concentration, integrity, balance.

QUESTION 2

What are the key success factors of Clark, Steele & Carson?

1. Closeness of professional staff to clients and community.
2. Specialist expertise and services available within firm.
3. Ability to attract, retain, develop and promote good people.
4. Diversity of people and skills working well together.
5. Leadership of key people in Toronto office.

QUESTION 3

What major opportunities do you see ahead for CS & C?

1. No major opportunities. Growth of our small community is stagnant. Let's stay a large *small* firm.
2. Continue to do more of what we are already doing, and more effectively promote existing and new areas of specialized service.
3. Development of growth clients.
4. Growth must be achieved through mergers to develop a stronger national firm.
5. CS & C can become whatever its partners want it to be. It could be so successful it could become one of the "big eight."—I wouldn't mind that.

QUESTION 4

When you think about the future of the firm and your future in it, what problems or weaknesses particularly concern you?

1. The selling ability of partners. We don't have enough partners who will go out and bring in the business.
2. The lack of a basic philosophy for CS & C. Since our last merger, we need to develop a firm philosophy known to everyone, and implement it.
3. We have to get more efficient, improve staff effectiveness on the job, operate close to where the clients are, improve liaison between partners and clients.

EXHIBIT 5 (continued)

4. Lack of feedback. Don't know where we stand. People don't know whether the firm really wants them to stay or not.
5. Our lack of growth. CS & C needs to keep expanding into other areas and services.

QUESTION 5

What should the firm start doing in order to improve?

1. Keep doing what we are doing now.
2. Some type of in-house professional development in the audit field, computers, sales tax, new developments.
3. Improve our business development and promotion techniques greatly. Develop the firm's image in the community with well-directed advertising publications, participation of partners and managers in community events.
4. Give some direction about the best use of one's time for the good of the company. Management should sit down with each partner and tell him or her what he or she should do more of—selling, management consultancy, community service, etc.
5. Develop more cooperation from everybody. Start monthly meetings of task forces, work groups, etc., to come up with more innovative and exciting ideas.

QUESTION 6

What do you see as your role in these improvements?

1. Doing more of the same, only better, I guess.
2. I don't know. I haven't thought about it.
3. Try to get the partners to see things my way.
4. That's not my job.
5. You'll have to ask the executive committee about that.

CANADIAN MULTIPRODUCTS LIMITED (A)

Henry W. Lane and Eileen D. Watson

"Don, you know I've fought that compensation plan for four years already — why should I change my mind now?"

Tony Hyatt, national sales manager for the Housewares division of Canadian Multiproducts Limited, was speaking to Don Wainwright, the newly appointed general manager of the division. It was a mid-July morning and the two executives were seated in Don's comfortable office on the top floor of the Multiproducts building. (See Exhibit 1 for an organizational chart of the Housewares division.)

"Our divisional sales record is good," Tony continued, "and I don't see why we should make any changes in the compensation package we've used for four years. I think this Objective-Based Incentive Compensation Plan is simply an attempt by International to standardize one more aspect of our operation. Corporate headquarters seems to want everybody in the organization to use the same buzz words...and Payroll wants all the divisions to use identical business forms, too!"

"Tony, I used to be as skeptical as you," Don responded, "but after I introduced the OBIC plan in Industrial and Commercial Equipment, the results convinced me. Now that I've moved to the retail group, I'd like to see your people get similar results — because in my opinion, Housewares' sales aren't as good as they *could* be, particularly in a few specific product lines." (See Exhibit 2 for a description of Don Wainwright's former division.)

"But Housewares is a unique division — completely different from our company's industrial division, especially in sales personnel and techniques..."

"Is that your main objection to the plan, Tony? Because if it is, I can show you how to adapt it to suit your situation in Housewares...and remember, there's no rush to get the new plan working properly. It took us a couple of years to iron out all the wrinkles in the equipment group, and I don't expect you to have 100 percent success overnight!"

"That's one objection—but frankly, Don, your plan is just too busy, too full of detail, for my people. In my opinion, an incentive comp plan should be simple and easily understood...and above all, it had better be fair and equitable, with measurable targets—no wishy-washy non-volume objectives."

After a short silence, Don said, "Well, Tony, the basic dilemma has to be faced—Housewares has got to improve its profitability picture, and Sales must bear a large part of the responsibility for doing that. If you're not going to go along with the Objective-Based Incentive Compensation Plan, what *are* you going to do?"

"I don't know, right now," Tony replied honestly. "Let me think it over and get back to you. I'll take another look at the material you sent me, and see what I can come up with."

Walking back to his office, Tony thought, "Don is the third person in as many weeks to approach me about using that confounded OBIC plan. First Payroll asked me about it, then my counterpart in Dallas, and now my new boss. I've got to make a decision soon."

Company Background

The company was a subsidiary of Multiproducts International, a U.S.-based, diversified manufacturer and marketer of more than 51 major product lines of industrial equipment and supplies.

Multipro's active program of research and new product development made the company an acknowledged leader in several basic technologies. In cooperation with Multiproducts International, the Canadian company produced hundreds of manufactured items for markets at home and abroad. Industrial markets accounted for 85 percent of the company's annual sales, with consumer product markets mainly responsible for the remaining 15 percent.

During Multipro's early years of growth and expansion, each division was headed by a division manager who was responsible for a specific group of products and all associated marketing activities (production and packaging coordination, sales, quality, and profits) and who reported directly to the president. Each division operated like an individual company, pursuing its own objectives within the framework of established company policies.

Several organizational changes were made over the years. The latest change modified the structure of Canadian Multiproducts Limited to align it organizationally with Multiproducts International. Each of the original divisions became a member of a product group having similar technologies and/or market capabilities. Each division manager reported to his group vice president, who was responsible in turn to the president of the Canadian company. A major objective of this change was to reduce the president's span of control, and to draw the various Multipro divisions together into a more cohesive whole. This facilitated the standardization of some company policies (e.g., divisional sales policies, terms of payment, commercial allowances, incentive rebates, etc.) in line with policies already in effect within the organization internationally.

The Housewares Division

One of the product groupings which resulted from the company reorganization was the Retail Products group, composed of two divisions — Housewares, and Lawn and Garden Products. Don Wainwright was appointed vice president of the Retail Products group, as well as general manager of the Housewares division (the previous GM had recently been promoted to the Dallas head office). No changes were made in the internal structure of the division. Tony Hyatt and Roy Elliott continued to share national sales and marketing responsibilities (Roy developed the marketing plans and programs which Tony implemented).

Describing the function of the Housewares division, Tony Hyatt stated, "We're a single dedicated sales and marketing group attuned to the consumer product marketplace, directly responsible for the sales and marketing, product and package design, procurement and production arrangements, and pricing and profitability of Multipro Housewares products." The division marketed dozens of products like audio cassettes; sealants and glues for bonding ceramic tile, metal, plastic, drywall, glass, rubber, and wood; home cleaning products; "Fix-It" household repair kits; home smoke detectors; aerosol fire extinguishers, "Camp 'n' Car" first aid products, medical tapes and bandages; antiseptic and protective creams and lotions.

In many ways, the Housewares division was considered unique within the Multipro organization. Most other divisions, like Industrial and Commercial, sold their products through authorized distributors or directly to individual industrial customers. Housewares sold its products to chain stores and buying groups, for resale in various types of retail accounts: grocery, drug, hardware, discount, paint, retail automotive, lawn and garden, and rental stores; and home improvement and building supply centers. Unit margin opportunities were not as great for houseware products as for most industrial products. One salesman remarked, "We sell nickel and dime items — we don't sell high ticket items."

Another unique feature of the Housewares division was the fact that none of its products was originally designed for the retail market it served. Multipro's research and new product development was directed toward highly-engineered products for specialized industrial markets, such as a new chemical foam for fighting industrial fires, and an instant high-strength glue developed for the furniture-manufacturing industry. Scaled-down versions of many industrial products were specially packaged in a variety of sizes, grades, and/or application types to fit the home consumer's needs precisely. The industrial foam product was packaged in small aerosol cans for extinguishing kitchen fires, and the instant glue was packaged in tubes of various sizes and applicator tops, for home use. One executive remarked, "Our products are usually spin-offs from the industrial marketplace. Ironically, the special features engineered into our products are often unnecessary for the home consumer's use. This high level of quality may not be necessary. Our competition may sell a lower, but adequate, quality product and cut into our volume. Then if you consider the costs of attractively packaging the product in small units, you can see why it's difficult for us to make a profit in the retail environment."

Other differences between the two types of divisions were apparent. Selling directly to industrial customers, sales staff in Multipro's industrial divisions needed to be technically trained, skillful in communicating technical data and knowledgeable about the industry. The sales reps in Housewares did not need the same degree of technical skill and knowledge. However, retail sales staff were expected to be able to communicate well, and to discuss business topics intelligently with key management people in sophisticated, large department store chains. A retail sales manager mentioned another point: "Industrial selling requires a lot more patience and persistence than I've got. I can't spend six months to a year calling on an engineer in the aerospace industry trying to convince him or her to spec a Multipro product into the plans. There's no sense of satisfaction in that, for me...I can't move that slow!"

Distribution and service requirements of industrial and retail divisions varied. A regional manager for industrial products stated,

> The main thrust of our company is to serve industry well. If a plant manager has ordered ten fabric filters, and it's a critical situation — unless he gets one of those filters tomorrow, he'll have to shut down — we'll ship him one filter right away, and the other nine when they're ready. Whereas in the retail business, Zeller's may say, 'We'd rather get the ten units all at once, because every time we receive goods from you it costs us money!'

A relatively recent development affecting the Housewares division was the computerization of many of its largest customers. Sophisticated computerized warehousing and distribution operations allowed many companies to be aware of the exact status of all its stock, at all times. Multipro's national sales manager remarked: "Canadian Tire knows exactly how often they turn a particular product in stock, and how many dollars are involved. When we fail to supply them with an order quickly, they lose "turns" — dollar sales. An industrial account doesn't think that way....unless there's an emergency, industry is inclined to wait."

The National Sales Manager

Tony Hyatt joined Multipro 12 years ago, when he found that travelling as a salesperson for a national grocery chain took him away from home and his three young children too often. After a short term selling in an industrial capacity ("I was frustrated—I'm a retail guy, and I prefer the action of the retail market place!"), he was transferred to a retail territory in Winnipeg. Within a year Tony was appointed a regional sales manager and became the sales manager for the entire western region five years later. Two years after that, he was transferred to head office as national sales manager for the Housewares division. About his work, Tony said:

> I enjoy most aspects of my job, especially the free-wheeling face-to-face negotiations involved in coming to a satisfactory compromise with a major account...a compromise which suits both parties. I believe in democratic management, but I can be a bit of an autocrat at times—the boss still has to boss, and make final decisions that may not be popular—but I think my people respect me, and I respect them, too. And I use common sense, and can empathize with people. I know my sales reps and regional managers pretty well, and deal with everybody differently....each has his or her own eccentricities, like I have! I want to treat people fairly, and yet I've had to fire some "square-peg-in-a-round-hole" individuals. And I think twice about transferring people from one major center to another.
>
> I want to be sensitive to their needs, but I have needs too. I want to serve this company well, earn my keep, do the things I have to do. I've no desire to be president of the company, but I'm hoping for some increased responsibility within the next one to five years.

Concerning the work of the sales personnel in his division, Tony said, "In today's retail environment, we don't sell products, we sell return-on-investment (ROI). We are businesspeople dealing with other businesspeople. A lot is demanded of our sales personnel, and they should be rewarded for their efforts. We've always used some form of extra compensation plan as a reward, and as a motivator, too." Tony's plan for his regional sales managers and sales reps consisted of salary plus incentive compensation (or bonus). (See Exhibit 3 for a memo describing Tony's compensation plan for the Housewares division.)

Tony wanted to provide an incentive system which was fair to everyone, and he was concerned about some inequities which surfaced in his plan. He noticed that bonus amounts depended on the nature of each individual's territory, and other variables such as price. Not all large-volume sales were directly attributable to a particular salesperson's efforts. For instance, although a Housewares sales rep made the initial contact, a sale of several carloads of home health care products was concluded, to a large degree, on the basis of the good price set by Tony—yet the salesperson made a handsome bonus on the deal. In addition, sales reps in centers like Toronto or Montreal selling to key national accounts could be credited with large dollar sales, although the products sold were shipped to locations actually serviced by other sales personnel, where the order might have been generated originally. Tony also observed that his sales people tended to concentrate their efforts on the highest-priced items, or on sure large-volume immediate sales. His request that they try to improve facings or get new listings[1] to give future benefits to the division, met with little success — new listings wouldn't "pay off" for the sales rep in dollar benefits right away.

The General Manager

Don Wainwright's career with Multipro began with summer employment during his university years. At the time of his quarter-century anniversary in 1978, Don had held various positions (sales rep, customer service representative, sales manager, marketing manager, project manager, and divisional manager) in departments located across the country. Each position represented a new and interesting challenge to Don, through which he attempted to live his personal philosophy that "work should be fun."

Five years ago Don was appointed general manager of the Industrial and Commercial Equipment group, which comprised two divisions: Air and Water Processing Equipment, and Commercial Display and Audio. One of his first tasks was to investigate ways of boosting sales in his new group. Previous experience had convinced Don that a strong extra compensation plan tended to motivate sales personnel to achieve divisional sales objectives, and he felt that the plan he had inherited from the former general manager (an annual plan, based on sales increases over the previous year) was not consistent with current market opportunities. Don soon switched to a territory management bonus — "Slightly more successful, but it still didn't meet our needs." He recalled what happened next.

> By this time, Dallas was on our backs. International's marketing personnel were trying to persuade us to use their OBIC plan on the assumption that whatever worked well in the States would work well for us. I always listen with respect to International's ideas, because I've often benefited through exchanges of information with U.S. personnel — so I investigated their plan pretty thoroughly.
>
> I finally decided to go with my own version of the OBIC plan. I worked on developing it for three months. I asked for a lot of input from my regional sales managers — what they wanted a plan to do, and what the plans they were currently using, couldn't do. Also, Payroll told me what they could handle — information systems in a large company like ours are very standardized and inflexible. Dallas gave me all their information too. Then I hired a sales manager, and turned the

---

[1] Any new listings with a dealer provided the opportunity for future orders. Changing suppliers' listings on the dealer's computerized equipment was a costly process, only done when the dealer intended to place future orders.

whole thing over to him. I'm glad we introduced OBIC in Industrial and Commercial Equipment. The plan wasn't perfect — no plan really is — but results were excellent.

Now as VP of the Retail group and GM of Housewares, I'm hoping to improve our profit picture — and I think some version of the OBIC plan would help. I've already talked to the retail sales managers, and sent them a list of benefits. There's no value in trying to legislate changes, so I'm not going to play the heavy and insist they give it a trial. The question isn't so much what I want, as what is decided through give and take with my people, and through their intuitive reasoning processes. I think the OBIC package is better than the one Tony's using now, but how he goes about getting results is really his decision.

The Objective Based Incentive Compensation Plan

On July 23, Don held a meeting of his two national sales managers in the Retail Products Group. Some of Don's remarks during the two-hour meeting are summarized below.

The purpose of this morning's meeting is to look at the OBIC plan with a view to implementing it in your divisions. To be effective as a management tool, a compensation plan — like the sales rep it rewards — must be chosen to suit the division's selling job, management objectives, and the marketplace. Each of you has budgeted a fair amount for annual payout in various kinds of extra compensation, and I'd like to see those dollars used to get the best results possible. Otherwise, we can't justify that expense. Personnel would like us to abolish extra comp altogether, and pay straight salary — easier bookkeeping, fewer loopholes and inequities, and so on — but I know sales reps! They need the extra motivation that a good compensation package can give, and they need recognition for individual effort.

I'm convinced there's room for improvement in the extra comp plans you've got in operation now. I've talked with the two of you individually about general reasons for adopting the OBIC package. Now I thought it might make sense to show you some specific examples of target sheets from my former division. Also, I've asked Barry Mills from the Equipment Group to drop by a little later to explain how he implements the plan with his salespeople.

Generally speaking, the plan works like this: at the beginning of each quarter, each regional sales manager and sales representative establishes for his or her own region or territory a list of objectives — a combination of sales volume objectives and non-volume objectives. Points are assigned to the objectives, depending on their degree of importance to regional and divisional plans. The more important the objective, the higher the point value. The total number of targeted points never exceeds 50, and the maximum earned stops at 100. It's important that realistic volume and non-volume objectives be set, so that only an extraordinary performance will be rewarded with maximum incentive compensation.

The OBIC plan offers enormous flexibility and potential for individualization. In Industrial and Commercial Equipment, each of the national sales managers adapted the plan to suit the particular needs of his or her own RSMs and sales reps. We considered many factors in setting objectives such as differences in regional markets. For instance, there's a very limited market for our 'Humidaire' line in Alberta, which we took into account when setting targets.

Don switched on an overhead projector to show the first of a number of transparencies he had prepared. He explained that the same target point summary sheet was used for regional sales managers and sales reps alike. However, the RSMs' targets were related to divisional sales objectives, while the sales reps' targets were related to regional sales objectives. Don commented on Visual A (see Exhibit 4).

Karl Lieberman's target sheet indicates that 44 of his 50 targeted points relate to the official sales forecast. When RSM or sales reps are at 100 percent of their sales forecast, their points will be at the target level — 50. If their extra compensation kicks in at 80 percent of forecast [see item #2 in Visual A], this means that at 120 percent of forecast they will have reached their maximum extra compensation. Incidentally, you can see how Karl's results were actually calculated. His boss had assigned an annual amount of $2700 incentive comp to him — about 15 percent of his total pay package, if I remember correctly. So his quarterly target was $675, with a possible maximum payout of $1350 per quarter.

You can see profitability objectives of the Air and Water Processing Equipment division in the weighting of target points in Visual A. Our air cleaning equipment is extremely profitable, and that's reflected in the preponderance of points assigned to that line.

Also, we discovered that we could vary the targets depending on the particular strengths and weaknesses of each sales rep. For instance, Visual B [see Exhibit 5] is the target sheet of an experienced sales rep, one of our best, who loves selling for the pure joy of the chase! There's no need to emphasize volume with her because she always tries for volume objectives whether or not the reward is in dollars. So, all her third quarter objectives are non-volume ones, heavily weighted in terms of the most profitable lines . . . thus meeting divisional objectives.

Visual C [see Exhibit 6] is another example of individually-tailored targets. This is the summary sheet for a new, inexperienced sales rep during his first quarter with the company. His targets will be beefed up each successive quarter until training is fully completed and he is pulling his weight with the rest of them. Incidentally, that unusual first objective was necessary because Hal's territory is 1200 miles away from his regional sales manager!

Besides flexibility, OBIC brought good sales management results in the Industrial and Commercial Equipment group. I'd like to see as good results in Retail Products next year! The most important benefits of the plan, though, relate to its ability to help the sales reps direct their efforts to those areas which will pay off for them, while at the same time meeting divisional marketing plan objectives.

At this point, Barry Mills arrived. At Don's invitation, he described his method of arriving at quarterly objectives with his salesmen.

The first step I take is to get each sales rep to develop his or her own list of planned sales by product and by account for the coming year. For each dealer account, which requires a special kind of management, the sales rep does a dealer resource analysis from a dealer work plan developed to serve as an operations base for the coming year. The plan may include product training seminars, sales training for dealers, order department training, or even making calls with the dealers' sales people. Our Air and Water sales reps also set personal targets for upgrading their territories, which they commit to paper on the 'Territory Management Objectives' form (see Exhibit 7).

Using all these planning tools, each sales rep selects, from his or her annual targets, quarterly objectives. Then we sit down together to come to mutually agreeable final objectives. I check to make sure that the objectives are set where they're reasonably attainable with maximum effort. This is when I assign points based on the relative importance of an objective, not the degree of difficulty in achieving it. Profitability of the objective is very important, together with its potential to gain other product business for the account.

Barry summarized the types of targets which might be developed for his sales staff as follows:

Profit Targets   Targets can be set up on specific profitable products, or whatever sales objective is currently important to our national or regional objectives.

National or Regional Sales Drives — Contests, etc.   Set up special promotion targets, as in our "4 for 3" program.

Equipment Sales   Develop targets to lockup major users of our treatment chemicals — sell specialized equipment to ensure future orders for supplies.

Dealer Business   Objectives to upgrade dealers — quarterly seminars on selling skills or products and calls with dealer sales reps.

Cost Control Objectives   Objectives applied where needed to help control discretionary spending.

Performance Management   Targets to upgrade questionable areas: time management, sales calls, communications, reports on time — general territory administration.

Barry admitted there were some problems with the implementation of the system, including difficulties in selecting realistic targets. Some sales reps were inclined to be overly optimistic, listing target account sales prematurely in a given quarter and consequently losing points on "no sale." There was also a tendency to list "sure targets." However, this could be combatted by the regional manager's knowledge of his or her individual sales reps and their accounts. "Over-payout" — payments above the amount budgeted for extra compensation — was another hazard. The visiting sales manager concluded his presentation with a visual which listed the benefits of the OBIC Plan for sales reps and managers (see Exhibit 8), and the meeting adjourned.

A Post-Meeting Conversation

Talking with Don over a cup of coffee in the company cafeteria, Tony admitted that he was impressed with what he had heard that morning and he could see the value of the OBIC plan for an industrial division. "Housewares is so different from Industrial and Commercial Equipment though — and I don't believe in change merely for the sake of change. There's got to be a really good rationale for shifting from what we have."

Don nodded in agreement, adding, "You'll need some time to think about today's presentation, and to come up with some ways of dealing with the profitability issue I mentioned before. Let's meet again in a few days and see where we go from here."

Glancing at his watch, Don was startled to see that he was almost late for an appointment. He excused himself and left the cafeteria hurriedly. Tony thoughtfully sipped his cold coffee, considering all he had learned that day. He wondered if the Objective-Based Incentive Compensation Plan might provide the best answer to the requirements of his boss, his sales personnel, the company, and himself. Tony thought, "I've got to make a decision within the next few days.... What should I decide?"

Canadian Multiproducts Limited (A)

EXHIBIT 1

CANADIAN MULTIPRODUCTS LIMITED (A)

Organizational Chart, Housewares Division, Retail Products Group

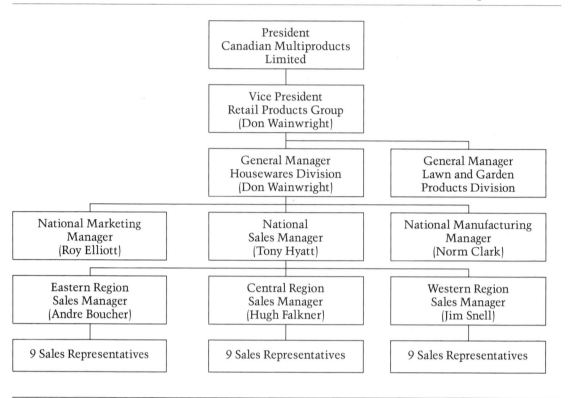

EXHIBIT 2

CANADIAN MULTIPRODUCTS LIMITED (A)

Industrial and Commercial Equipment Group

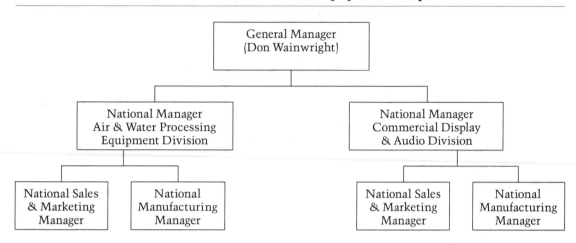

Air and Water Processing Equipment Division

Manufactures and markets equipment and supplies for industrial and commercial use: air and water pollution control equipment, fabric filters, bag houses, electronic air cleaners, air conditioners, humidifiers, dehumidifiers, heat pumps, water softeners, distillers, filtration systems, treatment chemicals.

Commercial Display and Audio Division

Manufactures and markets professional color and black and white video monitors, commercial large-screen projection systems, commercial audio and recording equipment, surveillance monitors, educational TV receivers and monitors, data display monitors.

EXHIBIT 3
CANADIAN MULTIPRODUCTS LIMITED (A)

Internal Correspondence

Personal and Confidential

194

TO: Peter Lawson
FROM: Tony Hyatt
RE: COMPENSATION PLAN
DATE: January 1

For the fiscal year beginning January 1, your Multipro Sales Bonus Plan includes:

1. A base salary expected to yield $18 000 per year and payable monthly.

2. A bonus calculated on an annual basis at the end of the year as follows:
   (a) 1% on all sales in excess of an annual base of $200 000 up to $400 000.
   (b) 2% on all sales in excess of an annual base of $400 000 (to yield up to a maximum of 50% of base salary).

3. For each of the first three quarters of the fiscal year, an advance payment on the annual bonus will be calculated on a year-to-date basis as follows:

   1.5% on all sales in excess of a quarterly base of $100 000 accumulative.

This Compensation Plan provides the opportunity for you to earn Incentive Compensation up to a maximum of 50% of your base salary on a year-to-date basis. Please bring any questions concerning this plan to our next divisional meeting.

TRH/jl   Housewares Division

EXHIBIT 4
CANADIAN MULTIPRODUCTS LIMITED (A)

Visual A

QUARTERLY POINT SUMMARY

R.S.M

SALESMAN Karl Lieberman   **PREPARED BY** E. M. Smith

DISTRICT South Western   **DIVISION** Air & Water Processing Equipment

DATE Dec. 29,   **FOR YEAR**

QUARTER   (1ST QTR)   2ND QTR   3RD QTR   4TH QTR

DESCRIPTION OF OBJECTIVES AT TARGET ATTAINMENT LEVEL	ASSIGNED POINTS		
	MAX	TARGET	EARNED
TARGET POINTS EARNED WHEN Y.T.D. F.C.S.T. ACHIEVED POINT AWARD COMMENCES AT % OF ATTAINMENT AS INDICATED*			
Y.T.D. TARGETS ($000'S) BY PRODUCT GROUP AT END OF QTR.			
VOLUME OBJECTIVES 1st 2nd 3rd 4th *			
#1 COMM. AIR CLEANING EQPT. (ALL MAIN CODES EXCEPT 853, 822) 382 582 878 1189 75%	40	20	14
#2 WATER PURIFIERS 13 28 42 56 80%	12	6	6
#3 PUMPS & AERATING EQPT. 84 178 270 365 85%	20	10	10
#4 HUMIDIFIERS (CODES 853, 822) 18 35 53 75 85%	12	6	6
RELATED SELLING COSTS			
#5 ALL CAN: WATER TREATMENT CHEMICALS 73 151 229 314 80%	8	4	4
#6 % OF COST INCREASE (DEPT. 406, 426) NOT GREATER THAN TOTAL SALES INCR. = TARGET. FOR EACH PERCENTAGE POINT COST INCR. (VS. PREV. YR.) LESS THAN SALES INCR., ONE POINT AWARDED TO A MAX. OF 4	8	4	4
TOTAL POINTS	100	50	44

CALCULATION FOR PAYROLL USE

QUARTERLY TARGET INCENTIVE COMP $675   TOTAL BONUS POINTS EARNED 44

CALCULATION   44 x 2% x $675

(POINTS EARNED X 2% X QUARTERLY TARGET BONUS)

AMOUNT OF INCENTIVE COMP $594

EXHIBIT 5
CANADIAN MULTIPRODUCTS (B)

Visual B

QUARTERLY POINT SUMMARY

SALESMAN N. Armstrong   **PREPARED BY**   L.A. Overton

DISTRICT Central   **DIVISION**   Air and Water Processing Equipment

DATE June 30,   **FOR YEAR**

QUARTER   1ST QTR   2ND QTR   (3RD QTR)   4TH QTR

DESCRIPTION OF OBJECTIVES AT TARGET ATTAINMENT LEVEL	ASSIGNED POINTS		
	MAX	TARGET	EARNED
1. "CLEAN-AIR" EQUIPMENT PROSPECTS: ESTABLISH 44 QUALIFIED "CLEAN-AIR" PROSPECTS. EACH MUST HAVE A PROPERLY COMPLETED ACCOUNT RECORD FORM, SHOWING: (A) AT LEAST $150 MONTH IN SUPPLIES POTENTIAL, AND (B) NAME OF DECISION MAKER. EACH ADDITIONAL PROSPECT WORTH 1 POINT TO "MAX."	20	10	
2. WRITE SELLING PROPOSALS: WRITE 3 WATER PURIFICATION SYSTEMS PROPOSALS PER MONTH (COPY TO L.A.O.). TARGET IS 5 PROPOSALS IN QUARTER. EXTRA POINTS EARNED AT 2 PER PROPOSAL (OVER TARGET) TO "MAX."	20	10	
3. CONSUMER SPOT ORDERS: TAKE 27 SPOT ORDERS (AT %55.00 MINIMUM VALUE) FOR CHEMICAL SUPPLIES; WITH AT LEAST 1 ORDER EACH FOR KRONO AND XR17. EXTRA POINTS EARNED AT 2 PTS. PER ORDER (OVER 22) TO "MAX." LEVEL	40	20	
4. NEW ACCOUNTS: SELL 5 NEW ACCOUNTS (EXCLUDING "CLEAN-AIR" ACCOUNTS) WORTH 1 PT. EACH. ADDITIONAL NEW ACCOUNTS WORTH 1 PT. EACH TO "MAX."	20	10	
TOTAL POINTS	100	50	

CALCULATION FOR PAYROLL USE

QUARTERLY TARGET INCENTIVE COMP   TOTAL BONUS POINTS EARNED

CALCULATION   X   X $

(POINTS EARNED X   X QUARTERLY TARGET BONUS)

AMOUNT OF
INCENTIVE COMP

EXHIBIT 6
CANADIAN MULTIPRODUCTS (A)

Visual C

QUARTERLY POINT SUMMARY

SALESMAN Hal Jobin   **PREPARED BY** Bill Barnes

DISTRICT Northern   **DIVISION** Air And Water Processing Equipment

DATE January 2,   **FOR YEAR**

QUARTER   (1ST QTR)   2ND QTR   3RD QTR   4TH QTR

DESCRIPTION OF OBJECTIVES AT TARGET ATTAINMENT LEVEL	ASSIGNED POINTS		
	MAX	TARGET	EARNED
1. SALES TRAINING BECOME THOROUGHLY FAMILIAR AND COMPETENT WITH MATERIAL IN BASIC TRAINING KIT. FINAL TEST CONSISTS OF 85 QUESTIONS. SHOULD GET 75 CORRECT. EACH CORRECT ANSWER ABOVE TARGET (i.e. 81-85) IS WORTH 4 POINTS EACH.	40	20	
2. TERRITORY REBUILDING USING NEW "ACCOUNT RECORD" FORM, PERSONALLY INTERVIEW ALL CONSUMER ACCOUNTS POSSIBLE IN DESIGNATED TERRITORY. TARGET IS 100 COMPLETED ACCOUNT RECORDS. EACH ADDITIONAL ACCOUNT RECORD IS WORTH 1 POINT TO MAXIMUM LEVEL.	40	20	
3. SPOT ORDER SALES DE-EMPHASIZE THIS UNTIL MARCH, DURING MARCH, TRY TO WRITE SPOT ORDERS. TARGET IS 10 ORDERS WITH VALUE OF 10 POINTS. EACH ORDER ABOVE TARGET IS WORTH 2 POINTS TO MAXIMUM LEVEL.	20	10	
TOTAL POINTS	100	50	

CALCULATION FOR PAYROLL USE

QUARTERLY TARGET INCENTIVE COMP   **TOTAL BONUS POINTS EARNED**

CALCULATION   X   X $ | **AMOUNT OF**

(POINTS EARNED X   X QUARTERLY TARGET BONUS) | **INCENTIVE COMP**

EXHIBIT 7
CANADIAN MULTIPRODUCTS LIMITED (A)

M.B.O. Sales Plan

TERRITORY MANAGEMENT OBJECTIVES

198

Part One
The Effective
Organization

Through the following objectives I plan to upgrade my territory
1. To increase my daily call average and maintain a minimum standard of ___8___ calls per day.
2. To increase my call activity on <u>new prospects</u> and maintain a minimum of ___3___ new calls per week.
3. To increase my spot order dollar volume by ___10%___ percent over the previous year on a quarterly basis.
4. To upgrade my dealer liaison work and dealer volume, I plan to work a minimum of ___12___ days each quarter with dealer salesmen and/or order departments.
5. To achieve listed targets I plan to organize and present ___2___ "Group Selling" Seminars per quarter.
6. To ensure "Penetration Selling" I plan on making a minimum of ___64___ physical product demonstrations per quarter.

Name: ___J. Moeller___

EXHIBIT 8

CANADIAN MULTIPRODUCTS LIMITED (A)

Benefits of OBIC Plan

BENEFITS OF OBIC PLAN FOR THE SALESPERSON

Salespersons feel more committed and responsible towards making their contribution to district forecast attainment.

They know they are being measured on their own effort and results.

They know the system is fair because they were part of the objective-setting process.

They know they will be rewarded for specific over-accomplishment.

They know their plans are flexible and can be changed.

Opportunity to double planned extra compensation.

BENEFITS OF OBIC PLAN FOR THE MANAGER

Quarterly objective-setting sessions create a good climate of understanding between manager and salesperson on district sales and other performance targets, which can be tailor-made for salesperson.

Creates opportunity to challenge salesperson towards achieving specific profitable territory goals.

Necessitates a quarterly performance and results review—provides opportunity to revise and/or upgrade target objectives for subsequent quarter.

Serves as progressive performance appraisal. Ties in with company performance review system and lends itself to appropriate performance management projects.

Gives the manager latitude to motivate achievement of specific sales objectives which can be tailor-made for each sales person, product, or marketing situation, according to need.

NOREX ELECTRIC *

Jeffrey Gandz and Eileen D. Watson

Larry Bedford, general manager of the Norex Electric plant in Peterborough, Ontario, was thinking about an improved profit-sharing scheme for his company. It was mid-August, and he hoped that a new profit-sharing plan could be ready for introduction at the plant by the following April.

The Company

Norex Electric (NE) was a subsidiary of Norex International, a large multinational corporation engaged in the manufacture and distribution of a broad range of industrial, engineering, electrical, and heating equipment and supplies. Among the electrical products manufactured by the Norex plant in Peterborough were wall sockets, light switches, and other injection and blow-moulded plastic components. The company was generally considered to be a successful operation, and its management group believed NE's profitability record was the best in the industry.

Constructed under the supervision of the chief engineer, Tom Manning, the plant housed a large manufacturing and assembly area, a warehouse and distribution area, and offices. Approximately 80 people worked in the manufacturing plant, which operated three shifts a day, six days a week. Another 25 were employed in the warehouse and distribution center, which shipped Norex products from the Toronto and Peterborough plants to the company's customers in eastern Canada. Goods manufactured in the Peterborough plant accounted for approximately 10 percent of the corporation's sales and pre-tax profits.

A sophisticated electronic computerized system linked the operations of the

*All names in this case have been disguised.

Norex International head office in Toronto with Norex Electric in Peterborough. As the NE general manager, Larry Bedford once remarked, "We just fill the orders that are processed in Toronto — we don't have a marketing function at all. That drives me up a tree, sometimes! I'd like us to be a complete operation — but I can't argue philosophically with the way the parent company's running this business."

The Industry

The types of electrical components made by NE in Peterborough were also made by five other Canadian companies engaged in this capital-intensive industry. The technology of the industry had not changed since its inception in the mid-1960s, and the products of all six companies were basically the same. Manufacturing standards were tightly controlled by the Canadian Standards Association through committees staffed by industry people. Larry Bedford observed, "That kills innovation. No changes can be made until everybody is ready. And the business is extremely incestuous. The six of us buy our materials from the only two sources of approved material available in Canada. Also, we all buy our tooling and technology from the same source, and we all use the same type of equipment."

The growth of the market depended to a large extent on housing starts. Concerning long-term prospects for the industry, Larry Bedford said, "Demographic data indicate a declining need for new housing. We're certainly not in a growing industry...and we'll do well to hold our own."

The General Manager

Larry Bedford received what he termed "an utterly useless degree in mathematics and physics" in 1970, and immediately joined the marketing staff of a small, aggressive Calgary firm. Through a series of promotions he became general manager of the company within three years. The firm was taken over in 1974 by a large multinational corporation, and Larry left eight years later. He explained, "I left because I ran out of ideas, and had some capable people nipping at my heels, and felt I couldn't contribute any longer. At that time, the company was extremely profitable — a little gold mine — but I had done and learned all I could."

In October, 1983, Larry became general manager of Norex Electric in Peterborough. Two operations — manufacturing and distribution — functioned as separate organizations within the plant. The manufacturing operation was supervised by the plant manager, Adam Weir, assisted by his general foreman, Roy Campbell. Karin Haust was in charge of the warehouse and shipping operation. The management group also included Dave Vickery, the plant accountant, and Tom Manning, manager of engineering services. (See Exhibit 1 for NE's table of organization.)

In July, 1986, Larry met Brad Markingham (an old friend from university days) for lunch. Brad was a human resource consultant for a management consulting firm, and the lunch-time conversation reflected the business interests of both men.

Brad   How's the business going, Larry?

Larry   We're as good as anyone else, Brad. We have the business under control as well as any of the competition. Our market share is very respectable — about 25 percent — and I don't see any reasonable expectation that it should be higher. You're probably aware that in our type of industry we can't market product features. We can only sell the talents of our sales force in Toronto, our good inventory control, and good service ... and that's somewhat limiting.

Brad   I've wondered how you happened to get this job. If I remember correctly, you had no previous connection with Norex.

Larry   My predecessor, the founder of this plant, retired suddenly because of illness — he was only 56. I'm not sure why they chose someone from outside to take his place, but I think it had something to do with the mix of personalities here. The parent company wanted someone to come in and keep the existing competent and productive organization together, with no disruptive upheavals.

Brad   Do you like working for Norex?

Larry   It's a good company, Brad, and I'm fortunate to have very competent people working for me. When I first came here and was feeling my way around, I talked with the guys and asked them, "What's your biggest fear about my coming here?" They told me that they were afraid that I'd take their work away from them! They had absorbed my predecessor's duties during the eight months since he left, and loved it. I made a solemn promise that I'd never take my work away from them, and I've kept that promise. I delegate everything — and as a result, I do very little work myself.

Brad   Sounds great! But you must have some problems ...

Larry   Actually, the plant operates very smoothly. Even though the United Electrical Workers Union has been in here since NE started, we have not had one grievance in the entire life of the plant! The main credit goes to the plant manager, but _all_ the managers have the confidence of the employees, rather than the union. Oh, the union people come out of the woodwork at negotiation time, but there's little interest otherwise. Union positions are always filled by acclamation.

Brad   Can you describe a typical NE employee?

Larry   Our employees are mostly female, primarily immigrant women working at unskilled occupations. It doesn't make much sense to hire better
educated, more highly-skilled people, since most of the jobs are simple
and machine-paced.

Brad   What kind of jobs are most people doing?

Larry   About one-half tend machines, checking that they are running properly, feeding materials into them, for example. Others work in warehousing and shipping, keeping the place clean, and so on. Pretty menial jobs.

Brad   What are the big influences on the profitability of your company?

Larry   We fight for our market share on the basis of price — but there are no
secrets in this business. If we cut our price five percent, everybody
matches it the next day — or the same day! We *do* get into price wars, but
they're totally non-productive. We expect to return approximately 20
percent pre-tax on investment this year. We exceeded that in '84 but did
only nine percent in 1985. Now to me, those aren't brilliant figures. In a
cyclical industry, we should do better in the good years.

Brad   How about absenteeism and turnover?

Larry   We think we've got those pretty well controlled. Actually, absenteeism here is the lowest of all Norex plants. We get some turnover, about 20
percent of the plant jobs per year, but that poses no problem since it's easy
for us to hire people and the training is minimal.

Brad   Larry, I'm interested in your ideas about profit-sharing schemes — I
know you've given the subject a great deal of thought.

Larry   It's been a long-standing interest of mine. Anything related to motivation and what makes people tick fascinates me. I've read a lot about profit-
sharing because it's fun for me. It's much more enjoyable leisure-time
reading than any other business topic.

   More importantly, there was a profit-sharing plan in place when I
started here, and I was employed on the basis of one. It's a profit-sharing
scheme on a mathematical basis, where I receive a fixed percentage of the
profits, as do the four people who report directly to me, plus the general
foreman. Percentages vary — how they were set up originally, I have no
idea. They seem highly arbitrary. But it's a significant percentage of the
individual's income; an average of seven to 15 percent, paid in a lump sum
each April.

Brad   Sounds like a pretty good scheme...

Larry   The problem with it is, it's supposed to motivate people to produce
more, to work harder and better. Our scheme doesn't.

Brad   Why not?

Larry   Because the relationship between the profits of this division and our
efforts is very remote. The market prices over which we have no control

play a much more significant part in the bottom line results than our efforts here; so our profit-sharing scheme has become a sort of deferred income plan whereby the company kicks in some money in April of the following year to pay for summer holidays, or whatever! It's almost like an arbitrary bonus, given by the company in its wisdom and because it is kind.

Incidentally, the company has recognized over the years that the scheme is faulty, because they have chickened out in poor years. Their rationale seems to be, "It really wasn't the fault of the guys at NE, so let's abandon the formula this time and pay a good bonus anyway."

Brad   When did you decide that you wanted to make a change?

Larry   We never talked about it — never thought about it, for that matter — my first year with Norex. 1984 was a very good year, and the bonus was gratifyingly substantial. As 1985 went along, it became increasingly apparent that we were going to have a poor year, and yet I felt that the people who were reporting to me were performing much better than in 1984. Then in the early spring of this year, even though the profit-sharing scheme should have paid much less for 1985's washout, the company once again decided to raise the ante.

Brad   I guess you've reached some conclusions about that...

Larry   Everybody agreed — myself, the managers at Norex Electric, and my head office superiors — that the plan stinks. It's not serving any valid purpose at all.

Brad   So what do you think should be done?

Larry   The alternative is to replace it with something better, or just make some agreement to roll it into income, and forget about the whole thing.... I've had many lengthy discussions with the others about developing a better plan. They finally asked me to put something in writing, to help them reach a more intelligent conclusion. I talked with my boss, and he agreed to let me do some research and try to come up with some alternative suggestions. I spent some time in libraries, and talked to people knowledgeable about profit-sharing concepts, and came up with a report.[1] I sent a copy to my boss, and copies to my four key people at NE. Here's an extra copy for you.

Brad   Thanks, Larry. What does your boss think about profit-sharing plans?

Larry   He indicated that he would be receptive to anything intelligent we might propose, but I don't think he's really committed to incentive schemes or profit-sharing. I believe that he and the company would probably rather dispense with the whole thing... perhaps leaving only myself on an incentive scheme, and dropping it for everybody else.

_____

[1]See Appendix for Larry Bedford's report.

Brad   What do you want?

Larry   I'd like to have a broadly-based profit-sharing plan in which everyone has an equal share, including the hourly-paid people. And that's my overt prejudice — I shout it from the rooftops!

Brad   Do you think you'll get what you want?

Larry   If we at Norex could come up with a unanimous recommendation, I know we'd get what we want! However, I was careful to be objective in preparing my report. I resolved that I would not prepare a proposal, but simply provide background information to the people who report to me.

Brad   What did you do with the report?

Larry   I passed it on to my four key people — the general foreman was on the plan, too, but I'm not sure if he got a copy of the report or not. In effect, I said, "You guys have to work with this. This is background information only. Use it. Pick a plan, or let's debate, or do something...but it's your plan, not mine. You make a proposal." Seemed to me that it would be more effective if I didn't have to sell it to them — and besides, they're the people who can make or break it, anyway.

Brad   So what's the current status of the plan?

Larry   I made it very clear that I'd be available to assist if I could, in any way. They held a couple of meetings at my suggestion. I chose not to be present, but we've all discussed the topic publicly, from time to time — they know my opinions. Well, guess what has happened? The whole thing has died! I haven't heard a peep from them.

Brad   I wonder what's going on...

Larry   I know they're not totally uninterested, but I'm surmising that they're overwhelmed by the complexity of the thing in terms of what motivates people. They know what my prejudices are, but they recognize that their individual goals are different, and their chances of coming to some unanimous agreement are relatively slim.

Brad   So you think their decision is to do nothing?

Larry   Yeah — and I'm reluctant to press them. But they'll be the losers. The median salary of the group we're talking about is around $33 000, and that's $5000 to $7000 in profit-sharing benefits per person per year — and it appears that they're not interested!

Brad   I guess you're trying to decide what to do next.

Larry   Well, I've already made the first decision — to get rid of the existing plan, which serves no useful purpose. My superior and the people who report to me are in agreement with that. Now, it hasn't been formally stated, "If you guys don't come up with something by date X the plan will be scrapped in favor of some adjustment to straight salary," but that's clearly what will happen. I'm curious to know what's going on — if anything — among my subordinates.

205

Brad   Sure is difficult for a boss to find out, sometimes .... Say, here's an idea! I've been intending to investigate the whole area of incentive schemes for my firm. Why don't I meet with each of your key people, and ask them for their thoughts about profit-sharing?

Larry   Fine! Then you could give me some feedback about where they're at. I'll ask them if they'd be willing to talk to you about the need for a profit-sharing plan at NE, and the form it should take .... You know, I'm pretty certain that I can predict right now what each will say. Tom Manning, the engineering guy, doesn't want ripples in his income — no surprises. He's fifty years old, has always worked for Norex, is extremely security-oriented, and is against incentive schemes of any kind, because they cause waves.

Adam Weir, the plant manager, seems to be interested. Now Adam believes that anything that happens to this company is primarily because of his efforts — he's largely correct, by the way — and I think he considers me a necessary evil. That doesn't mean that we don't get along, but I'm a nuisance. As long as I stay out of his plant, everything's cool! His hang-up about incentive schemes is that there's no plan which guarantees that only the righteous would benefit and the slackers would suffer. He can't figure out a system whereby some undeserving soul in here — perhaps like me! — wouldn't benefit from his efforts. That bothers the hell out of him!

The accountant, Dave Vickery, is relatively new and insecure. He replaced an experienced older man who was promoted to a head office job. Dave's just a young guy, and I think he feels that his opinion doesn't matter much. And Karin Haust, in charge of distribution, believes that there's no way we could come up with the arithmetic to suit her.

She's afraid to commit herself to a formula, because all formulas have pitfalls — and basically, she's afraid of being treated unfairly by the company. She thinks that this is all a plot, in a sense.

Those four are the key personalities involved, plus Roy Campbell, the general foreman. And I'm already curious about the impressions you'll receive when you talk with them.

Brad   I'm looking forward to that — should be really interesting! ... Larry, I've been glancing through this report while we've been talking. How did you choose the particular types of plans you wrote up?

Larry   That's all I could find, in a fairly broad search of the literature. As far as I could see, "There ain't no more." And of course there's no ultimate proof in this area, no studies comparing the bottom lines of similar companies who are using different motivational schemes. It's still like putting a Bible in front of someone and saying, "Believe this." You can always question the validity of the concept. You know, Brad, the technique and the arithmetic aren't terribly important to me. I prefer whatever plan the people who report to me prefer. The vital question is, how do you get everybody to care, and to understand where we're going, and what's important and what's not?

Following his conversation with Larry Bedford, general manager of Norex Electric, consultant Brad Markingham arranged to visit the Peterborough plant. He spent the afternoon talking with individual members of NE's management group about profit-sharing plans.

Tom Manning, Manager of Engineering Services

We've always had bonuses, ever since I started at the Toronto plant in the late 1950s. Sometimes they'd only be $5, sometimes $50 — and since coming to this Peterborough plant, I've received anywhere from $200 to $1500. There's no rhyme nor reason to the amount we get. The year we busted our necks, we only got $200. One easy year, the company gave $1700. The very next year, when sales were bad and the profits down, the company coughed up $1700 again. When Larry came here, he said that wasn't right — and I agree.

Frankly, I just don't like bonuses! I enjoy getting the cheque in the spring, but I don't like the idea of it being widespread. I'd only go as far down the line as the foremen — they really affect cost savings, making sure materials aren't wasted. But if a worker's standing around all day, doing nothing, and still gets the same bonus I did — well, that's not fair. Larry, Adam, Dave, Karin and I each have power in our own ways to make savings, and affect the profits — but how do you judge who's made the biggest contribution? Is it someone who, with the stroke of a pen, saves ten thousand dollars in the cost of materials, or is it someone who scraped and sweated for a month to earn the company an extra thousand?

I work really hard, and I love my job. Jobs, really, because I look after purchasing, quality control, estimating, selling, and customer complaints as well as engineering. Many people estimate my salary as being much higher than it really is, because of the range of responsibilities I have. Still I'm not terribly dissatisfied with my salary... Larry sets it after our annual evaluation meeting, and he's very fair. I don't know, or choose to know, what the others make. For one thing, I'd be told that it's none of my business. Besides, I'd be unhappy if I found out that theirs is more than mine! Seriously, though, I'm very busy, and I don't want to take the time to think about it.

Dave Vickery, Plant Accountant

I'm not really sure if profit-sharing plans are good or bad. This is the first time I've had a position where a bonus system is in effect (I've been at Norex for two years) and it was nice to get my cheque last April for .3 percent of the profits. Trouble is, the arbitrary nature of the system is confusing — somebody so far away puts a value on what you do. At raise time we tend to treat the bonus as found money, but, in fact, the expected amount was probably deducted from the raise each manager asked for at his December salary review.

They've been talking profit-sharing ever since I started at NE, and in my opinion they'll never do anything about it. For one thing, we're a manufacturing cost center, not a sales organization, and we can't have a great effect on profits. My job is not at all measurable on a profit scale, although I work hard for the good of the company. At busy times of the year I put in a lot of overtime hours, but the policy at NE is that if you're in the profit-sharing plan, you don't get overtime pay. Larry says that overtime is *never* justifiable — but in accounting, it *is* obviously necessary. But I'd get shot if I suggested overtime pay instead of a profit-sharing plan!

The managers have strong differences of opinion about what kind of plan would be suitable. Standards here are sloppy, so the plant manager is opposed to using manufacturing standards as a base for a profit-sharing plan. If we use a plan based on costs there would be other problems related to the fact that our parent company is our biggest customer, and cost figures can be manipulated. And even if a good plan were presented by the managers it's debatable if it would be accepted at head office. I have to say that a profit-sharing plan is outside my duties and my interests, right now — especially since I'm so busy in my time away from work, studying for my CGA exams.

Karin Haust, Distribution Manager

The basic concept of profit-sharing systems is very good, although what we have now is useless — no formulas, no measurement, no incentive! I'd like to share in the ups and downs of the company, but my bonus just increases every year. I don't know how my amount differs from the others, but I think the other managers are tied in with Norex profits, while mine is just a straight bonus scheme. I asked about this once, and Larry explained it as "additional income."

The nature of my job makes it difficult to say exactly how much I contribute to the profits of Norex Electric. Our Peterborough plant is the warehouse and distribution center for the Toronto plant too, which means that many variables affecting NE profits are out of my control.

My reaction to Larry's report is that corporate management would resist — Larry wouldn't have a chance to push it through. Adam and Tom seemed to react to the report with indifference, but I feel that a real profit-sharing plan would help develop team spirit. We'd feel more like contributing members of the management team, effectively sharing in the management of the company.

Adam Weir, Plant Manager

I want to have an incentive system at Norex, but only if it means something. The system in place hasn't worked in the past, and still doesn't work. What happens now is that the company says, in effect, "You're a good boy," and gives us a handout. We've discussed many times how to change it to reflect what it's supposed to do — to separate out those people who *are* putting in major effort, while leaving out those who are not pulling their weight. It's really difficult to measure effort at the management level, but I want to make sure I get recognized for what I do.

We had a good plant-wide incentive system where I worked before coming to Norex. It took a lot of policing, but the workers in the plant speeded up production, and put extra effort into turning out good parts. In our injection molding type of operation at NE, the workers don't have the same opportunity to improve. We set the time on the machines, and the only variable is the time it takes to remove the finished parts.

Norex is a good place to work. We have a good relationship with the hourly-rated employees, and there hasn't been a grievance in the history of the plant. We have some excellent, experienced people here — the general foreman has been with us for ten years, the plant electrician for twelve. I think that a profit-sharing plan could be extended to include them, and other foremen and set-up people.

The management group works well together, now — we try not to step on each other's toes. Larry and I discuss things once or twice a day. We've improved operations to the point where we now manufacture the same production as two years ago, with half the number of people. We run a tight ship, and it could be tighter. If we don't get into an incentive scheme soon, things will be too tight to improve! Something has to be done before the next bonus comes up in the spring.

Roy Campbell, General Foreman

The present plan is OK as it is. The only change I can think of is that the people with more responsibility, who are really producing, should benefit more. Some people under me shouldn't even be here. And people who leave at five every night...I don't leave the plant at night until I'm positive everything's running smoothly. Adam and I used to get calls all night long to come back to the plant when we were starting up — but that doesn't happen too much any more.

I'm a company-minded man. A few years ago, I was off work with a serious illness for eight months. Mr. Bevin, the former general manager, was really good to me. He kept my pay coming, and told my wife not to worry about a thing — and I got a promotion when I came back! I see my bonus as being tied to my performance, and it sure affects my work. When Larry asked me for ideas about a profit-sharing plan, I told him my thoughts about different measurements we could use — Larry's a good listener — but there were different loopholes in each one. I really can't think of anything better than we have, that's workable.

* * *

Later the same week, Brad Markingham reported the gist of these discussions to Larry. It was the conflict between the negative reaction by his managers and his own enthusiasm which made Larry Bedford wonder what his next move should be and whether or not he should push for implementation of some form of plan.

Larry Bedford's Report on Profit-Sharing

Introduction

The purpose of this report is to study the feasibility of installing an effective profit-sharing plan at Norex Electric. It is clear that the current profit-sharing scheme is not effective, and should either be eliminated or replaced by a plan that would enable NE employees to better achieve their personal goals while improving the return on investment.

Although the topic is important, it would be overstating the case to say that a profit-sharing scheme at Norex Electric is crucial at this time. On the whole, the organization functions reasonably well and the management group is better motivated than average. It is also true that we are not very labor-intensive, and therefore the gains from a more highly motivated work force are potentially less than in a company which has a lower ratio of material and capital cost to payroll dollars.

Nevertheless, I believe that a well-designed profit-sharing scheme is highly desirable. The level of motivation decreases rapidly in the lower ranks of our company, and our ability to cope with future challenges can be jeopardized by the resistance to change which is evident in most organizations. Also, it might be useful for Norex International to gain first-hand experience through the installation of a broadly based profit-sharing scheme at Norex Electric. The risks of failure here are less, and the lessons learned may be useful elsewhere in the organization.

The subject is extremely complex, and the literature in the field is far from unanimous in recommending a single proven approach. While trying to maintain objectivity, I must confess to a high level of personal enthusiasm for broadly based group incentives. To me, they have a great emotional appeal and appear to offer the greatest potential. They probably also carry the greatest risk of failure, and are the hardest type to "sell" in this organization.

Objectives of a Profit-Sharing Scheme

The following are frequently mentioned reasons for establishing profit-sharing schemes:

- to install a sense of partnership
- to provide a group incentive
- to improve employee security (especially deferred plans)
- to be fair
- to give supra-wage benefits without fixed commitments
- to attract desirable employees and reduce turnover

- to encourage employee thrift
- to provide flexibility in compensation
- to give tax advantages
- to provide economic education for employees
- to stimulate initiative
- to establish better employee relations
- to strengthen loyalty
- to increase productivity
- to increase profits

Motivational Effectiveness of Incentives

A. Money as an incentive

The effectiveness of financial incentives is not well understood. Salary administration policies and practices within the company are undoubtedly important — how the employee's income is determined, how the salary or pay levels compare to others in the organization, the level of secrecy in income levels, and the individual's income history. An incentive plan is not a substitute for sound salary administration.

There is considerable evidence that the installation of incentive plans often results in greater output per work hour, lower unit costs, and higher wages, in comparison to straight-payment systems. However, the installation of an incentive system is usually accompanied by changes in work methods, management policies, improved communication, etc. Can these changes be instituted without an incentive scheme? Perhaps so, but the presence of a financial incentive probably greatly facilitates the process.

B. Current trends in behavioral science

I conclude from reading McGregor, Herzberg, Gellerman, Likert, Maslow, Vroom, Drucker, and others, that behavioral scientists generally rate factors such as achievement, recognition, growth, advancement, responsibility, and challenge more highly than money as a motivator. Business executives are urged to change their management styles from "Theory X" to "Theory Y," to utilize the creative abilities of their employees in a more effective way, to give them the "big picture," to employ job enrichment and enlargement techniques, etc. However, the experts warn that these changes will not work without an equitable income policy in the firm.

C. Company results

It is somewhat difficult to assess the effectiveness of profit-sharing schemes because there is more information available about successful plans than about failures. There seems to be some evidence that companies with incentive schemes are generally more successful than others. It may be argued, however, that only the successful ones can afford it!

Surveys of firms with profit-sharing schemes show that the vast majority of companies with plans are satisfied. In a survey conducted by D & B and the Profit Sharing Research Foundation,[1] management rated their companies' plans as follows:

Very successful. . . . . .25.7 percent
Successful. . . . . .56.4 percent
So-so. .15.6 percent
Disappointing . . . . 2.3 percent

D. A consultant's viewpoint

U.S. consultant Mitchell Fein says that roughly 85 percent of the labor force is weakly motivated, and that traditional management styles and techniques have failed to find a way to "turn on" these employees. Conventional incentives tend to accentuate the worker's narrow self-interest and are not designed to encourage cooperation. Merit increases for productivity are not seen to be objective by the group and often operate on the "squeaking wheel" principle. According to Fein, the behavioral science approach also has been a failure. For instance, job enrichment fails because the job market is more selective than generally thought. The employees who end up with boring, repetitive jobs are the ones who prefer that type of work. Traditional management is left with only one alternative — to apply more and better controls, and give tighter supervision. Full responsibility for improved productivity is left with management, and as time passes, more costly controls, support staff, computers, etc., are required.

Fein surveyed 400 U.S. plants and concluded that work measurement increases productivity by 14.6 percent, and wage incentives give a further 42.9 percent increase, for a total gain of 63.9 percent. The survey indicated a labor cost reduction of 24.6 percent. The employees in this survey received an average of 23.5 percent incentive pay. Despite these potential benefits, only 26 percent of the industrial workers in the U.S. participate in incentive plans. Why? According to Fein, the major deterrent is management. Some managers believe that incentives will diminish their ability to control their operations, and that the incentives will deteriorate over a period of time. Some managers are convinced that productivity improvement is mainly created by management efforts — there is no need to share gains.

IV. Requirements for a Successful Plan

In order for a plan to have a reasonable chance of success, the following conditions should prevail:

- Confidence of most of the employees in the integrity, good intent and ability of their management. (It's difficult to know what the average union employee thinks about management at Norex Electric. In Toronto, there's a lot of union-management strife.

---

[1]A non-profit publicly supported educational foundation based in Evanston, Illinois. Its stated purpose is to discover and publish facts about the experiences of companies with profit-sharing, employee stock ownership, and participative programs, to serve as a practical guide for those designing/operating such programs.

We've fared better in Peterborough, but we may encounter more problems with the forthcoming change in union leadership.)

- A management with a constructive and friendly attitude, and respect for employees as individuals and as contributing members of a productive team. (We talk a good game in this area. However, there's a tendency at times to think of our employees as replaceable tools. A change in attitude towards more participative management would be difficult for some of our supervisors and managers.)

- The payment of wages and salaries equal to those prevailing in the industry or locality.

- A formula which has a good chance of producing significant employee benefits and meeting the company's needs.

- An effective program of administration and communication.

- Top management initiative and support. (Top management enthusiasm at Norex International is probably at a minimum because of current problems.)

- Emphasis on incentives to efficiency.

- Allocation to individuals on the basis of their annual earnings.

- Flexibility to meet changing conditions. (A successful scheme at NE would require a "handle" other than profits. We'd need sophistication in accounting and systems which we don't have now. Would we be willing to invest the time and effort required to debug the system, and would head office be available to help if required?)

- Some form of loss-sharing.

- The desire to make the system work. (There's no point in attempting to install an incentive system if we do not have a clear and firm commitment to make it work and to be patient enough to wait for positive results.)

V. Types of Incentive Systems

All incentive plans can be classified into two major categories: non-financial plans, and financial plans.

Non-financial incentives are motivating factors that appeal to an employee's emotions, rather than his or her wallet. Feelings such as pride in workmanship, recognition of achievement, affiliation, gratitude, shame in poor performance, pride in superior performance, spirit of competition, and many others, can provide a powerful adjunct to financial incentives.

Financial incentives may be subdivided into two major types — indirect, and direct.

Indirect financial incentive plans apply on a company-wide basis, and are not directly dependent on the individual employee's performance. Included are such things as equitable pay structures, merit increases, retirement plans, group life and health insurance, workers' compensation plans, and a variety of "fringe benefits" ranging from inexpensive cafeteria meals to subsidized recreation programs.

Direct financial incentive plans give higher pay for better performance, and can be administered on an individual, group or plant-wide basis. Methods used to reward increased effectiveness or productivity vary greatly, and include many different piece-work plans, standard minute (standard hour) plans, profit-sharing plans, and multiple-factor incentive plans. Many managers have promoted the idea of plant-wide incentive schemes, with the result that several simplified, overall plans such as the Scanlon Plan, the Lincoln Incentive Management Plan, the Rucker Plan, and Improshare have been developed.

The reaction of organized labor to the introduction of incentive systems varies. For example, the United Steelworkers tend to favor the use of incentives, while the United Automobile Workers usually are opposed.

I now propose to put forward some specific information about representative group incentive plans. In describing the essential elements of the various plans, I will deal more with the philosophy and principles than the accounting manipulations. There is no doubt in my mind that the mechanics can be worked out.

The Scanlon Plan

The Scanlon Plan is a company-wide or plant-wide incentive plan which shares the extra profit made possible by the efforts of the work force. It was developed in the 1940s by an official of the United Steelworkers of America, Joseph H. Scanlon. The "heart" of the Scanlon Plan is the necessity for union-management cooperation. The plan consists of two elements: a suggestion system, and a plant-wide incentive scheme.

The suggestion system provides the opportunity for every employee to contribute to the improvement of essential elements of production: operating methods, machinery and equipment, and paperwork. Suggestions are received and evaluated by representative production committees, and are disposed of by acceptance, rejection, or implementation.

The second essential part of the Scanlon Plan attempts to solve the problem of establishing universal standards by introducing a measure to reflect the results of everybody's efforts. This measure is the sales value of a company's production. In effect, the plan acknowledges that if production sales values are increased with no change in labor costs, productivity rises and unit costs are lowered. Thus, the universal standard becomes the ratio of labor costs to sales value added by production. As the labor percentage of the value added to production decreases, a plant-wide bonus is earned. Each employee's share is distributed monthly — frequent distribution is thought to increase the motivational value of the scheme. A bonus reserve is established to help stabilize monthly fluctuations. The profit-sharing feature of the Scanlon Plan is based on cost reduction rather than profits. Joseph Scanlon thought that cost reduction was an area where employees could exert some control, whereas profits were usually dependent on factors beyond their control. This type of profit-sharing might result in a situation where employees receive bonuses when the company is losing money, or do not receive bonuses when company profits are high.

The Lincoln Incentive Management Plan

Lincoln Electric Company of Canada Limited follows the example of its U.S. parent, which has successfully operated a combination profit-sharing and incentive plan on a company-wide basis since 1934. Substantial end-of-year bonuses are paid to its employees from profits which remain after dividends are paid to stockholders and money is set aside for the future (seed money). The remaining amount is divided as a bonus among all employees on the basis of three factors: the employee's merit rating, base salary, and the size of the bonus pool.

Lincoln's incentive plan, termed "incentive management," involves the use of standardized merit-rating cards for employee evaluation. Performance standards for employees are set by time study techniques, but an overall assessment or merit rating of the individual employee's performance and attitudes is used in determining bonuses. Each employee is rated on "supervision required," "workmanship and attitude toward quality," "output," and "cooperation," with a different supervisor assessing each category. The results are shared with each employee. On a company-wide basis, provision is made for management and employees to regularly discuss common problems and concerns through the forum of an advisory council.

According to Allan Fenton, in his article, "Incentive Management: How and Why it Works," the plan's payoff has been substantial. The prices of Lincoln's welding machines, for example, are basically the same as in 1940, despite a large increase in prices of materials and wages. The shareholders have received regular dividends since the inception of the plan, and earnings of employees have more than tripled over the period.

The Rucker Plan

Developed in the early 1930s by Allan W. Rucker, this plan is a company-wide incentive scheme with an emphasis on employee-management communication and cooperation, somewhat similar to the Scanlon Plan. However, the Rucker Plan's financial incentive is based on a different measure of productivity. This measure, economic productivity,[2] adds savings in materials and supplies to the considerations influencing the amount of the financial incentive.

The Rucker plan guarantees the work force a fixed percentage of the company's economic productivity, or production values. When the guaranteed percentage of production values exceeds payroll, the difference is distributed to the employees. Each employee's share is distributed monthly by a separate extra cheque; if there is no gain in a particular month, no extra cheque is forthcoming.

Plant productivity groups, with rotating memberships from all areas, meet monthly with key managers to review and analyze past performance, and to discuss plans for the future. A continuing flow of information (by way of frequently updated bulletin-board reports, paycheque stuffers, posters, quizzes, contests, etc.) stimulates employee interest, participation, and commitment to company goals.

Improshare

Improshare is the name given by originator Mitchell Fein to an incentive package which embodies many of the features of the older plans. Everyone in the plant or group

---

[2]Economic productivity is defined as the output of value added by manufacture (the difference between sales income from goods produced, and all costs excluding payroll costs) for each dollar of input of payroll costs (all employment costs related to whatever employee group is being measured).

participates, and productivity improvement is shared 50:50 between the company and the employees. The measurement base used for Improshare is the past average productivity level. The average work-hours required during a base period to produce a unit of product is established as a standard. Work-hour standards are frozen at the past average. Standards are not changed when operations are changed by either management or the employees (except for capital equipment and technology changes, which are specifically defined).

Gains are calculated weekly, with a moving average to minimize the fluctuations. Productivity is shared and paid weekly, and any losses are absorbed into the moving average. An agreed ceiling is established on productivity-sharing earnings. Any excess over the ceiling is carried forward to future weeks, and can be "bought back" eventually from the employees by cash payments. Fein believes that job security is essential to gaining cooperation from employees in the implementation of the Improshare plan. He recommends that all possible effort be made to keep the work force as static as possible.

Other Plans

In addition to the above, some companies distribute profit to employees in specific ways. Usually a fixed percentage, about 20 percent, of pretax profit is distributed on an annual basis, either equally to each employee, or as a percentage of base earnings, which might vary with status, seniority, or other criteria. Some plans pay cash in the period when profits were earned, others have deferral of payment to some future period or even to retirement.

VI. Pros and Cons of Group Incentives

I have reached some conclusions about the advantages and disadvantages of group-incentive systems.

Pros of group incentives

1. Easy to install; past performance can be easily used as a yardstick. One does not have to rely on arbitrary or complex measurement of what a "fair day's work" is, or what a company should produce.
2. Broad coverage; indirect, supervisory, clerical and management employees can be covered.
3. Promotes teamwork; by including everyone on the same basis (usually, percentage of earnings), common goals are created for the whole organization and the thorny question of who really was responsible for a given performance improvement is avoided to a large degree.
4. Encourages group discipline.
5. If done properly, promotes economic education and the free enterprise system.

Cons of group incentives

1. Poor incentive for some; slackers and inefficient employees awarded equally if social pressures do not work.
2. Rewards uncertain; and if too small, plan may fail.
3. Pressure on management; plan is likely to fail if management is unable or unwilling to accept a new way of life in the organization.
4. Lack of confidentiality; to be credible, *all* relevant information must be shared with employees.
5. A great deal of work; the communications effort required, the committees to screen employee suggestions, and the administration of a group plan may all be very time-consuming.
6. Some plans, such as Scanlon, need union approval.

EXHIBIT 1

NOREX ELECTRIC

Organizational Chart for Norex Electric

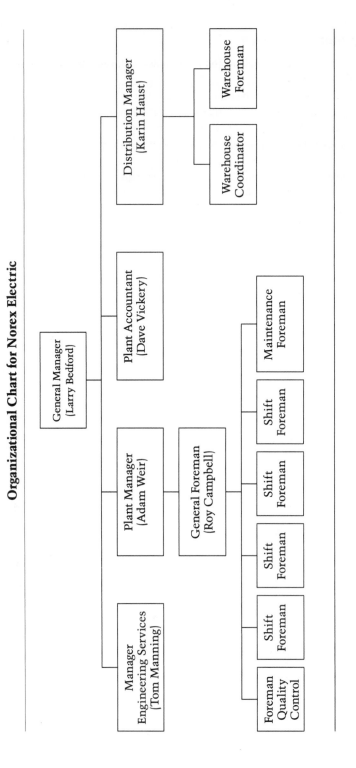

EXHIBIT 2

NOREX ELECTRIC

Example Profit-Sharing Formula[1]

Assumptions:

1) Total income for period*	$175 000
2) Total payroll of eligible employees**	$ 35 000
3) Net profit before taxes	$ 25 000
4) Management decides to contribute 20%*** of net profit before taxes to profit sharing, i.e.	$ 5 000

Calculation of profit-sharing rate:

$$\frac{\$5\,000}{\$35\,000} = \text{Profit-Sharing Rate of 14.3\%}$$

Application of profit-sharing rate:

Employee A earning $20 000 p.a. receives $2860 in profit-sharing
Employee B earning $30 000 p.a. receives $4290 in profit-sharing
Employee C earning $25 000 p.a. receives $3575 in profit-sharing

---

*Most profit-sharing plans provide for once-a-year sharing. Some plans share semi-annually or quarterly (rarely, if ever, monthly).

**The payroll of eligible employees excludes those who, because of insufficient service, do not qualify for participation. Consequently, the profit-sharing payroll is usually lower than the actual payroll.

***The percentage of profits to be shared, once decided upon, should remain unchanged from year to year so that profit-sharing rises and falls within the amount of profit. Notice that the percentage shared relates to the ratio of payroll to sales in this example.

[1]From "Profit Sharing—A Concept which Creates Winning Teams," p. 8, distributed by the Institute of Profit Sharing, Toronto, Ontario.

GARRETT TRUCK CO. LTD.

David Burgoyne and Olga Richardson

Frank Barton, manager of the London branch of Garrett Truck Co. Ltd., had decided to hire an extra salesperson. He believed that the three salespeople he currently employed were doing a good job but felt they were not able to give intensive enough coverage to their areas and, as a result, the potential of the district was not being fully exploited. In adding a fourth salesperson, however, Barton was faced with the decision of how to redefine sales areas and/or sales duties for the four people. (Exhibit 1 shows the existing geographic divisions of the sales district.)

The Garrett Truck Co. manufactured and sold heavy-duty diesel trucks and parts as well as providing maintenance and repair service. The product line was limited to larger units (tractor only) in the price range of $27 000 to $53 000 with an average selling price of $35 000. This was somewhat higher than the industry average for comparable-sized units and, in the company's view, was maintained through the high quality of the trucks and the level of personal service and attention accorded each customer. In the year ending September 1980, the London branch sold 107 new and 64 used trucks, which, with parts and service, made up a sales total of $5 541 000 (see Exhibit 2). Garrett trucks were sold throughout Canada to large and small fleet operators as well as one-unit operators; however, the London branch traditionally generated 90 percent of its sales from very small fleet operators that were located in nonurban areas and used trucks for local and long distance runs to haul a wide range of items including grain, cattle, sand and gravel, lumber, petroleum products, and freight. They tended to utilize the local servicing facilities in London provided by Garrett.

The city of London itself was not a large market for Garrett trucks, mainly because of the relatively small amount of heavy industry. In 1980, thirty-three new and twenty-one used trucks were sold to customers located within the city limits.

The London branch of Garrett Trucks had enjoyed little success selling to the major freight carriers and other fleet operators such as oil companies, ready-mix cement firms, and large manufacturers. One reason always put forward was that many of the large operations had their headquarters in Toronto and Montreal, and truck purchase decisions were made there. Another often suggested reason was that the "Big Three" auto manufacturers, with 50 percent of their total Canadian manufacturing capacity in Barton's sales area, had captured a large part of the major freight carrier business in the district, since deliveries of raw materials and supplies to their plants represented significant volumes for truckers.

The normal selling process was initiated by a Garrett salesperson calling on a potential customer. As most new truck buyers were fairly knowledgeable about the performance characteristics of different trucks, they generally did not need to view the truck itself but bought according to quotes given on their required specifications. In only perhaps 25 percent of sales, a customer wanted to see a truck before buying it. The salesperson's prime task then was to sell a buyer on the value of Garrett's higher-than-average quality and price. Maintenance and repair services were provided in a number of ways. The largest number of major overhauls were done at the London branch. However, two service dealers, one in Sarnia about 96 kilometres to the west, and one in Windsor about 192 kilometres to the southwest, had franchise rights to repair Garrett trucks in their area. The London branch also had a small service truck to dispatch for minor work on trucks that could not be brought to the main depot. A small number of customers had maintenance contracts with Garrett whereby for a certain fee, assessed either per hour or per kilometre, the trucks were overhauled on a set preventive maintenance schedule.

When Barton was transferred in 1977 to the London branch, which had one salesperson, he almost immediately added another. In the fall of 1979, he added a third person and simply subdivided the two existing territories to create the third territory. However, his decision to hire a fourth salesperson in the fall of 1980 involved a more complex situation, and Barton was currently considering three alternatives:

1. Divide the district into four territories as evenly as possible to give each salesperson approximately equal potential sales. The new territory would include a westerly portion of territory 1, an eastern part of territory 2, and southern part of territory 3.
2. Divide the territories, excluding the London city market, three ways, and make one salesperson the used truck manager plus giving that person sales responsibility for the city of London.
3. Leave the three territories basically unchanged geographically but assign one person the exclusive responsibility for fleet sales for the entire district.

Trade-ins were a necessary, integral part of new truck sales. Over the past three years, used trucks had accounted for just over 40 percent of all units sold by the London branch. At an average selling price of $8900, this represented over $500 000 in 1980, and yet the price barely covered the used truck department's out-of-pocket expenses (repairs, commissions) incurred plus the trade-in price. An additional factor was that used trucks were being carried in inventory for an average of one and a half months, which required a considerable amount of funds. In contrast, new truck contributions for the London branch were significant and well above the corporate average.

Frank Barton personally had been acting as the manager for both new and used truck sales, and all the salespeople had been selling both new and used trucks. With the growth of the branch, Barton felt he needed to reduce some of his commitments and for this reason had considered establishing the position of used truck manager. In addition to relieving some of his own responsibilities and giving one of his salespeople some management experience, it would also give focus to the selling of used trucks. Under this approach, all salespeople would continue to sell used trucks at the present commission rates. However, they would need to have the deals approved by the used truck manager, who would receive an overriding commission of 1 percent on all used truck sales, plus the normal salesperson's commission on any personal sales. This manager would also be responsible for the profitability of the used truck department and thus would have authority over the price at which trade-ins would be accepted, the extent of repairs to be made, and the selling price to be charged. This meant that on any new truck sale involving a trade-in, the used truck manager would have to test and inspect the old truck and advise on an acceptable trade-in value. In addition to the foregoing, the used truck manager would be responsible for new truck sales in the city of London.

"Fleet sales" had never been high in the London branch. Barton's definition of a fleet customer was any company that operated twenty or more trucks. Although quite often these were the products of a single manufacturer, this was by no means always the case. Barton estimated that there were fifty such potential customers spread over the total district. These figures did not include those companies that bought their trucks through a Toronto- or Montreal-based head office, or those companies that were committed to buying from one of the Big Three manufacturers. The territory estimates reflected Barton's best estimate of real market potential based on truck registration data and his knowledge of the market. The number of trucks purchased by these companies annually would amount to about 25 percent of their fleet size, some as replacements and some as additions. Of the fleet customers, six operated in the order of 150 trucks, ten operated around 50, and the remainder operated, on the average, about 25 trucks. Only 10 percent of the London branch's 1979 sales were to fleet customers, but by mid-1980 fleet sales had already exceeded that level. Barton felt that the London branch should be able to get at least 10 percent of the available fleet market. Since he felt they had 20 percent of the single-unit owner market, he was convinced that it would be difficult, but it was both possible and necessary to increase the branch's penetration of the fleet market segment. One salesperson with primary responsibility for this activity might be the answer.

One of the problems was that fleet customers not surprisingly expected larger discounts than the ordinary customer. The necessary discounts would probably exceed 27 percent. This could have considerable effect on a salesperson's potential commission earnings and Barton accepted that he might have to adjust the base salary to compensate.

One of Barton's concerns was the reaction of his existing salespeople to any changes in their territories. These salespeople, with their expertise, experience and personal ties with the customers, were the backbone of the branch's operations. They earned $400/month base salary plus commissions for an average total of $35 000/year. The structure of commission payments is given in Exhibit 3, and a typical month's sales by one person are shown in Exhibit 4.

Fred Graham, the salesperson in the southwest region (territory 2), was thirty-six years old and had sold Garrett trucks for two years. Before joining the company, he had owned his own small trucking operation. Graham was not a high-pressure salesperson but sold on the basis of personal knowledge of trucks and truck driving and his understanding of the needs of small truckers. Barton characterized him as a hard-working salesperson with little ambition for, or interest in, a management position.

Alan Myers, also thirty-six, had the London city and east region (territory 1). He joined Garrett Truck in 1976 before Barton was made branch manager. Previously in insurance sales, Myers had a charming personality and a polished style but at times was considered a little "pushy" by some customers and prospects. He had no previous experience with trucks before joining Garrett, yet with what Barton considered to be at best average effort, was the branch's highest paid salesperson.

Harvey, twenty-eight years old, became the third salesperson in the branch in the fall of 1979 and had the northwest region, an area not well covered previously (territory 3). He initially joined Garrett as an apprentice mechanic and, after achieving his Class A standing, rose to service foreman at the London branch before entering sales at his own request. His likable personality and knowledge of Garrett trucks had made him a good salesperson earning a respectable commission.

Before Frank Barton could start his search for a salesperson, he would have to receive approval from the head office. From prior conversations with his superiors, he knew that they were in favor of adding a salesperson but he still had to submit a formal proposal outlining the specific details of the job and his reasons for asking for someone to fill it.

EXHIBIT 1
GARRETT TRUCK CO. LTD.
LONDON BRANCH

Salespeople's Territories

━━━━━━━ County Line

••••••••••• Territory-Boundary

EXHIBIT 2

GARRETT TRUCK CO. LTD., LONDON BRANCH

Income Statement for the Years Ending September 30

(in 000's of dollars)

	1978	1979	1980
Total sales	$2865	$2988	$5541
Cost of sales	2310	2437	4700
Gross margin	$ 555	$ 551	$ 841
Expenses	505	499	676
Profit (loss) before tax	$ 50	$ 52	$ 165
Breakdown of Total Sales, $ (Units)			
New trucks	(61) $1760	(47) $1635	(107) $3689
Used trucks	(54) 390	(42) 362	(64) 555
Total trucks	(115) $2150	(89) $1997	(171) $4244
Total parts	545	731	963[a]
Total labor	170	260	334[b]
Total sales	$2865	$2988	$5541

a. Margin on parts sales about 35 percent.
b. Margin on labor about 50 percent.

*Garrett Truck
Co. Ltd.*

Sales Commission Payments on New Trucks

Percent Discount[a]	Rate of Commission (percent)
Under 19	5
19–19.9	4.5
20–20.9	4
21–21.9	3.5
22–22.9	3
23–23.9	2.5
24–24.9	2
25–25.9	1.5
26–26.9	1
27 or higher	0.5

The average commission earned on new trucks in 1980 was 2.1 percent.
Used trucks: 2 percent on selling price.
[a] Sale price on new trucks is quoted as a percentage discount for company-estimated list price.

EXHIBIT 4

G A R R E T T T R U C K C O . L T D .

Average Monthly Commissions

Current average sales and commissions for one salesperson in one month:

Units sold

New	3
Used	2

Sales dollars

New—3 × $35 000 (avg.)	$105 000
Used—2 × $ 8 900 (avg.)	17 800
	$122 800

Commission earned

New—105 000 × 2.1% (avg.)	$ 2 205
Used—17 800 × 2%	356
	$ 2 561
Monthly salary	400
Total monthly compensation	$ 2 961
Expenses paid to salespeople	$ 270
Total selling expenses to branch	$ 3 231
Cost to sell—% of sales	2.6%

LADBROKE VALVE CO. INC.

Jeffrey Gandz

The Ladbroke Valve Company manufactured two lines of valves, flanges, and spigots. One of these lines was sold to industrial users such as refineries and chemical works, the other to the dairy industry. Its office employees were members of the UAW, Local 9275. Although they were generally assigned to work either in the Industrial or Dairy divisions, they were all members of the same local and there was one seniority schedule covering all unionized office employees.

John Jeremy was an estimator who worked on the dairy line of products. He had been employed with Ladbroke for 25 years and had been one of the first employees to become a member of the UAW when it organized the office staff twenty years ago. He was a former president of the local and had served in other local offices for most of the last 10 years.

During the previous year, sales of the dairy line of products declined sharply and, as a result, there were only about 20 hours a week of estimating to be done. The company assigned additional estimating and scheduling duties on the Industrial product line to Jeremy. This resulted in a more junior employee, Mary Wilson, being placed on temporary layoff. However, after about one month the sales supervisor in the Industrial division complained that Jeremy was unable to cope with working on both the dairy and industrial products. He was returned to the job of estimating the dairy products only, and Wilson was recalled.

Jeremy was clearly underemployed in this job. The office manager, Frank Webster, decided to place him on a shortened work week; he would work (and be paid for) only 20 hours per week although he would continue to receive full company benefits, including vacation entitlements, as if he were working full time. This would continue until sales picked up in the dairy division and Jeremy could return to full-time estimating. In Webster's view, the company could do this since the Management's Rights clause of the collective agreement stated:

> The union further recognizes the undisputed right of the Company to operate and manage its business in all respects in accordance with its responsibilities and commitments. The products to be manufactured, the schedule of production, the methods, processes, and means of manufacturing and office methods are exclusively the responsibility of the company.

When advised that this would happen, Jeremy and his union representative spoke with Webster. They pointed out that, according to Article 9 of the collective agreement, Jeremy had the right to displace (or "bump") a more junior employee who was doing a job that Jeremy was qualified for. There were several jobs in the production scheduling office which Jeremy was qualified for and which were filled by employees with much less seniority. Article 9 of the Agreement said:

> In the event of a reduction in the working force, employees will be laid off in inverse order of seniority provided there are available other employees able and willing to do the work of the employees to be laid off.

Webster spoke with the supervisor of the production scheduling office before responding to this request. The supervisor was opposed to allowing Jeremy to "bump" one of the production scheduling clerks. He pointed out that the four production scheduling clerks had full workloads and that the department was running very smoothly. Webster also realized that if Jeremy was allowed to displace one of those employees, he would not have time to do the 20 hours per week estimating on the dairy line of products. Jeremy was the only qualified person who could do that estimating.

At a meeting that afternoon with Jeremy, the union representative, and the industrial relations manager, Webster denied Jeremy's request. He also pointed out that no reduction in working force was taking place. Jeremy was not being laid off; he was only being placed temporarily on a short work week. There were still the same number of employees in the office. Therefore, the question of layoff and the "bumping" of less senior employees did not arise.

Neither Jeremy nor his union representative were prepared to accept this decision, and they indicated that a formal grievance would be filed. In the event that such a grievance was not resolved to its satisfaction, the union could refer it to a neutral arbitrator who would render a decision which would be binding on the company and the union.

FOODSPLUS

Steven Cox, Henry W. Lane and Roderick White

Mr. Julius Mwanza, Managing Director of FoodsPlus, was considering a proposal to reorganize the company. FoodsPlus was an African holding company that managed investments in six operating companies. In its early history it had been a centrally managed company. Three years ago FoodsPlus had decentralized much of the management responsibility and control to the operating companies in order to reduce the influence of headquarters executives and to develop the local managers in the operating companies.

Decentralization had served its purpose, but Mwanza now was not certain it was still appropriate. He felt that the operating companies were running too independently and that he did not have sufficient oversight and control. Although his role now was more as a strategist, evaluator and coordinator, he did not seem to be getting the information he needed to accomplish these tasks.

There were no standardized operating reports coming to him, but that bothered him less than the inter-company coordination situation. No one seemed to have information on, or to be in control of, the numerous inter-company transfers of raw materials, by-products or other transactions. All the operating companies wanted more capital, but he could not tell to where it should be allocated. Mr. Mwanza wondered whether or not these companies were being managed effectively. Maybe it was time to re-centralize the whole corporation.

Background

Prior to the creation of FoodsPlus, there had been one large company known as Premier Brands. Premier had been founded early in the colonial period by European and Indian businesspeople to provide basic dietary foodstuffs: wheat and maize meal. Twenty years ago, Premier came to the financial aid of a major customer, Ace Bakeries Ltd., and shortly assumed control as majority owner. The acquisition was Premier's first major expansion. Several years later, because of the imminent retirement of some of the founders, controlling interest in Premier was sold to FoodsPlus which had been incorporated by local African businesspeople.

FoodsPlus and Ace Bakeries both traded on the national stock exchange. However, effective majority control of all operating companies was held by FoodsPlus (see Exhibit 1). Each company was a separate legal entity with separate management teams, and separate (although with some overlap) boards of directors. The operating companies were all in the agro-processing and food industries.

The FoodsPlus group of companies faced numerous challenges inherent in African food and agro-processing industries. Many of the company's products were staple food items and subject to stringent government price control laws. Price controls were established on the raw materials, often its by-products and the final products' selling price. These price control regulations affected the individual company's costs and revenues, and were often cited by managers as the reasons for poor performance.

A continuing problem was shortages. Due to unpredictable weather, maize and wheat shortages occurred frequently. These commodities were controlled by the National Cereals Councils, which in turn sold them to processing companies. Political factors affected many of FoodsPlus' products. When there were shortages the politics became severe. Accusations of windfall profits and illicit trading often were levelled at the companies. The government would step in with its own teams and closely supervise the allocation and distribution of cereals. One recent example highlights this problem. The government had purchased spoiled yellow maize. The maize contained a toxic fungus which, if consumed, could potentially harm humans. Very quickly, customers stopped buying maize as rumors circulated concerning its quality. One manager commented on the effect of shortages, "We lost good distributors. Some didn't come back to us." In times like these, Mwanza seemed to work continuously at managing relationships between FoodsPlus and organizations in its external environment — government, suppliers, and customers.

The Former System

Until recently FoodsPlus had expatriates in the top management positions and had operated with a centralized management system. FoodsPlus also had large investments in companies in neighboring countries but had lost most of these as a result of nationalization or operations had been discontinued during periods of social turmoil. Supervision of these companies across national borders had required the skills of an experienced executive group; and a centralized management system was needed to coordinate communication, co-operation, and resource sharing among the widely dispersed companies.

The former managing director staffed the group office with other expatriates to oversee the operating companies. Mwanza commented:

> After independence most of the operating managers were new to their positions. Africans were finding their way into management jobs during the last ten to twenty years, but because we lacked experience we required specialized assistance to perform effectively. The experienced advisors from corporate headquarters provided guidance and advice.

The centralized structure is shown in Exhibit 2. It had been set up so that the group managing director headed an office of 14 senior executives. These 14 executives had links with functions at the operating companies, but only in an advisory capacity. Direct line responsibility was between the group managing director, and the various general managers of the operating companies. The centralized structure was designed to provide assistance services, and theoretically FoodsPlus executive advisors had no power to implement policies, only to offer advice. FoodsPlus operated with its subsidiaries under revolving 10 year management agreements, whereby it earned a management fee of one half of one percent of gross sales to cover its overhead.

This system began to break down. The nationalization of assets in neighboring countries took away much of the responsibility and work from the expatriate advisors. Although they supposedly had no implementation power, some tried to impose their authority. The group managing director attempted to police this behavior and to minimize its occurrence. However, some operating company general managers felt their authority was usurped by the advisory group. On occasion, an advisor would tell his counterpart in an operating company what to do without ever informing the general manager. Conflict was common. One of the original advisors still working with one of the operating companies recalled the old system:

> We supervised the assets in four countries from headquarters. At times it was frustrating. The turnover rate among government personnel in some of those countries was high — a Minister in the morning, a nobody after lunch. Also group advisors were expected to fill in for vacationing personnel at the subsidiary level in all the countries. There was frequent travel.
>
> In theory, we were supposed to communicate with our counterpart executives in the operating companies through the respective general manager. In practice, this was difficult. We had to talk directly since the issue was often too technically detailed for the general manager to understand. I suppose that is how a communications problem started.
>
> On routine technical and purchasing matters, our advice was usually taken. On controversial matters, that was another story. Controversy usually erupted over quality or pricing of by-products exchanged between the companies. In those days transfer prices were set at an agreed amount. Changes in these transfer prices were then related to the percentage change in the price of cereals. A 10 percent price increase in maize translated to a 10 percent increase in the maize by-product.

Under the centralized system there was no formal performance evaluation system in place, at either the holding company or operating company levels. Group advisors and general managers received their compensation increases from the group managing director, and general managers awarded increases to executives and staff at the operating company level.

De-Centralization

Julius Mwanza began his career at Premier Brands and rose to the position of general manager. He was the first group managing director to be promoted to the holding company level from an operating company. Prior to his appointment, the group executives had been mostly expatriates. When Mwanza first took over, his impression was that there were roughly a dozen executives who did not have enough work, and who occupied themselves criticizing the existing system in place and causing unnecessary conflict. Since he had been general manager of Premier Brands and had experienced the problem first hand, he felt strongly that the system had to be changed in order to improve organizational effectiveness.

The Structure

> Under the old system we were over-centralized: too many chiefs, and not enough tribesmen. (operating company executive)

This feeling had been widely held at the operating company level. Julius Mwanza and the FoodsPlus board decided that a change was necessary. They announced a policy of decentralization and disbanded the advisory group. All the advisory group executives were offered positions in the operating companies, and the practice of downward advice ended. They were promised that no one would lose their position or take a decrease in compensation as a result of the transition. Although some former group advisors earned more compensation than their respective general managers, this situation was gradually corrected. All of the secretarial staff were also moved with their respective former group executives. The management agreements in place with the operating companies were nullified. All of the boards of the subsidiaries had outside directors removed, and the general manager and group managing director were installed, together with an independent, outside chairman. The operating companies were to be given independence and autonomy.

Prior to the decentralization, Premier Brands had become very large and was now profitable. However, management did not know which of the four business areas profits were coming from (flour, maize, animal feeds, or food products); and whose performance was responsible for the profit. The company had grown large and the general manager did not have the time to pay attention to detailed operations. The solution was to split the company into four separate entities: Premier Flour, Premier Maize, Gold Seal Feeds (animal feeds), and Kariba Brands (consumer foodstuffs). Senior department managers at Premier were chosen to take charge of the new companies. The idea was to give these managers more responsibility and the time to manage smaller pieces of the company. These general managers would have increased operating responsibility and decision-making would be located closer to the action in operations. One of these individuals spoke of the change:

> My mandate was to make my division a viable entity. If it made money, FoodsPlus would keep it. Otherwise, they might sell it off. I was told to go in there and if I made the company lose less money I would be doing a good job. If I got it to breakeven, that would be really good. If it made money, that would be outstanding. I was given the privilege of picking the ten best people from Premier to join my company with me.

Reporting Requirements

For budgets and investment decisions, new executive committees (in operations, personnel, finance and marketing) were formed, comprised of the functional executives from each of the companies. These committees were chaired by the group managing director, and took over the functions formerly held by the advisory officers. Approval for capital decisions rested at the board level of operating companies and then required ratification by the FoodsPlus board. FoodsPlus' overhead was allocated approximately on the basis of company size and gross margins, not on the amount of FoodsPlus time or effort spent with the company.

Each company was responsible for preparing its own budgets for approval by FoodsPlus. General managers forecast revenue and expenses and set their profit budgets, which went to the company board for initial approval.

The new decentralized organization was monitored through the following reporting systems:

- All general managers were required to submit a monthly written report to the group managing director. This report presented an overall assessment on profitability, budget variances, and other company issues such as security. During the times of shortages, the general managers reported once a week.
- There was a monthly meeting of all general managers with the group managing director. The meeting discussed each of the subsidiaries and their current problems.
- There was also a monthly meeting called the "finance and general purpose meeting." This was a meeting of the group managing director and group financial director with all of the senior executives of a subsidiary (general manager, production manager, finance manager, marketing manager). These meetings discussed management decisions specific to the subsidiary. Any

capital asset that had to be bought, improved or demolished was discussed and decided upon and then referred to the board of the subsidiary for approval.

Mwanza offered his views on the impact of change:

> The change was necessary and possible at that point because the subsidiary general managers were experienced enough to operate on their own and their management teams didn't need advisors.
>
> However, the transitional year was very rough. The former group advisors still felt like group officers and tried to behave the same way. They continued to take the major decisions to the group managing director and "go over the head" of their respective general managers. Although there were no serious power struggles, I had to bridge a lot of meetings. Most of the 14 former group executives quit soon after the decentralization was announced. Now only four former group executives remain within the organization, and all are at the operating company level. None have yet been promoted to the general manager level.
>
> On intra-company pricing, my role is to act as the arbitrator to make sure the boys are not killing each other. If there is a dispute over pricing, we will hold a special meeting.

One of the original group advisors, now an executive at one of the operating subsidiaries, talked about the new system:

> When decentralization occurred I was asked what position and title I wanted. My salary remained the same, and my salary and benefits were still paid by FoodsPlus, although this amount is crosscharged to the subsidiary company. I am classified as executive level. This distinction includes general managers, financial managers, and some marketing managers.
>
> Now, in general terms, I report to the general manager, since part of my function is to help the general manager. I now have very limited contact with the group managing director.

Performance Evaluation

There were two levels of management employees: the executive level and the graded management staff. Appraisals were only completed on a formal basis for the graded management staff in grades 4 (middle grade) through 8 (top grade). The appraisals were done by the personnel manager.

On the other hand, executive level employees (production, finance, marketing, personnel managers) were responsible to the general manager. One general manager stated:

> I cannot evaluate them. All I can do is "devaluate" them. I can only say that certain executives in the company are not doing their job. If I don't say anything, then they are assumed to be doing their job by the FoodsPlus board.

Remuneration packages for executive level employees included a base salary, house, car, servants, security service, and substantial educational allowances for children.

Mwanza shared his perspective on performance evaluation in the new system.

> At present there is no system for assessing the general managers at the subsidiary company level. Basically, to date we have been surviving. It's very unfair to grade executives on corporate performance when most of the companies were just arbitrarily spun off from Premier Brands. They have no control over their raw material prices from the Cereal Councils.

A senior executive in one of the companies talked about his perception of performance evaluation.

> I am paid by FoodsPlus. The FoodsPlus board determines my raises, but I have no idea how they are calculated. I don't even know that the increases have any relationship to performance. You just know if you are not performing — you'll be asked to leave.
>
>   The most rewarding thing I get is when the auditors have signed the accounts and I have shown a contribution to FoodsPlus and the board says "thanks" to us for getting their books done on time and operating within budget.

One former group advisor had not noticed a change in performance evaluation with the new system. "I have no idea how performance is assessed. My budgets are always approved without change. My annual salary review is signed by Julius Mwanza. I guess that means I am doing good work."

The Operating Companies

A brief description of each of the operating subsidiary companies' activities follows.

Premier Flour

Premier was the country's largest wheat milling company and had a 74 percent market share. Although market demand was relatively stable, wheat supply was unstable because of unpredictable drought and pestilence problems. Since bread was one of the country's major staple foods, it was strictly price controlled. Decisions on flour pricing, quality and distribution were very sensitive. Premier had rebounded from recent losses in a year of drought, and exhibited minor liquidity problems. Premier sold 54 percent of its annual flour production to a sister company, Ace Bakeries, at a small discount from "market price"[1] for bulk purchases. Most of the remaining output was sold to

---

[1]Market price was defined as the price that a FoodsPlus subsidiary would receive from another non-related company for both final products and by-products.

other bakeries, but a small part was sold through distributors for use in the home. It also sold its entire by-product supply of wheat bran to another sister company, Gold Seal Feeds. Sale of this by-product accounted for less than ten percent of total revenues.

Premier Maize

Premier Maize was newly created from the breakup of Premier Brands. Its primary business was production of another staple food — maize meal, and it held a 60 percent market share. The maize was milled to produce maize meal (83 percent), maize bran (7 percent) and maize germ (9 percent). Maize meal was price controlled. Its production and prices were scrutinized closely by politicians and the public, and this pressure had led to very small profit margins. Although profit margins were low, volumes were high. Premier Maize had just gone ten months without operating because of a drought and the resulting maize shortage, but still had managed to earn a profit. At full capacity this company was expected to be very profitable. It sold maize bran to a sister company, Gold Seal Feeds, at roughly 65 percent below its market price. Another by-product, maize germ, was sold to Black Eagle Foods, for extraction of refined cooking oil.

Gold Seal Feeds

Gold Seal, founded two years ago, was the largest animal feeds company in the country. Its final products were not price controlled. In addition, Gold Seal produced animal veterinary products and mineral supplements. Most of its raw materials were by-products from sister companies' processes. These by-products were not price controlled. It purchased 100 percent of its wheat bran from Premier Flour at prices 16 to 18 percent below market price, 100 percent of its maize bran from Premier Maize at prices 65 percent below market price, and 100 percent of its maize cake from Black Eagle Foods. Gold Seal had the greatest return on capital, largely because it benefited most from low intra-group prices. It also had a low equity base (mostly loans from other companies with low payback terms). In the view of FoodsPlus management, Gold Seal had outstanding long term growth potential.

Kariba Brands

Kariba Brands started operations at the same time as Gold Seal, and was the smallest company in the group. It produced breakfast cereals, pet foods, specialty animal feeds, sausage filler and other consumer food products. It also acted as distributor of Black Eagle oil, produced by its sister company. It purchased at a discount all of Ace Bakeries' stale bread for use in its animal feeds. It also was viewed as having very good potential for growth and increased profits.

Black Eagle Foods

Originally a joint venture with a European company, Black Eagle was one of the older companies in the group. Its sales were roughly evenly divided between spaghetti and other pastas, and edible corn oil products. About two-thirds of the flour for the pasta came from Premier Flour, the rest was imported. Corn oil products were a staple commodity made from maize germ and were especially sensitive to price control. All price increases required approval. A recent price increase application had taken four years to get approved. Black Eagle purchased 100 percent of its maize germ needs from Premier Maize at prices 45 percent of market price, and sold all of its maize cake to Gold Seal Feeds at prices 52 percent less than market price. Sale of this by-product represented less than five percent of total sales.

Ace Bakeries

Ace was a long established company, acquired by Premier 25 years earlier. It was the country's largest bakery. Although its market share hovered around 50 percent there had been a steady decline over the decade. Ace produced only one product — a 500 gram loaf of bread. It had very small margins, and was closely price controlled. Its performance was highly dependent on selling large volumes of bread and operating economies of scale. Ace bought 100 percent of its wheat requirement from Premier Flour at bulk discount rates, and sold all of its stale bread to Kariba at discounted rates. Ace's falling market share was a source of concern to the management of FoodsPlus.

Inter-Company Transfers

FoodsPlus operating companies sold numerous final products and by-products among themselves. A flow chart indicating the flow of products and by-products between subsidiary companies can be found in Exhibit 3, and a chart indicating which products were price controlled can be found in Exhibit 4. A summary of each company's financial performance is listed in Exhibit 5.

An important issue that FoodsPlus faced was intra-group pricing. The general managers were responsible for setting the price of their by-products. The operating companies sold significant products and by-products among each other, at prices that ranged from market value (commercial prices) to as little as 35 percent of market value (preferential prices). Given that most sales were at preferential prices, it was difficult for FoodsPlus to accurately assess financial performance of the various group companies. Intra-group pricing methods were based on the two following methods:

- *The negotiation method* normally produced a contract between two companies. Some of these contracts had been in place for long periods of time. Prices were below market prices and were now in need of revision. These supply contracts set forth prices, quantities, mode of transportation and costs of transportation. If agreement could not be achieved then the directive method had to be used.
- *The group directive method* was used in cases where an operating company requested a raw material pricing assistance. For instance, in a case where Premier Flour applied for a price increase from FoodsPlus for by-products sold to Gold Seal Feeds, Gold Seal might be able to persuade FoodsPlus not to approve the increase.

A New Organizational Structure?

In assessing the decentralized system, Mwanza worried that the change had led to too much general manager independence, and that maybe FoodsPlus was too removed from its investments. He was aware of the serious implications that yet another organizational change might have, but he wanted to come up with a structure that would operate smoothly, and yet still allow him to monitor the overall corporate performance on behalf of the FoodsPlus board of directors. He was having difficulty keeping track of all the company data that he was receiving and would probably need new staff to assist him. He wanted to improve communications and integration between the various operating companies — in marketing, finance, production and planning. Mwanza did not want to return to the bygone days of advisors; instead, co-ordinators or administrators might be a better head office group. But, what would ensure that a repetition of the earlier dissatisfaction with a centralized system would not occur again?

Mwanza also wanted to formulate a policy on price control management, intra-group pricing, budgeting, capital investment and long-term planning. FoodsPlus had long desired to diversify into new business ventures, but lacked the organizational system to plan for them. A recent foray into real estate development had in Mwanza's words "taken a few years off my life." What industries should be investigated, and should the new business ventures be mergers, acquisitions, or new startups? Would it be better to shift emphasis out of price controlled foods, or was FoodsPlus management too specialized in food-related industries?

EXHIBIT 1
FOODSPLUS

Organizational Chart

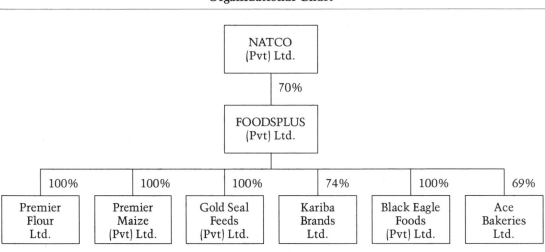

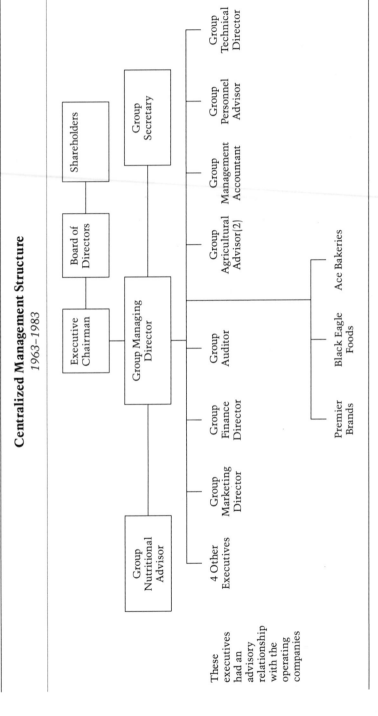

EXHIBIT 2

FOODSPLUS

Centralized Management Structure

1963–1983

Shareholders

Board of Directors

Executive Chairman

Group Managing Director

Group Secretary

Group Technical Director

Group Personnel Advisor

Group Management Accountant

Group Agricultural Advisor(2)

Group Auditor

Group Finance Director

Group Marketing Director

Group Nutritional Advisor

4 Other Executives

Premier Brands

Black Eagle Foods

Ace Bakeries

These executives had an advisory relationship with the operating companies

EXHIBIT 3
FOODSPLUS (Pvt.) LTD.

Flow of Products and By-Products

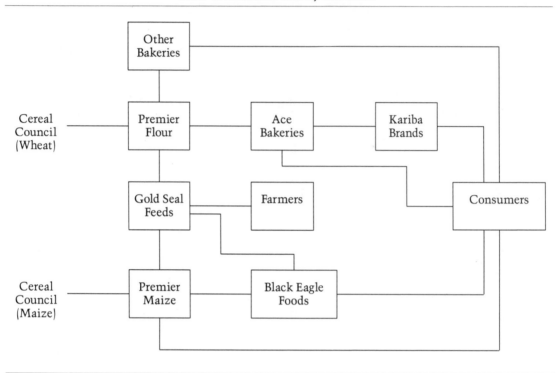

EXHIBIT 4
FOODSPLUS

Scope of Price Controls

Company	Price Controlled	Not Subject to Price Controls		
			By-Products Sold	By Products Purchased
	Final Products	Final Products		
Premier Flour (PF)	Flour		—wheat bran to GSF	
Premier Maize (PM)	Maize Meal		—Maize bran to GSF —Maize germ to BE	
Gold Seal Feeds (GSF)		Animal Feeds Animal Veterinary Products Mineral Supplements		—Wheat bran from PF —Maize bran from PM —Maize cake from BE
Kariba Brands (KB)	Black Eagle Corn Oil (distribution)	Breakfast Cereals Pet Foods Animal Feeds Sausage Filler Other Consumer Food Products		—Stale bread from Ace
Black Eagle (BE)	Black Eagle Corn Oil	Spaghetti, Pastas	—Maize cake to GSF	—Maize germ from PM
Ace Bakeries	Bread		—Stale bread to KB	

EXHIBIT 5
FOODSPLUS

Subsidiaries Performance

	Return on Capital		Profits After Tax		Gross Margin	Current Ratio
	This Year	Year Ago	This Year	Year Ago	This Year	Year Ago
Premier Flour	11.53%	−1.24%*	25 372 440	(2 731 420)*	13.6%	0.73
Premier Maize	25.50%	N/A*	12 438 120	N/A*	8.9%	1.45
Gold Seal Feeds**	71.28%	17.86%*	3 777 860	946 320*	13.1%	1.00
Kariba Brands	1.85%	−12.30%*	46 760	(309 840)*	16.6%	0.97
Black Eagle Foods	9.18%	11.90%	447 140	579 440	9.8%	1.32
Ace Bakeries	11.17%	45.30%	3 825 860	15 519 180	7.2%	1.00

*Figures are for seven month period only, from the date of the breakup of Premier into the four separate entities.

**The capital invested in Gold Seal was low, and a long term loan, which was not being repaid, was regarded as quasi-equity. This inclusion would reduce the ROC figures.

PART TWO

The Effective Manager

INTRODUCTION

In Part I we sketched the elements of the effective organization and tools the manager needs to understand and use effectively, in order to build and maintain such an organization. In these chapters the emphasis is on the micro level of analysis, that is, the manager and the people around him or her. We will examine what an effective manager needs to do in order to get work accomplished with and through other people.

At this level of analysis the building blocks are the manager, and the jobs and people that are managed. The manager needs to:

- understand the organization that he or she is in and interpret that organization to the people who report to the manager
- lead these people by implementing many of the systems instituted as part of the organizational design described in Chapter 2 and in many of the cases following that chapter
- exhibit a style through his or her behavior in implementing these systems which will have a significant effect on the people and their performance.

Similarly, the jobs the manager asks the people to perform will also affect the performance of the unit of which they are a part.

Just as the concept of "fit" among organizational elements was central to the idea of an effective organization, the manager must also worry about the fit among the elements in his or her immediate environment. Thus, the manager must match the right person to the right job and must design the right jobs to fit together to perform the tasks of the department or team being managed. And the manager's style of interacting with the people must fit with their needs if the best performance is to be expected. Each of these notions of fit will be explored in the cases and text which follow. The overall framework within which we are operating is shown in Figure 1. Note that this framework incorporates the elements of the effective organization which were developed in Part I.

Figure 1
A FRAMEWORK FOR ANALYSIS

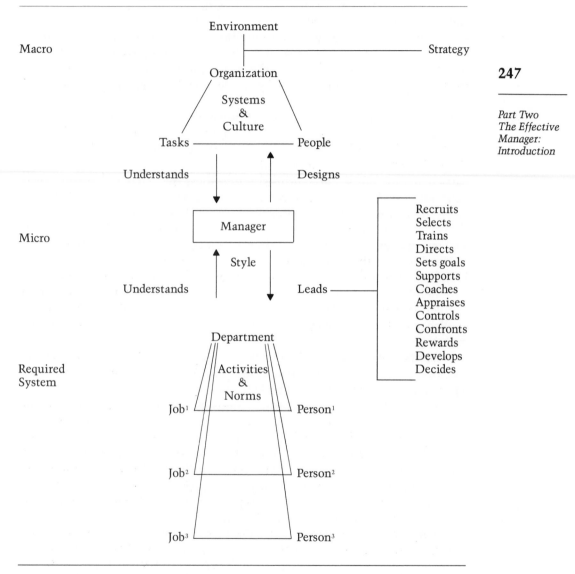

Elements of the Manager's World

In building the idea of the effective organization we assumed that for our purposes some elements of the manager's world, *viz* the external environment and the organizational strategy, were outside the manager's control. In this section we will make a similar assumption; we will take as given the basic organizational structure and systems. What is capable of being affected by the manager is his or her own style and behavior, the structure and layout of jobs, the selection and development of the people, and the response of the people to the manager.

The extent to which a manager's style is variable is a contentious issue in the literature of management, as is described in the chapter on Leadership. Suffice it to say that our perspective is that it is unlikely that a manager can make major changes in his or her basic propensity to respond to events in a particular way. But we are optimistic that most managers can modify their behavior in such a way as to eliminate the extremes of dysfunctional behavior and to refine those behaviors which produce desirable results. Managers vary in their individual ability to alter their behavior and those with the greatest adaptability have a significant advantage over those who are more rigid.

The design of individual jobs is also a key responsibility of the manager. Deciding what tasks are to be assigned to an individual job is as fundamental to building effective groups as is deciding how an organization is to be divided into departments. Similarly, once jobs are differentiated there is a concomitant challenge to integrate them into an effective package in order to meet departmental goals.

Most managers spend much of their time every day dealing with individual employees. In order to be effective in such interactions the manager must have a good understanding of individual behavior.

In Part I, which dealt with organizations as systems, we pointed out the complexity and interdependence of such systems. There is a parallel complexity involving individuals and their relations with managers and with each other. Both managers and the people they manage are complex. Indeed, one aspect of this complexity is the apparent contradictions in people, but Rogers points out that contradictions are part of being healthy human beings, and the acceptance of others' contradictions as part of normal behavior is part of what managers have to build into their own system.[1]

Having said this, we also acknowledge that in some ways all individuals are the same. As managers we need to understand that the behavior of people is *caused*; it doesn't occur randomly, and the causes in themselves are complex and multiple. (Again, in our desire to simplify behavior in order to more easily

---

[1]*On Becoming a Person*, Rogers, Carl R. Boston: Houghton Mifflin Co., 1961, Chapter 8, "To Be That Self Which One Truly Is": A Therapist's View of Personal Goals, pp. 163–182.

manage it, we often assume a single cause for a person's behavior). As Leavitt has noted, we are likely to improve our understanding of individuals if we assume that their behavior is caused, motivated and goal-directed.[2] In the chapter which follows we will see how to better conceptualize the underlying similarities and to identify the particularities which differentiate individuals.

There is an interconnectedness among individuals supervised by a manager, just as there is among departments in the larger organization. Three aspects of the relations among individuals are noteworthy. First is the link between the manager and an individual. Second is the one-to-one relationships among the individuals supervised by the manager. Third is the more complex interpersonal network of the group of people making up a department, task force or team.

The perspective pervading these chapters is managerial, so the focus is on understanding these elements of the manager's world in order to accomplish tasks effectively and efficiently. We are not studying people or advocating approaches to dealing with people as an end in itself, but as an essential part of managing performance.

This is not to deny, however, that people have important parts of their concerns and lives outside of the organization. And just as it is important to examine and understand the external environment to formulate strategy for the organization, it is important for a manager to understand the significant forces which exist for his or her employees outside the work context. If we see organizations as open systems, we can also conceptualize the constellation of roles for an individual as part of an open system. That part inside the organization is the managerial or employee role. But it is affected by and affects the host of other roles assumed by the person. These aspects of a person's life we will call "background factors" in subsequent discussions and are among the many influences on behavior which managers need to attend to in predicting and explaining behavior.

The final element treated in this section of the book is that part of the manager's behavior which parallels the administrative systems element described in the chapter on effective organizations. While it is essential to design systems which fit with the strategy, structure, key tasks and people in an organization, in this part of the book we are reminded that people, after all, are what make the systems work, or not work. Managers are charged with *implementing* the systems, and the *behavior* of managers and the aggregate of their *actions* (style) is critical to success. And the skill with which the manager behaves across a host of activities (see Figure 1) is a major determinant of this success.

Although most of the activities listed in the Figure have parallels in

---

[2]*Managerial Psychology*, Levitt, Harold J. Chicago: University of Chicago Press, 1978 (4th Edition), p. 10.

organization systems (as mentioned previously), it is worth noting that we have included one general activity essential for all managers: *deciding*. This is so obviously a crucial activity for managers that it seems almost unnecessary to mention it. Yet the ability to make decisions is one of the key talents which differentiate managers from others. The level of comfort (or discomfort) you feel in making decisions about the issues in the cases might be a clue to your own suitability for a managerial career. For example, put yourself in the place of Peter Roberts in the Canada Council case. Faced with a host of complicated issues and a sensitive and important meeting with your boss, the Minister of Communications, immediately after arriving back in Canada from your post as Ambassador to Russia, can you sort through the details and set the priorities you need to address in order to be effective. The more you are able to assume the role of the decision-makers in the cases, the more you fully identify with what needs to be done and make your analysis and recommendations from the point of view of the manager, the more likely you are to add to your actual ability to manage, as distinct from *planning* or *talking about* managing.

Summary

The effective manager, then, deals with individuals and groups of individuals for whom he or she has designed appropriate jobs and matched appropriately to those jobs. The manager interacts with a style appropriate to the people and the situation through a broad set of activities. All of these elements presuppose a fundamental ability of the manager to *make decisions*. The sections which follow are intended to help improve the quality of those decisions and actions and to lead to better performance by the manager and those whom he or she supervises.

C H A P T E R   2

Managing Individual Performance

Managers are interested in improving the performance of individuals on specific tasks and in designated roles within organizations. They are concerned with both the individuals' short-term performance and their long-term contributions to the organization. The managerial task is to recruit and select the right people for the job, ensure that they understand what needs to be done, provide the right training and resources, and establish conditions that lead to high employee motivation. In doing this, managers recognize that individuals vary in many respects and that different tasks and roles offer different challenges and rewards.

Task Performance

The way in which an individual performs a specific task or role is determined by four variables:

- the perceptions they have of the required tasks
- the effort they expend on the tasks
- the task-related abilities that they have and
- the resources available for task performance.

Perceptions

There is an old saying that an optimist may see a glass of expensive wine as being half full, whereas a pessimist sees the same glass as half empty. Similarly, when one person is told that a job must be given top priority he or she may believe that it must be done within the next half-hour; a second

Figure 2.1

MANAGING INDIVIDUAL PERFORMANCE

Determinants of Task or Role Performance

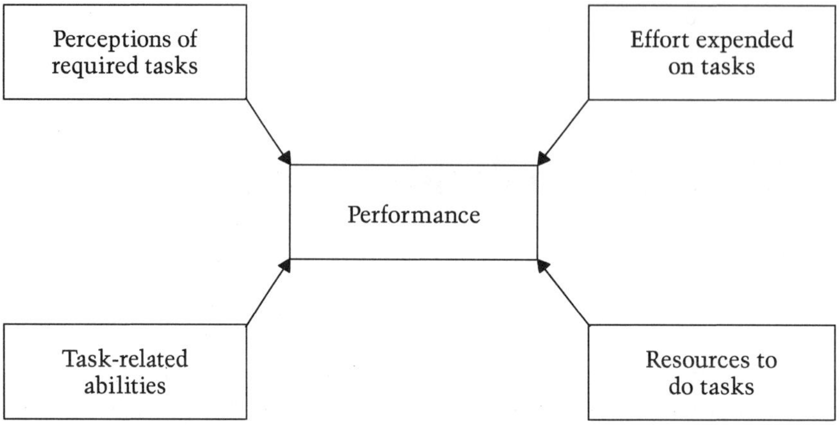

```
┌─────────────────┐                    ┌─────────────────┐
│ Perceptions of  │                    │ Effort expended │
│ required tasks  │                    │    on tasks     │
└─────────────────┘                    └─────────────────┘
                     ┌─────────────┐
                     │ Performance │
                     └─────────────┘
┌─────────────────┐                    ┌─────────────────┐
│  Task-related   │                    │  Resources to   │
│    abilities    │                    │    do tasks     │
└─────────────────┘                    └─────────────────┘
```

person may interpret this as being sometime within the next week or two. There is considerable variance in the ways in which different people perceive the same situation, request or instruction. A lack of task performance may well be attributed to the individual not understanding what is required, to what standard, when, and by whom.

Individuals tend to interpret requests, instructions, or other stimuli in ways which are consistent with their assumptions, values, beliefs, and feelings. These may be shaped or conditioned by their previous experiences in work, education, or life in general. The programmer who has been praised and rewarded for completing five complex programs in a month is likely to develop the belief that he or she is a good programmer, and will assume that five programs is an appropriate quantity to be produced each month. Most people believe that they are competent and are satisfying organizational expectations.

When a supervisor attempts to tell such people that they are good programmers but that five programs per month is an unsatisfactory rate, the second message may not get through. The individual may hear the compliment about being a good programmer, but not the supervisor's complaint about the quantity being produced. The individual is subconsciously striving to maintain agreement, or consonance, between existing beliefs and the message the supervisor is sending. He or she *selectively perceives*, blocking out the dissonant messages which conflict with their self-concepts, and accepting the consonant ones, those that reinforce their existing beliefs.

While the message may actually be received, its true meaning—the one intended by the sender—may be distorted so that it fits the pre-existing patterns of beliefs held by the receiver. Someone who believes that a supervisor is out to get them may perceive a complaint about inadequate program quantity as a personal attack. Or the message might be distorted by some stereotypical view that the programmer holds such as "All supervisors in this place criticize you all the time."

One key factor which influences how people perceive things is the *source-credibility* of the message. The complaint about program quantity may be perceived and accepted by an employee if it comes from someone the employee respects and considers a legitimate authority; it may be rejected if it comes from someone that the programmer feels is unqualified to express a valid judgment.

Another important factor affecting one's perceptions is the *meaning* that people give to certain words, phrases, or even verbal or non-verbal expressions. "Tomorrow" in one culture may mean the following day; in another culture it may mean "not today but several days in the future." The various barriers to someone receiving a message sent by another are detailed in Figure 2.2.

Figure 2.2
MANAGING INDIVIDUAL PERFORMANCE

Barriers to Effective Communication

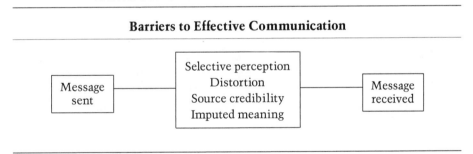

Effort

If employees know what has to be done—the task and the acceptable standards of performance, for example—a second determinant of performance is the amount of effort that they will choose to expend. Conventionally we talk

Figure 2.3

MANAGING INDIVIDUAL PERFORMANCE

Key Variables in Cognitive Motivation Theories

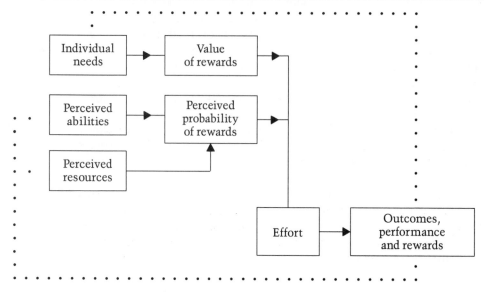

about the extent to which the individual is *motivated* to perform a required task or in a required role.

According to cognitive theories of motivation, in considering what motivates people to perform managers must consider their employees' physiological, social and psychological needs and how these determine the rewards they value from successful task performance, and their perception of the probability of actually receiving those rewards if they try to perform the required tasks (see Figure 2.3).

Needs and Rewards

Individuals have physiological, social and psychological needs. *Physiological* needs refer to hunger, thirst, warmth and shelter, and those other basic things which support physical life. *Social* needs refer to the need for the respect of others, and to be wanted and liked by other people. *Psychological* needs include the need to achieve and the need to self-actualize, or to achieve one's developmental potential and to exercise power and influence over others.

It is the strength of these unsatisfied needs which determines just how valuable a particular *reward* will be. The person who is hungry values food highly and will attempt to secure food; the person who is not hungry will value it less and exert less effort to find it. The person who craves the respect of others will be motivated to succeed at tasks which will earn that respect; another, caring little about what others think, may put little effort into those tasks. Someone craving power may expend great effort to succeed at a job because that success will put them in a powerful position; another person may not put effort into the same job because the elevation to a position of power may alienate them from others whose liking and respect they cherish.

The performance of any particular task may bring several possible rewards, and the reward may have both negative and positive values. When asked to work overtime, for example, an employee may positively value the extra pay and the praise and recognition which the employee will get from his or her supervisor. On the other hand, he or she may negatively value the displeasure of the children who expect to be taken to the ball game that evening. It is therefore important to consider the net reward associated with successful task or role performance.

A person's need structure, and therefore the rewards they value, may appear to change considerably from time to time, and from one stage in life to another. The high need for achievement in youth may become tempered with other needs — for friendship or social esteem, for example — in later life. Personality theory would suggest, however, that individuals' actual needs are relatively fixed by the time they reach early adulthood, and that these apparent changes in need structure are really the result of individuals coming to grips with what their true needs are. However, a growing body of research on adult development does suggest that changes do occur in the general, overriding issues of concern to employees (as distinct from specific needs).[1] One such formulation and its managerial implications are described at the end of this section.

Perceived Probability of Getting Rewards
Sometimes there is some question about whether putting in maximum effort on a task or in a role will actually result in rewards being received. There are actually two components to this probability. Consider the salespeople who are offered a free trip to Fiji if sales are increased by 50 percent. First, they may believe that no matter how hard they work and how skillful they are, there is a very low probability of increasing sales by 50 percent, since the market is declining. Second, they may put a low probability on actually getting the trip

---

[1] See, for example, the following books: *Transformations: Growth & Change in Adult Life*, Gould, Roger L., New York: Simon and Schuster, 1978; *The Seasons of a Man's Life*, Levinson, Daniel J. et al, New York: Alfred A. Knopf 1978; *Development Through Life*, Newman, Barbara M. and Philip R., Homewood, Illinois: The Dorsey Press, 1979, Chapters 9, 10, and 11; *Lives in Progress: A Study of the Natural Growth of Personality*, White, Robert W., New York: Holt, Rinehart and Winston, Inc., 1966, 2nd Edition; also *Adaptation To Life*, Vaillant, George E., Boston: Little, Brown and Company, 1977; and the more popular treatment of the subject, *Passages: Predictable Crises of Adult Life*, Sheehy, Gail, New York: E.P. Dutton & Co., Inc. 1976.

to Fiji if they do increase sales by 50 percent because the company has a habit of promising these things but then cancelling them when corporate profitability is not satisfactory, or some other excuse can be found. The probability of getting the reward is therefore determined by two probabilities; the probability that effort will lead to successful performance and the probability that successful performance will lead to the desired net rewards.

The perceived probability of getting the task done successfully is influenced by many factors. Individuals may perceive themselves as lacking the skills and knowledge, or they may feel that they have inadequate time, budgets, or staff to complete the task successfully.

The probability that successful performance will lead to the desired net rewards is heavily influenced by prior experience, which may have taught them that the company or their boss does not actually "deliver" on promises made or, conversely, that the rewards are usually even bigger than those which were promised and are invariably forthcoming.

Reinforcement

Continued or repetitive successful performance of a task or role depends to a large extent on the appropriate reinforcement of successful performance or, conversely, the extinguishing of behaviors associated with unsuccessful performance. *Positive reinforcement*, the distribution of rewards such as money, praise, recognition, or promotions following successful performance, is considered more effective in improving performance than *punishment* for failure.

Ability

While an individual's perceived ability may influence the effort expended on performing a task or role, his or her actual ability will also influence the outcome of this person's efforts. The clumsy person will seldom make a competent neuro-surgeon, no matter how much effort is expended; the person who tries to program a robot without knowing which commands control which functions is unlikely to be a productive technician.

Ability can be thought of in two ways. *Inherent ability*, sometimes referred to as aptitude or talent, may be inherited or acquired very early in life. A musical ear, a sense of perspective in drawing, fluency in speech patterns and manual dexterity are all examples of such inherent abilities. People may also have *learned abilities*. These are the skills and knowledge acquired through education, training, and experience. To some extent a lack of inherent ability may be compensated for by training, education, or experience. The person who has early problems speaking may benefit from elocution lessons; the employee who is naturally shy and retiring may overcome this through assertiveness training. However, some jobs may require such things as hand-eye coordination which simply cannot be taught, or would require enormous amounts of training before the individual could achieve competence.

Resources

Successful performance depends not just on required task or role perception, effort, and ability, but also on the actual resources available to do what is required. The appropriate tools, assistance, documentation, working conditions, and so on must all figure into the task or role performance model. It is too easy to pin the blame for non-performance on effort or ability when the problem is inadequate resources.

Person-Role Matching

Intrinsic and Extrinsic Rewards

Tasks and roles vary in the extent to which they require certain abilities and offer *intrinsic* and *extrinsic* rewards for their successful performance. The intrinsic rewards are those derived from doing the task or job well. The sense of achievement from building a beautiful cabinet, the sense of accomplishment that a manager may derive from seeing a subordinate complete a task for which the manager has trained them, or the pride from completing a major corporate marketing plan are all intrinsic rewards. The bonus that is received for completing the plan, or the pay that the cabinet-maker gets on completion of the work, or the promotion the manager receives for training subordinates well are extrinsic rewards. They are given *for* doing the job rather than *from* doing it.

Certain rewards, such as a bonus, may be rewarding to individuals in many ways. They may satisfy material needs for food and shelter; they may be tangible ways of signalling recognition of a job well done and are therefore cues which create satisfaction of needs for achievement and self-esteem. Alternatively, they may satisfy a need for high comparative status when one is known to have received the biggest bonus in the company.

Roles or jobs themselves vary in characteristics. A painter can readily see the results of his or her work and the chief executive officer can see the results of many of his or her decisions in the bottom line. There is a tangible end-product and an identification of that product with one's own endeavors. This is satisfying to someone with a high need for achievement. On the other hand, being the expediter in an engineering department or a product assistant in a marketing department, or any small cog in a large and complex organization, may be dissatisfying to someone with high needs for achievement since the relationship between efforts and some tangible achievement is hard to see. Even if the role has high status — a vice-president, for example — the link between effort and performance may be tenuous, and the job may satisfy social and esteem needs but not the need for achievement.

Certain jobs are more structured than others; some offer greater degrees of

Figure 2.4

MANAGING INDIVIDUAL PERFORMANCE

Role-Person Matching

Role	Person
Variety	Needs:
Autonomy	Physiological
Task identity	Social
Feedback from job	Psychological
Feedback from others	Abilities:
Associated extrinsic rewards	Innate
	Learned skills & knowledge

variety and autonomy; in others individuals can see the beginning, the end, their own contribution, and so on. The responsibility of the manager is to achieve the best, cost-effective match possible between the abilities and needs of the individual and the characteristics of the job. Sometimes this means changing the individual to match the job requirements, and sometimes it can be done by altering the nature of the job to suit the individual. This "matching" requirement is summarized in Figure 2.4.

Job Satisfaction

An individual experiences job satisfaction when that job satisfies needs and when the rewards from the job are perceived to be fair.

The person with a high need for achievement will tend to be more satisfied, other things being equal, when the job is challenging and allows the results of the work to be seen, rather than with an easy job with outcomes which are seldom seen. The person with high social needs will be more satisfied with a job involving working with others than with one in which the individual has to work largely alone. The matching of the needs of the individual with the characteristics of the job and the work environment can be a source of satisfaction.

But even if there is some satisfaction from doing a particular kind of job or performing in a certain role, dissatisfaction can come from the ways in which the extrinsic rewards for performance are distributed. When there is merit pay but people in a department perceive the distribution of pay to be unrelated to real merit, it may evoke similar reactions to that of the "B" student who sees someone who has done less work and "borrowed" another's notes receive an "A." While the B student may be satisfied with getting a B in and of itself, the comparison with the A student results in dissatisfaction.

Job satisfaction has been linked to a number of individual and organizational outcomes that managers are interested in. Generally speaking, highly satisfied employees tend to stay with organizations longer, attend more regularly, and experience less job-related stress than dissatisfied people. Although the research on these linkages is still somewhat equivocal, there is little doubt that job satisfaction has benefits for both the individual and the organization, and that it is a reasonable objective for managers to strive for.

One assumption that managers often make is that job satisfaction leads to good performance. However, some research indicates that the reverse is true... good performance actually leads to satisfaction. It is the unsatisfied need and the expectation of getting some valued reward or avoiding some undesired punishment which motivates the individual to perform. The performance which generates the reward satisfies the need. When people perform and get satisfying rewards they learn the linkage between effort, performance and reward. It is this repetitive learning which leads to the development of the expectations described in the motivation model outlined in Figure 2.4.

Development As a Variable

Another basic assumption we are making is that people grow and develop over their adult lives. While the people who appear in the cases all are described at a particular time in a particular situation, it is important to underscore that the stage of their development is a hidden factor affecting their behavior. In this regard, White's formulation of natural growth in adulthood is useful.[2] In a large scale, longitudinal study of normal adult male and females, five stages were identified. These are summarized below.

Stabilizing of the ego identity

Following the erratic swings of adolescence, most people go through a phase in which their basic self-concept as an adult is settled. They emerge from parental dependence and become their own persons. Most employees are through this period by the time managers have to deal with them, although "late bloomers" might still be dealing with this problem of development into their early twenties.

Freeing of personal relationships   Even after one's sense of oneself has stabilized, the pull of family in defining relationships with others is strong, and this stage involves overcoming the habit of treating others as if they were

---

[2]White, *op. cit.*

family members. It is during this period that we stop treating authority figures as if they were our parents and deal with peers as peers, rather than as siblings. Managers need to be aware of this stage, especially if they are supervising younger adults. Sometimes young managers themselves are still dealing with this issue, and it complicates their task, to say nothing of confusing those whom they are supervising.

Deepening of interest   Typically starting in the mid-to-late twenties, adults start to focus on their own competence in their jobs and careers. This stage is characterized by people emphasizing their own uniqueness and developing their professional and technical skills. It is also during this time that forming their own family becomes a preoccupation. Since both activities take considerable energy and attention, it is not surprising that people at this stage often feel the stress of time pressures. As two-career families become more and more common, the stresses associated with this stage of development are likely to become more pointed for both men and women.

Relativity of values   During the previous three stages of development the person tends to be preoccupied with the self. In the deepening of interest phase, which stretches into the forties, there is a strong component of personal conviction as the person demonstrates his or her strengths. A pathological tendency during that stage is dogmatism. But during the subsequent phase of development, people increase their appreciation for the grey areas, as distinct from the black and white way of perceiving the world in earlier development. Other people's values and perspectives become more relevant and are seen as enriching, rather than challenging, one's own views. This is the start of going outside of oneself.

Expansion of caring   In the late forties and early fifties, the concern for others, which starts to emerge in the "relativity" phase, now blossoms. During this period the focus is on developing others; in Jungian terms the concern is with generativity. The manager at this point is the mentor to others and puts less emphasis on his or her own accomplishments which were so important in defining the self at earlier stages.

Later stages   In a continuation of the study of the same group of individuals, Vaillant writes of further development in mid-life and beyond.[3] Although the subsequent stages are not as neatly categorized as the foregoing phases, two

---

[3]Vaillant, *Op. cit.*

types of behavior seem to emerge. One group has difficulty with accepting the curtailing of physical and mental powers and seems to wish to recapture their youth. These are characterized by marriage breakups, usually associated with teaming with younger partners, and sometimes accompanied by alcohol or drug abuse. Another group is labelled "coping." Their behavior is adaptive to aging and is associated with the adoption of hobbies and recreational activities. A "re-potting" kind of behavior is exhibited, and is associated with a positive mind-set, not one of passive or negative acquiescence to old age.

In this connection it is worth noting that another student of managers has written about the use of old age.[4] His own experience suggests that people who are successful in moving through the transition to old age seem to start their preparation for this phase of their lives as early as their forties. He also notes that effective use of old age requires the person to anticipate and develop the aspects of their talents which can only be fully employed by old people. In his own case that meant starting a career in writing and publishing essays based on his careful observations of organizational life through a long career at AT&T and an expansion of his experiences starting at mid-career. At 82 he is still writing challenging and inspiring essays on institutional and societal leadership.

The implications of these phases in adult development need to be considered by all managers. Reflections on their own motivations and behavior could be enriched by these ideas, and the supervision of others can also be informed by consideration of these stages. Of course, there is no guarantee that all people are successful in making the transitions from one stage to another. The pathologies of extreme behavior which magnifies characteristics associated with a particular phase, or the "freezing" at a particular stage might be usefully considered in analyzing and dealing with so-called problem employees.

Managing Individual Performance: Points to Remember

The key to getting good performance from individuals within organizations rests with managers who:
- understand each employee's need structure; what those physiological, social, and psychological needs are at any point in time
- understand each employee's basic, inherent abilities and recruit, select, train and educate employees so that they have or acquire the skills and knowledge to perform the required tasks

---

[4]"Life's Choices and Markers", Greenleaf, R.K., Newton Center, MA: The R.K. Greenleaf Centre, 1987.

- match individuals with jobs, tasks, or roles which suit their needs and abilities and provide the intrinsic rewards they desire
- clearly communicate the role or task requirements, checking that the employee actually understands what the job requires and the standards of performance which are acceptable
- build self-confidence among employees and so encourage them so that they will perceive their efforts as likely to result in successful performance
- manage rewards such as pay, recognition, praise, and promotion in such a way that employees' salient needs are satisfied, and they perceive rewards as being related to performance and to be distributed equitably
- understand the effects of various stages of adult development on others and on yourself and incorporate this understanding into managing individual performance.

C H A P T E R   3

Managing Interpersonal Behavior

At the end of the chapter on Managing Individual Performance the manager was seen to be key in obtaining good performance from individuals. Most of the activities engaged in by managers to obtain performance involve some type of interaction with employees: to understand each employee's needs and abilities; to recruit, select, train and educate; to communicate task requirements; to build self-confidence among employees; to manage rewards, and so on. Thus, the success of the manager in these myriad of exchanges with others depends to a great extent on his or her interpersonal competence. Our objective in this chapter is to provide some insights to increase managers' understanding, and some tools which managers can use to increase their skills.

Since so much of interpersonal exchange depends on our perceptions, we will start with that topic. Then we will discuss communication and some of the factors which contribute to effectiveness in our exchanges with others. We will explore some of the fundamental orientations in interpersonal dynamics and some general principles which emerge from these considerations.

Assumptions, Perceptions and Feelings [1]

In understanding individuals the centrality of perceptions in affecting behavior was firmly established. We saw that individuals vary in how they perceive, but that all are likely to select and distort their perceptions. We read of the importance of source credibility in what we perceive and of how we impute meaning to what we see. The impact of these phenomena on our interpersonal

---

[1] This section draws heavily on the work of authors H. Lane and J.J. DiStefano, from their book, *International Management Behaviour, From Policy to Practice*, Toronto: Nelson, 1988, Part 2, The Impact of Culture on Management.

behavior and effectiveness as managers is significant because of their link with our assumptions about others, and we act on the basis of these assumptions.

Our notions of what underlies whatever we are observing, thinking about or experiencing very much influence our perceptions. If we did not make such assumptions about our world, we would be hindered by the need to review the meaning of everything we perceive. But the fact that we are predisposed to see events or others in a way that is consistent with our assumptions is one of the bases of selective perception or distortion. The expression, "We see what we want to see and hear what we want to hear" is not only a statement of the influence of our needs on our perceptions, but a reflection of how our assumptions affect our perceptions. There is little difficulty if what we perceive fits with what we assume. But if our perceptions do not fit with our assumptions, problems occur. These difficulties are usually reflected in our feelings and behavior.

In each of the *cognitive* states (consistency or inconsistency between our perceptions and assumptions) we have different *emotional* states. When assumptions equal perceptions, the associated feeling is one of comfort, harmony, or neutral feelings. When assumptions do not equal perceptions we usually feel uncomfortable. It is the feeling of discomfort that provokes the reaction, and the usual response is to distort what we are perceiving to make it consistent with our assumptions (see Figure 3.1). Why do we do this? The simple answer is that we seek pleasure and avoid pain. Since there is a clash between what we see and what we assume, we manage to reduce the negative feelings associated with the "clash" by distorting what we see.

Although the usual mode of reducing the gap between assumptions and

Figure 3.1
MANAGING INTERPERSONAL BEHAVIOR

Cognitive and Emotional States

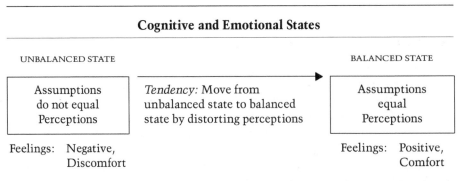

UNBALANCED STATE		BALANCED STATE
Assumptions do not equal Perceptions	*Tendency:* Move from unbalanced state to balanced state by distorting perceptions	Assumptions equal Perceptions
Feelings: Negative, Discomfort		Feelings: Positive, Comfort

perceptions is to distort perceptions, there is another option. We do not normally consider altering our assumptions, but it is a clear possibility. Unfortunately, it is usually an unexamined alternative. Furthermore, the closer the relation between the assumptions in question and our self-concept (the view we have of ourself), the less likely we are to consider changing our assumptions.

Descriptions, Interpretations and Evaluations

One way of increasing the accuracy of our perceptions is to be aware of the distinctions among *describing, interpreting,* and *evaluating* what we see. At the level of description, we are responding to, or communicating about, the objective facts of a situation. Keeping in mind the programmer mentioned in the previous section on individuals, we might comment that he or she has been on the job for four years and three months, has been absent only six days in this period, regularly meets quantity and quality standards, and has trained three new employees. Each one of these descriptive statements can be independently verified.

Interpretations, on the other hand, ascribe meaning to what we are perceiving. They also often impute motives to the actor in a situation. Using the same data as noted above, we would say that the programmer is experienced, highly motivated, technically competent, and interested in others' development. These may or may not be appropriate inferences from the data and may or may not be verified by inspection of these or other data available. The point is that the observer of the programmer has *interpreted* what he or she has perceived independent of any attempt to verify the meaning ascribed to the observations.

Evaluations depart even more from the objectively verifiable data being perceived and add a judgment about the description or interpretation as to its positive or negative qualities. Thus, we conclude that the programmer is a good employee and is ready to be promoted to a supervisory position.

Unfortunately, we seem to want to jump very quickly from the level of description to interpretation and evaluation of events which we perceive. It is unfortunate in the sense that we then act on our interpretations and especially on our evaluations before checking on agreement of the descriptive base. To some extent this tendency is functional in that it is efficient; but it often gets us into trouble as managers, because our judgments are premature or are based on distorted or selective perceptions. It also makes for a lot more interesting conversation and exchange than straight description. But we cannot overemphasize the usefulness of being aware of the distinctions made here. Managers can avoid a major source of interpersonal problems if they make a conscious effort to stay at the descriptive level prior to making decisions.

Avoiding Misunderstandings

Even if we manage to minimize errors due to perceptual inaccuracies, misunderstandings often emerge in our exchanges with others. Managing the misunderstandings which do occur, and trying to avoid them when possible, requires the ability to understand the other person from that person's point of view. This requires empathetic skill, the capability to perceive as the other person perceives, which adds to the demands on the manager's talents. One way to increase our empathetic ability is to make explicit the descriptive level data we know about a person. We infer much about what and how others perceive, just as we do about other characteristics, based on what we know about them. So if we consciously attempt to analyze objective data about our programmer using the conceptual framework described in the earlier chapter, we are more likely to have a stronger base for our inferences. If we are also aware of subsequent interpretation as a process distinct from the description, we add to the likelihood of accurately projecting ourselves into the other person's shoes.

However, the reader should be cautioned that it is not easy to develop these skills. The next time you find yourself in a group discussing even moderately complex ideas, try to restate another person's opinion in slightly paraphrased terms. Introduce your comments with "If I understand you correctly, you mean..." or "In other words..." or close your comments with these, phrased as questions: "Is that what you mean?" or "Did I hear you correctly?" You will perhaps be surprised at the frequency with which the other person responds by saying, "Not quite" or even "Not at all!" The number of iterations before others feel that we have completely understood their meaning is grounds for pausing to think about how well we listen. Test your empathetic skill and you are likely to want to improve it.

As is illustrated in Figure 3.2, this interpersonal technique is not the only factor in misunderstanding. Even if we employ these kinds of approaches to our exchanges with others, another element in the equation of communication is whether we really want to understand the other person's perspective. To grasp the reality of our desires in this regard, we need to apply the individual model to ourselves. In particular, it is likely that our need structure will significantly affect our attitude and behavior. For example, if we have strong needs to control others (high power or influence needs) we are less likely to employ whatever empathetic skill we do have. Or we might use empathy primarily as a manipulative instrument: "If I sense how other persons think and feel, they will be more likely to agree with me." On the other hand, if we have high social needs it is likely that our empathetic skills are well-honed and used in a non-threatening manner, because people are more likely to like us if we behave that way.

The third component, as illustrated in Figure 3.2, is an organizational level variable, the climate in which the interpersonal exchange occurs. If the

Figure 3.2

MANAGING INTERPERSONAL BEHAVIOR

**Managing Misunderstandings: Some Determinants of
Effective Communication**

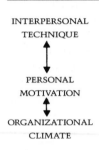

INTERPERSONAL TECHNIQUE	— Taking the point of view of others
	— Adopting the internal frame of reference of others
	— The skill of empathy
PERSONAL MOTIVATION	— Desire to see own or other's view
	— Personality dimensions (e.g. nAch, nAffil, nPower)
ORGANIZATIONAL CLIMATE	— Trust, respect, understanding
	— Cooperation, support

"Risk" of fully effective communication:
having your own view changed

context is supportive, then people are more likely to want to see another person's view and are more likely to employ all the empathy which they can develop. If the climate is filled with mistrust or if the reward system punishes people for taking a wider view, then empathetic skills are discouraged and open behavior is discouraged. All three components are important and they interact with each other. So if we want to minimize misunderstandings and maximize effective communication with others, we will manage all of these factors. Of the three, the one most amenable to the manager's direct control and therefore the most easily changed is that of empathetic skill.

Finally, it is important to note that one potential consequence of developing empathy, wanting to see the other person's perspective and operating in a safe and supportive climate, is having one's own ideas changed. Whether or not this possibility represents a risk or an enrichment depends both on the situation and the person's flexibility. But it would be inappropriate to advocate that managers consider applying these ideas without noting that change in oneself, as well as in the other person, is a possible outcome.

Congruence

Another significant factor in two-person relationships is what *congruence* one person experiences and demonstrates in exchanges with others. Carl Rogers, the noted psychotherapist whose writings have been so helpful to practitioners in many disciplines besides psychiatry, has suggested a powerful law of interpersonal relations.[2] Slightly paraphrased, the idea is that the more a person is congruent in what he or she experiences, is aware of, and communicates, the more it is likely that the other person will reciprocate with congruence, and the more likely that the relationship will develop in a positive way. The congruence notion is not a complex one; it simply implies a matching of each level of the person's experience, consciousness and behavior. For example, imagine that our programmer is frustrated by typing errors which lower the speed and quality of the output. If the programmer is fully congruent, then the individual is aware of what he or she is feeling and knows he or she is communicating the frustrations by the words, gestures, tone, etc. being used.

To understand this concept and its consequences more clearly, imagine *incongruence*. The programmer experiences the frustration, but is not in touch with his or her feelings. Perhaps the frustration is repressed or it is displaced onto something or someone else. Rogers notes that "when there is an incongruence between experience and awareness, it is usually spoken of as defensiveness, or denial to awareness. When the incongruence is between awareness and communication it is usually thought of as falseness or deceit." In the latter case, the programmer would be aware of the frustration, but chooses not to communicate it.

What gives rise to the law of interpersonal relations is the fact that others are often in a better position to recognize the incongruence in us than we are. We sense the lack of matching of the various levels in a person. And the consequence is that we develop a wariness with a person who is often incongruent. Similarly, when we interact with a person who is consistently congruent or integrated, we develop a sense of trust which enables us to be more congruent in return.

As managers we can work to be more fully congruent in all our interactions with people. This requires the will to be honest in our communications. But it also requires us to be aware of what is going on with us at the physiological level. Most of us have idiosyncratic cues about our body states and these can be used to signal what we are experiencing, especially if we have a tendency to block certain types of information from our awareness. For example, when we are nervous do our palms get sweaty, or our neck or stomach muscles tighten, or our voices quiver? If we know some of our patterns, then we can use our bodies to remind us that we are experiencing something which we would prefer to keep from our consciousness. While fuller awareness of what we are experiencing does not automatically lead to congruence at the level of communication, it puts us in a much better position to make the choice of being congruent.

[2]*Op. cit*, Chapter 18, A Tentative Formulation of a General Law of Interpersonal Relationships, pp. 338–346.

Interpersonal Orientations

A final set of concepts or tools for us to consider is the idea of fundamental interpersonal relations orientations (FIRO)[3]. The three orientations are Inclusion, Control, and Openness and are obviously related to personality characteristics. But the value of these particular variables is that they can be related both to interpersonal and to group dynamics. At the interpersonal level, we can conceptualize each variable as a twofold phenomenon. On one hand we express our inclusion, control or openness towards another person. And conversely, we want or are willing to accept demonstrations of these elements from another person. The inclusion variable has to do with membership and the initiation of interaction. The control variable has to do with influence or power, and the openness variable has to do with affection and interpersonal closeness. Figures 3.3 and 3.4 illustrate the ideas in tabular form.

Figure 3.3
MANAGING INTERPERSONAL BEHAVIOR

Extreme Types on the Three Interpersonal Dimensions

EXPRESSED BEHAVIOR			WANTED BEHAVIOR	
		DIMENSION		
EXTREME HIGH	EXTREME LOW		EXTREME HIGH	EXTREME LOW
Oversocial	Undersocial	Inclusion	Social-Compliant	Countersocial
Autocrat	Abdicrat	Control	Submissive	Rebellious
Overpersonal	Underpersonal	Affection	Personal-Compliant	Counterpersonal

Figure 3.4
MANAGING INTERPERSONAL BEHAVIOR

Schema of Interpersonal Behaviors

EXPRESSED BEHAVIOR	DIMENSION	WANTED BEHAVIOR
I initiate interaction with people	Inclusion	I want to be included
I control people	Control	I want people to control me
I act close and personal toward people	Affection	I want people to get close and personal to me

---

[3]For the latest version of Will Schutz's formulation of these ideas which he originally published in "The Interpersonal Underworld," *Harvard Business Review*, July–August 1958, contact University Associates in Canada or the U.S. The latest version of the questionnaires is copyrighted in 1982.

The theory suggests that each of us has a developed propensity to express and to need a certain amount of behavior on each variable. It has been our experience that the FIRO for any given person is subject to change over time, at least partially conditioned by the task and role requirements of the person. For example, imagine an employee with high expressed and wanted inclusion, low expressed and wanted control, and low expressed, but high needed openness. Promote this same person to a manager in a competitive environment where his or her peers operate highly independently, where the boss is authoritarian and expects a similar style from the managers dealing with their subordinates. After several months in the new job it is likely the manager will either modify his or her orientations or be very frustrated.

Instead of a job and situation influencing a person, we can consider the compatibility of two people's FIRO profiles. For example, what would you predict the relations to be if Persons A and B were put together?

Situation	Person A	Person B
1)	Hi expressed control Low needed control	Hi expressed control Low needed control
2)	Hi expressed inclusion Low needed inclusion.	High expressed inclusion Low needed inclusion.
3)	Hi expressed control Low needed control	Low expressed control High needed control

Most people would expect A and B to be in conflict in situation 1, to be resentful of rebuffs to each other's invitations in situation 2, and to be in harmony in situation 3.

These imaginary people illustrate how managers can use these concepts in analyzing conflicts and in modifying their own behavior to meet the needs of others. Test the applicability of the ideas by recalling an interpersonal conflict you have witnessed or been a part of. Do these variables help you to understand the causes and assist you in thinking of ways to alleviate the conflict?

Another area for applying the ideas is in selection. The manager can think of what the task or situation requires of a person and consider if the behavior of candidates suggests a compatible FIRO. Or if you are organizing a task force or committee to take on a particular problem, you might want to think of the FIRO profiles of potential members and "calculate" their compatibility.

The usefulness of the scheme is broad (the links of FIRO to group dynamics will be dealt with in the next chapter), but it is important to remember that these are orientations, not immutable characteristics. It is also worthwhile to remember our earlier caution about perceptions. If we are inferring a person's FIRO profile from our observations of past behavior, we should be tentative about our conclusions. Nevertheless, the ideas are powerful tools with which to organize our thinking about interpersonal relations.

Summary

In concluding this brief review of some of the important dimensions of managing interpersonal relations in the work place, it is important to remind the reader that the purpose of developing and using these ideas is to improve performance. We are not suggesting that managers become clinicians or amateur psychiatrists, but we do believe that it is necessary for them to understand and know how to use some elementary concepts from social science in order to develop and maintain a climate of concern for individuals and a productive organization.

Points to Remember

To obtain performance from others requires managers to be interpersonally competent. Managers must:

- be able to accurately perceive behavior and communicate thoughts and feelings
- be aware of differences between describing, interpreting and evaluating others' behavior
- be empathetic; understanding others from their point of view
- be more aware of their own needs and behavior—how congruent they are and how these mesh with others' needs and behavior.

Finally, we caution that we have not tried to be exhaustive in covering the interpersonal literature; dozens of books have been written just on the subject of listening. Rather, we have attempted to introduce a few key ideas which can be effectively applied to the cases which follow and to your real experiences.

Managing Workgroups

Most managers spend significant portions of their days managing groups of people or participating as members of workgroups. Because of this, we often hear managers complaining about the time they spend in committee or group meetings, yet few managers make much effort to organize their thinking about group behavior in order to improve their performance. This chapter is intended to provide a way of thinking about workgroups that will improve the effectiveness of managers who take the time to understand and apply it.

Workgroup Formation and Development

Many groups in modern work organizations are put together on a temporary basis as task forces or project teams; other groups are formed or reformed as a consequence of reorganizations. In most cases, when people are first put together to accomplish some defined tasks, a common set of issues arises which the group has to resolve before they can be effective as a team. If managers become aware of these issues, much can be done to facilitate working through them with a minimum of wasted energy or time.

One way of thinking about the process of group formation has been developed by the social psychologist, Will Schutz, based on his observation of hundreds of groups.[1] His research suggests that most groups first encounter issues of membership. Who is "in" and who is "out"? Sometimes the boundaries of in/out are not clear, as can be the case when a person is not fully committed, or where one's commitments are divided (as in a matrix structure or with a project supervisor who oversees several workgroups). If managers

---

[1] The formulation described here parallels the interpersonal orientation material cited and presented in the previous chapter. For a more complete description see Schutz, W., *The Interpersonal Underworld (FIRO)*, Palo Alto, California: Science and Behavior Books, 1966.

realize that most groups need to move through the ambiguity of membership during this *forming* phase, they can accelerate it by clarifying who is in or out, including themselves, reinforcing membership through formal means of identifying the group, designating a name or location for the group, celebrating the launch of the group's work and so on.

As a group becomes more clear, with respect to the inclusion or exclusion of its members, the second issue it often faces is one of control. Who is in charge, who has power, and who has influence over others are the questions next addressed. Because this stage is often filled with tension or conflict, many call it the *storming* phase. Again, managers can help a group to resolve these issues more easily and quickly if they recognize that such a phase often occurs as groups develop. Clarifying the formal authority structure can be of assistance in some cases. In other cases, acknowledging the multiple sources of influence in the group, because of diverse skills among members or the variety of tasks required, can help the group through this difficult stage.

Once the group has settled issues of inclusion and control, the third set of issues which often emerges involves openness and liking. "How open can or should I be?" and "Whom do I like/who likes me?" are the questions faced in this *warming* phase. This is the period when group cohesiveness is developed and reinforced. Here, too, managers can facilitate the working through of the issues in this phase by being open and friendly themselves, and by recognizing the group's existence as a social entity as well as a work team. For example, when the group is working late, a manager who orders in sandwiches is satisfying the group's appetite for cohesiveness as well as for food.

Finally, this third stage also involves the forming of norms, the unwritten rules of behavior in the group. The *norming* aspects of the group's development relate to the other stages, also. For example, a member's compliance to (or deviance from) the group norms often influences his or her membership in the group (forming stage) or the member's status (storming stage). Also, norms about how open or closed people should be often develop during the latter phases of group development.

To check the usefulness of these ideas about group formation, think about your own experiences in work groups. If you are in a study group as part of your managerial education, review your first few days. Were all members equally "in"? What cues do you use for judging who was more or less included? What might you have done to get your study group through the forming stage more effectively?

Similarly, how did issues of control and influence get settled, or are these questions still unresolved? When disagreements emerged over case problems or over when the group should meet or how it should tackle the cases, how did you settle them? In considering how you might help your group manage the storming phase, examine your own attempts to influence, and your responses to others' attempts to influence you. Do your recollections of your own behavior on these issues (as well as those dealing with the forming and norming/warming stages) fit with your FIRO profile from the previous chapter?

Finally, with respect to the openness or warming phase, one indicator of your group's development might be whether you are expressing your feelings (as distinct from your ideas) on the issues facing the group. If so, it is likely that you have formed a fairly cohesive group. If not, you can raise this issue and help the group move to more effective teamwork.

Figure 4.1, Issues in Group Development, summarizes this set of ideas, and suggests that the three phases tend to re-emerge in reverse order when groups start to break up. Managers should be alert to marked changes in a group's behavior on these dimensions. If a group is otherwise stable, indications of trouble in the areas of openness, control or inclusion can be investigated as possible signs of more serious problems in the group.

Figure 4.1
MANAGING WORKGROUPS

Issues in Group Development*

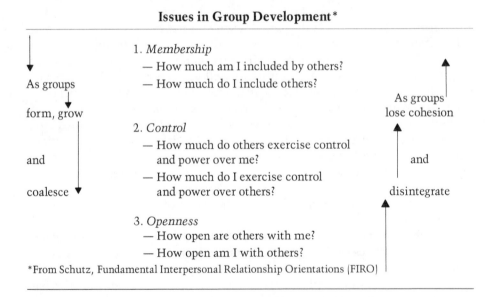

*From Schutz, Fundamental Interpersonal Relationship Orientations (FIRO)

Group Dynamics

The predictability of the stages which groups go through as they are formed depends on the relative uniformity of groups. But just as differentiation occurs in our large organizations, differentiation also occurs within groups (giving rise to differences across groups) which also needs to be understood and managed. And just as we conceptualized organizations as socio-technical systems in an earlier chapter, we can also view workgroups as socio-technical systems. The social systems are made up of the individual, interpersonal and

Figure 4.2

MANAGING WORKGROUPS

A Work Group Conceptual Scheme

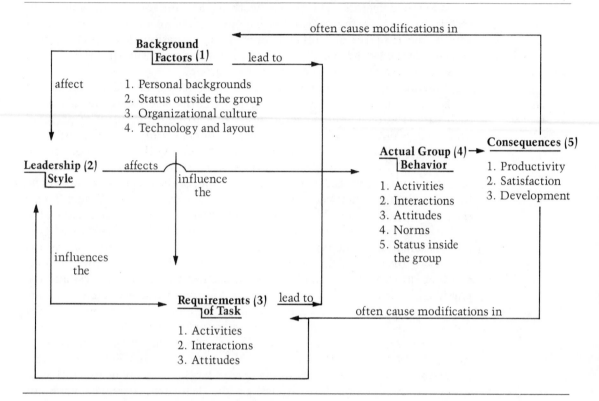

often cause modifications in

Background Factors (1)   lead to

affect

1. Personal backgrounds
2. Status outside the group
3. Organizational culture
4. Technology and layout

Leadership (2) Style   affects   influence the

influences the

Actual Group (4) Behavior

1. Activities
2. Interactions
3. Attitudes
4. Norms
5. Status inside the group

Consequences (5)

1. Productivity
2. Satisfaction
3. Development

Requirements (3) of Task   lead to

1. Activities
2. Interactions
3. Attitudes

often cause modifications in

group behavior of the members. The work requirements, tasks assigned, technology employed, rules, and so on form the technical system. The interaction of these two subsystems produces a given level of performance of the work group.

We now turn our attention to understanding the factors leading to group productivity and satisfaction. Figure 4.2 illustrates a conceptual scheme for understanding workgroup behavior based on the work of several authors.[2]

[2]Cohen, Allan R., Fink, Stephen L., Gadon, Herman and Willets, Robin D. *Effective Behavior in Organizations*. Homewood, Illinois: Richard D. Irwin, 3rd Edition, 1984, Chapters 3–6, pp. 54–150.

Homans, George C. *The Human Group*. New York: Harcourt Brace Jovanovich, 1950.

Turner, Arthur. "A Conceptual Scheme for Describing Work Group Behavior" in Lawrence, Paul R. and Seiler, John A. *Organizational Behavior and Administration*. Homewood, Illinois: Richard D. Irwin, Inc. and the Dorsey Press, revised edition, 1965, p. 154–164.

As a way of working through this framework, consider three different bank managers...the head of a credit card collection operation, the head of a large branch operation, and the manager of a team of account officers. In each case, the manager is likely to have a particular leadership style shaped by a number of background factors. The people working for him or her are subject to specific task requirements, and these requirements, together with the leadership of the manager and other factors in the situation, lead to the actual behavior of the workgroup. This behavior is what results in the productivity, satisfaction and further development of the group.

Following the order shown in Figure 4.2, let us consider each of the categories of the scheme as it applies to the three managers suggested above. In each case, the *background factors* are likely to be different. The personal backgrounds of the people reporting to a credit collection operation will need to be compatible with routine, repetitive tasks, while those working in marketing will need a different mix of personality, training and skills. Similarly, the status (as judged by the external world) of these people is likely to be linked to their personal backgrounds and will also vary across these different settings. Imagine, too, the differences in organizational culture associated with a credit card, branch or marketing operation. The formal rules are likely to be different, as is the type of organizational structure, reward systems and other elements which help make up a work culture. Finally, consider the level and type of technology usually found in each of the three settings, and the physical layout in which it occurs. Taken together, these background factors need to be consistent with each other if their combined effects on the leader and on the task requirements of the group are to be optimum.

How might the background factors affect the *leadership style* of a workgroup manager?[3] As we saw in the sections on Managing Individual Performance and Managing Interpersonal Behavior, there are a large number of factors influencing our behavior. From these discussions it is clear that personal backgrounds are important in shaping one's leadership style, but the formal organization and cultural context in which a manager works also influence his or her style. It does not take much reflection on the various managers in your work history to understand the rich truth in that assertion. And from there, it is a short step to imagining how leadership style influences the activities, interactions and attitudes which make up the *requirements of the task* for a particular workgroup.

Consider, for example, how a hard-driving kind of manager who is likely to head up a collection unit might affect the attitudes and behavior of the staff. In contrast, a more sensitive manager of account officers is likely to have quite a different effect on the task requirements for the officers. Finally, the wide variety of demands on a manager of a large, complex branch is likely to call for

---

[3]A broader discussion of leadership follows in a separate chapter on that topic.

a leadership style marked by coaching and probing skills mixed with a delegating orientation. These are likely to have quite a different effect on the task requirements of subordinates, as compared to the other examples cited.

While we are used to thinking about the impact of management style on task requirements and on people directly, the effects of background factors on task requirements are often less direct and less visible. The hidden dimension of space or layout, for example, has overwhelming effects on the ease of interaction between people. If the task requires significant interactions, but the layout inhibits them, the *actual group behavior* is probably going to deviate from the required. Once again, we see that, underlying the scheme, is a concept of "fit" which is associated with positive outcomes, or lack of fit between variables, which is likely to lead to less favorable results. Rather than exhaust all the possibilities for illustrating this idea of fit in this text, the reader is encouraged to take the three types of bank units and think about the mix of background factors and task requirements that might be congruent or conflicting with each other. For each set which you consider, project the effects of the fit or lack of fit between variables on the actual behavior of the workgroup.

The actual group behavior is a function of all three sets of factors discussed above. The activities, interactions, attitudes, norms (unwritten rules of behavior) and status of members inside the group all emerge from the combined effects of style, background factors and task requirements. If the actual behavior fits that required by the task, the group is more likely to be productive. If the emergent attitudes are consistent with those rooted in the members' personal backgrounds, the result is likely to be positive for the group's satisfaction. But if the external status a member brings into the group does not fit with the role imposed by the task requirements, then the member's status inside the group is likely to conflict with his or her external status. Under such conditions, the member's actual behavior is unlikely to match that required by the task, and productivity, satisfaction and development are all likely to suffer.

Another consequence of a good fit among these variables that emerges as part of the actual behaviors of people in the group is *cohesion*. The cohesiveness of the group is likely to be stronger if the group has settled the issues of membership, control and openness described earlier. And if the group is cohesive it is more likely to provide satisfaction to its members.

However the issue of group productivity *vis-à-vis* cohesiveness is more complex. Much depends on whether the basis of the cohesiveness is rooted in the task or in the social activities of the group.[4] The relative emphasis of the group is, in turn, dependent on the personal backgrounds of its members and

---

[4]For a full discussion of this issue see Mikalachki, A., *Group Cohesion Reconsidered*, London, Canada: School of Business Administration, The University of Western Ontario, 1969.

leader(s) and other background factors, and their interaction with the task requirements. The leader can shape the orientation of the group's cohesiveness and needs to keep in mind this basic distinction.

Again, the reader is asked to play out in his or her mind the dynamics of these variables in a credit card collection, branch or marketing scenario. How might the actual behavior of workgroups in those settings be affected by background factors of the members of the organization, by the leadership style of the manager, by the task requirements, or by any combination of these factors? As you project your ideas, is there any underlying notion of fit at the core of your predictions?

Finally, consider the feedback effects of the *consequences* on each of the other factors. High levels of productivity, satisfaction and/or development are likely to increase the sense of self-worth of the members and give the leader increased confidence in the group. These effects could conceivably lead to a more participative style by the leader, and greater competence in participation by the workers. This, in turn, might mean that the task's requirements are altered to include more decision-making. But if the reward system does not reinforce the expanded responsibility, the actual group behavior may not evolve in the way the leader would like. Thus, we can see how the feedback effects filter through the conceptual scheme.

Group Decision-Making

The issue of the degree of group decision-making was introduced, not only as an example of feedback effects, but also as an important element of managerial discretion. Although organizational culture and leadership style are obvious antecedents of how much group decision-making is encouraged, managers can shape the participation of group members in decisions by their deliberate choices.

There are some well-established conditions under which group decision-making is more useful and these will be included in the chapter on leadership (see especially the discussion of the Vroom-Yetton contingency model).[5] But in general, when the quality of decisions depends on the *combined* expertise of specialists, managers should encourage more participation. Similarly, when the implementation of the decisions is crucial and can be blocked by group members, managers are advised to be more participative.

Factors suggesting less participation include time pressure and members' incompetence in decision-making. These elements can be mitigated by training. Figure 4.3 lists the behaviors associated with effective group decision-making.

---

[5]"A New Look at Managerial Decision-Making", Vroom, Victor H. *Organizational Dynamics*, Spring 1973.

Figure 4.3

MANAGING WORKGROUPS

Effective Decisions in Groups

More effective groups tend to:

- Share and build on each other's ideas and information.

- Openly examine and resolve differences.

- Be conscious of their own operations and processes.

- Discuss objectives and tasks of group until well understood and accepted.

- Reach decisions through examination and comparison of differences and alternatives (consensus *vs.* voting or "steam-rollering")

- Develop supportive relations which promote
  a) listening to divergent ideas
  b) suppressing of ridicule
  c) respecting of others in giving and receiving information.

Managers whose personal preferences lean more towards authoritarian modes of decision-making need to consider two societal phenomena, largely outside our control, which tend to favor group decision-making. The first is the increasing complexity of our organizations. New technologies, larger organizations, and new applications of technology all increase the number and narrowness of specialists. For the increased differentiation associated with these phenomena, there is a concomitant need for integration. One means to integrate at the level of workgroups is group decision-making.

Secondly, there seems to be an increased level of desire for participation. This may be partly related to increased education among managerial trainees, but also seems to be a value issue. In either case, keeping talented people may require more participation by group members.

Conclusion

Notwithstanding these broad, external changes, managers need to manage their particular workgroups as effectively as possible, for the reasons stated at the outset of this chapter. This conceptual scheme and accompanying discussion are intended to help managers organize the complex realities of workgroup behavior and increase the accuracy of their explanations and predictions.

However, the real test of the usefulness of the framework rests with the individual manager. The scheme has the potential to be helpful because it is both simple enough to understand and apply, yet complex enough to capture important determinants of behavior. But its usefulness still depends on the individual manager's ability to observe the behavior around him or her and to relate that behavior to the concepts contained in the scheme. Both the observational and "mapping" skills require practice and development. We hope that this brief summary of ideas on managing workgroups will assist and encourage managers to practice such skills and to improve their effectiveness as leaders of teams.

Points to Remember

- Most groups go through a series of developmental stages before they are performing effectively.
- Group behavior is a function of the background factors, the style of the leader and the requirements of the task.
- Groups can make better decisions than individuals in some situations if certain conditions are met (e.g. open flow of information, supportive relations).
- As increased complexity requires more specialists, managers will be called upon to develop and apply group management skills which assist in the integration of these specialists into effective teams.

C H A P T E R 5

Leadership

There are few topics that have interested as many people from as many walks of life over such a long period of time as the concept of leadership. How often have you heard statements such as this: "What this (organization, school, group) needs is a good leader"? Or attributions of success made such as this: "Their ability to turn it around was largely due to his or her leadership ability." How often do you think leadership ability has been an espoused selection criterion for senior positions in organizations, or as the goal of a training and development program? How many studies have been conducted to discover what leaders do or where they come from?

Up to this point we have been talking about management. To oversimplify, we have positioned the manager as someone who assesses situations (specifically the fit among elements in a situation) from both a macro and micro perspective, decides what to do (to bring about a fit) and then does what is required. Although that sounds mechanistic, we have stated and shown through earlier cases that that is not so. The task of management is complex, often ambiguous, and requires great judgment.

We view leadership as something different from management, however. It is a process of influence — influencing others to follow a course of action or adopt a set of values. It requires a different set of skills and different behavioral patterns than management.

Zaleznik[1] suggests that leaders differ from managers in several key respects. He suggests that leaders shape ideas, while managers react to them. Managers, in their rationality, see work as a process of bringing people and ideas together to establish strategies and make decisions. They work with people but retain a psychological distance from them. Leaders see work as developing new approaches and enlarging the set of options. They relate to people with empathy,

---

[1] Zaleznik, A. Managers and Leaders. *Harvard Business Review*, May-June, 1977.

concerned about what situations mean to them. Managers see themselves as part of organizations trying to strengthen them; leaders are separate from these organizations, searching out opportunities for change.

This is not to say that both tasks cannot be done by the same person. In fact, many jobs require both leadership and managerial roles to be executed. It may be useful to review briefly the history of the study of leadership in the work place and project a profile of a future leader to more fully understand these differences.

Early research in the area of leadership was based on the assumption that leaders are born, not made — that they possessed some quality or set of qualities that differentiated them from others. This notion sent researchers in pursuit of those traits that accounted for the difference. Studies focused on personality, abilities and even physical characteristics. Stogdill[2], in summarizing research up to 1970, suggests the following as characteristics of leadership:

The leader is characterized by a

- strong drive for responsibility and task completion
- vigor and persistence in pursuit of goals
- venturesomeness and originality in problem solving
- drive to exercise initiative in social situations
- self-confidence and sense of personal identity
- willingness to accept consequences of decision and action
- readiness to absorb interpersonal stress
- willingness to tolerate frustration and delay
- ability to influence other persons' behavior and
- capacity to structure social interaction systems to the purpose at hand.

Much of the research from which this list was generated and that done subsequently suggested that the presence of these characteristics did not always lead to desirable outcomes. In fact, situations often determined which of these qualities or even others might account for success.

Another school of research concentrated on what the leader actually does. This behavioral approach focused on the reaction of subordinates to leader behavior — more specifically how effectively followers performed their tasks and how satisfied they were with their work. The outcome of much effort in this area was a number of two-factor theories, each factor representing a cluster of leader behavior. One factor could be labelled a *concern for people*, the other a *concern for task or productivity*.

---

[2]Stogdill, R.M. *Handbook of Leadership: A Survey of Theory and Research*. New York: The Free Press, 1974.

Most representative of this school is the series of studies conducted at Ohio State University.[3] These researchers labelled their factors *consideration* and *initiating structure*. Consideration is the degree to which a leader communicates with subordinates, respects them and their ideas, trusts them and is considerate of their feelings. Initiating structure, on the other hand, is the degree to which the leader is likely to define tasks for the group and structure their roles toward goal achievement. Any leader can be positioned on a grid with these factors as axes — from low on both to high on both, and anywhere in between.

The major weakness of both the trait approach and the behavioral approach was their relative lack of attention to the situation faced by the leader. This was shown by the inconsistent relationships between leader behavior and measures of performance or satisfaction.

Contingency theorists evolved to fill the void. They attempted to isolate situational variables that would suggest under what conditions certain leadership behaviors would result in improved productivity and satisfaction. Fiedler[4] suggested that these situational moderators were:

- *group atmosphere* — the degree to which the leader is accepted by the group and inspires their loyalty

- *task structure* — the degree to which the task is defined and ways of accomplishing it are known

- *position power* — the degree to which the leader has power accorded him or her as a result of the position held (reward and punishment power).

Fiedler's theory would suggest, for example, that a task oriented leader performs better when the group atmosphere is good, when the task is structured and the leader's position power is strong. When the task becomes unstructured and the position power is weak, a relationship oriented style is preferable. In general, Fiedler's theory suggests that a task oriented leadership style is most effective when conditions are either very favorable or very unfavorable. Conditions in between the extremes warrant a relationship oriented style.

Vroom and Yetton[5] present another contingency model which stipulates the situational variables that determine how leaders ought to use their groups in making decisions. Leaders can make decisions by themselves or by involving group members. The level of involvement can range from just using the members as a source of information, to getting their consensus on the

[3]Ibid., Chapter 11 ff.

[4]Fiedler, F.E. *A Theory of Leadership Effectiveness.* New York: McGraw-Hill, 1967.

[5]Vroom, V.H. and Yetton, P.N. *Leadership and Decision-Making.* Pittsburgh: University of Pittsburgh Press, 1973.

decision. The situational variables posited a series of decision rules to protect the quality of the decision and its acceptance by the group. Where the quality of the decision and acceptance are enhanced by group involvement, a more consultative style is warranted.

Hershey and Blanchard[6] have developed another contingency model which they labelled *situational leadership*. This model posits that leadership style ought to vary with the maturity of the followers. Maturity is defined by the ability and willingness of people to take responsibility for directing their own behavior. As maturity increases, the appropriate style moves from telling, for the unable and unwilling, to delegating, for the able and willing followers. They posit that selling and participating are the appropriate styles for the unable-but-willing and able-but-unwilling followers, respectively.

The contingency approach was popular in the 1960s and 1970s. It assumes that leaders can adapt their style to fit a situation, or alter the situation to fit their style. Implicitly they incorporate the behavioral approaches, and potentially some of the trait theory. But it too has fallen well short of being the panacea. Research has not shown overwhelming support for any of them. Many managers have seen them come and go as the "hot new way." Despite this, they remain intuitively appealing. At a minimum, the kinds of situational criteria raised in all three have a heuristic value for managers as they evaluate the appropriateness of their behavior.

Current Interest

The current focus on leadership seems, on one hand, as if we have come full circle and, on the other hand, as if we are extending ourselves into an entirely new domain. From the profile presented later in this chapter you might feel that the trait theories are back in rage. Yet there is one fundamental difference — these leaders are not born, but either train themselves or are trained. And the effects these leaders have are qualitatively different from those who were considerate or could initiate structure in the right situation. Organizations, whose strategies call for improved productivity, more innovation and steerage to new waters need to be led, not just managed. Reaching these goals will have to be done in structures and with systems that have changed in accordance with these strategies and to accommodate the new worker — those ready to commit themselves to providing their full talents at full energy in exchange for more say in the business affairs, a role that allows more of a contribution and whose contributions are fully appreciated.

[6]Hershey, P. and Blanchard, K.H. *Management of Organizational Behavior: Utilizing Human Resources.* (4th Ed.) Englewood Cliffs, N.J.: Prentice-Hall, Inc., 1982.

Leaders who are up to the task are being called charismatic[7], transformational[8], change masters[9] and servant leaders[10]. Let us look at each separately
and then roll them together.

Charismatic leaders are those who have profound effects on their followers,
commanding intense loyalty and devotion, and who cause followers to accomplish outstanding feats. They show very high levels of self confidence; they are
dominant in situations and dominant of others. They believe strongly that
what they are doing is morally right and they have a strong need to influence
others.

Charismatic leaders lead by example. They model the kinds of behavior they
wish their followers to exhibit, with no double standards. They image-build;
they take many opportunities to tell others of the things they and their groups
are doing and accomplishing. They are excellent communicators. They clearly
articulate their goals and frequently send messages about their mission.
Charismatic leaders expect a great deal from their followers but show every
confidence in their ability to succeed. We probably think of political or
military figures when we think of charisma — Ghandi, Kennedy, Trudeau,
and Hitler.

Kanter (1983) talks about those in leadership positions who have brought
about great innovations — who create processes for bringing new ideas into
use. She refers to them as *change masters*. These leaders have a vision — a very
clear sense of direction that can be represented pictorially. They share power,
information, support and resources. They are persistent, even dogged in
pursuit of their goals. They influence through persuasion. For them, change is
exciting and challenging.

These innovative leaders are not necessarily the ones who have the ideas
themselves. They recognize them, encourage them and help bring them to
fruition. They do so by building teams around the idea generator for additional
expertise. They build coalitions among teams for broader support. Everyone
participates and everyone shares in the rewards. Throughout, this leader has,
and instills in others, a desire for action, for movement and progress.

The third type of leader is the *transformational leader*. Bass defines these
leaders as the ones capable of bringing about large scale, higher-order change.
He contrasts that with the marginal and incremental change we have learned
about from study and experience. Like the two types of leaders mentioned

---

[7]House, R.J. A 1976 theory of leadership effectiveness. In J.G. Hunt and L.L. Larson (Eds.),
Leadership: The Cutting Edge. Carbondale, Illinois: Southern Illinois Press, 1977.

[8]Bass, B.M. *Leadership and Performance Beyond Expectations.* New York: Free Press, 1985.

[9]Kanter, R.M. *The Change Masters.* New York: Simon and Schuster, 1983.

[10]Greenleaf, R.K. *Servant Leadership.* New York: Paulist Press, 1977. See also, "The Leadership
Crisis", *Humanitas*, Vol. XIV, No. 3, Nov. 1978, reprinted by AT&T, 1987 and distributed by The
Robert K. Greenleaf Center, 210 Herrick Road, Newton Centre, MA 02159.

above, these individuals are visionary, and communicate that vision so that others can see the value and importance of goals and ways to achieve them. They are inspired and inspire others to forsake self interest for the benefit of the group. They are considerate of individuals, helping them to develop and grow.

Greenleaf (1977, 1987) characterizes the leaders needed for our time as *servant leaders*. The premise for his view is that there is an emerging ethic among followers. He suggests that increasingly people will give their commitment and loyalty only to those who care about them in a genuine and sincere way. The test of the leader's caring is that those served become more competent, capable, confident and whole — more likely themselves to become servant leaders. The acid test of servant leadership is the effect on the least powerful and least competent. Are these people also aided to grow, or at least not diminished by the leader's actions?

What differentiates the servant leader from the other types mentioned above? This kind of leader is a seeker who listens and observes with exceptional keenness. The servant leader processes the insights gained by such seeking and is prophetic; he or she sees ahead. This is what gives the "lead" in leadership and provides the substance in his or her vision. And the vision is primarily motivated by concern for the followers. This type of leader, too, has the confidence to say "come follow me," but the power used by the servant leader comes from persuasive skill rather than coercion or manipulation.

Greenleaf argues that servant leadership is especially critical in modern times because of the following chain of influences. He notes that the quality of a society is measured by the quality of care given to individuals, and such care is now mediated by large institutions — big schools, big churches, big business, big government — whereas it was formerly provided on a personal, one-to-one basis, primarily through families. Therefore, the leadership of large institutions is critical to the quality of our society, and Greenleaf finds it significantly below what is reasonable to expect, given the resources available to leaders and their large organizations.

Quite arbitrarily, we have rolled the characteristics and behaviors of the four types into one profile, which follows. It might provide an interesting parallel to profiles that are selected, trained or rewarded in most organizations.

Tomorrow's Leaders: a Profile

- Those with visions, who are able to communicate them to others clearly and frequently.
- Those who have high levels of self confidence such that they can share power with, and build teams and coalitions of very diverse types of people.

- Those who can set high expectations for others, show confidence in their ability to do it and reward the hell out of other's achievements.
- Those who have a high need to influence and dominate others yet can do it through persuasion rather than telling, coercion, or manipulation.
- Those who can inspire others through strong personal convictions in the moral righteousness of their work.
- Those whose purpose and results of leadership includes the followers becoming more competent, capable, and confident.
- Those who can create, manage and institutionalize change.

Summary

Have we come full circle? Are we back to finding "the great person"? Those questions are for you to answer. Whether we have or not, several issues have been clarified. Leaders are not just individuals with certain characteristics. They adapt their behavior to fit the situation. Leaders are not born. They develop and refine skills through formal and informal mechanisms.

JANIS JEROME*

Jeffrey Gandz

Janis was sitting in a corner of the bar, scribbling furiously on a pad of paper, when Denise showed up for their meeting at six o'clock. It had been awhile since Denise had seen her sister. It was almost ten months ago, in fact, when Janis had called to talk over how unhappy she was in the marketing department at Executive Financial Services and how she had been thinking of leaving. Later she had decided to accept a transfer into corporate planning and, the last time Denise had heard from her, she thought that her sister had settled into that job very well.

Background

Now age 40, married to a medical researcher and the mother of three children, Janis Jerome would have described herself as having had a pretty normal childhood. Very bright as a youngster, she had invariably been at the head of her class in primary and secondary schools. With a full scholarship to university she had completed an honors degree in languages. She met David while at university and, soon after graduation, at the age of 22, they were married. David was in medical school and Janis got a job teaching English and French in a community college. After two years, while David was still an intern, they had their first child, Andrea. Janis became a full-time homemaker looking after Andrea and then John and Chantal, born two and five years later.

The Early Career

When Chantal was five, Janis found herself with considerable time on her hands during the day, particularly during school hours. She responded to an

---

*Some names, places, and other potentially identifying data in this case have been disguised.

advertisement in the newspaper for an assistant in the communication depart-ment of a major bank. Despite the fact that she had little knowledge of the business world, she thought that the job might be interesting. Besides which, since David had chosen to go into medical research, and although he loved his work, it was not very well paid. With three children to bring up they could use the extra money.

She was interviewed by the vice-president of marketing and he hired Janis. Over the course of three years he gradually gave Janis as much responsibility as she could handle. In addition to preparing internal and external communica-tions, she wrote speeches for the executives and directors of the bank, maintained relationships with the press, and edited the internal bank newspa-per. She received excellent performance reviews, and the maximum amount of salary increase available for her grade.

After about three years however, Janis realized that she wasn't getting as much of a charge out of her job as she had gotten in the first place. The learning had stopped. Instead, one day was much like another, and one task was similar to others that she had performed before. And, more than that, she didn't seem to be getting anywhere within the organization. People she had seen come into the bank right out of university — usually people with business degrees — seemed to be being promoted, to be building their careers, much faster than she was. And she was aware that although she thought she was as bright or brighter than most of these people, and certainly harder-working, there was much that she didn't know about the world of business. Their language, the "buzz-words" they used, often left her wondering what they were talking about.

Business School

She talked over these feelings with Bill Simpson, her vice-president. At first he was surprised. But, after a lot more discussion, Bill recognized the problem for Janis. She was no longer content to fill a job, however well she did it. She wanted more . . . more responsibility, more challenge, more recognition, more advancement. And he was honest with Janis. "It's the MBAs who have the fast track now. I seriously doubt that you will be able to move ahead in this bank, or in other financial institutions without a business degree."

Depressed but determined, Janis applied for an MBA program. She knew that at 36 she would be one of the oldest students and that, unlike many others, she had very limited exposure to the world of business, other than the bank she had worked for. She waited until she had been accepted before even raising the issue with David. There would be problems. She had heard how intensive the business program was. There were classes, reports to write and exams to sit — often on weekends — and she would have to work most evenings. And they would miss the money that she had been earning at the bank. Telling Denise later how David had reacted, Janis had said:

> I don't think he likes business people very much. He's at home among scientists, other researchers, people like himself. He thinks business is trivial, unimportant. He doesn't treat my business friends well, often showing impatience or contempt for the things that interest them — and me! But I told him that it was time that I had the opportunity to pursue something that interested me.
>
> And basically, David is fair. He understands my needs, although he had little idea what had happened to change my outlook on life. I had some investments, stocks and bonds and things, and, somehow, we'd manage financially.
>
> After three weeks at the business school I was convinced that I'd made the worst mistake in my life. It was terrible. I thought I was pretty smart but I was doing terribly. Debits and credits didn't make any sense to me. The management science stuff went right over my head; production techniques were incomprehensible and the capital asset pricing model was sheer mystery. And everyone else seemed to know exactly what was going on. David was miserable, Chantal was crying a lot and claiming that Mommy didn't love her any more because I wasn't around often to play with her. Andrea was at the age where she needed attention and I wasn't around to do things with her, and occasionally I was working late at the library and wasn't even there to spend time with the children at night.

When Denise had seen Janis, at Christmas of Janis' first year in the MBA program, Janis was convinced that she was a failure at the business school. Then it all started to come together. A finance exam yielded an A, then followed other As and Bs in all subjects. Toward the end of the year she was helping other students with management science projects, and she was emerging as a natural leader in groups and project teams. The only disappointment was that at the end of the year she hadn't made the Dean's list! During the summer between first and second years of the business program, Janis decided not to take a job. It was, she had told Denise, "time to spend with my family — to try to make up for what I put them through the last few months." But by September she was ready to be back at school. Denise remembered talking to her at the start of the new school year. What a difference! She was confident, self-controlled, obviously in command of her abilities.

A New Career

The year was a good one for Janis, both academically and personally. She waltzed through courses, organized a concerted job search effort, and finally landed a job in the marketing department of a financial services company in her home town. She was a little ambivalent about the job when she and Denise had met for lunch a few months after she had started.

> I recognize that it's a pretty good starting job for a newly-minted MBA. The pay's good — about $42 000 — and the job certainly calls for me to use much of the material and analytical process I developed at the business school. There's lots of

interaction with the sales and investments people. But the thing that keeps getting to me is that I don't really feel like a new, wet-behind-the-ears graduate. I know that I've just earned my degree, but I'm so much older than the average entering MBA. And I feel that my previous experience is not being counted for much. I really feel that I should have more authority and responsibility than I do.

After she had been in the job about nine months, Janis called Denise to ask for some advice about her career. She wasn't getting along particularly well with her boss whom she thought was far too timid and ineffectual to establish the marketing role in the company as a driving force. Much of her work seemed to involve the coordination of details rather than the central, innovative, and creative function that she thought the marketing department ought to serve.

She had heard that there was an opportunity to move into central, corporate planning, working for a hard-driving manager of corporate planning — a real mover and shaker. But there were some clear disadvantages to the job. Although she would get tremendous exposure to all corporate functions, it was clearly a staff job. It would make great use of her analytical skills and would require excellent communications abilities — but she would be in the role of coordinator, evaluator, analyzer...not the action-oriented line work she really wanted. Furthermore, it was not a step upward in the hierarchy, and Janis was feeling that an upward move was essential to maintain her progress toward her goal — a vice-presidency within the next five to seven years.

On balance, Janis concluded that the move to corporate planning made sense. She didn't think that the marketing job was leading anywhere and she wasn't learning anything more from her boss. So, making sure not to burn any bridges, she moved to corporate planning.

Once in a while, Janis would call Denise to let her know how things were going. She was having a tremendous time. Put in charge of the company's computer-based planning models, she was learning a great deal about the operations and about the corporate planning functions. She was also meeting regularly with the senior corporate officers, getting involved in strategic decision-making, feeling close to the action. All of this newness, the challenge of being out of her depth and then mastering the difficulty, was exciting. She was experiencing the same sense of achievement as she had at the business school, and was working every bit as hard, often going into the office both Saturday and Sunday each week. She liked the people she was working with, and seemed set for an upward career path through corporate planning.

A Potential Move

It was bit of a surprise, therefore, for Denise to get the phone call that day and to find Janis in such turmoil. Three things had happened to her recently. First, a new person had joined her department, an economist without much experience in business, no business degree, and little knowledge of the company's operations. Janis had discovered that her earnings were almost $20 000 a year less than this new person, despite the fact that she was responsible for helping and training this newcomer. Second, recent conversations with several managers in the firm had left her with the distinct impression that, while she was highly valued, the chances of promotion within the firm were very low. She was not an investments expert and had no actuarial qualification. Third, she had met a senior partner in an international consulting firm in the U.S. at a conference and he had suggested that she might find consulting interesting. However, it would require her to be based a couple of hours drive from home and would involve extensive travel in North America and, conceivably, internationally.

Janis had been to see the vice-president of human resources about the disparity in salaries between herself and the new hire in the department. She felt that he had been less than totally candid with her. He had explained that it was necessary to offer him a high salary because of the difficulty attracting financial services executives. What Janis had come away with was the conviction that they could underpay her relative to this newcomer because the company thought that there was little possibility that she would move because of her family commitments.

The scribbling on the paper that Denise noticed as she entered the bar, was Janis jotting down the pros and cons of staying where she was or taking the job with the consulting firm. She went over them with her sister.

> The money is terrific. I'm making about $48 000 now. They are offering a base salary of $60 000 which — together with profit sharing and a bonus I could earn — it could come to about $75 000 in the first year. Apart from the money itself, I think that it represents a major upward movement in recognizing my worth. Second, it's a great opportunity. They want me to open up a whole new area of business for them here; it's a field in which they have very few clients now, but they have a lot of expertise in the U.S. and I'd have access to that. I'd have to make the contacts here, but I think I should be able to do that if given enough time. Third, the guy I'd be working for is first-class. He's very well respected in the industry and I think that I'd learn a tremendous amount from him. Although he would be based in Chicago, and I'll be technically reporting to the head of the Toronto office, he would be my real boss.
>
> The firm seems to want the kind of people who have been through MBA programs. Altogether, my profile seems to match those who have been successful with the firm. They seem a very results-oriented group and I think that I'd have an opportunity to move ahead quickly.
>
> But what about the personal issues, Janis? Where would you live? What about David and the kids?
>
> Obviously I've been thinking about them a great deal. If I got a small apartment, I could commute on weekends — I'd be back home Friday evening and I could head out either Sunday night or early Monday morning. I've figured out the finances

[and here she went through some of the numbers she had been working out] and, even though the commuting cost and the expense of maintaining a second home would eat up much of the difference between what I'm earning now and what I could make in the new job, I'd be a little bit ahead with much more potential for quick improvement.

Longer term, I think that if I was really successful with this firm there's a chance that David would move to be with me.

Is that realistic? After all, he's deeply involved with his research. Do you expect him to give up that to follow you?

I don't really know. But, realistically, the chances for me to get ahead here are really slim. I spent so many years earning money in less-than-exciting jobs so he could concentrate on his work. Don't I deserve a chance now?

What about the children? Aren't you going to miss them, and won't they miss you?

You know, it's funny. I love the children. The time I spend with them is wonderful. They are at that stage where they are developing their own distinct personalities, and it's fascinating. But I see very little of them now. I'm out early in the morning and it's usually David who gets them ready for school. Barbara, our housekeeper, is in the house when the children get home, and she prepares the evening meal. The kids get themselves ready for bed. I know that I'll miss seeing them, and I won't be there sometimes when they need me. But there will be the weekends. Actually, I'll probably end up spending more time with them at the weekends than I do now! I think that I've been in the office the last three Sundays!

The other side of that coin is that I wonder what impact it would have on the children if I stayed, failed to move ahead in my business career, and never realized my own potential. Wouldn't I be bitter? And what kind of role model would I be? Wouldn't it be good for them to see their mother as a successful, independent individual rather than as someone tied to her job because of her family?

Actually, if I take this job it might be harder to explain to my folks and to David's family than it would be to explain to the children. They tend to see me as the dutiful, home-loving wife and mother. I think they would have great difficulty adjusting to me living in another city, away from the family. I'm not sure what they'd think.

What about persevering a little longer with E.F.S.? After all, they know your value and surely they will see if they can move you ahead faster.

I doubt it, Janis had responded. I think that the top management of the firm are dead set against seeing non-accountants and non-actuaries in the executive offices. And, also, I think it's pretty clear that they intend to exploit the fact that I'm not very mobile because of my family commitments. The salary they're paying this guy is evidence of that. . . .

What about other options here? Is it absolutely essential to move?

With many firms' head offices moving away from here, I don't think the opportunities are very great — certainly in financial services. There may be some opportunities in consulting, but who knows if I'll ever get an offer as good as this one again?

In her work as a corporate lawyer, Denise had met many business consultants and knew some with the major consulting firms quite well.

> Janis, are you sure that you've really looked carefully at this consulting business? It seems to me that a lot of what consultants do is really helping firms deal with very elementary problems, the kinds of things that won't pose much of a challenge to you. Sometimes they're employed to do the dirty work that management doesn't want to take the responsibility for — you know, have a consultant to blame. It seems a long way from the type of 'line' challenge that you've been looking for.

> You may be right. But what options do I have? I'm dead-ended where I am now, and this offers me an opportunity to break out.

It was clear to Denise, from both the content and tone of what Janis was saying, that she was having a lot of difficulty deciding what to do. Denise was wondering what she could do to help Janis think through her situation clearly and reach the best decision. She had talked with David some months previously and she was sure that Janis announcing that she would be taking a job out of town would come as a tremendous surprise to him.

Al Mikalachki

"Hell, times like this make me wonder why I ever wanted to be vice-president of manufacturing," thought Tom Fuller as he sat down at his desk. "It seems that the biggest problems in this company are with people. Why can't two good men learn to get along with each other? If I don't quickly resolve the conflict brewing between Harry Smith and Jim Jones, the whole department is going to be in trouble."

Background

Martin Brass was an established manufacturer of industrial products. Tom Fuller was responsible for the manufacturing operations and had a number of people reporting to him, including Harry Smith, supervisor of the maintenance department. Jim Jones, foreman of building maintenance, reported to Harry Smith, and the on-going friction between the two men was what Tom Fuller was now considering.

Harry Smith's maintenance department included machine, building, and electrical maintenance. Harry was 52 years old and had 26 years' service with Martin Brass Company. He was a graduate civil engineer and, outside of his work, belonged primarily to technical organizations such as the association of professional engineers, foremen's club, and a management club. Harry and his wife had been married for many years.

Jim Jones, foreman of building maintenance, was 52 years old and had 19 years' service with the Martin Brass Company. Jim was married and had three sons. One of his sons was a chartered accountant, another was a minister, and the third was still in high school. Jim completed public school, apprenticed six years as a tool and die maker, and worked 22 years in that trade. Before he became foreman of building maintenance, he had been an assistant foreman of the tool room at the Martin Brass Company. For the last 14 years he had been an elected councillor on the local municipal school board. During the past three years on the board he had held the post of chairman.

Harry Smith Talks About Himself

As far as my home life is concerned I am fortunate in having a wife who is easy to get along with. We have had an unusually happy life. Although we have no children of our own, on various occasions we have probably adopted most of the youngsters in our neighborhood. Most of them feel free to come and go at our house anytime they like. My wife has always shared my ambitions and she takes great interest in the university courses that I am taking in the evening. It is my ambition to get a Master's degree to prove to myself that I can do it and to feel the satisfaction that I've accomplished something.

When I started in Martin Brass Company there were only three other people in the engineering department. During this period each of us worked individually in whatever project he was doing at the time. When we started to grow by engaging in defense contracts, the company persuaded me to take on a Navy project, and I more or less became the engineer in charge of the project. I had absolutely no contact with the company's engineering department at that time because the project was kept separate. I handled a great deal of the work on that project without having to go through anybody else in the company.

Later the company set up a new plant in Lansing, Michigan and I was sent there to work with an American engineer. I've always felt that I was sent to keep him in line. This American engineer was to take over supervision of the plant, but he soon asked for a transfer because he became disgusted with the smallness of the operation and with all the needling he was getting from people in the plant. I remained in charge of the plant until it was closed seven years later.

After the company closed the Lansing plant, I returned to this plant [Martin Brass] and got another lone wolf assignment. Along with a couple of other people, I was asked to plan a revised layout for the plant. It was a difficult and exciting challenge, and I think we did a good job. There are many things that we did then that are still here and are still good. But that again was pretty much of a lone wolf job. It demanded working with the foremen, of course, and getting across my ideas about the layout. Any time you have to do that it calls for a lot of horse trading. But it was a good assignment and I enjoyed it very much.

I have no objection to working with a group, but I do prefer a small group to a larger one. The satisfaction that I get out of a lone wolf approach to things is in terms of accomplishment. Recognition doesn't worry me a heck of a lot. It doesn't matter a darn to me what other people think about the work I do. I have a job to do and I know I do a good job. The disapproval of others never enters my mind. I get a great deal of satisfaction in watching the accomplishment of the group I am working with. I am particularly delighted when plans that I have worked on have gone through.

In my present job the main objective is to keep the shop running with a minimum of down time. It is pretty difficult for me to delegate as much as I would like. Maintenance is a business in which none of us can be too expert in any of the particular jobs. I probably keep my finger on the pulse of things a little closer than I should. I begin a normal day by discussing whatever problems the leader of the night cleaning group had. From there I go and check with the various foremen for what is going on and if nothing needs further discussion I check to see if the overnight work has been completed satisfactorily. During the day I might have the odd bit of conversation with the sales people or I might have a discussion with the cost people as to how we are going to follow through on the charges of certain jobs. These sorts of things generally carry on all day—just going around seeing that everybody is managing to get along all right.

I become involved in a lot of activities. Unfortunately, I've been working quite a bit on the technical end of things. I wish I could get away from this but there is a reluctance among the foremen to assume responsibility. I believe this is because of the dissimilarity of pay among them resulting in the "why should I do more work than another person who is getting the same or more pay" syndrome. I know one foreman in particular who disagrees with and gets quite annoyed at this dissimilarity. Now there may be other reasons for this reluctant attitude, but I certainly don't know what they are.

I also get caught up in some direct supervision when I shouldn't. For example, I have some people who go around their foreman to talk to me. Now I would prefer that they deal with their foreman; however, you can't throw a person out of your office when he or she comes to talk to you. I do know that all of our foremen at the present time object strenuously to this sort of thing happening. I feel that the only thing I can do is gradually to wean them away from the habit. I honestly believe that in time we will eliminate it.

There are times when I find the work here really interesting because of the various types of jobs that arise. At other times, though, I also find myself wondering if there is not something missing. We run into periods, I guess everybody does, where there isn't too much new coming along. I think this job has lost its challenge for me and I really need a challenge to stay perfectly happy. I don't want to say that Tom Fuller doesn't give me enough opportunity here, because he does give me a lot of opportunity and a lot of freedom. However, when you're in a company like this, which isn't big enough to have a real plant engineer, you naturally have limits to your job. There are things I'd like to do and can't—things I'd like to do, for instance, in developing new practices for factory maintenance. I can't do that because everybody wants me to hold off while they keep the machines in production. They want to take another six months' production out of a machine before letting it go for repair, and so it goes. I need a chance to grow, to be challenged, to think more for myself. That is probably the reason I went into a Master's program that will make me work. And when I get done I will feel satisfied that I have accomplished something.

Jim Jones Talks About Himself

I come from a very poor family. From the age of ten I bought my own clothes with money obtained from paper routes and working in market gardens. When I was 14, I had to quit school to help support the family because there just wasn't any money. Things were even more difficult when I was a little older. I was laid off so I stayed home and pulled stumps out of the muck, cleared land and plowed for nearby farmers. I grew vegetables and sold them at the local market and did odd jobs.

Raising my family has been very difficult. My first youngster was born with a harelip and a cleft palate. Two weeks after he was born it was discovered that my wife had a malignant tumor and a specialist had to operate on her. We had two more children after that, on my wife's insistence. Some complications set in after our last son was born and my wife had to have another operation. That operation was not successful and she had to have a third within a year.

I feel that education is the key to success nowadays. I have always tried to talk my boys into getting all the education possible. My second lad came to me two or three years ago and said, "Dad would you put me through university." I said, "Boy, if you pass your public and high school, I will see that you go to university if I have to put a mortgage on the house. You just show me that you're interested and keep your end of the deal up."

It was my interest in education that prompted me to run for the school board. I was successful on my fourth attempt and I have been serving on the school board ever since. I have chaired the school board for the past three years. When I stand for election I stand on my own record. I've always believed in running as an independent. In the last two elections I got the highest vote of any trustee in my district. Although the school board people don't run in parties, under the surface there is a lot of party politics. I know that Conservatives back different Conservative trustees and the Liberals back different Liberal trustees for the board. I don't like to be tied to a party. I feel that it is the independents like myself that build this country.

I am happy in the work I am doing on the school board. I deal only with the building end of things and leave the academic side to the PhDs. I spend long hours at committee meetings. At times things become monotonous and boring. I am tired when I get home and I am tired the next day. But when I think back about all that we have done in the last 14 years, it all seems worth it. The number of buildings and schools that we have put up is amazing. Financing these buildings, making them attractive, seeing to it that we use the taxpayers' money the best way — these have been big challenges and I am proud of what we have done.

I often speak to graduating classes. There is nothing more rewarding for a trustee than to address such a gathering. When I attend these commencement exercises and see the students receiving their grade 13 diploma, I begin to realize that this is the real reward for the work I do. Why, I get as excited at one of these commencements as I did the day they honored me by naming a new school after me — the James Wilson Jones Public School.

I like working on the building end of things. I have built three cottages at one country place already, and I would build more if my wife would let me. I have always been interested in building. Ever since I was a little kid I played around designing buildings and constructing them. I get a chance to do this type of work in connection with my school board and church activities.

I have worked for a number of firms in my lifetime. The most difficult firm I worked for was General Motors early in my career. The regimentation there was unbelievable. You just couldn't keep up with the rules and regulations of that company. That job taught me a good lesson. I realized that if you kept wearing people down with rules and regulations, you would never get their cooperation. I try to get the most out of my workers by endeavoring to get them to work along with me, rather than bulldozing them. Maybe I am not tough enough at times. I don't think human beings like to be pushed around, yet I realize that my way has its limitations. I'll give you a little instance of this. The other day we had new signs to put on the fence so as to designate the parking areas. I said to Jerry, one of my workers, "Jerry, go out and take those old signs down and replace them with these new signs." I thought that was a very simple assignment. When I went out to check on the progress, I found that he had another chap working with him. They were using the fence posts as the limits between the cars. I said, "Do you realize what is going to happen? By the time you get down to the end, you are going to be five parking spaces short. Now, get those signs off the fence and put them back where they belong." These are the things you run into. You give a worker a simple assignment and you don't say, "Make sure that you do this, that, and the other thing." You just say, "Replace the signs." You simply have to be a little more detailed and forceful with some people and say, "Now you must do exactly this." But I like to hold those orders to a minimum. Some people say that is a weakness in my supervision.

To do a little reviewing of past history, I was employed as a tool and die maker — that is my trade — prior to coming on the maintenance staff. I was an assistant foreman in the tool room for a time doing job evaluation and estimating. A slow up in business necessitated a change and they put me back on the bench. This was no reflection on my work, but rather on the economic conditions, which did not warrant the company carrying an assistant foreman in the tool room. After another year on the bench, I was approached by the industrial relations department about the job as maintenance foreman. I took it over on the understanding from the company that there was not to be a repetition of what happened in the tool room. If there was going to be a repetition, I wasn't interested in the job. Going back on the bench in the tool room was very embarrassing for me. It was embarrassing to be an assistant foreman and to be involved in doing job evaluations and then to have to return to work on the bench beside these fellows. Many of them didn't want job evaluations in the first place and were a little annoyed with me.

As far as my future plans are concerned, I am hoping to work out my pension at Martin Brass Company. I am 52 now and if I am in a favorable position I would like to retire at 65.

Jim Jones Talks about Harry Smith

Harry Smith is the cause of my biggest problems. I feel that in my own department I would be more effective if I were only given my head. Unfortunately, Harry Smith just won't let me run it. He makes it very difficult for me to contribute fully in my work. You see, he has cut back in my department quite a bit. At one time the electricians and machine repair people used to report to me, and I, in turn, would report to Harry. Harry Smith has them reporting directly to him. Well, the result of this is that he has more people calling him and telling him about little things. I wouldn't think that he would want to be bothered by these little things. As a matter of fact, once he was bawling me out for not telling him about something that had happened and I said to him, "Harry, I thought that was so little and insignificant that you wouldn't want to be bothered with it."

For some reason or other he is the only person I know with whom I just can't get along. I try hard in the job to please him and to work along with him. I keep trying to tell him that if things go wrong in the work that I am doing, it's not because I am trying to buck him. He thinks that I am constantly trying to annoy him. It's rather a miscommunication or my not understanding what he wants me to do. Instead of giving clear orders to do things, he will talk around the subject and toss out the odd hint. I never know for sure when he is tossing a hint or simply making a comment. For example, we were out looking at a hand rail going up in front of the shop one day when he said, "I would like to paint this pipe black but I don't know whether I should." He hemmed and hawed this way for a while and then left. Well, I didn't know whether to paint the rail or leave it.

Harry Smith doesn't like my working with the school board. Well, I've been working with the school board for 14 years and I intend to continue. If Harry Smith would only listen to me he would see that I pick up some good ideas for the company through my association with the school board engineers. But Harry Smith gets all uptight when I suggest a new idea and mumbles something about being a good engineer himself and that he will work out any new ideas.

There are other ways in which the company benefits from my work with the school board. I worked hard to get the school board to adopt an agreement that they would purchase materials from companies that produce within the municipal school area; consequently, we put Martin Brass products into the schools. The plant manager even came down personally and thanked me for this.

It is hard working with Harry Smith because you can't tell him anything. He has an awful temper. I have seen him pound the desk, holler, shout, and almost burst a blood vessel over some little triviality. For example, it was around New Year's and my son, whom I hadn't seen for about 18 months, was coming down to visit us. He was going to fly in about 5 o'clock in the morning and he was going to leave at 7 o'clock the next morning. Well, that was a bad period of time around here. I had three or four of my men off sick, so I came in and got things started the night my son arrived. After I got things started one of the men called me into the office and said that it smelled as though something was burning. We checked around everywhere and we could find no burning wire. I said that if it were something serious it would be showing by then, and I left. Well, I no sooner got home than one of the men phoned me and said that they noticed smoke coming from one of the fluorescent lights. I called Harry immediately and informed him of this. He jumped on me over the phone and asked me why I hadn't called sooner.

After that he called the electrician to come in and take care of the light. This was fairly late at night, actually about 3 o'clock in the morning. I saw my boy off at the airport about 7:00 that morning and then came straight to work. Upon my arrival Harry immediately called me into his office. He gave me a terrific tongue lashing for not being on the job that night. Well, I had had it. I said, "You just hold on a second, Harry. I came in yesterday to get the job going as I should. We looked around for the burning wire and we didn't find it, so I left. As soon as I heard about it I called you. Now, I spent most of the night up with my boy whom I haven't seen for about 18 months and I haven't had much sleep. I am not about to come in here and have you jump all over me." Well, he continued, so I just got up and walked in to see Harry's boss. But after I told him the story, all he said was that he would look into it. Of course, he didn't do anything.

The people around here just think it is a standard joke the way he pushes all of us around. Harry Smith is continually blasting away at me in front of my workers. Being undermined like that in front of my workers makes it very difficult for me to maintain discipline around here. As far as I am able to ascertain around the plant, I think the man is greatly frustrated. He doesn't get along with anybody too well. If you look at his history you will find that he has had difficulty with supervision all along the line. They sent him to Lansing, years ago, to operate a plant. At the same time they brought in an American who was going to build electrical fixtures. This chap was quite an expert in this field. Well, he wasn't there two months, before the two of them locked horns and the result was, I understand, that this fellow packed up and left.

There was another chap who had worked for Harry as a foreman at Lansing that quit, too. I met him recently in the shopping plaza and he said, "Are you still working for Martin Brass Company?" I said, "Yes, I am working for Harry Smith." He said, "Don't get me started on that, please."

My predecessor also quit after two years on the job. He told one of the millwrights, "I just can't stand it any longer. The man won't give me any latitude at all. He won't let me think for myself. Everything I do is wrong."

Well, I have tried my best to please Harry, but a man can only stand so much. He has abused me about as much as I can stand. It is getting to the point where the job just is not worth the hassle that I am subjected to. Although I sincerely want to stay at Martin Brass, if things don't soon shape up around here I am going to have to find another job where my contribution will be more appreciated.

Harry Smith Talks About Jim Jones

I have a situation in which the saying, "If you treat someone like an S.O.B., he will act like an S.O.B." is applicable. In my relationship with Jim Jones I am sure he sees me as an S.O.B., and it has been this way ever since he came into this department three years ago.

I know this is partly related to his outside interests. His position on the school board is a big job which takes a lot of time. Some of this time is taken away from his work. I admire the guy for the position he has and for the work he does in it. But I do believe a person should give his first responsibility to the job, and that is all I ask of Jim. I've told him that I'm happy to have him take time out for the school board meetings provided he lets me know he is leaving. But he invariably refuses or forgets to tell me that he is leaving. If he just leaves and I go looking for him and can't find him, then that makes me mad, although I don't say anything to him. I just can't figure out why he feels he has to leave without telling me.

Another thing that really bothers me about Jim is why he can't do a better job here than he is doing. There is no question that Jim is great as chairman of the school board, which is a big job. It is a big job — a lot bigger than he has here — a bigger budget than for this whole company, more buildings, more people, and so on. But when it comes to his foreman's job he just can't seem to cope. He is either calling me on the telephone or stopping by the office nine or ten times a day for my approval or advice on a situation. Why I almost see more of Jim than I do the rest of the foremen combined. I've wondered at times that maybe the guy is near a nervous breakdown. For example, once I had him in the office when I had a salesperson explaining equipment to us. I always like to get the foremen in, so that when we get a new piece of equipment we don't have to go through it more than once. Well, Jim fell asleep right in front of the salesperson who was trying to explain the equipment. I was embarrassed as hell!

I can't depend on Jim in emergencies either. I can think of several occasions when I have called Jim to attend to some emergency repairs on the plant, and Jim has let me down by not appearing himself. You see, one thing that has resulted from Tom Fuller's way of operating is that we have been given a lot more freedom than we ever had. All that Tom asks in return is that we maintain this plant so that when work starts in the morning, the plant is ready to go, that it stays in operation until the end of the day, and that this happens every day. Any time anything happens at night, I feel it is my responsibility to come out here to oversee the job. That is what gets me about Jim. I don't know how he sees this.

I've quietly tried to talk with Jim about these problems, but he has given me no real answers. I have had him in here; I've had him sit there in silence. I can't break through to him; I can't get any response from him. Jim and I talk about the school board. I disagree with some of the things he has done with the school board. We can talk about those; but when we come to talking about his job here we can't get anywhere. He just clams up and makes me feel very uncomfortable.

A Foreman's View

As Tom Fuller mulled the problem over in his mind he felt it might be wise to get an outside view on the problem. With this in mind he called on Jeff Sprout in production, a foreman who knew both Harry and Jim well enough to comment on the situation. After a little hesitation Jeff Sprout said,

Harry Smith is one of the weaker members of our top management staff. He has no respect for anyone. With Harry Smith, it's only what's in it for Harry Smith that concerns him. He's been a problem for a long, long time. He had a foreman a few years ago who was one of the finest men that anybody will ever find in any job, anywhere. Harry absolutely abused him and rode him until the fellow quit.

On the other hand, Jim Jones has talked to me so often about Harry Smith that I'm fed up with hearing the stories. It's the same story over and over again. I've been hearing it from Jim now for years. He spent 30 minutes with me yesterday just telling me the same story over again. You see, Jim Jones does an excellent job for the municipal school board, but he can't do anything right for Harry Smith. Harry Smith rides him and abuses him and Jim doesn't know what to do with him. I told Jim that he ought to invite Harry out to dinner, get him away from the plant, and then lay it on the line. "Tell him just exactly what you think and if that doesn't work," I told him, "the next time Harry says anything to you in the company, you just talk right back and say, "Now listen here, mister, you can't talk to me that way. If you want to fight we'll go out in the yard and we'll have a fight." But Jim said he couldn't do that because he'd be afraid he'd lose, and I said I was afraid he would too!

Harry has undercut and pushed Jim around for so long that Jim can't do anything right. Yesterday I had some maintenance work that I wanted done in my department and I asked Jim to do it. He said he had direct orders from Harry not to touch anything that wasn't in the schedule, and consequently he wouldn't be able to do it for me because Harry had laid it on the line that the schedule was not to be budged. So Jim said that if I wanted anything I would have to go to Harry. So I went to Harry and, oh, Harry was nice as pie to me and said, "Of course. Sure, we've got to have that done." Then he went down and lambasted poor old Jim with both barrels. Jim said to him, "But Harry, I thought you told me we weren't to change anything on the schedule today." But Harry just blasted Jim up and down until he was really a sorry sight. Then Jim came to me and said, "What am I to do?" Well, these sorts of things have been going on for a long, long time.

As Tom Fuller reflected on Jeff Sprout's comments and thought about all that he knew about the two men and their relationships, he pulled out a pad and pencil. "I really think the time has come for me to intervene. Given the nature of the men and the importance of maintenance to the plant's operations, I had better plan my words and actions carefully.

PETER GIFFEN

Jeffrey Gandz and James C. Rush

Joy Legrange, warehouse supervisor at Prince International, faced a potentially tense confrontation. One of the warehouse employees, Peter Giffen, with a history of episodes of absenteeism, had failed to show up for work again this Monday morning. He had missed three days in the previous month, and she wondered what, if anything, she should do to stop what she saw as an emerging pattern.

The Company

Prince International was a large, multinational consumer products company with operations in over 40 countries. In Canada it manufactured a full line of products in several plants, the largest and oldest of which was in Kitchener.

The large warehouse operation which Legrange supervised was critical to the efficiency of the Kitchener plant. As products came off the manufacturing and packaging lines in the north part of the plant, they were sent by conveyer belt across the main road to the south warehouse. It was a non-stop, two shift operation. If the warehouse operations were interrupted or slowed, the whole system jammed up, and problems were experienced trying to find room to stack finished product in the manufacturing plant.

Peter Giffen

Age 28, single, and with seven years' service with the company, Peter Giffen worked in the south warehouse. His duties usually involved palletizing and stacking finished products using hand dollies, or a fork-lift truck.

Giffen still lived at home with his mother and father — that is, when he slept at home at all. It was widely known that he liked a good time, and for him a good time meant lots of girl friends. He often boasted to his workmates how infrequently he had to sleep in his own bed.

His love of socializing apparently cost a fair amount, since he often complained loudly about how broke he always was even though his living expenses at home were low, and his parents were not financially dependent on him. He also made additional income from part-time jobs, refereeing men's softball in the summer and women's basketball in the winter. He played a lot of sports himself — some "pick-up" hockey in the winter and usually some bowling in the summer. He seemed to enjoy the fun afterwards — getting together with the guys and gals — at least as much as the sport itself.

Peter Giffen's Absences

Peter Giffen had a long history of sporadic absences stretching over several years. He seemed to go through spells in which he missed a lot of time, usually over several episodes. During the last three years he had missed:

Yr 1.	12 days	—	5 episodes
Yr 2.	9 days	—	7 episodes
Yr 3.	10 days	—	8 episodes

In addition, there had been numerous occasions when Peter was late for work — once or twice resulting in disruption in the warehouse operations.

Although Joy Legrange did not think that excessive drinking or womanizing were the reasons for the absences, she wasn't sure. She had heard of his late nights from his frequent boasting about how late he was out and what a great night he had, when he showed up for work the day after his frolics.

Several episodes of absence had followed hockey games. These, Giffen claimed, had aggravated a bad back condition which he had a few years previously. When she examined his personnel file, Joy Legrange noticed that two years before he had been sent to see the plant doctor about his back, following return from one of these sports-related absences. The only notation from the doctor was that Peter had been examined and there was no reason why he could not be at work in the future.

Joy Legrange was the third supervisor that Peter Giffen had worked for over the last three years. Others had made comments about his attendance in the file. Each had allowed a record of absences to build up and had then confronted him about it. In all of the sessions Giffen had agreed that his attendance could be improved, while claiming that all his absences were genuinely related to illness or injuries. After each of these counselling sessions his attendance had improved markedly.

During the period of good attendance between the spells of absenteeism, Giffen was a good worker. He did his job without complaint but never really went "the extra mile." As she looked over the file Joy Legrange recognized all of the three previous supervisors; — two were "hands-off" types of managers, letting the employee get on with the job with a minimum of supervision; the other was a real "hands-on" type, always keeping tabs on how things were going, coaching and helping his crew, and criticizing them when they didn't do a proper job. He was tough but well liked by most people in the plant. It seemed to Legrange that Giffen's absenteeism tended to be higher when he was on this "hands-on" supervisor's crew, and less when he was left alone to get on with his job in his own way.

The Current Problem

At 8:00 a.m., Monday, January 7, Peter Giffen was absent again. And this was going to leave the warehouse crew shorthanded. As she dug out his file, it looked to Joy Legrange as if he was about to commence another one of his absence spells — he had already missed three days earlier in December. She thought she should do something, but wondered what action to take and when to initiate it.

HELEN MALLEY (A)

Jeffrey Gandz

Valerie Hyatt, the new manager of Federation Bank's Mid-Town Mall branch, started to work through the pile of paper that she had found waiting for her on her arrival at the branch a week ago. The previous manager, who had recently left the bank to work for a trust company, had left a number of things which required fairly urgent attention. One of the items was a performance appraisal form for Helen Malley. To her dismay, Valerie Hyatt saw that the form had been completed about two months previously, but it had not been discussed with Helen Malley.

As she read through it, it became clear that her first impressions of Helen Malley were being confirmed by her predecessor's appraisal. The performance was rated as "low competent," and it stated that Mrs. Malley was deficient in a number of areas of her work. In the last week, as she surveyed the operation, Valerie Hyatt had noticed how slowly Helen Malley, a liability clerk, appeared to work and how uncertain she was in her actions. Just the previous day she had asked Malley a rather simple question about where a particular account should be placed, and Malley had appeared not to know. A recent inspection report by the bank's internal auditors had shown a number of problems emanating from Malley's area. Malley appeared to be the source of many of the problems.

Helen Malley

Before she sent for Malley to discuss the performance appraisal, Valerie Hyatt decided to review Malley's file. This, in itself, was a major task since the material in the file was extensive. Helen Malley had been with the bank for 16 years and had worked in a number of clerical positions, starting off as a junior teller and rotating through several jobs including customer service clerk, liability clerk, deposits clerk, and back to teller. She had been in the position of liability clerk at the mall branch for 18 months.

Aged 59, Malley was separated from her husband and had three children, one of whom — a teenage son — still lived with her. She lived just a few hundred yards from the branch.

In her early years with the bank, Malley had always been considered a competent employee. All her performance appraisals, conducted at annual intervals, had indicated competent, although not outstanding performance. There was one exception to this. Four years ago she had a series of disagreements with her administration manager at a former branch, culminating in her request for a transfer from that branch. The reasons for the conflict were not explained in the file, nor was there any documentation other than her request for transfer for "personal reasons."

Two years ago Malley had a total of 23 days of absence, most of these in one or two day episodes. This was noted on her subsequent performance appraisal but did not, apparently, justify giving her a "low competent" appraisal. In the summer following the appraisal Malley complained of severe back pains. She said that she had been hurt the week previously when the steel gate of a vault swung closed behind her and hit her back as she was bending down to open a drawer. No one in the branch had noticed this accident and she had not complained to anybody about it at the time. During the past year Malley again had a total of 23 days of absence, 15 of which she attributed to treatment for this back condition. Her physician had certified that she required that time off work.

As far as Valerie Hyatt could tell from the records in the file, a pattern of sporadic absence had continued through the following winter. Starting in March of this year, Malley was off work for a total of six weeks for what was described in the file as a "nervous disorder." There was a good deal of correspondence in the file indicating that the bank's medical director had been in touch with her physician and had agreed to continue short-term disability benefits until she returned to work. Following her return to work there was some evidence of a deterioration in work performance. Malley appeared much slower at her job, hesitant and nervous, and this had been noted on her performance appraisal by the previous manager. This manager had left the bank in September before discussing the appraisal with her, and this is the situation which Valerie Hyatt had inherited.

The Performance Appraisal Interview

Having reviewed the file she decided that it was appropriate to conduct a performance appraisal interview with Malley. In Hyatt's mind there was absolutely nothing to be gained from glossing over the inadequate performance. Therefore, she confronted Malley with the performance appraisal that the previous manager had written up.

Malley burst into tears when advised that the evaluation was negative. She claimed, apparently with considerable sincerity, that she had never received an inadequate performance appraisal in all her years with the bank. This was the first negative feedback that she had apparently ever received. When Hyatt reviewed each dimension of performance with her, Malley's comments were always the same. She stated that she had never been adequately trained in any of the functions of the liability clerk. Furthermore, she stated that her absenteeism in the previous two years had been due to the fact that her back gave her a great deal of difficulty when she had to stand or move around, and that she was often in pain. While it wasn't sufficient for her to stay at home in bed, she said it was adversely affecting her performance.

One aspect of the performance appraisal that Hyatt brought to Malley's attention was her apparent brusqueness and curtness with customers and with fellow staff. Malley explained that she was in pain a lot of the time and really didn't feel that she was able to work.

Malley also said that for years she had felt incompetent when having to deal with customers. She had never felt that she had been adequately trained for her jobs. Most times, when she had been assigned to a new task, she was just "thrown into the deep end and expected to swim." She said that this treatment had made her very nervous, and she never felt that she really knew what she was doing.

Malley refused to sign the performance appraisal review that Hyatt had conducted with her. Hyatt stated that the review would be sent to head office anyway. She indicated clearly to Malley that she had six weeks to significantly improve her performance in a number of dimensions, otherwise her employment would be terminated. In response, Malley said that she really didn't think that she would ever be able to do the job of liability clerk. Throughout this interview, Malley was crying and it was clear that she would not be able to work any more that day.

Subsequent Developments

The following morning Miss Hyatt received a telephone call. Malley's family physician, Dr. Reginald, told her that Malley had experienced an extreme stress reaction and had come close to a nervous breakdown in his office the previous afternoon after her conversation with Hyatt. He advised Hyatt that Malley would be off work for a number of weeks and that he would write to the bank's medical director explaining the circumstances. Hyatt also received a letter signed by Malley which she thought had been drafted by a lawyer. This letter refuted the "charges" of poor performance made in the appraisal and reiterated Malley's exemplary record.

Throughout the fall Malley remained off work. Every few weeks her physician would contact the bank's medical department indicating that she was still unfit to return to work. Meanwhile, at the Mid-Town Mall branch, she had been replaced by another employee who took over the liability clerk's job, and the operation was running much more smoothly. As she got to know the people in the branch well, it was clear to Hyatt that they were all relieved that Malley was no longer there. She hadn't been doing her share of work in the branch for some months, and the staff really felt some animosity toward her because of this. Several customers mentioned in passing that they were quite pleased that she was no longer there and felt much more at ease discussing their loan details with her replacement. On the other hand, a number of customers commented that they missed Malley and preferred discussing their problems with an older person.

In early December Hyatt heard directly from Malley that she was feeling much better and expected to return to work early in the new year. Hyatt did not look forward to this, since she was convinced, from her discussions with Malley, that she just couldn't perform the job at a competent level. But she didn't really know what she could do under the circumstances nor how she should treat Malley when she returned to work.

ELIZABETH HENDERSON (A)*

Joseph J. DiStefano

Elizabeth Henderson clenched her teeth and stared distractedly at the pile of untouched paperwork on her desk. Moments before, she had completed a short, tense meeting with a member of her clerical staff, Helene Bouchard. For the second time that month, Helene had approached Elizabeth with a request to make changes in her work schedule. Elizabeth's annoyance with these increasingly frequent requests was mounting daily, as was her frustration with her own apparent inability to deal with Helene's desire to alter her work schedule to her convenience. Elizabeth thought angrily that she had just lost another battle in what was shaping up as a major war.

Elizabeth had recently picked up signals from Helene's co-workers and from other supervisors that the schedule changes were causing administrative and relational problems. Elizabeth knew that she would have to discuss the problem with Helene, and with that in mind, she pushed her paperwork aside and began to analyze her situation and options.

Comtel Inc.

Elizabeth and Helene worked in the Information Resource Center of Comtel Inc., a firm which manufactured and sold high-tech components to the telecommunications industry. A major part of the company's activities was directed toward research and development efforts. Over 600 people worked in the Montreal headquarters of the company. Of this group, approximately 400 were directly involved in research and development project work. The remaining 200 employees performed administrative and other support functions. Comtel had specialized branch operations in Edmonton, Alberta;

---

*This case was prepared under the supervision of Professor Joseph J. DiStefano by a student who wishes to remain anonymous.

Maidenhead, England; and in five centers in the United States. In total, the company employed over 2000 people.

The Information Resource Center assisted the research and development program by collecting and organizing the latest relevant technological journals, newsletters and other publications of scientific agencies; maintaining up-to-date files of legal statutes, regulatory requirements and proceedings of hearings or Commissions; classifying and protecting proprietary documents which described the technical aspects of research carried out at Comtel; and performing data base searches for scientists who required knowledge of literature that might be available in publications other than those purchased by the information center. The center also maintained a large collection of books and periodicals on finance, management and North American business practices.

Comtel's upper management considered the information center to be a vital support service to the company's scientific community. When the company built impressive new facilities outside of Montreal in 1980, the information center had been given a prominent position on the ground floor of the six storey building. The center was located near the company's cafeteria and eating area, which was frequently used for informal meetings and think sessions. The eating area, with its spacious design, comfortable setting and numerous small tables and chairs, often functioned as an extension of the center's limited meeting and reading facilities. Scientists, project workers and management frequently met in the center to gather information or to do research, and then proceeded to the cafeteria where ideas and concepts could be discussed over coffee or lunch. As one manager said, "It's amazing how many of Comtel's new products and practices find their start on a white paper napkin!"

Information Center Organization

Responsibility for the operation of the information center was in the hands of the center's director, Mark McTavish (Exhibit 1). Mark had extensive training and experience in information systems, and had been lured away from another company when the directorship had come open 18 months before. Mark was well liked by all the center's staff. His technical knowledge was appreciated by the center's clients and his gregarious, easy-going manner quickly made him a favorite in the organization. The staff of the center found him fair and considerate, but Elizabeth had noted his reluctance to deal with difficult personnel matters. Otherwise, she found him supportive, analytical and enthusiastic about the center, and receptive to suggestions for its improvement.

Elizabeth was one of five managers who reported to Mark. The other managers included Robert Boisvert (French Services); Arlene Heller (Reference Services); Jean Tomlinson (Circulation) and Alexander Terry (Acquisitions and Cataloguing). Elizabeth managed Audio-Visual Services. With the exception of Robert Boisvert, each of the center's managers supervised at least three, and some as many as eight, clerical employees.

Audio-Visual Services

The role of AV Services was to acquire, organize and manage the center's collection of film, videotapes, cassettes and slides; to ensure that all equipment was in working order and to coordinate bookings of equipment, materials and viewing rooms. In addition to overseeing these operations, Elizabeth also had responsibility for the unit's budget, scheduling of clerical staff and service development. Her work required frequent contact and coordination with Comtel's Training and Development Division, which consisted of a staff of fifteen.

Elizabeth supervised two full-time clerical workers, Catherine Hill and Sylvie Richard. Helene was the only AV employee who worked on a part-time basis of 18 hours per week. She was also the only AV employee to have responsibilities in another unit. Approximately half of Helene's time was spent in the AV unit and half in French Services. But her reporting relationship was to Elizabeth, who was responsible for supervising her.

Work in AV Services was often stressful. Bookings had to be made with care, since most resources were in short supply and often in high demand. Conflicts in the use of rooms, equipment or materials could create major problems and much ill-feeling among users. Consequently, Elizabeth felt that it was very important that staff members who made bookings were not distracted or disturbed by needless inter- or intra-unit conflicts or controversies.

Except for the recent problems with Helene, Elizabeth felt that she had established an excellent working relationship with her staff. Elizabeth credited her staff with innovations and improvements in services and procedures, and made every effort to maintain a supportive, encouraging and trusting relationship with them. The atmosphere within the AV unit was open and friendly, and conversation ranged easily from business related topics to social and domestic concerns.

Elizabeth's relations with other supervisors in the center were more mixed. Although she had no overt conflicts with any of her peers, she found that she liked some decidedly more than others. With those she did not like, Elizabeth tended to remain cordial and professional, but also somewhat distant and reserved. Fortunately, it was easy to minimize contact with these people. Except at formal staff meetings, Elizabeth rarely had to interact with any of the other supervisors for extended periods of time.

Clients

The clients that Elizabeth and her staff served varied widely. Clients included new recruits who needed to see films and videos as part of their orientation to the company, training and development staff who needed to check on the appropriateness of new material, scientists who had acquired material on new technical procedures, and administrative/managerial staff who sought tapes or films on management practices or career development.

Elizabeth found that each client group had different needs and different ways of approaching and dealing with AV staff. Of all the groups, the scientists tended to be the most problematic and the least tolerant of the unit's rules and procedures. The scientists often seemed to feel that their needs took precedence over other users and that their desire for equipment, materials and viewing space should be accommodated immediately. Other users were generally more considerate and easy-going, requiring more or less instruction and assistance depending on their familiarity with the center and the AV unit.

Elizabeth attempted to be sensitive to the differences in the unit's clients, and to adopt an approach appropriate to each. She felt that both she and her staff were largely successful in providing a high level of service, with a high degree of personal contact. Indications from both upper management and clients suggested that people enjoyed coming to the AV unit and that the unit's performance was more than satisfactory.

AV Unit Scheduling and Duties

Catherine Hill and Sylvie Richard, the full-time AV employees, each worked 35 hours per week. Their duties were divided informally between cleaning and checking materials and equipment, arranging bookings, assisting with AV presentations, and developing programs in conjunction with the Training and Development Division. In arranging the work schedule for the unit, Elizabeth had to ensure that there was always at least one person available to take bookings. This activity took precedence over any other task that needed attention.

Helene Bouchard's role in the AV unit differed slightly from that of Sylvie and Catherine. Helene acted as a secretary to both Elizabeth and Robert (French Services), typing reports and letters as required. While in the AV unit, however, she was also expected to take bookings and assist with the maintenance of equipment and materials. Even when she was working in the French unit she could be called to assist with AV matters if that unit became unusually busy. The AV unit had priority because client needs were usually more urgent. French services performed by Helene were primarily clerical and could be completed on a more flexible schedule.

Because of Helene's part-time status and shared responsibility in French services, she was almost always working with either Catherine or Sylvie when she was in the AV unit. Thus she had the help of at least one of the women when client pressure was high. However, the reverse was not true. When Helene was not there, Catherine or Sylvie had to handle peak periods by themselves. They saw Helene as having more freedom and flexibility. Furthermore, there was rarely a sense of urgency in her secretarial work. Occasionally a letter or report had to be typed on the same day, but usually it did not matter whether typing or other clerical tasks were completed one day or the next.

Helene Bouchard

Elizabeth Henderson (A)

Helene was 29 years old, married with two young children. She was born in a small, rural center outside of Dorion, Que. With the exception of the one year she had attended secretarial school in Montreal, Helene had spent her entire life in her birth place. She met her husband, Bob, a construction worker, while she was in Montreal. After they were married, they moved into a house which Helene's father had given to them. Bob and Helene both travelled at least one half hour to work. During the winter, blocked roads and difficult driving conditions were not uncommon, and as a result, Helene's absences and schedule changes increased by approximately 25 percent from early December until March.

Helene's was a closely knit, traditional French Canadian family. Her immediate and extended families were the center of Helene's life, and although on snowy winter days she often thought of moving closer to Montreal, she knew that she would miss the frequent, convenient contact she had with her sister and mother, each of whom had homes within a block of Helene's. Helene's four brothers lived within a 200 kilometre radius of their birthplace and visited the family frequently.

Helene had worked at Comtel for eight years. Until the birth of her first child, six years earlier, she had been a full-time employee in the information center. After her daughter was born she took a four month leave of absence and upon her return persuaded the then director of the information center that her work load only warranted part-time hours. The director agreed and assigned Helene an 18-hour-week schedule (Exhibit 2). All of Helene's benefits and seniority were prorated to reflect her new status.

Helene generally liked her work and her co-workers. She was considered by other members of the center to be a diligent, conscientious worker and somewhat of a perfectionist. Now, with two active children at home, she frequently found that she was tired and stressed. Though generally healthy, the children were at an age where they were susceptible to colds and the usual childhood diseases, and Helene's sleep was often interrupted. She also had to cope with the stress of her husband's irregular schedule and the almost constant worry about finances. Maintaining two cars and feeding and clothing two young children exhausted their resources — mental, physical and financial.

Helene was relieved that her job permitted a degree of flexibility. She appreciated Elizabeth's willingness to accommodate schedule changes. On the other hand, Helene believed that, given the nature of her work, there was really no reason why she shouldn't have her schedule the way she wanted it. "I'm here when I absolutely have to be," she said, "and for the rest of the time, it really doesn't matter."

Elizabeth Henderson

Elizabeth, 27, was born and raised in a Montreal suburb. Her parents, originally from western Canada, had lived in Montreal for 25 years. Elizabeth's father was a professor at McGill University; her mother, also a university graduate, stayed at home with Elizabeth, her brother and two sisters. Elizabeth was married and had an infant daughter.

By the time she was 25, Elizabeth had completed an undergraduate degree in economics and political science, and a Master's degree in library and information science at the University of Toronto. Her job as supervisor of the AV unit was her first full-time position. Elizabeth had been with Comtel now for two years. Prior to joining the company, she had taken one general course in administration as part of her library degree. She had taken no further instruction in administration or management, although she knew that courses were available both within the company and at nearby universities and community colleges.

As she analyzed her present conflict, Elizabeth realized that there were several factors relating to her background that contributed to her reluctance to discuss the problem openly with Helene. Elizabeth had grown up with a strong social code requiring that people outside the family unit be treated with politeness and consideration, but also, a sense of reserve and distance. This was coupled with a strong norm, which operated both inside and outside of the family, regarding emotional expression. All of Elizabeth's family, herself included, exhibited tight emotional control, especially where negative emotions, such as anger, fear, resentment, and hostility were concerned. Other values which dominated Elizabeth's home environment included a strong sense of duty and responsibility to work, independence, education, and professional status.

Because of her family orientation, Elizabeth found it difficult to handle situations that were potentially or actually emotionally charged or confrontational. At best, she tended to avoid such situations, but if caught in one, she would often withdraw and become silent, or become defensive and aggressive. Other times she would take on extra duties or responsibilities herself, simply to resolve a problem or smooth over rough relationships. Afterwards, she would frequently regret her actions, but the desire to escape from conflict usually dominated her behavior.

Recent Events

In the past four months, Helene had requested some twelve changes in her schedule. Some were as inconsequential as coming in half an hour later than usual, but others involved complicated shifts in both days and hours worked in the week. Elizabeth had agreed to virtually all of the changes, recognizing the lack of urgency in Helene's work and reasoning that Catherine and Sylvie could adjust their own work around Helene's presence or absence. Helene's reasons for wanting the changes usually centered around domestic or social needs, or to facilitate the travelling she and her husband did to get to their respective jobs.

Elizabeth had agreed to Helene's requests for two additional reasons. First, Elizabeth had seen displays of temper from Helene in the past, and she hated the thought of being in a confrontation with a staff member who could vent her anger in such a fiery manner. Second, Elizabeth recognized the differences in job orientation between herself and Helene. Elizabeth's job was a top priority in her life and the focus of much of her energy and interest. Helene's job was a necessary evil and little more. Despite her annoyance, Elizabeth felt that she had no right to impose her own values on Helene.

Initially, Helene's changes seemed to cause little reaction from Sylvie, Catherine or Robert. Lately, however, Elizabeth had noted that Sylvie and Catherine were reacting to Helene's irregular appearances with displeasure. They had not directly spoken to Elizabeth about their feelings, but now, when Elizabeth informed either one that Helene would not be in at the expected time, they reacted with stony silence, or the query, "What's wrong this time?"

It was obvious that Robert, who had joined Comtel just one year before, was also finding Helene's schedule problematic. Usually quiet, easy-going and amenable to every suggestion, Robert had taken to regularly asking Elizabeth when Helene would be in this week. In part, this was necessary because Elizabeth sometimes neglected to inform Robert of Helene's revised schedule. Keeping track of Helene's hours was becoming an administrative headache, and with other matters pressing on her mind, Elizabeth sometimes found it difficult to tell all those who needed to know exactly when Helene would be in and when she would not.

Elizabeth knew that the problem had progressed beyond the point of personal differences in values and attitudes between herself and Helene. Other people were now involved, and if the situation was not resolved soon relations would continue to deteriorate, and the administrative hassles would only increase.

Elizabeth felt that she had to figure out whether she should talk to Helene now, or wait until another request was made. She also had to determine what approach to take with Helene. Finally, she wanted to understand the basis of her own annoyance with Helene, and learn more about herself, if for no other reason than to avoid this kind of problem in the future.

EXHIBIT 1
ELIZABETH HENDERSON (A)

Organizational Chart, Information Resource Centre
Comtel Inc.

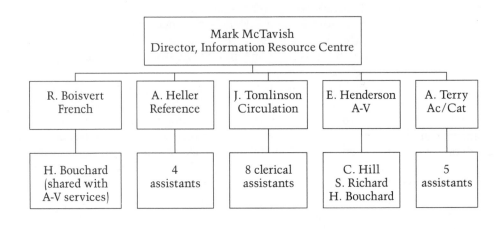

EXHIBIT 2
ELIZABETH HENDERSON (A)

Typical Schedule for Helene Bouchard

Two Week Rotation:

Week 1 —	Monday	12–5	(5 Hours)
	Wednesday	9–4	(6 Hours)*
	Thursday	9–5	(7 Hours)*
Week 2 —	Tuesday	9–5	(7 Hours)*
	Friday	12–5	(5 Hours)
	Saturday**	9–4	(6 Hours)*

*1 hour off for lunch
**Normal hours for all Information Resource Centre employees, except the director, included a 9–4 Saturday every other week.

A and D, INC. (A)*

Joseph J. DiStefano

In April, Ron Stevens, foreman of the testing laboratory at A and D, Inc., had a difficult decision to make. Two of his laboratory technicians, Louis Lamarche and Lise Moreau, seemed to be ending a love affair which was seriously affecting the work of the lab. He was wondering whether he should get involved or let the personnel officer, Jean Leduc, take care of it. Ron knew that if he ignored it, he would have more time to deal with other pressing technical and supervisory problems. Ron was uncertain about people's reactions if he did get involved. Neither did he know how serious the falling out really was, nor how much of his time he could afford if he got involved. Ron was concerned about the impact on the technicians' productivity because there had already been several hours of work time taken for discussions between Jean Leduc and Louis and Lise.

Environment

The Plant

The testing laboratory was situated in a brand-new, continuous process, agricultural fertilizer plant located near the rural town of Varennes. The plant had only started operating a year previously. Upper management was drawn from other operating units of A and D, Inc. First-line supervision consisted of recent university graduates (see Exhibit 1). Management maintained a strong focus on the implementation of corporate personnel policies which emphasized line management responsibilities, building an image of a company family and care for employees.

---

*This case was prepared under the supervision of Professor Joseph J. DiStefano by a student who wishes to remain anonymous.

The Region

The community of Varennes was a small, French-speaking town composed of families in the low to low-middle income bracket. The region was newly industrialized but farming remained a major occupation. Traditional social values of family respectability and job security prevailed.

The plant management was not involved in the community, but the local community always knew what was going on inside the plant. The local townspeople were always interested in watching how the new managers would act in novel situations.

The Laboratories

The testing laboratory was the most modern plant lab in the company. The lab ran on a 24-hour, seven-day per week basis as an autonomous service unit to the plant. The quality of the analyses were critical for process control. The analyses were done at several stages in the production cycle.

The laboratory, (with a book value of $500 000 in assets), was air-conditioned and colorful, with an ergonomic design. The employees considered the testing lab an excellent place to work because of the high skills required, the clean, quiet environment, the mix of men and women, and because there was little direct supervision in the day-to-day shift work. The average analysis of two or three samples took about an hour.

The technicians in the maintenance laboratory cleaned, repaired and tested the metal parts for process pumps and miscellaneous machinery. The lab was hot and noisy because of heavy machinery and poorly placed ventilation equipment. The metal parts weighed from seven to twelve kilos and were covered with graphite. At the end of their workday, the technicians were black to their elbows. This work area was called a lab because the technicians had to work to specifications of one ten-thousandth of an inch.

The quality control laboratory was dedicated to final product testing. It was similar to the testing lab except the work was very routine. A technician would run 50 to 100 consecutive samples through the same five tests in about two hours.

The three labs participated in a rotation system for technician cross-training. The technicians would be trained by pairs in each lab. For example, Louis and Marcel had just recently started their ten-week training in the testing lab. They would then work eight months in the testing lab before moving to the quality control lab. All the technicians had to follow the program which would take three years to complete the full cycle of cross-training. The system had been completely planned and the training dates had been communicated to the technicians. The majority were enthusiastic because the system offered novelty and higher pay as they became more skilled.

Personal Backgrounds and Performance

Ron Stevens

The head of the testing lab was Ron Stevens' first job since graduation with a B.Sc. in chemistry. He was 26 years old, married to a francophone and had a 3-month-old daughter. Ron had lived around Montreal for the past eight years. Previously, he had spent all his high school years in Colombia, South America, where his father had been an executive with a major multinational metal company. His parents had always encouraged learning other languages so he was fluent in both Spanish and French. As a child, he had attended a French language Swiss public school for a year and he had been enrolled in French language Cub Scouts.

In his youth Ron had originally thought that he would become a physician and would return to Latin America to practice medicine among the poor. His idealism had been inspired by his four uncles, each of whom was a physician, and by his mother, who had been a nurse. Ron had done volunteer work in a veterans' hospital and with retarded children. As he matured his interests had shifted from medicine to other areas of science and technology.

Ron had been hired before the actual plant start-up so he had selected and trained the technicians as well as actively managing the complete lab start-up. He was one of four anglophones in the staff of 100. However, Ron was the only fluently bilingual anglophone as well as being the only anglophone with direct supervisory responsibilities for hourly employees.

Ron's job performance was good. He had recently been upgraded from a 3 to a 2 (scale of 1 to 5) with a raise in salary. He had a high profile position to the plant management because of a published commendation from the divisional vice-president just prior to the plant start-up.

Ron's management style focused on group discussions and an open-door policy. He was friendly and on good terms with the technicians. He engaged in public congratulations, back-slapping and coffee-buying as techniques to encourage the employees. Ron emphasized personable relations as a goal, since he recognized that people spend as much waking time with their co-workers as with their spouses. Nevertheless, Ron also stressed high performance. Only six months previously Ron had convinced a poorly performing technician to quit on the basis that the man would be more satisfied in another work environment. This action had been the first forced turnover in the plant, but not everything had gone so smoothly. When Louis rotated into the testing lab, Ron did have some questions about Louis's ability to adapt. Ron had made a joke to Louis and Marcel about their having to work harder in the testing lab. Ron made the same type of jokes to other technicians and they even returned them to Ron. However, Louis had taken it personally. During Louis's first week of training, Ron had spent a half-hour discussing the misunderstanding with Louis in Ron's office. As a result Ron had given Louis a private apology.

Louis Lamarche

Louis was 28 years old and married with no children. Prior to moving to Varennes, Louis had been unemployed. Louis had worked one year in the maintenance lab where his performance had been good. His ex-foreman characterized him as steady, dependable and hard-working with good relations with co-workers both on and off the job. Louis had received a community college diploma in chemical analysis but he had yet to work in that field. At the time of the love affair, Louis had been training for three weeks in the testing lab.

Ron's initial reactions to Louis were unfavorable because of the latter's appearance and manner. Louis was overweight, frequently unkempt, and shuffled when he walked. Although Ron realized that his dislike for Louis was based on superficial qualities, he could not eliminate his feelings entirely. Acknowledging what he took to be a personal bias, Ron vowed to suppress any negative feelings in dealing with Louis.

Lise Moreau

Lise was 23 years old, married to the same man she had dated since age 16, and to this point had no children. She was considered to be very pretty. Both her family and her husband's family came from the town of Varennes.

Lise had worked sixteen months with the company in the testing lab. She had a diploma in chemical analysis with some experience in a hospital lab. Lise was one of the high performers in the testing lab. She was a very organized person who had achieved low variance in her analytical results. She had an outgoing personality. Ron recognized that he was attracted to Lise and knew that he would have to guard against favoritism in supervising her work. Lise was scheduled for rotation to the quality control lab in six months.

Jean Leduc

Jean was 35 years old with a high school education. He worked in personnel at a level equivalent to a foreman. He had transferred to the Varennes plant from another company plant where he had worked his way up from an hourly position to foreman and finally into a personnel position.

The plant management had put Jean into the role of plant "priest." His main task was to listen to the employees about their job-related and personal problems. He had little authority to make decisions, but created solutions by discreetly advising line managers. Employees trusted Jean because of his confidential treatment of their problems. Prior to the problems with Louis and Lise, Ron and Jean had not worked together.

A Problem Development

The training was not going well for Louis. He was not learning at the same rate as Marcel. Louis seemed distracted and he often had to repeat analyses. Louis's training was several days behind the relatively fixed schedule.

Jean had been coming frequently to the lab during the past several days. He had been talking to both Lise and Louis. Just that morning, Lise and Louis had individually requested separate half-hour periods to go talk with Jean in his office.

Lise was working on a special set of analyses which Ron was using to help the engineering group trouble-shoot a quality problem. These analyses were slowing down because of the time spent with Jean. Ron was aware that process quality was currently a major upper management concern. The process was having too many interruptions and divergences from the stringent specifications, familiar problems for a plant start-up.

The affair between Lise and Louis was having an impact on the other technicians, too. They had started taking longer coffee and lunch breaks a few days ago. There appeared to be heated discussions in the lab which quickly faded when Ron entered.

In an attempt to find out what was going on, Ron cornered Marc (Lise's co-worker on shifts) and pulled some information from him. Lise had been accepting Louis's offers to drive her home and she had even gone to Louis's for a drink after work. Louis seemed convinced that Lise loved him. However, Lise had rejected Louis's suggestion that they both leave their spouses and move in together somewhere. Recently their disagreements had become more visible and the lab technicians were starting to take sides.

Unsure about Marc's reliability, Ron went to Jean and received confirmation of Marc's information. As well, Jean told Ron that Louis had come to the plant at midnight a few nights ago to see Lise. Lise had refused to see Louis who, in turn, refused to leave the plant. Marc had called Jean, who then drove 25 kilometres to the plant. The four had spent three hours in the cafeteria trying to reach a compromise. They did not come to any agreement because Louis refused to accept Lise's claims that she did not love him and that she would not leave her husband.

Plant Labor Relations

Some production workers had recently started a drive to unionize the hourly employees. Such a drive consisted of convincing people to sign a union card until the government-stipulated minimum for union accreditation was achieved. Labor laws made it extremely sensitive for management to express an opinion about the pros or cons of unionization, so the plant management was urging first-line supervisors to keep building a reputation of concern for employees and of open discussion without the need for third party interference. Ron did not want to create an issue with Louis or Lise which could embitter the plant employees or affect their position regarding the desirability of a union.

The Decision

As Ron drove home at six p.m. after a 10-hour day with only a fifteen-minute lunch, he mulled over a number of questions and concerns. He knew he had to decide between letting Jean handle this dispute or getting involved himself. Ron was uncertain how long the affair would continue to affect productivity and morale. How could he control the effect on the workplace when so much was happening outside of normal hours?

In a general sense, Ron wondered where management's prerogative to step into private lives started. How would the technicians react to his involvement? Alternatively, where did the employee's right to privacy end?

Ron asked himself, if he did get involved, what could he do to get people's trust in such a delicate issue. How long would it take to build trust? Ron was well aware that he was already putting in most of his time to current problem areas such as the engineers' needs, equipment failures and necessary technician training sessions.

Whatever his decision, Ron wondered what he would tell his own supervisors at tomorrow's daily session at 8:30 a.m. They would want a complete analysis and some recommendations for action.

EXHIBIT 1
A and D, INC. (A)

Partial Organizational Chart

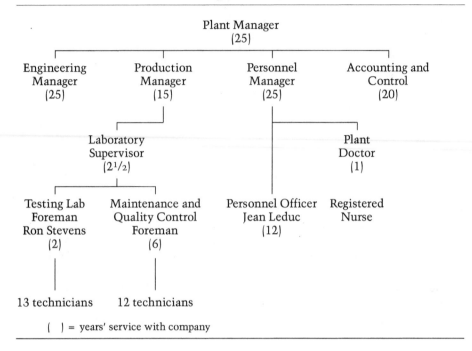

( ) = years' service with company

A and D, INC. (B)*

Joseph J. DiStefano

In May, Ron Stevens, foreman of the testing laboratory, reflected upon his decision to get involved in Louis and Lise's tumultuous love affair (see A and D, Inc. (A). It had taken him about two weeks to gain the trust of all the technicians and Jean Leduc. Ron had engaged in innumerable, separate meetings with Lise, Jean, Marc, Louis and others over coffee in the cafeteria as well as in his office. Ron had spent portions of each morning, sometimes even at 3 a.m., on the phone whenever someone wanted to talk.

Ron was faced with a new decision because the whole situation had taken a turn for the worse. Louis's working ability had deteriorated to the point where he had been given a temporary medical leave by the plant doctor, with a recommended visit to a psychiatrist in town. Louis was diagnosed as a paranoid schizophrenic so he had received the full pay, medical leave which lasted three months. Several interested parties were awaiting Ron's decision on how much contact Ron and the technicians should have with Louis. Essentially the question was how much should they respond to Louis's problems during this time when he was officially out of the plant receiving periodic treatment.

Louis

Jean had found out from Louis that he was under several pressures. Louis was having problems moving into his recently purchased trailer home and he was carrying $3000 in credit card debt. Louis felt very insecure with his new task and foreman, and he had been having serious marital problems for several years in addition to the recent involvement with Lise.

---

*This case was prepared under the supervision of Professor Joseph J. DiStefano by a student who wishes to remain anonymous.

To Ron's surprise, Louis was very receptive to discussing all his problems. However, Louis continued to insist that Lise loved him. He frequently attempted to talk with Lise by phone at her home and at work.

Louis had begun complaining of being followed by Lise's husband and another man. Louis had begun evasive tactics by speeding around town in his Corvette to lose his imagined followers. He also carried a baseball bat in his car for protection. Lise was categorically denying the allegations about her husband's following Louis.

Louis claimed to be suffering from a lack of sleep, loss of appetite and extreme nervousness. Prior to his medical leave, his performance had deteriorated to the point where he was two weeks behind in his training. In his last few days he was doing only routine waste water analyses, which he had learned in his first week.

Lise

Lise had remained somewhat reticent to discuss her part in the affair. However, her performance had returned to her previous standards. She maintained that Louis was imagining love and that she wanted to stay with her husband. Lise had expressed concern to Ron about her reputation at work and in the community. She wanted the whole affair kept quiet with a minimal impact on her marriage. Lise had complained of insinuating comments from some of the employees in other parts of the plant. When pressed about the details of her involvement, Lise denied that anything had actually occurred between her and Louis. She convinced Ron that her initial relations with Louis had been innocent and that the love affair was only a fantasy on Louis's part.

Plant Situation

Many people throughout the plant had heard about the falling out between Louis and Lise. All the principals (Jean, Marc, Ron, Lise and Louis) were under pressure to divulge information for the rumor mill. For the past two weeks, Jean and Ron had been concerned about giving information to anyone, even upper management, in the fear that leaks would occur. They did not want Lise, Marc and Louis to lose trust and start to resist management's involvement.

Management's Involvement

Ron had prepared a six-page, point-form report detailing meetings, phone calls and other important incidents. He discussed this document with his lab supervisor, the personnel manager and the plant manager when Louis went on the three month leave. They were satisfied with the update and encouraged Ron to keep up the good work. They offered no concrete advice and admitted to never having witnessed such a personal breakdown before. A copy of the document went into Louis's file.

Ron's lab supervisor had been promoted into that position during the initial two weeks of the problem. Compared to Ron, he had only six more months of seniority with the company in another department of the plant. He actually had less direct supervisory experience than Ron. The lab supervisor was heavily involved in one of the production manager's major projects. The supervisor was the coordinator of a novel inter-plant testing and quality program which would facilitate diagnosis of quality problems. The expected outcome was an annual income improvement of several hundred thousands of dollars.

Involvement of Personnel and Medical Staff

Jean's manager was pressuring him to decrease his involvement. Jean had been putting numerous hours into communicating with all parties. The time commitment included a four-hour evening discussion with Louis and his wife at Louis's urgent behest. Jean's manager wanted the lab management to take control of the whole problem because the corporate philosophy emphasized line management's total responsibility for their employees. Personnel staff were available to point out problem areas and verify that line management practices were in line with corporate personnel objectives.

As Louis's condition worsened, Ron and Jean had convinced him to talk to the plant medical staff, a registered nurse and a part-time staff doctor. The doctor had arranged the few days' leave and the psychiatric appointment, which resulted in the diagnosis of paranoid schizophrenia.

The medical staff were very reluctant to divulge their opinions, and advised Ron that Louis was now a medical problem. The staff maintained that they could withhold information under the terms of the Hippocratic oath. They had little sympathy for Ron's position even when Louis started coming into the plant often and was calling many people at all hours.

The medical leave meant that Louis was remunerated under an insurance plan. He was only nominally an employee of the firm. The spirit of the plan was to eliminate unnecessary financial worries while ill employees received medical treatment. The medical staff determined who qualified for leave and decided when people were medically fit to return to work.

Jean had reluctantly divulged to Ron that Louis had discussed his marital problems while his wife was present. Louis had found his wife having sexual relations with his best friend several years before. This had caused severe stress to Louis and he continued to use it to dominate his wife. Ron was unsure whether he should let his supervisors know of this.

The personnel group had done a thorough research of Louis's background when he went on temporary leave. They discovered that Louis had actually been fired from a Shawinigan company several years before because he had "beat up" his foreman. The police had been called and Louis had been forcibly committed to a mental institution for several months for violent paranoid schizophrenia. He claimed that it was his wife's infidelity which caused his problems. Louis admitted to falsifying his employment record.

The Present Situation

Louis had continued coming to the plant at odd hours attempting to see Lise, even though he was on medical leave. Ron had taken the unusual step of instructing the guards at the gate not to admit Louis into the plant unless Ron came to escort him. Louis appeared to resent this. Ron was unsure whether this would affect Louis's medical treatment or whether it would jeopardize the fragile trust between them.

At least the immediate problem of getting lab work done was solved. A summer student was being trained sufficiently to complement a skilled technician on the two-person shifts. She would fill in for Louis and the formal rotation could continue for the next few months.

Since Louis insisted on maintaining daily contact with many people, Ron wondered whether he should create a role as primary contact point. As a focal point, he could assess Louis's progress and orchestrate responses to Louis. The lab technicians were looking to Ron for guidance now that Louis was diagnosed as mentally ill. But Ron thought he needed some support from the medical staff, who appeared unwilling to confide in him.

The efficacy of the treatment seemed dubious to Ron. Louis was seeing the psychiatrist only one hour each week. Although the plant doctor had indicated that every person's contact with Louis was a part of his treatment, Ron had doubts about being involved in the medical treatment of paranoid schizophrenia. He not only had to resolve the question of his own role, but also felt the need to provide some guidelines to his lab technicians. He really wondered what he should do now.

A and D, INC. (C)*

Joseph J. DiStefano

In July Ron Stevens, the testing lab foreman, was taking a rare opportunity to sit at his desk and review Louis's continuing saga (see A and D, Inc. (B)). Ron's attention to Louis had been sandwiched into ten- to fifteen-minute periods every other day since he had decided to follow Louis's treatment for paranoid schizophrenia more closely. Faced with several other on-going managerial problems, Ron found himself dealing with discrete events where the connecting links had to be forged from his perceptions, analyses and decisions over time. Recently, Ron had begun to detect evidence which suggested a change from his playing a supportive role. He increasingly felt that Louis was manipulating people and wondered if he could take a more confronting stance in dealing with Louis. In light of the medical staff's readiness to declare Louis functionally capable for work, Ron decided to review the past six weeks and reexamine what he ought to do with Louis now.

In dealing with Louis's problems earlier, Ron had decided to promote a supportive attitude. As guidance for his technicians, Ron encouraged them to listen attentively to Louis and to advise Louis to seek professional medical help, including self-hospitalization. As well, Ron encouraged them to relay to him the substance of their contacts with Louis. The medical staff had come to trust Ron as he channeled information to them and only gradually sought their reciprocal support. Recently, they had begun voluntarily to inform Ron of their contacts with Louis more fully.

Louis

At the beginning of his medical leave, Louis had spent ten days in hospital on the ward for the mentally ill. He had left the hospital under relatively mild

---

*This case was prepared under the supervision of Professor Joseph J. DiStefano by a student who wishes to remain anonymous.

medication in the care of his supportive wife. However, Louis continued to insist that Lise loved him and that she should leave her husband and live with him. He had started to follow Lise and wait for her outside her apartment, which had caused her to go from work directly to her mother's, where her husband would join her. Antagonism was building because of this inconvenience and because Louis attributed some damage to his Corvette and pick-up truck to Lise's husband. Louis had complained to the police, whose investigation and report described only minor scratches to the paint, similar to that often caused by carelessness in parking lots.

More recently, Louis appeared to be enjoying his medical leave. He had acquired a superb tan and, when he wasn't in the sun, he was driving around and visiting people at their homes to discuss his problems. Ron had started to notice that Louis would give someone some information and then carefully crosscheck with Ron or the medical staff for knowledge of the same information. Every other day for the past two weeks, some previously uninvolved technician would call Ron to describe a fifteen minute doorstep discussion he had just had with Louis.

In addition, Ron had begun to detect a new note of defiance in Louis's attitude during recent discussions in Ron's office. Louis insisted that he had a right to work in the testing lab and so he asserted that he would refuse an assignment to the maintenance lab. As well, he had thoroughly researched the company medical leave policies, so he knew that only medical staff could authorize when he could return to work and that the full-pay, medical leave period was only half over.

Ron's Other Problems

While trying to sort out these issues Ron felt under intense pressure to reduce severe quality problems being experienced in the plant. The warehouse was piled to the ceiling with several million dollars of off-standard and waste product. The process engineers were often demanding new types of analyses and long series of re-sampling and testing. As if this were not enough to occupy his attention, it seemed that every day at least one of the major lab instruments would develop a new technical problem which caused both backlogs and a scramble to solve the problem. As well, the technicians were all trying to jockey their vacation times to coincide with long weekends.

In the midst of all this activity, Ron identified several important elements which affected his thinking. First, to his relief, the Louis affair had not become an issue in the intensifying unionization drive. There were few leaks, and many people were either not aware that Louis was on a medical leave or didn't care. Secondly, during Louis's frequent visits to the plant he would talk with Ron defiantly and proudly about his physical strength, about his love for Lise, and about his variety of personal problems. During these face-to-face talks in Ron's office Ron slowly became aware of his fear of Louis and his

A and D, Inc.
(C)

protectiveness for Lise. Thirdly, Ron suspected that Louis was not disclosing all of his activities during his weekly meetings with his psychiatrist. The psychiatrist and the medical staff believed that Louis was functioning nearly well enough to do some lab jobs, but that he would never lose his mental problems. But the medical staff would suspend their treatment of Louis once he returned to work. Finally, Louis's paranoia and record of past violence had led Ron to send his wife and baby daughter away for several days after Louis had claimed they were following him while Ron was at work. Ron's superiors had been shocked at the involvement of Ron's family, but still offered very little support.

The Decision

In light of Ron's suspicion that Louis was manipulating people and withholding relevant information from his psychiatrist, Ron was worried about the medical staff's impending decision to declare Louis competent enough to return to work. In view of the uncertainty he was alarmed by his lab supervisor's recent request for Ron to plan for Louis's return to work. Ron wondered what his options were. One relief was that the foreman of the maintenance lab was not averse to having Louis back in his lab. His only condition was assurance that Louis would not cause him any problems.

In the back of his mind, Ron was also relieved by his recent acceptance to the MBA program at a well-known business school. The MBA seemed like an avenue out of all these operating emergencies, and he hoped that his request to the company's executive committee for a leave of absence would be accepted. But he also knew that his own pride would not permit him to evade responsibility for addressing the problem with Louis. Should he fight against his return, try to engineer Louis's transfer to the maintenance lab, or face resumption of the problem by having Louis return to the testing lab where Lise was working? As he pondered these options he knew that his supervisor would expect justification for his decision and a plan for how to minimize future problems.

A and D, INC. (D)*

Joseph J. DiStefano

After consulting with Jean and the plant doctor, Ron decided that Louis was playing games. Further, Ron also decided that Louis was not yet manageable. He began an intensive lobbying campaign to convince the plant medical staff to continue the medical leave up to the end of the three month period. Ron met with the plant doctor and the nurse several times over the span of two days. He presented summaries of his knowledge about Louis's activities and attempted to prove to them that Louis was not following the psychiatrist's recommendations. As well, he proved that Louis was misinforming all medical staff about his actions. Ron made a case that a return to work at this time would severely disrupt the lab operations, as well as being highly stressful for Louis. With Ron's encouragement several technicians, including Lise, discussed Louis's activities with the doctor. The psychiatrist concurred with the extension of medical leave when he was fully informed of the facts by the plant doctor.

Another result of the discussions was a decision to change the communication tactics with Louis. The medical staff and Ron started discouraging Louis's contacts by being more brusque and paying less attention to him. This switch from patient listening and encouragement precipitated Louis making a series of aggressive phone calls. After one such call from a phone booth, Ron called the police to protect Lise because Louis threatened to hurt her. However, the police would neither incarcerate nor commit Louis because he had not yet become a public danger, according to their criteria.

Louis never became physically aggressive, but within a few days he committed himself to the mentally ill ward for one week. Louis left the ward under severe medication and ceased to bother Lise.

Louis returned to work in the maintenance lab when the medical leave was finished. He was told in no uncertain terms to cause no problems or he would

---

*This case was prepared under the supervision of Professor Joseph DiStefano by a student who wishes to remain anonymous.

be fired for misrepresentation on his job application. His performance was acceptable and he engaged in virtually no social contact except with two close friends. One technician from the maintenance lab was moved early to the testing lab for training to replace the summer student.

The unionization drive ended with the organizing group having insufficient votes to claim representation for the whole plant. Because the percentage was close to that required, the certification issue was referred to an arbitrator. However, not a single lab technician had signed a union card, so the lab technicians were excluded from the proposed bargaining unit. Ron believed that his delicate management of both the love and insanity issues had actually contributed to better communications without the need of a third party.

During the last two weeks of the medical leave, Louis had talked with Ron and the lab supervisor for fifteen minutes in Ron's office. This was the first time that any management other than Ron or Jean had talked with Louis. Ron had found Louis to be no more cocky, aggressive or abrasive than usual. However, Ron had to spend a half-hour cooling off his supervisor, who had been ready to fire Louis on the spot. Ron realized that his management had little conception of what he had been through. As he reflected on their apparent ignorance of the severity of the problems he had faced, he wondered whose fault their isolation had been; his for not communicating enough, or theirs for not paying enough attention?

At the end of the summer, Ron received his leave of absence to study for the MBA. It was only the third approval for study leave in the company's history, and Ron felt he had earned it.

THE CANADA-CHINA
COMPUTER CRISIS CASE (A)*

Joseph J. DiStefano

John Stevens, Director of the International Division of Software Services, Ltd., was attempting to clear up his desk before leaving for a week's selling trip. As he left his office to clarify a question with a programmer, he was nearly bowled over by Dr. Paul Horn, who was striding down the hallway in the opposite direction. "You're just the man I want to see," the project leader blurted out with uncharacteristic intensity. "We've got a very serious problem with Yulan Sun. She's deliberately erased the whole program for the interactive graphics package for the multi-shift scheduling problem we've been working on, and I'm madder than hell! It will take us several months to reconstruct the work. Worse than that, I'll miss the deadline for the project's completion and for the upcoming annual trade fair, which would give our work the perfect publicity we need to launch it successfully."

John was stunned, since he knew that Yulan Sun, a visiting expert from China, had spent several months working on the project. He felt his own blood pressure rise as he replied, "I guess I had better see her right away, Paul. What's behind this and what do you want me to do?"

After a brief explanation of what had transpired over the past week, Paul Horn suggested that John sit tight. "Before you talk to her, I want to get to the bottom of the story myself and try to resolve the problem. I'll talk to her and put something on paper for you before you get back."

By the middle of the next week, John was on the telephone listening to his secretary read the letter Paul Horn had written to Yulan (See Exhibit 1). He shuddered at the probable consequences, not only for Paul's project, but also for the overall agreement with the People's Republic of China (P.R.C.) which John had been working on for the past 15 months. In his letter, Paul presented his view of the events leading to the present crisis, and challenged Yulan to reply by the end of the week and to turn over the floppy disk on which he knew

---

*All names and locations in China and Canada have been disguised.

she had saved a copy of the program. John's secretary had learned from Lindsay Tan, a Software systems analyst, that Yulan had refused to reply to Paul's letter until she met with John, preferably the day he was to return from his selling trip. John knew that on his first morning back at Software he faced a major presentation to the executive committee of one of his important customers, so he asked his secretary to defer the meeting with Yulan until the next day. He wanted time to confer with Lindsay and Paul before meeting with Yulan. Furthermore, he worried about meeting alone with Yulan. Prior experience had taught him that misunderstandings were likely to increase, rather than be resolved, if all parties weren't present. But as tempers seemed to be rising in this situation, he wasn't sure if a joint meeting would be productive either. He knew that, whatever he decided to do, the stakes were high, and that he had better think through his approach carefully.

Software Services and the P.R.C. Cooperation Program

Software Services, Ltd. was a successful computer software company. The company had grown rapidly from its founding in the early 1970s and had carved a special niche developing custom programs for particular clients which could be generalized to other related problems and sold more widely. An example was Paul Horn's current project in multi-shift scheduling, which had been started for a hospital client interested in improved scheduling of its nursing staff. Software's competitive edge derived in part from their decision to invest in the latest hardware and to develop software for this equipment, which they thought would likely be adopted by their current customers. Suppliers of the new technology understood that they could take advantage of Software's programming skills and market network, so relations between Software and its suppliers were excellent.

Currently the company had about 60 full-time technical specialists with advanced training and skills and about 20 other professional staff, most with BSc. degrees, who were contracted on a part-time basis. Another 15 professionals served the marketing and commercial functions in the company. About half of these had moved from the technical areas as the company had grown. The balance of the sales and marketing ranks consisted of MBAs with technical undergraduate degrees or experience. Support functions (accounting, technicians, clerical staff, etc.) consisted of about 40 full time employees, and the senior executive team made up the balance of the personnel in the company.

To operate efficiently and to keep the highly-skilled employees challenged and occupied, the company had adopted a matrix structure. The marketing side was organized by industry specialization. The industry managers drew project leaders from the technical groups, which were oriented toward specialized products and applications such as modelling, decision support systems, and operations research. As part of the market differentiation, the company also had an international division which, in recent years, had added to the firm's ability to attract and retain bright, young professionals in an increasingly competitive market.

The international division was the home for the P.R.C. Cooperation project, where it was now causing considerable frustration. About 15 months earlier Software had been approached by a non-government organization (NGO) in Ottawa which provided placement services for the Canadian International Development Agency (CIDA). CIDA had sponsored a project at the request of the Ministry of Foreign Economic Relations and Trade of the P.R.C., and the NGO was seeking to place in Canadian industry advanced computer experts, some less experienced programmers, and recent graduates of Chinese technical universities. It was to be a four-year program, the objective of which was to update the experienced people who had fallen significantly behind during the Cultural Revolution between the mid-1960s and mid-1970s. The less experienced graduates were to get exposure to modern equipment and techniques and to gain experience in dealing with real-world problems. The program would simultaneously provide the participants with an understanding of the capitalist system and forge potential commercial links with Canada. Both of these results were consistent with CIDA's policies, which had increasingly shifted toward trade-related aid in recent years.

In this particular project CIDA provided a contribution in overhead to the companies, and travel money, salaries, living allowances, language training, and medical insurance to the Chinese visitors. The company was expected to provide facilities and management time in return for the work and output of the Chinese during each visitor's one-year stay. As one of the companies cooperating with CIDA, Software had agreed to accept ten advanced specialists and twelve inexperienced programmers over the four year contract. In addition to CIDA's paying for this additional staff and providing overhead allowances to the company, Software executives also hoped, perhaps naively, they acknowledged, that establishing direct relationships with the people and government of the P.R.C. would provide them with business advantages in the future. The dramatic opening of China to the West and increasing trade activity might offer new market opportunities for Software's international division.

While reading the newspaper, John Stevens had learned of a similar strategy by one of Canada's leading law firms. The firm had hired and paid the expenses of two Chinese law students for each of the past four years in the hope that the law firm would learn about Chinese regulations and evolving legal system, and make important connections with the trainees who would be among the few Chinese to know Western laws, and through them be well-placed to serve the emerging markets for corporations doing business with the P.R.C. The firm had initiated the idea because of Canada's long relationship with the P.R.C. Canada had been one of the earliest Western nations to recognize the P.R.C. and China had reciprocated by establishing an embassy in 1972. John believed that establishing relationships with Chinese experts of high standing made excellent marketing sense for the long run. He therefore had urged his own firm to accept CIDA's request for cooperation and had been happy to assume the responsibility for the agreement as an additional activity.

The People

Paul Horn

Dr. Paul Horn, one of Software's most competent technical specialists, was an extremely valuable member of the Software team. Paul had been with the firm for several years. He joined the operations research department and soon established himself as a high producer who met deadlines. He often worked simultaneously on a number of different projects and frequently saw new applications for the techniques he developed. In addition, Paul was highly visible in his profession outside the company. He was a regular contributor to professional meetings and published in the most prestigious academic and managerial journals in the world. This was seen as highly desirable by the Software executives, who were anxious to expand the firm's reputation internationally. Because of Paul's record of accomplishments, he had recently been promoted to a project leader. Further, the R & D committee, consisting of the vice-president for R & D and two industry managers and department heads, had responded positively to Paul's frequent requests for equipment, assistants and financial support for new ideas. The company encouraged such proposals, but the R & D committee scrutinized the requests carefully and demanded clear evidence of performance before extending or renewing its support. More recently, Paul had extended his sources of support by obtaining special grants from various levels of government to help businesses acquire new technology. He had also hired assistants for his work through government-supported training programs.

Paul had obtained an Honors BA and an MA from Oxford University and had come to North America to pursue his MBA and PhD at the University of Chicago, where he specialized in operations research. As many other doctoral candidates had discovered, the process was painfully long. In spite of the financial support from the university, he found it necessary to obtain employment before his dissertation was completed. For a year he worked part-time as an instructor in a nearby institution and then full-time as a lecturer in a university in the southwest. Paul finished his doctorate and quickly came to enjoy his comfortable life. Both of his children were born while he was a faculty member at this university. However, it was primarily the deplorable state of the local schools that prompted his decision to join Software and move to Canada. Paul Horn, determined to see his children in a good educational environment, reluctantly left his idyllic situation at the time his older child approached school age.

In switching to the private sector from a university and to Canada from the U.S., Paul expected to make some adjustments. But holding impressive degrees from prestigious universities, Paul also expected more rapid advancement than he initially received at Software. He attributed the delay to misrepresentations by Software, whom he felt had not always lived up to its initial agreement with him. Because of this, he had had sharp exchanges with some of his supervisors and had aired his disagreements openly. However, the strong R & D support, his recent promotion to project leader, and visible successes during the past two or three years had seemed to overcome his earlier frustration. Only rarely did flashes of his earlier feelings break through. His testiness when impatient was no secret in the company, but there was no question that his colleagues enjoyed Paul's company and respected his knowledge, skill and commitment to his work.

Throughout the company Paul had a reputation as a very hard worker who was frequently seen in his office or the lab facilities early in the morning and on weekends, as were all of Software's most successful project leaders. Within his department he was known as particularly helpful to the young technical specialists brought in by the company on a contract basis. Paul also regularly joined his fellow workers at the staff lounge for lunchtime and coffee break conversations. Paul could always be counted on for incisive and cutting comments when the repartee and humor became good-naturedly competitive, as it often did when friendly rivalries surfaced.

Paul and his wife, Joan, seemed to enjoy life in the suburbs. Paul played golf and, as president of the local chapter of the Optimists, he had led the efforts to raise money to buy micro-computers for elementary schools in his area. He was equally active in his professional societies and served as an officer in one of the national organizations of computer specialists. When the P.R.C. project had been discussed in the company, Paul had been one of a dozen or so technical professionals who had expressed to John an interest in becoming involved.

Yulan Sun

Sun Yulan had been quick to suggest that her Canadian hosts reverse the traditional Chinese ordering of surname first and call her by her given name, Yulan. She had arrived in Canada late the previous July. CIDA had provided a six-week orientation to Canada at the University of British Columbia for a large group of Chinese ranging in age from their early 20s to late 40s. These people were all participating in development programs of varying duration across the country. Yulan's first few weeks were spent adjusting to an incredibly different world from that which she had known in China. The abundance of consumer goods, the richness of the homes and apartments, the conspicuous wealth, the many yachts in Vancouver harbor, even the expanse of the boulevards, highways, bridges and neon signs, all overwhelmed her senses. Initially she struggled with her comprehension of English; the speed, accents and colloquialisms used by the woman in whose home she was billeted and by her teachers and acquaintances at the university confused her. They were so different from the part-time, textbook training in English she had had in Beijing. In addition to the disorienting language and cultural differences, Yulan struggled with her dislike for Western food and learned to cope in a city that experienced a public transportation strike which lasted nearly the whole time she was there.

Gradually she became accustomed to her new surroundings, but she felt contradictions in most of her observations and experiences. The bungalow where she lived was modest by Canadian standards, yet seemed wasteful with so many rooms, color TV, telephone, appliances and furnishings all for the one owner who lived there. Yulan wondered about a society which could generate such wealth, but still leave her host so financially insecure that she had to rent a room to Yulan in order to survive her divorce and unemployment. The media surprised and shocked her, too. How could a country allow insulting commentaries about government officials to appear in print and on TV? How was it possible for radio stations to broadcast music with lewd lyrics and for TV videos to display even more suggestive dancing and revealing costumes?

Yulan experienced this mix of thoughts and feelings from the perspective of living 48 years in China. Born just before World War II of reasonably well-to-do parents in Shanghai, Yulan showed a keen aptitude for science and engineering during her middle school years (1948–1954) and was among the few to attend university in the tumultuous years following the revolution. Even more special was her selection to a prestigious Chinese university known throughout North America as "China's MIT," which drew its student body from among the best students in the country. Yulan majored in engineering in the automatic controls department and graduated in 1959. She was immediately taken onto the faculty and was active in research and teaching until 1965 when she was transferred to the computer engineering department. There she quickly established her special talents by teaching and doing research in a variety of areas dealing with both hardware and software. Yulan was the author of two books and several articles on computers.

During her years on the faculty, Yulan met her husband, also an engineering professor. They had their only child, a daughter, in 1968. Their happiness as a family was short-lived, however, because the Cultural Revolution dramatically disrupted their lives. The university was closed for almost a decade, and Yulan was "sent down." This euphemism meant that she had been forcibly removed from her family and sent to a rural area where she had done manual labor in agriculture and had undergone "re-education" and "self-criticism." She had not seen her husband or daughter for three years. No sooner had she been pronounced "rehabilitated" and permitted to return than her husband had been subjected to two years of the same treatment, during which he had fallen victim to a parasitic disease while planting rice. The debilitating effects of his illness were still visible in his physical frailty, but his spirit remained undiminished.

Perhaps as a consequence of such difficult experiences, Yulan often appeared rigid to John. Particularly when her wishes were thwarted, she became impatient and did not hesitate to raise her voice in anger or to use the traditional Chinese technique of "shaming" the source of her aggravation into acquiescing to her will. This aggressiveness seemed especially marked in her dealings with individuals she perceived as lower in status than herself. Occasionally she seemed slightly paranoid, but John dismissed most incidents as misunderstandings caused by language or cultural difficulties. Notwithstanding these annoyances, John also saw Yulan as an adoring and devoted mother to her daughter and a dedicated, hard-working professional, much admired by her colleagues.

As she emerged from the difficult period of the Cultural Revolution, Yulan's fortunes improved. She and her husband returned to the academic life which they enjoyed. They were provided an apartment in a five-storey walkup, typical of the many such blocks which housed faculty and staff on the university campus. The campus itself represented a work unit or *danwei*, the basic structure around which all society was organized in the P.R.C. Everyone who worked or studied at the university lived on campus under the authority of the work unit.

In 1978 as China opened to the West under the leadership of Deng Xiaoping, the university began to develop a capability in the field of management. From a fledgling department of economic management engineering (in North American terms, a bit like a combination of industrial engineering and economics) a rapidly expanding faculty was being built and a need for computer expertise was identified by the senior university administrators. In 1981 Yulan was transferred to the Economic Management Engineering Department as its first director of the Management Information Laboratory. It was in this capacity that she was also selected as the first visitor to Canada on the CIDA-sponsored program with Software.

John Stevens

John Stevens had been with Software almost from its inception. He had joined the firm after graduating with an MBA. His interests and studies had emphasized international business and marketing. Prior to beginning his MBA, John had completed a mathematics degree and had worked overseas as a volunteer in a developing country. He followed this internship with an extensive period of world travel. Upon returning home, he developed an interest in electronics and computers which led him to a challenging job in computer sales. Ambitious and hardworking, John was a natural achiever in business, but soon recognized his need for more formalized training in order to make it into the upper echelons of the corporate world. On the advice of his many contacts and friends, he applied to and was accepted by the MBA program at The University of Western Ontario.

Upon graduation John started in a general marketing job at Software before the company had grown so large. The industry specializations had not been as distinct then and the relations between the marketers and technical specialists were not as formalized. Few people in the company had heard of a matrix organization. John's gregarious style and broad education made it easy for him to relate to the variety of people working at Software. His success at marketing the firm's products and securing cooperation from project leaders and their team members gave him significant informal influence in the organization. As the company grew, John's career advanced steadily and he became a manager of one of the industry groups soon after the matrix structure was adopted.

A few years later the size and complexity of the company required a full-time manager of the human resource function and John was asked to take the job. Seeing the opportunity to do something new and challenging, John agreed, but indicated that he would eventually want to move back into a marketing job.

Seen as a basically easy-going person, some of his tough decisions and recommendations about the careers of some of Software's less outstanding performers surprised some managers. Others were disconcerted at John's volatility in expressing his anger when things didn't go well. During the first two years in the job, John took pride in the policy initiatives he had taken, in the talent that he had helped recruit, and in establishing a relatively smooth-running organization. But he also chafed under the mounting paperwork and regulations imposed by various governmental agencies concerned with human resource issues. What had seemed like a challenging job, tapping some of his natural abilities and core values, had turned into an exasperating routine.

Fortunately for him, the senior executives of Software were just about to create the International Division as a separate entity when John's frustrations crested and he informed the president of his desire to be reassigned to a line job within the next year. The timing and match with John's interests and background were perfect, and he jumped at the opportunity to head the new division.

John undertook his international responsibilities with renewed vigor. At the end of the first year he had been successful in building a solid team and doubling Software's international billings. He credited much of the growth to the excellent performance of the technical professionals in the company, the Paul Horns and Lindsay Tans who turned out exceptional work. They, in turn, commented on the reappearance of the more relaxed John Stevens they had known earlier.

Just at this point, the P.R.C. Cooperation project surfaced and the president asked John to join him on an exploratory trip to China just before Christmas. John had long ago developed an interest in China. As a teenager John had read about China with fascination. When the P.R.C. embassy was first established in Ottawa and a few Canadians had reported on their travels, John had written several inquiries trying to arrange a visit. Although none of his letters had been answered, his interest had remained undiminished. Over the previous two years he had read four books dealing with Chinese political history from the time of World War II through to the excitement of the "Democracy Wall" posters of the early 1980s. No one was surprised at the president's selection of him, nor at his quick reply of "When do we leave?"

The exploratory talks were so successful that he and the president returned with a signed agreement that they had negotiated during their five-day stay. They knew that such a quick agreement was unusual. But they also knew that the Chinese had everything to gain and very little to lose. So they understood that their closing a deal quickly ought not to be seen as a special achievement. Nonetheless, John returned from the trip personally exhilarated and enthusiastically took on the P.R.C. project in addition to his regular duties. Since then John had handled a number of difficult problems and many routine issues. His low tolerance for bureaucracies led to renewed frustrations in dealing with the Canadian government's and Chinese demands for paperwork and reports. As the first year of the project wore on, some of John's enthusiasm abated. But the appearance the following August of the first visitor, Yulan, regenerated his interest. Now that her visit was culminating with a difficult problem, John had a sense of deja vu.

Lindsay Tan

Lindsay Tan was a systems analyst with Software who had been close to Yulan since her arrival. Lindsay was born and raised in Hong Kong and educated in Australia and Canada. She had taken her undergraduate degree in computer science and had been involved in some project work for Software through her senior thesis. Her work had been helpful to the company and her enthusiasm had caught the attention of several people. She was offered a permanent job upon graduation and after a few months' vacation in Hong Kong with her family, she had joined the company full time. Although she did not speak Mandarin, the fact that she was Chinese provided a natural rapport with Yulan. During the first few months they were often seen together during breaks, and after work. Lindsay spent a number of hours introducing Yulan to the area, helping her get settled in her apartment, and generally being friendly. During this time she often relayed information about Yulan's progress to John and her role as an objective and helpful intermediary came to be accepted and relied on by both John and Yulan. Her voluntary call to John's secretary about Yulan's reaction to Paul's letter was typical of the informal role she had played.

Yulan's Arrival and Early Months of P.R.C. Cooperation

Yulan Sun had arrived in Vancouver in late July and was due to fly East to start work with Software in mid-August, following the orientation. John was scheduled to go to the Far East in early August and would not be in Toronto for her arrival, so he arranged to see her in Vancouver. John arrived late in the evening and had clients to see from 10:00 a.m. until his flight to Tokyo later that afternoon. Yulan had orientation meetings also, so they met at the hotel to get acquainted over breakfast. Although Yulan was a bit nervous and hesitant, John had no trouble understanding her English and they exchanged pleasantries about her experience during the orientation and joked about enduring the "Canadian disease" of strikes. John noted her discomfort with the food, but was encouraged at her curiosity about his pancakes and blueberries and her apparent willingness to try them when he offered a taste. After talking about plans for her first few weeks at Software, John gave her the airplane tickets that she needed. He received a package of pictures, audio tapes and letters to take to China for Yulan and arranged for a taxi to return her to the university.

John had decided to stop in China during his trip to meet the first two programmers and an experienced systems analyst whom the Chinese had proposed as visitors starting the following January. He also expected to interview a number of recent computer graduates who would be potential candidates for a subsequent period at Software. Yulan said that the authorities would either arrange for him to meet her husband and 16 year old daughter, or they would deliver the photos and other personal items on his behalf.

The visit went well. John was impressed with the two young computer graduates. They were bright and outgoing and acted as translators during his stay. He quickly approved their projected arrival in Toronto the following January. He was also very favorably impressed at the extensive experience of the second expert, a colleague of Yulan's who had managed a very large factory. But he was worried about her English abilities and urged that she be given more time in the intervening months to strengthen her communication skills. He emphasized that this was important so that both they and Software could obtain the full benefits of the cooperation. He underlined this point about language preparation by rejecting the other graduates because of inadequate English. The Chinese had surprised him by proposing that some additional programmers join the other two who were to go to Canada in January. But he was sure that it would be impossible for them to function in English, so John was firm in his refusal.

In addition to these interviews and the sightseeing that his Chinese hosts graciously provided, John discussed the desires of two senior officials to visit the Software offices the following November. As part of the original agreement, they were to spend a week with Software and a second week visiting other companies in related industries throughout Canada.

At the end of John's stay, Yulan's husband and daughter met him and extended an invitation for lunch in their home which he accepted with pleasure. When he arrived in the spartan apartment, his thoughts raced back to Toronto and the accommodations he had arranged for Yulan. Even though he had deliberately picked the smallest, least expensive three room plus bath and balcony apartment near the office, he knew it would be luxurious compared to her home. He had thought it would be larger than her home, but had rationalized that since two visiting experts would be in it for most of the time, it wouldn't be embarrassing. Now his stomach tightened in the realization that he had probably erred. But knowing there was little he could do, he turned his attention to his hosts. They provided him with a seemingly unending flow of delicious dishes. He was stunned at the end of the meal by homemade ice cream. He discovered that making ice cream was one of Yulan's hobbies and promised to treat her to the surfeit of flavors at Baskin-Robbins when he returned. At the end of the meal, Yulan's daughter played the violin for him and then proudly played a rock tape on her radio cassette player. She had just returned from a youth camp with American teenagers and had received several tapes as gifts.

The two multi-use rooms were small, grey concrete cubicles and it had shocked John to realize that Yulan would undoubtedly have the best of what was available. Glad for the privilege of being invited, he walked down the four flights savoring the experience and still sensing the genuine warmth that overcame the drabness of the blocks of apartments through which he wound his way back to the university for his final afternoon of meetings. He had had doubts about the worth of taking time from his business calls to stop at the university. But given the special hospitality he had just enjoyed and the importance of face-to-face meetings with the proposed visitors, he was convinced that the detour had been invaluable.

On the same evening he returned to Toronto, he picked up his children and drove to Yulan's temporary room to deliver photos. Two nights later John and his wife took Yulan out for ice cream, starting a close relationship which built over the early months of her stay. Initially, John saw Yulan briefly two or three times a week at the Software offices, often running into her in the halls or seeking her out for an informal brown-bag lunch. Yulan was quickly immersed in the activities of two different project groups to which she was assigned to learn the computer languages and hardware. She learned quickly and worked long hours on her own. She also attended English classes for recent immigrants in a nearby branch library once a week.

Yulan quickly became accustomed to the fast pace in the company and was invited to several homes for dinner during the first few weeks of her stay. By mid-September she had moved into the apartment which John had sub-let for her. She obtained the few essential items of furniture with Lindsay's help and seemed to be adjusting to her new environment. John and his family had her to their home several times, and his wife and Yulan seemed to get along especially well. Both were extremely direct people and often laughed about their tendency to ask questions which others found either intimidating or impolite.

In October Yulan attended a course called "Computer Technology, Management and Change." The course was part of a program funded by CIDA to expose the Chinese to Canadian managers and industries across the country. The company visits took place in November.

Fall was also a busy time for John. But he received positive reactions from Yulan, from the two project leaders with whom she worked, and from Lindsay and other Software employees who had made her acquaintance. So he was satisfied that things were going according to the plans and objectives that had been described in detail in the CIDA agreement.

Visit of Senior Chinese to Software

John received the shock of his life when the two senior Chinese, with whom he and Software's president had signed the agreement, tried to renegotiate substantial parts of the contract during the very first meeting. They wanted to use the Software contract as the vehicle to send eight of their experts and new graduates to other companies and industries in Canada. They claimed that shifting priorities in China made it critical that different technical specialties be developed. But they wanted all the arrangements to be conducted through Software!

John had been through a few negotiations in his years, but was unprepared for this. He had read and reread Lucian Pye's *Chinese Commercial Negotiating Style*, a study of U.S. and Japanese executives' experience in China. Although it warned that attempts to renegotiate were normal, John thought he had settled the issue in August when it had also arisen. Then the Chinese had opened it as a possibility, but had not specified the numbers of people or the fields of specialty. John had said "no," but wondered in retrospect if he had been direct or firm enough.

He explained carefully to his counterparts that Software's primary objective in the cooperation project was the direct and extended contact with the Chinese visiting experts. The Chinese visitors pushed their demands and then backed off; then they repeated the cycle of pushing and backing off several times. After a stalemate, the conversation turned to Software's assistance in purchasing a minicomputer for the Faculty of Economic Management. CIDA limited its contribution to $150 000, but the equipment the Chinese wanted was estimated to cost about $200 000. The Chinese tried to reduce the number of trainees to make up the differential. After four hours of discussions, other equipment funds in the contract were used and John agreed to give up a less-experienced visitor to fund the balance needed for the computer purchase.

Then the Chinese returned to their original request to divert several of the trainees to other companies and fields. Again John explained and argued about preserving Software's interests in the agreement. The Chinese finally relented and the meeting ended. The next morning when meetings resumed, John listened incredulously to their raising the issue again. During the previous evening he had thought a lot about his responses to their pressure and had developed a contingency plan which he now acted on. Standing up, he slammed the table, raised his voice and said in a steely tone, barely controlling his anger, "Look, if that is what you want, you should have negotiated contracts with those companies. I am not going to do all the work for the benefit of our competitors. If you want to do that, fine. But I will tear up the contract and you can start again with them. I am prepared to rip it up right now. Tell me yes or no, but let's settle it now." Evidently he had gotten through to them, because after some agitated discussion among themselves, they quickly retreated and pronounced the issue closed.

The Multi-Shift Scheduling Project

As the year progressed, Yulan's adaptation to the technical aspects of Software's activities was excellent. Although she showed some signs of impatience during management and planning meetings of the project groups, she clearly was a very capable professional with the ability to make a significant contribution to Software's business. So at the beginning of the new year, about half way through her stay, John asked Paul Horn if he would be interested in Yulan's joining his team as a full partner in their activities. Paul knew of Yulan's work and he agreed to have her help devise a visual interactive system for scheduling several shifts of workers. It was a problem that Yulan was keenly interested in since China had many enterprises which had three-shift operations. She knew that enormous amounts of time were spent in doing workforce scheduling and that the results were often sub-optimal.

After an introductory meeting with Paul, she met with the full-time project member who had been working with the latest SAGE equipment and received a series of briefings on the project, the state-of-the-art hardware, and the software requirements. Then Paul took Yulan to the research site, where he introduced her to the supervisor who did the scheduling of the nurses. As he explored the problem with the scheduler, Paul tried very hard to include Yulan in the conversation so she would be able to start her part of the work. He found the exchanges went very slowly, with much head-nodding from Yulan, and lots of pauses. When Paul thought they were finished, he asked Yulan if she had any remaining comments. Paul was shocked when she responded by asking the scheduler what the problem was. This required going back over the previous 45 minute conversation, which embarrassed Paul. Paul concluded from this experience that Yulan understood very little of a casual conversation, but he also felt that she was unlikely to admit it.

Yulan retreated to her cubicle and began to learn about the sophisticated system. With help from the project team members and a major effort from her (she still continued working on two other projects), she pushed ahead. By late March she had done an enormous amount of work in developing the basic equations for solving a specific problem of scheduling shifts of nurses over several weeks, and in programming the solution to be displayed in color in a visual interactive model. This provided the scheduler with the ability to make adjustments easily to several variables and to see the results in graphic form instantly. To translate the accomplishment into terms that John Stevens could easily grasp, Yulan explained that the program was 1000 lines of FORTRAN, and the results converted work currently taking one scheduler a full month to complete into an hour's task. At the same time, it provided much greater flexibility for subsequent manipulation of various decision components.

Even though the work was only partially complete, Yulan's demonstration for John and Lindsay proved to be most impressive. John was doubly pleased because Yulan had been able to describe the context of the work and set up the demonstration of the model in clear, succinct terms. It was also very important to the success of future Chinese visitors that the first collaboration yielded positive results. John was so happy at what he had seen that his first stop after leaving Yulan's presentation was to the president's office to report the results, and his second stop was to Paul's office to laud the progress. He also dictated a brief note of praise to Yulan's superior in China. Then he left for home feeling that it had been a most encouraging day.

The results were even more important in light of a meeting which Yulan had initiated with John two or three weeks earlier. She had come into his office obviously tense. She felt overwhelmed with the tasks needing to be completed in the short time remaining before her departure. She was negotiating with vendors regarding the purchase of the minicomputer, which took enormous amounts of time detailing the specifications, coordinating with the purchasing department, and reviewing the proposals. She had project work through early April with the other two teams and had another three-week project management course she wished to attend in May. In June she planned to spend time at Waterloo University's computing center, and she was fitting in industry visits near Toronto whenever she could. She also wished to see Montreal and Ottawa and to return to China via Boston, New York and Washington.

John tried to help her think through priorities and to make trade-off decisions, but everything seemed to be top priority to her. Yulan knew she had much more work to do on the project for Paul if it were to be fully completed, but she also realized that she was running out of time. This pressure was reflected in her eyes, which filled as John talked through the activities with her. Although her reserve and her pride kept her from crying, it was the most emotion Yulan showed at any time other than when she spoke of her daughter. John finally ended the meeting by suggesting that she work on the scheduling project until she and Paul thought that his team could take over her portion and complete it. John agreed to set up a three-way meeting as soon as Yulan thought she had progressed sufficiently to pass on her work to Paul and his assistants.

Two weeks later they had such a meeting in Paul Horn's office. Prior to the meeting John had described to Paul the pressures Yulan was under and the approach he had suggested. In the meeting he summarized the issues and asked Yulan to describe the status of her work up to that point. She did so and indicated that she was not happy to stop then. She realized more testing and debugging was needed, but just didn't have enough time. Paul indicated that if Yulan were to provide briefings to his assistant and to the project member with whom Yulan had worked most closely, they would probably be able to complete the work. He pointed out that she would still be available if questions or problems emerged during the final stages. Although all three recognized that it was not the ideal solution, they also seemed to agree that it was practical.

The discussion included Paul's plan to include the work in the company's presentation for the upcoming trade show on decision support systems. It seemed clear to John that this had been the plan from the beginning, but he also noted that Yulan and Paul had difficulty in understanding each other throughout the meeting. Their accents seemed impenetrable to each other and John had found himself translating several times during the meeting. He had been surprised in the meeting that neither Yulan nor Paul had acknowledged their difficulty. Several times he noticed Yulan's blankness at Paul's comments, but Paul only tended to repeat his comments when this happened. Similarly, he spotted Paul's puzzlement at Yulan's pronunciation, but she seemed oblivious to his inability to understand her. So John intervened by testing their understanding and rephrasing and repeating their comments until they each indicated comprehension. The incident dissolved in his memory when, soon after this meeting with Paul, Yulan put on such an impressive display of her work. He had also heard from both Paul and Lindsay that Yulan had conducted a similarly successful demonstration for the scheduling manager of the client hospital. The health administrator had spotted one or two problems in the algorithms and had requested some color changes in the graphic displays, but had been overwhelmingly positive in her reaction to the work and to its potential for scheduling nurses. Although Paul and Lindsay independently had reported the enthusiasm of the hospital administrator to John, they also both had noted that Yulan had not seemed satisfied with her presentation. Each told John of Yulan's denials when they had commented on the success of the presentation. Each had been puzzled by her apparent dismissal of their genuine compliments. Paul had reported with a combination of annoyance and puzzlement that Yulan had abruptly cut him off with an "I don't think so!" when he had observed that her presentation had gone very well. Again, John recalled these comments which only now seemed significant, even though he wasn't at all sure how to interpret them.

Other Concurrent Events

Between January and April two other events occurred which John thought influenced what was going on between Paul and Yulan. First, an additional expert and the first two computer graduates had arrived at Software in early January. Although their presence provided instant relief for Yulan's loneliness, complications about financing arrangements and housing had arisen. John held a series of meetings to explain the budgets in greater detail and to work out equitable financial arrangements to cover furniture purchases and rental fees now that Yulan had been joined by another woman who was sharing the apartment. Although he tried hard to be fair, there was no question that Yulan had borne a disproportionate amount of financial burden by being the first visitor and by living alone for the first few months. Another possible inequity might have been that the new graduates were provided the same monthly stipends as the older, more experienced visitors. John wasn't sure how this was perceived, but thought that it might have irritated Yulan.

However, a series of abrasive exchanges between Yulan and John left no ambiguities as to her feelings. In a meeting with John many months earlier, Yulan had expressed an interest in visiting the University of Waterloo, which she knew to be a world leader in computers. By March, she held a firm opinion that John had guaranteed a two-month visit at the University of Waterloo. But John distinctly recalled only promising to try to arrange such a visit and recalled the duration as being much more open-ended, more like "one or two months." He was sure about only saying he would attempt to arrange a visit, because he had no close friends there and was uncertain of the faculty's willingness to spend time with Yulan. But when these differences in perceptions surfaced, Yulan was adamant about her view being accurate and was very angry with John, even when he repeated that he would do his best to help. At one point in their discussions the exchange got quite heated. John understood how such a misunderstanding could occur, but was baffled at Yulan's anger and at her apparent lack of appreciation of John's point of view or his willingness to attempt to set up the visit.

After this incident they had had an even more explosive disagreement over the funding of Yulan's intended Montreal and Ottawa trips. Several significant budget overruns had occurred and John felt as if he had given in on many items. So when Yulan pressed him to cover all expenses for these visits he balked and then added some conditions to which she reacted with extreme displeasure. At one point they were shouting at each other and both took some time to recover their composure. The amount at stake was not large, but John saw the principles and precedents as critical. Similarly, from Yulan's point of view, she felt strongly that her understanding of the agreement was being violated, so she too felt it to be a matter of principle. Neither had had much ability to see the other's perspective and it remained the single point of unresolved rancor during the nine months. So John wondered if this had any bearing on Yulan's erasing the disk. "Perhaps," he thought, "Paul is paying for my sins!" But as he puzzled about the possible connection, he doubted its relevance. His experience with Yulan suggested that she was inclined to be direct on such matters, at least with him. Still, he had prevailed regarding the funding and reporting arrangements for the visits, so the possibility remained that she was displacing her anger onto Paul. Even if this were the case, John wasn't sure how it would help him to deal with the current problem.

The Impasse

Paul had discovered that Yulan had erased all traces of her program from the system disks when he had sent his young assistant to Yulan's cubicle to pick up the program and to be briefed on the project. This was part of the previous agreement that Paul would manage the necessary follow-up and completion of the work which Yulan had done. Yulan had refused to give the program to Paul's assistant. When Paul subsequently met with Yulan he learned she had taken a copy of it and erased the original. She said she wanted a guarantee that Paul would credit her work and have the presentation made at the trade fair. When Paul demurred and said that he wanted to have a successful display at the trade fair as much as she, but that he couldn't promise it would be accepted, Yulan became even more insistent. She defended her actions by stating several times that the programming was her work, and as such she had the right to do anything she wanted with it. Paul reminded her with some force that his earlier efforts had secured the equipment, his project team had supplied the briefings, and that he and his team members had worked with her during the writing of the program. He added that it had been his negotiating skill and his reputation which had secured the license for the software. Their exchange had deteriorated to an impasse shortly before Paul had run into John in the hallway. Shortly afterwards, Paul sent the memo in Exhibit 1 to Yulan.

After his secretary read the memo to him by telephone, John called Lindsay. Lindsay confirmed Yulan's refusal to respond to Paul or to his memo until she met with John. But Lindsay also added that in her view Yulan was also annoyed at Paul's claim that the research was a joint, cooperative effort and was offended at the implication in his memo that she would violate the copyright or licensing arrangements. In conversations with Lindsay, Yulan had repeatedly referred to the long hours of extra work on nights and weekends. She noted that she had done so even without the possibility of bonuses the others would likely receive if the project was successful. She seemed adamant about her position.

From his conversations with Paul he knew, too, that Yulan's work was important to the project. Although it would be possible to reconstruct the programming for the model, it would take three or four months and critical deadlines would be missed. Of importance, too, was the fact Paul had planned on showing the evolution of the ideas and programming as part of the trade show in July. It was there that the package would receive the critical exposure it needed for commercial success.

John knew he had to act before too long, since Yulan would soon be leaving for her three-week management course. Paul's project and trade fair deadlines loomed as additional pressures to act soon. John also knew that the future of the P.R.C. Cooperation project would also be seriously threatened if the problem were not solved. He even wondered if he should threaten to pull the plug on Software's China activity as a way to indicate the gravity of the situation to Yulan. John felt intense loyalty to Paul and appreciated his willingness to have Yulan join his team. At the same time he felt personally committed to the P.R.C. activity and to Yulan's success as the first visitor. He wanted very much to see the collaborative effort between Yulan and Paul yield the rich results which up until a few days ago had looked so promising. From his perspective, neither party could have done what had been done without the other, and the best results could only be obtained by getting this impasse resolved in a cooperative way.

"How to do it?" was the question which confronted him now. "That's what I'm paid for," John thought, as he turned his attention to framing the approaches he should consider in order to make a decision and plan its implementation.

EXHIBIT 1
SOFTWARE

Paul's Memo to Yulan
Software Internal Memorandum

DATE: May 8
TO: Yulan Sun
FROM: Paul Horn
SUBJECT: Your VI Model for Nurse Scheduling

Following our conversation on May 6, I think it advisable to lay out my expectations in writing.

First, let me congratulate you on the OPTIK Visual Interactive (VI) Nurse Scheduling model that you have written during your stay at Software. This model represents a useful initial step towards a VI decision support system to address this important and difficult problem. I'm sure, however, that you recognize that the work is still incomplete. In particular, the system does not meet the needs of the manager and further development and testing must take place to prove both the approach and the model.

To continue development of this model, we require the source code (program) that you have developed. While there is no question that the program itself is your work, let me remind you that the project idea was mine, I provided the team of people already experienced with the SAGE equipment and OPTIK software and Software's goodwill secured the cooperation of Ms. McLeod at the Hospital. Further, we worked together during your writing of the program and you used Software's computers and the OPTIK software licensed to the company through me. In short, there is a substantial investment of Software's resources and my time in your program. I, THEREFORE, EXPECT YOU TO PROVIDE US WITH A COMPLETE VERSION OF THE SOURCE CODE FOR THIS MODEL.

EXHIBIT 1 (continued)

I further expect that, when we have completed this work, (hopefully later this summer) a decent presentation for the trade show will result. Your contribution to this work will be recognized in this presentation. Of course, it is not possible TODAY to guarantee that this presentation will be ready or will be accepted by the trade show—technical or managerial problems could still occur since considerable work remains to be done.

Finally, I restate our agreement concerning the OPTIK software. This is a valuable, privately-owned commercial product which we use under license. You must not take away from Software any OPTIK manuals, copies of any manuals, any machine readable OPTIK programs, subroutines or floppy disks or ANY LISTINGS OF OPTIK PROGRAMS OR SUBROUTINES.

We are now upgrading the operating system on the SAGE IV to the new version. The object program that you left on the SAGE will not run after this upgrade. Further, any floppies written under the old OS are not readable under the new OS.

It is, therefore, imperative that we have THE SOURCE CODE FOR YOUR MODEL BY FRIDAY, MAY 10. We can then down load it to our mainframe using the existing OS and reload it to the SAGE under the new OS.

I look forward to your cooperation in providing this program.

PH:lm
c. John Stevens

SUPERIOR SHIRT COMPANY (A)*

James C. Rush and Eileen D. Watson

Tony Barnard, district sales representative for the Superior Shirt Company, was on his way to Lancer's Menswear Store in Peterborough. He was about to make his first sales presentation of Superior's new line of spring and summer sport shirts to the store owner, Fred Lancer, and his son Rick. As he wheeled his late-model station wagon into Lancer's parking lot, Tony wondered how Fred and Rick would react to his presentation. Would his sales results show any improvement over the old approach? And would his boss, VP Sales Hal Ebert, be satisfied that the latest policy changes were producing desired results?

The Superior Shirt Company

Superior was a well-established clothing firm which specialized in manufacturing three types of men's shirts:

- Dress shirts — "Superior" label, known for reliable fit, dependable quality, and middle-of-the-road prices (retail prices $28 to $40);
- Sport shirts — "Superior" ($25 to $35), "Topper" ($35 to $45), and "Gentry" ($45 and up) labels; and
- Coordinates — two lines of "mod" casual shirts and sweaters, recently introduced under the "Boris Romanov" ($60 and up) and "Personal Best" ($80 and up) labels.

Superior Shirt Company employed approximately 25 salespersons, each representing either the dress and sport shirt lines or the relatively new line of coordinates to a broad range of customers, including single-owner rural general stores, large urban independents, and department stores. The Superior

---

*All names and locations in this case have been changed.

dress shirt market was well established. Following a twice-yearly presentation of the upcoming dress shirt lines, sales reps simply counted and filled depleted dress shirt stocks once every month or six weeks. By contrast, the sportswear market was, with a few exceptions, spotty and undependable. The new coordinates were rapidly gaining in popularity, registering significant sales increases with each new season.

Until the previous year, Superior Shirt sales representatives for dress shirts and sportswear had sold both types together during the same sales presentation, with generally unsatisfactory results for sport shirt sales. Buyers complained about the length of the presentations; after two hours of viewing and ordering their dress shirt selections, they "turned off." They weren't interested in sitting through another two-hour presentation, so gave scant attention to Superior's new sportswear lines.

Hal Ebert, Superior's VP Sales, remarked, "Our volume in men's casual shirts is a drop in the bucket to what we used to do, and what we can do . . . yet I saw recently, in a 25 year old magazine published for Superior Shirt, something about 'our major thrust this year is to make new inroads in sportswear.' Some things never change!"

In a bid to improve sportswear sales, Hal decided to introduce a policy change. Sport shirts and dress shirts would be sold separately — sportswear in July and August, dress shirts in September. He told Superior Shirt salespeople,

> I expect greatly improved leisure wear sales volumes this year. We have a meaningful new line, and I know you'll experience a lot of pleasure selling it. Separating dress shirt presentations from sport shirt presentations should find our buyers in a much more receptive mood. You can be genuinely enthusiastic about what we're offering. Also, keep in mind the need to educate retail buyers away from their usual focus on market share, to understanding Superior's contribution to their bottom line performance. We're ahead of the competition in that area.
>
> It's time for Superior to regain sportswear sales lost in the last few years. An expanded urban and rural distribution will permit us to increase the production budget next season. And I don't have to remind you that better volumes will be reflected in substantial increases in your incomes! Forget the decreasing number of retail outlets, the increasing competition, all the negative factors. Concentrate on improved sales, which will be good for *everybody*!

Tony Barnard, Salesperson

A well-groomed, youthful-appearing man in his mid-thirties, Tony Barnard had joined the sales department at Superior Shirt immediately after college graduation. Tony started off on the order desk, and worked his way up through various positions until he became district sales representative in the western district. He moved to the eastern district, selling dress shirts and sportswear in a territory which included 55 independents and nine department stores.

Tony's office was located in his large, comfortable Peterborough home in a suburban area close to the school attended by his four young children. He liked most aspects of the Peterborough location:

> From a business point of view, the eastern territory's about the same as any other territory — maybe slightly better, when you're in the clothing business, because many people here are clothes-conscious, especially in urban areas. If I look at it from a personal point of view, Peterborough's a gorgeous place to live and raise my family. It's ideal in so many ways.

Describing the customers in his district, Tony said,

> I classify my customers as two types of accounts. There are those in the rural areas, mostly owners, and those in the major centers. We've done fantastic business with the rural buyers, both in dress and in sport, because of the way the lines were structured — we had what they were looking for. But in the major centers where people are more fashion conscious, they're looking for something different. We don't seem to have captured those people.

Before calling on Lancer's Menswear with Superior's sportswear samples for the upcoming spring season, Tony talked about his reaction to the company's new sales presentation policy:

> I'm really pleased that we're trying something new this year with the sportswear line. In past years we've taken our casual wear out in September alongside of our dress shirts. I would take a display room for my samples in a hotel, and run appointments for all my customers from that area, from eight o'clock in the morning until about midnight. Some of our buying sessions have run five hours... easily five hours. But when buyers come in to buy our line and it takes such a long time to work it, they kind of lose their concentration. Once a buyer's been sitting there for two hours, I think I'll lose whatever I bring out after the second or third hour. This way, I should be able to keep their attention throughout the entire presentation... and increase sales, of course.
>
> This season, we probably can do sport shirts in two hours, saving the dress shirts for a later date. It's such a hectic time of year — we're trying to beat the competition, who seem to be coming out with their lines earlier and earlier. With fewer retail outlets every year, and the growing competition, we've got to be aggressive. But we're not only competing with the competition, we're also competing with our own sales staff — the company has purchased only a limited stock, and once a number sells out, it's gone!
>
> Because we're coming out early, we'll do the presentations for our best customers right at their store locations, instead of in hotel display rooms. And Lancer's Menswear of Peterborough is our first appointment. In the past, Fred Lancer and other buyers really haven't looked at Superior as a sport shirt house. The last couple of seasons I think our image has started to change — we've put out a few items that have knocked them dead! At least, in certain parts of our sportswear... there is still a lot lacking.

Driving the few blocks from his home to the recently constructed mall location of Lancer's store, Tony thought about the store, its people, and the upcoming sales session:

Lancer's is an amazing business! From the little corner store started by Fred's dad in the early 1930s, it's now a million dollar operation. Lancer's is the biggest single account in eastern for many sales reps. It has the largest volume per square foot of any independently owned men's clothing store in the country. With 50 employees in addition to family members, Fred's dad still comes to the store daily and mingles with customers. He often talks about his grandchildren, who work there part-time, and says, "I'm proud of what we've done here, and I'm proud of the family."

I guess they had a rough time in the early years, but the business grew steadily because of the owner's uncompromising philosophy of giving excellent personalized service. His son Fred joined the firm about 20 years ago, and they've just brought in Fred's son Rick — the one with the MBA. Because Lancer's is a family business, they like to see the young family members coming in and taking on the major responsibility. The work is shared — if something has to be done, they'll all pitch in. Obviously Fred would like to spend more time on the golf course . . . but when it comes to retirement, none of us in this business seems to know when to quit. There are sales reps on the road who have been at it for 40 or 50 years, and they are still on the road. And there are long-term retailers who are still holding on to their businesses. It becomes a way of life. But when Fred can see that the business is running smoothly, then I think he might step back . . . but never completely out!

Fred will be doing the buying today, together with his son Rick. However, Rick is a young fellow who really hasn't been exposed to the buying process of the business yet, so my presentation will be made mainly to Fred. I'll show the complete spectrum of Superior sportswear, in the small sampling room they built in the basement of their new store. Fred made room for an in-store sample room because it's such a busy store that he finds it difficult to get out to a hotel display room. I'll show him samples of the new leisure wear line, along with swatches.

I think I'm at the point now in my rapport with most customers that they place a lot of trust in me and in what I think is going to sell — even to my establishing quantities with them. You get this more in the rural territories — they place a lot of faith in sales reps, and there are some who take advantage of it . . . but the bad apples don't normally last long. With this territory I have gotten to know the owners fairly well; so I can quite accurately predict where they're going to go, and I can lead them pretty well into what is selling and what is not.

But other than our popular Suprablend and our old standby flannel shirts, Superior Shirt hasn't previously had a casual line we could sell to the metropolitan customers — that's where we can make some inroads this year. This time around, the company's telling us that they've injected more color into the line. I think they're trying different fabrications. The biggest problem for us is getting over the retailer's mental block — "Superior" means "dress shirt." The average consumer thinks the same way, too.

I'll mention the spring advertising campaign Superior will be mounting — 30-second TV spots, selling sportswear in a very different way from the past. But I wish they had delivered the colored posters they promised, showing the complete look for this year, in time for my presentation at Lancer's today. Well, I'll have to influence their thinking by what I say and do...I am my only sales aid!

Being one of the owners, Fred is always looking at profit. He's always looking at how much money he can actually make on each item. This Lancer's account has changed in the last couple of seasons, because Fred has only just come back to do the buying. Prior to this, he was out of the buying function, by choice. However, the other fellow who was doing the buying left to open up his own store, which forced Fred back into that function. But eventually I think Fred wants to get out of buying and have his young sons take it over. He'd like to be able to sit back and concentrate on other things.

I enjoy selling to Fred. Aside from the department stores in my district, Lancer's is my biggest account. Fred is sharp and professional. He always lets me know, very directly, how he's reacting to what he sees. And his son is learning fast — he's bright and responsible.

I know that Fred has already booked sportswear with some competitors. I have a pretty good idea what direction he's going in, and where he's putting most of his emphasis — Lancer's Menswear expects certain companies to provide certain looks. I'm putting the line together today, and I'm excited...firstly, because of the fact we are coming out early, and I believe in that. Secondly, Fred and Rick will be able to concentrate on the sportswear line; and thirdly, I think there are some nice looks in the line. I haven't had enough time to really analyze it, but I see a lot of interesting things in the new line — we should have a good season.

Fred Lancer, Owner/Buyer

In his luxurious office tastefully furnished in shades of grey and burgundy, Fred Lancer completed a business call, adjusted the volume of soothing background music, and glanced at his watch. A distinguished-looking man in his mid-50s, Fred was an impressive embodiment of "what the best-dressed business man should wear." He thought:

I've a dozen things to do right now, but I don't want to keep Tony waiting too long for today's appointment...even though it's the same story every year. When a new line is introduced, every salesperson has been told by his or her principals that this year's is the greatest line ever produced by their particular company! I assume that Hal Ebert, and probably the Superior president as well, have given their sales reps a very high level of motivation. Tony will be full of enthusiasm!

Superior shirts are primarily noted for being, in my opinion, a dress shirt line. Superior has its greatest power as a dress shirt line — people will come in here and ask for a Superior shirt, a dress shirt. They do not come in and ask for a Superior sport shirt *per se*, although we're getting some call for the Suprablend, because the fabric is exceptional, and it has had good advertising and exposure for six or seven years. That's a lot longer than some products Superior has brought out in the past — introduced with great hype one year, gone the next.

What's new this year, thanks to the decision-making wisdom of the Superior people, is the division of the placing season into two sessions, one for sportswear and one for dress wear. Normally, we'd sit through Tony's presentation of the dress shirts, after which he'd start to show us the sport shirt lines — but by then, we'd be so tired we wouldn't feel like even watching. So because of that change, I think Superior will probably sell more sportswear...just because of that.

And probably the most important aspect to a retailer is markup. Of course, we've got to like the product; but providing that we do like the product, markup is extremely important for big retailers. Especially with rising expenses of staff and whatever, markup is the only salvation of such a company as ours.

It'll be interesting to hear Tony's story. Compared to other sales reps we see, his presentations rank in the high average. He's a quality presenter, always carries himself with dignity. There are some very talentless people who are trying to sell some good products; there are some very talented people trying to sell some poor products; and there's everything in between — we get them all. Tony is a talented, knowledgeable one...he's not going to stay here long. My best guess is that Tony will probably be moved up into more important decision-making positions with Superior Shirt, as most of the good ones are.

I always keep Lancer's customers in mind when I'm buying. Before our most recent expansion, our typical customer was the established, mature man. I think we have a very good hold of the older men's market in Peterborough, due more to our size than anything else, and for this marketplace, we're over-selling. But with the advent of our Young Men's Shop, we're reaching the youth — the fast-track, rock-and-roller types. We're now capturing a cross-section of the entire male spending population of Peterborough and district. That's really exciting! And we've also introduced a section that deals exclusively with the high end of the spectrum — the $600 suit, the $70 dress shirt, the $40 tie.

Men are the main buyers of our shirts, but men and women usually come together to our store — men rarely shop alone, as women do. In most cases, the woman accompanies the man whether he's buying dress wear or casual wear. She seems to be the great guider. We have to sell to both. The customer today is absolutely bombarded with ticket shock. Even Superior shirts today are $28 and up! Whatever happened to the $10 shirt? A lot of people haven't bought a shirt since the price was $10 — men are very funny that way. Women are a little bit more attuned to what's happening. But men can't fathom some of today's price points.

Rick Lancer, Son/Employee

Twenty-six years old, dressed in tailored slacks and color-coordinated shirt, tie, sweater, and jacket, Rick Lancer hurried downstairs to the sample room. He thought about the presentation to come, and about the implications for himself, "the son as learner."

My father is a very dominant buyer, and he dominates every meeting. He has an incredibly vast knowledge of the market — he knows Peterborough and the mens-wear market completely. Basically, the Superior line deals with gentlemen's fit, gentlemen's cut; and as far as knowing what elderly men and the mainline people want, my knowledge of that market is very limited. I'm just starting out, but I'm learning fast. My father has always gone on a gut feeling about what he feels is going to sell. That's the way he buys. There is really no budget that he sets for himself — if he sees something that he likes, he's going to buy it. Sometimes he's wrong, but most of the time he's right.

We have a very good rapport with Tony, which has been built up through the years. There isn't a nicer guy on the road. He's honest, and tries to be up-front with you — if there's something that isn't selling, he'll tell you, "I didn't do so well with that one." And he tries to keep things in their proper perspective . . . yet he is a sales rep. As good a friend as Tony is to us, he's still only a sales rep, and even though he's a nice guy, we're the ones who have to sell the product when it leaves his hands. Sales reps on the road always say, "This is the sharpest, freshest, best line we've ever had!" We chuckle inwardly, and always ask ourselves, "Well, is that line going to go for us?" In my experience with sales reps, you've got to decipher that approach right away, because they all use it.

Superior is a very important name for Lancer's of Peterborough. The name Superior is number one for us, as far as dress shirts go. It's for the particular customer who is not willing to spend a lot of money — he's looking for something that is not the cheapest price, but not the most expensive . . . something right down the middle that really hits home. The Superior line is basic, like baseball and apple pie. It is the same thing each year. They may introduce some new colors, some different patterns, some slightly different styles. But basically it's for the customer who doesn't like changes. For the customer who, if he buys a Superior shirt this year, he'll come back and buy a Superior shirt again next year. It doesn't vary in its fit. It's as "solid as Sears," as they say.

There's nothing different with Superior, whereas, when you're dealing with high fashion, there are different things coming five times a year! For the customer coming into our Young Men's Shop, we have to ask, "Is that line going to be different enough?" The Young Men's Shop customer wants to see something different every time. I don't want to see that customer walking down the street with the same shirt that I've got on. Whereas mainline customers just want to have something comfortable, that looks nice, and is dependable and washable.

From my point of view, coordinated color packages of more than one item are the most sellable. A shirt can be sold more easily with a coordinating pant or sweater than all on its own . . . I wonder what Superior has to offer, this time?

The Sales Presentation

Tony and Rick chatted quietly as they waited in the downstairs sample room for Fred to arrive. Tony had previously arranged a large display of sports shirts (approximately six dozen, each attractively exhibited on its own hanger) on a long rack at one end of a huge display table. Two smaller racks stood empty at the other end of the table. Tony quietly moved about behind the display table, readying his sample cases of packaged shirts for the presentation to come. He had removed his jacket, and was wearing a closely-fitting shirt, muted blue-patterned tie, and blue trousers. He joked with Rick about having forgotten to bring the shirt he had intended to wear, and so had been forced to put on an old knock-about number—an ironic twist of luck, for a shirt sales rep!

Fred entered swiftly, with apologies for lateness, and sat down beside his son. Standing on the opposite side of the display table, one hand behind his back and appearing quietly confident, Tony began immediately: "Before I take you through the line, I'll explain the new pricing structure. This year, we're giving a 58 percent markup—two percent better than last year. That's 56 percent plus two percent advertising—I know you'll be pleased with that!"

Tony began showing the spring line, three or four to a dozen shirts at a time, beginning with the shirts on the rack. He presented the shirts by taking them off the rack to his right, and laying them out carefully in color groups on the long table. Then Fred (closely watched by his son) quickly chose those from each group that he wanted to consider later. His choices were removed and hung by Tony on the empty racks to his left; the rejects were returned to their original place.

Tony constantly drew the buyers' attention to new features and trends: "In the striping end of it, notice the famous maker influence here. Notice the open collar, great colors, new patterns. Very sellable!... Youth is going to wovens, not knits. The knits are still going to gentlemen."

(Interruption—Fred was needed in the main office, and left the room. Tony continued briefly with Rick, then sat down and waited for Fred's return.)

Fred returned in a few minutes, and Tony resumed his presentation. He responded directly to all questions about details of price points and markup, Superior's involvement in and support of Lancer's advertising programs, and fine points of product manufacture, fit, color, fabric, and so on. For example:

Fred   Do you have a good program in Oversize? Competing lines have good Oversize programs.

Tony   Yes. I'll show you our cards with the fabric swatches. You'll see they're all available in Oversize.

Fred   About sizing—exactly how big are Superior's Tall and Oversize? And what's the range of Oversize? And Stout?

(Tony quickly brought out reference books and read aloud the specs for sizing.)

Fred   I wonder what the rate of success is with this lay-down collar?

Tony   We had great success last year with that collar.

Fred   What about Suprablend? I hope you still have that line.

Tony   Yes. They continue to be very popular.

Tony   (*Approximately 15 minutes into the presentation*)   We're changing our focus from sportswear to casual wear, which better describes our new image. You'll notice a brighter label, and the packaging will change. And what we've done with the Suprablend fabric is to provide new contrasting colors. Blue is an important color this year.

Fred Nice! These are some wild colors. But positive!

Tony I've never been so enthusiastic about a line — and you haven't seen anything, yet!

(Interruption again — store employee talking with Fred. Tony moved some shirts off the table, then sat down quietly, waiting for Fred's attention.)

Fred (*Returning after brief exit*) I'm always excited about the Suprablend.

Tony You're always excited about the Suprablend . . .

(Another interruption — store employee conversing with Fred re advertising plans. Tony sat down again, talking with Rick about fabrics: "60 percent cotton, 40 percent poly is this year's success story. And the really different looks for next season are in 100 percent cotton — the 'bells and whistles!' ")

Fred (*Attentive again, reacting to Tony's presentation of a line of patterned shirts*) Are those the only colors?

Tony What you see is what we own!

Fred chose five patterned shirts — three whites, a grey, and a yellow. He rejected all shades of blue.

Tony (*Holding out a teal-blue shirt for Fred to see*) What about a blue?

Arranging and rearranging his choices, Fred made no reply. He stayed with his original color choices. Tony next introduced a colorful new line of 100 percent cotton shirts.

Fred I can't say I like that cotton line — it's just not exciting. And the $40 price point for 100 percent cotton, the Superior "Cadillac" . . . the label doesn't warrant it. Customers for that price want the horsey! [Polo] Also, last year we had far too many lines at that price point — five manufacturers. They all started to look alike!

By this time, Fred had chosen 16 shirts. With fresh enthusiasm, Tony introduced the "Singing Sands" line, touting their past success and popular price point of $26 to $28, depending on collar style.

Fred We're buying according to color now, not according to collar style.

(Another interruption — Fred took an urgent call on the phone in the display room.)

Tony (*Talking to Rick*) Coming up is a group for the youthful market — very appropriate for your Young Men's Shop. I wish I had our merchandising materials with me, but the portfolio photos weren't ready in time for this presentation. They show some great lifestyle illustrations, to create that image of Superior as quality, dressier leisure wear for the young professional group.

His telephone call completed, Fred rapidly chose a few shirts from the selection on the table.

Tony　Tell me what you're thinking so far. Give me some feedback.

Fred　I'm seeing nice colors, some sellable patterns, some fabrication differences.

Tony next presented a colorful, youthful Superior line:

Tony　Notice the texture...these are suitable for the Young Men's Shop.

Fred　The open weave makes sense. These are good...

Tony　We consider these mesh.

Fred　We like to be able to give customers a story along with good color preference. Suprablend and mesh have a story.

Tony　Look at these two novelty Hawaiian shirts — they're selling like crazy to university kids in Kingston!

Rick　I just couldn't sell the Superior label in the Young Men's Shop. But I could sell the Topper label...

Tony　Everybody knows Superior — quality, fit...

Rick　Youth wants style, and Superior has the reputation of being Mr. Straightline. We can sell Superior in the mainline business.

Tony　To get you by this line...I'll talk about Topper. It's just gorgeous! I think this shirt will sell. I like it very much.

Rick　You've got good taste, you dress fashionably — but these will sell mainline.

Fred　What else are you selling? And why not double up on the tissue paper? Customers buying in the higher range expect the sound and plushness of a thick tissue paper handle. They shouldn't feel the cardboard.

Tony produced from a sample case a different group of 100 percent cotton plaid sports shirts. He lovingly placed each on the display table: "Notice the beautiful styling. And the colors are perfect."

Fred　That's nice!

Tony　Now do those look like traditional Superior shirts?

(Fred to son — "We have already ordered similar shirts, sold with coordinating pants..." Fred quickly chose three of the group.)

Tony　(*Showing samples of the Gentry label*) More 100 percent cotton, lighter weights. Feel the handle on that — we're doing exactly what you mentioned! And the focus here is on color. You're looking at color, quality, and style.

Fred We're obligated to four other groups. Before making our selection of at-random shirts, we need to select color dyed-to-match...

Tony *(Sitting)* Let me understand what you're saying. Gant and Polo dye pants and shirts to match. Boris Romanov and Personal Best put out sweater-shirt coordinates...

Fred I can sell the Gant program very easily, pants and shirts. And Gant shirts are about $10 less than Gentry. It's difficult to sell a $45 shirt alone — there's more flexibility with a $35 shirt. Superior Shirt has more clout, yet pricier shirts must have meaning...

Tony I advise you to book today — these won't be available for long. Don't wait until after you've seen Polo.... *(Showing next group)* This is where you want to be! *(Holding out a blue stripe on white cotton/ polyester blend)* Notice that in this group, all eight are in different fabrics. We've gone for texture and color, to capture a brand-new look.

Fred *(Eliminating and choosing certain patterns and colors.)* All one price, huh?

As Fred eliminated one shirt, a muted stripe, brown on beige, Tony exclaimed, "That's my favorite!" Rick responded, "Not for us..."

Fred You've saved all the good stuff for last. Is there anything else you want to show us?

Tony That's it. We're done.

Rick What, no Superior pant?

Tony began writing Lancer's order. With his son attentively watching, Fred made quick choices of colors and sizes from the shirts previously selected, calling out the style number on the card attached to each shirt and stating the number of units of each size and color he was ordering. Tony rapidly noted these details in his order book. Fred arranged and rearranged packaged shirts to see how they'd look together on a store shelf; and he also paid close attention to how these choices would coordinate colorwise with his selection of shirts on hangers. He consulted Rick occasionally about color.

Fred *(About one model)* Teal or blue?

Rick If I were buying for the Young Men's Shop, I'd choose teal. But for the gentlemen's line, I'd choose blue. *(Volunteering about one shirt)* That's a terrible color — the beige is too pinkish.

Fred What about the brights, Rick?

Rick The brights are a harder sell.

Fred Soft shades sell much nicer.

Tony *(Trying to influence buyers to order the rejected beige color)* Not one beige? That color has sold before...

Fred   It's an awful color!

Rick   That pale turquoise is a great color.

Tony   Bright blue would be good with a khaki pant...

Fred   *(Reducing his selection of mesh shirts by three)*   I have too many mesh. *(Referring to the Suprablend line)*   This is a basic shirt. You fill in the columns with the usual order, Tony. You know what we want...

As Fred quickly and decisively made his choices, Tony remained alert and attentive, quietly suggesting additions. Rick occasionally asked his father about his reasons for a certain order. The final order totalled 70 dozen shirts, two dozen more than the previous year. Tony noticed that Fred's choices of styles and colors were approximately the same as last year's.

Two hours had elapsed from beginning to end of the sales presentation. As Fred and Rick prepared to leave, Tony thanked father and son for their order, and briefly discussed delivery details. He added, "I'll be upstairs in a few minutes to fill out your Superior dress shirt inventory, just as soon as I put these samples back in my car."

On his way out of the display room, Fred noticed a discarded shirt at one end of the table. He exclaimed, "This is the famous shirt we didn't buy — the striped one Tony was pushing!"

CARIBBEAN SUGAR MACHINERY LTD. (A-1)*
(Ron's View of a Workgroup in Conflict)

Joseph J. DiStefano

Ron Moore and his "policy group" of students at the business school faced a serious problem. It was near the end of the first term and the critical report for Business Policy, the only required course in the senior year, seemed in jeopardy because of interpersonal conflicts within the group.

The policy report required a group to study an on-going company and prepare a note on the industry involved, a case on the company and an analysis of the company's situation, together with a set of policy recommendations for its future. This complex task necessitated not only long hours of hard work, but also significant cooperation and teamwork within the group. As Ron reflected on the past several weeks of growing friction, he wondered what realistic alternatives existed for the group. Knowing that they would soon be meeting with Professor Forsyth in an attempt to resolve the last blow-up, he realized that a workable solution was needed if they were to meet the project deadline in late February.

Background of the Group

Late in September (in Ron's words "when stragglers rush to find a policy group"), Ron Moore asked four classmates if he could join their group. Joe, Ian, Alice and Stan had already begun discussions with Carling Breweries. By mid-October the group received a negative reply from Carling management, who stated that a professor was going to do a case study on the company. Stan was the most upset in the group since, as Carling's campus representative, he had felt assured that there would be no problems in securing the company's cooperation.

Now the scramble was on to find another firm. Ron saw it as an opportunity to suggest Caribbean Sugar Machinery Limited (CSM) which his father had

---

*All names in this case have been disguised.

started ten years previously. CSM was one of ten companies the group considered. Earlier during the summer Ron and his father had discussed the possibility of using CSM as a policy company. Mr. Moore's reaction had been somewhat negative, on the grounds that CSM wasn't a "normal" company. At that time Ron had agreed, realizing that the company locations in Winnipeg and Trinidad would present formidable problems. But now, if CSM were to be a serious possibility, Ron felt it necessary to convince his father personally that the group could do a useful job for the company at relatively low cost.

Approval from several people would be necessary before starting the project. Initially Alice and Stan expressed more interest in CSM than did either Joe or Ian. It was also necessary for their policy professor to approve the project. Fortunately, Mr. Moore planned a trip to Toronto on October 18 and he suggested that Ron meet him. In giving his approval in principle to the project before Ron went to Toronto, Professor Forsyth expressed some concern about Ron's being the only group member with direct company contact. He was apprehensive that the other members might not be able to participate on an equal footing. Ron felt Professor Forsyth's worry was unnecessary and, in any event, didn't deserve further consideration until his father's approval was secured. Ron's meeting with his father was successful and he returned to London on the following Monday with considerable material about the company.

About the Company

CSM had a revolutionary, patented method for processing sugar cane, which resulted in animal feed and versatile fibre by-products in addition to sugar production. The production process meant that CSM had the potential to operate in the sugar, animal production, pulp and paper, building products, and chemical industries in 75 tropical countries.

At this point in the company's history it had minimal production facilities, top management, market information and sales. The firm was starting to move from an R&D stage to an international marketing and production stage in which yearly sales would be at the multi-million dollar level. Ron was personally convinced that the group could do much useful work for the company.

The Group Makes a Decision

The morning after Ron's return from Toronto, Professor Forsyth gave his approval for the project, provided that the workload and experience were shared equally among the group members. The next day, October 24, all five of the group sat down to pick one of the three possible companies which they had screened from the original ten possibilities. Although all knew Ron's preference, he said he would go along with the majority vote. However, all knew Ron would be a reluctant participant if CSM were not chosen. Stan voiced the group's appreciation for Ron's efforts in securing CSM's cooperation. Ron felt this was Stan's way of saying, "You're forcing us to accept CSM." But Ron didn't respond. He said to himself, "If they feel I've railroaded them, that's their problem. I've worked damn hard to get CSM's agreement, and if I don't weaken my position now, I'll get the majority vote."

The vote came out 3 to 2 with Alice and Stan joining Ron in approving CSM. Ron felt that neither Joe nor Ian were set against CSM, but were hesitant to get involved because Ron would treat the project as a job that had to be done exceptionally well. But since the group had previously agreed to abide by the majority vote, CSM was chosen.

Ron's Views on the Group and Its Members

Ron's initial attitude toward the group was that its members had an above-average ability to reason both facts and opinions. Ian was the exception to this generalization. Last year Ian was designated by their class as the braggart of the year, an appellation Ron felt had been more than adequately earned. But basically he was confident that the group could do the project effectively and efficiently. He felt he could work much better with these four than with highly emotional people who had fixed ideas and refused to budge even in the face of contrary facts.

Ron realized he was entering a group whose members already had established social ties apart from the business school. Alice and Stan had dated during the previous year, were now living together and planned to get married after graduation. In earlier years Stan, Joe and Ian had lived together at Huron College. In addition, all four had worked together in project groups during their junior year, so Ron felt somewhat like an outsider from the beginning, even though he had been with them all in the same section. Of the four, Ron felt closer to Joe and Stan only because he had talked to them more frequently during the previous year. He viewed them both as very amicable with consistent personalities. Although he had heard from others that Alice's stubbornness made her pure hell to work with, he felt no particular apprehension as they started the policy project.

Starting to Work

With approval secured, Ron was very anxious to start organizing and working. By then he had almost finished a set of data sheets for a preliminary marketing study of the 75 countries with which the company would be involved. Ron had undertaken this work on his own initiative late in the summer. Ten years of thinking about CSM's problems plus working on these data sheets gave Ron a good understanding of the company. Since mid-August he had spent at least two or three hours a day thinking about the company, and Ron felt he was in the best position to direct the project group in the initial stages. Aside from the fact that he knew most about the company, Ron also felt much more motivated to do an excellent job. Everyone understood that Ron's higher motivation stemmed from his having more to gain, or to lose, than the others. His father's approval plus a job in April depended on the quality of the report.

October 26 marked the first time the group met to discuss how the project should be approached. Ron was unable to attend, due to a course conflict. He suggested that the others each study the feasibility studies, consultants' reports and data sheets which he had brought to London. He hoped that each would quickly learn as much as possible so they could get down to work.

Mr. Moore's Visit

Mr. Moore came to London to meet with the group early the next week. Before then the importance of the group's meeting Mr. Moore had frequently been raised. This time it was Stan who couldn't attend the meeting. Because Stan had high influence with the other three members and because Ron had good rapport with him, Ron felt Stan's absence was most unfortunate. Ron saw Stan's support as crucial if later Ron needed to persuade the others to his point of view. By missing that meeting Ron felt that Stan would probably rely on Alice's interpretations of what went on rather than on what actually transpired. A tape recorder had been brought to the meeting for Stan's benefit, but it didn't work.

From the outset Alice took the lead in asking Mr. Moore questions. Most were an attempt to discover how much information and time would be available to the group. Ron knew the answers to the questions and had already tried to explain the limitations to the group. He felt that his father's answers supported what he had told them previously.

As Ron drove his father to the airport after the meeting, Mr. Moore remarked that he was quite impressed by Alice and the questions she had asked. Although Ron felt a bit put off by the compliment, he said, "Alice puts all her energy and enthusiasm into everything she does." But privately he felt that his own questions and comments during the meeting had been somewhat more relevant to the project than Alice's.

Drafting the Proposal

At the end of the week of Mr. Moore's visit to London the group met to draft the project proposal. Alice had told Mr. Moore that he would receive a copy of the proposal, including a budget, within ten days. This meeting marked the first major confrontation between Ron and the other four members. Alice assumed the role of group leader by copying down the main points for the proposal. Ron started to get annoyed at the procedure. He wanted to get a framework up on the chalkboard in order to discuss the company's entire operations.

As the discussion progressed Ron saw that the direction of the other four was fundamentally opposed to his ideas. "This won't do," he thought. "I know damn well that I know more about CSM than all of them put together." Each time the other four agreed on a point that Ron disputed, he tried to convince them it was the wrong approach. He raised his voice and used every bit of logic available to him. But he felt as if he were hitting his head against a brick wall — they refused to budge.

In an attempt to gain control over the meeting, Ron then walked up to the chalkboard and wrote down in bold letters, the headings: *marketing*, *finance*, *personnel*, *production*, and *control*. He suggested that the ideas be put under the proper headings for logical discussion. His action went over like a lead balloon, and he was indirectly requested to sit down.

Recollecting this meeting Ron said, "Needless to say, I was mad. The others were annoyed and probably surprised at the way I was acting. Normally I contain my emotions quite well and give others the impression that I have everything under control."

The others responded by saying, "We all realize that you're very deeply involved in this project, but maybe a more unbiased approach is best." By this time Ron was feeling embarrassed by the way he had been acting and agreed to continue with the original approach. He half-heartedly assumed his normal role as a logical, unemotional participant. When the meeting was over, everyone left feeling frustrated and a little shaken by what had happened.

Ron's Apology; Alice's Reaction

After cooling down and thinking over these events, Ron decided that he owed Alice an apology. Whether or not anyone knew it, his blow-up had been directed at her. He wanted to explain to her why he had lost his temper and how he felt about the project.

That same night Ron approached Alice at a business school dance. He told her how seriously he was taking the project and apologized to her for his actions that morning. He added that he realized that she enjoyed playing the leader and was the type who put all her energy in her efforts. "But," he cautioned, "I'll still continue to oppose strongly anyone who tries to lead the project in a direction that I think is wrong. If you continue to attempt leading the group, more meetings like this morning's are inevitable."

Alice appeared uneasy to Ron. But she replied, "Ron, you can't lead unless others are prepared to be led. Furthermore, you shouldn't talk to me alone. If you feel that way, tell the whole group."

Additional Meetings

On the following Wednesday the group met with Professor Forsyth to review the proposal which Alice had typed. Ron didn't think the professor was very impressed, but thought that the proposal was approved because it was general in nature and didn't contradict the conversations held between Mr. Moore and Professor Forsyth. Although Ron felt reservations, it didn't seem worth going over the objectives in the proposal again.

It was at this meeting on November 7 that a suggestion was made that the group go to the University of Guelph, renowned for its agricultural emphasis, to find information on sugar cane. Ron objected since the group hadn't yet discussed information which he had already obtained from the company. But it seemed to Ron as if the decision had already been made. The vote was four to one, and soon afterwards Joe, Ian and Ron went to Guelph.

The next meeting was held at Alice and Stan's apartment on November 13. The purpose of the meeting was to discuss the industry note and to split up the workload. Because of a course conflict Ron arrived late, and the group had already decided that the sugar industry was the one to study. Since discussions concerning the content of the note were well under way and running smoothly, Ron thought it appropriate to assume a low profile. For the first time it appeared that some progress was being made. Ron accepted his portion of the prescribed workload with little disagreement.

It was then that Ron became aware that, unless the conflicts in the group were resolved, he wouldn't achieve his objectives. That night he sat down, thought things over quite carefully and composed a letter in which he expressed his feelings in the best way he could. After typing it up and making four copies, Ron gave two copies to Alice and one each to Joe and Ian (see Exhibit 1). He distributed rough drafts of the data sheets at the same time (Thursday afternoon, November 15).

Tensions Build Anew

During "Happy Hour" in the faculty lounge that same afternoon, Joe and Ron discussed the group. Joe spoke for the others in saying they felt Ron was too involved in the project and was prepared to let his other courses slip. When Joe noted that Alice had told him that Ron had frequently been coming to classes unprepared, Ron became annoyed. He and Alice shared only one course, and Ron could only remember once when he was unprepared to answer questions. He really started to wonder why Alice would say such a thing. It was the first time he consciously recognized that she might be taking the issue of group leadership in a very personal way. Her previous comment about "leading only if others wanted to be led" took on new significance.

The meeting the next day started in a relatively low-key atmosphere. Stan said that he had thought the group had reached a consensus on procedures and objectives for the project. "But," he added, "from the looks of this letter from you, Ron, I was wrong." Ian said that he didn't think the group needed a leader, and Joe added that he just wanted to get on with the work. Both admitted that they weren't prepared to do an excessive amount of work on the project. Ron agreed that their position was most reasonable. Ian and Joe said that they only viewed the project as a course requirement to get finished. If the company obtained any benefit, that would be a nice bonus. Alice didn't say much except that she didn't really think that there was any conflict between her and Ron.

After this discussion they moved to the second item on the agenda, which was discussion of the data sheets Ron had just completed. These consisted of a covering note plus 13 pages of legal-size paper listing possible variables for investigation by the group or by the company at a future date. Exhibit 2 contains the covering note and an outline of the variables covered.

At the previous meeting they had suggested the group spend a few minutes choosing the variables which should be investigated for each of the 75 countries. Alice and Stan had already drawn up a short list of variables to research. Ron didn't think that their list was comprehensive enough, while the others thought Ron's list was too lengthy, too complex and would require too much time to complete. Ron agreed, but said that each variable had to be investigated either by the group or the company. Therefore he thought it was desirable to have a set of data sheets for each country so the blanks could be filled in if any of the members happened to find pertinent information.

The others felt that the cost of printing 75 copies would strain the budget. But Ron countered by saying that he would pay the bill himself if they didn't want to spend the budgeted money for copying. The merits of the data sheets were discussed but no decision was reached. The subject was dropped when it became obvious that Ron was going to have the copies made regardless. The meeting then broke up, and they all went to the library to gather information for the groups of countries which had been allocated to each member.

Frustration, Brainstorm, and Blow-up

By this point Ron was really feeling frustrated. He hadn't been able to direct the efforts of the group. No facts had been assembled, and he felt that they were working on the wrong industry note. To top it all off, the group wasn't enjoying its work. The first term was almost over, and Ron thought the group still didn't know where it was going. With all of these negative feelings, Ron found himself losing an incredible amount of sleep worrying.

One night he had a "brainstorm" in which all the problems facing CSM became clear. He wrote down all the questions that came to his mind. The next day he asked Joe and Stan if they would object if they spent about an hour and a half at the Friday meeting answering the questions he had written out. Neither objected to Ron's request.

After an hour of argument about basic project objectives at the beginning of the November 23 meeting, Ron suggested that some headway might be possible if the group could individually answer his list of questions. He suggested that he read the questions one-by-one and that each spend five minutes writing down his answers or thoughts. He had three reasons for the approach — 1. to get everyone's ideas down quickly, 2. to see how the group was thinking, and 3. to eliminate arguments which would inevitably develop if they discussed the questions. Ron tried to communicate his reasoning, but he felt that his explanations fell on deaf ears.

 He was grudgingly allowed to ask the questions, but the group insisted on discussing each one to eliminate duplication in the written responses. It soon became apparent to Ron that the others were going to let him answer his own questions. He tried to say as little as possible but felt forced to put forth his ideas when no one else contributed. As they went through the questions serially, Stan copied down the answers, Joe remained silent and Ian made occasional comments. Alice and Ron lightly discussed his ideas. Slowly Ron's blood pressure rose.

When there was no response to question 14, Ron laid out several alternative answers. One was immediately discarded by Alice and Ian concurred. Ron asked their reasons and was told, "It just won't work, so let's get on to the next question." Ron argued that the alternative they were rejecting might be useful in certain circumstances, but was again rebuffed with a "No, no. Forget it." With his anger mounting Ron said, "O.K. Let's forget it."

Alice picked up his tone and said, "Don't say that if you don't mean it." Ron leaned forward and gave vent to his anger... "Listen, Alice, I'm getting a little pissed off at your throwing out my ideas after only giving them *that* (snapping his fingers) much thought." Amazed at Ron's outburst, Alice threw her pencil across the room, broke into tears, and ran out of the room saying that they could consider her out of the group.

Ron sat back stunned. Trying to figure out what he had done, he felt about an inch high. "A real male chauvinist pig," he thought, "I've really done it now!"

Joe and Ian left, and Stan and Ron started to talk. Ron was really feeling sorry for what he had done, but couldn't figure out what had provoked such an extreme response in Alice. He had always treated her as "one of the guys" and felt that he would have done exactly what he just did if Alice had been a guy.

Stan told Ron that Alice had really broken down when she had read Ron's "talking paper"... even to the point of thinking about dropping out. She had taken the letter as a personal assault on her by Ron. Since that had hardly been Ron's intention, events seemed to be getting more and more distorted each minute.

As Ron's feelings hit rock bottom, Alice came back into the room to get Stan. Ron apologized for upsetting her, saying that he had never intended to do so. Alice replied that she didn't mind people criticizing her ideas, but that she couldn't take Ron's constant attacks on her personality. Although he knew he

Caribbean Sugar Machinery Ltd. (A-1)

hadn't consciously meant to do so, Ron felt increasing guilt for his behavior. On the verge of tears himself, he tried to make her understand why he had written the letter and why he had lost his temper. It seemed to Ron as if she couldn't or wouldn't believe him. It soon became evident that none of them had any energy left to patch up the hurt feelings. On that note they decided to leave.

The Aftermath

The next week Ron met with three of his professors, including Forsyth, seeking advice and guidance. He really wanted to salvage the group. Professor Forsyth wanted to talk to each of the other group members before discussing the project with the whole group.

On November 30 they all met at Joe's place to discuss the industry note which Stan had been trying to put together from the individual efforts. As he pieced it together it became clear that the whole note was useless. Agreement was reached that CSM was in the sugar machinery and building-board machinery business.

It was also evident that it would be futile to continue if more useful and comprehensive information were not obtained. The group decided right there to call Mr. Moore in Trinidad to see if he could bring to Canada information on the sugar machinery industry. He said he would try, but Ron thought the information would be minimal at best and useless at worst. During the past month Mr. Moore hadn't even contacted the group. In this pessimistic atmosphere, Ian said he might be able to find another company before Christmas.

Ron was disturbed. It was late in the year to start a new project, yet considering recent events the outcome of CSM looked uncertain and relations with Alice and the others were strained. He felt that some thought should be given to specifying the alternatives available to the group and to establishing the preferences of the members before the meeting with Professor Forsyth which they had scheduled for the following Sunday. But Ron wasn't sure what he should do or what was likely to happen.

EXHIBIT 1

CARIBBEAN SUGAR MACHINERY LTD. (A-1)

Talking Papers

November 16

It is my personal feeling that, within our policy group, we have some very basic problems which must be resolved before we can attain our group objectives in an enjoyable manner. Furthermore, I'm not sure whether or not these problems are procedural or personal in nature. The problems which are bothering me now are:

1. Do you feel that I will jeopardize the group's objectives for my own personal objectives? (e.g. Are mine in conflict with yours?)

2. Am I correct in thinking that you do not wish to address questions which inevitably must be answered in the future because the workload may appear to be monumental? (e.g. crossing the bridge when we come to it attitude)

3. What solutions can you suggest to resolve an evident personality or role conflict? (e.g. Alice and myself)

4. What do you feel the objectives of this policy group should be?

I believe that, if we can discuss these questions at the meeting tomorrow, we might be able to avoid the frustrations which we have all experienced in every other meeting.

Sincerely,
Ron

EXHIBIT 2

C A R I B B E A N   S U G A R   M A C H I N E R Y   L T D .   (A - 1)

Data Sheets Covering Note

The purpose of this National Market Data paper* is to provide a framework of variables which, in the future, can be used in assembling a total sales package. This paper is not to explicitly lay out those areas which must be covered by the Project Group. The extent to which we investigate these data areas will be solely left up to the discretion of the group.

*The paper covered 13 pages of legal-sized paper and contained the following items with appropriate space to fill in the desired information. For many of the main items there were sub-categories including breakdowns for historical data dating back to 1968. The paper was organized as follows.

    I. Market Environment
        A. Political—7 main items
        B. Economic—9 main items

    II. Inputs
        A. Sugar Cane—11 main items
        B. Animals—7 main items (with 37 sub-categories)
        C. Feed Supplements—13 main items

    III. Outputs
        A. Meat—9 main items
        B. Fibre—4 main items

CARIBBEAN SUGAR MACHINERY LTD. (A-2)*
(Alice's View of a Workgroup in Conflict)

Joseph J. DiStefano

Alice Macintyre and her "policy group" of students at the business school faced a serious problem. It was near the end of the first term and the critical report for Business Policy, the only required course in the senior year, seemed in jeopardy because of interpersonal conflicts within the group.

The policy report required a group of students to study an on-going company and prepare a note on the industry involved, a case on the specific company, and an analysis of the company's situation, together with a set of policy recommendations for its future. This complex task necessitated not only long hours of hard work, but also significant cooperation and teamwork within the group. As Alice reflected on the past weeks of growing friction, she wondered what realistic alternatives existed for the group. Knowing that they would soon be meeting with Professor Forsyth in an attempt to resolve the last blow-up, she realized that a workable solution was needed if they were to meet the project deadline in late February.

Background of the Group

The policy group for the senior year was originally made up of four group members from the same section in the previous year. These four had been part of a larger project group during that year. The three men, Stan, Joe and Ian, had had close associations since their first year at university. They had lived in the same residence and had joined in social and athletic activities. Alice had become part of the group when she began dating Stan during the year. They lived together during their senior year and intended to get married after graduation.

Ian was outgoing and outspoken and came from Kitchener, Ontario. He was often looked upon as being a show-off and overly frank. Joe, from Kincardine, was more quiet and conservative. His social life centered around his female

---

*All names in this case have been disguised.

roommate, a recent university graduate. He was well-liked and a relatively soft-spoken young man.

Stan was the brawny, football player type who was well-liked by his classmates and respected by the faculty. He had set very high career goals and was working as a campus representative for a beer company while attending business school. Although he was outspoken, Stan was sometimes sought for guidance by his peers. Because of his emotional involvement with Alice, he was often teased by male classmates. But this involvement also affected Stan and Alice's work. When they discussed business problems, criticisms of each other's viewpoints were often mistaken as personal. After business meetings Alice was often upset, feeling she had been too stubborn in her views. Stan found it difficult to understand her reactions.

Alice was outgoing and heavily involved in extracurricular activities both in and out of the school. She had had more business experience than the other group members through her summer jobs and rarely hesitated to speak her mind. She was extremely happy living with Stan.

This original group of four formed spontaneously as soon as the project was assigned in mid-September. Ron Moore from Winnipeg joined the group two weeks later. A classmate from the same junior year section as the other four, he was outgoing and well-liked. Ron enjoyed most things he did and appeared to enjoy being an opinion leader. He was constantly busy with his Human Relations course and his girl friend in Waterloo.

Finding a Company

In early October the members had several ideas as to possible companies that could be studied. Many of these had been studied in recent years and were therefore unavailable to them. Others simply indicated that they did not wish to be studied. The group therefore decided on Carling O'Keefe Breweries. Since Stan was a sales representative, he had access to much relevant information. Furthermore, Carling's marketing department seemed anxious to have the policy study done and was apparently ready to co-operate.

Then the bubble burst with a phone call from Stan's boss. The company had also been approached by a business school professor who wanted to write a case. Carling had opted for the case study as opposed to the student group's efforts.

By then it was mid-October, so an emergency meeting was called, and Alice drafted a letter to be sent to companies by each member. The letter described the project and requested the company's cooperation. Alice and Ron suggested one company each and the other three each contacted two companies. From the eight letters sent, two companies responded favorably by mail within one week. One was located in Owen Sound and the other was a small hosiery company in London.

In the meantime, Ron was pursuing his company contact in much more depth. He went to Montreal to meet with the president of Caribbean Sugar Machinery Limited (CSM). His access to top management was facilitated by the fact that the president was Ron Moore's father.

While Ron was in Montreal other group members began discussion of the merits of each company. They were reluctant to choose the Owen Sound firm because of its distance from London and the likelihood of bad road conditions during the winter. They agreed that the London hosiery company was more attractive. No travelling time would be required. The firm was small and newly-formed, and management apparently had some serious problems it wanted solved. Then, after almost a week away, Ron returned with news that CSM agreed to co-operate in the study. He said that it was urgent that the group give him two hours that day to explain. Time was crucial; most other groups had already found a company and begun their study.

Since Professor Forsyth had just told the group that the hosiery company was too small for a five-member group, they immediately assembled at Alice and Stan's apartment to listen to Ron. He explained that CSM was a relatively new, but totally revolutionary, company which had invented a new way to process sugar cane. The company had financial connections in both Canada and England and was on the verge of breaking into the world-wide market. Its main operations were in Winnipeg and Trinidad. Ron's presentation was extremely disorganized. His descriptions of the company, its services and its marketing plans were quite vague.

The group members were highly skeptical about using CSM as a project company. Except for Ron most of the others didn't feel that enough information was available. Ron presented piles of notes, textbooks and product samples to the group after his four-day meeting with his father. None of it was organized, but it was evident that Ron had spent considerable time discussing CSM. It was also clear that Ron very much wanted to pursue the project with CSM. He was hoping to work with the company after graduation and had spent his past summer working with his father on CSM problems. Since the hosiery company had been eliminated, the group decided on CSM, but insisted that Ron's father meet with them within two weeks.

The Start of Work and Friction

Ron met with Professor Forsyth to explain CSM's operations, and then the group met with the professor to decide on methods and directions to take on the project. On October 26 the members, except for Ron who was unable to attend the meeting because of a course conflict, read through the material Ron had brought and tried to find out as much as they could about sugar cane production and processing.

It proved to be a most difficult exercise. The sugar cane industry was next to impossible to research because of the diversity of the information and the enormous quantity of information in the university's libraries. The members were going around in circles looking for a place to begin.

Ron came to the next meeting with file folders for 75 sugar-producing countries and announced that this was the starting point. "We have to research in depth these 75 potential customers for CSM," Ron said. The others were still uncertain of the direction to take, but Ron assured them that this was the most important thing his father had insisted upon. The report began to look more like a marketing research project than a policy report.

Alice listed some important facts about countries in a chart form which would summarize the aspects of each country. It basically consisted of 14 criteria upon which all countries could be compared. Ron felt that too much information was left out, but the other three agreed with Alice's criteria. The list was well-defined and at last the group had something concrete.

Over the next several days meetings were frequently held. The questions were always the same — "Where are we headed?" "What should we be doing?" The meetings went in circles and no decisions were made. It became more and more clear that Ron was very concerned about collecting more market data. It appeared as if the rest of the group wanted more data on the company itself. This information couldn't be found in books; although he felt he was well-informed, Ron was unable to supply it to the others' satisfaction.

Mr. Moore comes to London

Finally Ron announced that his father would be arriving in London on October 30 for a two-day stay. Group members were to prepare questions for Mr. Moore. As the time for the visit grew nearer, the group's skepticism grew. On October 29 Ron told them that his father would only be able to meet with the group for one evening. When they met with Mr. Moore, they learned he would be leaving London four hours later. This came as a shock to everyone. They did not feel that it was enough time to collect all the data on CSM that they needed.

Ron and his father came to the meeting at 6:30 p.m. after having discussed the project and CSM with Professor Forsyth for two or three hours. Stan was unable to attend, so a tape recorder was set up. Unfortunately it failed to work. In opening the meeting Mr. Moore said that he had been impressed by what George Forsyth had said about the business school and the policy project. He did, however, appear extremely tired. He had had nothing to eat and therefore did not seem really prepared or enthused about the meeting. Mr. Moore asked about the background of the group members and this was followed by questions from the group about CSM and its plans. The questions posed were well-stated and most were answered effectively. It appeared as if Mr. Moore thought the students were well-prepared. Throughout the meeting the students knew

Mr. Moore had to catch a plane at about 9:00 p.m. and so were aware of the time pressure.

After Mr. Moore left, Ian, Joe and Alice felt much more confident. He had provided some background on CSM and had told them more specifically what he wanted done for the project. To him the collection of market data was not of primary importance. He did feel, however, that the group needed to investigate the market before they attacked policy decisions for the company.

The group promised Mr. Moore that he would receive a proposal stating project intentions within ten days. The proposal was to include a budget, objectives, and methods the group would employ. He agreed that the proposal was necessary before he could officially approve their efforts and left the impression that he was glad the group was doing the study. Mr. Moore was reluctant, however, to give the group all the data they wished. For example, he thought financial data and information about organizational structure were irrelevant to the project.

The following day all five members met to work out a format for the proposal. Alice tried to take notes. The meeting resulted in conflicts and disagreements, especially from Ron. He did not feel that his father wanted such a detailed proposal, but Alice interjected, "If we make a good proposal and it's very specific, we'll be able to use it as an outline as we work on the project." Joe and Ian (Stan to a certain extent, too) seemed rather complacent during the whole discussion. They were glad, however, to have something on paper—a concrete guideline which could be followed throughout the project.

On the other hand, Ron objected both to the general format and the points being included in the proposal. As the issues were discussed, he would first object and then, when he saw he was outnumbered, simply stop talking and sit glumly watching the other four. When they asked his opinion or requested an explanation of his objection, his response was, "You're totally off-track; but if that's what you want, it's O.K. with me." Alice repeatedly asked Ron to be more specific. In the absence of such clarification the group left the meeting frustrated. It was obvious that there was disagreement, but no clear idea of what specifically was desirable emerged.

Because Alice had taken notes she went home and wrote out a draft proposal. It included specific objectives, the methods they intended to use and a proposed budget. Stan read and approved it and they took it to be typed. Within a few days copies were distributed to each member, and one was mailed to Mr. Moore. In an accompanying letter they asked for immediate confirmation of their objectives and plan of action. They hoped that this approval would be in their hands in ten days.

Until the group received Mr. Moore's reply, their activities were rather limited. The meetings continued for the collection of data on both the sugar industry and the 75 sugar-producing countries. Basically this involved filling in the blanks on the form Alice had drawn up. With the four members of the group still trying desperately to find direction, they finally agreed to divide the industry note into five sections and each member was given responsibility for a section. At this point the process of dividing the work seemed promising, but once each tried to collect data they either were overwhelmed or discovered a lack of information in their section.

No one really knew what they were supposed to be doing. Finally, on November 7, it was decided that much of the data on the 75 countries was agricultural data that came from United Nations statistics. The group decided that the best place to collect this data was at the University of Guelph. Therefore, they decided that on the following Friday all members would go to the Guelph library. At the last minute neither Alice nor Stan could go because of a death in the family. The other three went to Guelph, although apparently very little actual data were collected. Other than sending some books to U.W.O. in interlibrary loan, nothing seemed to have been accomplished. Feelings in the group were mixed. Alice was getting progressively more frustrated because of the lack of participation by Ian, Joe and Stan. They appeared disinterested and didn't seem to be doing their share of the work.

A Fundamental Disagreement

It was becoming more and more evident that there was direct conflict between Alice and Ron. They both seemed keenly interested and involved in the project, but they had basic differences of opinion. Alice felt that the group should take a general overview of the company and concentrate on formulating a strategy for CSM in both the short- and long-term. This would mean making some very gross assumptions unless Mr. Moore provided more input. Ron, on the other hand, wanted to be very specific and collect reams of market data in order to formulate a short-term policy. He always seemed to think in specifics and to tend not to take a general policy view. The difference of opinion was deep and fundamental in nature.

In spite of this, their interest in the project led them to discuss the study occasionally outside of the group meetings. However, their ideas about what should be done were so different that these exchanges ended with both of them going away even more frustrated and angry. Alice's reaction was to turn to Stan and try to explain these incidents with Ron. Stan always shrugged the situations off as unimportant and tried to convince Alice to be less involved. But this ran contrary to Alice's basic nature, which was to give all she had to a project. She couldn't understand being apathetic to anything.

Stan became concerned over Alice being so upset — often in tears — after her exchanges with Ron. He tried to support Alice, but didn't want to alienate Ron. Ian and Joe seemed to agree with Stan, but didn't appear prepared to say so. They were definitely followers who appeared to have chosen sides, but wouldn't do so explicitly.

Ron's strong devotion to both CSM and the project was now clear, especially in relation to the others. The difference in goals between them seemed to imply inevitable conflict. His motivation stemmed from family involvement and the personal benefits of a job at graduation; their orientation was a concern for a meaningful policy project from which they could obtain relatively good grades.

Meanwhile they were all still waiting for feedback from Mr. Moore on the proposal. They had heard nothing, although more than two weeks had passed since he should have received it. No one, including Ron, could understand his lack of response.

Mounting Friction

On November 15, the afternoon before an all-day Friday meeting, Ron handed Alice a pile of photocopied papers. He gave her an extra copy for Stan and also distributed copies to Ian and Joe. The first page, entitled "Talking Papers," was written in point form as an agenda of issues to be discussed the next day (see Exhibit 1). The points outlined the problem areas that needed discussing, as Ron saw them. Attached was a thirteen page questionnaire which Ron felt, once answered, would give the relevant information on a comparative basis for each of the 75 countries. (See Exhibit 2 for the data sheets "Covering Note" and summary of the questionnaire contents.) Ron wanted approval of the questionnaire. Then he would make 75 copies of these thirteen pages and the group would proceed to collect the needed data. He proposed writing to the 75 countries to get the data. This seemed to be in direct conflict with what had been decided in drawing up the proposal and in collecting data on the countries according to the criteria listed in Alice's chart.

Alice was the first to get one of Ron's Talking Papers. She quickly skimmed over page 1 in her marketing class and stopped on the third point. It stated something to the effect that the interpersonal conflict between her and Ron would have to be resolved the next day. She was shocked and surprised to have Ron approaching the whole group about it before initially seeing her. She felt it unfair of Ron not to warn her of his plans to raise the issue this way. Alice was really hurt and hurried out of class. Her one thought was to meet Stan and she avoided everyone she knew.

Stan was furious. He said, "Ron had no right to prepare either the questionnaire or the Talking Papers unilaterally without consulting all the other members." Alice was still upset and just wanted to be alone. Trying to calm and reassure her, he said, "Ron was wrong to focus on you as the problem. We've all been to blame."

That same evening both Ian and Joe phoned Stan. After reading Ron's packet, they had reactions similar to Stan's... "Ron should not have gone ahead on his own. After all, the summarized chart of country criteria served the same purpose as his questionnaire and we've been working on it for weeks! Does this new questionnaire mean all our work was in vain?" they asked. Furthermore, they agreed that Alice had been unfairly attacked. They felt, as Stan did, that all this must be discussed thoroughly until some conclusion was reached. While they had been aware of the conflict between Ron and Alice, they, too, seemed to feel they were involved.

Later that night Alice and Stan discussed the problem further. Stan felt that Alice was overreacting to the situation. "Perhaps I am," she thought, "but I'm being hurt once again just because I really and truly believe in and care about this project. If I didn't care so much, I wouldn't bother taking such an adamant stand against Ron." She had another group which she could join and offered to do so in order to resolve the problem. But Stan would have no part of that solution. He persuaded her just to wait and see what would happen the next day. She didn't really even want to attend the meeting, but she knew that if she didn't go, the inevitable conflict would only be postponed.

The next morning they went to the meeting together. Alice did so with great reluctance only after pledging to herself that she would keep her mouth shut. At the meeting she tried to remain quiet until called upon for her opinion. The group of five went over the points in Ron's Talking Papers.

The conflict between Ron and Alice was talked out by them. It was decided that neither would take the initiative to lead the group. Both would be heard with equal weight. It appeared that the interpersonal difficulties mentioned in Ron's note had been resolved.

Then they decided that no one (especially Ron) would undertake any new project direction or extra workload without consulting the whole group for approval. It was agreed that all future meetings with Professor Forsyth be held as a group. They agreed further that neither Ron nor anyone else was to discuss the project with anyone without including the rest of the group members.

Ian and Joe then tried to get the meeting moving more functionally. The deadline for the report was getting closer and no progress was in sight. They hadn't even heard from Mr. Moore yet.

Another Try

The next meeting was a week later, on November 23. Prior to the meeting Ron said that he worked out several key questions and wanted the individual members to write down their responses at the meeting. He said he thought many of the key problems of CSM could be isolated this way. The suggestion was received unenthusiastically, but the group agreed to co-operate as long as some discussion took place in addition to the individuals writing out their answers.

This process went on for some time until, all of a sudden, the discussion was right back where it had been at earlier meetings. On about the 13th or 14th question Alice couldn't hold back her frustration any longer. It seemed as if Ron was talking about collecting more market data again. She objected strongly to Ron's point. She was frustrated more than ever by the mediocrity resulting from the lack of direction within the group. She told Ron that he should see the project as a group effort and that he should accept the proposal and chart form of country criteria as given and work within those constraints. Gaining momentum she added, "Those guidelines were laid and agreed upon by all five of us. When you had your chance to give specific objections, you should have. But you didn't, and now you'll just have to work within those criteria and guidelines!"

Ron was visibly upset and becoming very angry. Finally, he burst forth, "Alice, you really tick me off. Why do you always have to object to everything I say?"

Alice was unprepared for this and tried to defend her position. She knew the group needed direction and some guidelines. She felt that they had been well-established in the first few meetings in late October. But somehow none of this came out very well. She was fighting back tears and couldn't stand being attacked by Ron any longer. She wanted some of the others to support her with their viewpoints, but they didn't. With her rising tension she jumped up and ran out of the room leaving her books, notes, and papers.

Taking a long walk around the campus, Alice tried to sort out her thoughts and feelings. She didn't feel she had been wrong; she believed in every stand she had taken. She had frequently invited disagreement from the other members, but more often than not they had remained silent. She took this to mean that either they just didn't care or else they totally agreed with the criteria and the proposal she had prepared. She couldn't understand why they didn't express their opinions.

Alice felt Ron had been unfair in attacking her in writing, and especially in front of the others, without actually trying to understand why she was the way she was and why she said what she said in the meetings. While she understood why Ron was more involved in the project than the others, she thought she had tried hard to respect his viewpoint. Either she had failed to understand his involvement, or Ron had not wanted her to understand. Another possibility was that he had been unwilling to admit his total involvement and its effects. Whatever the reason, she knew she would have to deal with this latest incident.

An Attempt to Resolve the Problem

Alice went back to the meeting room to find Stan and Ron. She said she thought it would be better for her to join another policy group and leave the four others to continue the CSM project. But both Ron and Stan objected and the three tried to talk the problem out.

Alice tried to tell Ron how hurt she had been by the Talking Papers, and how much she wanted this group to hand in a very good project. Ron listened and apologized. Stan insisted that Ron stop going to talk to professors without the project group as a whole. Ron agreed, and it was decided that all would try again — this time as a group effort. A meeting was scheduled at Joe's house the following day.

Alice and Stan went home. Alice was still upset; she wanted badly to do everything right. She was afraid of breaking up the group and causing problems for everyone else. She was also afraid to be too opinionated and wanted to avoid aggravating Stan any further. So far she had been the one to speak up for what she believed, while Stan had backed her up. But she knew he didn't like this role, so she wanted to step back into a more quiet and unobtrusive position within the group. She vowed to both herself and Stan that she would never lead another meeting or become so deeply involved in this or any other project.

The next day Ron spoke to Professor Forsyth about these events and the group problem, including Alice's running out of the meeting. This discussion was in direct violation of what he, Alice and Stan had agreed upon the very night before. Ron telephoned all the members to say that Professor Forsyth wanted to see each of them individually. In view of their previous agreement Stan and Alice couldn't believe their ears!

The next day Stan and Ian went to see Professor Forsyth. From what Alice understood, they tried to explain her feelings, especially how disappointed she had been when she learned Ron was consulting a few other professors (besides George Forsyth) about his interpersonal conflict with Alice. Professor Forsyth suggested Alice talk with him, but insisted that he had not told Ron that all the members should see him. Rather he had offered to see each one if they so chose. He wanted to avoid hearing only Ron's side of the problem and wanted the others to have an equal opportunity to express their feelings.

In her meeting with Professor Forsyth Alice suggested that the major conflicts were probably now over, because everyone had at last been frank. Professor Forsyth offered to call the other professors that Ron had involved to request them to stay out of the situation. However, Alice said that she preferred to handle the problem herself and let it pass by easily. She thanked Professor Forsyth for his concern and felt reassured that the group could now handle most events. At last Ian and Joe were becoming involved in the problem.

Back to the Task...and the Next Blow

On November 30 the group next met together to proceed with the project work. All went well, but everyone, including Ron, was still anxious to hear from Mr. Moore. They had still heard nothing from him and had no concrete data from the company to use in the project. They finally decided to call him in Trinidad that afternoon. When they telephoned Mr. Moore gave his approval to the proposal, but said he had some modifications to make. However, he did not and would not state them to Stan over the phone. He said he would be in London for one day in about a week's time. But he told them that he would be unable to provide most of the information the group needed.

After the phone call the group discussed the future of the project. How could they proceed without more input from Mr. Moore and CSM? They were lost and confused. Mr. Moore had said at the original meeting, "Yes, I'm interested," and "Yes, I have data for you." But now they were uncertain whether he really did have the data or whether his enthusiasm for the project had waned since receiving the proposal. In this pessimistic atmosphere Ian said that he might be able to find another company before Christmas. They decided that the best way to cope with the situation was to seek help from Professor Forsyth. A meeting was arranged for the following Sunday, at which time they intended to ask him what he expected of them as a project group and what he thought Mr. Moore's obligations to the group were.

Alice was concerned. It was late in the year to start a new project. Yet, considering recent events, the outcome with CSM looked uncertain and relations with Ron were strained. She felt that some thought should be given to specifying the alternatives available to the group and to establishing the preferences of the members before meeting with Professor Forsyth, but she wasn't sure what was likely to happen or what she should do.

EXHIBIT 1
CARIBBEAN SUGAR MACHINERY LTD. (A-2)

Talking Papers

November 16

It is my personal feeling that, within our policy group, we have some very basic problems which must be resolved before we can attain our group objectives in an enjoyable manner. Furthermore, I'm not sure whether or not these problems are procedural or personal in nature. The problems which are bothering me now are:

1. Do you feel that I will jeopardize the group's objectives for my own personal objectives? (e.g. Are mine in conflict with yours?)

2. Am I correct in thinking that you do not wish to address questions which inevitably must be answered in the future because the workload may appear to be monumental? (e.g. crossing the bridge when we come to it attitude)

3. What solutions can you suggest to resolve an evident personality or role conflict? (e.g. Alice and myself)

4. What do you feel the objectives of this policy group should be?

I believe that, if we can discuss these questions at the meeting tomorrow, we might be able to avoid the frustrations which we have all experienced in every other meeting.

Sincerely,
Ron

EXHIBIT 2

CARIBBEAN SUGAR MACHINERY LTD. (A-2)

Data Sheets Covering Note

The purpose of this National Market Data paper* is to provide a framework of variables which, in the future, can be used in assembling a total sales package. This paper is not to explicitly lay out those areas which must be covered by the Project Group. The extent to which we investigate these data areas will be solely left up to the discretion of the group.

*The paper covered 13 pages of legal-sized paper and contained the following items with appropriate space to fill in the desired information. For many of the main items there were sub-categories including breakdowns for historical data dating back to 1968. The paper was organized as follows.

    I. Market Environment
        A. Political—7 main items
        B. Economic—9 main items

    II. Inputs
        A. Sugar Cane—11 main items
        B. Animals—7 main items (with 37 sub-categories)
        C. Feed Supplements—13 main items

    III. Outputs
        A. Meat—9 main items
        B. Fibre—4 main items

CANADA MANPOWER: STUDENT EMPLOYMENT CENTRE (A)*

Joseph J. DiStefano

By the end of July Barbara Carroll's mounting frustration with her work situation at the Student Employment Centre (SEC) office of Canada Manpower had reached the point where she felt compelled to take some action. Performance in the assigned tasks had not only become ineffective and inefficient, but the indifferent behavior of her student colleagues was causing hostile reactions from customers who sought help at SEC. Slowly, her initial enthusiasm for her summer job of assisting area employers to hire students had been transformed into anger. The other counsellors and their supervisor seemed neither to notice nor to care about the deteriorating service. In the month she had left to work, Barbara was determined to do something to improve both the operations and image of the office.

Background: Student Employment Centre (SEC)

Student Employment Centre (SEC) was a program designed by Canada Manpower to help students find summer jobs and assist employers to find summer staff. Canada Manpower allocated funds to each of its large offices throughout the country for the SEC program. These offices, in turn, hired recent college or university graduates to manage the local SEC program which itself employed several students in its operations.

The staff of these centers were responsible for three major sets of activities — promotion of SEC, processing of clients, and record-keeping. Promotional activities involved planning and implementing informative and persuasive campaigns directed toward potential employers and employees.

---

*All names in this case have been disguised.

Students had to be reached in the high schools as well as colleges and universities. Both they and potential employers had to be informed of the SEC program itself, location of local offices, registration procedures, and so on.

As clients responded to the promotional campaigns a series of processing activities were initiated. Requests from employers were received and processed. Students were registered and applications were coded and filled by educational level and job interest. Students were interviewed for specific jobs, and job referrals were made. Liaison with employers was maintained until openings were filled or cancelled.

Throughout the period of SEC activities accurate records were to be kept. Statistics on employer visits, job vacancies, registrations, referrals and placements were compiled for Canada Manpower. These data were used to help evaluate the performance of the current SEC staff and to plan allocations for the following year.

The Kitchener Office

For the summer the Manpower office in Kitchener was allocated funds to hire eleven staff consisting of three assistants and eight counsellors. However, since the Kitchener Manpower office itself needed extra, short-term staff for the summer, they used some of the monies from the SEC allocation for their office.[1] This action reduced the SEC complement by one assistant and two counsellors.

Staffing for the SEC program was started in early February by Art Hodes, community liaison officer for Kitchener Manpower, who was also responsible for SEC activities. He held a competition for the two assistant positions, each of which called for a college graduate. Marion McPartland and Tommy Flanagan were hired and enjoyed joint responsibility for all office duties, which they informally split between them. Marion was responsible for internal office operations and Tommy was in charge of publicity and other external activities. Both received the same pay and were considered on equal levels in the office hierarchy (see Exhibit 1 for an organization chart of the office). Tommy was to work through September, but Marion was scheduled to leave at the end of June since she was expecting a baby in early July.

From February until the end of April, Marion and Tommy were the only employees in the Kitchener SEC office, which was located in a building separate from Canada Manpower. Minimal supervision was given by Art Hodes and they were expected to organize and carry out the three basic functions for which they had been employed. Because of heavy student traffic,

---

[1] According to Barbara's information, the regional headquarters of Manpower, if aware of this situation, chose to disregard it.

Tommy spent considerable time helping Marion receive and screen students while Marion coded and filed the registrations. Only a quarter of Tom's time was devoted to planning and conducting a program of employer visits and student publicity. The mix of activities at the office varied considerably over this period and was largely dependent on the number of students registering and the jobs available. Exhibit 2 shows the relative emphasis given to the various activities from February to September.

At the end of April another competition was held for the six counsellor positions. Manpower intended these jobs to be filled by candidates who had been full-time students during the current academic year and who intended to return to college or university following the summer recess. It was for these counsellor positions that Barbara Carroll, Claude Williamson, Lorraine Geller, Pete Jolly, Hank Jones and Mary Lou Williams were hired. All six positions were considered equal in job responsibility and carried equal pay.

Once the counsellors were chosen, Marion allotted the initial assignments within the office. Pete, Claude and Mary Lou were given the tasks of interviewing and counselling students, making job referrals, and maintaining employer contact. Marion and Tommy also performed these functions. Barbara was assigned to the reception counter which involved greeting students and explaining how to best use SEC and, when the counter was free, helping to code and file applications. The counsellor at the reception counter also showed students a list of jobs available and directed them to the proper counsellor for interviewing if they were interested in any jobs on the list. During the heavy registration period in May at least one, and sometimes two, additional counsellors were required for coding and filing. Lorraine requested and received the switchboard assignment.

Because of the changing demands on the office these job responsibilities were subject to change and were treated as informal guides rather than rigid descriptions. When the counsellors were hired, Marion indicated that the assignments would vary and that helping each other as the need occurred would be expected as part of the job.

Barbara's Background

Barbara came to her job as a student counsellor with high expectations and enthusiasm. She had done exceptionally well during her first year of business administration at the University of Western Ontario and was anxious to apply some of the skills she had developed there.[2] Her anticipation of using her training was encouraged by Art Hodes in the orientation he gave when he

---

[2]One of her professors described her as "an attractive, ideal student — earnest, disciplined, and highly analytic with succinct, penetrating and organized contributions in class."

informed the counsellors that any special promotional activities or new methods of accomplishing the basic tasks at SEC would be welcomed. "As long as you contribute to accomplishing our objectives, you're free to do whatever you can to improve our operations," he said.

The youngest of four sisters, Barbara came from a very close family and grew up in Ottawa. Aged 22, she intended to return to Western to complete her business degree following the summer work at SEC, after which she planned to seek a career in government. Her father was a successful manager in the federal Department of Revenue-Taxation where he had earned several promotions although he had come into the civil service with only a high school level education. Her oldest sister was a public school teacher married to a business executive. Her second sister was working as a legal librarian in the federal Department of Justice after earning her B.A., B.L.S. and M.L.S. The third sister, who had both a teacher's certificate and a B.A., was secretary to the manager of a government office in the Kitchener area.[3] Mr. and Mrs. Carroll were proud of their daughters' accomplishments. They felt strongly about trying to do one's best in anything attempted, especially in education and employment.

Other SEC Personnel

Art Hodes, 27, the community liaison officer for Kitchener Manpower, was responsible for the SEC operations for the first time. Because of his regular responsibilities at Manpower, the SEC program represented only a fraction of his activities. During the course of the summer he spent about an hour a week in the SEC office, although he was on the selection board which hired the assistants and counsellors.

Tommy Flanagan, one of the two graduate assistants, had been a student counsellor in the Kitchener SEC program the previous year. During the past year he had been studying political science at The University of Waterloo in preparation for entry into the masters degree program. Tommy was 24 and married to a school teacher in Kitchener.

Marion McPartland, in her second year as graduate assistant, was the senior staff member in both age (28) and experience. She had graduated with a masters degree in mathematics and taught high school for a few years; then she worked in the placement office at The University of Waterloo. During the previous summer Marion had also been a graduate assistant at SEC. Her husband was completing his masters degree in political science at Waterloo. Neither she nor Tommy had been involved in hiring the counsellors.

---

[3]This was not a factor in Barbara's obtaining the SEC job. In fact, she was almost disqualified because of the close association of Manpower with the department in which her sister worked.

Lorraine Geller was the youngest student counsellor (21) although she had been a counsellor in the previous two years. During the previous year she had completed her second year of journalism at The University of Western Ontario.

Claude Williamson was 26 and came from Toronto. He had worked for Canada Manpower in their placement booth at the Canadian National Exhibition the previous summer. Following that experience he had enrolled in the final year of a social welfare course at Ryerson Polytechnical Institute. This was his first work with SEC as a counsellor.

Barbara Starts Work

After a two or three week breaking-in period Barbara got into the job routine and became immersed in her work. As she gained familiarity with the various activities of the office, she became aware of areas where more effort was required. "There seemed to be no overall plan for employer visits," she noted. "Visits up to this point had been conducted by Tommy and seemed to have been done mostly on impulse. He would think of a large employer and would go out to call on them and a few nearby companies. Few visits had been conducted and even fewer had been effective."

Therefore Barbara asked to be relieved from her office duties for awhile in order to plan a campaign of employer visits. "I felt there was little sense in accepting, even encouraging, hundreds of student applications each day if we didn't make an equal effort to convince employers to hire through SEC." In addition Barbara felt there was some pressure to move quickly. "Since most employers had either already hired students or would do so very soon, our visit campaign had to be planned and implemented immediately or it would be futile."

Tommy gave her the go-ahead and Barbara got to work. She learned from those who had worked the last summer at SEC that an extensive visit program had been run the previous year, and she decided to base her plan on that experience. However, she soon found that all the records from the previous campaign had been lost, so she quickly began work on her own.

After the plan was completed, it was cursorily examined and approved by Tommy. Barbara then scheduled the staff members for a series of employer visits with each counsellor responsible for one day, and gave the schedule to each counsellor and explained the call program. However, the schedule was often interrupted by the heavy demands of the day-to-day office work. Absences also caused problems, since the internal work load meant that no one could be spared for an employer visit when the office was shorthanded. In addition the visits were usually tiring and disappointing experiences. Many employers had already hired for the summer and so did not respond positively at the time of the visit (although later in the summer several of those visited hired through SEC when they needed more staff). Since making visits was not mandatory — the decision was left to the individual counsellors — in the face of such discouragement, the visits were given second priority. Claude and Lorraine never called on any potential employers.[4]

The other staff conducted a fair number of visits in late May and in June. In July and August, however, few visits were made. Barbara explained this drop-off in terms of staff shortages and diminishing interest. The office was under pressure when Marion left in June and soon afterwards Pete Jolly, one of the counsellors, left to take a permanent job. The assistant position was left vacant and a counsellor replacement wasn't hired until August. Also Barbara felt that most staff questioned the value of the visits at that time in the summer. They wondered if the effort would be fruitful that late in the season. And since most did not plan to work at SEC next year, there was no incentive in terms of seeing the benefits of their effort in the following year.

Barbara's Views of the SEC Staff

After two months at the office Barbara's observations of her colleagues and supervisors left her with several impressions and opinions. She saw Art as a very social person, but she wondered why he provided so little guidance for SEC. "It was either because he had so little time to devote to SEC or because he simply did not realize guidance was required," she said.

She viewed Tommy as very "straight" and thought he must have been a good counsellor the previous year. He had a very friendly manner and spent hours talking to students and to staff. But he was a poor organizer and was very reluctant to assign duties and to direct or correct staff in particular activities. She noted that Tommy never reprimanded any of the staff, although Marion did not hesitate to do so if she thought it appropriate.

In Barbara's judgment Marion was a good manager. She was good with people — both students and staff. She knew what had to be done in the office because of her previous year's experience, and she made sure it was completed. She assigned duties, directed staff and dealt with problems effectively. "Marion worked very hard herself," Barbara emphasized, "and thus provided a good example of what she expected from us. More than that, she really was concerned about the students who were looking for work and about the SEC reputation. Even after her baby was born, she came back to see how we were doing."

---

[4]Before she left SEC, Marion warned the two of their responsibility to make these calls, but it did not change their behavior. Barbara openly showed her negative feelings, but felt powerless to supervise them. Mary Lou indirectly made her position known by avoiding unnecessary interaction with them. Whatever response Hank had was hidden, since he was often separated from the others because of the interviewing he did.

Barbara saw Lorraine as an extremely social person whose propensity to talk often interfered with her work. She spent much of her time talking with Claude or friends who dropped into the office. Her conversations often ran to fashions and the latest rock groups. She avoided the demanding counselling work in favor of the switchboard or statistical tasks which were considered the slack jobs in the office. This pattern of doing a minimum of work also showed by her consistent lateness for work and taking long lunch hours (up to two and a half hours instead of the 45 minute break allowed). This was especially true after Marion left. Lorraine planned to travel to Europe for a year after finishing at SEC in August. Barbara thought that her ineligibility for a SEC job the next year was part of the reason for her low performance (government regulations required that all student employees be enrolled the year before and after their summer jobs.)

Barbara's most negative opinions were directed at Claude. He never wore a suit as did the other male staff; his long hair and beard fit with his sandals and casual dress. Barbara had particular scorn for what she felt was his hypocrisy. "He was always bad-mouthing the establishment and the government — he continually spoke of 'screwing the government' — yet he was on the payroll of the very institution he pretended to loathe. He seemed to have an inflated opinion of himself," she added. "He once said to me that he didn't write his final exams at Ryerson because it would have been an insult to him to graduate from such an institution!"

Rising Frustration

It was against this background of observations and experience that Barbara entered her third month of work at SEC. Soon after Marion left Barbara noticed that the talking started to reach dysfunctional levels. Claude and Lorraine, but also Tommy, spent an increasing part of their working hours talking to each other and to their friends. Whenever there was no obvious or immediate demand for work, such as a student client at the counter or a phone ringing, they would sit and talk despite the fact that there were always filing and coding to do. So the backlog mounted.

This aggravated Barbara because from her interviewing of students she had become sensitive about the office image. She knew that the students who came in looking for work were acutely aware that they were unemployed, but the SEC staff who were students like themselves had secure jobs that paid well. Furthermore, many of the students had very low opinions about Canada Manpower and came to SEC with expectations that the help would be more effective than Manpower.

Barbara was very anxious to meet these expectations and was angered by the wasting of time by staff. She felt that visible neglect, quite possible since students at the counter had a full view of the office activities, except for the interviewing which was done in separate cubicles, would perpetuate the students' view of Manpower and SEC as useless. On the other hand, if staff gave students the impression that they were really trying to create and fill jobs, Manpower's reputation would improve. Since students often came into the SEC office and sat several hours waiting for employers to phone in requests, she felt that staff behavior was important.

Barbara described an incident to show what she meant. One day in July when a group of these students were sitting and waiting for jobs, Lorraine, Claude and Tommy were talking at their desks. After observing their behavior for some time with mounting anger, one of the students finally stood up at the counter and announced, "This place isn't a student employment centre; it's a student social centre and I'm leaving!" With that he stomped out, slamming the door as he left.

397

*Canada
Manpower:
Student
Employment
Centre (A)*

The Final Straw

During this period Barbara was kept busy interviewing students about jobs that were available and making referrals. In late July the situation worsened and some staff were not even meeting the immediate demands of work. Students were often left standing at the reception counter waiting to be attended to while staff sat and talked. At the same time Claude's usual behavior deteriorated even more. Several times he sat in the office without a shirt on, and Lorraine and Tommy responded with amusement. The final straw for Barbara was an afternoon at the end of July when Claude rode his bicycle up and down the aisles in the office.

Her anger at this behavior and at Art and Tommy's inaction to correct it was heightened by the fact that she knew that both Claude and Lorraine had deliberately lied to the hiring board about their plans for next year. If they had admitted that they were not returning to school, but were travelling abroad instead, they would have been ineligible for the jobs. She was especially bitter since she had since had occasion to speak with some of the other applicants for the counselling jobs who had been rejected. She knew that many of these candidates were superior and could have made significant contributions to the SEC project.

Angered and frustrated by a situation which she felt was destroying SEC credibility and having a serious impact on the morale of students who came in seeking help, Barbara decided to take responsibility herself for improving the office. Although she was determined to do something in the next week, she was unsure of what to do or who to see.

EXHIBIT 1
CANADA MANPOWER: STUDENT EMPLOYMENT CENTRE (A)

Organizational Chart

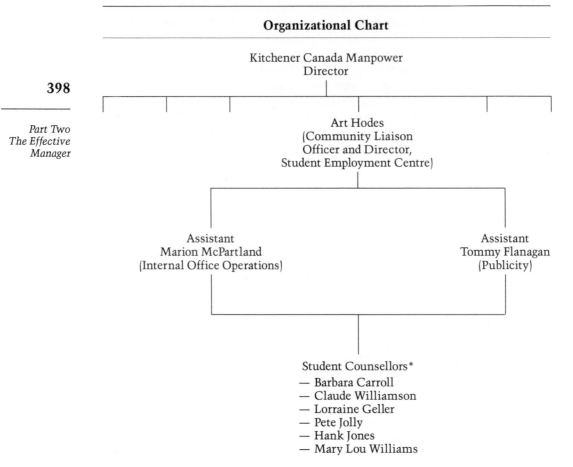

Kitchener Canada Manpower
Director

Art Hodes
(Community Liaison
Officer and Director,
Student Employment Centre)

Assistant
Marion McPartland
(Internal Office Operations)

Assistant
Tommy Flanagan
(Publicity)

Student Counsellors*
— Barbara Carroll
— Claude Williamson
— Lorraine Geller
— Pete Jolly
— Hank Jones
— Mary Lou Williams

*The reporting relation of the student counsellors was not rigidly prescribed. The individual counsellors tended to report to the assistant who happened to assign work to them at a particular time and/or to whichever one with whom they felt most comfortable.

EXHIBIT 2
CANADA MANPOWER: STUDENT EMPLOYMENT CENTRE (A)

Kitchener Office Activities: February to September

| | ACTIVITIES | | | |
Time Period	Visits, Employers and High School Publicity Campaign	Student Registration, Coding and Filing of New Applications	Handling Employer Requests, Interviewing Students. Job Referrals, and Follow-up Activity	Preparation of Statistical Report
Feb. to April	About 1/4 Tommy's time spent on this activity	Heavy emphasis, large volume of registrations meant coding and filing work was substantial. Marion full-time and Tommy 3/4 time on this activity.	Very light. No requests for summer employees until late April. Only part-time jobs after school and on weekends were available.	Weekly reports (requiring a few hours on Friday) and a larger monthly report (took about 1 day to prepare) were compiled throughout this period.
May	Little attention given to this activity until late May due to heavy registration and placement activity plus the need to train new staff.	Very heavy.	Moderately heavy. Two staff working on this activity full-time.	
June	Attempt made by Barbara to plan and implement visit campaign.	Extremely heavy. Peaked in June.	Extremely heavy.	
July	Due to loss of staff and heavy demands of registration and placement, little time spent here.	Very heavy.	Very heavy.	
August	Almost nil	Very light. Only part-time of one employee required.	Moderately heavy. Vacancies hard to fill. Most students not interested in working. Required more time to fill fewer jobs.	Weekly and monthly reports as above. In addition, many summary reports were required by Canada Manpower in Ottawa, Toronto regional office and Kitchener.

WARWICK CHILDREN'S AID SOCIETY (A)*

David A. Peach

Ed Masters, executive director of the Warwick Children's Aid Society (CAS),[1] faced a decision which might result in conflict with his staff or problems in his relationship to his board of directors. A committee of staff members had developed a proposal for formalizing an experimental flex-time arrangement about which he had serious reservations. Faced with different proposals from him and this committee, the staff had voted to support the committee's report and asked him to submit it to the board of directors. Now he had to decide what to do for the upcoming board meeting.

Background

The Warwick CAS was the agency responsible, under the Child Welfare Act of Ontario, for the protection, care, and adoption of children, and for counselling and other services to families in the city of Warwick and the County of Northampton. Located to the east of Metropolitan Toronto, Northampton County had a population of 275 000, while the city of Warwick itself contained about 100 000 residents.

The Warwick CAS was governed by a board of directors with 15 members. Three of these members were city councillors and represented the city of Warwick, while the county had two members. The other ten members were elected from the general membership of the Society. Membership in the Society, which like other similar institutions in the province was essentially a private corporation, was open to any interested citizen who paid the $5 annual membership fee.

The board was responsible for establishing local policies for the Warwick CAS, within the framework of the Child Welfare Act, for appointing staff, for

---

*All names and locations in this case have been disguised.

establishing salary scales and other employment practices. Funds for the operation of the Society came from the city, the county and the province, and the board was responsible for the annual budget plan for the dispersal of these funds.

The board delegated some of its authority to its standing committees. Besides the executive committee of the board, these standing committees were: Services; Personnel; Finance and Property; Public Relations and the Constitution and Nominating Committees.

The Warwick CAS was administered by Ed Masters, who had the title of executive director. His services coordinator was responsible for the activities of 25 professional staff members. His office manager was responsible for eight clerical personnel constituting one department. The office manager acted at the same time as controller. The professional staff was divided into three departments: Family Counselling, Family Service and Child Care.[1] Each department was under the direction of a departmental supervisor and each, with the exception of the Clerical Department, held regular meetings for purposes of case assignment and for discussion of service concerns. A staff development committee representing each department arranged programs throughout the year. An independent and voluntary staff association existed which included all staff who wished to belong, exclusive of the director and his secretary. Exhibit 1 summarizes the organization of Warwick CAS.

The Schedule Problem

Over a number of months, Masters had been concerned with the hours being worked by CAS's professional staff. Because of the nature of the work, all client transactions could not be handled during the agency's nine to five, Monday to Friday, regular work hours. Under existing policy, work outside of regular hours was to be compensated for by having time off work during regular hours in the same week.

However, because of the individualized case loads, most staff members found it difficult to take compensating time off, and found their work time encroaching on their personal time.

The Warwick CAS had tried a work schedule in which the office was open until 9 o'clock on Wednesday nights, with the staff who worked late on that

---

[1]The Family Service Department administered the Child Welfare Act, responding to complaints and concerns made known by the community (e.g., schools, police, hospitals, public health nurses, welfare department staff, clergy, relatives, and neighbors) to CAS about the welfare of children. Family Counselling had no legal responsibility under the Child Welfare Act, but simply responded to requests from clients where there seemed to be, at the moment counselling commenced, no child in jeopardy. The Child Care Department supervised the actual foster care of children.

evening taking a half-day off work on another day of the week. However, the staff had not found it possible to concentrate appointments on that one evening, and the practice had been discontinued in favor of the present policy.

In June the staff development committee arranged a general staff meeting to discuss the subject of a shortened work week. A staff member had learned informally that the office manager was to attend a managerial conference outside the agency at which this topic would be an agenda item, and had encouraged the staff development committee to ask the director if the office manager could report on the subject to all staff. The director agreed.

At the close of the June meeting, the staff appointed an *ad hoc* committee to explore the possibility of a four-day work week at Warwick CAS. This *ad hoc* committee consisted of one representative from each of the four departments, the coordinator, and the director, *ex officio*.

Around this time, the director summarized his thinking about a four-day work week in a memo to the entire staff. He noted that it would:

- provide the client with more opportunity for face-to-face contact with staff
- require acceptance of a more structured expectation upon staff
- impose even closer scheduling of staff meetings and conferences
- provide a more concentrated work period in each week, reduce "free time" mid week, increase "free time" at weekends
- be implemented experimentally on the basis of a commitment for a minimum period of time which will provide the basis for a realistic review.

The Committee's Work

At its first meeting, the committee defined its objectives as follows:

a) to make service formally available to the public during hours over and above 9 a.m. to 5 p.m., five days per week,

b) to rationalize the overtime being worked at present into a recognizable pattern

   i) so that workers due compensatory time off would actually get it;

   ii) so that workers could anticipate when they would be off-duty;

   iii) so that administrative functions (staff meetings, conferences) could be planned;

   iv) so that the profile and logic of the structure would be fair and easy for all staff to follow.

Each departmental representative was to bring from and carry to his or her colleagues questions and concerns specific to that department's area of service. The committee also investigated the modified work week schedules at two larger CASs.

Operationally, the committee decided to rotate the chairmanship for each meeting. Finally, it re-christened the object of its endeavors "ModWeek."

At a general staff meeting held on July 3 the staff heard the report from this *ad hoc* committee and decided to try the proposal offered by the committee. This proposal was based on a work week with two 11 hour and two 7 hour days, with either Friday or Monday off. The proposal, which was to take effect August 1, provided that the board approved, read:

a) ModWeek hours will be arranged by each department.

b) At least half staff will be on duty in each department at all times.

c) Tuesdays, Wednesdays and Thursdays will never be off-duty days for anyone.

d) The office will be open until 9:00 p.m. on Tuesdays & Wednesdays.

e) Where a statutory holiday coincides with an off-duty day, this will be added to annual leave.

f) Only one off-duty day may be taken in one week. These days are not cumulative.

g) ModWeek work schedules shall be organized and altered in each department once only, each month. These will be issued by each department no less than 48 hours before the new schedule is due to operate. Distribution will be to: reception desk, each department, noticeboard, each supervisor, coordinator, office manager, executive director.

h) Responsibility for making out the monthly schedule shall be taken by department staff members in rotation.

i) One hour for lunch and one hour for supper will be the general meal time allotments. Where staff are working 4 days per week, these staff will adjust their meal times on the short work days to provide a minimum 35 hour work week.

j) There will be no change in out-of-hours duty hours. The receptionist will use her discretion to notify out-of-hours duty workers of calls.

k) Receptionist relief will be arranged by the office manager. Probable supper time for receptionist will be 4 to 5 p.m.

Exhibit 2 shows a proposed work schedule for two of Warwick CAS's departments for August. Any individual working a four-day week had to make arrangements with a co-worker to cover emergencies in his or her cases on the day he or she was off-duty.

The ModWeek proposal was accepted from August 1 as a six-month experiment with a review to be held in three months. Masters had submitted the proposal to the Personnel Committee of the board. The Personnel Committee had approved the proposal and forwarded it to the Executive Committee. This committee approved the proposal and also approved the cost of an additional part-time receptionist, to share the extended office hours.

At this point the *ad hoc* committee members became the ModWeek Committee, continuing to meet approximately once a month. In August the ModWeek committee considered the problem of the light workload that clerical personnel who were working during the evenings seemed to have. They developed a system of pooling dictation tapes so that this work would be centrally available.

After a month's operation, the staff of Warwick CAS seemed relatively satisfied with the operation of ModWeek. The committee considered and approved request of some staff to work 9 a.m. to 6:30 p.m. daily hours, with a Friday or a Monday off. Some other personal variants of the basic schedule were also permitted. The committee considered complaints that the absence of certain clerical workers on their Friday or Monday off impeded some agency work or resulted in an overload on some individuals. They decided that these were problems inherent in any schedule and that the CAS and the individuals involved would just have to live with them.

However, later in September the committee decided that individually flexible work hours, such as 9 to 6:30 daily, especially among clerical personnel, were causing service gaps in the office. Consequently, the rules were changed so that only three options were available to all CAS staff: a) full ModWeek (four-day week, with two eleven hour and two seven-hour days), b) half ModWeek (one eleven hour day per week, with a Friday or Monday off every other week) or c) a regular 9 to 5 schedule. As before, any member of staff who worked other than a 9 to 5 schedule had to find a "buddy" to cover for days off. An inability to find a buddy or having a job which could not be covered adequately meant that the individual had to work a 9 to 5 schedule. Although the difficulties Warwick CAS was experiencing with schedules other than the above were all in the area of clerical services, the committee decided to impose the restrictions on all social work personnel in the agency as well.

This proposal was put before a meeting of all staff in October. Some of the professional social workers objected to the restrictions, saying that the new ModWeek schedule was just as rigid as the schedule before ModWeek was adopted and was also incompatible with service demands. With the charge that the ModWeek committee attempt to find some way to provide for more personally flexible work hours, the staff approved continuing ModWeek until the end of the formal experimental period at the end of January.

Ed Masters' Dilemma

The ModWeek system continued through the end of the year. Although the ModWeek committee had been unable to develop a system of personally flexible working hours, it believed that the continuing three options of full ModWeek, half ModWeek and regular 9 to 5 schedule provided most individuals on staff with more flexibility than they had before. Consequently, in

January they were preparing to propose to the full staff that the experimental nature of ModWeek be changed and that ModWeek become the established option.

Ed Masters had some misgivings, however. While in general the system seemed to work well, at times its operation meant that certain jobs did not get done on time. For example, the absence (on her ModWeek day off) of a key person had caused a 24-hour delay at a critical point in the development of the budget for the year.

Masters believed that the Warwick CAS was presently operating with an absolute minimum of clerical staff, and that in order to assure that the agency would continue to provide full service to the public, it might be necessary to require some staff to work particular hours, rather than allowing individual choice. Since he was responsible for the operation of the society, Masters believed he should have that right.

He believed that the department heads were carrying too much of a burden because of ModWeek. He also believed that it would be necessary to abandon ModWeek during the summer, when most staff members took their vacations. At a minimum, Masters did not believe that Warwick CAS should irrevocably commit itself to the automatic year-round operation of ModWeek. In general, Masters was doubtful about making a total commitment to ModWeek, at least as it was currently practiced.

Masters was also concerned about the amount of time that the whole ModWeek program had taken. Two general staff meetings in June and October had been devoted to the subject, and another was scheduled for January. At the most recent ModWeek committee meeting, 33 person-hours had been taken to make a decision that Masters believed he could have made in five minutes.

As a result of his misgivings, and in preparation for the general staff meeting on January 8 which was to review the first six months of operation, Masters sent the following memo to the staff:

WARWICK CHILDREN'S AID SOCIETY

MEMO

TO: All Staff   FROM: Executive Director
RE: ModWeek   DATE: January 8

1. I support the concept.

2. I recommend continuation as follows:

    a) the basic work week be five days per week with provision for compensatory time off,

    b) ModWeek be considered a variation of the basic work week,

    c) ModWeek be reviewed by the board next May and annually in May thereafter, provided that special review may be made at anytime,

    d) ModWeek be not applicable during the summer months which will mean June, July, August.

We have no documentation as to the actual benefit of ModWeek to clients by way of face-to-face encounter after 5:30 p.m. This should be provided for by simple procedure to be devised by Executive Director during February, March, April. We should provide the board with this data before making the system permanent.

The preponderance of annual leave is in summer when we also have most staff turnover; under these circumstances we cannot guarantee the absolute minimum one-half staff coverage on any given day.

Beyond the foregoing I am not satisfied that the Supervisors are not bearing an extra burden during the day which interferes with their regular responsibilities.

At its December meeting, the ModWeek committee had prepared the following proposal to present to the staff at the January 8 meeting:

> The staff has completed six months' trial of a shortened work week offered to staff as an option since August 1.
> During this period, a committee representing all departments has met regularly to discuss problems. The staff now proposes to the board that this shortened work week be regarded as the established option in the agency. It will therefore no longer be regarded as experimental. The committee is unable to suggest ways of extending the options to include personally flexible work hours largely because of the small number of staff.

Faced with different proposals from its executive director and the ModWeek committee, the staff voted to support the committee's report and asked that it be submitted to the board of directors.

Masters was faced with what he thought was a bit of a problem. He wondered whether he should simply submit the proposal to the board or whether, at the same time, he should voice his own strong misgivings about ModWeek and ask for the board's consideration of them along with the proposal.

EXHIBIT 1

WARWICK CHILDREN'S AID SOCIETY (A)

Organization Structure

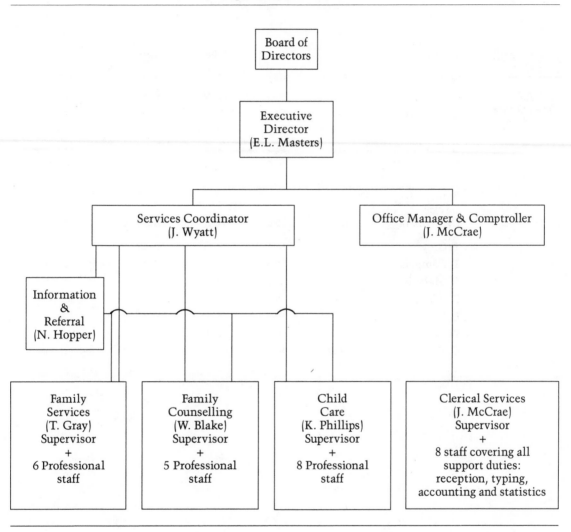

EXHIBIT 2
WARWICK CHILDREN'S AID SOCIETY (A)

Proposed Work Schedule

Family Counselling Service	Mon.	Tue.	Wed.	Thurs.	Fri.
W. Blake	9–5	9–5	9–5	9–5	9–5
E. Spenser	9–5	9–9	9–9	9–5	OFF
G. Herbert	9–5	9–9	9–9	9–5	OFF
G. Hopkins	OFF	9–9	9–9	9–5	9–5
G. Gordon	OFF	9–9	9–9	9–5	9–5
M. Moore	9–5	9–9	9–9	9–5	OFF

Family Services Department	Mon.	Tue.	Wed.	Thurs.	Fri.
T. Grey	9–5	9–5	9–5	9–5	9–5
T. Campion	9–5	9–5	9–9	9–5	9–5 alt. OFF
A. Marvel	9–5	9–5	9–9	9–5	9–5 alt. OFF
P. Sidney	9–5	9–5	9–9	9–5	9–5 alt. OFF
E. Barrett	9–5	9–9	9–9	9–5	OFF
W. Scott	OFF	9–9	9–9	9–5	9–5
C. Rosetti	9–9	9–5	9–5	9–5	9–5 alt. OFF

BELL CANADA (R)

J. David Whitehead and Eileen D. Watson
Revised by Jeffrey Gandz

Betty Gauthier, newly appointed section manager in Bell Canada's London district business office, was worried. After only three weeks at her present job, Betty had just received a grievance signed by all non-management personnel in her unit. The grievance was concrete evidence of widespread dissatisfaction with the amount of work required, the pressures to produce, the way the work was organized, the way performance was measured, and the way the work was managed — in short, "abdication of managerial responsibility" and "management by computer."

A response was required within five days. "This is really serious," Betty thought. "I've got to act fast on this, and I'm still not sure I have a handle on all the things I need to know about my new job. Funny...having just got started on the identification of my long-run priorities and an action plan, I thought I was on the right track. But now this grievance arrives on my desk — it sure gives a new urgency to the resolution of problems in this office. I must act right away; I wonder what I should do first?"

Company Background

Bell Canada was a federally regulated telecommunications company which supplied local and long distance telephone service to 5.6 million customers in Ontario, Quebec, Labrador and parts of the Northwest Territories. The company employed 48 000 men and women throughout its regional, area, and district operations. As a result of recent corporate restructuring, Bell Canada was now part of the holdings of Bell Canada Enterprises (BCE), along with Northern Telecom, and several other major enterprises.

During the early 1980s, many issues arose which seriously challenged the company's ability to remain profitable and competitive. Sweeping technological, economic, and political changes threatened every aspect of the business.

Following the deregulation of Canadian telephone companies by the Canadian Radio-Television & Telecommunications Commission (CRTC), the company lost its monopoly status. As a result, rival interconnect companies were challenging Bell Canada's market share. Vast technological changes were in progress, affecting product lines, office automation, computerization of equipment, and aspects of the business. As one Bell manager remarked, "We must keep ahead of tomorrow's requirements." Adjustments related to management of the company's human resources were being made, such as large-scale staff reductions, hiring freezes, and staff retraining for newly created jobs.

The day-to-day interface between the company and its customers took place at the level of the district business office — either through telephone conversations, or personally at a Bell Phonecentre. Accounts for all residential and business services within each district (a large geographical area, covering five counties in the case of London district) were processed in the business office by service representatives (SRs), their supervisors, and the section manager.

Each customer call was dealt with initially by a service rep — a residential SR for a customer with anywhere from one to three residence lines, and a business SR for a business/commercial customer with more than three lines and/or a PBX system. Instructions then were relayed to the network of departments affected by a particular service order — accounts, billing and records, sales, installation and repair, operator services, engineering, and others as required. The work of service reps in the business office was recognized as an important and valuable contributor to the company's success.

Customer Services (London District)

Located in western Ontario, the London business office serviced 140 000 customers and grossed $83.8 million in revenue. The district manager, W.L. Murray, was in charge of all Bell sales and service in a designated five-county area. The district served both residential customers (one to three telephone lines) and business customers (more than three lines, and PBX systems). Reporting to Betty Gauthier and handling all residential accounts were four business office supervisors, who supervised a total of 26 service representatives (SRs), and four relief service reps, as well as clerical staff and the manager of the Order Bureau and her staff of 10. This group of 46 worked in a large, open office which occupied half of the third floor of a modern office tower in downtown London. Accounts for business and commercial establishments were the primary responsibility of a second group of supervisors and SRs who worked with their own section manager one floor above. Staff functions serving the entire district were housed, along with the regional general manager's office, in a brand-new ultra-modern office complex (the Bell Building) three blocks away.

General responsibilities of a business office service representative were described in an employees' handbook:

> Represents the company in dealings with the public, including customer-initiated contacts relating to applications for service and collection of accounts; compiles information; provides input for publication of telephone directories; is responsible for service revenues; administers tariffs; sells residence and business service.

Brief descriptions of the functions performed by other London district customer services departments with which Betty's residence business office worked were given as follows:

Accounts, Billing and Records
Sets up and maintains customer accounts, makes up the payroll, and keeps the company's books and accounts.

Sales
Studies and evaluates business customer needs and sells telephone equipment and services to meet these needs; recommends development and adoption of new services; assists in forecasting requirements; reviews and recommends rate treatment.

Installation and Repair
Constructs, rearranges and removes outside plant; installs, rearranges and removes customer equipment and services; maintains all plant; rearranges inter-connection of central office equipment; makes direct customer-contact sales; services buildings.

Operator Services
Handles all local and long distance telephone calls, including the provision of information and other assistance services; determines quantities and arrangements of equipment and facilities involved; instructs customers in the use of services.

Engineering
Prepares long- and short-range plans of future plant and service needs; engineers telephone plant, buildings and structures; provides advice of an engineering nature to other departments.

The Service Rep's Job

The service rep played a key role in this total customer service system. The work of Bell's service representatives was considered an extremely important determinant of the company's public image. "The SR is the primary link between the company and the customer, and between the customer and the company," one manager said. "When the customer calls — be it an order for new service, a question about a long distance phone call, or any one of a thousand other requests — the service rep must help in an efficient and friendly way."

The SR was responsible for quickly completing the paperwork for each customer contact. "The handwritten memos must be both neat and accurate, correctly identifying in our own special code the exact nature of each customer contact. Service orders then are typed from the SR's memos; and from these we have the plant department installing or repairing equipment, the accounting department issuing bills, operator services arranging a listing on information records, and so on. Any error in the rep's paper work can have innumerable negative consequences . . . not the least of which is a possible loss of customer confidence."

Service representatives were also responsible for collecting overdue telephone accounts as well as offering customers appropriate suggestions for additional telephone services. Both these responsibilities — account collections and sales of equipment and services — required "tact and judgment," said a customer service supervisor. Service reps' salary levels were the highest of all Bell's clerical personnel, reflecting the skill requirements for the job.

Sweeping changes had occurred in the job of an SR within recent years, reflecting the intense new focus on increasing productivity. Manager Betty Gauthier recalled, "We actually used to sort long distance calls manually! And service reps had to pull all overdue accounts manually from their bins to make their collection calls — so some accounts would not be pulled, through SR neglect or overwork, and some accounts simply would not be treated. Today, accounts at risk are presented automatically to the reps within a predetermined time frame each month."

Turnover among London service representatives was low. A hiring freeze was in effect, with little or no recruiting taking place. Training opportunities had become infrequent, although the complexity of the SR's job had increased. As Betty noted,

> Due to extreme growth in the number of products available, the amount of detailed knowledge service reps and sales people must have is phenomenal! They need to know not only their own but their competitors' products as well. And where residence service reps used to be able to quote package rates, now we have only individual product rates, making each contact more complex. Repair complaints can be very complicated now, too. The cause of a problem could originate with someone else's equipment, not ours, necessitating our getting more detailed information, quoting different rates, explaining endlessly.
>
> Automation provided the opportunity to establish different-sized work units as required — a change from the former huge, centralized locations. "An operator in Scarborough now takes calls for Hamilton. And now we can close smaller offices, and the personnel and equipment can be established elsewhere . . . .But when we close small offices, where will we put those so displaced? And since we can no longer hire the cream of the graduating crop, we're trying to take surplus people from other jobs and train them to be service reps, or take surplus service reps and train them for other jobs."

The office layout also had changed frequently through the years to accommodate the information storage and retrieval needs of business office personnel. As one corporate HR executive recalled,

> Traditionally, the physical layout of the office has been the responsibility of the section manager. There was a time back in the 1960s and early 1970s when it seemed that we were always changing the way the service reps' desks were positioned, now this way and now that way. AT&T experts would recommend this way or that way as ways to increase efficiency. I hate to think of how many thousands of dollars were wasted then, changing desks around to new positions! Time study consultants were okay, but their experiments cost us a fortune. And afterwards, we'd set them up the way we wanted, anyhow.

Residence Section Manager

Betty Gauthier, a 16-year employee of Bell Canada, had joined the company after high school graduation. Betty worked at first as a long distance operator in Ottawa. She soon became a trainer on special assignment to the marketing department, transferring to the Ottawa business office as a service representative in 1970. Management positions followed in rapid succession; temporary training administrator, assistant manager, Order Bureau, and assistant manager of an Ottawa business office. Moving to Kingston, Betty became business office manager, supervising six management and approximately 50 non-management personnel.

Following her marriage, Betty and her husband moved to London, Ontario. For a short time she managed two London Phonecentres; but soon the transfer to Saudi Arabia of London's residence section manager provided the opportunity for her to become a business office manager once again. Three years later, Betty transferred to the Bell's Budget and Results department, developing and reviewing budgets for the entire western Ontario area. A year later that department was moved to Toronto, so in September Betty accepted the challenge of returning to the London business office as manager of the residence section — a lateral move, in terms of job level.

As residence office manager, Betty was responsible for supervising the operations of her office "to the satisfaction of customers, shareholders, employees, and the community which she serves."[1] She was accountable to the district manager for achieving company and office objectives; developing her supervisory staff through setting and measuring performance objectives; administering all personnel matters relating to the residence office; and arranging office facilities and equipment to produce the highest efficiency and best customer service.

---

[1]From the official job description for a business office manager as detailed in Bell's Business Office Management Guide (B.O.M.G.).

In addition to her responsibilities as office manager, Betty was an enthusiastic, energetic participant on company committees and in community organizations—for example, the Bell Public Relations Committee, the Grand Theatre Board, and the United Way Personal Gifts Committee. Betty also attended university classes in the evening as a part-time student.

Regarding the management of her staff, Betty voiced many thoughts and concerns:

> I'm determined to do an excellent job of managing my people here, and I've given a lot of thought to my management style. Before going with the Budget and Results group, I came from a job where I supervised six managers, 50 non-management people, and had a district manager who was very much in favor of letting you do your own job. He let you be the one to initiate changes and be the one in control. And being given that responsibility, I felt really committed to getting the job done and done right!
>
> Going into a staff position in the B and R job, I felt as if I had neither responsibility nor authority. It seemed I was a paper pusher and number cruncher—an interesting experience! Word would come from the executive VP as to what productivity he expected for the next year. Then his regional budget and results group would decide who got what piece of the area pie and then western Ontario would say, OK, here's what we've got and where do we go from here? We dealt with the results of someone else's decisions.
>
> Whereas now, my objectives are very clear to me, and I must manage my people effectively in order to achieve them. My collection objectives, for example, are simply to accomplish the least bad debt losses with the least customer irritation. *In Search of Excellence* says it very well—that book should be required reading for every manager! Hands-on, value driven, productivity through people...all excellent guidelines.
>
> But taking over as office manager again a week ago, I'm finding so much trouble that I don't know where to start. All the reps are unhappy, the managers are in bad moods, and no one seems to care about doing a good job. Although considerable downsizing has taken place since I left eighteen months ago, no office reorganization has been done—the extra work has simply been dumped on individual SR positions. CTEA[2] union reps have become very active on behalf of dissatisfied SRs...and now, I must deal with pressures from senior management to greatly improve our productivity and profitability as well.

Office of the Future

Added to all the other changes Bell managers and employees were dealing with, increased automation of all business offices was right around the corner. A gradual process of technologically transforming every business office into a "paperless office of the future" was already underway. The Guelph office had

---

[2]Canadian Telephone Employees' Association, a union representing all Bell's clerical employees.

installed BCRIS[3] computerized equipment, and the office furnishings and lighting had been improved to provide an ergonomically sound work environment. Improved productivity and profitability of Guelph district business office operations had become an established fact; and plans were underway for BCRIS equipment and procedures to be introduced in London within 2 years. Betty Gauthier anticipated many benefits from the new system:

> The introduction of BCRIS will speed up the service rep's job — for instance, it'll eliminate the order-writing job. Orders will feed directly into accounting and other departments, so the clerical function of entering an order and other details will not be needed. The assignment of telephone numbers in the plant department will be automated, too....A ripple effect will occur throughout *all* our district customer service operations.

London Business Office, Residence Section

The residence section of the London district business office was located on the third floor of a modern downtown office building. Thirty-six service representatives and their four supervisors were located in one large open room, with Betty's office and the order desk at the end nearest the security-locked entrance door. Movable four-foot partitions divided the SRs' desks into pods of four (see office floor plan in Exhibit 1). The four supervisors' desks were carefully positioned for easy observation of the service representatives' activities.

Visitors to the office were impressed with the continual noisy hum of telephone conversations, which permeated the large room in spite of sound-reducing carpeting and partitions. They also noticed constant apparently random (but actually quite purposeful) movement of SRs throughout the office space, passing to and fro between their desks and central record bins or "tub files" to retrieve records relating to the current caller's telephone service.

The desks of all service reps were organized alike. To the SR's right were drawers containing microfiche records for every customer in her section — directory listing and equipment records, credit records, and long distance statements. A microfiche-reading machine occupied a prominent position to the right of each desk top. To the left was a holder containing reference manuals and books, and a set of earphones used by his or her supervisor to monitor customer contacts for appraisal and training purposes. Directly in the center of the desk was the heart of the work station — a telephone system with several indicator lights enabling the SR and supervisor to determine the status of the line. "When I see no light at all," said one supervisor, "I know the SR's position is closed — that the rep is busy on paper work and not taking calls.

---

[3]Pronounced "Bee-Kris" — acronym for "Bell Customer Record Information System."

Then if the SR makes an outgoing call, a blinking light goes on. A flashing light indicates that all incoming lines are filled, and customers are either getting a busy signal or a pleasant voice asking them to hold the line until a business office SR is free to take the call. That flashing light serves as a warning to SRs to finish current calls as quickly as possible — customers are waiting! Those lights give me a good idea of what each of my employees is doing at any given time."

Affixed to the right-hand partition of each work station were four receptacles, each labelled with a number corresponding to a type of order form. As an SR completed the procedures required for a contact, he or she filed her handwritten memo in the appropriate receptacle. These forms were picked up periodically by the order desk clerk, who typed service orders for distribution to other departments. An order clerk stated, "We type information from the handwritten memos on a nine-page fanfold, which goes out to many departments. For instance, to install a new service we must notify central office equipment to assign a telephone number and the accounting department to start billing, as well as the installers, repair service, directory department, statistical department, and others." The average elapsed time from the writing of the initial service order by the service rep to the receipt of departmental copies was four hours.

Typical Telephone Contacts

Three calls received one September morning by service rep Marilyn West were typical of the hundreds received in the London business office daily. One caller was a man who denied any knowledge of a particular long-distance call billed to his number — a seven-minute call to Hamilton, Ontario, on Saturday morning, July 28. Marilyn quickly located the relevant microfiche and placed it on the reader, verifying the facts about this particular call. Marilyn then kindly but firmly insisted that the call had in fact been made from his number, that the details must be correct, and that he was indeed responsible for the charges. When the customer switched to a complaint that "the Bell keeps changing the rates without telling people," the SR patiently explained the weekend rate structure "...which has been in place for many years; regular rates before 12 on Saturday, two-thirds off from 12 noon Saturday to 6 p.m. Sunday."

Throughout the five-minute conversation, Marilyn's hands were busy — first noting the details of the customer's name, telephone number, and nature of the complaint on an "1109" form, then completing paper work relating to previous contacts. The call concluded on a reasonably happy note — the customer seemed satisfied with the rep's explanations, and the SR's desk top was clear!

Marilyn received another incoming call immediately. She answered at once, in a pleasant tone, "Good morning, Mrs. West here. Can I help you?" The customer responded, "This is Mildred Rand, out Thamesford way. I want to get my party off my line."

West You're having difficulties with your party?

Rand I've had five and a half years of nothing but trouble — my party hogs the line, cuts in when I'm talking, and won't let me call out in an emergency. And my 10-month-old son is sick in the hospital now, and I just know the hospital won't be able to contact me if they need me to come into London in a hurry!

West Sounds as if that's a bad situation — please give me your telephone number, and I'll get your records.

Mrs. Rand gave her phone number. Marilyn placed her phone on hold, quickly walked three metres to the central tub file, and retrieved the card containing the Rands' telephone service records. Marilyn wrote her own name and the Rands' number on a pink card and placed it in the tub file — if another SR came looking for those particular records, she would know where to find them. Marilyn returned to her desk and withdrew from her desk-top file the fiche map of the rural area in which Mrs. Rand's house was located. It was first necessary to ascertain if the equipment to provide a private residence line actually existed in this out-of-the-way location.

West I have a map here of your area, and am trying to pinpoint the exact location of your home. Are you located south or north of R.R. 3?

Rand On the north side. *(Marilyn hurriedly reached for another fiche map and placed it on the reader).* On the west side of Concession 11, y'know.

West I see your house is the second one from the corner. When your service was first installed...

Rand That was ages ago! The MacPhersons built their house since then, and a new city couple put up an A-frame last year...guess we're fourth from the corner, now.

West We'll change our records here. At any rate, we have the equipment available to install single line service for you this week...

Rand ...today?

West Not that soon, because we have to arrange in advance to send an installer out to do the work, Thursday or Friday this week.

Rand Thursday would be better...but I might have to be at the hospital most of the day. Tell your installer that if there's nobody at the house, to go out back to the barn. My dad will be there, and he'll let him in. My dad's hard of hearing, so he'll have to yell pretty loud.

West I'll make a note of that on your order, Mrs. Rand.

Throughout the remainder of the conversation, Marilyn consulted various data bases, and scribbled notations on her "1109" memo pad. She viewed a microfiche containing data needed to calculate the service charge for Mrs. Rand's rate group; she looked at another fiche for London rate areas; she added columns of figures to obtain the correct monthly service charge; and quoted the price for installing two jacks along with the new service.

West Although there's an installation charge for the jacks, as I mentioned, there's no charge for the change to a private line . . . and I know you'll enjoy the security of your new service. I hope your little boy is better soon.

Rand This is his third time in hospital this year . . .

West I'm sorry to hear that . . . goodbye, Mrs. Rand.

Rand Goodbye.

Marilyn had barely begun writing an order to change the Rands' service records to indicate the two new houses on Concession 11, when her telephone rang again. A customer was calling to make payment arrangements for a large outstanding bill. The customer had received a final notice, and was anxious to forestall the disconnection of her telephone service. Marilyn had difficulty locating the records for this account — another SR had them at her desk, and had neglected to place a pink indicator card in the tub file. Marilyn eventually found the records, and satisfactory payment arrangements were negotiated.

Marilyn glanced up at the centrally located office clock. "Almost time for my coffee break — the morning is flying past, as usual. Guess I'm lucky to have such an interesting and busy job, even if I never quite catch up with all my paper work. I wonder if I'll have time between incoming calls to get through today's scheduled treatment of my delinquent accounts? Hope so — the backlog builds up at an incredible rate, and has a disastrous effect on my personal performance rating."

Service Reps Talk About Their Job

The London business office service representatives were knowledgeable and experienced people — none had less than three years' experience, and one had been an SR for twenty-five years. Their qualifications included higher levels of education; some had university degrees, and many had acquired some university or community college credits. A sampling of their opinions concerning the SR's job was obtained through personal interviews:

The pay is good. I report to the office at 8:30, open my position for calls at 9, and work till 5, although my key is pretty well closed off around 4:15. We all get one hour for lunch, with two break periods. I enjoy most parts of my job — the people I work with, the atmosphere, customer contact, my supervisors...I love talking with people, though we're the ones who take the brunt of all errors, even those made by other people, other departments. Right now, I'm happy here. I don't want to go anywhere else.

What I like least about my job is sometimes we're incredibly busy and there's no time between calls. And customers are so "brave" over the telephone. I can't stand rude people who yell at me without reason, and I get at least one a day. I'll go out of my way for most people — we're here to help. However, if there's no time between calls and we're receiving one order after another, we're bound to forget something and make mistakes.

I was married two years ago, and moved to London with my husband. I expected to be a full-time service rep in London, as I was in my home town, but there were no positions open. I had to take the only job available, as regular part-time SR. Only one full-time job has come up in the meantime, and I didn't get it — someone was transferred in from out of town. I've been told that I will likely never be able to work as a full-time service rep again — the jobs just don't exist. I'm resigned to this situation at the moment, since I'm now pregnant and expecting my first child in a few months.

What I like about my job — doing so many things, the variety. I'm a real organizer, and I like planning my work from minute to minute. I like the challenge of thinking all the time. I'm a perfectionist, so I'm constantly challenging myself. I like to do a good job for my own satisfaction, so I study my results each month. What I dislike is irate customers, and the number I get can vary according to the time of year and how busy we are — they may react strongly to being on hold for awhile. Most of all, I dislike whiners whose minds are made up before they call. There's quite a difference between residential and business office customers... this residence office often gets lonely people who want to talk for hours.

I wouldn't want to be a manager here. They get the worst of the irate customer contacts referred to them, and they're in between — have to satisfy both the SRs and the people above them. I have experienced two opposite kinds of management...I was over-managed in my former location, where I was the only new SR for years, and my manager was delighted! She managed me by the book — uniform procedures were used throughout that office. There was a daily "turret check," when the manager came around to see if she could help with any particular items that I had stuck up there to question her about. Coming into this office was a real shock to my system! Here I only get a message from my manager when I'm doing something really wrong. So sometimes I ask the other reps about a procedure, or they just tell me "That's not the way we do it here," or I just take a chance that I'm doing the right thing in a particular situation...I'm on my own, so to speak.

I was a member of a task force (four representatives, one from each section, plus a manager) which met last year about morale. We talked with each section about their problems, and we came up with some solutions. But the managers are so very busy. However, Betty always keeps us informed of what is happening, and tries to keep us in the picture. Before Betty, it was them versus us! However, CRTC often announces big changes to the media before Bell headquarters has time to pass the

419

Bell Canada (R)

information down the line; so customers sometimes ask me about some new policy before I've heard about it myself...that's just the way it is.

We have a formal annual review called the JPR — Job Planning and Review. Your manager writes up a report and assesses you in the various areas you're supposed to be competent in, and looks at whether you're ready to move up into management or not. She reads it off to you, and discusses it, and you can change any part if you wish. Then all the managers meet in a review board situation, where everybody talks about all their own SRs, and input is given by all other managers about each rep. However, I'm distressed that only one year's JPR is kept on file — all previous JPRs are destroyed.

I am evaluated by the number of queries about my work (no queries is my goal), how long customers are on hold (my use of the "not-ready" key), length of my calls, my written vouchers, adjustments to customer accounts returned with errors, and sales — how much revenue I'm making for the company. Although I'm supposed to be evaluated on quality of customer contacts — the amount of accurate service that I give my customers — my manager listened to only three of my contacts all last year.

It seems to me that the type of training I got 15 years ago was superior to what the new reps have received. Training used to be done in London, an eight-week training program operated by special instructors. We would be trained thoroughly in one aspect of the job, then practice receiving that type of call at a real rep's desk in the office. This provided a gradual easing into the job, which I liked very much. I also liked the classroom discussions, a half-dozen of us with our own instructor — it gave me a chance to air my difficulties, and hear others' responses. Now, they have computerized programmed learning in Toronto. SRs get their practice lessons on tape, using a self-teaching method. They read the theory from books, then do a practice lesson on the phone with unseen training people, then take the tape of this practice customer contact to a supervisor for evaluation. Talk about individualized learning — everyone advances by herself, at her own pace, but all alone.

My workload, the amount of paper on my desk, has increased incredibly over the years. We used to have slow periods, but no more! Now there are more people calling in and fewer people to answer their calls. It is absolutely necessary to do a lot of overlapping work. At the same time as an SR is talking to a customer, he or she has to be posting orders, pulling records out of the desk, doing two and three things at once. When I get home, I'm still spinning at top speed!

What I like best about my job is customer contact — such variety! I never know what I'm going to get when I answer the phone. I am measured on the number of calls I make a day, the number of calls I receive a day, the amount of time per call, the time I keep customers waiting, my collection index (the percent I collect each month). My sales are tracked, too; and I get positive or negative feedback on Mondays through my individual results.

It's impossible to do a good job when I'm doing two things at once. I am bound to make clerical mistakes, or adding mistakes. What I find really difficult is sales — I dislike selling. We receive training on the products, so we know the facts about all of the Bell products. But we don't actually receive tips to help us sell, although I ask the other reps who have been doing a lot of selling for their tips at our meetings. Sometimes I hear one of them use a phrase that's better than the one I've been using, so I'll adopt it myself. And I could use some help in bridging contacts — for instance, when someone calls in about installing a phone, how can I sell them a long distance gift certificate?

Service Reps Talk About Impending Changes

Bell Canada (R)

Most of the service reps and their supervisors were highly enthusiastic about the prospects of a "paperless office of the future" made possible by the introduction of BCRIS computerized equipment, although a few reservations were expressed:

> My reaction to information about BCRIS is totally positive. It will get rid of all the paper and most of the files. That irritation will be done. Even though we'll have problems in the changeover period, the end result will be well worth the effort.

> The service reps are used to moving around during the day. Once the automated process takes over, they're going to be sitting still. We will get increased productivity, for sure...but at what cost?

> The Guelph people are so positive — they're the initiators of this change, and by the time it gets to us, all the bugs will be worked out. And Bell has promised us that no one will be laid off as a result of the change. Of course we're not hiring now, either; even though the workload here is almost beyond us, temporary part time people are filling in from now until BCRIS is installed.

> When BCRIS comes in, I will certainly miss the clerical part of my job. However, it will be an interesting change. It will be less frustrating work — I won't have to chase floating records! My only worry is about my eyes, and the possible detrimental effects of looking at that screen with its peculiar kind of lighting for long periods of time.

> When Bell mechanizes a function, the grade for a job goes up. A friend of mine, a Repair Centre Clerk 6, changed to a Clerk 7 when new technology was introduced. Will we be upgraded too?

The district union representative was encouraged by the way Bell was approaching the introduction of more change:

> The "paperless office of the future" will be marvellous for individual service reps. The company promises that although fewer bodies will be required, no one will actually lose their job. Attrition will take care of some, and if a service rep is absolutely unable to get onto the mechanics of the new job, a transfer can be arranged. SRs have been assured that the hunt-and-peck method of typing entries will be okay, and during a trial period no great expectations will be held for a perfect performance. That seems fair to me...and the union is watching closely to see that the company keeps its promises.

Performance Management: Measurement and Feedback

The productivity and effectiveness of business office service reps were tracked continually using intricate systems of measures or "key indicators." London results (individual, group and district) were made available daily to Betty Gauthier, who posted relevant performance statistics in a central location in the office. She explained,

The number of key indicators has grown tremendously in the past decade or so, due to pressures resulting from loss of our monopoly position. Greatly improved productivity is a must. Results in the London office have been good, compared with the rest of the region; but we're always striving for better numbers.

We get our results after each business day, and I make a monthly summary. There are 30 or so performance measures, key indicators, on which my performance is judged; but the two most important are productivity[4] ("work units," on my summary sheet) and my SPMP—Service Provisioning Measurement Plan.[5] Collections are important, too. And I also have the Outward Movement Performance Measurement Plan [OMPMP], designed to recover our telephone sets when customers disconnect and move out. My office has a sales objective for each month, leading to the calculation of revenue per hour. I also have on-duty and off-duty injuries objectives. I have incidental absences objectives, payroll errors objectives, first-aid training objectives.

We're good in the area of efficiency, and our work units results compare favorably with other offices. We average about four and a half minutes a call, which is less than other small offices. But because we have so much work to do and only so many people to do it, then on the customer access side the results aren't as good. What I need is more staff to answer the calls faster. But if I get more staff, I have more paid hours, which reduces my productivity. Is there a happy medium? I don't think any office has it. In offices that are achieving their SPMP objective, they're not achieving the productivity results we get.

My management performance is evaluated formally every October [see Exhibit 2 for details of the management appraisal form], and we keep excellent records of our service reps' performance for their annual evaluation sessions [see Exhibit 3 for details of the non-management appraisal report]. My performance objectives are given to me 'top down,' and I try to meet them 'bottom up.' I'm given my total objectives for the year each December, when the new budget comes down. If they're impossible objectives, I'll explain why I can't meet them; and then we discuss it, and come up with final objectives. On a monthly basis, it's a matter of monitoring the results as they come in to make sure the SRs are achieving those

---

[4]Productivity measurement was based on a factor or number of work units assigned to each type of telephone contact, depending on the degree of complexity and amount of time usually required to complete the work (e.g., final account collection, a highly complex procedure, rated 14.99 work units; account maintenance rated only .16 work units).

[5]SPMP measurement was the average length of time (seconds) required for SRs to respond to customers' calls, independently measured by the CRTC.

final objectives. And if they're not, I talk to their managers and review progress with the service reps. I try to find out why, and then develop appropriate action plans to correct the situation.

To improve my SPMP measure, I first do my own analysis. If I can't find anything that could be causing the problem I go to the manager for another opinion. He/she may have an answer: "Well, we've been inundated with customer calls about the bill reformat. We didn't have any idea how much of an impact that would have! We forecast that it would maybe increase our calls by about five percent, but they actually increased by 14 percent." Or maybe there was a large-scale error in long distance tapes, or some other unusual occurrence.

But if we don't know the answer, we start looking at every aspect of the reps' work. Has their time between calls narrowed so much that they can't complete one contact before the next customer is on the line? Has the time that they spend in "not ready" mode doing clerical work exceeded the office average for the past year or so? That's wasting time. Are they adhering to the coffee and lunch break schedule? That's all recorded on our machine — when they logged onto the system, when they came off for coffee, when they went to lunch, all of those things. We look at all aspects of what we measure, and see what is different this month from last month, and from the month previous, if we don't already know.

And usually I already know, since I always review our results from the previous day. Weekly I provide an assessment of what I think our month-end productivities are going to be. If we aren't going to meet productivity objectives because the work load has fallen below our forecast, we get rid of hours — I loan people to other departments, grant unpaid "excused time" or whatever. We react daily to the results; if daily monitoring our SRs shows an average speed of answers of 100 seconds, and I know that if I get any more than 30 seconds I'm not going to meet my month-end objective, we don't wait till the monthly report comes in to react.

We post the daily results on boards in each section. Also, we post the monthly review with the total office results together with the reps' individual results — how many calls they took, . . . their average in comparison to the total office, . . . their average length on calls, . . . their average closed key time, how they are doing on collections, and so on. We also post results of our monthly product promotion campaign. We have a different incentive each month. Last month, the SR with the highest sales won a Contempra telephone . . . she did her job well, sold effectively, and received a perk. She was happy about that!

I have four managers here who depend on me for supervision. Although they don't need a lot of supervision, it's still my responsibility to ensure that they are performing at the required level. I have to assess their performance and make recommendations about their potential to advance to a higher level of management, and to give them a yearly increase if they deserve it. And I review quarterly with each of my managers what they are doing for non-management people, to make sure that they are performing their functions to keep their section informed of on-going results. There should be a strong communications link between the managers and the SRs.

I guess communications is one of our major problem areas. I've just returned to this office, and everybody is fighting with everybody else. They're saying that management's blind devotion to computer statistics is causing severe morale problems with the staff in the office. They're saying that we have no feeling for employees, we're just looking at numbers. Something must be done to improve this situation—the tension is growing daily, and now they've filed this grievance.

The Grievance

London district SRs were represented by the Canadian Telephone Employees' Association (CTEA), one of two unions representing all of Bell's clerical workers, who comprised more than 50 percent of total company employees. (Other non-management employees, craft and services workers, had been represented by the CWC—Communications Workers of Canada—since 1976). Organized 35 years ago, the CTEA General Council (composed of 50 district chairmen) employed field officers to serve as watchdogs for the collective agreement and to process grievances. In the opinion of a Bell executive, "the CTEA is quite a responsible union, really interested in solving problems for its Bell members. It is made up largely of people who are or have been Bell workers, who are loyal to both the company and its employees."

Historically, relations between the London local and management had been cordial and cooperative. However, recent events were producing a stronger union stance on behalf of its members, as explained by an elected representative of the local:

> For at least a year and a half, our union has been dealing with individual grievances, and dealing directly with the manager involved. However, morale has become so bad that, in order to deal effectively with so many common problems, we have finally put in a group grievance. There are stress problems, incidental absence problems, overwork...these all came up in a recent members' meeting. Previous attempts to resolve problems from the bottom up—unit meetings, and a task force on SR problems—have failed. Employees are frightened to say anything, and managers don't encourage openness.
>
> Different work groups are going different ways, because all four managers are displaying markedly different interpretations of management policies. Some reps are resorting to cheating to beat the key indicators, in order to get their work done without being hassled. Two new reps are being hired, and the old staff isn't receiving any training.
>
> The equipment is in place to provide performance data—how much closed time, outgoing calls, other criteria—but it's not being used to manage the SRs, it's more like a club over their heads. Our work standards are inappropriate too; for instance, standards designed to be used by Wardair provide a two-minute average elapsed time between calls as reasonable for doing paperwork. At our office, the average time between calls is zero to 13 seconds—though it should be higher.
>
> So we've drafted a grievance which focuses on our conviction that management is abusing its rights through its current practice of managing by statistics alone, causing unwarranted stress and morale problems among the reps. We've identified

five main issues: pressure on reps to finish contacts hurriedly when the "customer waiting" light begins to flash, lack of sufficient dedicated time for completing paperwork, unequal distribution of work loads among SRs, too few full-time staff, and abdication of managerial responsibility — management by computer, rather than by consistent, person-oriented direction. All of the residence office SRs signed the grievance.

We presented the grievance to the four first-level managers. When this group gave indications of resolving only one of the major issues, the union decided to take it to the next level. We delivered our grievance to Betty Gauthier today. She has five days in which to respond.

425

Bell Canada
(R)

EXHIBIT 1
BELL CANADA (R)

Floor Plan, London District Business Office*

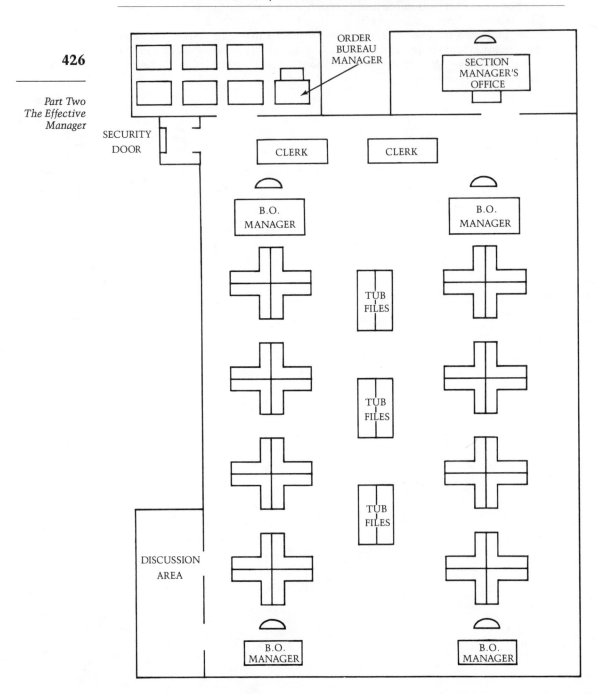

*September 1984

EXHIBIT 2

BELL CANADA (R)

Management Appraisal Form

Contents of Page 1

Should be typed

ONTARIO REGION MANAGEMENT APPRAISAL
BELL CANADA/RESTRICTED
(G.C. 203.7 APP. B)

19__

BC 760 P/R (O.R.) (84.06)

427

PERFORMANCE
CLASSIFICATION [   ]

RESOURCE
CLASSIFICATION [   ]

*Bell Canada
(R)*

SURNAME:_____ INITIALS:_____

TITLE:_____

DIST:_____

A.V.P. GROUP:_____

EDUCATION:_____

LANGUAGE SKILLS: R   W   C

   ENGLISH
   FRENCH
OTHER (SPECIFY)

SAL.
CLASS._____ NCS DATE:_____

APPT. DATE
TO LEVEL:_____

APPT. DATE
PRESENT JOB:_____

PREPARED BY:_____

_____

Main Responsibilities (Past 12 months)

Performance (Past 12 months)

Contents of Pages 2-4 (abridged)

DEMONSTRATED MANAGERIAL SKILLS AND QUALITIES

INTERPERSONAL SKILLS
   Leadership:
   Behavior Flexibility:
   Oral Communication Skills:

STABILITY OF PERFORMANCE
   Resistance to Stress:
   Tolerance of Ambiguity:

ADMINISTRATIVE SKILLS
   Organizing and Planning:
   Quality of Decisions:
   Decisiveness:
   Creativity:
   Written Communication Skills:

WORK MOTIVATION
   Inner Work Standards:
   Energy:
   Work Involvement:

RESOURCE SUMMARY
EMPLOYEE CAREER INTERESTS
DEVELOPMENT ACTIVITIES DURING PAST 12 MONTHS
CURRENT DEVELOPMENTAL NEEDS AND RECOMMENDATIONS (NEXT 12 MONTHS)
PLACEMENT RECOMMENDATIONS

Year	Qtr.	Plcmt. Code					
19__	____	_____	or	_____	or	_____	
19__	____	_____	or	_____	or	_____	

SIGNATURE: _____
TITLE: _____
DATE: _____

EXHIBIT 3

BELL CANADA (R)

Non-Management Appraisal Report

Contents of Page 1

NON-MANAGEMENT
PERSONNEL APPRAISAL REPORT
(G.C. 203.10)
19___   YR. MO. DAY

1 – SURNAME_____ INITIALS_____
                           CLASS
2 – TITLE_____ GRADE_____   8 – N.C.S. DATE_____

3 – AREA/DEPARTMENT_____   9 – APPT. DATE TO GR./C.L._____

4 – DISTRICT_____   10 – APPT. DATE TO PRESENT JOB_____

5 – EDUCATION_____   11 – ABSENTEEISM (12 MTHS. PRIOR TO REVIEW

                R W C   R W C   INCIDENTAL TIMES_____ DAYS_____

6 – LANGUAGE SKILLS   E   F   S.D.B.   TIMES_____ DAYS_____

7 – OTHER (SPECIFY)   PREPARED BY:_____

12 – SUMMARY OF MAIN RESPONSIBILITIES AND RESULTS (PAST 12 MONTHS)

13 – DEMONSTRATED POTENTIAL

Contents of Page 2

DEVELOPMENT PLANS

15 – OTHER DATA

16 – DEVELOPMENT RECOMMENDATIONS – PREVIOUS REVIEW

17 – CURRENT DEVELOPMENT NEEDS

18 – PLACEMENT RECOMMENDATIONS
  SPECIFY QUARTER

19 – CODES

  [   ]   [   ]   [   ]
  PERF.   RES.   PCMT

_____   _____   _____
        DATE   SUPERVISOR'S SIGNATURE   TITLE

428

MANAGING CHANGE AT NTC (B): TEAM PLAY

James C. Rush and Eileen D. Watson

The atmosphere in the office of the Harmony project manager at Northern Telecom's Station Apparatus Division (SAD) plant was tense. Jim Retallack's weekly meeting with project staff was due to begin in less than an hour, and Retallack was only half-way through the stack of progress reports and milestone sheets piled on his desk. Jim rapidly scanned each report, looking for critical information to help him gauge the stage of completion of each component of the total project.

The Harmony telephone was slated to be in full operation in eight months and Retallack was determined to meet that deadline. In the face of criticism from some detractors, Jim wondered if he should be doing something differently in order to complete the project on time and under budget. As he scrutinized the reports he thought, "I'm certain that project teams are the best way to organize... but how can I make team efforts more integrated, more productive?"

Retallack was aware that differences of opinion existed among certain members of the 10 working groups (teams) which constituted the Harmony project staff. Many urgent issues were awaiting his immediate decision, including the thorny problem of whether to build or buy the Electret transmitter. The Harmony project would significantly affect the lives and livelihoods of many SAD employees.

Harmony's History

Doug Clark, new product manager at the Station Apparatus Division (SAD) in London, had been named acting eBasic project manager fifteen months earlier by Alan Lutz, General Manager of the plant. (The eBasic name — "e" for "electronic" — was used to identify the new basic residential telephone prior to the creation of the "Harmony" name.) The project involved building the

Harmony prototype and manufacturing the finished product. Automated manufacturing and assembly processes were assumed from the beginning.

Clark became the driving force behind extensive market research which was used to formulate NTC's strategy *vis-a-vis* the new product:

> To design, develop and introduce a new family of high quality electronic single-line telesets which will be low cost, have wide consumer appeal, have high volume sales, employ flexible, common technologies and manufacturing processes, have low labor content, and be introduced by January 1984 for global roll-out.

As a result of intensive study and research by Clark and other key staff, the best design was chosen for the first member of the family. This was the Harmony telephone, a basic residential set. It was to be the first of the complete eBasic (800) line of Northern Telecom products, which would also include a partially featured residential telephone (Signature), a basic business telephone (Unity I), and a full-feature business telephone (Unity II). It was proposed that Harmony be in production by November 1983, for introduction in January 1984.

Corporate approval had to be sought for the recommended expenditure of $12 million in additional research and development and capital investment. At first, the corporation was reluctant to grant approval. For an organization which for two decades had mainly concerned itself with one basic model, the idea of a massive change "from a serial, technology based, product development process to an iterative, market-focused integrated team approach" was greeted with skepticism by some. Also, many engineers tended to believe that NTC should be in the switching business, not the terminal business.

Resistance was encountered on the basis of other objections as well — the product was wrong, the market had been improperly read, basic phones weren't needed, sales projections were too optimistic, other sets (e.g. Contempra) would be cannibalized, the London plant would be unable to deliver on time, the product would cost too much, and the project was not part of the corporate strategy.

Within the plant itself, morale was low — "doom and gloom" prevailed. Concerns were expressed about probable effects of automation on the 1300-member workforce. The union executive was opposed to introducing new manufacturing processes that would render obsolete all the knowledge and expertise of experienced workers, and which surely would reduce the number of jobs available.

The proposal finally was accepted on the basis of establishing a cost-effective manufacturing process for all NTC terminals. The project was given a do or die mandate — "Do it right, or you're dead!" Lack of success at any stage ultimately would result in plant closure, affecting 1300 employees.

Official approval had the effect of silencing objections inside and outside the London plant. When it was made clear to SAD workers and management alike that the only alternative to introducing new products and manufacturing processes was to close down the London operation entirely, the union and management agreed to work together toward a successful Harmony launch. The plant would continue producing the old 500 line throughout the developmental period for the new model.

Staffing the Project

Doug Clark (acting project manager) brought engineering manager Jim Baker on board shortly after his own appointment. Controller Kathy Flanagan and technology manager M. Alikhan were added later, completing the core group of four.

When official approval of the project seemed only a matter of time, plant manager Alan Lutz was considering going outside the plant to hire a full-time project manager. He talked with Jim Retallack (a PhD in Electrical Engineering who was working at BNR in Ottawa) about the job. Retallack recalled the circumstances of his move to the London plant:

> After three and a half years in R and D, I wanted to broaden my experience in the business side of NTC, and...get some production under my belt. I called the general manager in London, to tell him I was interested in moving — he and I had talked together in the past. The outcome of this was an interview with Al, and an offer to head up the Harmony project team!
>
> As I thought about the opportunity, I sought the advice of John Roll, then president of BNR and himself a former general manager in London. He suggested, "If you think you can succeed at the job, you should do it." So I wound up my Ottawa job in a month or so, and arrived in London early in December.

Retallack immediately began a campaign to establish the definition of the Harmony project team as a unique, high-status group composed of dedicated people with exceptional talent and motivation. One of his first acts was to acquire separate office space reserved for the use of the Harmony project group only. He was successful in commandeering an area which came to be known throughout the plant as the "eBasic office."

He got to know the people already assigned to the Harmony project, and came to appreciate the initial personnel selection. Divisional general manager Al Lutz had put many new people into positions of responsibility; and Doug Clark and Jim Baker had hand-picked the best group of "maverick nonconformists" they could find within SAD. They felt that special talents and skills were needed for such a unique and innovative project.

Speaking about his early days in his new position, Jim Retallack recalled,

> My first week on the job, I attended an important value analysis session where we discussed a significant cost reduction. We were talking $20 minimum to $27 maximum to produce Harmony — almost 60 percent less than the old basic 500 set. It seemed to me that $23 was the number to shoot at.

And I relied heavily on Doug in the beginning — so much so, that I was only there for a short time before I took off for six weeks of previously scheduled vacation. Some people never quite figured out how I could do that . . . but I had made a point of working with them quite intensively before I went away.

Organizational Structure

Al Lutz made it clear from the beginning that the new project manager was to be given people and resources from other departments who would be dedicated to the Harmony project full-time as required. (See Exhibit 1 for a partial divisional organization chart). Jim was to have the freedom and the authority to structure every aspect of the project his way. Talking about his early impressions of the organization already in place when he arrived, Retallack said,

> The financial and marketing aspects seemed to be in good shape when I took over — I needed only to ensure that Clark and Flanagan and their people were kept informed and involved. Alikhan had just come on board, replacing the former design head; and both he and Baker had chosen excellent people for their teams, starting with Jim's key man, Jim Kilpatrick. However, I felt that their functional roles should be more sharply focused, making for greater accountability and increased effectiveness.

Retallack believed that in order to design and develop every component and complete the final assembly simultaneously within severe time and cost constraints, cross-functional teams were necessary. So responsibility for product development was broken down among 10 teams, each comprising technology (design) and manufacturing (engineering) people (see Exhibit 2 for team lists). Test staff, quality control, and materials control people were to be added later, as needed.

Each team was responsible for one key component of the product, and for meeting the following objectives:

- developing a reliable design that could be manufactured within cost objectives;
- maintaining a close liaison with other cross-functional teams;
- maintaining close liaison with marketing, quality control, production control, and purchasing;
- producing a design that would lend itself to automation.

Retallack's strategy was to nail down a tough, uncompromising structure and rigid reporting systems. He said,

> To get the product to market quickly on time and on budget means getting it right the first time! I know we can do it . . . but it's going to take a lot of discipline, and strong control and leadership from the top.

Jim was aware of the strength of his position as a dedicated full-time project manager reporting directly to the general manager. He thought it was advantageous that he had been brought in from outside the plant, so he had no prior reputation in the plant to contend with. "However," Jim remarked, "it helps that the common assumption is that I am a good personal friend of Al Lutz, a popular and competent GM. This isn't the case; but I'll never tell that to anyone!"

Jim believed that effective management of change was critical to the project's success. He felt that a key success factor was having superior personnel on the Harmony team, representing the major functions. About half of the team members were dedicated to the Harmony project; but Jim remarked, "I have to fight very hard with some other guys to keep these people dedicated. Some other managers try to steal them back; and I can't allow that to happen."

Negative reactions to various aspects of the project were being expressed by skeptical detractors throughout the division, including a few members of the existing Harmony team. As one manager recalled, "We had many non-believers in our midst. Retallack faced a severe attitude problem — 'Here's another new boy — he'll soon learn! Harmony will never be completed on time, and costs will escalate out of sight.' "

Reporting Procedures

From the beginning of his tenure Retallack insisted on a strict reporting schedule involving report forms, regular meetings, sign-off procedures, memos, work orders, and other means of tracking the progress of every Harmony component toward completion. Initially, each team was asked to produce a detailed schedule of the tasks or steps required to develop and source their assigned component (see Exhibit 3 for the detailed tooling schedule for Team 10's receiver). These steps were then listed on the team's "milestone chart," giving planned start and completion dates. Actual start and completion dates were added when known, and any slippage was monitored (see Exhibit 4 for a section of Team 9's milestone chart).

By early February 1983, an overall eBasic milestone chart had been developed by manufacturing manager Jim Kilpatrick and technology manager Alikhan, and distributed by Jim Retallack (see Exhibit 5 for a memo and accompanying eBasic milestone chart). Because all of the Harmony components were interrelated, no single team could complete its job alone, without reference to the others' work. To keep all teams fully informed, Retallack kept up a constant stream of communication — information updates, deadline reminders, announcements, program reports, etc. Retallack's on-going preoccupation was with prodding everyone to complete each step on time, on or under budget.

Jim believed in written commitments, "enforced personally," to engender a high realization of personal responsibility. Every team was required to make a formal report once a week on its progress to date, based on a report form outlining:

- status to date with respect to scheduled milestones (including outstanding, current, and future milestones)
- problems and suggested solutions
- interaction with other teams.

These were delivered to Jim each Thursday morning, and formed the basis of "in person" reporting at weekly Harmony team meetings.

Meetings, Meetings, Meetings

Weekly project review meetings were held Thursdays at 3:00 p.m. Retallack demanded strict punctuality at every session, and anyone who was late was chastised publicly. The meetings were opened by the project manager with some overview statements ("I tried to inject some humor," Jim said), and then were chaired by either the engineering manager or the technology manager. This freed Retallack to track progress manually on a master chronological grid chart, and to focus on the issues raised by each team.

Project review meetings also included reports from the product manager and the controller on market issues and the financial status of the project. There were generally 30 or more people in attendance, from the level of manager down to the working levels. Directors were not permitted at these meetings. Other meetings were held on a regular basis, implemented later in the project development as they became necessary.

- Senior Management Status Reviews, Mondays at 8:15 a.m. — information sessions for managers of project staff.
- Production Reviews, Tuesdays at 1:00 p.m. — status reviews for Production, Material Control and Engineering of Manufacture personnel not directly involved in the cross-functional teams.
- Field Trial Reviews, Mondays at 9:30 a.m. — status reviews, focusing on short-term action required as a result of new information.

Decision, Decision, Decisions

Among the many urgent issues competing for Jim Retallack's attention was the Electret transmitter "build or buy" decision. The electroacoustics manager in charge of transducers for the Harmony project was Bill Greason, an electrical engineer and 5-year Northern employee. Bill was responsible for two key handset components (the Dynamic receiver and the Electret transmitter) and for the tone alerter which was to be installed in the base assembly.

Bill Greason's reputation as an excellent manager was well-established. His team had been successful in developing the new Dynamic Receiver prototype, to be manufactured in Penang; but how to install it in the plastic handset package was a problem. Greason's people maintained that a difference of $1/10''$ diameter in the plastic cup size would improve acoustical properties of the Dynamic receiver. The BNR industrial design crew adamantly refused to change their specs, which were optimized for appearance. (Eventually, a satisfactory installation method was worked out, leaving both sides satisfied.)

However, this was a relatively simple decision compared to the human and other issues surrounding the pending decision about the Electret transmitter. Greason summarized his concerns as follows:

> I've got the team that built the first Electret. Originally, this type of transmitter component was BNR's idea, but BNR couldn't build it — and we did! I'm proud of my team; and I envision delivering the "perfect Electret" as our quality contribution to the Harmony project.
>
> However, at our last value analysis session, our preliminary cost estimates came in at $1 over our original goal. When Jim Retallack asked what else we could do to lower costs, the finger was laid on the Electret.
>
> And an alternative exists. One Japanese supplier manufactures pre-packaged microphones by the billions, at 25¢ each — much below our cost. We've run a "shake and bake" analysis[1] on samples we purchased from the Japanese supplier, and they seem OK.
>
> But talking with my people, I find reluctance to go with the imported Electret. They worry about jobs being lost in the plant. Also, it would seem a slap in the face of a good team to reject our own product, particularly when the common perception is that Japanese quality and reliability will be uncertain. My team has voiced the concern that "we're selling out to the Japanese"... and yet Retallack keeps pushing cost constraints, and insisting on an answer today, if not sooner!

Other pending decisions involved the resolution of differences among the various teams, each of which depended on one or more of the others to complete its own work satisfactorily. For example, the jacks were to be built in the SAD plant (it had been ascertained that no alternative source existed); but absolute cooperation was essential between the jacks' team and the teams for the circuit board and transmitter. Only one model of jack would be produced, and it would end up on the modules for both the transmitter and the printed circuit board; and problems had surfaced when two different teams with two different philosophies tried to come to some mutually acceptable conclusions. While the original jack design satisfied the needs of one, the needs of the other weren't satisfied. For instance, the holes drilled in the circuit boards to make

---

[1]Tests indicating the product's reaction to extremes of temperature and different types of impact.

contact with the jacks were different sizes than those for the transmitter—the transmitter team wanted a larger opening than the circuit board team's requirements.

Another issue dealt with the installation of the new piezo-electric alerter which had been built by one of Greason's teams (Team 3). It tested as a good product, and was already being manufactured in the London plant. However, certain problems were awaiting resolution with the base assembly team (Team 1). Modification in the design of the alerter or of the Harmony base might be needed to complete the assembled "fit" of the two components. Also, Team 1 was insisting that one of the four pedestal feet supporting the base be installed in the back of the acoustic cavity. Team 3 was resisting the placement; the quality and volume of alerter sound might be adversely affected.

Occasionally, differences of opinion surfaced between the design and manufacturing elements within the Harmony teams. When design engineers submitted a new design, the reaction of some manufacturing people tended to be, "It can't be done that way!" Where any of the technology was already in production, the temptation was to "Just take it and put it in, as is," in the new set. However, the existing manufacturing technology had not been built to be automated; and automation of all possible Harmony processes was an absolute necessity.

As he thought about the many issues which needed to be resolved, Jim Retallack wondered how to dispel the atmosphere of gloom and doom he kept encountering. He was uncomfortably aware that old patterns of non-communication between professional management and the rest of the plant had exacerbated the anxieties of people throughout the organization. The plant grapevine was rife with rumors of production changes, layoffs, and even plant closings. Jim wondered what could be done to improve morale and develop a positive spirit of cooperation and commitment to a successful Harmony launch.

The Next Step

Jim Retallack scanned the last report, noted the team's progress toward its goals for the week, and plotted its current status on his master chart. He was pleased to see that the cords group had achieved its on time, under budget goal and the keyboard and line switch teams appeared to be on target for next week's deadline. The upcoming Electret transmitter decision was a major source of concern, however.

His mind still grappling with aspects of the Electret issue, the project manager strode purposefully through the office area of the plant to the eBasic meeting room, bulging file folders in hand. It was precisely three minutes to the hour. The weekly meeting was about to begin.

EXHIBIT 1

MANAGING CHANGE AT NTC (B): TEAM PLAY

Partial Organizational Chart, SAD Plant

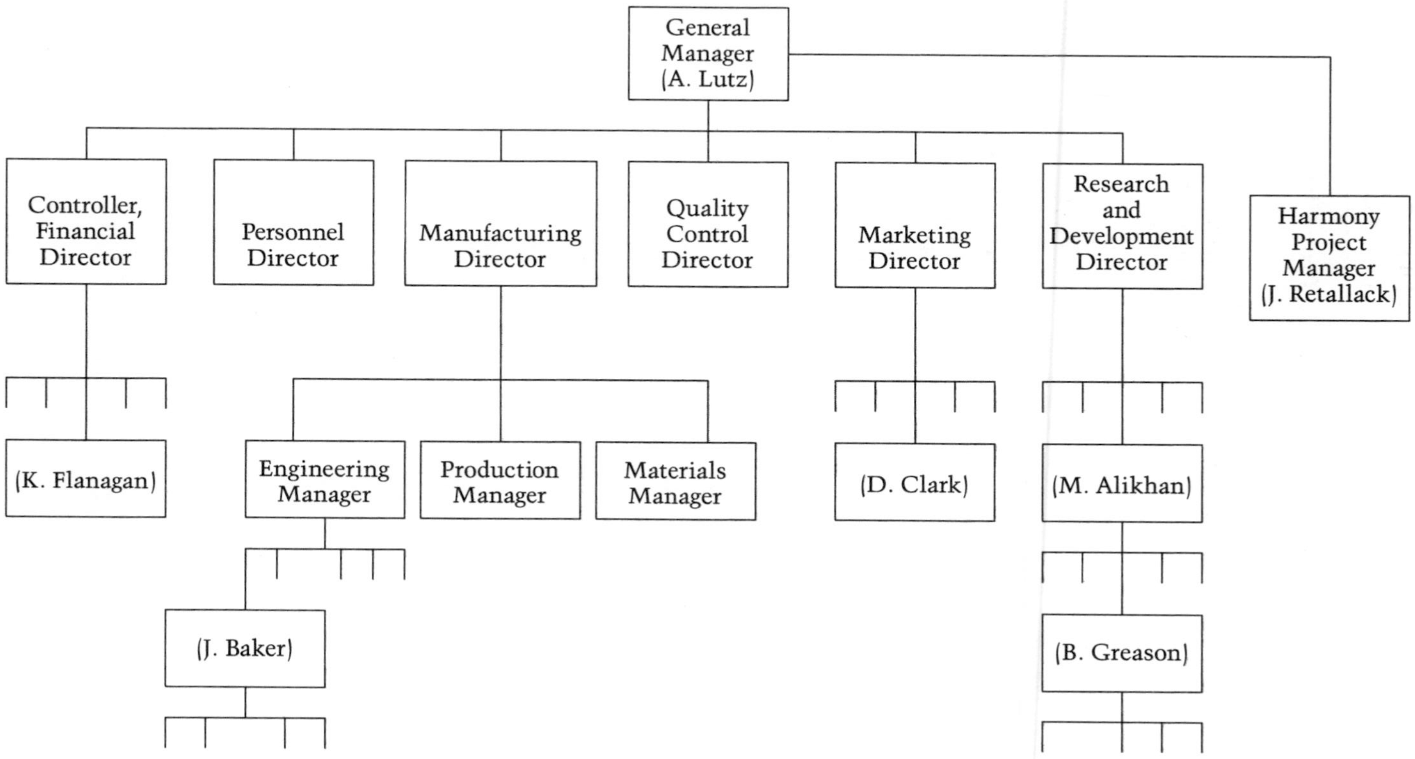

EXHIBIT 2

MANAGING CHANGE AT NTC (B): TEAM PLAY

Harmony Team Chart

Project manager:	Jim Retallack
Manufacturing/Engineering manager:	Jim Baker
Design/Technology manager:	M. Alikhan
Controller:	Kathy Flanagan

	Responsible for	
Team	Design	Manufacturing
1. Base and housing assembly	Kuhfus Charchanko	McGowan
2. Circuit board	Turner	Darling
3. Alerter	Heyward	McGowan
4. Keypad	Kuhfus	Neate
5. Line switch	Walker	Kilpatrick Romano
6. Jacks	Walker	McAlpine
7. Cords	Walker	McAlpine
8. Handset assembly	Kuhfus	Robinson
9. Transmitter	Gumb Freeman	Foster
10. Receiver	Freeman	Foster

EXHIBIT 3

MANAGING CHANGE AT NTC (B): TEAM PLAY

Tooling Schedule

Drafted: 83-01-13

DYNAMIC RECEIVER

Review Date 83-03-10

E. Foster 2320
Ext. 7336

Description	Schedule		Cost	R.M. #	Tool # and Supplier
	Original	Present			
Lower pole piece	June 1 83	June 1 83		107958	N.T. 513492
Upper pole piece	June 2 83	June 2 83		107955	N.T. 513493
Center pole piece connector	Jan 3 83	Feb 3 83 comp.	16K	107954	N.T. 513484
Terminal	Feb 1 83	Feb 3 83 comp.	16K	107956	N.T. 513486
Diaphragm	May 1 83	May 1 83	11K		N.T. 513448
Acoustic resistance	Use	B.A.R.	Machine		
Ferrule	June 3 83	June 3 83		107957	N.T. 513485
Encapsulation	83-05-05 83-09-	May 2 83 Sept. 83	106K		N.T. 513481-1 N.T. 513481-2
Cover	May 3 83	May 3 83	36 K		N.T. 513499
Housing	83-05-16	May 4 83	41 K		N.T. 513494

EXHIBIT 4

MANAGING CHANGE AT NTC (B): TEAM PLAY

First Page of Team 9's Milestone Chart, March 10, 1983

DATE: _MAR II_ SUB PROJECT: _TRANSMITTER (9)_

PAGE _1_ OF _6_

TECHNOLOGY _B. GUMB_

E of M _E. FOSTER_

TEST _R. MILLER_

BASIC SINGLE LINE TELEPHONE (800 SERIES)

1983

LINE	ITEM — ACTIVITY	WEEKS	RESP.	J	F	M	A	M	J	J	A	S	O	N
1	DESIGN CONCEP.	3	B.G.	▶										
2	DESIGN	10	B.G.		△--△									
3	ALUMINUM VS. GRAPHITE	3	B.G.	◀										
4	LINER VS. GASKET	4	B.G.	◀										
5	MODEL	2	B.G.	▶◀										
6	PRINTING PROCESS DEVEL	10	T.R.	▶	▶									
7	PROTOTYPE TOOLING	14	E.F.				△	◁	△--△					
8	FIELD TRIAL PIECE PARTS	6	E.F.				▽	△						
9														
10	FIELD TRIAL SAMPLES (500)	6	E.F.						▽	△--△				
11														
12														
13	PRINTED CIRCUIT BOARD													
14	TACK FOOT PRINT	13	G.K.	▶		△△								
15	DESIGN	13	B.G.	◀◀										
16	ARTWORK DESIGN	5	S.L.	◀			△							
17	PROTOTYPE	3	B.G.	▶				◀	△					
18	FIELD TRIAL BOARDS	3	E.F.							△				
19	PRODUCTION TOOLING	23	E.F.							△--△				
20	PROCURE P.C.B.	22	2170								▽	△		
21														
22	CAN													
23	DESIGN	13	B.G.		△									
24	FIELD TRIAL PARTS	13	O.S.		▶						△			
25	PRODUCTION TOOL	10	O.S.		▶			◁						
26	DESIGN	10	O.S.											
27	ORDER	2	O.S.					▽						
28	BUILD	17											△	

LEGEND: ▽ PLANNED START △ PLANNED COMPLETION ◇ PLANNED SLIP ▽▲ ◀ ◆ ACTUAL

EXHIBIT 5

MEMORANDUM

83 02 02

To: eBASIC Project Team

From: L.J. Retallack

Subject: *eBASIC Schedules*

"The time has come, the Walrus said, to talk of many things", and the most painful of all is schedules. Attached is the preliminary version of the eBASIC schedule generated by Jim Kilpatrick and Alikham. A number beside some of the entries references them to sub-projects as defined in my recent memorandum. Note primarily that Development MDA* sign-offs scheduled for March/April (with the Dynamic already completed in January) are in agreement with our original schedules, and hence we are on track with respect to the overall Product Plan.

It is extremely important that we meet the MDA sign-off dates in order to meet January 1984 shipment commitments. I am proposing that we complete the MDAs to their full extent even if we have not fully optimized the design. EofM can then use the MDAs to start production planning and the Technology team can step back to iterate the design as required to further improve cost/performance.

Over the next week, ie. by February 11, 1983, each team must meet with Jim Kilpatrick and Alikhan to finalize detailed schedules for each sub-project. We are getting off the ground and now is the time to consolidate our activities into a solid team effort.

L.J. Retallack

LJR/Ms
att.

---

*Manufacturing Design Authority = design OK'd for manufacturing the prototype.

BEFORE THE AXE (A)

Richard C. Hodgson and Eileen D. Watson

" . . . and we're asking for your resignation, effective immediately."

Matt Gruber, president and CEO of Quorum Limited, stood transfixed in shocked disbelief. Was the Kapco chairman and CEO, Henry Young, really asking him to resign after 21 years of devoted service? Matt's mind raced — what had gone wrong? And why? What should he say? What could he do? As he listened to Henry's voice detailing seemingly inconsequential reasons for his dismissal, Matt gathered himself to respond. (See Exhibit 1).

Four Decades

Matt Gruber was born to a prosperous European land-owning family which was tragically disrupted and separated by events of World War II. After the war the six-year-old boy arrived in Canada, where he was reunited with the remnants of his family. The Grubers were stateless, penniless immigrants in a strange country — they knew no one, spoke no English, and were unfamiliar with the Canadian culture. However, they were determined to overcome all difficulties and make their way successfully in an unfamiliar environment.

Matt admired the resilience of his parents. "Starting off fresh after such major setbacks, they acquired a small business and sent all their children to school. We all did well, and my father was very, very proud. He's never taken a cent from the government. And at age 73 he still actively manages the business."

Graduating from the University of Toronto with a B.Sc. in mathematics, Matt Gruber joined Calgary-based Kappa Equipment Ltd. when he was 23. During the next six years he worked closely with several key people with whom he remained closely associated throughout his entire 21-year career in the organization. Matt talked about his early years in marketing research, working as a general researcher (one year), sales research manager (three years), and consumer research manager (two years):

> I went to Calgary at a significant time in Kappa's history, marked by the retirement of a long-time president, T.R. Maloney. He was a tyrant — a typical old business tycoon — and following his retirement the company took the chance to do something new and modern. The VP personnel, an engineer, became the new president. He brought in an organizational development specialist, a great human relations type — John Annet, a personnel wiz. And during that period under Annet, they brought in all the big guns of organizational behavior for courses and workshops. So when I was hired there was a lot of experimentation going on at Kappa. There were many new faces, or old faces in new positions.

> Besides Annet, the two key players at that time were Henry Young, VP marketing for Kappa, and Don Kershaw, president of a Kappa subsidiary company. When a company-wide shakeout occurred several years after I joined, Henry Young and John Annet became competitors for the top job. Henry won, and John disappeared. So Henry Young became the president, Don Kershaw became the VP marketing, and together they created an environment at Kappa where there was no point in playing any politics. They were both relatively young, and once their positions were locked in, all jockeying for top executive slots disappeared — and everyone focused on getting on with the business.

> The company then went into a very active, fertile time. The senior people were confident in their positions, and therefore, I guess, tolerated mavericks...I think I could have been called a maverick. I was a challenger — I challenged the status quo. I was really turned on by achieving, not necessarily the target achieved. My boss, Don Kershaw, liked that. And I hit it off well very early on with Henry Young, and in fact became an instrument for him in changing some of the existing practices.

> Existing practices were basically historical. Many people didn't know why they were doing what they were doing. My philosophy was that if you don't know why you're doing what you're doing, you shouldn't do it. I was analytical, of course — I mean, I didn't have the experience. I brought to the job an intellectual approach, a common sense approach, "KISS — Keep It Simple, Stupid!" And a philosophy that "bullshit doesn't baffle brains"...and, perhaps, young audacity and incredible guts and courage to go along with it! I know people thought I was going to be turfed out several times, but I was not.

> After six years in the company I went back to school full-time for an MBA. Unexpectedly, Henry Young said he wanted me back at Kappa after I finished school...here's how it happened. One day, as VP marketing, Henry asked me to produce some statistics for the next day. The man who usually did that was not myself, but another guy, Marc, and he was away. So I said, "Yes, of course I can do it. In fact, I provide all the material that allows Marc to do the stats anyway." I said, though, that I was studying for a university exam the next day, and I couldn't give it to him till a day later — I couldn't give it to him tomorrow. That's how Henry found out that I was going to school, and he asked me what I was intending to do in

the future. I said I was going to go back to school full-time. He asked me if I was going to leave the company. I said, "Well, I guess I can't go back to school full-time and also be here." He wondered if I was going to ask for a leave of absence. I said, "I hadn't intended to — my objective is simply to go back to school. But if you'll give me a leave of absence, thank you very much!" He asked if I planned to come back to Kappa Equipment. I said I hadn't thought about it, and he said, "Well, we'd like you to come back, and we'll pay you a salary to go back to school." And I said, "Thank you very much, but I don't want any strings attached." He said, "No, no, there'll be no strings attached." So my going back to school was to be paid for!

Now, three months later Don Kershaw became VP marketing, and Henry became president. I got into some conflict with Don, who was my boss, around that time. I was telling him that I was going back to school, and he said he knew, and he thought that Henry Young had over-stepped his bounds! Don said there was no company policy re schooling — they had no provisions for that. Then they made up the ruling that they'd pay 75 percent of the salary for those employees they wanted back.

But that wasn't the big argument between Don Kershaw and me. What happened was...Don wanted to put on a big presentation, his first presentation as VP marketing, to a group of visiting bigwigs. He asked me to put out a forecast that would indicate that we were going to achieve 50 percent share of market in every segment. I told him that it didn't make any sense, because in some segments we already had more than 50, and in others we had only 25 percent; "So to say within one year you're going to have 50 percent overall is ridiculous — the competition is not going to drop dead!" Don challenged me, and asked what my job was; and I said it was to issue forecasts. And he said that's what he was asking me to do. And I said I didn't believe in his method — it didn't make any sense.

Don got very upset. I then suggested to him that I would work his numbers out, but he would have to sign the forecast, not me. It would go out under his signature. Alternatively, he could send it out as an objective only. But I couldn't send out that forecast — I would not put my name to it. I guess you could hear us down the hall, two floors up, everywhere in the building! And I went back to school a month later...so people were very surprised when I came back — they thought I'd been fired!

So I've had that kind of open, honest rapport with Henry and Don all the way along, and clearly it did not detract from my progress in the company. If anything, it enhanced it. I've worked closely with Don for 21 years, and reported directly to him for part of that time, so I know him much better than Henry. I've been told that Henry is a very snobby, rude person, but I've never seen him that way. I think that he is just a very shy person. He's not good on the one-to-one chitter-chatter at all. But on the people side, he has had a history of having love affairs with people, so to speak — in the corporate sense — and then when they have finished their usefulness, he's found someone else to have a love affair with, and dropped them.

Matt Gruber graduated from the MBA program and returned to Kappa Equipment in Calgary as new products development manager reporting to Don Kershaw, VP marketing. The structure of the organization was rapidly growing and changing; a new holding company called Kapco Ltd. was formed, with Henry Young as chairman and CEO. Kapco Ltd. controlled Kappa

Equipment (with Don Kershaw as president) as well as Vancouver-based Quorum Ltd.

Two years later I became group brand manager at Kappa Equipment and was so successful in the job that Don Kershaw appointed me VP marketing four years after that. I produced results the company badly needed. I turned Kappa's declining market share around, raising it from a low of 37 percent to 45 percent within three years. Momentum carried this forward to 50 percent within the next three years.

I was pleased with my other achievements at Kappa, like introducing nine-for-nine successful new products in a three-year period, representing 25 percent of the company's sales volume. And I established effective interdepartmental relationships, permitting corporate-wide productivity programs. I really restructured my marketing division so that people had more flexibility to try their own ideas, and apply their own creativity. We were able to hold our selling costs constant, and our operating earnings were increased by 100 percent. Also, I co-developed a strategic position for marketing our equipment on a world-wide basis.

Four Years Before the Axe

Then a difficult issue came up for me during another major re-structuring of the corporation. Henry Young became chairman and CEO of the Kapco organization, focusing on the 'outside publics,' and Don Kershaw became president and COO of Kapco Ltd., focusing internally as an operator. That left the presidency of Kappa Equipment open. At that time, Henry asked me to go to Vancouver as president and CEO of Quorum! I didn't really want to go to Vancouver; I wanted to continue at Kappa in Calgary. I indicated to Henry that it would be very natural for me to succeed Don as the president of Kappa, and have someone else run the non-equipment division, Quorum.

Henry explained his reasons for a move to Vancouver: he wanted me to apply the same type of creative and innovative thinking to the reorganization of Quorum that I had used in Kappa Equipment; and he wanted me to broaden my experience base, so that within four or five years I would return to Calgary and be in a position to logically succeed Don Kershaw or himself as leader of the company! Henry said, "You can't do much more at Kappa than you've done already — sure, you could fine tune it, but other people can carry on from where you've taken the company. I want you to get more experience in non-equipment areas . . . and of course, I'm thinking about our succession needs."

After much careful consideration, Matt agreed to accept the presidency of Quorum. He wrote a long memo to Don Kershaw, outlining his thoughts and feelings about the proposed change. (See Exhibit 2.) The official announcement of Matt's appointment was made by Henry at an advance briefing session of the key Kapco management group:

Our president and CEO at Quorum, Charles Stone, will be retiring not later than the end of next year. Charles has served our corporation with devotion, distinction and effectiveness on a world-wide basis. I know of no one who has soldiered and led with greater professional competence, human qualities and sage advice than Charles — supported, I might add, by a wonderful wife.

Charles' successor-elect at Quorum is Matt Gruber. Matt's track record at Kappa is legendary even in this day. The marketing team he has built in the equipment division and the teamwork he has continued to establish within Kappa are the envy of all those who know him and have worked with him as their leader. He is young and has the confidence of all of us. If I have a regret it is in asking his teammates to accept his departure. If I have a conviction it is that he will be a worthy successor to Charles.

Matt will have the opportunity to share in the research and analysis that will be devoted to the new areas of growth through acquisition. He will have an opportunity to express his views not only about the continued growth of our present non-equipment assets, but about the nature and management of the assets we will acquire in the future. Matt's appointment is extremely significant in our long-term staffing plan, because it involves a commitment to succession to Charles, and represents an area in which the major thrust of our future growth is expected.

Matt talked about what happened next:

So I moved to Vancouver early in the new year with my wife and kids, and restructured Quorum Ltd. I followed the principle that the corporate office of Quorum was not going to over-direct or over-subsidize the operating units. The division was actually composed of six companies, each with its own president. The divisional superstructure served as a holding company. So in effect you had a holding company, Quorum Ltd., with operating units underneath it, reporting to an operating function of another holding company, Kapco Ltd. — which was inefficient. So I began building Quorum into an operating division, getting away from its holding syndrome.

Then an interesting and puzzling thing happened. After I had been in Vancouver for less than a year, my boss asked me to return to Calgary! Don Kershaw, president and COO at Kapco, had been my boss for many years. I had always worked closely with him, and helped him. He always needed someone with him, and I had been that guy for a long time. However, my job with Quorum was not complete, and I felt it would be wrong to leave at that time. I sent Don a memo outlining my thoughts about the development of Quorum Ltd., refusing the move for the good of the company.

I wrote Don that with respect to the Calgary alternative, while it certainly would enhance the necessary interface between my office and his, as well as with the rest of Kapco, the penalty to the effective integrated operation of Quorum would be so great that I found it difficult even to consider it as a rational alternative. Without a resident leader, how could he in practice still have a single Vancouver-based operating division? Even though I fully appreciated the gist of our discussions on this subject, surely within the current divisionalized structure of Kapco Ltd. the Vancouver divisional president's mandate is such that he must spend by far the majority of his time and efforts with his divisional management...within the parameters of previously approved plans, objectives and budgets, of course.

I suggested to Don that if he felt that I was not participating and/or inputting sufficiently to the total Kapco operating and future development process as much as I should be because of availability and distance, I would come to Calgary on whatever periodic basis he wished, to meet with him and anybody else, to participate in overall operational affairs. With respect to acquisitions and strategic planning, I suggested that a committee of Don, Henry, myself and others be formally instituted with mandate, responsibility, issues, timetable, etc. clearly established—and I assured Don that I would do my part. Without this formalization, I doubted very much if my mere physical presence would have much impact on the ongoing process.

So I remained in Vancouver, and worked very hard on Quorum's reorganization. I had been gradually weeding out the smaller and less-profitable companies within the division, aiming for a reduction to three companies—Quorum's three giants. Don likes getting involved directly with all parts of the Kapco organization; so I said to him last year that maybe what we should do, since these companies are all pretty well self-sufficient now, is wipe out the Vancouver head office and have the companies report directly to Calgary. But we'd have to get rid of all the small chains first. You can't have large units like Cornucopia Inc. and Supreme Stores and Universitile mixed in with the little companies—not that they're no good, but they're too small; it's an imbalance. And of course that was spoken in the context of the succession scenario...actually, one of those small units was no good—Dandee Ltd.—but it was Henry's baby, and I was trying to nurse it back to health. I recommended we sell it when I first moved to Vancouver, and recommended the same thing several times since, but Henry was adamant. And what the heck—Dandee is peanuts in the context of total Quorum.

In January of this year we were told that Jerry Lanark had been appointed executive VP of Kapco Ltd., with no specified responsibility. When I asked Don what Jerry Lanark's role was to be, he told me that as far as he was concerned, "Jerry Lanark is my legs. I've got a lot of responsibility and do a lot of travelling, so he's my legs." Henry said when he made the announcement that the position is best described by what it's not than by what it is: "Jerry is not to get in the way of the existing structure, he's not to usurp authority in any way, he doesn't have any. We want him to be able to roam widely, and get a broader operating exposure." I wondered at the time, "Is he being groomed for a top position?" But it didn't really bother me because I was 43 or 44 at that time and he was over 50, and there's plenty of time for me. Still, I questioned his suitability—I heard that he once said, "It's too bad that an organization has to have people, because it would be so much easier to operate without people." To me, of course, what is an organization but its people?

I like my people to be creative. It's creativity in the context of entrepreneurship—in other words, it's not good enough to do well in what you're doing unless you know why you're doing it. If you want to grow and build and make a good organization better, or make a lousy one good, you should apply your judgment, your creativity. So you have to have people with sufficient intelligence to be able to do that. Secondly, and probably much more importantly, you have to have an organization structure and environment that supports and encourages this; whereas many organizations actually prohibit it because it's not in the book. And my view is that with 18 000 people in the Quorum division...heck, I'm only one of them! My job is to make sure that every one of those people can act and get on with it, and not get held up. If I can do that I'll have made a great contribution. If I try to tell everyone what to do the whole organization will go at the pace of one guy, instead of the pace of 18 000.

And I like my people to be outspoken, because I don't want to guess what's in their heads — I want them to say what they're thinking. Most of my communication with people is done verbally, not by memos. I write very few memos. I spend most of my time outside of my office. Now I don't visit all the individual stores, but I spend a lot of time at the head offices of our various retail chains.

Recently, when we were about to make some major organizational changes in Retail, Jerry Lanark made some statements to our people which absolutely horrified me. He let some key people know that their organizations were going to be divested, and they hadn't even been told! I was really angry and upset. I said to him, "As long as the current structure exists, I don't want you to say anything about our plans. It's none of your business to say anything like that." And I added, "Besides, Jerry, it's time we talked about your position, so that we don't step on each other's toes — a minister without portfolio can be rather a delicate position."

So we had a conversation one evening. Jerry had a lot to drink, and he said, "Look, Matt, the two top executives are going to be retiring soon. I know you're very good on organization structure and have lots of ideas — why don't we put together a recommendation about forming a new structure after they leave?" I said, "You've got to be kidding! They're still in charge! Sure I've got lots of ideas. If they ask me for my ideas, I'll give them. But I'm not stupid — being the executive VP has got to lead to something, and if you're going to be tomorrow's president, we'll work it out then. And we'll do it aboveboard!" Jerry replied, "Suit yourself, Matt — either we'll do it together, or I'll do it myself." I said, "Fine!"

Henry and Don responded positively to my suggestion about aiming to have Quorum's three biggest companies — Cornucopia, Supreme, and Universitile — report directly to Kapco Ltd. They accepted my recommendation, but added, "We want to let you know that we are going to go after acquiring Ereo International!" That puzzled and disturbed me. They were acquiring a huge corporation like Ereo, and although we were involved in the preliminary identification of companies to be considered, we had not been included in the detailed assessment of that potential acquisition. And obviously this giant would have to report directly to the president, and be represented on the board, and everything else.

Well, that gave even more support to my recommendation that Quorum's head office be disbanded. We would get rid of the little companies and keep the big ones, which would report directly to Calgary. I would clear out my office and be in a position to be back in Calgary by the end of the year, to assume a senior position there. I speculated that they wanted me to come up there and look after Cornucopia and Ereo, not from an operating level but from a corporate level. I thought of several other possible alternatives...but what happened was, we didn't get Ereo! They refused the terms of our offer. Some major shareholders and corporation managers balked.

Interesting procedural developments occurred around that acquisition attempt. As a board, we were called by Henry on a conference telephone call with no prior warning. Most board members were completely in the dark. With no documentation in front of us, we were asked to approve a resolution giving Kapco management the authority to make an offer for Ereo International that would cost a billion dollars — over the phone! And this was the first time we were going to make an acquisition which was larger than our entire company, and if the thing didn't go right, we could sink the whole corporation...and to do it over the phone like that...but Henry received approval in principle. I didn't want to embarrass him publicly during the conference call, so I raised my questions privately with him after the fact...and there were no hard feelings. At our next board meeting at the end of the month, everything was hunky-dory between Henry and me.

On July 26, Henry Young, accompanied by Jerry Lanark, arrived in Vancouver at the head office of Quorum Ltd. Matt was called out of a management meeting by Henry, who announced, "Matt, I've got some bad news for you — I'll be very short and brutal. We're making some necessary position changes, and we're asking for your resignation, effective immediately."

EXHIBIT 1
BEFORE THE AXE (A)

Kapco Ltd.
Partial Table of Organization

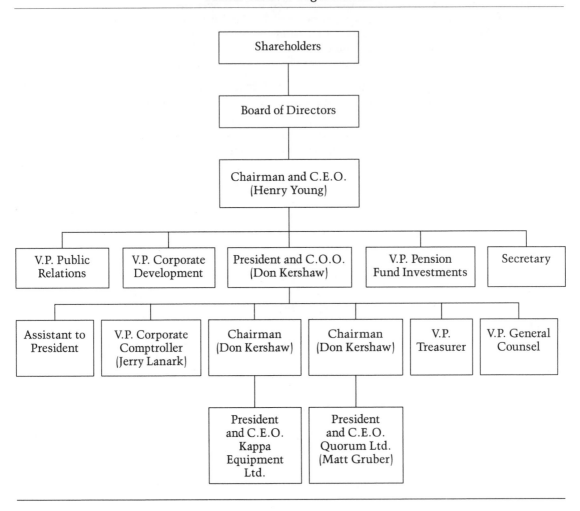

EXHIBIT 2

BEFORE THE AXE (A)

Mr. Kershaw: c.c. Mr. Young

The implications (both business and personal) of the proposition that Mr. Young laid before me last Friday are becoming more clear to me following a couple of days' thinking and discussions with my wife.

I see it as a career decision like none other in the past and most probably like none other in the future because it deals not only with what I will do tomorrow but reaches out to include events which will unfold 4–5 years from now.

My understanding of the Friday discussion is that the corporation (Kapco) has begun to lay down a "people" plan which currently leads to my assuming the leadership of Kapco upon the withdrawal from active duty of Messrs. Young and Kershaw. Furthermore that in the meantime (with suitable transition time) I would take on the responsibilities of President and CEO of Quorum Ltd. in order to acquire specific operational experience essential to the effective leadership of Kapco, experience which could not be as readily acquired should I continue my progression through the Kappa Equipment route.

As I indicated on Friday, I am certainly appreciative of the corporation's "vote of confidence" in me as an individual as well as my abilities; however, I could not immediately grasp the full implications of such a proposition.

Having had some time to reflect upon it I see both a challenge that excites me as well as some risks; however, no challenge is worthy of acceptance (indeed may not even be considered a challenge) if there is no associated risk of failure.

It seems to me that both of us (the company and me) are playing for very big stakes here—the company in ensuring the future well-being of the corporation for its shareholders and its employees, and in my case ensuring the future well-being of my family and myself. The object of the game obviously is that both of us come out as winners; and to ensure this outcome, as little as possible should be left to chance.

I believe a significant factor in my effective leadership of the Kappa Equipment marketing division besides my dedication, hard work and knowledge of the area, is the acceptance, trust, and respect of myself in that leadership role by my peers, subordinates, superiors, and outside contacts. In the Kappa context, this acceptance and respect was developed over an extended period of time through direct personal interaction—in fact I believe the respect I have earned among my co-workers within Kappa Equipment is such that a move of myself to the presidency of Kappa would be seen as a logical and expected progression.

The above variables do not initially carry the same weight in my move to Quorum, yet they are just as important in ensuring an effective operation.

To stack the odds in our favor in my quickly establishing effective leadership of Quorum, and hopefully subsequently of Kapco Ltd., it is imperative that apart from

EXHIBIT 2 (continued)

whatever I can and must bring to the job, that there be no confusion or speculation among my peers, subordinates, and outside contacts as to what my role is the day I walk into Quorum. The worst of all situations would be that people within the Vancouver-based groups and even the staff group of Kapco would see me as a threat to their personal ambitions and/or a source of outside interference. On paper (ie. a casual glance at the organizational chart) it could easily be perceived as such without the benefit of awareness of future appointments/changes.

I would ask you to consider therefore that in conjunction with my appointment as Executive VP Quorum Ltd, I also be appointed to the Kapco Board of Directors. This would help in more clearly positioning my role within Quorum, its group of six companies, and outside contacts. Moreover it seems quite logical to have the vacant directorship replaced by myself.

Since it is planned that I will assume Mr. Stone's position within a year, then here again it may be more appropriate to announce this future intention now and thus assist in the orderly transfer of responsibilities, rather than leaving it open to unnecessary, idle speculation.

I believe that both my immediate appointment to the Board of Directors and the announcement that I will replace Charles upon his retirement would reflect the confidence the CEO of Kapco has in me, and would therefore go a long way in allowing my associates and contacts at Quorum to immediately extend a certain level of confidence in me which they would have if they knew me more directly, and which I will confirm for them in due time.

On the personal side I guess it is only natural that the initial reaction would be somewhat biased by the familiar present which looms large in comparison to the future unknowns:

— I will miss the happy personal relationships at Kappa Equipment.

— There is a lot of satisfaction being at the head of a marketing success story, the momentum of which will carry us forward for quite some time.

— There is a lot more I wanted to do at Kappa—it's almost as if I was walking off the course after completing only 9 holes of a super round. I am certainly not bored yet.

— There are of course all the logistical problems associated with a move to another city, e.g.
   — schooling—we certainly want to continue our children's education in Montessori schools.
   — my wife's job at the community college
   — all my community associations and involvement
   — my wife's mother (74) moved to Calgary to be near us

EXHIBIT 2 (continued)

Lest this sound like a litany of negatives or building a case for a "turndown," let me assure you that was not the intention. I merely wanted to be honest with myself and honest with you in considering all the variables at play. I am expecting that the above dislocations and disruptions will be more than offset in the job satisfaction of the new challenges to be met and the financial rewards to go along with the heavy responsibilities I am expected to shoulder.

I know this note (you asked me to jog your memory) is already very long; however it wouldn't be complete if I didn't make some comment about "bucks." Rightly or wrongly, I can't help but feel I got somewhat "short changed" in this aspect of my current position. When I was appointed V.P. Marketing, my salary was less than what I thought it should have been, and less than at least one of my subordinates. The explanation given was that I was still young and that I had to first of all demonstrate I was capable of doing the job. When I proved myself there was a freeze on salary increases. Furthermore I noted with great interest that the person coming in to replace me will be an executive V.P. Marketing.

When I go to Quorum Ltd., I would hope the same situation will not repeat itself. I have already been told that in the case of Alec Browne, when he steps down as Director, his financial compensation will continue for a period of time since this is customary for "services rendered." Well, I too have "rendered services" to the company and therefore do not think it unreasonable to expect appropriate rewards. As far as age is concerned I consider that irrelevant—if you consider me old enough to do the job, then I consider myself old enough to accept the pay.

This all sounds very mercenary and not really my style, however I felt you should know my feelings at the outset so that we can dispense with them in a mutually agreeable fashion and then get on with the job.

Matt

THE CANADA COUNCIL (A)

Joseph J. DiStefano, Joseph N. Fry and Eileen D. Watson

Fighting off the effects of jet lag, Peter Roberts carefully drove through the hazy Sunday morning sunshine toward Parliament Hill. The newly appointed director of the Canada Council had arrived in Ottawa from Moscow the evening before; but an early morning phone call to his residence had dispelled all hopes of sleep. An unfamiliar voice had urgently requested his attendance at an emergency meeting: "I know you don't officially take over as director until tomorrow [October 7/85], but something has come up. Can you meet with us in two hours?"

Roberts agreed to his caller's urgent appeal, after finding out that the purpose of the meeting was to deal with an unusual government request to assist with a financial bailout of a major arts organization. "What a start," Roberts mused, fully realizing that this was likely only one of a number of issues that had been put on hold pending his arrival.

Origins of the Canada Council

The Canada Council was created in 1957 by the Canada Council Act, following a recommendation by the Royal Commission on National Development in the Arts, Letters and Sciences. The Council's mandate was "to foster and promote the study and enjoyment of, and the production of works in, the arts..." It was to be concerned primarily with the fine arts — "art for art's sake" — not only with existing but also emerging new artists, audiences, arts organizations, and works in the arts.

Although it was to be financed with public money, the Council was set up as an independent body modelled in part on the Arts Council of Great Britain. The Canada Council Act stated that Council employees were not to be part of the Public Service of Canada; and the Council itself was to have overall responsibility for the organization's policies, programs, budget allocations, and grant decisions.

At the time of writing, the Council reported to Parliament through the

Minister of Communications, along with several other government-assisted agencies for the dissemination and perpetuation of Canadian culture. (See Exhibit 1 for a listing of cultural organizations and gross federal expenditures for each.) Canada Council staff members maintained a close liaison with all federal cultural agencies and departments (especially Communications and External Affairs), with provincial arts councils and ministries of cultural affairs, and with arts organizations across the country.

Organization and Services

The Canada Council was governed by its 21-member board, often referred to as "the Council." The board[1] consisted of 21 unsalaried public trustees, including a chairman and a vice chairman, appointed by Order-in-Council for limited terms. The members were drawn from every province, and each received an honorarium for attending meetings four or more times a year, for two to three days each time. Members of the board considered and approved grants, and established the direction for Council policy (assisted by advice and recommendations from the Canada Council staff, the disciplinary advisory committees, and the artists and arts professionals who served as Council jurors and assessors).

The organization's executive staff was headed by a director and an associate director appointed by a Cabinet Order-in-Council. A management team of five — director, associate director, and three assistant directors — supervised the operations of the corporation. In 1985, professional and support staff of the Council numbered approximately 235, organized into four divisions — Arts, Administrative, Secretariat, and UNESCO (see Exhibit 2 for an organization chart). The UNESCO Division provided supporting services and channels of communication in Canada for UNESCO's international cooperative programs; the Secretariat provided secretarial, communications, translation/terminology and official languages services, and assisted with the work of the Atlantic regional office; and the Administrative Division was responsible for administration, finances, information services, research and evaluation, the reproduction centre, the central registry and archives, and the Killam Program of research fellowships and memorial prizes.

Of all the Council personnel, those in the Arts Division had the highest public profile. They were specialists in the artistic activities supported by the Council — writing and publishing, visual arts, media arts, dance, theatre, music, arts awards, art bank, touring office, and explorations program. (See

---

[1]Within the Canada Council organization, the governing Board usually was referred to as the "Council." However, to avoid confusing readers of this case study, we have used the term "Board" to describe the group of 21 appointed trustees, and "Council" when referring to the organization.

Exhibit 3 for details of Arts Section programs.) Knowledgeable and experienced concerning their art forms, they maintained constant contact with funded and non-funded arts organizations and individual artists. To facilitate the council's funding activities, they travelled widely throughout Canada, met annually with hundreds of members of the arts community, chose assessors, organized juries (see "Evaluation System" description below), prepared grant recommendations for the board, and advised the board on policies and programs.

Grants were awarded to individual artists and programs in other arts sections (through the Arts Award section) and to arts organizations (through the six disciplinary sections — writing and publishing, visual and media arts, dance, theatre and music.) Grants to artists were made according to "artistic excellence"; and all applicants "must have completed basic training or have the necessary competence to be considered as professional." Financial need was not a criterion (for individuals, though it is for organizations.) Applicants could accept Council grants while having received grants from provincial agencies as well, although frequent Council-agency consultations made duplication unlikely. Generally, one out of five applicants was successful in obtaining a grant.

Evaluation System

A complex system of advisory committees, juries and assessors had been developed in an attempt to ensure impartial judgment of the relative merits of each grant application. The following groups and individuals performed regular evaluations:

- Six *disciplinary advisory committees*, one for each art form, advised on policy and programs. Forty professional artists were selected each year by Council section heads to serve on these committees. (These artists were not eligible for grants while serving their one-year terms.)

- Eight hundred *jurors*, all professional artists, were invited by Council section heads and officers to judge grant applications. New juries were selected for each competition.

- *Assessors* were selected by Council section heads to judge the grant applications of arts companies (for example, dance companies or symphony orchestras). Assessors were drawn from the same list of about 1700 names from which jurors were chosen.

Financing the Council's Activities

The Canada Council was a statutory foundation, deemed a charitable organization for purposes of the Income Tax Act. When the Council was first established in 1957, the Parliament of Canada endowed the organization with

$50 million. The revenues from this endowment financed all Council programs for the first few years by providing approximately $1.5 million each year for the arts. By 1964, this income was clearly inadequate to meet even the most pressing needs of the artistic community, and Parliament began to make annual appropriations to the Council.

In the 1970s and 1980s, the annual parliamentary appropriation became the Council's chief source of income. During the fiscal year 1984–85, approximately 86 percent of the Council's $84.2 million budget was a parliamentary appropriation (see Exhibit 4 for 1984–85 financial statement). Other sources of Council funds were donations and bequests for special purposes, totalling $29 million in 1984–85.

Distribution of Council Funds

Approximately 80 percent of the Council's annual expenditures represented direct grants in support of professional artists and arts organizations. The balance was directed to services to the arts, the Canadian Commission for UNESCO, and operating costs. During 1983–84, about 3900 grants with a total value of $64 million were awarded to individual artists and arts organizations through the Council's various programs (see Exhibit 5 for the numbers and amounts of grants). This figure rose to $70 million in 1984–85.

In the opinion of one staff member, the achievements of the Canada Council far exceeded its original mandate:

> The Canada Council was supposed, in an elitist sense, to promote Western European and North American opera, ballet, symphonies. There was no Canadian art, no Canadian culture; yet now we have 230 theatres, 103 symphony orchestras, and three major ballet companies! They've materialized through guile, policy, hard-nosed attitudes, and lots of help from our friends. A remarkable achievement is that there are established artistic media in 160 medium-sized Canadian communities — for instance, in Thunder Bay, a city of 115 thousand people 500 miles from anywhere, there is a credible symphony. We even had a request from a hamlet in the Yukon to send the National Ballet for a stint of local cultural uplifting!

Troubled Times

During its 30-year history, Canada Council personnel had weathered many political storms; but the tenure of Council director Timothy Porteous (1982–85) seemed more troubled than most. A one-time aide to former Liberal Prime Minister Pierre Trudeau, Porteous narrowly escaped being fired by Trudeau in the summer of 1984 after he and the Council successfully opposed Council's inclusion in the Liberals' Financial Administration Act (Bill C24).

Bill C24 was designed to strengthen the government's control over the operations of large commercially oriented crown corporations. Inclusion of the Council in this bill would have overturned the advice of the 1957 Massey Commission that the Canada Council should be an "arm's-length agency," and of the Federal Cultural Policy Review Committee, whose report (1982) confirmed the findings of the Massey Report.

The chairman of the board, singer Maureen Forrester, spoke about reactions to the proposed bill:

> Thousands of artists in Canada were opposed to the Council's inclusion in the bill, and their representatives appeared before the Standing Committee on Miscellaneous Estimates to argue that compromising the Council's independence would compromise the freedom of the arts in Canada, and would diminish the status of every artist and arts group in this country.
>
> A few days after the artists spoke to the committee, I appeared before its members as well, along with other board members and staff of the Canada Council. We presented a brief urging our exclusion from the provisions of Bill C24.
>
> Parliament was responsive to the representations of artists, arts groups, the Canada Council, and other cultural agencies, and amended the bill to exclude the Council, as well as the National Arts Centre, the CBC, and Telefilm Canada (formerly the Canadian Film Development Corporation).

Grant Cuts

Canada's Liberal government was defeated during the 1984 federal elections. Following the landslide victory of Brian Mulroney's Progressive Conservative party, the new Minister of Communications, Marcel Masse, announced his intention to reduce spending in the Department of Communications (DOC). In November 1984, Masse ordered the Canada Council to cut $3.5 million from its budget. Council Director Porteous and Board Chairman Forrester strongly resisted Masse's directive, but were unable to change the Minister's mind.

Accordingly, Porteous regretfully implemented across-the-board grant cuts to artists and arts organizations, and announced other money-saving measures: the Council's toll-free telephone line would be cancelled, as would the fund-raising and subscription advisory services to performing arts organizations; Stanley House in New Richmond, Quebec (used for arts meetings) would be closed; the Arts Advisory Panel would be suspended; services of the Canadian Commission for UNESCO would be reduced; Council staff would be cut, up to five percent; a reduction would be made in the costs of administering grants programs; and the Council's only regional office located in Moncton, New Brunswick, would be closed. (However, in the face of objections from the Atlantic provinces, Council decided that the Moncton office should remain open until at least March 1986.)

Changes in Council

Working with the government-appointed group of people who formed the 21-member board, presented both problems and opportunities to Porteous and his staff — especially during the period of transition which followed the 1984 elections. The board's composition altered drastically during that time. Four members, Liberal appointees, ended their terms in 1984. In February 1985, seven Liberal appointees ended their terms (six of them their second term, thus making them ineligible for reappointment). Another Liberal appointee ended his term in April 1985.

The new Progressive Conservative government appointed two new members in November 1984, four in December 1984, one in March 1985, and five in April 1985. Integration of the 12 "new" (PC-appointed) members with the nine "old" (Liberal-appointed) members was a serious problem.

The sometimes-sympathetic, sometimes-antagonistic media commented extensively on appointments to the board. Among the newspaper headlines of the day were "Tories Bypass Forrester in Making Appointments to Canada Council" (Montreal Gazette, May 9/85), and "Patronage Mars Canada Council Appointments" (Calgary Herald, June 4/85). Director Porteous was reported to be "A Cultural Mandarin Under the Gun" (Globe and Mail, May 25/85). He was held responsible when "MP (McDonald) Claims Council Discriminates" in awarding grants (Calgary Herald, May 31/85).

Relationships between board and staff were degenerating. Staff members suspiciously questioned the motivations of a body of "political appointees," so maintained a wary, almost defensive, stance. Board members often felt manipulated to rubber stamp decisions previously made by staff. They also complained about inconsiderate administrative procedures, such as the too-late delivery of hundreds of pages of material (agendas, reports, proposals, etc. packaged in a "hotel book") the night before quarterly board meetings.

The Beleaguered Director

Timothy Porteous had been appointed to the Council as associate director in 1973. When he was appointed director in 1982, he continued to hold his previous divisional responsibilities as well — there appeared to be no obvious successor, and monies to support administration salaries were scarce.

Porteous was perceived by staff members as passionately committed to the Council and its work. It was said that he had great trouble delegating responsibility to others. He worked extremely hard, putting in long, tedious hours personally reviewing applicants' files and signing approximately three thousand grant submissions annually.

Porteous sought to resolve problems affecting Council personnel. Staff turnover was high, although that was thought not to be detrimental, necessarily. Several senior positions were vacated in 1984–85, and new appointees were being sought. A staff member described somewhat stressful working conditions:

> There's a fair amount of burnout at the Council. We feel the unease of change and
> budget restrictions. It's hard to sustain one's energy much more than five or six

years, with constant demands, constant questioning, and a constant sense of having to explain and justify. And travelling across the country takes a toll. Many officers come from the milieu, do a stint in the Council and then go out again into their artistic sector.

A strong believer in the Council's independence from government, Porteous sometimes took a vocal, public position against the government. He was a loyal defender of staff members against frequent criticisms from "outside." He described the position of the Council as "halfway between the arts community and the political community, and there's pressure from both sides — you can't abandon yourself to either!"

On July 2, 1985, Porteous hastily convened a press conference. He announced to assembled reporters and others that he had just received a phone call from the DOC Deputy Minister informing him his position as director of the Council was terminated! Porteous went on to say that Communications Minister Marcel Masse had been abusing the arm's-length principle of government funding for the arts by increasingly handing out funds to arts groups himself, instead of letting the Council do its job.

A hundred or more artists and representatives of cultural agencies who had gathered at the news conference, applauded Porteous's criticisms of the government. Chairman Maureen Forrester also supported him, as did cheering Council staff members.

Denials that Porteous was fired came immediately from Masse, Deputy Minister Marchand, and Prime Minister Mulroney. They said the director had been offered another job; but on July 18, Porteous wrote,

> I did not have to interpret Mr. Marchand's statement to me over the telephone on Friday, June 28. He told me that the government had decided to replace me, and that it wished to announce the name of my successor in the week of July 1 . . . . The job that was offered to me was not consul general in Los Angeles (as reported in the press). That position is already held by Joan Price Wisner. The job was a secondary level, and the responsibilities and other details were only vaguely defined.

Summer of 1985

Throughout July and August, Porteous continued to "lay everything on the line to defend the Council." His position, however, remained in limbo. Rumor had it that Masse had approached several prominent Canadians to take the directorship of the Council, without success.

The press conference of July 2 triggered a spate of activity on behalf of the Council. A telegram was sent by 33 prominent Canadians to Prime Minister Mulroney, warning of the danger posed to the Council by Masse's actions. Serious charges were made against Masse, accusing him of forcing reductions in operating grants to arts organizations by the independent Council, while at the same time continuing to increase direct funding through his office of other arts projects with little regard to support for their future operation. Other statements were made: Masse did not consult Council chairman Maureen Forrester about these actions; he ignored her recommendations about appointing new board members; and he discussed nothing with her between November of 1984 and July 1985.

Other issues were becoming more urgent during that troubled time, and all were given extensive media coverage. Some arts groups were angry about the Council's apparent unfair judgments on standards. Diane Milligan, executive director of Dance Nova Scotia, said "No Canada Council money comes east of Montreal for dance, because companies must obtain a national standard of excellence that is rooted in Central Canadian taste" (Halifax Chronicle-Herald, August 31, 1985: "Canada Council Told It's Ignoring Atlantic Dancers"). After a meeting between representatives of Atlantic Canada's four modern dance companies, officials from the Atlantic provinces' cultural departments, and Council staff, Milligan reported, "We definitely have the feeling they have no intention of funding any of the existing companies in their present form."

A Successor to Porteous

In August, Masse telephoned Peter Roberts (Canada's ambassador to the Soviet Union) in Moscow, asking him to assume the directorship of the Council. Roberts was a Calgary native, an amateur musician, a University of Alberta graduate, and a Rhodes scholar (Oxford, 1953). He had joined the External Affairs department in 1955, and subsequently held postings in Hong Kong, Saigon, Washington, and Brussels. He had been Press Secretary to Prime Minister Trudeau from 1970 to 1973, working alongside another Trudeau aide, Timothy Porteous.

Roberts had an extensive general knowledge of the arts, having served as Assistant Undersecretary of State for Cultural Affairs in the Secretary of State Department from 1973 to 1979. In that position, he was responsible for promoting cooperation between federal cultural agencies and formulating cultural policies and programs. Rejoining External Affairs in 1979, he served as Canadian ambassador to Romania (1979–83) and to the Soviet Union (1983–85).

Roberts decided to accept the director's position, to be effective in October. He later remarked to an acquaintance,

> I was interested in the Canada Council job because I knew many of the people there, I knew what the Council did, and I knew many of the clients from past associations. Most of all, I felt it to be an important organization in this country. The Canada Council may be controversial, but it still provides 84 million dollars to support the arts! It achieves a lot — it keeps the arts going, it helps initiate many cultural activities. I knew it would be an interesting job, and the timing fits my personal planning schedule — my wife and I wish to be established in Ottawa prior to my retirement.
>
> When the appointment of Peter Roberts was announced, the reaction of the board

and members of the arts community was immediate, and supportive of the government's choice. Roberts was described variously as "someone the staff can look up to," "a diplomat's diplomat," "a solid, political neutrally person," "a man who can hire and fire and write tremendous reports," and "an external man who knows how to deal with institutions — well placed to take that job."

Roberts' First Impressions

Peter Roberts talked about some of the obvious difficulties which existed when he assumed office:

> I walked into a hornets' nest my first day at work! I had decided the previous day to go along with the Acting Minister's request that the Council serve as a conduit for a government-funded bailout of the Vancouver Symphony Orchestra. The board chairperson and the associate director had supported our participation; but the entire senior staff of the Council descended on me the next day, telling me in no uncertain terms that my decision was unacceptable!
>
> The head of Music resigned the day I arrived, on principle. He had resigned before, many times, but had always been talked into staying. He was very shocked when I accepted his resignation, even though he was a very able person. The head of Theatre had just left to take a job in the theatrical world. I was aware of other vacancies, actual and pending.
>
> I could see that there was great alienation between senior arts officers and management. The management team of five — director, associate director, and three assistant directors — were the people who ran the operations, but the heads were excluded from this club. I wished to correct this unfortunate situation as soon as possible.

Roberts initially sought information and suggestions from the four senior people who, together with the director, formed the Council's management committee — Gilles Lefebvre, Jocelyn Harvey, Peter Brown and Shirley Thomson (see Appendix for brief biographical sketches). Some of their thoughts and opinions are summarized below:

Gilles Lefebvre

Gilles Lefebvre (associate director) talked about his impressions of the growth and development of the Canada Council:

> It has been interesting to observe how the number of Canadian artists grew immensely, beginning in 1964. This cultural explosion started in preparation for the 1967 celebrations. At that time we opened ourselves to the world and gave confidence to Canadian artists — especially Quebec artists. They became much less isolated. The most extraordinary things happened to our country that centennial year... but in having to request money from the government, artists lost part of their independence.
>
> I have observed a very natural evolution of the existing managerial process at Canada Council. In the beginning, management did not need to be large... but then as each art form grew there had to be an organization, a structure around the granting process, requiring a financial officer for each section. Other structures

arose around new programs — Arts Awards, Touring Office, Art Bank, Explorations, etcetera; and to make sure that each art form or section would be well publicized, a Communications section was established. Now there are 235 people employed at Canada Council, with still the same senior management structure as before — the five original positions!

For the last six or seven years, people from government have been wanting more control over the Canada Council. They could not see that the objectives were well served by the established systems. They wanted quantitative measurement — the MBA mentality. And yet, for years to come we will still be funding the TSO, chamber music groups, the National Ballet, and so on. These organizations will endure.

This year has brought much turmoil. It has been very demanding for me, 24 hours a day. In the interim before Porteous left, establishing closer relations with the Minister of Communications became vitally important. Peter Roberts is the best man I can think of for the top job. He knows the situation in Canada from experience; and it is obvious he'll have to make some changes and experiment with some solutions for our problems.

Jocelyn Harvey

Jocelyn Harvey (assistant director and newly appointed Council secretary) spoke of several areas concerning her dealing with the Board which needed immediate consideration, including an appalling briefing book for new members. Other priorities demanded her attention:

> The policies manual must be revised — it doesn't reflect existing Council structures. And documentation delays are so frequent that we're receiving complaints from board members about lateness. For instance, there are objections to the infamous "hotel book" of 400 pages being delivered to members' hotel rooms at the last minute, the night before board meetings! I intend to tighten things up, immediately.
>
> At present, we report all grants, no matter how small. The board has delegated authority for grants to be approved and signed by officers (director, associate director, assistant directors) to the limit of $20 000 or $25 000. The board approves other larger grants.
>
> There is some feeling that the board shouldn't be kept as remote as in the past — for example, it should have a say in deciding to increase our endowment fund. Our new board sees its role as creating policy, and is impatient with grants procedures. A current issue is the large dollar value of continuing grants to the big institutions which are taking high percentages of our budget. The economic impact on some communities of withdrawing some of our support could be disastrous if not devastating — but how do you judge between the Canadian Opera Company and a little group in Stephenville, Newfoundland? Incidentally, a number of board members come from small towns.

Peter Brown

Peter Brown (assistant director and treasurer) described his early experiences at the Canada Council:

> I arrived at a difficult time for the Council. Funding was frozen — actually cut — when I arrived. There was much turnover of Council members, and the director's

job was on the line. This was healthy in the sense that arts specialists were being returned back to the community, but unhealthy in that there was no continuity remaining within the central organization of the Canada Council.

Now, with a new Council and a new director, we're experiencing a lot of stress due to all the changes. We're undergoing a grilling about our administration costs. Why are our costs higher than the Ontario Arts Council's, for example? Many factors contribute, of course — official languages, expensive travel (Ontario Arts Council people live in Toronto, but our people have to travel to Toronto, and beyond). And Canada Council research is used by all organizations — they don't have the expense of generating their own.

Most financial allocations go to urban areas, with the result that there has been a backward movement in underfunded places. This is most noticeable in the performing arts. For instance, in the Maritimes there is no funded dance company, and the symphony needs help. How should we address this issue? Should we set regional standards as opposed to national standards?

There is a question as to whether the Council should be more pro-active. But how can you quantify artistic works, allocating funds fairly across disciplines? Which deserves the funding: a Harry Somers work, or a production of *As You Like It*? There's such a different nature of various art forms. And there's pressure to force a Canadian bias on disciplines, which is impossible.

The "Big Twelve" (actually, 23 large, ongoing performing arts organizations like the Toronto Symphony Orchestra) are actively lobbying...even a one percent change in allocation can work wonders. It costs relatively little to support an individual. For instance, a $2000 commission can fund a choreographer to choreograph a dance work, or a composer to create a musical work; but $2000 is only a drop in the bucket of the total budget of the TSO!

Museum Boycott

Shortly after Peter Roberts' arrival at the Canada Council, a long-simmering controversy regarding museum funding boiled over in the press. A group of Canadian art museum directors announced their intention to boycott Council juries, because of a new policy introduced in 1984 which discontinued annual funding in favor of project-by-project competition for funds to mount their exhibitions. This policy change was introduced in fairness to smaller galleries; but the staffs from 25 of Canada's major art museums and galleries reacted angrily to the new system — they claimed it would quadruple the time they spent drafting grant applications.

Seeking background information on the controversy, Roberts talked with a member of the Visual Arts section, who said:

> We are in the business of funding contemporary art, by agreement between the Canada Council and the National Museums Corporation. Prior to 1985, 18 galleries received funding annually — the Vancouver Art Gallery, Art Gallery of Ontario, etc. Of our limited $2.5 million budget to give in grants, the 18 galleries got $2 million, and all others had to compete for the balance. The galleries have been coming in once a year, assuming they would receive their grants without

question. Our committee evaluated past years' applications, compared the galleries, and saw inequities. The idea came about that all money should go into a pot, and all galleries should compete on an equal basis, project by project. We talked about this for two years, and we made it clear that the change was coming up.

We have never funded art galleries for operations, always just for program assistance as in specific exhibitions. Our fund is supposed to be a contribution only, but what was happening was that certain galleries lacking adequate provincial support were dependent on our funds for everything, and juggled funds to make use of our support in ways other than it was intended. We're in a difficult situation, of course, feeling the unease of change, budget restrictions, always explaining to people.

Policy Issues: Some Opinions

In his early days, Peter Roberts made it his business to learn as much as he could about key members of the Canada Council staff. Hugh Davidson, acting head of Music and general manager of the Touring Office, said:

> Council is now addressing issues of regionalization and excellence — but assessed by whom? We have no national music standards, for example. Now costs are up, bucks are thinner, support is down 16 percent in the last five years. The trend seems to be toward less support. And if other people own the entire distribution of our films and books, if we weaken our national broadcasting, and if we make sure our arts don't have enough funds and centralize what's left, we might as well give the whole thing away.
>
> But we live in hope. Council is at a crossroads right now. There is not enough money to support big organizations adequately, and new growth too. I don't know how the government and rich people will address this issue of providing enough funding.

Robert Kennedy, Arts Awards head, remarked:

> The Council gets caught when dealing with large organizations and their blue chip boards, which have great political clout. It must continue its support, even if its contribution is only 10 percent of the budget. But many middle to small sized organizations are producing the best contemporary art work — new, fresh. Large organizations can't afford to take the same risks on new work, yet take the lion's share of the Council budget.
>
> With new board members and a new director, many legitimate questions are being asked. Staff have strong opinions but must not get cornered into an adversarial relationship with the board, or have to lobby the board as the accepted means of advancing one's point of view. There are always slippery issues — our juries, for instance, since there's always someone not represented. And we have to turn down 75 to 80 percent of applicants. Regionalism is an issue, naturally, because most artists live in big cities, so most of our grants go to cities.
>
> Our role is basically passive, non-directive — but programs have to be established and defined, and this inevitably raises difficult issues. What should be Canada Council's responsibility to older, more established, experienced artists,

young up-and-coming artists? What price innovation versus excellent traditional work?

Monique Michaud, head of the Dance section, stated:

> Organizationally, the 10 section heads have been accustomed to going directly to the top—there has been no other way to go! The director had to take too many decisions himself. This proved to be ineffective, although his heart was in the right place, and he knew the arts community intimately. Tim loved the organization, and battled everybody when we had to fight for our lives.
>
> None of us are trained managers, though management to me is common sense. My role is to represent Council to the artistic community, and vice versa. We're the front line for the Council and have to deal with the flak from the artistic community and the board. I won't release confidential information from juries' reports. If a case becomes notorious (when I am accused of discrimination) I inform the board; and if it wants more information, it will form a committee and get together with the Dance Panel. In such cases I keep the director aware of every step of the process.
>
> Giving money away means you have no friends. You're in turn identified as villain or angel. Organizations tend to request more money than they need or the Council can afford. If they have confidence, they end up levelling with the officers. In the end, they get an honest allocation.

The Auditor-General's Report

In mid-October Peter Roberts received his confidential copy of the "Comprehensive Audit Report to the Board of the Canada Council." The report was the result of a special audit conducted by the office of the Auditor General of Canada (OAG) between March 1984 and January 1985, and was based on observations pertaining to the 1983–84 fiscal year. Roberts read the document with a growing sense of concern.

The Auditor-General's report dealt with three areas of the council's activities: program management, financial management and control, and management and use of human resources. The following is a summary of observations and recommendations made by the OAG:

Section 1: Program Management

The objective of the section on program management (the management of grants and assistance programs) was "to ensure that the Canada Council is establishing priorities, systematically evaluating the effect of its sponsorship activities, and following an effective and impartial process for awarding grants." Five aspects of program management were assessed, giving observations and recommendations for each.

(1) Council Board

Board members should have more than just cultural and artistic expertise, they should also have administrative and financial abilities. The report recommended, "To assist in the appointment of future members, the Board of the Canada Council should identify the knowledge and skills it needs to carry out its mandate, and make recommendations accordingly to the Governor in Council."

The report was critical of the number of Council employees who attended the quarterly board meetings (an average of "more than double the number of board members"), and recommended that the Board establish a list of staff that may be called on to appear as necessary.

Various types of documentation produced by Council staff for the board (e.g., the briefing book for new members) received unfavorable comment. The report recommended that documentation for the board should "inform members about the Council's policies, strategies and processes; be updated regularly to eliminate outdated and redundant material; be presented in a format that facilitates reading and assists decision making; and that minutes of board meetings should be available within a reasonable time after each meeting."

(2) The Adjudication Process

This was judged to be generally satisfactory. However, the report questioned the fact that 57 percent of the value of grants given in 1983–84 was based on evaluations by Council staff, not juries and independent assessors. In addition, the documentation in grant files (evaluation criteria, reason for granting/refusing applications, amounts awarded) was criticized. It was recommended that "the Canada Council should document the evaluation criteria used to assess grant applications and the method by which applications are weighed against them, and justify its decisions about awarding grants on the basis of these criteria."

The report noted a lack of in-depth evaluations of all organizations receiving grants, as well as a tendency to award grants "automatically" to past recipients based on amounts given in previous years, thereby creating a "historical bias" in the adjudication process. The report recommended that the Council should "review its methods of awarding operating grants, and conduct in-depth evaluations of the organizations receiving operating grants on a multi-year cycle."

(3) Resource Allocation Process

The criticism was made that the Council's decisions about apportioning funds were being made on the basis of historical and evolutionary factors, and responsiveness to the artistic milieu. The report supported a strategic planning approach, with the Council establishing priorities and contingency plans. The Arts Division was singled out especially as being "hampered by the fact that no minimum standardization of planning activities exists, so...only some of the sections make detailed and explicit budget proposals and link them with their plans." The report recommended that "the Canada Council should document how it allocates its annual budget within each artistic discipline and each of its services, so as to establish and demonstrate its priorities and the choices it has made in relation to them."

(4) Evaluating Program Effectiveness

The report recommended a tightening up of evaluation criteria and processes. Empirical data, both qualitative and quantitative should systematically be gathered to ensure that specific corporate objectives to Council programs were being met: "To be in a position to account for its activities, the Canada Council should define clear links between its programs and activities and the results envisaged in its statement of objectives."

Systematic evaluations should be conducted (perhaps by outside consultants) for management's use; and the resulting evaluation reports should be submitted to the Audit and Evaluation Committee of the board.

(5) Program Coordination

The degree of independence with which each of the 10 sections of the Arts Division operated was criticized as resulting in ineffective Council operations and confusion for clients. A formal central co-ordinating progress was recommended: "The Canada Council should co-ordinate policy development and review, as well as its activities in the various artistic disciplines, and should facilitate its clients' approach to the Council's services."

Section 2: Financial Management and Control

The financial management and control section of the report was designed "to verify that budgetary controls are adequate and are being adhered to, and that investment activities of the endowment fund and other funds are properly controlled." The Treasurer's role in preparing, controlling, and monitoring budgets (especially of the Arts and Administration divisions) was termed inadequate, and administration costs (14.2 percent of the annual budget) were deemed excessive.

Signing authority delegation was described as unclear, showing redundancy and repetition, and lacking dollar limits on each administrator's signing authority for the purchase of goods and services as well as payments to employees. The report recommended that "the Council should define clear roles, responsibilities and accountability for managers with respect to financial management."

Section 3: Management of Human and Material Resources

The third objective of the Auditor-General's Report was to ensure that the Council's human and material resources were being managed and used effectively and economically. No agency-wide operational objectives of performance indicators were found by the Auditor-General's representatives, who were critical of the lack of work load indicators and monitoring structures to apply to human resource management. It was recommended that the Council "should rationalize its process for allocating human resources, and controlling their use, by determining its real needs with respect to human resources, starting from a budget base of zero, basing the annual allocation of human resources on operational objectives arising from actual needs and expected work load, and re-examining its personnel needs through the use of work load indicators."

* * *

October 16, 1985

Peter Roberts pushed back from his desk, deep in thought. "I'm getting a much clearer picture of the magnitude and scope of the problems," he mused. "The question is, where do I go from here?"

The ringing telephone interrupted his thoughts, a staff member walked in with a sheaf of papers to be signed, and an out-of-town visitor appeared at his door. Peter sighed, thinking, "I'll have to have an effective action plan to carry me through the next few weeks."

EXHIBIT 1
THE CANADA COUNCIL (A)

Gross Federal Cultural Expenditure, 1979–1985

Department	1979–80	1980–81	1981–82	1982–83	1983–84	1984–85	1985–86
Communications	95.1	95.1	94.5	94.6	94.6	94.1	94.9
•Agencies•	93.6	93.0	91.8	92.4	92.3	92.1	92.4
Canada Council	5.2	4.9	5.1	5.3	5.0	5.0	5.1
CBC	67.7	67.5	66.0	66.5	65.2	65.2	65.3
CRTC	1.7	1.8	1.8	1.7	1.6	1.7	1.7
Can. Film Dev. Corp.	1.4	0.9	0.7	0.7	2.8	3.3	4.4
National Arts Centre	2.0	2.0	2.0	2.0	1.7	1.6	1.7
National Film Board	5.2	5.2	5.2	5.1	4.9	4.9	4.5
National Library	1.9	2.0	2.4	2.5	2.5	2.3	2.1
Nat. Museums Corp.	5.9	5.7	5.5	5.4	5.3	5.1	4.8
Public Archives	2.7	3.0	3.3	3.3	3.1	3.1	2.8
•Department•							
Arts & Culture	1.5	2.1	2.6	2.1	2.3	2.1	2.5
Other Federal Departments							
Environment Parks Canada—							
Historic Parks & Sites	4.1	3.9	4.4	4.4	4.1	4.2	3.6
Secretary of State Multiculturalism	0.8	1.0	1.2	1.0	1.3	1.5	1.5

SOURCE: The Canadian Council Trends in Support to the Arts Technical Tables, Research & Evaluation, June 1985.

EXHIBIT 2
THE CANADA COUNCIL (A)

Organization Chart, October 1985

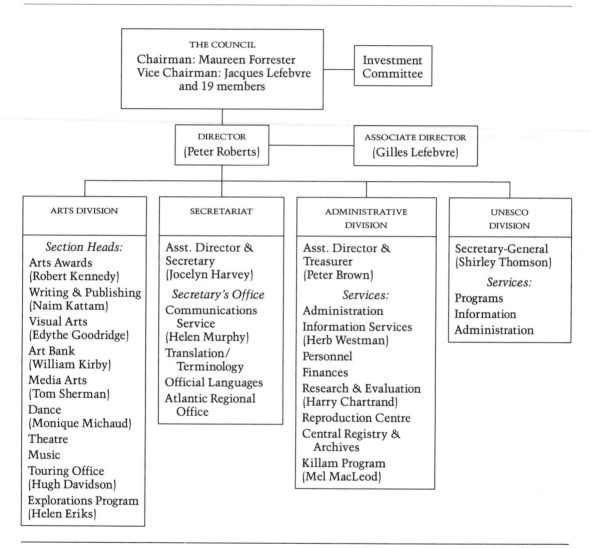

THE COUNCIL
Chairman: Maureen Forrester
Vice Chairman: Jacques Lefebvre
and 19 members

Investment
Committee

DIRECTOR
(Peter Roberts)

ASSOCIATE DIRECTOR
(Gilles Lefebvre)

ARTS DIVISION

Section Heads:
Arts Awards
(Robert Kennedy)
Writing & Publishing
(Naim Kattam)
Visual Arts
(Edythe Goodridge)
Art Bank
(William Kirby)
Media Arts
(Tom Sherman)
Dance
(Monique Michaud)
Theatre
Music
Touring Office
(Hugh Davidson)
Explorations Program
(Helen Eriks)

SECRETARIAT

Asst. Director &
Secretary
(Jocelyn Harvey)
Secretary's Office
Communications
Service
(Helen Murphy)
Translation/
Terminology
Official Languages
Atlantic Regional
Office

**ADMINISTRATIVE
DIVISION**

Asst. Director &
Treasurer
(Peter Brown)
Services:
Administration
Information Services
(Herb Westman)
Personnel
Finances
Research & Evaluation
(Harry Chartrand)
Reproduction Centre
Central Registry &
Archives
Killam Program
(Mel MacLeod)

**UNESCO
DIVISION**

Secretary-General
(Shirley Thomson)
Services:
Programs
Information
Administration

EXHIBIT 3
THE CANADA COUNCIL (A)

Summary of Arts Section Programs

WRITING AND PUBLICATION

The Canada Council Writing and Publication Section administers numerous programs of support for Canadian writers and publishers of poetry, drama, fiction, non-fiction and children's literature. It offers programs for book publishers through block and project grants, translation grants, a book purchase program, and aid for the promotion of Canadian books and periodicals. Programs for periodicals include grants for publishing, for promotion, and for the remuneration of free-lance contributors.

The Section also helps promote Canadian books and writers through a variety of other programs, including the book donation program and the National Book Festival. In addition, national professional associations of writers and publishers are eligible for grants. Individual Canadian writers are assisted through a public readings program for organizations in Canada and the United States, and through writers-in-residence programs in Canada.

Writers planning writing projects in poetry, drama, fiction, non-fiction and children's literature are funded by the Arts Awards Service.

MEDIA ARTS

The Media Arts Section is the most recently formed section at the Canada Council. Its objective is to provide support for the direct, creative use of conventional and new technologies and related media by independent, professional artists. The section administers three major programs: film and holography, video and audio, and integrated media (computer processing, imaging—audio and video—or system control, videotex and teletext, laser techniques, video disc and optical storage media).

By encouraging artists to explore many technologies and media, the Council hopes to contribute to the defining and disseminating of new esthetic criteria in the expanding field of media arts.

The Arts Awards Service also funds individual filmmakers, video artists, and critics and curators.

MUSIC

The Canada Council Music Section funds nearly 200 music organizations including orchestras, opera companies, choirs, instrumental ensembles and service organizations. It also supports some training, Canadian recordings, contemporary music and a commissioning program which stimulates the composition of Canadian music. Most of the funding is directed to professional classical music and musicians. Other types of music may receive limited funding under some Music Section programs or may be eligible for assistance from the Explorations Program or the Arts Awards Service.

Individual musicians are funded through the Arts Awards Service. They may apply for grants in the following areas: performance and composition of classical music: opera stage direction; composition; arrangement, songwriting and performance of jazz, rock and folk music; instrument-making; and orchestral and choral conducting.

DANCE

The Canada Council Dance Section funds ballet, modern and experimental dance. Other types of dance such as folk or jazz may be eligible for assistance from the Explorations Program or the Arts Awards Service. The Dance Section administers programs of assistance to professional companies, schools, independent choreographers, small-scale presenters and service organizations.

Individual dancers are funded through the Arts Awards Service.

VISUAL ARTS

The Canada Council Visual Arts Section focuses its programs on exhibitions of contemporary Canadian visual art in all its forms including film, video, architecture and crafts. Exhibitions of art other than contemporary Canadian also may receive Council assistance. Support is provided to non-profit public art galleries, museums and artist-run centres. (Artist-run centres are production and exhibition spaces run by professional artists.) The Visual Arts Section also funds print workshops and production and service centres as well as service organizations in the visual arts. Performance art created by individuals, groups and organizations also may receive support. Other funding includes a program for visiting artists in Canada and the maintenance of two studios in New York for Canadian artists.

Individual visual artists are funded through the Arts Awards Service. These may include sculptors, painters, graphic artists, artists working with mixed media, installations and crafts, architects, photographers, critics, curators, and multi-disciplinary and performance artists.

The Visual Arts Section also includes the ART BANK, located at 2279 Gladwin Crescent in Ottawa, which was created in 1972 to complement the programs of the Visual Arts Section of the Council. Its objectives are to provide recognition and direct assistance to professional Canadian artists through the purchase of their work; to present contemporary Canadian art to the public in everyday environments through a rental program; and to stimulate the private and corporate collecting of art.

The Art Bank collection, which is the most comprehensive of its kind in the world, consists of over 12,000 works by over 1,500 artists. It has art by both well established artists and those in the earlier stages of their career. The collection includes works on paper (prints, watercolors, drawings, photographs), which form the largest group: paintings, sculptures and three-dimensional works (including outdoor pieces); ceramics; wall hangings; and installations. More than 70 per cent of the collection is rented at any given time.

THEATRE

The Canada Council Theatre Section funds professional theatre companies and organizations, an English-language playwrights-in-residence program, independent French language theatre groups, training, theatre writers' travel and service organizations. All forms of theatre are supported including mime, puppetry,

EXHIBIT 3 *(continued)*

theatre for young audiences, music theatre, comedy, drama and collective creations. The Theatre Section encourages companies to hire Canadian artists and administrators, and to include Canadian plays in their repertoires.

Individual theatre professionals are funded through the Arts Award Service. These may include performers, mimes, directors, playwrights, administrators, designers, technicians and critics.

TOURING OFFICE

Touring is a way of developing audiences, extending the employment of artists, and giving communities access to performing artists. The Touring office was established in 1973 to stimulate touring by Canadian performing artists and to ensure access to performances by the widest possible Canadian audience. It provides touring information and consultation services to artists, managers and administrators, and helps to offset revenue shortfalls of performing artists and arts groups on tour. The Touring Office Advisory Board helps develop policy and provide technical guidance. It is composed of 16 members drawn from all the provinces and territories as well as the Canadian performing arts industry.

ARTS AWARDS SERVICE

The Arts Awards Service of the Canada Council offers a competitive grant program to individual artists and arts professionals in the following disciplines: architecture, arts administration, creative writing, criticism and curating (visual and media arts), dance, film, multidisciplinary work and performance art, music, non-fiction writing, photography, theatre, video and visual arts. The first four grants listed below are offered in each of the preceding categories, with the exception of arts administration where no "A" Grant is offered and non-fiction writing where one type of grant is available.

All grant applications are evaluated by juries or assessors according to the following criteria: the artistic background and potential of the applicant, the applicant's contribution to the art form, the merit and artistic quality of the project, and the relevance of the project to the applicant's work. Applicants for all grants must be Canadian citizens or landed immigrants who have lived in Canada for five years as landed immigrants.

Arts Grants "A": Arts Grants "A" are intended to provide free time for personal creative activity by artists who have made a significant contribution to their discipline over a number of years and who are still active in their profession. Grants cover living expenses and project costs to a maximum of $20,000 (1985), for periods of up to 12 months. In visual and media arts, the maximum is $28,000 (1985) for periods of up to 12 months.

Arts Grants "B": Arts Grants "B" are intended to help artists to improve their skills or to work on personal creative projects. Professional artists who have completed their basic training and who meet the eligibility requirements set for their disciplines may apply. Grants cover living expenses and project costs to a maximum of $14,000 (1985) for periods of up to 12 months.

Project Grants: Project Grants are intended to enable artists to continue their work, and/or to undertake a specific project of work or study. Grants cover living expenses and project costs to a

maximum of $4,000 (1985), for periods of up to 12 months. (These grants, in effect from 1 April 1985, combine and replace Short-Term Grants and Project Cost Grants.)

Travel Grants: Travel Grants are intended to enable artists to travel on occasions important to their professional career, for example, to take part in international competitions, to attend solo exhibitions of their work or to attend a first or major performance of one of their works.

Non-Fiction Writing Awards: These grants are intended to promote writing of non-fiction by providing free time for authors to write a new work. Writers who have at least one book professionally published may apply. Works are assessed mainly on their literary value, subject matter, and the writing background of the author. The grants cover living expenses, project costs and travel costs to a maximum of $15,000 (1985) for periods of up to 12 months.

Classical Music Artists in Mid-Career (Pilot Program): These grants are intended for classical singers, instrumentalists and composers applying for Arts Grants "B" who are 30 years of age or over, and are well established professional musicians. A special adjudication procedure exists to evaluate these candidates.

Artists' Studios in Paris: Three studios, with living accommodation, at the Site international des arts are available at moderate cost to Canadian musicians and visual artists who wish to pursue advanced studies or creative projects in Paris. These spaces are available to Canadian artists through an annual competition.

Visiting Foreign Artists: The Canada Council, in cooperation with the Department of External Affairs, administers a program of visits to Canadian cultural institutions by distinguished foreign artists. The visitors direct advanced workshops or give master classes.

EXPLORATIONS

Explorations is a multidisciplinary and project-oriented program which may introduce new approaches to creative expression, extend the limit of an existing art form, cross disciplines, or fulfill specific needs to the development of the arts. Through a flexible mandate, it covers cultural and artistic activities not normally eligible for funding under other Council programs. Applications for Explorations grants are not restricted to professional artists or to people who have had formal training in the discipline represented by their project. The intent of the program is to stimulate arts and culture—to provide initial support to innovative, unusual or unproven ideas that otherwise might not be realized. Explorations grants have funded film scripts, craft workshops, research and writing on a variety of cultural issues, performing arts projects, animation projects, film, video and audio experiments and a variety of other arts- and culture-related projects.

The grants cover travel and other direct costs of a project and frequently provide a subsistence allowance. Applications are assessed by six regional selection committees representing Northern Canada, British Columbia, the Prairies, Ontario, Quebec and the Atlantic provinces. Regional committee recommendations are then reviewed by a national committee composed of representatives from each regional committee and members of the Canada Council.

EXHIBIT 3 (continued)

PRIZES AND AWARDS

1. Molson Prizes
2. The Izaak Walton Memorial Prizes
3. The McLuhan Teleglobe Canada Award
4. Governor General's Literary Awards
5. Canada Council Children's Literature Prizes
6. Canada Council Translation Prizes
7. Canada-Australia Literary Prize
8. Canada-French Community of Belgium Literary Prize
9. Canada-Italy Literary Exchange
10. Canada-Switzerland Literary Prize
11. Virginia P. Moore Award
12. Sylva Gelber Foundation Awards
13. Jules Leger Prize for New Chamber Music
14. Healey Willan Prize
15. Victor Martyn Lynch-Staunton Awards
16. Jacqueline Lemieux Prize
17. J.B.C. Watkins Prize
18. Peter Dwyer Scholarships
19. Theatre Scholarship in Great Britain

THE KILLAM PROGRAM

The Killam Program supports scholars of exceptional ability engaged in research projects of broad significance in the humanities, social sciences, natural sciences, medicine, engineering and studies linking any of the disciplines within these broad fields. The program is financed by a donation and a bequest to the Canada Council by the late Mrs. Dorothy J. Killam. Two categories of awards are offered under the Killam Program.

The Izaak Walton Killam Research Fellowships: The Izaak Walton Killam Research fellowships are offered annually to support independent scholars in the fields listed above, who are doing research at a university or other research institution.

The Izaak Walton Killam Memorial Prizes: The three Izaak Walton Killam Memorial prizes of $50,000 each are awarded annually to eminent Canadian scholars in natural sciences, engineering and health sciences who are engaged actively in research in industry, a government agency or a university. The prizes, for which each nominee must be named by three experts in his or her field, are given in recognition of a distinguished career.

THE CANADIAN COMMISSION FOR UNESCO

The United Nations Educational, Scientific and Cultural Organization provides in it constitution that each member government establish and maintain a national commission. In Canada, this responsibility has been delegated to the Canada Council.

EXHIBIT 4

THE CANADA COUNCIL (A)

Statement of Revenue and Expenditure of the Endowment Account
for the Year Ended 31 March 1985

(in thousands of dollars)

Revenue		1985	1984
Parliamentary grant		$72 614	$65 581
Interest and dividends		10 601	9 816
Art Bank rental fees		596	580
Cancelled grants, approved in previous			
years, and refunds		334	437
	TOTAL	84 145	76 414

Expenditure		1985	1984
Arts:			
Grants and services		69 396	64 661
Administration		6 042	5 611
Works of art		712	844
	TOTAL	76 150	71 116
Canadian Commission for UNESCO:			
Administration		852	813
Grants		189	115
		1 041	928
General Administration		6 011	5 928
	TOTAL	83 202	77 972
Excess of revenue over expenditure			
(expenditure over revenue) for the year		$ 943	$(1 558)

EXHIBIT 5

THE CANADA COUNCIL (A)

Council's Support to the Disciplines, 1978–1984

Discipline	1978–79 (1)	1978–79 (2)	1979–80 (1)	1979–80 (2)	1980–81 (1)	1980–81 (2)	1981–82 (1)	1981–82 (2)	1982–83 (1)	1982–83 (2)	1983–84 (1)	1983–84 (2)
CANADA COUNCIL	3 161	41 074	3 085	41 795	3 006	43 693	3 486	51 557	3 580	59 549	3 902	63 905
Individuals	1 076	4 662	1 046	4 819	991	4 912	1 142	5 813	1 121	6 997	1 111	7 497
Organizations	2 085	36 412	2 039	36 976	2 015	38 781	2 344	45 744	2 459	52 552	2 792	56 408
Dance	101	4 870	88	5 518	99	5 727	125	7 230	143	8 764	154	9 168
Individuals	53	201	42	189	56	238	57	275	61	327	65	382
Organizations	48	4 669	46	5 329	43	5 489	68	6 955	82	8 437	89	8 786
Music	592	10 600	574	10 533	519	11 111	590	12 594	498	14 206	603	15 229
Individuals	294	1 254	281	1 172	256	1 205	256	1 205	201	1 267	247	1 604
Organizations	298	9 346	293	9 361	263	9 988	334	11 389	297	12 939	356	13 625
Theatre	274	9 760	293	9 936	289	10 679	344	11 998	318	13 985	333	14 842
Individuals	84	376	106	413	98	466	110	449	92	556	100	524
Organizations	190	9 384	187	9 523	191	10 213	234	11 549	226	13 429	233	14 318
Visual Arts	680	4 880	708	5 051	643	5 271	726	6 430	826	7 516	841	8 224
Individuals	364	1 574	347	1 785	343	1 744	407	2 154	422	2 773	420	3 081
Organizations	316	3 306	361	3 266	300	3 527	319	4 276	404	4 743	421	5 143
Media Arts (2)	211	1 721	191	1 887	167	1 949	205	2 493	244	3 018	250	3 189
Individuals	83	259	82	307	53	202	72	308	77	462	60	306
Organizations	128	1 462	109	1 580	114	1 747	133	2 185	167	2 556	190	2 883
Writing	943	7 563	899	7 083	974	7 027	1 143	8 580	1 236	9 791	1 262	10 041
Individuals	157	823	147	752	134	878	174	1 111	198	1 216	141	1 089
Organizations	791	6 740	752	6 331	840	6 149	969	7 469	1 038	8 575	1 121	8 952
Other	53	219	61	380	76	504	94	561	132	929	158	1 084
Individuals	41	175	41	201	51	261	66	311	70	396	78	511
Organizations	12	44	20	179	25	243	28	250	62	533	80	573
Explorations	302	1 461	271	1 407	239	1 425	259	1 671	183	1 340	301	2 128

(1) Number of Grants
(2) Thousands of Current Grant Dollars

Biographical Sketches of the Senior Members of the Canada Council Staff

(1) Gilles Lefebvre, Associate Director.

Gilles Lefebvre was a distinguished gentleman in his early 60s who had been appointed Associate Director of the Canada Council by Order-in-Council on March 7, 1983. His early musical education had led to a notable career spanning almost four decades. He founded Les Jeunesses Musicales and served as its Director General from 1949 to 1972. Other positions included Director, Canadian Cultural Centre in Paris (1972–79); Director General, Bureau of International Cultural Relations (1979–81); and Assistant Undersecretary, Bureau of International Cultural Relations, Department of External Affairs (1982–83).

Among his many other activities, M. Lefebvre had founded the JMC Orford Arts Centre, served as Associate Artistic Director of the World Festival of Expo '67, was Chairman of the Canadian Conference of the Arts, chaired the Finance Committee of the International Music Council, and audited the Musicians' International Mutual Aid Fund. He had organized national and international music competitions, and received many honors for his achievements:

Officer of the Order of Canada for outstanding service, 1967

Honorary doctorate from the Universite de Montreal, 1978

Diplome d'honneur of the Canadian Conference of the Arts, May 1978

Honorary membership in the International Music Council (other members included Yehudi Menuhin, Maureen Forrester, Ravi Shankar, Henryk Szeryng, etc.)

Canadian Music Council Medal, 1982

Medal and plaque from the Kodaly Institute in Kecskemet, 1982

JMC Medal, 1983

Honorary Doctorate of Sherbrooke University, 1986

(2) Jocelyn Harvey, Assistant Director and Council Secretary.

After serving several years as Executive Assistant to Timothy Porteous, Jocelyn Harvey began her new job as Secretary shortly before the arrival of Peter Roberts. Her natural directness, warmth, and manner of gracious personal authority were assets in aspects of her work requiring that she be responsible for all dealings with the council; and her educational background and professional experience helped her deal with other aspects of council communications and "print outreach."

Ms Harvey's undergraduate and graduate degrees in English Literature (from Wisconsin and Ohio State Universities), and Ph.D. in English Literature (Cornell University, 1964), led to a variety of university teaching posts until 1969. A writing career beckoned, and she began working in entrepreneurial fashion as a free-lance contract writer and editor (1969 to 1976). Other professional positions included: Editor, Transport Canada, (Ottawa, 1976–77); and Co-Editor, *Perception*, and English Editor of non-periodicals, The Canadian Council on Social Development (Ottawa, 1977–78). She joined the Canada Council as Senior Writer in 1978, and from 1982–85 served as Executive Assistant to the Director. In October 1984, Jocelyn assumed her new position of Assistant Director and Council Secretary.

(3) Peter Brown, Assistant Director and Treasurer.

An urbane and cosmopolitan business administrator, Peter Brown had come to the council in January 1985 from the private sector position of Assistant General Manager (Finance and Administration) for the Corporation of Massey Hall and Roy Thomson Hall (1983–85). A graduate of McMaster University (BA Economics and Business), Mr. Brown had held a variety of responsible financial positions from 1957 to 1970. After studying international industrial management in Switzerland (1971), his career activities included several senior-level positions in international business: Vice President, Traders Finance and Leasing Inc., and Panama Director, Traders Liberian Companies (1972–76); President and Director, Traders Finance S.A., Luxemburg (1976–78); Vice-President and Deputy Vice-President (Finance), Acres International Ltd. (1978–83).

Mr. Brown was an accomplished vocalist. He had studied music for nine years at the Royal Conservatory of Music, Toronto, and performed with many orchestras and opera companies. Other activities included his membership in the Boards of Directors for the Shaw Festival and the Mainly Mozart Festival, and Massey Hall's Board of Governors.

DMR GROUP, INC. (B)*

James C. Rush and Eileen D. Watson

During his conversation in the fall of 1986 with executive vice president Alain Roy, the president of DMR Group, Inc., Pierre Ducros, remarked:

> I believe we have to re-create the excitement and commitment of our entrepreneurial start-up in the 1970s. I have an intuitive feeling that to survive in this business, we need to have 'value added' to the services we offer, and we must expand worldwide. The logical way to do that is through acquisitions — which means a focus on attracting the best professional people, educating our management, and broadening their experience base with lateral moves.
>
> Excellent management is the key ingredient of our future success... and while we're talking about changes in our management style at DMR, my mind keeps turning to Marc Girault. We have many dedicated, hardworking managers throughout our organization, but the Quebec City office manager is truly unique. If everyone in this organization thought and behaved like Marc, there would be no need for us to have this conversation.

"I suggest that we study the way Marc operates," replied Alain. "One answer to our problems lies in developing managers who all can be as good as our best — and that means Marc Girault!"

Marc Girault became a partner two years after joining DMR. In another two years he was made manager of the Quebec City office. Under Marc's leadership this office rapidly became the largest and most profitable of the entire DMR organization.

When Girault took over the office, he was managing 70 professionals, and generating revenues of $4 million. Ever-increasing profitability goals were achieved each year; and soon the office's profitability exceeded its 30 percent

---

*All names in this case have been disguised, except those of the founding partners of DMR.

target. Currently, the Quebec City office employed almost 200 people, with revenues for the year forecast at $10 million.

Praise from the President

"Let me share with you what I wrote about Marc for the last awards banquet," said Pierre, drawing a copy of his speech from a desk drawer. He read excerpts from his notes:

> I believe that it is Marc Girault's *attitude* — his profound respect for people — which underlies his successful management style. He sees a client as an equal partner; and he works hard to support the client's success. He insists that it is the client who must be the winner!
>
> Marc is somewhat reserved, never proposing a solution hastily. He is competent, honest, and humble. The quality of his work and his high standards of professional ethics inspire confidence. He treats all clients, big or small, equally — no one client is more important than the other. He is dependable — he holds to the agreed-upon contract price, and keeps his commitments.
>
> Marc is innovative, and does not hesitate to use his autonomy to overturn traditional methods. His people created a new management tool which failed to receive the approval of head office; but Marc persevered, and finally had it accepted, not only throughout the DMR network, but by clients all over the world.
>
> Because he has chosen high-quality staff, he accepts projects which other consulting firms judge too difficult. He insists that DMR proposals contain no surprises — no partial estimates, no loopholes. He takes significant risks in situations involving millions of dollars.
>
> Marc was our first DMR manager to implement structured professional development programs for everyone. He recruits personnel who can address the staff's weaknesses, and is careful to encourage initiative and innovation. I've heard him say, "Every person must find a way to establish themselves."
>
> There is no procedures manual in the Quebec City office because Marc communicates what he wants in other ways — he is not a man of power, but a facilitator, a motivator. He teaches by example, and involves his team in major decisions.
>
> The results speak for themselves — high market penetration, an office on the leading edge of technology, where the utilization of personnel is high. Marc above all wants to get concrete results — not just for the Quebec City office, but to meet the overall goals of the DMR organization.
>
> Marc is always on the go, but he manages his energy. He works hard — he dedicates eight to ten hours a day to his job, plus one or two nights a week. He expects others to do their part, and does not tolerate mediocrity around him. But Marc is not a slave to the office. He balances his professional and his personal life, spending quality recreational time with his family.

"He sounds too good to be true," exclaimed Alain, "and yet, I know you've accurately described Marc Girault."

What Other DMR Managers Said About Marc

I think he's the best leader I've ever seen. He respects the style of everybody. The basic values here at DMR are *his* values — solve problems when they are small, see each person every six to eight weeks, respect the client. He spends a lot of time teaching us what to do — how to do a call on a client, how to sell our services. He tells us to implement *values*, not procedures.

Situational leadership seems to be the way he operates — I like that style myself. He stays very close to people who are working on hard and difficult jobs. If we are working on a tough proposal, Marc will stay close all the time during the preparation of the proposal; but once it is implemented, he becomes close to someone else.

Marc manages the office like his own personal things, with great concern. He encourages everyone to take responsibility and initiative, and he will back us up, no matter what decisions we have made. He has pride in us, confidence in us, listens to our ideas before making a decision.

He has a low-key approach: 'DMR wins if my people win!' He has surrounded himself with good people (he has grown them), although there are no superstars. Marc listens very well. He speaks very little at management meetings.

Marc is a good delegator, and makes one feel comfortable about delegating upward. Very people-oriented — when promotions come up, Marc asks, 'Who's on the list? Who is going to be frustrated about not getting a promotion?' And he is very concerned about quality.

Marc Girault's Approach to Management

Girault was a tall, dark-haired man in his mid-40s, with a youthful appearance, expressive face (eyebrows perpetually in motion!) and relaxed body posture. He spoke in a gentle, well-modulated voice, his conversation punctuated with frequent smiles. His dress varied from businesslike (well-tailored three-piece suits for meetings with clients, government officials, etc.) to informal (rolled-up shirt sleeves for managers' meetings).

Describing his personal philosophy of management to a visitor, Marc Girault said:

My job is simply a leadership-type job. That is, I define and sell objectives — and it's easier to sell my objectives if they are originally defined with members of a group. I also define and sell values. I communicate, communicate, communicate! About 98 percent of my time is spent interacting with people.

Managing an employee means helping him or her first to understand the project being proposed, then agreeing on the mandate, the budget...all very motivating. Most managers are grossly overworked; so people management is done over lunch, after work, whenever time can be found. I believe that if a manager would meet each employee once a month for lunch to address his or her personal situation, there would be no dissatisfied employees. And as a general rule, a manager should not give an employee an unacceptable assignment twice in a row.

I believe in autonomy. Autonomy is something that you take; but in order to be autonomous, you have to understand the objectives and values of upper management. You formulate your own plans to meet the values of the enterprise. DMR's values are transmitted by word-of-mouth. When a new consultant has to prepare a proposal for a given customer, strategies should be discussed at length with the supervisor — talk about the personnel to be used, financial limits, customer satisfaction, etc. He or she will gain his understanding of the company's values and priorities through these conversations.

For "people management," you begin with the principle that each employee is a professional. What is a professional? Someone who has stringent responsibilities, such as managing the quality of service to clients, giving leadership to DMR people, the financial aspects. Every manager is responsible for all four domains.

At the very base of our organization are "rock values" relating to the customer (respect for the customer) and personnel (we have to make sure that the consultants realize that their job is to fulfill the real needs of the customer). The customer may not need a complex system with all the bells and whistles that our people would love to provide. We have to convince DMR personnel of that; and it's very difficult to teach that value. We have many people who get great satisfaction from doing a sophisticated on-line system with all the bells and whistles, who are very disappointed when they finally understand that the real objective is simply to do an expanded system that will produce results in two months! Some consultants are deflated by this. The hardest job is to persuade them that it is not their needs but the client's that matter.

When a new employee is introduced to DMR, company values are stated explicitly — usually during an orientation session. And it's basically a two-way process at DMR. All kinds of good ideas come to me from others — they share their values with me as well.

I communicate values in a more formal way to my managers through meetings held every second Wednesday between 5 and 10 p.m. with everyone who manages personnel. The agenda is the same every week:

News of current/future happenings;
Business status — requests for proposals (RFPs) received, RFPs outstanding, status of RFPs;
Up-to-date client forecast and business developed;
Personnel development — hiring, salary planning, etc.;
Services — for example, a presentation on a new service, or a special project; and
Closing — an open session, with myself as moderator, dealing with topics interesting to the managers (e.g. how to help a young DMR person cope with problems caused by the large size of the company).

Besides the bi-weekly managers' meetings, general employee meetings are held every six weeks. At these, I cover financial results, introduce new employees and talk about departures, and include a presentation about some project or service-related subject. I'll often ask new employees (four or five at a time) to speak for five or ten minutes about an achievement.

I believe that motivation is not an inner thing; we can't motivate ourselves. Motivation has to come from our environment. You need to feel that you are loved; you need to feel that you are doing something that matters, something of importance; you need to feel that you are recognized and rewarded properly; you need to feel that you are doing something in which there is a challenge for you. How are those four things accomplished? Only through personal communication and contact. Just the other day a manager was telling me about a customer who provides none of those things for her employees, and the employees are suffering terribly.

Within our organization, as large as it has become, the way I can pass on these values is through making sure that my managers understand and practice good communication and personal contacts with their personnel. It is unbelievable what you can accomplish through "MBWA!" For instance, talking with a manager about giving a raise to a staff member, we can discuss this person's qualities related to a certain scale of values. We have many bright people who are quick to pick up what is needed and wanted in terms of motivating their people — you don't have to tell them twice.

What you do speaks louder than what you say. We unquestioningly pay overtime to our people out on operational sites, and we give bonuses for good effort. Good consultants are in short supply!

Performance cannot be managed on a project basis — it's too time-consuming. You manage performance on an exception basis — for instance, when you see poor performance, with negative results, you really step in. But positive feedback is very important, too; so if our managers and project managers are doing their jobs properly, employees should be getting positive feedback regularly.

If you manage the activities of your people on a daily basis — an *hourly* basis, actually — you don't get performance problems, unless someone lacks the capabilities. Then we give them opportunities to improve. We have customers now who are former employees, who for one reason or another were unable to do the work in this environment, and I had to more or less fire them — but when they quit, they were smiling!

There are many opportunities at DMR for employees to innovate. A successful company promotes innovative thinking and supports it — "intrapreneuring." For instance, getting money from the government to support education programs within the company was done by an enterprising employee. And we encourage ten days of educational opportunity or training for each employee.

I wish that the managers did not have to work so hard. Every six months I redistribute responsibilities throughout the management staff, to minimize their workloads; but six months later, the managers are still working too hard!

At the moment, we encounter the most difficulty with managing new graduates. With no prior experience, they cannot compare DMR to anything else; so if they run into difficulties, they may blow their problems out of all proportion.

I don't believe in a structured environment where, for instance, project reviews are done regularly every Monday morning at a regular 9 a.m. meeting. That's not an efficient way to operate — of ten projects that a manager has in progress, six really don't need to be reviewed. So why waste time doing reviews that are not needed? That's not to say we don't have reviews. We do, but only when they are required. You assess each situation. I know if a project is being managed by a particular person I don't need to review it at all. And for projects that are continuing successfully towards their goal, project reviews are not required unless that person asks for it.

How do individuals know they are doing well? It depends on the size of the office. In a small office, you're with people so much that you see all the opportunities to express appreciation for good work. If things are going wrong, you see that too, and can turn to a coaching mode as required. You can say, "That's a great job," or "That's a good idea," as opportunities arise. Good work deserves to be recognized.

PART THREE

The Management of Change

INTRODUCTION

In the previous chapters we have presented the concept of organizations as socio-technical systems. We discussed the glue that holds them together and gives them direction — strategy, structure, administrative mechanisms, culture and management style. We then discussed individual and group behavior and the relationships between individuals, groups and jobs.

We have now reached an understanding of organizations and management that permits us to think about how to make changes. A change may be necessary in any one or more of the variables we have covered to this point: strategy, structure, administrative mechanisms, job design, or people's behavior. Whatever the change, it will not take place in isolation from all the other variables. It will take place in a context that encompasses all of them. A change in one component of the system may require changes in other components. Managers cannot ignore, or forget, the systemic characteristics of their organizations as they undertake change.

Why will management want to make a change at all? New factors may have emerged in the firm's external environment, such as government regulations on health and safety, or equal employment. There could be an economic recession which forces recognition that the firm has become overstaffed and inefficient. Managers may be anticipating trends and trying to position the organization to meet them. Or they may be losing ground to competitors for any number of product- or service-related reasons.

The previous examples seem to suggest that the need for change originates in the firm's external environment, but that is not necessarily the case. There could be internal dissatisfaction with tasks or company procedures; employees may see ways of improving operations. Whether the originating factor is external or internal, as the manager and initiator of change you sense that something needs to be done differently. You see the need to move your organization from its current mode of operating to a new mode.

C H A P T E R   6

Managing Change

Requisites for Successful Change

Change must be managed. Although that may seem obvious, our experience suggests that it is not always so. Successful change in organizations requires commitment from the organization's leaders, a competent and motivated person responsible for managing the change, and a process for designing, implementing and institutionalizing the change.

Visible and stated commitment of the organization's leaders to the change is critical to successful change. These leaders control many of the actual variables which influence others' behaviors; they dispense rewards of many kinds (task assignments, promotions, or pay raises), and control the resources which people need to do their jobs. They will decide if required resources are allocated to change projects, if budgets for staff development and training will be made available, or if adequate staffing will be provided. The public statements of the leaders will be scrutinized by organization members to assess the sincerity of the desire to affect change. If the leaders are not perceived to support the change, then it is unrealistic to expect others in the organization to be enthusiastic, and any change is likely short-lived.

Championing Change

The reason for the failure of many change efforts is poor management. Change requires someone with conceptual, analytical and action skills, as well as great effort. The effective change agent or champion must understand the change process, be able to communicate effectively, and mediate or adjudicate conflicts which arise during the change process. The "champion" must attempt to get as many formal and informal leaders as possible to support the change openly and consistently. It is also important that the person responsible for the change be a respected individual, clearly identified with the leadership of the organization. Nothing is more likely to convey a sense that the leadership does not support the change than assigning responsibility for it to a low status individual, or to one who has no respect within the organization. Many changes involve the use of high-prestige consultants as change agents who may be intimately involved in all aspects of the change management process. They can bring expertise, credibility, and a high profile to the change. But, in our view, they can be only temporary change agents. At some point the process set in motion must be internalized by organizational members who assume responsibility for the change.

The Change Management Process

A process must be established for change design and implementation and ensuring that it persists for as long as it is appropriate. If the change agent manages this process well there is a better chance of the changes being successful. We propose to develop a three stage, seven step model by looking at the major elements of this process.[1 and 2]

Stage 1. Design and Impact Analysis

Step 1 • carefully selecting the change so that it is one which people will view as important and needed;

Step 2 • analyzing the potential impacts of the change;

Stage 2. Implementation

Step 3 • choosing the appropriate change strategy to gather support for the change and to defuse resistance to it;

Step 4 • planning the change so that the desired strategy is implemented effectively;

Step 5 • monitoring the change as it is implemented;

---

[1] Most three stage models of organizational change like the one we use and present in this chapter trace their conceptual lineage back to Kurt Lewin. His article "Frontiers in Group Dynamics: Concept, Method and Reality in Social Science; Social Equilibria and Social Change" was published in *Human Relations* Vol. 1, No. 1, in 1947. This article put forward a three stage model (unfreeze, move, refreeze) as well as the concepts of constancy and resistance to change, social fields, force fields and group decisions as a change procedure. Many of the conceptual elements of our model are modifications of Lewin's original ideas.

[2] Thomas A. Kochan and Lee Dyer developed a three stage model for analyzing change in a unionized environment in their article "A Model of Organizational Change in the Context of Union Management Relations," *Journal of Applied Behavioral Science*, Vol. 12, Jan. 1976, pp. 59–70. See also Thomas A. Kochan, *Collective Bargaining and Industrial Relations*, Richard D. Irwin, 1980, pp. 411–418. Another similar three-phase model can be found in A. Mikalachki and J. Gandz, *Managing Absenteeism*, University of Western Ontario, School of Business Administration, London 1980.

Step 6 • modifying the change and the change plan if responses and developments indicate that it is not producing the desired results.

Stage 3. Institutionalization

Step 7 • ensuring that fit among environment, organization, task and people exists.

Stage 1, Step 1: Selecting the Change

People generally have a limited capacity to change and there are many reasons for their resistance to change. Given the difficulties often associated with bringing about change, and the amount of time and energy required to drive the process, it is important not to waste these limited resources on changes unrelated to important problems or on changes which people will not see the value of. Changes should contribute visibly to achieving the organization's goals and/or improving routines and employee satisfaction.

Many writers on the subject of change would argue in favor of the "theory of the small win." It is the small incremental changes which stand the best chances of success.[3] Unless forced by a crisis into making major, system-wide changes, you may be wise to start small and let the change mature and grow. The diffusion of change beyond its initiation depends in large measure on perceived success — continuation of change is fueled by such success and, unless early success is apparent, the chances of realizing your goals are slim.

Stage 1, Step 2: Analyzing the Impact of Change

There are a series of questions that you should ask before launching into implementing a change. They involve defining those individuals or groups who will be affected by the change; identifying sources of support for and resistance to the change, and the reasons for the potential resistance; assessing whether the reasons are well-founded or are mis-perceptions; and estimating the shock-value of the proposed change and, thus the potential for reflex rejection.

We cannot overemphasize the importance of the impact analysis in managing change. It is the foundation on which your change management strategy and tactics will be built. It requires answering a series of questions:

Defining the Scope of the Change
• How much time do you have to make the change? Is it critical that the change take place immediately, or do you have time to avoid hasty actions?

---

[3] Quinn, J.B. *Strategic Change*. Dow-Jones Irwin, 1980.

- What individual or groups of individuals does the change focus on? Identify specifically who will be directly affected by the proposed change.
- What will these people have to do differently? What behavioral changes will be required? What changes in work processes will be necessary?
- Which peripheral groups will be affected by the proposed changes? Remembering the systemic nature of organizations, look beyond the immediate focal group to see if important constituencies like unions are involved, or if interdependent work groups will feel the effects.

Identifying Sources of Support for Change

- Who will see the need for the change? Can they, or will they, be able to influence others? If the informal leaders and opinion leaders of your organization see the benefits of the change, you stand a better chance of implementing it.
- Who will benefit from the change and how will they benefit? Do they understand how they will benefit?

Identifying Sources of Resistance to Change

- For whom is the change unpleasant or even terrifying? Who might be required to behave quite differently, abide by new policies, or interact with different people? From an extensive academic and practitioner-oriented literature, we know people resist change for the following reasons:[4]

Self interest[5]   Many changes threaten the real interests that people have in maintaining the status quo. They may lose power or influence because of a proposed change. They may have to give up some activity that they enjoy, take on some tasks which they don't like doing, or interact with people they dislike. Maybe the nature of the tasks they do will change considerably. The salesperson may see his or her territory as more difficult to work, the bank branch manager may see active selling as having lower status than financial counselling, and so on.

Misunderstanding and misinterpretation[6]   It is not unusual for those affected by a change to misunderstand what is happening, or to misinterpret

---

[4] a) Lawrence, P.R. "How to Deal with Resistance to Change." *Harvard Business Review*, May-June 1954, pp. 49-57.

b) Kotter, J.P. and L.A. Schlesinger, "Choosing Strategies for Change." *Harvard Business Review*, March-April 1979, pp. 106–114.

c) Watson, G. "Resistance to Change" in *The Planning of Change*, edited by Warren G. Bennis, Kenneth F. Benne and Robert Chin, New York, N.Y.: Holt, Rinehart and Winston, 1969.

d) Zander, A. "Resistance to Change — Its Analysis and Prevention." Advanced Management, XV, No. 1., January 1950.

[5] Shibbins, G. *Organizational Evolution: A Program for Managing Radical Change.* New York, N.Y.: Amacom, 1974.

[6] Kotter and Schlesinger, *op. cit.*

the reasons for the change and the motivations behind the move. A union may see automation as an attempt to replace people with machines; management may see it as a way to improve quality and may have no intention of laying-off people.

Violation of ideals, values or norms[7]   People have strongly held beliefs about many issues, including such things as appropriate service levels and quality work. Many changes, such as a decision to increase the pace of manufacturing or to reduce customer service levels to save costs actually threaten these values, ideals, and norms.

Disagreement with change   Strange as it may seem, not everyone will agree that management's bright idea is really bright! When someone tries to change something like an ordering procedure — perhaps to improve the ability to audit suppliers — someone else will think that the procedure is clumsy and time-consuming and may resist its implementation.

Jealousies and rivalries   When someone, or some group, benefits more than another from a change, the group which benefits less may oppose it. A move to a new location, for example, may be opposed by one department which sees another getting the prime office space or location.

Impact on relationships   People get used to interacting in certain ways, either cooperating or confronting each other for example. It is upsetting to try to adjust to different ways of interacting, to be nice to someone with whom you have traditionally argued, or to get tough with someone you have been dealing with on a friendly and informal basis.

Fear of failure[8]   Change may create feelings of incompetence. To be successful at demonstrating new behaviors, people must have the ability to perform them, as well as the motivation to do so. And whether or not they are motivated to try them will depend, at least to some extent, on their perception of the probability of success if they do try. To the extent that a branch manager of a bank perceives him or herself to lack selling skills, he or she will be fearful of trying. To the extent that he or she tries and then fails — because of a lack of ability — the bank manager will not be encouraged to persevere.

Pace of change[9]   Some people may resist change, even if it is in their self-interest, because it is unexpected, sudden, or radical in their view. An innate desire to maintain the status quo, or inertia, must be overcome. Lack of

---

[7] Shibbins, *op. cit.*

[8] Kotter and Schlesinger, *op. cit.*

[9] Stanislao, J. and Stanislao, B. "Dealing with Resistance to Change." *Business Horizons*, July-August 1983, pp. 74–77.

advance information and adequate preparation often seems to result in such a reflex rejection.

Incapacity to change Although people may agree that change is required, at the time that new behaviors are being demanded of them they may simply be overworked and lack the capacity to respond to the new demands. If a change requires membership in a new committee, or attendance in a new training program for example, this may be beyond the capacity of an administrator at a particular time. People may lack the time, the resources, or the ability to respond to new requirements.

Regardless of the scope, support and resistance can be found. Managers capitalizing on support and defusing resistance are more likely to be successful.

Figure 6.1
THE MANAGEMENT OF CHANGE

Stage 1 of the change process:
design and impact analysis

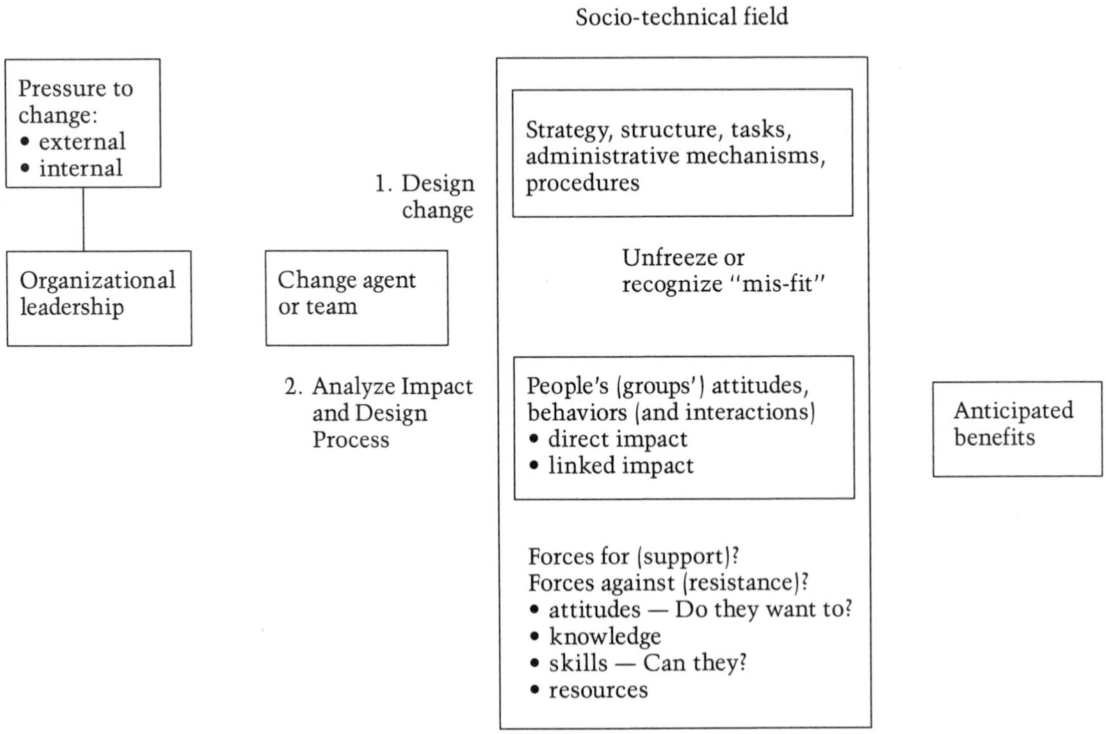

Socio-technical field

Pressure to change:
• external
• internal

Organizational leadership

Change agent or team

1. Design change

2. Analyze Impact and Design Process

Strategy, structure, tasks, administrative mechanisms, procedures

Unfreeze or recognize "mis-fit"

People's (groups') attitudes, behaviors (and interactions)
• direct impact
• linked impact

Anticipated benefits

Forces for (support)?
Forces against (resistance)?
• attitudes — Do they want to?
• knowledge
• skills — Can they?
• resources

Stage 1, as we have developed it to this point, is summarized in Figure 6.1. In Stage 2 we will look in more detail at why people may resist change, and tactics for overcoming that resistance.

Stage 2, Step 3: Choosing a Change Strategy and Process

The question always arises as to whether a top-down, authoritative approach to change or a participative approach that involves people in planning a change is the more appropriate strategy. There is no simple answer to the question, but there are a set of conditions that you should consider in choosing your strategy. A strong argument against involving people in a change usually is not having enough time, perhaps because a crisis situation has developed. This may be reasonable — if it is true and not just an excuse. A crisis usually makes the need for change more obvious to everyone and "unfreezes" the organization, giving management more freedom in designing and implementing the change it believes is appropriate. There is no question that it can take an extensive amount of time to ensure proper participation and to secure cooperation.

There are many different tactics which can be used to build support for change,[10] but they all amount to demonstrating the net benefits of the change relative to the costs. These are summarized below.

Education and Information
One approach is to educate and inform people as to the intent and purpose of a proposed change so as to ensure that it is clearly understood. Clearly, this is indicated where the resistance is based on misperceptions of a situation or where a lack of information and a clear presentation of the facts might help. Indeed, this is a necessary component in almost all change efforts.

Managers also must recognize that attempts to communicate in low-trust relationships frequently go awry and might actually backfire if the climate is poisoned to the extent that all communication is distorted. If this is the situation you face, then your first task is to build trust.

Consultation
Sometimes resistance to change can be overcome through the process of consultation, which includes two-way communication and education. Quite often, people who may initially resist change may lower that resistance as a result of having the opportunity to make their point of view known through a consultative process. They are able to live with the outcome — even if it is slightly distasteful to them — because they are satisfied that they had some role in shaping it. Consultation has the additional advantage of identifying possible problems and unintended consequences the change initiators may be

---

[10] This section draws heavily on the articles by Lawrence and by Kotter and Schlesinger, *op. cit.*

unaware of. Consultation tends to take time; although this may be a disadvantage under some circumstances, it does allow for adaptation to occur while it minimizes the surprise effect that can lead to reflex rejections.

Training and other assistance

We have suggested that people may resist change because they fear being incompetent or that they simply don't have the capacity to respond in the manner requested. It may be necessary to provide additional resources, training and development programs, some time away from the job to prepare for a new role, or perhaps just some encouragement and social supportiveness where the fear of incompetence is unjustified.

Negotiation

Faced with strong resistance to change, or the desire to have someone actively support a proposed change, it may be necessary to negotiate the change, agreeing to something in return for the change. The "want" might be positive — a reward, for example. Or it might be the avoidance of a negative, such as a punishment. There could be an agreement, for example, to allow a union to have veto power over the implementation of a new program in return for an agreement to waive traditional job classifications. Or a guarantee of job security may be given in return for some concession with respect to seniority.

Co-optation

Another possible approach is to co-opt resistors. This often involves making them such a key part of the change, involving them in a genuine power-sharing arrangement and extensive consultation, so that they begin to feel that they "own" the change. They may also start to lose sight of the reality that the change may not be in their long term interest. For example, one joint staffing committee in a unionized college worked so well and was such a genuine co-operative effort between union leaders and management that the teachers' representatives started suggesting a reduction in the number of teachers employed. It took a sharp reminder from others not involved in the committee to make these teachers realize that they were not acting in the best interest of the people they represented, at least in the short-run.

Manipulation and deception

It is sometimes tempting to manipulate or deceive someone to overcome resistance to change. For example, a union might be induced to give up some seniority protection to allow for the retention of some employees who are more junior but whose qualifications are better. And, once this breach in seniority is made, it might be used to get around strict seniority in recalls. Needless to say, once this tactic is discovered it results in a climate of hostility and mistrust.

Coercion

Finally, of course, there is always the option of trying to coerce someone into changing their behavior. Threats, explicitly stated or merely implied, are often made in the service of initiating or promoting change! They may involve telling salespersons that they will not keep their jobs unless they change their territory, or threatening to close down a plant unless employees agree to the introduction of new technology.

From the above discussion, we have identified seven factors that should be considered when designing a change process:

The amount of time which is available   Many of these strategies — consultation, for example — take considerable investment of time.

Potential support for the change   The more people who support change, the more senior and powerful they are, and the more openly supportive they are, the greater is the likelihood of success.

Potential resistance and the reasons for it   Is it a matter of some real or perceived loss, the violation of some value. If the resistance stems from ignorance or misperception, then communication and education is appropriate. If it is based on fear of incompetence, training might be appropriate. If it is based on the real loss of something, it may be necessary to negotiate some compensation.

The relative power of the change initiator and the people resisting change   Do the resistors have the ability to slow-down or totally sabotage the change effort if they decide not to cooperate or to actively oppose it. If the 'resistor' has power to resist, negotiation may be required. If there is no such power, coercion might be employed provided that the consequences of using coercion are acceptable. Remember resistance does not have to be active, formalized resistance. It can also take the form of a passive, withholding of support.

The locus of information required to design the change process   Specifically, where are the data to design the change? Who knows what has to be done? If the change manager does not have the right information, there may be no alternative to consultation. Remember, information is an important source of power.

The current climate within which the change is being initiated   Is there trust and acknowledged legitimacy in the relationship? Do people respect and like one another? Are people predisposed to cooperate? Where there is no trust, meaningful consultation is difficult and any communication or education efforts may well be interpreted as insincere and misleading.

The desired outcome in terms of the relationship between the change initiator and the change resistor   If the desired outcome is to maintain a trusting, cooperative relationship, the tactics of coercion, co-optation, manipulation, or deception are clearly bad choices.

In designing a change you must look at all these factors simultaneously, as is suggested in Figure 6.2, since they interact. For example, although it is

Figure 6.2
THE MANAGEMENT OF CHANGE

Choosing a Change Process

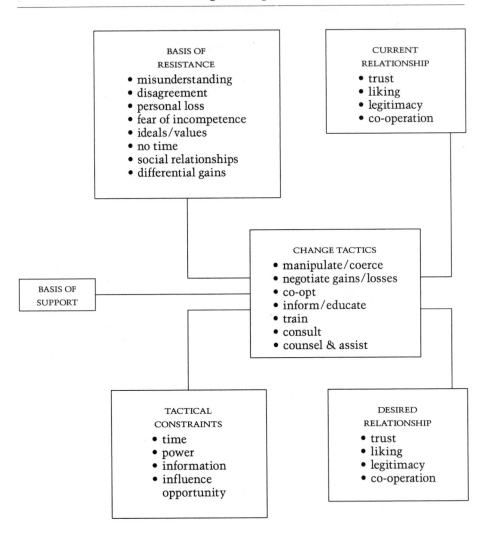

intuitively appropriate to use education and communication in cases of misperception leading to resistance, it may backfire if the current climate is one of mistrust and hostility. Although it may be expedient to try to coerce someone to change, they may have considerable power to withstand the coercion. In addition, the aftermath of coercion, in terms of the emergent relationship, might be dysfunctional. For example, trying to coerce a reluctant manager to change the way he or she handles performance appraisals may be difficult for a human resource director to do if that manager is highly influential with the president and if, as a result of the attempt to coerce, this manager subsequently attempts to block other changes.

There may be problems with the use of negotiations, particularly where they amount to appeasement. Giving in to the unreasonable request of someone in order to overcome resistance to a proposed change establishes a precedent. That person, or others who see the transaction as having taken place, may demand similar concessions for future changes.

Some people might argue that involvement is critical in any situation if employees are to comprehend the nature of the changes and to develop commitment to them.[11] Such writers tend to view commitment as a natural outcome of involvement or participation in decision-making. Furthermore, participation has the advantages of bringing more and different perspectives, views, opinions, and knowledge to bear on the issue, and there is much evidence that certain types of decisions are improved when there is involvement by those affected by them.

The advocates of participative change management also suggest that for true commitment to be obtained, people must be involved in all aspects of the issue, from participating in the analysis of the problem to deciding on the actions to be taken. And there must be some real degree of influence or power-sharing — a perceived opportunity to shape the nature of the change.[12]

There are very different forms of participation and different ways in which people define what participation means. Participation may mean just communication, or it may mean consultation, or involvement in decision-making in terms of some measure of co-determination to define problems as well as to solve them. Two-way communication is almost always required; consultation of some form is usually desirable, but true joint decision-making may not be crucial in all situations. One point of view says that change managers should be selective about the extent to which participative management is used and that participation is appropriate when: a) those affected share similar objectives as the change initiators, or at least can subscribe to some common, superordinate goal; b) they are affected by the change; c) the nature of the change is not cast in stone and there is a real, meaningful opportunity for those involved to shape it in some way; d) they have the information that is required; e) their acceptance is critical for implementation; and, f) there is time to engage in a participative process. If the decision has already been made

---

[11] Marrow, E., Bowers, D. and Seashore, S. _Management by Participation_. New York, N.Y.: Harper and Row, 1967.

[12] Greiner, L., "Patterns of Organization Change," _Harvard Business Review_, May-June 1967, pp. 119–128.

or if time is not available to allow for meaningful consultation,[13] attempts to get people involved in the process will be perceived as manipulative and insincere, as indeed they are. If people are not affected by the change, they will not become involved in the process and may resent the time that they have to spend participating in it. And, if the people do not share some common goals, they may well subvert the process and use it to pursue their own objectives.

We do not propose to go through each possible combination of change tactics, their advantages and disadvantages, and the situational conditions under which they might be effective. It should be recognized that it might be appropriate to utilize multiple strategies. What is clear, however, is that the choice of approach is a critical choice, requiring careful assessment of the task that has to be done, the individuals affected, the situation within which the change is taking place, and the desired short- and long-term outcomes. Since some strategies take longer than others — education compared with coercion is one example — it puts a premium on the type of analysis described previously. If the people affected by change are not identified early and their potential reaction to change is not considered, the only strategy that time may permit is coercion, deception, or buying them off through some major, costly concession.

Stage 2, Steps 4–6: Planning, Monitoring and Modifying the Change

The change plan should identify the actions which will be taken to obtain support for the change and to overcome resistance to it.

Many changes require long planning horizons and often involve considerable costs and it is therefore important to plan them well. Where training and development are required, for example, they should be specified in the change plan so that implementation is not held up unexpectedly while these are provided. Since change itself consumes time and energy, it usually requires resources. If someone is to attend a training session, who is available to do the work? If data-based problem-solving is to occur, who has the time to gather the appropriate data? If a decision is made to form some joint committees, who has the time available to sit on them? The change plan should explicitly recognize the need for additional resources where they are required. It is particularly important in those cases where long lead times are required to free up some resources — particularly to get well-trained people. Failure to

---

[13] In this context we are talking about involvement in decision-making beyond communication and consultation. A more elaborate framework for considering whether there should be such involvement is in V. Vroom and P.S. Yetton, *Leadership and Decision-Making*, Pittsburgh: University of Pittsburgh Press, 1978.

have the right people available can inject months of delay into any change project, especially if they have to be hired from outside the system.

As you think about moving your organization from its current state you need to have an explicit and articulated goal to move towards. This goal is the answer or solution that will eliminate your problems and produce the desired results. You may be considering changing your product or the market you serve, your sales territories or production processes, your compensation system or performance appraisal procedures. A dangerous assumption may be that once we change one of these factors, our people will naturally accept it and behave the way we expect. This is not always the case.

The other element you need to plan is the process of change decided in the previous step. Depending on the nature of your problem and the amount of information you have about it, you may also need to think about how to involve the right people in finding a reasonable solution. Thus, a manager has two separate issues to consider in implementing change. One is to develop an acceptable solution, and the other is to devise an acceptable process for implementing the solution. A complex problem never faced before, where no one person has all the information, may require that the solution emerge from a well designed process.

It is surprising how often major changes are initiated without enough thought being given to the issue of communications. The communications plan must be thought out so that the right messages are communicated to the right people. There will be those who will be directly affected by whatever changes take place and then there will be all the others who will hear about the changes in one way or another, and who, in the absence of definitive communication, will read their own interpretations into what they observe or hear.

Many organizational changes are undertaken without much prior thought being given to measuring the progress or impact of the change. Such measurement is necessary if people are to be convinced of the need for change, and to encourage them to persevere based on initial levels of success.[14] Where additional resources have been spent, an accounting has to be made, and this is the third reason for measuring the success or failure of the change. The change plan should identify the objectives of the change and indicate how the achievement of these objectives and progress toward their achievement will be assessed.

Modifying the change if progress does not match anticipated results requires the change agent to go back through the previous steps to determine whether the original analysis was insufficient or if something has changed in the meantime.

Stage 2 is summarized in Figure 6.3.

---

[14] Greiner, *op. cit.*

Figure 6.3
THE MANAGEMENT OF CHANGE

Stage 2: Implementation

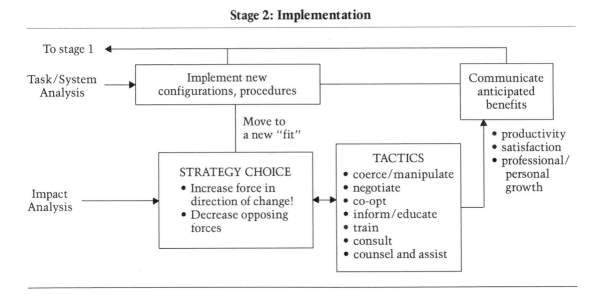

Stage 3, Step 7: Institutionalizing the Change

Once a change has been made, the next challenge is to ensure that these new practices and procedures are consolidated and established as the new norm. In part, of course, the reinforcement will come from the success of the change. If, in fact, the change reduces the problems for a manager, speeds order processing, results in better customer satisfaction, or improves an employee's job, the behaviors producing these results will be reinforced. However, people need to see improvement. The change manager should be aware of the various ways in which success can be highlighted and fed back to those involved in the changes, recognizing and rewarding the achievements with praise, recognition, or more tangible rewards, and celebrating significant milestones along the way.

For a change to stabilize and become institutionalized, it must be consistent with the rules, policies, and administrative mechanisms of the organization. Since many of these systems and practices take time to change, they must be planned for in advance so that they are ready to reinforce the desired, emergent behavior. Failure to do this may be the most important reason for a change effort failing to continue.

The creative part of change management is in the early stages: thinking about what types of change are needed, analyzing their potential impacts, and developing strategies and plans. The implementation often involves great

Figure 6.4
THE MANAGEMENT OF CHANGE

Stage 3: Institutionalization

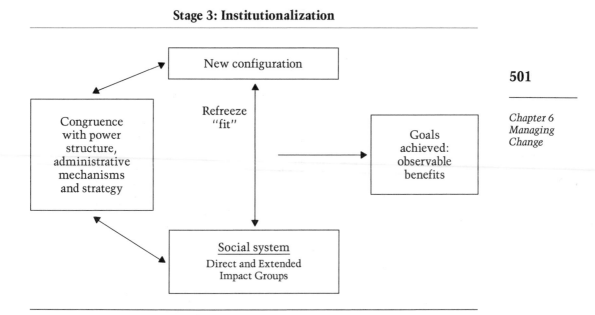

amounts of detailed work and may extend over a substantial period of time. By the implementation stage the change initiator — the original source of enthusiasm and energy for the change — may have mentally moved on to other things. The implementation may be abandoned to others who have less understanding of it, less commitment to it, and may be less skilled at doing it. Make sure you anticipate and provide for a continual infusion of replacement people and energy.

Although great effort may go into a good, comprehensive change plan, the probabilities of absolutely smooth implementation are remote. Persistence and flexibility are essential. Stage 3 is summarized in Figure 6.4.

The Model

All three stages are shown together in Figure 6.5. What is important about seeing the three stages together is the relationship between them. Proper design, implementation and institutionalization are necessary to achieve the anticipated benefits. As well, feedback from later to earlier stages suggests that change processes are iterative. It may not be possible to design the perfect change process. It is very likely that environmental conditions may change in midstream, rendering the original plan ineffectual. Thus, the three stage model is shown with feedback loops.

Figure 6.5

THE MANAGEMENT OF CHANGE

The Change Model

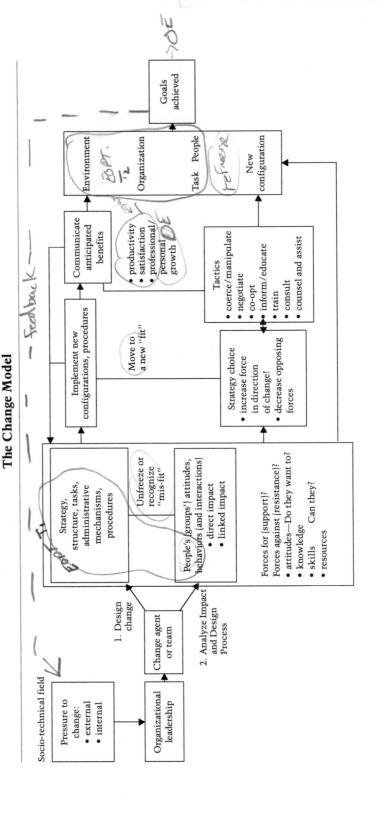

C · A · S · E · S

BANK OF MONTREAL: DOMESTIC DEVELOPMENT PROGRAM (C)

James C. Rush and Cheryl Harvey

Gord MacAskill, Executive Project Director, Domestic Development Project Team, looked around the conference table. Present were Mel Anderson, Operations and MIS Support Manager, Dave Cross, Organization and Methods (O and M) Implementation Manager, Bill Hodsmyth, Project Control Manager, and Deanna Rosenswig, Commercial Banking Project Manager. Gord was acting as the Domestic Banking project manager. November 1, 1982 was the date scheduled for the two-year conversion process to begin and now it was time to define precisely what had to be done. This early summer meeting of the core of the implementation team was planned as a brainstorming session to define its role in the upcoming restructuring.

Reorganization of the Domestic Banking Group

The final and broadest segment of the reorganization of the Bank of Montreal began in 1982. All the other bank groups had been restructured since 1976 to achieve three objectives: a focus on principal market segments, improved opportunities for the professional development of officers and staff, and improvement in the quality of service.

The Domestic Banking group served mid-market and small business customers as well as individuals through a nationwide network of about 1300 branches. The restructuring, as recommended by a task force, split the group into two: the Canadian Commercial Group to serve business and the Domestic Group to serve individuals. The Commercial Group was organized around the Commercial Banking Unit (CBU), while the branch remained the foundation of the Domestic structure. (Exhibits 1, 2, and 3 illustrate the 1982

503

Domestic structure, the Commercial structure, and the new Domestic structure respectively.)

The restructuring radically altered the jobs of the 20 000 employees in the old Domestic Group. Management positions had been based on the concept of the branch manager as a jack-of-all-trades. He or she was supposed to have the skills to gather deposits, make personal loans, loans to small businesses and mid-market businesses, to sell services and other products to retail and commercial customers, and to provide transaction processing services to other bank groups (Treasury, Corporate and Government, and International Banking). The new jobs reflected commercial-retail and credit-service dimensions of specialization and required the development of new career paths for all management personnel. Interim sourcing paths were developed to effect the transition from old to new jobs. Training programs for each new job were also developed.

Implementation of the altered structure would focus on each designated CBU and its associated branches. There were 98 designated CBUs and 1238 branches across the country (see Exhibit 4). To determine and locate a CBU, a branch by branch analysis of commercial business volume would be undertaken. All commercial portfolios would then be allocated to the CBU, which would be located in a high potential or core business area. The CBU would be physically situated in, or close to, key branches.

The conversion to the new structure demanded massive changes. Product- (versus branch) based financial reporting and the segregation of all processing services in cost centers required changes to the on-line system as well as enhancements to the mechanized system. Branch premises needed alterations to separate the processing functions from customer view where this administration function was not located in an ADCON center. The branch layout also had to reinforce the distinction between the various services offered to the retail customer. CBUs had to be identified and located in an existing branch or in a new facility, their associated domestic branches identified, their premises altered, and commercial accounts relocated. Operating procedures had to be rewritten, forms designed, and manuals prepared. Employees had to be told of the changes, selections had to be made for the new positions, and training had to be started. Furthermore, the entire system had to be functioning perfectly within two years.

Change in The Bank

The "henceforth" method of change had been typically used by the bank. A project was assigned to an individual or a group of people who, working in isolation, took as much time as needed to arrive at the best possible solution to the problem with which they were presented. When the solution was determined, it was proclaimed and henceforth put into practice.

A recent exception to the method occurred when the career path project began in 1980. Career paths were developed first in the Southwestern Ontario division through a process which involved corporate Human Resources staff, divisional HR staff, divisional executives, and outside consultants. The career paths were then explained to all divisional staff by the executives. A similar process was then undertaken to expand the program to the British Columbia division. There, slightly different paths developed and were explained to the staff in a series of meetings with divisional executives. The career path project was halted when Domestic restructuring became imminent.

Other changes, however, continued. The economic downturn of the past couple of years had developed into a recession. The bank was closing unprofitable branches; over 100 branches were scheduled to close over the 1982–1984 period. Productivity programs were carried out and automated teller machines (ATMs) were introduced. Some staff had to be laid off when customary turnover was curtailed by economic conditions.

The Domestic Development Project Team

The Domestic Development Team was charged with the responsibility of making the restructuring of Domestic Banking happen. The question was, how? What was the best way to convert from the old structure to the new? Gord and the other team members had been struggling for days with this question. They had made no decisions, but several considerations had emerged, although they had yet to place priorities on these.

Bill Hodsmyth had so far been able to identify over 500 discrete activities that had to be undertaken in the conversion of a CBU and its associated branches. He did not know how long it would take to complete these activities, how many of them could be worked on at the same time, or which ones had to be done first.

There was a question of where the process should start; should it start in Toronto where corporate headquarters was, or just about anywhere else in the country, where the complexities of a conversion would be fewer and the sheer volume of accounts would be less? That raised another question. Could Toronto be converted identically to Halifax, Regina and Victoria? Would metropolitan centers be the same as smaller cities, as regional centers? Could a division be converted all at once, or was it necessary to proceed in some sort of staggered fashion?

There were now 24 people on the project team. Seven were clerical staff, while the others had come up through the line banking system. Some, like Mel Anderson, Dave Cross and Bill Hodsmyth had developed particular technical areas of expertise, but none of them had ever done anything like this before. What should their role be? Was this enough people to manage the conversion? How should the process be managed? Should it be managed by the team itself or by some other group? How would they know if they had done a good job? How would senior management evaluate their performance?

Soon all Domestic employees would know about the planned reorganization. Their first concrete information would be circulated shortly (see Exhibit 5). That might put a stop to the rumors that had been prevalent for the past few months. But this was another signal that the team had to move quickly.

Gord's head was spinning with these considerations and a multitude of others as he glanced around the room. Today the project team had to define its role in the conversion process, outline a basic conversion strategy and determine what was essential to its own success.

EXHIBIT 1
BANK OF MONTREAL — DOMESTIC DEVELOPMENT PROGRAM (C)

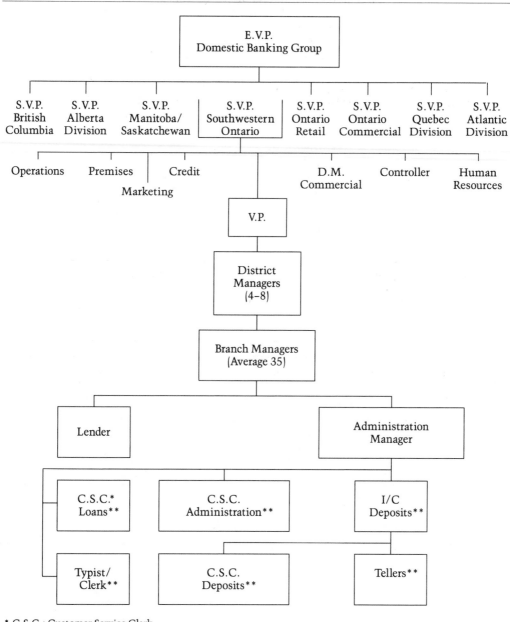

Domestic Banking Group
January, 1982

* C.S.C.: Customer Service Clerk

** Non-management position

EXHIBIT 2
BANK OF MONTREAL
DOMESTIC DEVELOPMENT PROGRAM (C)

Canadian Commercial Banking Group

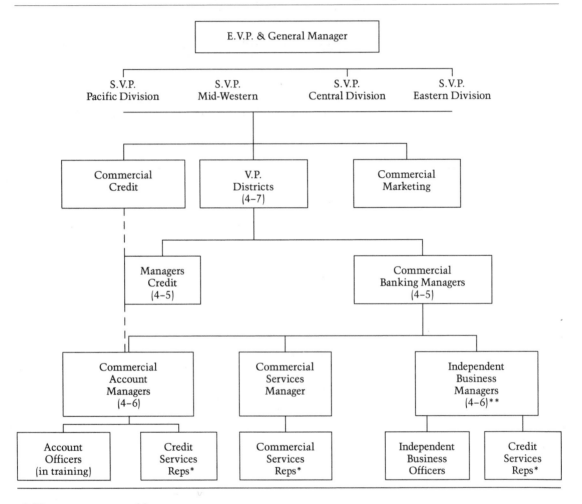

* Non-management position

** A senior independent business manager would exist where numbers warranted.

EXHIBIT 3
BANK OF MONTREAL
DOMESTIC DEVELOPMENT PROGRAM (C)

Domestic Banking Group

```
                        ┌─────────────────────────┐
                        │ E.V.P. & General Manager │
                        └─────────────────────────┘
          ┌──────────────┬──────────┴──────────┬──────────────┐
  ┌──────────────┐ ┌──────────────┐    ┌──────────────┐ ┌──────────────┐
  │    S.V.P.    │ │    S.V.P.    │    │    S.V.P.    │ │ Staff Support│
  │  Operations  │ │Consumer Credit│    │  Consumer   │ │              │
  │              │ │              │    │  Marketing   │ │              │
  └──────────────┘ └──────────────┘    └──────────────┘ └──────────────┘

          ┌──────────────┬──────────────────┬──────────────┐
  ┌──────────────┐ ┌──────────────┐    ┌──────────────┐
  │    S.V.P.    │ │    S.V.P.    │    │    S.V.P.    │
  │Western Region│ │Central Region│    │Eastern Region│
  └──────────────┘ └──────────────┘    └──────────────┘

     ┌──────────┬──────────┬──────────────┬──────────┐
  ┌─────────┐ ┌─────────────┐   ┌──────────┐ ┌──────────┐
  │Consumer │ │V.P. Executive│   │ Consumer │ │Operations│
  │ Credit  │ │  Manager    │   │Marketing │ │          │
  │         │ │   (4–5)     │   │          │ │          │
  └─────────┘ └─────────────┘   └──────────┘ └──────────┘
      ┊         ┌─────────────┐
      ┊         │Area Manager │
      ┊         │    (9)      │
      ┊         └─────────────┘
      ┊       ┌───────┴──────────────────────┐
  ┌──────────────┐                      ┌──────────┐
  │Personal Loans│                      │ ADCON**  │
  └──────────────┘                      └──────────┘
  ┌──────────┐          ┌──────────┐
  │ Personal │          │  Branch  │
  │  Loans   │          │ Manager  │
  │ Officer  │          │ (10–15)  │
  └──────────┘          └──────────┘
            ┌───────────────┼───────────────┐
      ┌──────────┐   ┌──────────┐   ┌──────────┐
      │ Tellers* │   │ Customer │   │Processing│
      │          │   │ Service  │   │Personnel*│
      │          │   │ Clerks*  │   │          │
      └──────────┘   └──────────┘   └──────────┘
```

* Non-management position

** Administrative consolidation unit. Exists as off-site processing facility servicing several branches. Only 55 exist; more planned.

EXHIBIT 4

BANK OF MONTREAL
DOMESTIC DEVELOPMENT PROGRAM (C)

Commercial and Domestic Structures
Summary Statistics

| | Commercial Divisions | | | | |
	Eastern	Central	Mid-Western	Pacific	Total
No. of Districts	6	7	5	4	22
No. of CBUs	25	33	22	18	98

| | Domestic Divisions | | | |
	Eastern	Central	Western	Total
No. of Districts	4	4	5	13
No. of Areas	34	36	42	112
No. of Branches	361	423	454	1238

EXHIBIT 5

BANK OF MONTREAL—DOMESTIC DEVELOPMENT PROGRAM (C)

Memo to all Domestic employees re planned reorganization

During any major change, employees naturally want to know what's going on and what's going to happen to them. Often, anxieties about change can be reduced by letting the facts be known and shedding some light on the future. This project bulletin is intended to communicate the facts regarding organizational developments in domestic banking. You can expect to hear about progress being made and the details as they become available.

I am writing to advise you that domestic banking is reorganizing to more directly serve our changing markets and the needs of our customers. The Bank of Montreal will remain a bank that is responsive, innovative and committed to its customers. The diverse needs of commercial and retail customers have been recognized, and separate groups, Canadian commercial banking and domestic banking, are being designed to best suit these distinct markets. At the same time, career opportunities will be enhanced for people working in these groups. Implementation will be undertaken on a region by region basis, with the initial steps planned for Ontario.

The success of our bank lies with people, those who bring their business to the Bank of Montreal and the employees who are the bank. It will take the efforts of all of us to implement these changes successfully.

You can expect the next bulletin to include information about the changes in organization structure and initial implementation plans.

Chairman and
Chief Executive Officer

Number 1
August 1982

BANK OF MONTREAL: DOMESTIC DEVELOPMENT PROGRAM (D)

James C. Rush and Rosslyn Emmerson

Early in 1984 Gord MacAskill, executive project director, convened a meeting of the Domestic Development Project Team at the Bank of Montreal. Gord had been a member of the original task force struck in March 1982 to design a revolutionary new structure for the bank's Domestic Banking operation. He was the only representative of that task force to sit on the project team responsible for planning and implementing the conversion of the branches to the new structure. By the end of 1983 many of the Ontario branches had made the changeover. Now the project team was meeting to review progress before the change began in Western and Eastern Canada. Gord was particularly interested in identifying any changes which could be made to the implementing process to facilitate the conversion of the remaining branches.

A New Structure for the Domestic Banking Group

The major aims guiding the original task force's redesign of the Domestic Banking Group were two-fold: (1) to gain market share by improving the quality of customer service, and (2) to increase profitability by improving the quality and volume of the bank's credit portfolio. The task force concluded that these objectives could be achieved best by increasing the professionalism of officers and staff specializing in serving particular market segments with distinctive servicing requirements. Two market segments, the commercial and the retail segments, were thought to have sufficiently distinct requirements to justify specialized service. The commercial segment consisted of mid-market and small business customers, whereas the Retail segment consisted of private individuals.

Under the old system both the commercial and retail segments of the market were serviced at each branch. Consequently, every branch manager was expected to be a jack-of-all-trades, with the necessary skills and resources to gather deposits, make personal loans as well as loans to small and mid-market businesses, sell services and other products to both retail and commercial customers and provide transaction processing services to other bank groups (Treasury, Corporate and Government, and International Banking).

Under the new system, personnel would specialize in servicing either commercial or retail accounts.[1] The commercial accounts would become the responsibility of a smaller number of Commercial Banking Units (CBUs), each associated with several branches. Most of the CBUs would be located in the same building as a branch, but some would be located in separate facilities. Managers in each group would follow distinct career paths within their commercial or retail specialization. The branch network would retain responsibility for the retail customer and handle simple transactions for both.

Planning Conversion to the New Structure

The new design was approved by William D. Mulholland, chairman of the bank, late in 1982. Top management was convinced that the change would increase market share and profitability by giving the Bank of Montreal a competitive advantage over other banks which were still operating under the old comprehensive branch banking system. Indeed, it was believed that any delay in the implementation of the new system would be very costly in terms of lost opportunities and profits. So in November 1982 the project team was given a mandate to have the whole new system functioning perfectly within two years.

The Role of the Project Team

Although MacAskill knew that the executive would hold him accountable for successful implementation, he came to the conclusion that his team could only control three areas directly. First, they could design a change program for converting existing branches to the new structure. Second, they could ensure that the proposed changes were explained to affected executives, staff groups and customers. Finally, they could monitor the change process and adjust the change program as required.

There remained the question of who should be responsible for the actual implementation of the change at the various branch locations. The project team considered two options: (1) the creation of permanent implementation teams to convert all branches and (2) the use of local teams supported by some training and guidance. The latter option won favor on the grounds that

---

[1]See Bank of Montreal — Domestic Development Program (A and B) for organization charts of the old and new systems.

resources were not available to handle the former and local managers would better understand and support a change they had implemented themselves. Therefore, the project team decided to delegate responsibility for the conversion of each branch/CBU to local teams comprised of the commercial banking unit manager, area manager, credit manager and personal loans manager (two commercial and two domestic representatives).

Having circumscribed its own sphere of responsibility, the project team concentrated on designing the conversion program. The location of each CBU was determined on the basis of a branch by branch analysis of potential commercial business volume. A total of 98 CBUs and 1238 branches were identified across Canada. The plan specified which CBUs would be associated with which branches and how the distinction between various banking services was to be reinforced by both branch layout and the location of the CBU.

The new structure entailed an extensive redefinition of existing jobs and career opportunities, within the bank. Some 20 000 employees would be affected by these changes. A revised operations manual was printed and, on the basis of new job descriptions, detailed procedures were developed to select, train, and evaluate personnel in accordance with the requirements of the new system.

The project team identified over 500 discrete activities which had to be undertaken in the conversion of a branch. A detailed schedule was drafted specifying what had to be done, when, and by whom. According to the schedule, appointments to each management team would be announced 65 days prior to change day at that locality. Thereafter, the local team would perform a sequence of activities to achieve an orderly transition to the new system (Exhibit 1). The local team would be responsible for managing the change, explaining it to local personnel, assigning jobs, helping staff work through any issues that arose and monitoring and reporting progress to the project team.

The project team decided that the first conversions should be made in downtown Toronto so that members of the project team would be on hand to assist the local managers work through any unforeseen problems in the change program. Then, on the basis of the Toronto experience, the project team would make any necessary revisions to the change program to facilitate conversions elsewhere. The entire conversion would be complete by September 1984 (Exhibit 2).

The Conversion to the New Structure

At the meeting convened by Gord MacAskill in January 1984, the project team reviewed its progress with considerable satisfaction. The conversion was proceeding ahead of schedule, under budget and for the most part, in accordance with the team's design. Some difficulties had arisen along the way, of course, and a number of problems had yet to be resolved.

Delays Preceding C-date

Delays occurred early in the selection of CBU managers when the chairman objected to a number of proposed appointments. He felt strongly that all CBU managers should have recent, high level credit experience and insisted that all candidates be screened over again according to revised qualification criteria. A new selection procedure was developed, tested and employed. Consequently, some CBU managers were appointed just a matter of days before the scheduled change day (C-date) for their units. These managers had no opportunity to be active members of their local implementation teams until their appointments were finalized. Moreover, there was insufficient time for them to undergo formal training for their new jobs although, relative to others' experience, most found that their previous credit management experience helped them to adapt quickly to their new responsibilities.

The days immediately preceding C-date were extremely hectic for some bank employees. The branch support staff, for example, had to work long hours to prepare the files to be transferred to the local CBU. Ann Jordan, a supervisor of Branch Support Services, observed that all the necessary preparations could have been made during slack time over a two month period, had sufficient warning been given. Instead, she and her staff spent three nerve-wracking days in the basement trying to prepare all the files at short notice.

A common complaint made by non-managerial personnel concerned poor communications with head office and inadequate training prior to C-date. Rumors of forthcoming changes began circulating weeks, often months, before any formal announcements were made at the branches. Meanwhile, employees became increasingly anxious about how the change would affect their jobs. The vast majority worried needlessly. It was necessary to transfer some employees to other parts of town, and a few (less than 10 percent according to one estimate) were down-graded or assigned to jobs which were not at all to their liking. Nevertheless, jobs were offered to all employees.

C-date and Its Aftermath

The members of the project team were able to monitor the conversion process more closely at the downtown Toronto sites than elsewhere. The initial conversions experienced some transactional and operational problems, but other downtown conversions proceeded more smoothly. But as the conversions moved outside of the Toronto core it was revealed that early conversions were not typical of branches located elsewhere. The downtown branches were all located within blocks of each other so that customers were not greatly inconvenienced by being redirected to a nearby CBU or another branch which had a personal loans officer on staff. Moreover, the downtown branches already had well-established, informal communication linkages which enabled staff to clarify any confusion arising over who was responsible for particular customer services. Other branches located elsewhere enjoyed none of these advantages because they were geographically spread out and isolated both from each other and from the project team in Toronto. Staff at the latter branches complained that disputes over the division of responsibility were often difficult to resolve and that their customers were seriously inconvenienced when redirected to other locations.

Confusion over the allocation of responsibility for various services was a recurrent problem in the days following conversion. Under the old system, disputes concerning the spheres of responsibility of branch employees were referred to the office administrator, a position that did not exist under the new CBU system. Often the commercial services managers found it necessary to take time away from their duties to perform the role of office administrator during the transition.

The division of responsibility between the branch and the CBU was another major source of confusion. Commercial clients, for example, wanting to know the balance in their personal accounts were redirected to the CBU only to be referred back to the branch for that information. Where CBU and branch employees had previously worked together, a phone call was often sufficient to clear up confusion over their respective responsibilities. In other instances *ad hoc* committees with representatives from the CBU and its associated branches were formed to address problems of coordination and responsibility. Tanner Marziali, the area manager in London, helped the London group set up an operations committee to handle all the operational problems, solve responsibility issues, clarify procedures for transactions and other issues. At first the committee played an important role in facilitating the changeover.

Several managers told the case-writer that C-date was an anti-climax in their units. In contrast, lower-level staff perceived the entire change process as a nerve-wracking ordeal. Karen Maslow, a commercial services representative, summed up the sentiments expressed by many of her co-workers when she said:

> The policy statement of the Bank of Montreal, you've maybe seen it in that frame on the wall there, says how the bank aims to give shareholders, employees and customers every consideration and assistance....Something like that. I used to believe it too until this happened, but now I think it's so much hypocritical hogwash. I'm not against the changes that have been made. Maybe they're a good thing. But the way the bank made the changes is just unforgivable. The management here did their best. It wasn't their fault. They were kept as much in the dark as the rest of us I think. None of us knew what we were doing and we had no time to learn. Head office just doesn't give a damn for any of us—not even our customers. All that stuff about consideration and assistance is a bad joke. The whole experience was very stressful for all of us. Morale really suffered.

As fears over job security waned, new fears took their place. Employees complained that the new job descriptions were worded in such a way that many people could not judge their qualifications or ability to do the jobs. As a result, some employees failed to apply for jobs for which they had the advantage of relevant experience. Others with no such dvantage applied for jobs in the belief they would receive adequate training prior to C-day. However, the training department was too overloaded to develop programs for the non-managerial jobs. When C-date arrived, employees had to learn their new jobs on the spot by a process of trial and error. Many employees described the procedures manual as too general and confusing. Others found it was inconvenient to read the manual while a customer stood waiting for service, and instead attempted to muddle through the requested transactions. Still others sought instruction from co-workers familiar with the transaction procedures, who were too busy learning their own jobs to be of much assistance.

As the queues lengthened and co-workers grew more irritable, the tension mounted and mistakes were made. Some customers were upset to discover that their transactions had not been correctly processed. Many more errors were discovered and corrected without customers ever learning of them. In one case $3 million was "misplaced" in a single transaction, only to be "found" a week later. Although few serious mistakes were irreversible, the employees felt they were continually working under a dark shadow of imminent disaster.

For most employees, the first days and months following C-date were the most demanding. Some reported they would have left the bank at that time had the job market been stronger. But gradually people gained confidence in their ability to do their new jobs. Alice Cravits, a customer services representative, described the experience this way:

> The first month is spent just discovering how much you don't know about the job. It's one surprise after another and you think there's no end to it all. Then you start working out ways of doing things during the second month and by the third month the work begins to fall into a routine.

Tanner Marziali found he had to do four jobs at that time, two jobs from the old system, one job in the new system and the job as a change manager. Like other managers, he regretted not having more time to spend talking with branches and clients about the reasons behind the change and what it meant to people.

Tanner Marziali's experience was not uncommon. The changeover required all participating managers to work long hours. Nevertheless, most managers believed that the changes would prove worthwhile, although some remained skeptical of the new system's advantages. Often branch managers regarded the loss of responsibility for the prestigious Commercial Lending operation as a most unwelcome change. Others expressed concern over how they were to be evaluated by the performance appraisal system tailored to the new job when they had been doing both old and new jobs during the transition.

The most major adjustment difficulties were experienced by the Personal

Loans job family. Under the old system personal loans were processed at every branch by customer service clerks (CSCs) with clerical support from typist/clerks. Any unusual applications were referred to the branch manager. Under the new system, personal loans officers were on staff at some, but not all, branches and visited other branches on certain days. They reported to the personal loans manager and, in addition to the evaluation of loan applications, were required to do much of the clerical work previously performed by typist/clerks. By mid-summer of 1983 sharp loan volume and dollar declines were reported in the Personal Lending operation in the Toronto area, despite the development and advertisement of a number of new products aimed to stimulate growth.

A similar problem emerged in the Commercial Lending operation. Credit service representatives reported that they were too busy with customer calls and clerical work to prepare pro-forma statements and financial analyses. As a result, the commercial account managers were taking time away from promotional activities to do financial analyses of existing business.

Mid Course Action Taken

In August 1983 a task force struck by the project team investigating the problems experienced by the Personal Lending operation in Toronto reported that the Personal Lending job family was suffering from "personal organization and management skills deficiencies" exacerbated by a heavy burden of paper work. Lenders were "buried under clerical routine" and were unable to perform their marketing and portfolio growth/control activities. The task force recommended that forms be revised to reduce paperwork, a work load reduction manual be circulated, and time-management training programs be developed and offered by the training department.

The project team took steps to improve communications. A series of video presentations and pamphlets were circulated. Special care was taken to describe the changeover realistically and give sound, practical suggestions for dealing with problems which had arisen in the early conversions. These materials were well received by bank personnel, although some managers complained that Domestic Development Man (a comic book suggesting how to deal with problem situations) was inconsistent with the professional image of the bank.

Workshops in customer-relations were held at a number of branches. Jane Burton, a customer service clerk who had attended one workshop, told the case-writer:

> It's all very well calling the customers by name and learning how to unruffle feathers when they can see you don't know how to complete a transaction. But it would be better to train us so we knew how to do our jobs in the first place. Then the customers wouldn't be upset.

Customer Response

During the early conversions commercial customers frequently complained that they received no notification of the changeover until they came to do business at their usual branch and were redirected to the local CBU. Some first heard of the changeover when they were telephoned by Royal Bank managers who solicited their business by intimating that commercial accounts would be adversely affected by certain changes underway at the Bank of Montreal. Many commercial customers, accustomed to arranging both their personal and commercial loans at the same time without hindrance, were seriously offended when told they would have to apply for personal loans separately through a personal loans officer, subject to a formal evaluation. Some loss of business resulted when many of these "high profile" customers withdrew both their personal and commercial custom to other banks.

Still other commercial and retail customers, in the habit of working with particular bank employees, were upset to learn that their accounts had been reassigned to other employees not familiar with their financial history. A few, mostly elderly, retail customers refused to discuss their affairs with anyone new. However, many of the larger commercial customers welcomed the more specialized professional attention their accounts received at the CBUs. In addition, the vast majority of the Retail accounts stayed with the Bank of Montreal.

Learning From Experience

The project team had learned much from the early conversions. Now, at the meeting in January 1984, team members were given an opportunity to discuss the major lessons. Gord MacAskill encouraged the team members to evaluate the change program with the aim of generating some concrete suggestions as to how it might be improved to facilitate the changeover in the remaining branches in Eastern and Western Canada.

EXHIBIT 1

BANK OF MONTREAL—DOMESTIC DEVELOPMENT PROGRAM (D)

Countdown to Conversion

Let's call the day conversion happens "C-Day". By the time it gets to your branch, you will have been through a sixty-five day process. Here's what happens in sequence, starting sixty-five days ahead of the big date.

C-65 You will hear who is going to be the Area Manager, Personal Loans Manager, Commercial Banking Manager and Unit Manager, Credit.

C-63 A Managers' meeting is held to spell out what their new duties are going to be.

C-60 Here is where you come in. The branch manager will hold a meeting to let you know what the conversion will mean in your branch. He will explain the new procedures and hand you a questionnaire. By filling it in, you help to explain just what you do right now. They will put together an organization structure that will deal with your needs and activities after conversion. You will also see the "Operations Guide" pocket book. It spells out in general terms what the processes will be in a newly converted branch or C.B.U.

C-55 If you are non-management and you have not had a performance review in the previous six months, you will get one. There is nothing sinister about it. It is to give the manager (if there is to be a change) an idea of who you are and how you are doing. It also helps in selecting staff for the new positions that will open up.

C-50 An analyst from the Domestic Development Task Force rides into town to study the operational needs and the workload. He or she identifies the staff requirements for both Domestic and Commercial Banking.

C-38 Organization charts prepared by the analyst are submitted for approval.

C-33 Each manager submits his recommendations for the staffing of each new post.

C-25 Appointments day! The branch manager in the new structure (if there is a change) and the Personal Lending Officer are appointed. Certain clerical jobs are posted. If you have a preference, submit it early.

C-20 The branch staff prepare Commercial Credit and Current Account Files for delivery to the new C.B.U.

C-15 From now until C-10, one whole working week, all staffing is completed and staff are advised of new positions. If you need training for your new position, it begins now.

C-Day This is the day you get the chance to show the public that the change is to their advantage. And it is! Your work will be more streamlined, the customer will be served with greater efficiency. Please help, we are counting on you.

EXHIBIT 2

BANK OF MONTREAL — DOMESTIC DEVELOPMENT PROGRAM (D)

Turnover Timetable

The conversion process now under way is the next step in a process which began in the mid 1970s. Most of the other changes will have been visible to most employees. They affect internal practices which don't have much impact on the day-to-day transaction with the average customer. The Domestic Development Program, however, is a major step—it changes the way you will work in your branch. Elsewhere in this newsletter we spell out exactly what happens (See "Countdown to Conversion") but just to keep you posted on progress, here is what the timetable looks like.

Present Time: By early October, all of Toronto will be converted except for two downtown C.B.U.'s.

October 31: All of Ontario converted, 400 Domestic branches; 32 C.B.U.s.

August 8–March 5, 1984: All branches in Alberta and Quebec will be converted.

December 21–June 28, 1984: Atlantic provinces, beginning with Halifax on December 21.

December 27–August 20, 1984: Conversion begins in B.C. in the Kelowna area. B.C. totally converted by August, 1984.

March 12–September 4, 1984: The last step, all branches in Manitoba and Saskatchewan converted.

Now read "Countdown to Conversion" and look for the early signs of conversion taking place at your branch.

Jeffrey Gandz and Jennifer Crocker

As he reflected on the morning's meeting with the president of Conprod Canada Inc., Martin Shawcross was excited and apprehensive. The proposed merger of the BioMedicus and Pharmasearch sales forces was the biggest challenge he had faced since he had taken over as marketing manager of the BioMedicus division of Conprod. The merger with the much larger Pharmasearch sales force involved many difficulties and he had less than a month to develop a strategy and plan for the merger.

Conprod Inc.

Conprod Inc. was a United States based multinational company with operations in 40 countries, and worldwide sales in excess of $4 billion in pharmaceuticals, health and beauty aid products, diagnostic reagents, surgical products, optometric equipment, and other related products. Its Canadian subsidiary had sales of $130 million and was one of the largest and most profitable of Conprod's international affiliates.

Although it had many successful pharmaceutical products, its intensive research and development efforts had failed to come up with breakthrough products such as Librium, Valium, Aldomet, or other rapid-growth, high-profit products. Consequently, the corporate management had decided to acquire a major, research-oriented company in the pharmaceutical business. Top management felt that with its marketing skills and the excellent Pharmasearch corporate image, the addition of new products could lead to a substantial increase in corporate growth.

Eight years earlier, Conprod acquired Pharmasearch, a large, multinational

---

*All names, locations, and dates in this case have been disguised.

pharmaceutical company based in the mid-western United States. The acquisition was so large that it drew the attention of the Federal Trade Commission in the U.S., which promptly ordered the businesses to be run separately, without merging operations, until such time as the FTC ruled on the propriety of the deal. This applied to all Conprod/Pharmasearch operations worldwide. For five years the Canadian subsidiaries of the two companies ran as distinct operations, with separate plants, separate financial and control systems, separate sales forces and separate management groups. Later, there was some limited merging of financial departments and production units and Martin Shawcross had been seconded from BioMedicus as executive assistant to the president of Pharmasearch. Over a period of two years, before returning to BioMedicus as marketing manager, he came to know the Pharmasearch operation well, including most of the people in the sales management group.

The FTC finally approved the acquisition of Pharmasearch by Conprod and the green light was given for operations to merge in the U.S. and abroad. Subject to approval of plans by the president of the international division of Conprod, the extent of integration and the strategies for it were to be left to the Conprod executives in the countries in which both BioMedicus and Pharmasearch operated.

The Canadian Pharmaceutical Industry

The Canadian pharmaceutical market, valued at about $1.1 billion at retail prices, has a very large number of manufacturers competing in its Ethical and Over-the-Counter (OTC) segments. These include major multinational firms such as Hoffman LaRoche, Ciba-Geigy, Ayerst, Glaxo, and Pfizer, as well as Canadian-owned enterprises such as Horner, Novopharm, and many smaller firms with a few products, often manufactured under license from one of the multinationals.

Ethical Pharmaceuticals

The Ethical segment of the market consists of drugs which are only available on a doctor's prescription and are dispensed by a pharmacist. They are promoted and advertised to the medical profession in medical journals, through exhibits at conventions, by medical representatives — sometimes known as "detailmen" — and through sponsorship of instructional videotapes, cassettes, and other audio-visual materials.

Medical representatives try to get a ten to fifteen minute interview with about seventy-five percent of all the doctors in their territories every three months; give the doctor details about the product, its uses, any contra-indications or side effects; and try to persuade the physician to prescribe the product. The representatives gather information about the product and the doctors' experiences with it and report these back to the company. They will often check with local pharmacists as to which of the doctors are actually prescribing the product so that future sales calls can be planned. They will also check that the pharmacists have supplies of the product, in good condition and not outdated, and that the pharmacists have all the required information about the product.

It may take several sales calls before a doctor decides to prescribe the product or even to give patients the free samples supplied by the representatives. Although there are statistics on the number of prescriptions written for different Ethical pharmaceutical products which are gathered by a prescription auditing service, it may be hard for detailmen to know what impact they are having on doctors in their own territories, since these data are aggregated into large regions. Dollar sales are hard to attribute to particular representatives since many drug stores purchase their products through wholesalers or central buying groups which then trans-ship to the retail stores.

Over-the-Counter Drugs

Over-the-Counter (OTC) drugs are those products such as Aspirin and Chlortripilon which are available without a doctor's prescription but which are mainly confined to drug store distribution, although some are sold through food stores and variety/convenience outlets. They are promoted to the consumer through advertising in mass media, in-store promotions, limited distribution sampling, and coupons. They are also promoted to pharmacists in the belief that the pharmacist might recommend them to customers. The drug stores are given inducements to stock and display products in the form of promotional discounts, attractive displays, point-of-sale materials, and co-operative advertising allowances.

The manufacturer's representative calls on wholesale and retail outlets on a regular basis, checks stock, takes orders, arranges the distribution of cooperative advertising money, builds in-store product displays, and makes sure the professional and non-professional store staff know what they need to know about the products.

Distribution Changes

A significant development in the industry was the growth of large buying groups. These were either chain or franchise operations such as Shoppers Drug Mart, Big-V, Boots, and independent stores which cooperated in purchasing arrangements. This put significant pressure on the pharmaceutical firms to give ever-increasing discounts for over-the-counter products. Because of the large orders involved, and the erosion of net margins as a result of these pressures, many firms — including both BioMedicus and Pharmasearch — had changed to shipping directly to large stores and buying groups as well as distributing their products through wholesalers, as they had done exclusively in earlier years.

Sales Force Organizations

The major pharmaceutical firms vary considerably in the proportion of their total sales accounted for by Ethical and OTC products, but most have some of each category. In general, their sales forces detail the Ethical products to doctors and also sell the OTCs to drug stores, buying groups, and wholesalers. However, some of the larger companies have specialized Ethical and OTC sales forces. BioMedicus had moved to this form of sales organization 10 years earlier, whereas Pharmasearch had stayed with the more traditional combined Ethical/OTC sales organization. The sales management group at BioMedicus believed that specialization had helped both their Ethical and OTC businesses considerably, allowing the sales and product training to be geared to the type of customer (drug store, physician) as well as allowing the representatives to do what they did best — detailing products to physicians or selling OTC products to drug stores, buying groups, and wholesalers.

The BioMedicus and Pharmasearch Sales Forces

There were some major differences between the BioMedicus and Pharmasearch organizations in Canada. Pharmasearch was larger, with sales of $26 million compared with BioMedicus' $21 million. Pharmasearch was known for its Ethical pharmaceuticals and had leading products in the antibiotic, cardiovascular, and respiratory disease segments. BioMedicus had some leading OTC products in the cough/cold market, sinus remedies, and cough syrups as well as a few, fairly old Ethical products which nevertheless accounted for over 40 percent of its sales and 65 percent of its gross profits.

Another substantial difference between the companies was in the composition and organization of their sales forces. Pharmasearch had one sales force which handled both Ethical and OTC products. All of its medical representatives had degrees in pharmacology, physiology, or related health sciences. Many had been pharmacists in retail or hospital service before joining the company. Emphasis in recruiting was placed on education in the health sciences and the company invested very heavily in extensive product training. This had resulted in a reputation as a highly knowledgeable, professional detailing force. The Pharmasearch representative was welcomed in doctors' offices, hospitals, and pharmacies. Turnover was extremely low, and over 80 percent of the 61 representatives had more than ten years of service with the firm at the start of the current year.

The BioMedicus sales force was split into two groups. The 33 medical representatives called only on doctors and retail pharmacies and were recruited from people with varied backgrounds; most were university graduates, many in health sciences, but others had engineering, arts, or other academic qualifications. The 18 merchandising representatives called on retail pharmacies and drug stores, wholesalers, and the major buying chains. They were, first and foremost, salespersons who used merchandising techniques, rather than detailmen who presented technical information on products to physicians. The sales organizations for BioMedicus and Pharmasearch before the merger are shown in Exhibit 1.

Issues in the Merger

There were some obvious attractions to merging the two operations. The BioMedicus management team thought that the highly trained and professional Pharmasearch medical representative could probably boost sales of its Ethical products, whereas the marketing and merchandising expertise of BioMedicus could almost certainly improve the sales of the Pharmasearch OTC products. An early estimate, made by Shawcross while he had been seconded to Pharmasearch, suggested that a total sales force of 90 representatives (55 medical representatives and 35 merchandising representatives), 13 district managers, 4 field and regional sales managers, and one sales director would be the best configuration for maximum cost-effective coverage of physicians, hospitals, and the retail trade. In total, the BioMedicus and Pharmasearch sales forces had 112 representatives, 15 district managers, 7 regional or field sales managers, and two sales directors. A total of 27 people would be in excess of requirements, representing about $1.9 million in annual salaries and benefits. Excluding management, five sales representatives would reach retirement age within the next year, four more the year after, and then four in the year after that.

The greatest surplus of people was at the field sales management levels and district management. There were major differences between the roles of the district managers in the two organizations. In BioMedicus they were heavily involved in recruiting and selecting representatives, motivating them, coaching and counselling them, and appraising their performance relative to objectives. The district managers did not have their own accounts, spending all of their time with the representatives. In Pharmasearch, the district managers had some supervisory responsibilities but were really just senior salespeople, without highly developed management skills.

From his experience in both the BioMedicus and Pharmasearch operations, Shawcross knew that there was a vast difference in the degree of sales management sophistication between the two organizations. Sales analysis, the careful calculation of territory potential, analyses of call frequency and cost effectiveness, and other scientific sales management methods had been commonplace in BioMedicus for many years; they were very limited in Pharmasearch. Whereas the BioMedicus sales force was used to the establishment of key account and territory objectives based on such analyses, negotiating these objectives with their district and field sales managers, and being appraised and rewarded on the achievement of objectives, the Pharmasearch salespeople were used to being allocated quotas — usually based on a percentage increase in dollar sales over the previous year — and, provided they came close to meeting these quotas, they received regular, annual salary increases.

Also, there could be significant distribution savings since BioMedicus and Pharmasearch orders could be batched together for shipment; this was estimated to result in annual savings of $250 000. However, it was also clear that there would be some significant additional training costs. Depending on who filled which jobs, some representatives might have to be retrained from detailing duties with doctors to direct sales duties in retail accounts, buying groups, and wholesalers. And representatives from each company would have to learn the product line of the other. Given that they were already experienced salespeople, Shawcross estimated that about two full weeks of product training would be required for each person in the new, combined salesforce.

Apart from this direct job training, a large number of people would have to be trained in the new systems — whether these were adoptions of one or other of the merging organizations' systems or some new, hybrid systems. There would be new expense accounts to learn, new call reporting systems, new performance appraisal systems, and so on.

Key Personnel Decisions

One issue which Shawcross knew he had to deal with very quickly was the selection of a director of sales. Both the BioMedicus and Pharmasearch directors were long-service, valuable executives who had built extremely strong personal loyalties among their sales forces and sales management teams. John Grayling, the BioMedicus sales director, was 50 and had been with the company for 22 years, working his way up from sales representative. Age 62, Bill Trilby had been director of sales at Pharmasearch for 15 years and had a total of 35 years of service with the firm. Their management styles were completely different, but they were both appropriate for their organizations. Trilby was formal, almost autocratic in style whereas Grayling was much more relaxed; he delegated a great deal of authority but was also hard-driving and energetic. There was a great deal of respect for Trilby among the Pharmasearch sales force, just as there was for Grayling among the BioMedicus people. What would be the impact on the salespeople from Pharmasearch if their director was not appointed to head the combined sales force? And, of course, what would the impact be on the BioMedicus sales force if he was?

There were also some overlaps in field sales management positions. For example, the regional sales manager for BioMedicus in the west, Jim Keyhope, was 54 years of age, had no intention of retiring early, and had turned down many promotional opportunities because he would not leave Vancouver. The western regional manager for Pharmasearch lived in Edmonton; he was 61, had told his sales director that he intended to work to normal retirement age, and was considered the best of the Pharmasearch regional managers.

Culture, Policies, Systems

The slow and steady amalgamation of other BioMedicus and Pharmasearch functions over the previous few years, together with all of the general news about the merger, had resulted in most of the head office management people being ready for some type of change, although no one really knew what form it would take. The situation was quite different for the sales forces. Each of the sales divisions had established its own, distinctive culture and systems. Each had a very large number of loyal salespeople used to their own systems and procedures. Although salary grids were comparable, benefits plans were much better in BioMedicus, with, for example, a generous stock savings plan. Car policies were different, with Pharmasearch providing deluxe models and BioMedicus providing more basic models. Expense accounts were handled differently; Pharmasearch reimbursed salespeople for all reasonable expenses, whereas BioMedicus gave salespeople a fixed daily allowance for hotels, meals, etc. The performance appraisal system, which was highly developed at BioMedicus, was quite primitive in Pharmasearch and it was not possible to compare the relative merits of the Pharmasearch and BioMedicus salesperson by comparing the performance appraisals.

There was also the problem of the image of BioMedicus among the Pharmasearch sales force. Although the Pharmasearch people would probably benefit significantly if they got the BioMedicus benefits package, Shawcross thought they might be very upset with the idea of abandoning the highly prestigious Pharmasearch affiliation. From the few Pharmasearch people he had met, Shawcross was convinced that "working for Pharmasearch" was really meaningful to them.

The South African Merger

Shawcross had visited the South African affiliate of Conprod earlier in the year and had looked at the way they had merged the BioMedicus and Pharmasearch operations. BioMedicus had never been a very successful operation in South Africa. With about one-quarter the sales of Pharmasearch, it had only been marginally profitable in the previous decade, and the Pharmasearch acquisition was really needed to give Conprod a viable base in the pharmaceutical market.

The marketing director of Pharmasearch had been offered an attractive early retirement package and had agreed to work with John Blount, the South African marketing director of BioMedicus, in designing the new sales organization. They sat down with the two sales directors of the merging companies, having advised the current sales director of BioMedicus that he would become western regional manager reporting to the sales director of Pharmasearch. They designed the optimum sales force from a coverage and cost-effectiveness point of view, then they went down their list of salespeople in each region and decided who would be offered jobs in the new organization. In reaching their decision they took a number of factors into account, including the individuals' performance appraisals, their locations, what they knew about their willingness to relocate if there were two good people in the same territory, their potential for future development, age and length of service.

Having staffed the new organization in this way, they called a national sales meeting in Pretoria. As the representatives checked into the hotel, they received an envelope telling them to report that evening to one of two meeting rooms in the hotel. Those in one room were advised of their new appointments in the sales force. Those in the other room were advised that they were no longer employees of BioMedicus or Pharmasearch. They were given personalized statements of severance pay and provisions, and asked to check out of the hotel immediately. Those who were remaining with the new organization were kept in session to prevent contact with people who were terminated. In total, one quarter of those attending the meeting, about ten people in all, were let go. Most of these were BioMedicus employees.

Shawcross had talked at length to Blount about this process and Blount staunchly defended the way it had been done. There were serious profitability problems with BioMedicus, and they needed to realize the advantages of the merger as soon as possible. The sales forces were young, and there was no way that attrition could produce the number of quits that they needed. A slow integration of the two organizations would have taken about five years, people would have continued to be uncertain about their places in the new organization, and he thought that some of the best people would have left under such conditions. While admitting that it was a bit of a blood bath, he was convinced that it was the best way of doing it.

Pension plan and Severance Provisions

The pension plans for Pharmasearch and BioMedicus had been consolidated for five years. The plan entitled employees to 2 percent of their final year earnings for each year of employment, to a maximum of 60 percent. Together with Canada Pension Plan benefits, an employee who retired at age 65 with 35 years of service would retire with total earnings (after-tax) about equal to pre-retirement earnings. However, there were substantial penalties for early retirement. Employees would, of course, be contributing for fewer years. If someone retired after 20 years of service instead of 25, they would be entitled to 40 percent (20 years × 2 percent per year) of their final year's salary instead of 50 percent (25 years × 2 percent). Also, since the pension would probably be paid over a greater number of years, it was reduced in amount by 3 percent per year for retirement between 60 and 65, and by 5 percent per year for retirement between 55 and 60.

BioMedicus also had an established corporate policy for severance payments designed, according to the stated purpose, "to assure fair treatment to an employee terminated by the Company as a result of job elimination, work performance, or other reasons of Company convenience except for violations of Company rules or regulations." The key terms of this policy are summarized in Exhibit 2.

Next Steps

Martin Shawcross recognized the importance of the steps he would be taking over the next few weeks. If the merger resulted in confusion, demoralization, and feelings of inequitable treatment by either sales management or salespeople, direction could be diverted from the selling task, trade inventory levels might well drop, and good people could decide to leave the organization. It was important to retain the best characteristics, skills, and abilities of both sales organizations in order to fully realize the potential from the merger. What was the best way of going about this? What additional information did he need? Who should he involve?

EXHIBIT 1

BIOMEDICUS CANADA INC.

Biomedicus

Sales force organization before merger with Pharmasearch

President — Conprod Canada Inc.
└─ Marketing Manager — BioMedicus Division
   └─ Sales Director (50)*
     ├─ Manager, Sales Training and Administration (61)
     │ └─ Sales Assistant (33)
     ├─ Supervisor, Sales Promotion — Ethicals (46)
     ├─ Supervisor, Sales Promotion — OTC (39)*
     ├─ Field Sales Manager — West (54)*
     │ ├─ District Manager — Ethicals (44) — 8 reps.
     │ └─ District Manager — OTCs (44) — 5 reps.
     ├─ Field Sales Manager — Ontario (61)
     │ ├─ District Manager — Ethicals (38)* — 12 reps.
     │ └─ District Manager — OTCs (44) — 7 reps.
     └─ Field Sales Manager — Quebec/Maritimes (51)*
        ├─ District Manager — Ethicals (53) — 13 reps.
        └─ District Manager — OTCs (59) — 6 reps.

Pharmasearch

Sales force organization before merger with BioMedicus

President — Conprod Canada Inc.
└─ Marketing Manager — Pharmasearch (63)**
   └─ Director of Sales (62)*
     ├─ Manager, Sales Administration (44)
     ├─ Regional Manager — East (52)
     │ ├─ District Manager — Hamilton (31) — 7 reps.
     │ ├─ District Manager — Moncton (49) — 7 reps.
     │ └─ District Manager — Toronto (45) — 7 reps.
     ├─ Regional Manager — Quebec (60)*
     │ ├─ District Manager — Montreal (50) — 8 reps.
     │ └─ District Manager — Quebec (50)* — 8 reps.
     └─ Regional Manager — West (61)*
        ├─ District Manager — Vancouver (53) — 8 reps.
        ├─ District Manager — Winnipeg (52) — 8 reps.
        └─ District Manager — Edmonton (47)* — 8 reps.

NOTES: Age of incumbents in parentheses. *indicates "outstanding" in last performance appraisal. **elected early retirement following merger.

EXHIBIT 2
BIOMEDICUS CANADA INC.

Extracts From Biomedicus Severance Policy

Employees under 45 years of age:

1 months plus $1/4$ month for each year of completed continuous service up to 6 years; thereafter, $1/2$ month for each completed year of service up to 25 years—maximum one year.

Employees 45 years of age and over:

In addition to severance pay provided above, a supplemental payment provided as follows:

Age	Additional Duration
45–50	$1^{1}/_{2}$ months
50–55	2 months
55–60	$2^{1}/_{2}$ months
60–65	3 months

Pay is based on employees' base pay at time of severance. This does not include bonuses, commissions, or other incentive payments.

During the period in which severance pay is being paid, the individual will also be covered by life insurance benefits, medical/dental/retirement plans.

The following benefits cease as of the day of termination:

    Long-term disability plan
    Accident insurance
    Workers' Compensation
    Travel insurance policy
    Stock option plan
    Management incentive compensation plan
        (no pro-rata credit for time actually worked)

531

*BioMedicus
Canada Inc.*

INNOVATION AT CHEMCAN

James C. Rush

In late 1983, Chemcan Inc. committed itself to excellence and innovation. An Innovation Advisory Board was formed and Bill Warner, director of administration, volunteered and was appointed chairman. The board endorsed and launched the Key to Innovation program in February, 1984 which represented a serious exposure on the part of Chemcan, first to its employees as a new way of managing, and second to its U.S. parent as a way of maintaining itself as an entity.

John Hanson, manufacturing chairman of Chemcan's Innovation Advisory Board, was asked to take over the role of board chairman. John had been an original member of the advisory board and was currently manufacturing manager. He and other managers felt that the program was waning, yet knew that it had the support of the president. He wondered how to revitalize the effort.

Background

Chemcan, a wholly owned subsidiary with headquarters in Toronto, is a diversified manufacturer and distributor of agricultural chemical, building, medical, and consumer products. It was founded in the early 1900s to manufacture agricultural materials. There were only 14 employees in the first plant at Guelph, Ontario, but expansion was rapid as other agricultural products and industrial chemicals were added to the line.

In 1934 a Canadian subsidiary of American Chemical Company was formed and, together with its affiliates, today employs 2000 people. In addition to manufacturing for domestic and sale export, Chemcan imports and markets many of the parent company's 2500 different products.

Parent Strategy and Performance

1983 marked the end of a five year period in which the American parent had concentrated on two basic strategies. First, they restructured and strengthened their research and development efforts. A separate research division was created for each business area, and over the period overall expenditures doubled to $225 million. Second, the company was divesting itself of low or non-performing product lines.

In 1984 Chemcan worldwide experienced net profits of $215 million on sales of $4.15 billion. New product launches in the Medical Group and Consumer Products Group accounted for substantial improvements. The Chemical Group, operating in a mature market, was in a cost reduction situation. The Agricultural Group was suffering from poor worldwide economic conditions.

The obvious market pressure for new products and product enhancements, and the economic pressure for more cost effective ways of producing and selling them, made innovation key for their Chemcan continued success.

As well, American Chem's chief executive officer had been influenced by the then current best seller, *In Search of Excellence*. He wanted to change the culture of his organization to a more innovative and more people-oriented one. He wanted this company to become an aggressive hi-tech company. American Chem responded with their own innovation program.

Chemcan

Chemcan too was in the midst of other strategic and structural changes at the time that the call for more innovation came. The company had had historical strength in manufacturing. Attention was turning away from production toward marketing and R & D. Structurally the organization was being broken into smaller, more manageable pieces; each of these pieces receiving more involvement and, in some cases, direction from their counterpart at American Chem. Department manager positions were staffed by marketing managers, reflecting the upgrading of the marketing functions. The structure of the organization and the typical department are shown in Exhibits 1 and 2.

Despite the stronger ties to the parent company, the president of Chemcan was committed to maintaining a strong Canadian company. He believed that employees wanted and needed a strong focal point with which to identify, and career opportunities that would keep them in Canada. He knew that many of his people did not view a move to New Jersey positively.

His view of the innovation program was that it was part of a larger plan to improve communication in the company. Other significant events were going on in parallel as part of this overall effort to affect the culture. These included:

- quality circles in two of the three plants[1]
- a management development program called Toward Excellence based on the book *In Search of Excellence*
- the appointment of a communications coordinator and the expansion of the company newspaper
- a philosophy of allowing managers to run their own business.

The Employees' View of the Company

Although people had, over time, seen changes in the company that they did not like, they generally felt it was a good place to work. It had been a family, socially-oriented company. As a result, turnover was very low. With a change in presidents the climate changed in the mid 1960s to a tighten-the-hatches, non-people orientation. Bottom line results were the most important consideration, and the organization became lean. The result of these changes was a very risk-averse, conservative culture. Entrepreneurial types left, seeing no match between themselves and the organization. Risk-taking and any mistakes resulting from it were perceived as punishable.

Employees were given several opportunities to express their views of the organization. One department held a conference in which participants were asked to describe the organization. Positive themes emerged around product quality, professional people and company image. Negative themes centered on being too conservative, not paying enough attention to people, and poor communication and cooperation among people and groups. These negative themes were the result of clustering items of dissatisfaction raised at the conference, and are shown in Exhibit 1.

As well, an employee attitude survey was conducted by outside consultants. This survey revealed that the areas where employees felt most dissatisfied were employee involvement and influence, communications and inter-group relations. The items showing the highest percentage of dissatisfaction read "enough effort is made to get the opinions and thinking of people who work here," "most of what I learn about what is going on here I get from other employees," and "I never hear about changes until after they are made."

Innovation Advisory Board

In response to the pressures to become a company with a new culture — one that supports innovation — an Innovation Advisory Board was formed. Mem-

---

[1] The Union rejected the idea in the third plant.

bership was established with each department having representation. The original objectives for the board were to:

- develop objectives, policies, and procedures for a program of innovation
- have members as liaison between the board and their departments
- recommend and provide motivational programs which encourage a climate of innovation
- develop an awards and recognition program
- maintain a commitment to the program
- ensure the maintenance of a corporate identity through the establishment of standards
- be an advisory body for employee communications.

Early meetings of the task force concentrated on definitions of innovation and awards for innovative ideas. Visits were made to other companies known by the members to have such programs.

The group decided on the following definition:

> An idea which, if adopted, would be a change in procedure, concept or operation which will result in a benefit to the company. It must propose a specific solution to a specific problem or situation.

Warnings of the need to get top management as well as grass roots commitment, and the short lived benefit of financial reward packages were made by some members. The members felt that to be most effective, responsibility for any such program should rest at the department manager level. Training and promotional programs would be necessary.

Departments were asked to form their own committees and develop action plans for ideas programs. They were also requested to hold monthly meetings to give direct reports on the status of the program.

The Program

In February the Key to Innovation Program was launched. Following a memo to all employees from the president, department managers convened meetings of all staff to describe the program. The announcement and the program details are shown in Exhibit 3.

By September, 1985, the program had generated 455 ideas with projected savings of just over $250 000 (out of pocket costs were almost $34 000).

The President's Award was given to a process engineer and a product manager who developed a new press loading technique with a potential saving of $150 000/year. A gold award was given to two plant foremen who suggested replacing a furnace ceiling cylinder with refractory material saving a minimum of $75 000 in down-time and materials. A sample of suggestions given awards and prizes is shown in Exhibit 4.

Reactions to the Program

The following represent a series of reactions to the program.

> We used to have a suggestion plan in the 1960s, but it was viewed as poorly administered and unfair. It died because of lack of attention. This time what we need is to present ideas to an objective group who will fairly evaluate and provide quick feedback. I see us going back to the old way — people do not have time to evaluate and respond to suggestions, let alone implement the good ones. *(manufacturing manager)*

> Marketing thinks the only savings to be made are by manufacturing. *(manufacturing manager)*

> We moved too quickly — we made too many assumptions about what people understood — we aren't sure where it is going ourselves — what it should be — managers were asking what should I do about it. *(marketing manager)*

> Mickey mouse ideas are getting awards — the easy to implement ideas are implemented — others are not. *(marketing manager)*

> I am skeptical. I've tried this before in other companies and it didn't work; it's another way to squeeze. *(salesperson)*

> We are trying to encourage openness. I like that but I am worried about quick fixes to a long term problem. *(product manager)*

> We need to keep a sustained flow of ideas. We've got to tie it into our performance appraisal and reward systems. *(product manager)*

> This is a bandwagon/follow-the-leader thing. It's bitching, not ideas, just like we had before. *(staff)*

> It won't work when you don't control your own destiny; we're too controlled by the U.S. now. *(staff)*

> This program was really needed. We need more innovation ideas. We were doing this before the program but this formalizes it; it is an honest way of implementing something important in the company. It signals a priority. *(product manager)*

> It is a good idea but wasn't properly implemented. We're not getting enough good ideas. As a program there is nothing to sustain it. It takes too much administrative time. *(senior manager)*

> Innovation for office is unnecessary. It should be at a plant level, but the plants are under too much pressure. There is no time to think, no time to socialize anymore; that's what's necessary for ideas. *(product manager)*

> Everybody is too busy and this place is too impersonal now for innovation — people aren't even getting recognized for what they do now, let alone something extra. *(administrative staff)*

> Why don't we spend the money used to develop this program to reward people for the levels they are already working at? *(administrative staff)*

I like the fact that they are asking for my input; it reflects a new style of involvement and participation in decision-making. We've had good ideas come in but need to reward people from time to time for submitting them. *(production manager)*

The Current Situation

John Hanson was not surprised by these reactions. He knew that a more innovative organization was necessary for growth. He wondered what else should be done to spur innovation at Chemcan.

EXHIBIT 1
INNOVATION AT CHEMCAN

Office of the President, Chemcan

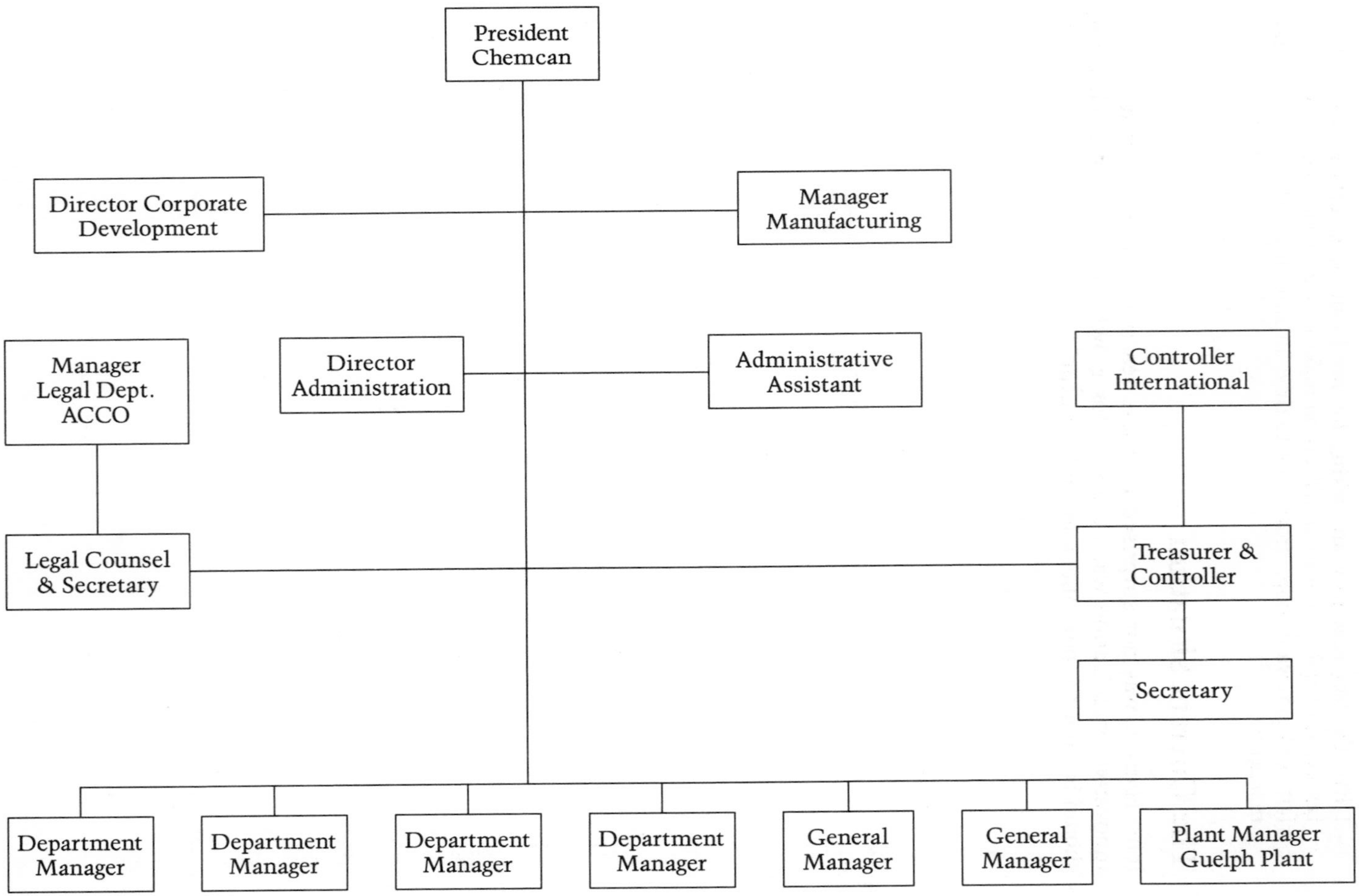

EXHIBIT 2

INNOVATION AT CHEMCAN

Chemicals Department, Chemcan

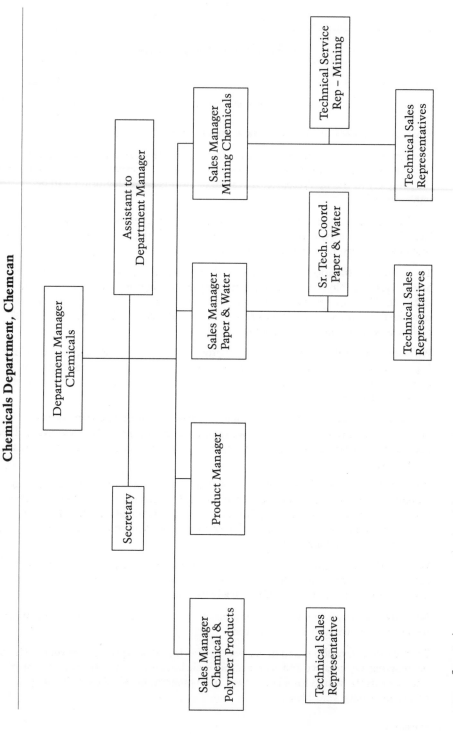

NOTE: Secretaries report to a supervisor Admin. support but are in dept. headcount

Assistant to Department Manager and one Technical Sales
Representative not in department headcount

Sales Manager — Paper & Water currently not in headcount — requested for 1985

EXHIBIT 3
INNOVATION AT CHEMCAN

Memo from the president

To All Employees   February 1984

ANNOUNCEMENT

The Key to Innovation program is now underway at Chemcan.

The opportunity exists for all employees to contribute ideas that have a positive influence on quality and productivity and the general effectiveness and reputation of the company in the marketplace. A system of awards and recognition will be implemented.

The Key to Innovation program was organized so that everybody at Chemcan will have the opportunity, in an informal, friendly way, to use their creative abilities to find new answers, new solutions and new ideas.

The values and traditions that have served this company so well in the past are not being discarded. No sudden changes are planned. Rather, we are building on our strengths. The Key to Innovation program is a recognition that as information comes into existence and circumstances change it's not always possible to solve today's problems with yesterday's solutions.

We believe you will find new ways to improve the work environment and continue your dedication to the company-wide concern for quality. Some people think of quality as costly luxury features; however, it simply means turning out excellent work the first time.

The objective of the Key to Innovation program is to stimulate and encourage everyone to contribute ideas which will improve our company. We hope to avoid too many rules or structures in our program as spontaneity and enjoyment are the essence of the program.

It's obvious why we called the program Key to Innovation, as all of us are seeking the combination (or key) to open the mental locks that stop us from thinking of a better way to do things. Most of us have difficulty getting our creative juices flowing because we tend to be either afraid of making mistakes or unwilling to look beyond our own area of responsibility.

We hope the innovation program will be the action that shakes us out of routine patterns, encourages us to think about new ways of doing things and stimulates us to ask new questions, possibly leading to a better way.

We know the people of Chemcan have many ideas to contribute to the company and the betterment of those who work here.

The Key to Innovation program is a way to give tangible expression to your desire to be imaginative, creative and searching as it encourages you to ask more "what-if" questions in the search for a better way. It's a program for all of us. What do you think? Let's have your ideas.

President

EXHIBIT 4

INNOVATION AT CHEMCAN

Awards and Recognition

Introduction

Awards will be granted for innovations of value, or benefit to Chemcan which are essentially outside the employee's assigned job responsibilities or above levels of performance expected in the job assignment.

The awards will be determined by your department Innovation Committee with emphasis being placed on recognizing the participants in the program.

When you submit an idea, you become an active participant in the program with your participation being acknowledged by the presentation of the symbolic Chemcan Key to Innovation Lapel Pin.

President's Award

You have an opportunity to try for the President's Award. From all submissions, an outstanding idea, or ideas, will be selected for the prestigious President's Award of the Year. The President's Award is for an idea which is truly innovative or has a value or benefit to Chemcan of $50 000 or more for the first full year of operation. The President's Award consists of:
— a tax free benefit of $1000
— a permanent member of the President's Innovation Circle
— a weekend for two
— photo and feature article in Chemcan News

Department Awards

The Department Awards are rated as Gold, Silver and Bronze. Recipients will receive recognition in Chemcan News.

Gold Award
The Gold Award is presented for an idea within the definition of innovation, which is innovative and has *significant* value or benefit to Chemcan. The award consists of:
— a weekend for two
— a plaque recognizing the achievement

Silver Award
The Silver Award will be presented for an idea, within the definition of innovation, which is innovative and has a *measurable* value or benefit to Chemcan. The award consists of:
— a dinner for two
— a plaque recognizing the achievement

Bronze Award
The Bronze Award will be presented for an idea, within the definition of innovation, which is innovative and has a *value* to Chemcan. The award consists of a plaque in recognition of the achievement.

EXHIBIT 5

INNOVATION AT CHEMCAN

Award Winning Ideas

Bronze

Yvonne Cameron—secretary, Legal (Administration)

— an idea to post personnel changes on the bulletin boards regardless of job level.

Margaret Brandt—secretary, Purchasing & Distribution

—ideas for product and location profiles to be published in the Chemcan News.

Beverlee Seeley—secretary, Treasury (Controllers)

—her second Bronze Award (first was for the Paper Work Reduction Task Force) for her plan for a reorganization of the Credit section office space.

Michael McManus (Chemicals)

—a recommendation that a company store be opened at the Guelph Plant. Presently, Guelph employees must travel to another location.

Don Cormier—rigger (Guelph Plant)

—an idea to use scrap stainless steel cable as a replacement for steel sash-chain and cable used in measuring the volume of cyanide in storage bins.

Carol Savage—assistant product manager (Consumer)

—an idea to imprint an Innovation message in the new pay stubs.

Silver

Howard Martin—department manager

—an idea to set up an in-house, joint-venture travel coordinator. Equipped with a video terminal, the coordinator will take advantage of the economies of scale by making all travel arrangements for company personnel at the Atria and Scarborough locations. A minimum saving of $12 000 per year is forecast by the travel agency.

Irving Applebee—supervisor, Pharmaceuticals Plant

—An idea to store off-site back-up diskettes of computer transactions in the pharmaceutical drug vault for a saving of $2200 per year.

Jean-Paul Vachon (Lasalle Plant)
Ernest Aumond (Lasalle Plant)

—an idea to recycle the inner cores of paper rolls with 3" cores by inserting the used 3" core into new papers which have a 4" core. This will reduce the down-time and the paper waste involved in the switch between paper rolls with different core sizes.

Bobby Eickmeier (Consumer)
Pauline Rocco (Consumer)

—a method of simplifying the procedure for identifying and resolving short payments from customers. The procedure will eliminate considerable paperwork, help keep customer accounts "clean", and potentially avoid future staff additions.

GULF CANADA LIMITED: RESTRUCTURING THE HUMAN RESOURCE FUNCTION

James C. Rush

David Sepsenwol, Director of Corporate Human Resources for Gulf Canada Limited, and Bob McIntyre, Director of Human Resource Planning, were thinking about the implications of a proposed new structure for their Human Resource function. This step was the latest in a process that had started eight months earlier in which David and Bob had been taking a hard look at Gulf's management company. To date, they thought that, in theory, the major contribution HR could make would be in:

- managing the corporate culture;
- managing the corporate property — that is those key players destined to be senior managers of the corporation;
- managing the external environment.

They had to decide whether this was feasible, and if so, how to do it.

Corporate Profile

Founded in 1906 as The British American Oil Company Limited, Gulf Canada Limited has played a major role in the growth and development of Canada's energy industry. Currently Gulf had approximately 37 000 shareholders, 9700 employees and assets totalling $5.1 billion. While 60.2 percent of the corporation's common shares were owned by Gulf Corporation, Pittsburgh, Pennsylvania, Gulf Canada Limited was a separate entity with its own board of directors.

History

In 1979 Gulf had separated into three companies, in order to take advantage of Alberta tax laws and to recognize the significant environmental and operating differences between upstream and downstream companies. Although this meant new legal entities, it meant nothing significantly new in the kinds of tasks performed. The company was still a producing, refining and marketing company. The three companies were Gulf Canada Limited, Gulf Canada Resources Inc., and Gulf Canada Products Company.

Gulf Canada Limited

The management company provided corporate strategic direction, basic policies, performance objectives, financial control and measurement criteria for the Gulf Canada companies. It handled the corporate planning and development, treasury, controller and internal audit functions, and provided services and coordination in human resources, information services, law, public affairs and research and development.

Gulf Canada Resources Inc.

The "upstream" subsidiary conducted a wide range of exploration and production activities. It was one of Canada's leading producers of crude oil, natural gas and gas liquids, and was a participant in the Syncrude oil sands project. The company operated 13 gas processing plants, had interests in 80 other gas plants and field gathering facilities, and was involved in coal exploration. Their land position in both western Canada and the frontiers provided the basis for aggressive petroleum and natural gas exploration programs. The company's new-technology Beaufort Sea Drilling System was owned and operated by a wholly-owned subsidiary, BeauDril Limited.

Gulf Canada Products Company

The "downstream" products division was responsible for manufacturing, marketing and logistics. Producing a wide range of petroleum and petrochemical products, it accounted for about 15 percent of Canada's refining capacity and refined product sales. It operated wholly-owned subsidiaries Superior Propane Limited, Commercial Alcohols Limited and Servico Limited, and had interests in several of Canada's principal crude oil and refined product pipelines.

The Culture

The culture of the organization could be described as risk-averse, compliant and family-oriented — "What's good for one is good for all." People inside the organization were largely unaware of the values, behavior and styles that guided the organization. Promotion from within had been the norm throughout history until the introduction of the National Energy Policy three years earlier, and the bad time that ensued for the oil industry. This policy forced reductions in staff. The company also chose to bring people in from the outside to fill key tasks. Performance became the key part of the psychological contract. The old notion of family was breaking down. Ambiguity resulted and many people felt frustrated.

The Role of the Management Company

The precise role of the management company was never clearly articulated. Without a clear mission and with the dramatic growth in the industry, the management company grew to over 1400 people. They found themselves largely in the business of providing services to both operating companies. Key senior managers found themselves dealing with more day-to-day problems than they had intended. This hands-on service role was not satisfactory; it was clear to most that the direction of the management company had to change. The responsibility for the company's future had to be assigned to one specific group.

Senior management decided that the new role of the management company could be described by the phrase "corporate development." In the most general sense, corporate development involved activities which answered the questions "What business are we in?" and "What businesses ought we to be in?" It identified and developed the organization's competitive advantage. It was referred to by some as having "the world at large" as its focus, and by others as the "eyes and ears of the beast." They decided it should be visionary and must have the responsibility for carrying the visions down to a business level, believing it is those activities that would broaden the base of the organization. This is the business of strategic management.

The Process of Change

Four people were heavily involved in trying to plan the change to the new management company role. David Sepsenwol, director of corporate human resources, was relatively new to the organization, having joined only a year before. David had spent time as a consultant to the industry on human resource and change issues. He was trained as an organizational development specialist, expert in the management of change. For him, it was most important to consider process when contemplating any change.

Bob McIntyre, director of human resource planning, had been with the organization twelve years and was the only person in human resources at the director level who had spent time in all its sub-functions. He had the knowledge of Gulf Canada from a human resource perspective.

Bert Walker, vice president of administration, had a long career inside Gulf Canada and had been part of several of the major change efforts that had gone on previously. He had at his fingertips a wealth of historical information about the company. He was the link between this group's efforts and the executive council—the ultimate decision-makers in this situation.

Donna Davis had worked on Bert Walker's staff for several years. Her strengths lay in the strategic planning processes and she was able to connect these planned change efforts to other strategic and operational plans affecting the organization. David, Bob and Donna were the major work team with Bert acting both as an information provider and as a sounding board for ideas.

For six months, this team spent most of its time trying to focus clearly on the management company as a whole—how to move the management company from its current operating role to the role of corporate development. They were not specifically defining this end state, but concentrating more on ways of moving to something uncertain. A great deal of time was spent testing the feasibility of change models. Several complex models of change were tested but, although interesting to the team, they proved unwieldy.

After considerable effort, the group decided it would be better to start small, to change the human resource department first and let that serve as a flagship to other functions inside the management company. This appeared sensible on several fronts. First, and probably most important, it was manageable. Second, it was Bert's notion, and agreed to by others, that with people being the strategic resource of the future that they become the lever for all other changes.

Corporate Human Resources

The structure of the department is shown in Exhibit 1. Over the period of late December, January and February, members of the department looked at themselves and their businesses from a variety of perspectives. This culminated in a conference of senior Corporate Human Resource managers in late February.

At this conference the three themes for HR's contribution to corporate development emerged. These themes were managing the culture, the shared-values of the corporation; managing the corporate property or those high-performing, high-potential individuals in senior management positions who are bound for officer level positions; and managing the external environment, those social, political, economic and technological forces requiring management attention. Although the themes sounded reasonable, there was much concern on the part of the HR directors and their staffs about what this would mean for the future of corporate HR, and for them personally in such a role. The conference also resulted in a plan for change shown in Exhibit 2.

In March, at Gulf's annual Human Resources Environmental Assessment Conference, three key factors were raised that had obvious implications for the new Human Resource Department role:

- given foreseeable economic conditions, particularly for employment, management is effectively in the driver's seat regarding both its union and nonunion staff. Traditionally, however, employers have responded to poor business conditions in ways that reduce rewards (particularly in imposing changes in the non-monetary dimensions of work) and thereby reduce employee motivation

- the need to change management systems/practices and structures to address the motivational problems of an increasing number of "stuck" employees in the workforce

- the potential impact of legislation such as pension reform, the Charter of Rights and employment and pay equity.

With the information raised by both conferences, Bob, Dave and Donna conducted interviews with every director. The interviews lasted two to three hours and followed essentially the same format. The questions asked were: What are you doing now that you could justify as being supportive of those themes? What is left over, things that you cannot justify in terms of three themes? What are those activities? How are they being organized differently? How much time are they taking? To what extent are they detracting from work that should be directed to the themes?

Thought was then given to two basic HR organizations at the corporate level: one group, small in size, that would devote its energies towards managing along the lines of three themes, and another group of people who, at least for the short term, would be involved in providing services such as staffing and compensation to the management company. This latter group would be highly centralized and smaller in size than before.

Each operating company had its own Human Resource function reporting to the line executives. This would leave the Human Resource groups in the operating companies to provide service to those companies, but conflict had often developed between them and corporate HR as to who was responsible for what.

The Task

The group was excited about this novel idea. They were concerned that others in the HR area did not share the same enthusiasm — but they wanted to move forward.

The time was right. Three of the four executive council members would retire within 18 months and succession plans were not public knowledge. Their U.S. parent was being taken over by Standard Oil of California. The new owners had indicated they might sell off Gulf Canada Ltd. Both these factors led the team to believe that now was the time. Tomorrow the opportunity may be gone.

EXHIBIT 1
GULF CANADA LIMITED:
RESTRUCTURING THE HUMAN RESOURCE FUNCTION

Corporate Human Resources Department

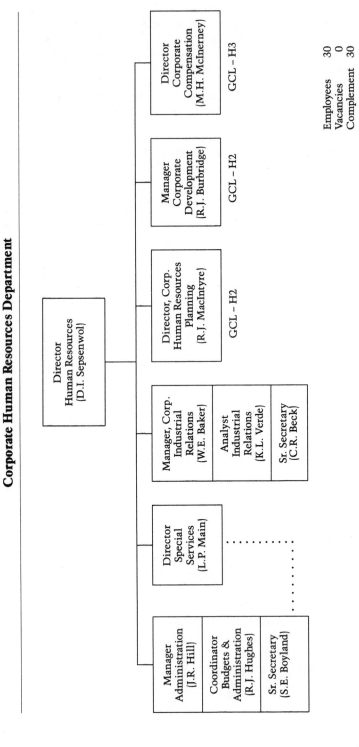

Employees 30
Vacancies 0
Complement 30

83-12-31

Chart GCL – H1

Corporate Human Resources Department

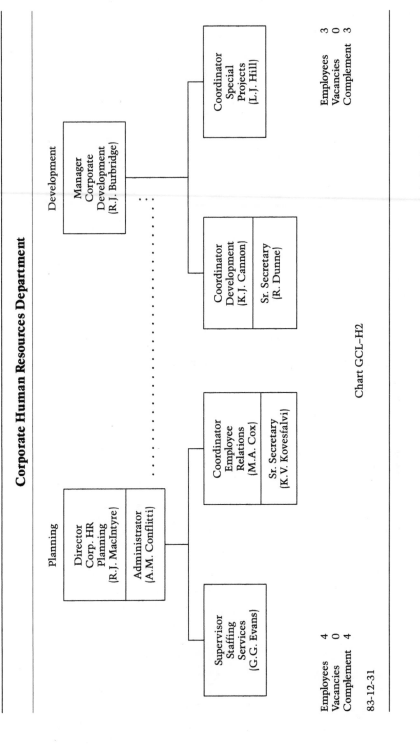

Chart GCL–H2

83-12-31

EXHIBIT 1 (continued)

GULF CANADA LIMITED:
RESTRUCTURING THE HUMAN RESOURCE FUNCTION

Corporate Human Resources Department

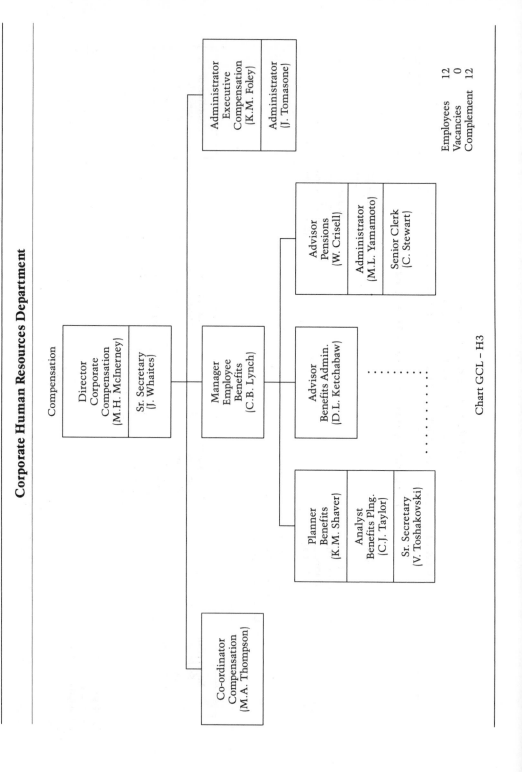

Compensation

Co-ordinator
Compensation
(M.A. Thompson)

Director
Corporate
Compensation
(M.H. McInerney)

Sr. Secretary
(J. Whaites)

Administrator
Executive
Compensation
(K.M. Foley)

Administrator
(J. Tomasone)

Manager
Employee
Benefits
(C.B. Lynch)

Advisor
Benefits Admin.
(D.L. Ketchabaw)

Advisor
Pensions
(W. Crisell)

Administrator
(M.L. Yamamoto)

Senior Clerk
(C. Stewart)

Planner
Benefits
(K.M. Shaver)

Analyst
Benefits Plng.
(C.J. Taylor)

Sr. Secretary
(V. Toshakovski)

Employees	12
Vacancies	0
Complement	12

Chart GCL – H3

EXHIBIT 2

GULF CANADA LIMITED

RESTRUCTURING THE HUMAN RESOURCE FUNCTION

Six-Step Plan for Change

1. Diagnose the present conditions, including the need for change.
2. Set goals and define the new state or condition after the change.
3. Define the transition state between the present and the future.
4. Develop strategies and action plans for managing this transition.
5. Evaluate the change effort.
6. Stabilize the new condition and establish a balance between stability and flexibility.

IPI (A)*

Jeffrey Gandz

Michael Parker, the human resources manager at IPI's Orillia plant, looked once more at the tables he had just compiled (Exhibit 1). He didn't like what he saw. While the absolute level of absenteeism did not seem unduly high by generally accepted standards — or so he thought, since the standards were not that clear — he saw very little improvement in the statistics. Although the first half of the year looked encouraging compared with the previous full year, he knew that absenteeism was usually higher in the peak summer vacation months and around Christmas, and expected that the year-end figures would likely be similar to last year's.

The previous week he had seen an article in a popular business magazine that had talked about the "lost weekday," the costs, causes and some of the cures for absenteeism. New to his job, and with a clear mandate by senior management to improve human resource management effectiveness, Parker was determined to tackle absenteeism at the Orillia plant.

IPI

With worldwide sales of over $10 billion, IPI was one of the world's leading consumer goods firms. Its products were not technologically complex and most were not protected by patents. The firm was widely recognized for its superior management in all areas, but particularly in marketing and production. The high quality of its products was essential to continued success. One

---

*All company and individual names and locations in this case have been disguised.

of the major challenges to the firm was to maintain this quality in the face of intense competition in the market place, often accompanied by deeply discounted prices.

IPI had also been in the forefront of the Quality of Worklife movement. Over 50 percent of its North American employees worked in modern plants, designed on a "socio-technical systems" basis. In these plants there were no time-clocks; controls were built into the work itself rather than externally imposed; supervision focused employee efforts more against business outcomes than in traditional plants; and all employees were on salary and received comparable benefits, whether they were in management or not. The older, traditional plants had hourly paid production workers, different benefits plans for salaried and hourly employees, time clocks, and closer supervision and controls.

IPI had been involved in manufacturing in the Orillia plant since 1921. The plant was traditional, employing 900 production employees in a three shift, 24 hour operation, and it produced 70 percent of IPI's sales volume for the country. There were four major production departments, a large shipping and storage department, and various support groups (Exhibit 2). Some departments were all male, while others had a high proportion of female employees; the supervisors tended to be under 30 years of age and college educated. The company had an explicit policy of keeping wages in the top 25 percent of comparable industries in the local area and, in addition, employees received profit-sharing. The work was safe, clean and not physically demanding. Turnover among supervisory and non-supervisory personnel was very low.

Although most of the major plants in Orillia were unionized, IPI was not. An elected Employee Committee represented the non-managerial employees in wage and benefits discussions, grievance processing, and on many committees dealing with health and safety, community relations, retirement pensions and other issues of joint concern. There were very few plants in IPI's worldwide operations with certified unions, and company managers viewed themselves as managing well enough to make certified unions unattractive to employees. The company had invested substantial amounts of time and money in carefully selecting, training and developing its supervisors and managers. They generally possessed highly developed interpersonal and group management skills as well as technical competence.

The other three IPI plants in Canada were of the more modern, socio-technical systems design, all having been established after 1962. It was well recognized among the Orillia plant's managers that senior corporate management planned to convert the plant to the newer style of management within the next five years, and expected the Orillia management group to be able to manage such a change, with appropriate corporate resources supporting their efforts.

Michael Parker

Age 34 with twelve years' experience at IPI following graduation from a business administration program, Mike Parker had excellent credentials for his job. Before being appointed to his present position of human resource manager, Parker had managed one of the largest departments, having started with the company as a first line supervisor. In that job he had developed a good reputation as an effective, people-oriented manager. His appointment to this new position was widely perceived as a promotion, and it was clear that he would play a major role in the organizational developments to take place in the next few years. Reporting to Parker were three employee relations officers who acted as resource persons to the department managers, and various specialists in compensation, benefits, safety, training, and community relations. Parker also had responsibility for the medical department (three nurses and a part-time doctor), security, and food services. Parker reported to the plant manager.

The Absenteeism Management Proposal

In his report to Richard Cross, the production superintendent, Mike Parker pointed out a number of concerns. Among them were;

- The 4.5 percent absenteeism was probably understated since some kinds of absences were not recorded or reported in the figures he received each month from the departmental secretaries. He was not sure how much understatement was occurring or what the impact on the total would be if authorized leaves of absence for bereavement or maternity leaves were included.

- The apparent variations in absenteeism might be a function of variations in reporting practices rather than actual attendance changes.

- At an approximate cost of 1.75 times the daily pay — a widely used yardstick of cost — absenteeism was costing the Orillia Plant over $1.8 million annually, of which he felt one quarter might be recovered if absenteeism could be reduced to levels of five years earlier.

- Some departments appeared to be running much lower absence rates than others. Females appeared to have about twice the absence rate of males.

- The proposed changes in plant management practices, benefits, and pay systems might prove very expensive if absenteeism continued at the current rate, or increased.

- He did not know if the current practice of paying employees for five hours for each of the first 10 days of absence in a year contributed to the absenteeism or not.

Finally, Parker suggested that he adopt improved absenteeism management as one of his objectives for the coming year, since he felt this was a way in which the human resource management function could contribute to improved plant performance in the medium and long term. His comments were very positively received and he was asked to develop a plan for improving absenteeism management. An initiative in this direction was endorsed by the production superintendent and plant manager at the month's department manager meeting.

Parker contacted the chairperson of the Employee Committee, Margaret Atkinson, to discuss the general problem of absenteeism and what could be done about it. She was wary of any immediate action. She thought that most people who were sick were genuinely ill and that any abuse of the sick leave plan was limited to very few people. They both agreed that they needed to know more about the incidence of absences of different types and also needed to understand why absences occurred. A few days later, Parker noticed an advertisement for a one day seminar on absenteeism conducted by two business school professors. He thought that this seminar might help him develop a plan of action.

EXHIBIT 1

IPI (A)

IPI—Orillia, Absenteeism Rates

Absenteeism Severity Rates Including All Sickness/Injury for Previous Five Years and 1st Half of Current Year

	Yr. 1	Yr. 2	Yr. 3	Yr. 4	Yr. 5	1st Half Current Year
Management Male	1.5%	1.6%	1.8%	1.9%	1.5%	2.2%
Management Female	—	—	—	—	1.2%	3.0%
Biweekly Male	2.6%	4.9%	3.1%	3.4%	2.8%	3.1%
Biweekly Female	2.4%	2.1%	2.1%	2.1%	2.2%	3.2%
Hourly Male	4.5%	5.0%	6.4%	5.4%	5.7%	4.4%
Hourly Female	7.4%	7.3%	7.8%	9.3%	9.4%	8.6%
TOTAL	4.1%	4.7%	5.5%	5.1%	5.2%	4.5%

Excluding Illness Over 3 Months' Duration

	Yr. 1	Yr. 2	Yr. 3	Yr. 4	Yr. 5	1st Half Current Year
Management Male	1.5%	1.5%	1.8%	1.6%	1.4%	1.7%
Management Female	—	—	—	—	1.2%	3.0%
Biweekly Male	2.5%	3.3%	2.8%	2.8%	2.8%	2.3%
Biweekly Female	1.9%	2.1%	2.1%	2.1%	2.2%	3.2%
Hourly Male	3.6%	3.5%	4.2%	4.0%	4.1%	3.1%
Hourly Female	5.9%	5.8%	7.0%	8.0%	7.4%	7.3%
TOTAL	3.4%	3.5%	4.0%	3.9%	3.9%	3.4%

EXHIBIT 1 (continued)

IPI (A)

Absenteeism Percentage of Time Lost Statistics—January–June Current Year

Including All Sickness/Injury

	Pet foods	Beverages	Toiletries	Food products	Shipping & storage	Engineering services	Testing	Chemical engineering	Pack	Human Resource management	Factory administration	Accounting	Plant Manager's Office	Central engineering	Orillia plant
Management Male	0.6	4.1	0.9	1.2	2.2	7.7	0.8	0.7	0.4	0.4	0.4	5.3	0.0	0.5	2.2
Management Female	1.9	4.8	0.0	—	—	—	—	4.0	—	—	—	—	—	—	3.0
Biweekly Male	0.4	2.4	2.4	0.0	2.7	1.1	3.7	1.1	—	0.0	2.9	7.9	0.8	3.3	3.1
Biweekly Female	1.6	0.5	1.6	4.0	4.0	0.0	4.4	0.0	—	6.7	2.8	2.9	0.0	1.3	3.2
Hourly Male	6.1	3.9	3.6	2.7	5.7	3.2	5.6	1.3	3.2	2.9	2.4	—	—	—	4.4
Hourly Female	8.5	13.2	9.8	4.8	—	—	3.2	8.3	7.3	5.1	0.8	—	—	—	8.6
TOTAL	5.9	4.4	5.2	2.7	5.2	3.6	3.8	2.4	3.6	3.7	2.2	6.3	0.3	1.4	4.5

Excluding Illness Over 3 Months

	Pet foods	Beverages	Toiletries	Food products	Shipping & storage	Engineering services	Testing	Chemical engineering	Pack	Human Resource management	Factory administration	Accounting	Plant Manager's Office	Central engineering	Orillia plant
Management Male	0.6	1.0	0.9	1.2	2.2	7.7	0.8	0.7	0.4	0.4	0.4	5.3	0.0	0.5	1.7
Management Female	1.9	4.8	0.0	—	—	—	—	4.0	—	—	—	—	—	—	3.0
Biweekly Male	0.4	2.4	2.4	0.0	2.7	1.1	3.7	1.0	—	0.0	2.9	2.0	0.8	3.3	2.3
Biweekly Female	1.6	0.5	1.6	4.0	4.0	0.0	4.4	0.0	—	6.7	2.8	2.9	0.0	1.3	3.2
Hourly Male	3.4	3.9	3.6	2.7	3.2	2.1	5.6	1.3	3.2	2.9	2.4	—	—	—	3.1
Hourly Female	8.5	13.2	6.7	4.8	—	—	3.2	8.3	7.3	5.1	0.8	—	—	—	7.3
TOTAL	4.1	3.9	4.2	2.7	3.1	2.7	3.8	2.4	3.6	3.7	2.2	2.6	0.3	1.4	3.4

EXHIBIT 2

I P I (A)

Partial Organization Chart

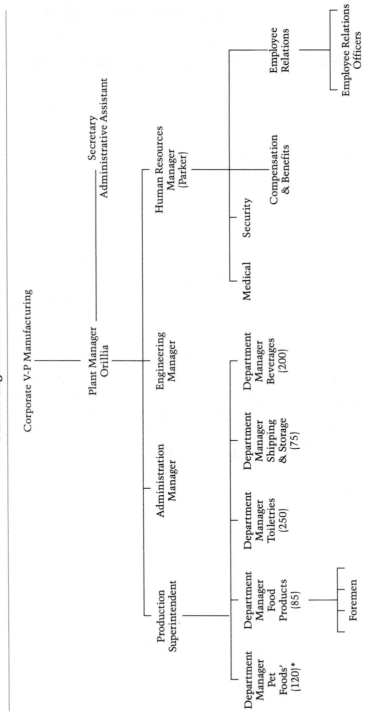

*Approximate number of hourly paid personnel in parenthesis

KELLOGG SALADA CANADA LTD. (A)*

John H. Howard and Gerald Ross

Management at Kellogg Company of Canada Ltd. had long been concerned with the welfare of its employees. Beginning in the late 1960s, Kellogg had started using techniques such as job enrichment as a means of improving the quality of work life. Already providing excellent wages, benefits and working conditions, Kellogg management believed it was important to provide meaningful jobs which met its employees' needs for growth, participation, and fulfillment through their work.

Kellogg Company of Canada Ltd. was a wholly owned subsidiary supplying the Canadian market with all Kellogg's products. It had captured over 50 percent of the ready-to-eat cereal market, producing several million pounds of cereals per year. Kellogg's recently completed corn mill was still unable to provide enough flaking grits[1] to meet production demands. To remedy the problem, up to 10 percent of the company's production needs for flaking grits had to be imported that year from the parent company in the United States.

In addition to production difficulties, there had been greater than normal problems with cleanliness and safety. All these issues were of concern to top management, and all seemed to be the type of problems which better mill operations could solve. Mill problems, however, were often difficult to isolate, since the conversion ratios in milling corn into flaking grits and other by-products were partly a function of the operations in the mill and partly a function of the quality of the raw corn available.

---

[1]Produced from raw corn, along with brewer's grits, #8 grits, corn flour, and hominy grits. Raw corn is first cleaned using a screening process, washed, and put into storage for future use. When taken out of storage, it is put through a "degerminator" to grind off the outer shell and extract the "germ" at the center. The shell and the germ are added into hominy grits, and the remaining grits proceed down the line. The grits are vacuumed to remove the fine powder on them; this powder becomes corn flour. The grits are then sorted by size, with only the very largest being used for cereals (flaking grits).

Fred Duncan, recently appointed supervisor of the corn mill, thought that these might be the types of problems which a job enrichment program could help solve, and which at the same time would be consistent with the corporation's genuine concern for its employees.

Job Improvement

"The people who are doing the work really make it happen," said Fred Duncan. Fred had recently introduced a job improvement program for the 19 hourly workers in the corn milling operation. The program had its impetus from a recent in-house seminar for managers. "Job improvement" was Kellogg's name for job enrichment, since the latter was felt to imply that existing jobs were tedious.

Job enrichment resulted from horizontal or vertical job enlargement, or a combination of both. Horizontal job enlargement is characterized by increasing the variety of functions performed at a given level. It reduces boredom, broadens employees' perspectives and prepares them for vertical job enlargement. Vertical enlargement permits employees to take part in the planning and control functions previously restricted to supervisors and staff.

Although unionized, the corn mill seemed an ideal place for such a program. It was physically separate from the rest of the plant and any changes would cause minimal interference with other production operations. The mill was small, with only 19 hourly workers spread over three shifts, and consequently was more manageable than a larger department.

Finally, the plant manager, George Sharp, felt that the workers were over-supervised and that, perhaps, the three foremen (one per shift, each earning $12 000 per year), could be eliminated. (See Exhibit 1 for a partial organization chart of the Kellogg plant.)

Just prior to starting the job improvement program, Fred Duncan, then shipping and warehousing supervisor, was asked, in addition to his existing responsibilities, to replace Art Johnston as supervisor of the corn mill. Since the seminar Fred had been interested in the concept of job improvement, and his acceptance of these new responsibilities was conditional on going ahead with a job improvement program in the mill.

His first step was to distribute the attitude survey which had been used by the consultant at the seminar. The last page of the survey contained a section for specific suggestions. When the results were compiled Fred found that one of the most common complaints was over-supervision — many of the workers felt that the foremen's jobs were redundant.

The attitude survey set in motion the process of job improvement which transformed working life in the corn mill.

The Removal of the Foremen

In the attitude survey, the workers expressed the opinion that not only were the foremen bad for morale, but they also added nothing to the performance of the job. A first miller, Tom McKnight, stated,

> The main thing in the whole setup is trust. When you're working with a foreman-supervisor relationship in a department, I think the whole overriding factor is that the company just does not trust you. And if they did, what's the need for a foreman to tell you what to do? You have to understand more of your job when you get along without supervision. Really, there's no other way of putting it, you just have to understand more of it.

Frank Sommers, another first miller, echoed similar sentiments:

> We all can't be doctors or lawyers and professional people. At the same time, there's no reason to feel that because people are not, they're incompetent to do the job which is given them without somebody watching over their shoulder. This whole idea of having that feeling towards ordinary fellows, that they may not be able to handle a job, is ridiculous! I'll prove it to you this way — in all probability, the people that they appoint as foremen are people who've just come off that job themselves.

As a follow-up to the survey, Fred Duncan called a meeting of the foremen, and they agreed with the hourly workers. During the discussions it was made clear that no one would be laid off from the company. As a result of these discussions, two of the foremen were shifted to other departments and the third became mill coordinator to assist Fred Duncan. (See Exhibit 2 for the new organization chart.) The decisions the foremen previously had made were now to be shared among the men.

Fred also instituted weekly Tuesday meetings with the day shift to discuss any problems. Since the workers rotated shifts, each shift met with Fred once every three weeks. These meetings became the vehicle by which future changes were to be made. The interchange was primarily between the hourly workers and Fred Duncan himself, although the union was invited to send a representative — an invitation that was rarely accepted.

The tone of the meetings was informal. There was never an agenda. The workers were encouraged to talk on any matter that concerned them. Tom McKnight described the atmosphere:

> When you set up these meetings and talk with the company, you don't know whether you're working with the blessing of the union or whether you're stepping out of bounds. In a lot of cases you say things at the meetings that the union wouldn't consider quite proper; but under the circumstances, the way the meetings were set up and the way they worked out was the best that could have happened. I think that any interference coming from the union could destroy it before it ever got off the ground. I think it has to be done with the complete cooperation of the union, and I think that the union has to be willing to overlook a

lot of things that could happen....In the areas of the contract that you work under, you just have to ignore them — there's just no other way you can do it. It has to be an agreement between yourselves that if something happens, you're going to ignore that for the benefit of everybody.

Such a situation was fragile and depended on mutual trust. Surprisingly, the union maintained a low profile with respect to the meetings and seemed to be content that the burden of dealing with grievances was now on the shoulders of the workers. The union steward, Jake Menard, commented:

It took us quite a few meetings. I attended a few of them and didn't want to get directly involved in making decisions....Let them make their own decisions... and make their requests directly to the company, because it's more effective that way and they feel more a part of making that minor change. All the small bitches that people had — they're gone. They don't exist any more, and it's hard to realize that...you have to almost see these people shift after shift, day after day, to realize this — the petty little arguments that go on there because somebody didn't sweep the floor on the shift before them, and so on. They don't exist anymore; they just aren't there, because there's no one there pushing them. Now, there's some explanation for it not being done...but with more involvement. In a period of 12 months, I haven't handled a grievance from that department on that issue...oh, there's been a few, as I say, I've attended some of their meetings, but most of all I have kept out of the thing as much as possible and let them file their arguments here, on paper, and give them directly to the supervisor, and then he handles them from there. I saw them afterwards, after they were filed with the supervisor, and supported them.

The increased sense of responsibility achieved from the weekly meetings also promoted a more cooperative atmosphere in the mill.

If we have a big problem, the packer may come up and pitch in and help. Before, they'd do it, but the general feeling was, unless the foreman told you to, you didn't have to do it, but...actually, most of the employees would if you went and asked them, they'd give you a hand. With the foreman there, it's a matter of, well, you had your job to do, and Joe Blow had his job to do, and you did it" (Ted McKie, second miller).

The men also began to find that with no foremen around, any extra time breaks taken merely added to the time that their partners spent at the job. As one miller said,

We have our relief periods. Well, here it's according to the contract, two 15-minute and one 30-minute break. It's no secret to anybody that they're well spent and an awful lot more. We were in the habit, with the foremen and the supervisor, of taking somewhere around 25 minutes for our first break in the morning, and 30 to 35 minutes for our lunch, and another 20 to 25...and do you know something, I don't think there's one of us damn individuals who leaves any later than we ever did before! With this system, I turn my job over to my partner and he or she looks after it. Now, if I overstay until the cows come home, that's who is gonna give it back to me — either that, or gonna say "Hey, I'm not going to go along with this —

smarten up!" You know, an awful lot of that "jailer and key" business is going to have to be taken out of that contract in the future.

Mill Clean-Up

Initially, the early meetings with Fred Duncan were primarily concerned with airing gripes. These were related to hygiene matters, and mechanical and safety problems. One of the first issues confronted was the weekly clean-up in the mill. Particular difficulties had been encountered in scheduling this clean-up, which generally took place on Saturdays. On one hand, the job was dirty and few wished to disrupt their weekends for such a task. On the other, overtime was paid. Attendance had been skimpy and there were no regular procedures to be followed.

In the meetings the workers proposed a solution — to put up a schedule for clean-up on a notice board where they could sign up in advance. They also agreed to draw up detailed procedures for clean-up, and assumed complete responsibility for scheduling their own participation. Those wishing to participate simply signed up and were allocated on the basis of who, on the day shift, had the fewest overtime hours.

This system resolved a long-standing grievance. Although it was strictly in violation of the union contract, it was mutually agreed upon by the workers and the company. Tom McKnight commented on the improvement:

> The clean-up . . . is normally considered the job nobody really wants to do, but it has evolved now to the point where the people don't mind doing it when they can do it within their own hours that they want to do it in — they're only too willing to do it. Under our old system, those areas like clean-up and that, it was thought that they had to be done at a certain time — and it just isn't so. As long as the work is done and done right, who cares what hours it's done in!

In the corn mill there was a battle not only to keep equipment clean but to control infestation. In the past, problems had been encountered in this area, thus jeopardizing product quality. Here too there was a marked improvement. The sanitation auditor wrote Fred Duncan a memo stating: "Regular cleaning of the interior of the equipment such as the grit abyer and the dust take-off stacks have been instrumental in keeping infestation to a minimum. Better daily housekeeping has also added to the improved appearance of the mill." The improvement appeared to be not only the result of better attitudes in the mill, but of the revised scheme of conducting clean-ups.

One interesting incident occurred when one of the workers, Dick Timmons, felt that he should have been chosen for clean-up the week before — he wanted the overtime. In a fit of anger, he went straight to the union steward and explained the situation. The steward agreed that Dick was entitled to the overtime, and prepared to confront Fred Duncan. Fred was somewhat surprised by a formal delegation, including union representatives and Dick himself. This behavior seemed to Fred to be totally out of proportion to the nature of the problem. He heard the complaint and readily agreed to the claim. To the surprise of the delegation he offered no resistance, but proposed to pay Dick the overtime to which he was entitled.

When Dick returned to the mill, the workers had heard of the incident and began to chastize him. After all, with the new clean-up scheduling system that they had proposed, it was the workers themselves who were responsible. Dick could just as well have brought his problem to them and it could have been readily sorted out. As it was, however, he had not only jeopardized the clean-up scheme but the whole job improvement program as well. The pressure was such that Dick went back into Fred's office to apologize for causing all the trouble and burst into tears. He had simply felt entitled to the overtime, and had acted inappropriately by going so quickly to the union.

Absenteeism

The job improvement program had other consequences. Absenteeism was reduced because the workers could regulate their own work loads. Fridays and Mondays had always been days of particularly low turnout. The workers discussed the problem in the weekly meetings and suggested that it was the inflexibility of the work week that was to blame. When a worker wanted to take a little extra time on a weekend, he or she had no alternative but to be absent from work. This was frequently the case when a person was going away for the weekend and needed either to get away early or to spend an extra day at the destination. They suggested as an alternative that, while still working a 40-hour week, they be permitted to arrange among themselves how the forty hours were to be broken up. For example, a worker might work six hours one day and ten the next. No overtime would be paid. This recommendation was instituted, and greatly reduced the rate of absenteeism.

Chronic absenteeism was also reduced. Ted McKie was an individual who had a drinking problem which had seriously interfered with his attendance. The job improvement program, however, appeared to contribute to his renewed sense of enthusiasm, with the result that he had stopped drinking.

> I did take an awful lot of time off. If I went out and had a few beers, well, I'd call and say, "I won't be in, I'm going to stay and have some more beers," you know. I'd get upset from too much drink. Well then, they'd keep a worker over, or if they had spare help, they'd bring someone over from spare. It cost the company a pile of money for absenteeism... but I don't do that anymore. I don't have that problem now. And I know that since the initiation of the job enrichment plan, I take a little more pride in my job. I feel I'm accomplishing more. It gives me an incentive to come to work, where before you had a foreman sitting behind you, looking over your shoulder, telling you what to do and what not to do.

Ted had recently begun to take evening courses to complete his high-school education.

Flaking Grit Yields

Probably the greatest single benefit from the company's point of view was the greatly increased yield of flaking grits (the prime ingredient in the process of making cereals) from approximately 28 to 42 percent. This increase meant that the mill could supply all the needs of the plant and that the by-products, some of which were selling at a loss, were drastically reduced. For example, the production of brewers' grits was reduced from 150 000 to 60 000 pounds per day. The price of raw corn used as the basic raw material in milling was approximately $9.46 per 100 pounds, while the brewers' grits (a by-product) sold for only $7.50 per 100 pounds. (See Exhibit 3 for data on flaking grit yields.) The company no longer had to import flaking grits from the U.S.

The innovation which caused this dramatic increase in yield came from a suggestion made in the weekly meetings by Tom McKnight, a first miller. He suggested that the screens used to sort the various sized grits could be rearranged to produce more flaking grits. Management was skeptical of the merits of such a plan, but was willing to encourage any potential improvement. Tom had his way and his suggestion worked.

The Wage Demands

The workers appeared to be satisfied with both the new freedom and the responsibilities that they had acquired — the atmosphere at work had changed. Frank Sommers commented, "Working in a factory...is not going to resemble anything that factory work was when I first started here. When we go over to the other side where the other departments are, we feel sorry that those poor buggers there can't do what is required of them to do without somebody telling them."

In spite of their enthusiasm, the workers recognized that the company had substantially benefited from the new arrangement. In particular, they emphasized the considerable savings stemming from the elimination of the foremen. Furthermore, they felt that the increased responsibility they had to bear as a result constituted a change in job content — a change which would justify an increase in pay under the union contract. In view of these savings Tom McKnight stated: "We felt the time had come to ask, as a group, for compensation for what we had achieved."

Fred Duncan sympathized with the demands, but recognized that the current two-year contract still had a year to run. He felt that the union, because of inflation, wanted to use this incident to reopen the whole contract — a precedent-setting event. On the other hand, he knew that the current improvements in the mill depended on the goodwill of all parties, and that the company had not only made substantial gains but stood to gain more in the future. Fred began to calculate just how much money had been saved by the improvements since the program began, and how he should respond to the workers' request for a compensation adjustment.

EXHIBIT 1
KELLOGG SALADA CANADA LTD. (A)

Partial Organization Chart Before Removal of Foremen

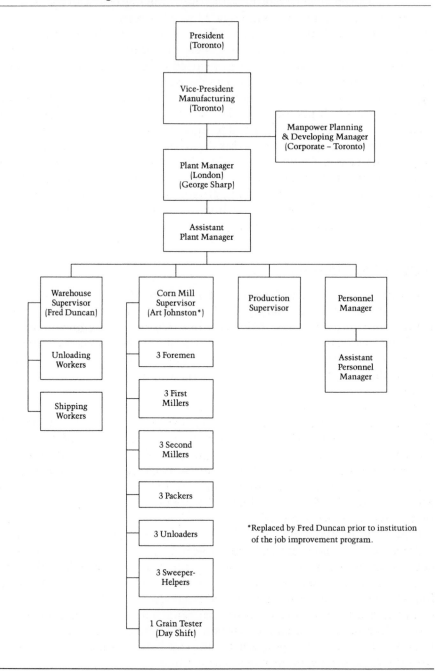

*Replaced by Fred Duncan prior to institution of the job improvement program.

EXHIBIT 2

KELLOGG SALADA CANADA LTD. (A)

Partial Organization Chart After Removal of Foremen*

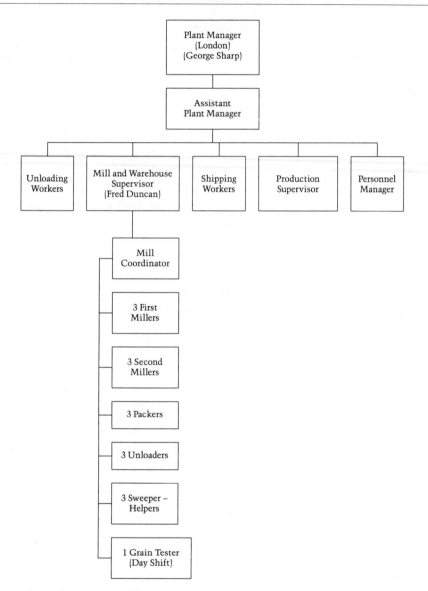

567

*Kellogg Salada
Canada Ltd.
(A)*

*Chart is the same as in Exhibit 1, except:
1. Fred Duncan controls both the milling and warehousing operations
2. There are no foremen, but one of the former foremen works under Fred as "Mill Coordinator".

EXHIBIT 3
KELLOGG SALADA CANADA LTD. (A)

Increase in Flaking Grit Yields*

Corn By-Products Before & After the Increase in Flaking Grit Yields * ~transfer prices~

	Previous Yield (Percent)	Current Yield (Percent)	Selling Price (per 100 lbs.)
Hominy Grits	1.8616 35.8	2.059 39.6	$5.20
Brewer's Grits	2.0775 27.7	1.035 13.8	7.50
Corn Flower	.3552 4.8	.2072 2.8	7.40
Total By-Products	68.3	56.2	
Flaking Grits	28.6	42.3	
#8 Grits	.1612 3.1	.078 1.5	5.20
Total Output	4.45 100	3.38 100	

*The company needs 30 000 000 lbs. of flaking grits annually. Raw corn costs $9.46 per 100 lbs.

EXHIBIT 4
KELLOGG SALADA CANADA LTD. (A)

Current Wage Scale (1973)

First Miller	$5.71/hr.
Second Miller	$5.55/hr.
Packer	$5.18/hr.
Unloader	$5.18/hr.
Sweeper	$4.92/hr.

"Any suggestions for improving our Participation Program?" Craig Fairley, manager of Kyron Motor Company's automobile assembly plant in Trillium City, Ontario, addressed his question to a group of senior managers gathered in the plant's training center.

> Everything was going so smoothly. Everyone seemed enthusiastic and committed—but what's happening now? With our new Prestige model launch next month, we need all the employee cooperation we can get, but our Participation Program seems to be falling apart. I'm still convinced it's a great program. Our coordinator is doing an excellent job. Other Kyron plants are doing it—why can't we?

The Motor Vehicle Manufacturing Industry in Canada[1]

The automotive industry in Canada began in southern Ontario in 1904. In the early years many thousands of automobiles were introduced but few survived infancy. These included the LeRoy, the Russell, the Tudhope, Thomas, Galt and others. From 1918 to 1923 Canada was the second largest vehicle producer in the world, and a huge exporter. By 1982 Canada boasted nine producers of cars and trucks, and was the seventh largest world producer.

The form and size of today's automotive industry was shaped by the first Canadian content legislation in 1926, the Tariff Board hearings of the mid-1930s, World War II, the Royal Commission on the Automotive Industry in 1960, and the subsequent Automotive Products Trade Agreement (APTA) of

---

*Some details in this case have been slightly altered, and all names have been disguised.

[1]Excerpted from "Selected Facts and Figures of the Automotive Industry in Canada," prepared by the Motor Vehicle Manufacturers' Association, Toronto, Canada, 1983.

1965, by which Canada's automotive industry became an integrated part of the North American industry. The APTA, or AutoPact, brought continental, conditional free trade in motor vehicles and original equipment parts. The agreement contained safeguards requiring that APTA producers in Canada maintain levels of assembly in Canada related to the value of their Canadian sales. Also there were provisions relating to Canadian value added, met through both domestic use and export of parts and assembly.

During the 1970s three events dramatically changed the North American automotive industry; the oil embargo of 1973–74, the Iranian oil crisis of 1979, and the emergence of Japan as one of the world's largest producers of motor vehicles. The fundamental result was the foundation of a global industry.

The Canadian automotive industry was almost completely restructured during the recession of the early 1980s, to compete with the greater productivity of Japan and the "new Japans" — Korea, Taiwan, Singapore, Thailand, and Brazil. Management methods and organization (including labor relations, as well as product development and supplier relationships) were rebuilt to improve productivity and quality. Key changes included: 1) new contracts with the United Auto Workers to reflect common interest and mutual problems and responsibilities; 2) the emphasis on "just-in-time" inventory control systems; and 3) the use of statistical methods to improve both quality and productivity.

To meet the global challenge presented by offshore manufacturers North American producers changed their products, emphasizing fuel efficiency and down-sizing, weight reduction, streamlining, front-wheel drive, and the use of electronics such as automatic mirror control, fuel and mileage monitoring, accessory power control, sleep and alcohol detection systems, and automatic braking devices. In making these drastic changes in product, investment by manufacturers in production facilities and equipment increased greatly. In Canada, over $4 billion was spent on new projects. In 1981 and 1982, twenty-nine new models were introduced.

Attempting to help the Canadian automotive industry, the federal government commissioned the Industry Strategy Task Force, which released a report in 1983 identifying priorities and formulating strategies and policies to support industry initiatives. In addition, the federal government built a $25 million test track and facilities at Blainville, Quebec. The Ontario government established six technology centers, including the Automotive Parts Technology Centre in St. Catharines and the Robotics Technology Centre in Peterborough, which were expected to provide the industry with innovation and technology to be used in future products and in the assembly process of vehicles. Management believed that the future promised many changes in a revitalized, restructured industry — changes in product design, alternate fuels and power sources, and in manufacturing.

Kyron Motor Company Limited

Kyron was one of the world's largest industrial enterprises, with active manufacturing, assembly and sales operations in 30 countries, on six continents. Although Kyron was better known as a manufacturer of cars and trucks, it also produced a wide range of other products — farm and industrial tractors, industrial engines, construction machinery, steel, glass and plastics. Also, Kyron was established in other businesses — finance, insurance, automotive replacement parts, electronics, communications, space technology and land development. In 1983, approximately 400 000 men and women were employed in Kyron factories, laboratories and offices around the world. Kyron products were sold in nearly 150 nations and territories by a global network of some 11 000 dealers, and the company's annual sales were in the $40 billion range, exceeding the gross national products of many industrialized nations.

Kyron of Canada was established soon after the founding of the original U.S. company, when a modest plant with the imposing name of Kyron Motor Company of Canada Limited opened in a converted wagon factory. Canadian operations expanded steadily. By the early 1980s, Kyron of Canada controlled many manufacturing and assembly plants, parts depots, distribution centers, regional sales offices and administrative centers. The company also had wholly-owned subsidiary operations in several foreign countries, as well as affiliated companies in Ontario.

As with the industry in general and Kyron's U.S. parent in particular, Kyron of Canada's growth was marked at times by immense difficulties. The company tottered on the brink of disintegration in the great depression of the 1930s and its aftermath. The emergence of a strong labor movement brought strikes marked by terror and violence to Kyron plants, in spite of (or perhaps because of) extremely repressive measures used by management. Ultimately, in the early 1940s, the UAW was certified as the bargaining agent for Kyron workers, and the company turned to manufacturing World War II tanks and other vehicles.

After the war, the Kyron organization seemed once more in jeopardy. Managerial ranks were full of gaps — deaths, resignations and discharges took their toll. Reconversion to effective peacetime production demanded great capital expenditures, but financial management was confused and almost chaotic. Kyron's auto products were not seen as quality-competitive with those of other companies, and negotiations with labor were becoming increasingly strained, taking place in an atmosphere of fear and anger and mutual distrust. However, new managerial leadership took hold, and steps were taken over the next three decades — shrewd financial measures were instituted, manufacturing facilities were enlarged, a new line of cars was introduced, and a more mature relationship with labor developed. Although adversarial in nature and marked with occasional strikes and tensions during the life of collective agreements, both union and management had developed some respect for the legitimate roles of the other, and some degree of trust. The autoworkers in the major companies had received steady increases in real wages as a result of automatic productivity[2] and cost-of-living adjustments. There was a common recognition that these wage levels placed the labor costs of North American manufacturers much higher than their Asian competitors. This opened the way for Japanese companies to import better value products, either in the form of lower priced cars, or competitively priced cars with more features.

Along with the rest of the industry, Kyron sustained enormous losses from 1979 to 1982, due to many factors; high interest rates, high unemployment and high inflation, together with the weak performance of the Canadian automotive market, the pessimism of Canadian consumers, and increasing competition from abroad. Company management declared that improving quality and productivity were the essential goals for bettering Kyron's position in the 1980s.

Kyron's Participation Program

To meet the competition Kyron executives visited nearly every major high-volume automobile manufacturing plant in the world. In particular, they studied the Japanese manufacturers, hoping to discover the reasons for their productivity and quality achievements. After investigating every detail of their operations, Kyron executives found a number of areas in which the Japanese way of doing things was different from the North American. Three of the principal differences were in workforce management, approach to quality, and the determination to eliminate waste in any form.

A Kyron vice president stated,

> We found their approach to workforce management unlike ours. Japanese managers assume that people, properly selected and trained, are competent, want to work, want to do a good job and take pride in their efforts. They make every employee feel part of the team. They conduct in-depth training programs for everyone. When problems occur, every employee who can contribute, participates in resolving them.
>
> Our system assumes that workers are lazy, generally incompetent and indifferent to the effect they have on the quality or cost of the product. We contribute to the individual's feeling of unimportance to the business by not training him or her adequately for the work to be performed, our indifference to complaints or

---

[2]The UAW collective agreements in the 1960s and 1970s had included a three percent annual 'productivity improvement factor' which was, in fact, independent of actual productivity improvement.

suggestions (except through a structured formal written suggestion or grievance system), putting people out of work with any downturn in volume, and using unpaid time-off the job as a form of discipline.

As a result, our employees have no feeling of commitment from the company, and have no commitment to the company or its goals. Their primary link with the company is through their union and their union contract. Their relationship with the company is basically adversarial, with disputes settled by an impartial referee who interprets the terms of the contract.

Where the Japanese system encourages the use of the talents and ideas of all of their employees, our system discourages or even prevents active and constructive participation by a large part of our workforce. Where Japanese workers are striving for continuous improvement in productivity for the common good, ours are resisting productivity improvements because they perceive them as a threat to their jobs.

So we've decided to undertake what might be called a "people revolution," involving our employees in a participatory, cooperative approach to management of our plants. We're calling it our "Participation Program," and plan to install it in all Kyron operations throughout the world. We know that the success of such a program depends upon a sincere effort on the part of both union and management. Sincerity is the key!

And it isn't going to be easy; we'll be plowing new ground. We don't have the benefit of experience. We will need strong leadership, support and commitment from all the people involved in the process. People Participation and our new approach to management provide both opportunities and risks. The process is too dynamic to be made to stand still; it will keep advancing. We need to keep leading it.

We know we must select and train members of management differently than we have in the past. But that is not all. We must seek out individuals capable of motivating and leading — not merely managing and directing. Tomorrow's leaders must be a new breed. They must have vision and an ability to foster enterprise inside the large corporation. They must be able to look into the future. Our success will be determined by how well we tap our human potential, our greatest competitive resource. Leadership is going to be based on our ability to govern, not merely command.

Trillium City Assembly Plant

In the late 1940s, Kyron of Canada constructed an enormous assembly plant on the outskirts of Trillium City. It was designed as a "swing plant" — an operation with maximum flexibility, able to change from producing one type of product to another (e.g. mid-size to small-size cars) with a minimum of downtime. Beginning production in 1950, Kyron's Trillium plant initially operated at full capacity, two shifts a day, assembling 30 cars per hour. By late 1982, 42 cars were rolling off the assembly line every hour; and with the projected launch of the new Prestige model in March 1983, it was expected that 60 cars per hour (260 000 per year) could be produced at maximum overtime.

In 1983, 3500 people were employed at the Trillium plant — 3100 hourly workers, of whom 50 were female, and 400 salaried employees. The average age of hourly and salaried employees was considerably higher than the industry average of 38 years of age, with 13 years of service. Production was organized into four departments — body, trim, paint and chassis — which were sub-divided into units called zones. (See Exhibit 1 for Trillium assembly plant's organization chart.)

From the beginning, union-management relations at the Trillium plant were adversarial. UAW members responded to every perceived provocation with wildcat strikes, many grievances, and a constant attitude of skeptical mistrust of all management initiatives. Managers, on the other hand, felt hard-pressed to do jobs which they felt were excessively complex and constantly changing due to the additional tasks involved in producing mixed product lines and changing products. (These changes were legislated by Kyron's U.S. product development group without prior consultation with the Canadian subsidiary.) By the late 1970s, constant labor-management confrontations had given Trillium a bad reputation throughout the industry for labor-management relations.

In 1978 the expected production goal of 42 units per hour was achieved, but operating costs were unsatisfactory. The plant's operating performance loss was $200 000 to $300 000 each week. An external auditor reported that Trillium's product quality was not competitive with other auto assembly plants — and in fact, there was a huge backlog of new cars just off the assembly line waiting in Kyron's lot to be repaired, which required much weekend overtime work. Frequent work stoppages were occurring, especially in the material handling and final assembly departments. The plant union chairman complained loudly and frequently about many areas of dissatisfaction, including the general environment of the plant, "prison grey, dirty and messy... rotten housekeeping."

The plant manager in 1978, an engineer with 30 years' service at Kyron, managed the plant's operations in a typical adversarial style. Daily management meetings were a series of name-calling sessions, with each blaming the other for faults of omission or commission. After each meeting blame and disciplinary action was passed down the line, as far as the hourly workers. As one superintendent summed up, "Shouting and screaming and "C.Y.A." was the way of life at Kyron." When the plant manager retired in 1979, Craig Fairley (formerly general manager of another Kyron assembly plant) took his place. Craig had started with Kyron of Canada in the mid-1950s as a tool and die maker, and became an industrial automotive technician two years later. He learned every operation on the assembly line; and through regular promotions rose to the position of Kyron plant manager 30 years later.

When he took over at the Trillium plant Craig was an enthusiastic advocate of the Participation Program promoted by corporate management. During

1979 contract negotiations the Canadian company and the union agreed to take part in a trial Participation Program, with the Trillium plant specifically named as the trial site. Craig hoped that the Participation Program would facilitate the resolution of many of the giant plant's problems. Reflecting on his work and his involvement with the Participation Program, he said:

I really like production. It's so interesting, though it's the toughest of any job. There are thousands of variables. You've got the people, number one — in this plant in production alone you've got almost 1000 hourly people on one shift, plus another 50 or 60 salaried people. You've got the parts — 3500 parts that are all variables. Everything is extremely complex — if the vendor doesn't send you good parts, you've got problems. If your hourly workers don't come to work today, or if someone doesn't show up for work to bolt trim parts on, you've got to find somebody else for the job. It's hell because there's always some new crisis every day. I like that! There's a real sense of satisfaction when you've corrected something or you can see you're making progress. There are a lot of downers, so you've got to take your satisfaction from ... well, we made our production numbers today, this part fits better now, we improved this quality defect ... those types of things. In your inner self it really does bring satisfaction, and that's one of my philosophies. That's what I tell people in production.

When I arrived here in 1979, I felt the working atmosphere had to be changed to a more participative style — a style I've practised throughout all my working life. People weren't involved — they seemed to have lost all initiative. Most people said they just didn't like coming to work. They'd try to get their eight hours over fast and get out. That year, the plant had changed over to manufacturing a van along with the car, building the van on the same assembly lines and with the same system as the car. As a way to run an assembly plant, that was not a good decision. And at the same time, nine robots were introduced in the body shop, an outside contractor was on strike, the material handling shop and the chassis department were having facility problems ... the organization wasn't ready for a major change. What a challenge!

That decision about the van led to unrest in the plant. People just didn't cope with it, and it kept getting worse and worse. We used traditional ways of trying to solve that problem, giving everybody hell, from the top all the way down until it got to the supervisor, and he got it too. So everybody was running around shouting at everybody else. When I first came here I couldn't believe it — I'd go to a meeting, and they'd say, "Bring in the badge numbers of the people that aren't doing the job!" and, "Who did you discipline today?" and, "Why can't you do this?" and, "This superintendent is no good, we should take him off the job." When the meeting was over, they'd received 20 assignments each, and they wouldn't do anything when they went out on the floor, and neither would I! They'd reached a point of paralysis.

I remember walking through the plant before I took over as manager. I couldn't believe the horrible environment the salaried people were forced to work in — dirty old desks 30 years old, dingy rooms — so as an example there, I upgraded the offices. I repainted all the desks, bought new tops for them all, got some plants and decorations...then we did the same thing in the plant. After we got the budget under control and had the money, I put 10 painters to work in the plant. That made the biggest physical difference in the plant, and to all the hourly employees — all of a sudden they could see that something was happening.

And from there we went into a line stop. We shut the assembly line down, which had never been done before in the history of Kyron. We had the supervisors talk to every hourly worker in their zone — they were amazed that the line actually stopped! And then we had a foreign car comparison display. We used a Japanese van against our van, and a Volvo against our car, and set them up in one area in the plant. We took everybody off the line in groups of approximately 20 people, and gave them an hour-long presentation of the quality levels of our competition. So things like that made the hourly worker a heck of a lot more aware of the state of our company and the state of our own plant, and how we were doing quality-wise compared to other assembly plants. That started a whole communication format with the hourly people in 1979, and was the beginning of my attempt to break down the mistrust which has always existed between the employees and the union and management.

I worked hard to improve communications. I myself spent a lot of time walking through the huge plant, getting to know the hourly people first-hand, reacting to individual operator problems. I was careful to avoid using management symbols — the golf cart for transportation, the suit coat, yelling and screaming. I conducted my management meetings completely differently. I had sessions with all salaried people in the first stages, especially first line supervisors, and then I'd tell them that we were in a lot of trouble, and I'd tell them exactly what the situation was — we were losing $250 000 per week, the quality levels were no good compared to the other plants, and communications had stopped. After I'd tell them the problems, I'd give them some of my philosophy. I didn't beat them over the head for not getting their production numbers today, but kept asking, "What can we do to get the numbers tomorrow?" There is a big difference in the approach. And I'd tell them to go home every day and think about something good that had been done, and to feel satisfied about that progress. And then gradually they kept making progress every day. It wasn't quite that simple — but it worked.

I really listened to my managers, and their suggestions. And because the biggest single problem at Trillium was union-management relations, I began listening to union complaints, too. The UAW plant chairman had been a thorn in the side of every manager for 30 years. He's the toughest plant chairman of any Kyron plant, U.S. or Canada! His name is Ed Trowbridge, and he was at the center of all our problems with the union. And did we ever have problems — there were three thousand outstanding grievances when I arrived! Trowbridge was yelling and screaming so loudly that it was just fights all the time, and management wouldn't listen.

So I must admit that I took a real gamble in my career — I listened to Trowbridge. And what I did was start to solve some of his problems — he wanted a fan in a certain location, a water heater fixed, a safety problem corrected — so I'd fix some of the easy problems for him. His bitches were legitimate in some cases, not all... and in those cases that were, I thought we had a responsibility. So, I'd get those things corrected fast. Now the management was sitting there watching, and they were muttering that this Fairley guy is going to get in trouble, and if he thinks that the union is going to start to run the place, he's wrong. So I had to talk to them about that...and it was a gamble that I wouldn't lose all my credibility with the management people at all levels.

So I started to get some trust going between the plant chairman and me. The Participation Program got going too, when the union, in 1979 negotiations, agreed to trying a workers' participation program at specified plants in the U.S. and Canada. They asked for the Canadian trial plant to be at Trillium City because of this plant's reputation for always being upside-down. Trowbridge got into that really deeply. He wanted it, he liked it, and there for about a year things were really super. He set up one area, Zone 15 in the final assembly department, as a specific Participation Program Group.[3] That worked really well, because the plant chairman who carried a lot of weight was deeply involved, and one of his stewards in the plant also got involved. And we set up an overall committee structure for management people and senior union people, and had regular meetings with quality of worklife government staff in Toronto.

So there was Trowbridge saying that the Participation Program was his program! The Trillium union really wanted a quality of worklife program, and that's essentially what they got. The Americans were saying that I was crazy to go that far! There are fundamental differences between P.P. in the States and an involvement program like Q.W.L. — quality of worklife is more along the lines of satisfying all the needs of production workers, whether they be environmental, personal or whatever. For example, a worker in Zone 15 wanted to take his coveralls home to wash, because he didn't like the smell they got from our vendor. So we said okay, if you want to take them home, go ahead. Whereas the company's idea for the Participation Program as I see it was more like quality circles, focusing on the quality of the product. The Participation Program is operations-oriented, quality of worklife is people-oriented. And you can see management thinking, "Watch that Q.W.L. stuff now, because what we really want is improvement in product quality." But you've got to have enough foresight to see that if you get the employees happy with their environment or whatever the problems are, you'll automatically get the quality! In Zone 15, for example, they dealt initially with some personal issues, then went out and tackled quality problems.[4]

And every time there has been a major change, for instance from one-shifting to two-shifting, or before a major new car launch, I've taken the opportunity to talk to all the hourly people. Prior to the launch of the 1979 car I held a one-hour meeting with all employees by department. I showed slides of the new product, covered the results of past year, emphasized the need to stay competitive with other locations, explained our launch plan in detail, and so on. And 18 months before we were supposed to build the new Prestige we brought in models from the design center in the States. We cleaned out a large storage area in the plant and set up seats for everybody. We had the car on display and then brought in the U.S. experts to talk about it. I made a speech, and told them that we wanted their input on how to build this car, thus involving the employees right from the start.

---

[3]See Exhibit 2 for steps in the development of Zone 15's Participation Program.
[4]See Exhibit 3 for an outline of Participation Program issues, results, and program evaluation for Zone 15, final assembly department.

We had them review the sub-assembly prototypes — for example, the front panel, doors, seats. And they loved that involvement. Let's face it; the worker who has been putting in door regulators on a production line for twenty years knows more about how that door regulator should be designed than anyone else! If anybody made a suggestion, it was recorded by an engineer from the corporate design center. They had to get back to us on every suggestion that was made, and then we in turn sent a memo out, signed by the assistant plant manager, the Participation Program coordinator, and myself, thanking them for their suggestion. And when someone had an idea that we knew would help from a reliability and a quality standpoint, we'd be quick to pick up on it, and make a design change in that area. In fact, out of 360 suggestions received, 200 were accepted and implemented.

We've taken a lot of actions related to Participation Program goals. We've done a lot of things right, by starting to listen, communicate, solve problems, and upgrade the workplace.[5] We looked at our progress and our accomplishments by the end of 1982 and thought we had done very well. Although we can't attribute all improvements specifically to the Participation Program, a changed atmosphere and P.P. did contribute to the fact we've had no walkouts or work stoppages during the past three years. Also, grievances on appeal to an arbitrator have been reduced from over 3000 three years ago, to 75 in 1982. Employees' use of the "hot lines" has resulted in both quality and safety improvements, and quality levels have improved dramatically — over 45 percent, as measured by warranty, uniform audits, and "things gone wrong." Overall plant safety/compensation performance has improved, along with overall union/management relationships, although some problems still exist in this area. Housekeeping has improved dramatically, and with very few exceptions, remains at a very good or excellent level consistently.

And I think we've made some progress with hard-line union representatives. In December 1982 I did a ten-day trip to visit assembly plants in Japan, and the plant chairman went with me. Before we left, Trowbridge went to a membership meeting at the union hall — told them he'd been invited to go to Japan with the plant manager, and wanted the workers to vote whether he went or not! He wouldn't make the decision himself. So they all, except one, voted him to go. We had a super trip, got along really well, had a few beers together and the whole works... but when we came back, people started bugging him about it, and unfortunately he can't take that. Our relationship has slipped back, almost as far as it was in the beginning, where he acts as if he doesn't trust me, and is openly antagonistic to my ideas. I don't understand it...

But in other areas we've made some progress — constant tension conditions between hourly and salaried employees have been eliminated. Also, the plant operating budget has been underrun by approximately $5.0 million over the past three years from 1979 to 1982, excluding funds spent to upgrade the plant. Yelling and screaming has almost disappeared as a way of getting things done — management is more effective, and we're seeing improved hourly participation and concern. A lot of this has to be due to the initial success of the Participation Program... but I'm worried about the future.

---

[5]See Exhibit 4 for a summary of Participation Program actions taken throughout the Trillium assembly plant.

We appointed a full-time P.P. coordinator in 1981. He's a very popular guy, formerly a production engineer in this plant. He's doing excellent work, but so far, we've only been able to install four functioning project committees in our production departments. That's just a drop in the bucket, in terms of the total plant. And one project committee dropped out early in the year due to lack of interest and involvement, leaving only three project groups. Steering committee meetings have been discontinued for a variety of reasons. The official status of the Participation Program is coming up to be voted on by the union, as specified in the contract, and I'm wondering which way the membership will vote. I can't fathom Trowbridge's position now — from being gung ho, he seems to have cooled off to the point of actively discouraging the workers from participating in the program.

So I'm concerned that the union might be throwing out the Participation Program. They started full of enthusiasm and participated well, and Trowbridge was happy, until suddenly two or three of his stewards started to get the idea that they were doing themselves out of a job here. They felt threatened, by a "union within a union," and they wanted to direct the program, not us. We wouldn't permit that, of course — it had to be a joint program. And there are so many other problems within the plant related to the P.P. — I'm fearful for its future. For instance, first line supervisors feel threatened by employees taking too much responsibility for their own work; and with full employee participation, the supervisors' job becomes more complex — they can't walk away from problems, can't hide, everything is in the open. There's a general resistance to change by both union and management — and I keep hearing that too much of the Participation Program activities in the plant are all Craig Fairley. That's a big problem, especially with the middle management people.

We gave them lots of training. All my supervisors went through a couple of days training session in P.P. awareness — managing by using your people's resources. We put on communication courses, which are absolutely super courses — they've got all the right things in them. We put a lot of attention on training management to do things in what I consider the proper way of managing. But you have to have the charismatic-type personality that holds them, that people will follow. The middle management people are not all believers. I'm dealing with people who've got 25 years' experience in the business, and the only way they got their job done in the past was using the two by four and getting their own way. It's hard to change those people around.

I get concerned when my management doesn't like the way I'm operating. I tell them, "Hey, you're the production manager, go do your job! I'm not going to tell you how to do your job!" In the old days they always expected that the plant manager would tell them how to do their jobs — but they've been doing their jobs for 25 years, they know how to do it. "When you get in trouble you tell me, and then you tell me how you are going to get out of trouble — I'm not going to tell you!" If it's their idea, they'll work hard on it. And they'll feel better about doing it if they do it themselves. That's my philosophy — and now I've got to get all the management people thinking the same way.

We were so successful in the beginning. Three or four key people in the plant have changed their way of operating, and the whole plant turned around, so everybody could see that managing differently really, really worked. But then when they got into difficulties again, when they see the Prestige launch is having problems, they say, "Well, it's back to the old system again." I hear things like, "The problem is, Fairley is listening to the hourly guys too much. Hourly workers think they don't have to do their jobs because Fairley's on their side." Well, that's a cop-out for not being able to do your job as a management guy!

Our Participation Program at Trillium for our salaried people is working very well. At their meetings in 1982 they identified some wants and/or needs: better communications, as in daily management meetings, two-way radios, and so on; a need for more training in interpersonal skills, and other areas; better measurement of first line supervisor performance, perhaps based on quality and cost factors; identification tags for all floor personnel; a dress code, with uniforms supplied; a locker room for supervisors; a special Participation Program activity center for supervisors; and a TV communication system. Actually, most of their major wants have been satisfied already, or actions are currently being taken to deal with their requests.

Wish I knew what to do to change the minds and attitudes of Trowbridge and the union and my management people to get them all working together to produce a terrific car. I want the Prestige to be the best car ever made by Kyron — why can't everybody see that the Participation Program would be a great way to help accomplish that?

EXHIBIT 1

KYRON OF CANADA (A)

Organization Chart—Trillium Assembly Plant

(February 1982)

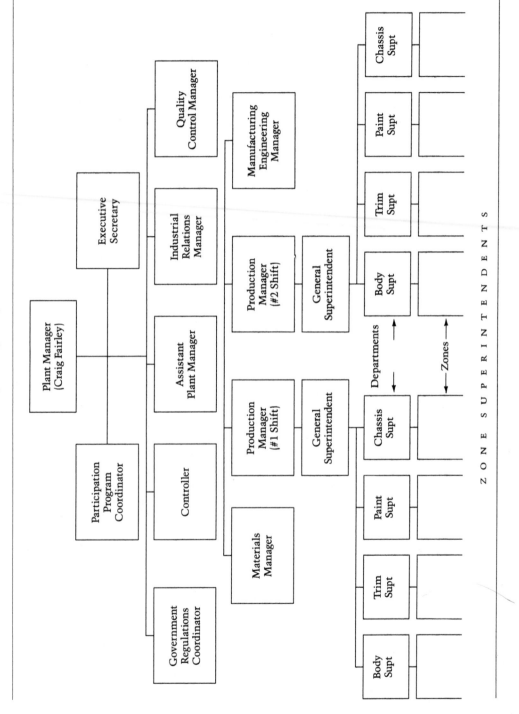

EXHIBIT 2

K Y R O N   O F   C A N A D A   (A)

Steps in the Development of Zone 15's Participation Program

1. Program implementation at Trillium Plant after 1979 negotiations:

   Jan./80 Management (operating committee & production superintendents) met with Province of Ontario Q.W.L. Centre representative.

   Feb./80 Similar meeting held with union leadership.

   Feb./80 Plant manager addressed all supervision regarding participation program and Q.W.L. (response favorable).

   Mar./80 U.A.W. confirmed interest in pursuing a trial project.

2. Sept./80 Steering committee formed (meets every 2 weeks)

   4 union reps: president, plant chairman, committeeman from Material Handling Dept., and steward from Final Assembly Dept.

   4 management reps: plant manager, production manager, superintendent, industrial relations manager.

3. Nov./80 First Zone meeting, Zone 15—Final Assembly (18 employees)
   — Plant manager explained, "We spend 20% of our lives at work—make it more satisfying."
   — Union president—covered history of union in area, and U.A.W.'s interest in program.
   — All employees volunteered to participate.

4. Nov./80 Project committee formed, 5 members (meets every 2 weeks).
   — Committee consists of a project chairman and 2 other members elected by zone employees, the supervisor, and union representative.
   — Project committee meets on a regular basis, attends steering committee meetings to report progress and request changes.

5. Fall,
   1981 Entire zone met several times after shift (training, or specific issues). Off-site training conducted (12 hours) for entire zone. Company paid for accommodation; other expenses paid by Q.W.L. Centre. Company also provided 8 hours straight time pay. Other miscellaneous training (e.g., how to conduct meetings) and off-site workshops were attended by zone members.

6. Oct./81 Participation Program Coordinator appointed.

EXHIBIT 3

K Y R O N   O F   C A N A D A   (A)

**Examples of Participation Program Issues and Results,
and Program Evaluation Comments: Zone 15, Final Assembly Department**
(December 1980)

EXAMPLES OF WANTS

Initial Issues:
1. job rotation
2. music in zone
3. freedom to go home after last relief
4. personal coverall issue
5. take out time clocks

Subsequent Issues:
— wanted access to phone for warranty calls
— wanted file cabinets
— wanted to participate in mix change allocations
— wanted better understanding of how organization functions
— wanted more training (project leader and all employees)
— wanted meeting of entire zone and industrial engineers (manpower issue)
— wanted radio station, not just music
— wanted to talk directly to vendors
— wanted more training on P.P. principles for organization (specifically first line
  supervisors and union representatives)
— wanted something done about heavy workload on park brake job
— wanted improved cooperation between shifts

EXAMPLES OF RESULTS

— warranty calls expedited
— mix change allocation
— reduction of two quality control and two seek and repair operators (reallocation
  involved)
— mini vent operation improvement (mix)
— park brake job improvement
— production loss improvement
— corrected undersize hole in door inner panel for regulator rivets
— versatility through job rotation
— accompanied wind noise audit team on road test and resolved problem
— some improvement in absenteeism

EXHIBIT 3 (continued)
KYRON OF CANADA (A)

Program Evaluation Comments
(December 1980)

Union Chairman: "Since the plant was built, the workers have never had so much attention. It's a bit difficult when you're used to nothing but fighting. But we welcome changes of a positive nature.

"Some of the old-school supervisors still think discipline is the answer to all problems, but this is changing. But the Participation Program is still on trial with many workers."

Shop Steward: "People have to be treated with dignity and respect, and we've made a start."

Zone Supervisor: "There's less personal pressure because the men are accepting more responsibility for their work. Instead of telling people what to do, we're sharing a common goal. Even supervisors from other zones in the plant show greater respect for the employees in the pilot project."

Chairman of P.P. Committee*: "Learning other jobs in the zone is a good idea. It creates some pressure, but all want to participate. Some want to learn more jobs than others, but I feel everybody can be accommodated."

Hourly Workers: "We are being treated as individuals, not just numbers on a punch card."

"I feel the difference as a person. I feel better."

"The atmosphere here is better. There seems to be less tension. The guys aren't uptight when they come to work, but we still have a long way to go."

"We seem to get along better with management, and the atmosphere is more friendly. I enjoy working here now."

Executive Director, Ontario's Quality of Working Life Centre: "The process will be a long one, and is potentially very significant. Its importance flows from the participation of a union such as the U.A.W. and from the assembly line technology involved.

"The project is difficult because of the massive size of the Trillium plant. So far, only a tiny segment of the assembly operation is involved. But I see both sides as committed, and I'm optimistic at this early stage."

*An hourly worker selected by other hourly workers in the zone.

EXHIBIT 4

KYRON OF CANADA (A)

Participation Program Actions Taken Throughout the Trillium Assembly Plant, 1979–1982

- Held a one-hour foreign car comparison program for all hourly employees. Individual groups of 20 to 30 hourly employees attended a quality comparison of foreign cars to our products.
- Meetings held with all production supervision in January 1980, on ways and means to improve service to first line supervision. All staff (services) assistance areas participated.
- All supervision completed an "operations analysis" of each hourly employee in his or her zone. This analysis was reviewed by department superintendent/production manager/plant manager. The object was to improve awareness and communications between senior management and the floor. The plant manager personally interviewed 35 first line supervisors.
- Assembly lines were held for 10 minutes on February 4, 1980 (following a down week), at which time each supervisor greeted his or her employees and reviewed with them improved environment (painting), housekeeping, methods improvement, quality and future production schedules.
- All departments continued conducting quarterly departmental meetings with salaried employees. Office conditions (a constant complaint) have been upgraded.
- Plant manager held meetings with all production supervision, etc., to update employees re 1979/80 costs and objectives, warranty costs, quality control points, and plans to implement a Participation Program at Trillium City.
- A quality information board was set up in the main aisle in the plant. Plant quality results, warranty information, plant performance comparisons to other assembly plants, etc., were posted.
- Plant supervision talked to their employees about the importance of meeting our control point objectives, as established through a new quality program.
- Emissions/F.M.V.S.S. hourly involvement program—a total of 16 inspectors were brought in during a down week for training purposes (including yard audits, classroom study, and a restructuring of inspection methods).
- Agreement reached with union on a method to make the change to one shift in 1980 more efficient and less disruptive. Agreement involved advance posting at both passenger and truck plants, with progressive layoffs. Marked first co-operative effort between union/company for a major plant action.
- As another example of the Participation Program, the joint union/company placement committee program proved very successful, with the placement of approximately 1000 hourly and 152 salaried employees who were laid off when the plant one-shifted.

(continued)

EXHIBIT 4 (continued)

- Communication sessions were held with all hourly personnel on May 27, 1980. All lines were stopped in all departments for approximately 3/4 of an hour between 10 and 11 a.m. Superintendents and general supervisors were used to give a 10-minute speech to all employees on quality problems at Trillium, and the necessity for improvement under one-shift conditions. Individual display units identifying quality concerns were then reviewed.

- Various video tapes were shown during the year ("State of the Company" video, etc.) to all salaried employees and the union committee.

- Quality hot line system was introduced in 1981 (24-hour reaction by plant manager or senior manager required).

- The plant manager continued to meet bi-weekly with the local union to solve some of their problems and further improve relationship between union/management toward achievement of common objectives (quality).

- Family Day was held Sunday, October 5, 1980. Various video tapes and films were shown to employees and their families. Showings included "It's Ready, It's Right," "If Japan Can, Why Can't We?" and "Employee Information Program for 1981."

- Plant tours for hourly employees reinstituted.

- The plant manager conducted information sessions (cost, quality and safety) for all salaried employees in October, 1980.

- Monthly meetings held with the local union president and his or her committee on quality indicators.

- As required by company management, a communications session was held with all management and the local union leadership on "Where We Stand" (slide presentation). Also shown to paint department hourly employees at their request.

- Automotive assembly division training staff visited Trillium and presented their "Awareness Training Program."

- All hourly and salaried employees were shown the Firestone "23–28" film.

- A safety hot line system was introduced in November 1980.

- "Season's Greetings" letters are sent to the homes of all hourly and salaried employees at Christmas. Letters are also sent prior to other major changes, such as two-shifting, Prestige introduction, etc. The letter highlights progress made during the year (e.g. quality improvements) and emphasizes our various Participation Program activities, and requests continued cooperation.

- Each department involves hourly employees in reviewing quality concerns found as a result of daily test drives, uniform quality audits and yard audits.

- An involvement exercise involving frame line employees was completed, frames as received from the "X" frame plant contained repetitive defects which resulted in assembly difficulties and repairs at Trillium. Through the efforts of our employees and a Participation Program group at "X" frame plant, several exchange visits involving hourly and salaried employees were held between the two locations.

EXHIBIT 4 (continued)

Problem areas were videotaped and presented to hourly employees at their plant. Quality levels improved dramatically.

- Safety tours initiated each Wednesday. Union safety representative joins tours.
- At employee and union request, several chassis vendors supplying substandard quality parts were invited to a meeting after shift with the hourly operators involved. Results were excellent.
- The Participation Program team (hourly/salaried) from "Y" plant (instrument panels) visit on a regular basis as a result of employee complaints.
- Contacts have been established and visits made to metal stamping division plants in order to report metal problems first-hand.
- Senior company officials now talk to both union members and hourly employees during visits.
- Plant environmental upgrade has continued, with many wood block floors replaced with cement, and all floors sealed with a bright clear finish.
- Participation Program Centre was built in the center of the plant to display units, provide information on our quality levels vs. other plants, and provide other information re company and plant activities.
- Line stop information sessions continue to be held.
- 1980 advertising campaign initiated, using plant personnel in commercials. A preview of the ad campaign was shown to all employees.
- President, Kyron of Canada, and hourly employees held press conference re 1980s program. Hourly employees participated in dealer visits, etc.
- One-day seminar held in May 1981, for salaried employees (160 supervisors, technicians, and specialists, and 26 U.A.W. representatives). This marked the first time that management/union had met together. The Toronto Q.W.L. Centre, with the assistance of 20 moderators, broke employees into groups which prepared lists of concerns and, subsequently, lists of proposed solutions.
- Project Zone 15 expanded to include 70 employees on two shifts in October 1981. The initiation meeting for the expansion was prepared and presented to the 70 employees by the outgoing committee of the original project group.
- A Participation Program facilitator was appointed by the steering committee in October 1981. The facilitator received Participation Program and problem solving training by national training staff.
- All union committee members attended a 2-day off-site seminar on Participation Program and issues raised at the May seminar.
- Material Handling initiation meeting for 60 workers was held in November 1981, with presentations being made by the steering committee members. It was unanimously adopted to form a P.P. group.
- Material Handling group elected project committees on both shifts which meet every two weeks.

EXHIBIT 4 (continued)

- U.A.W. plant chairman, a member of the steering committee, was appointed chairman of the Participation Program labor network.
- Three-day workshop for 60 members of management addressed unresolved problems and concerns from the May 1981 seminar. A Participation Program salaried project committee was established to resolve items raised.
- One-day workshop (off-site) was held for project Zone 15 to review progress, future direction, and outstanding concerns.

Re Two-Shifting:

- Agreements were reached with the union on a recall system prior to two-shifting. Union/company cooperation was very evident for the major task.
- One-day orientation sessions were conducted for all recalled hourly employees (approximately 1200). These sessions included a 1½ to 2 hour presentation by the plant manager, followed by an address by the union plant chairman. Employees were made aware of all the changes that had occurred while they were on layoff, shown the Firestone "23–28" film, etc.
- All first-line supervisors were provided with extensive classroom training which included a two-day employee awareness training program. This program covers the importance of making group decisions, and prepared employees for managing under Participation Program.
- After a very successful two-shift launch, a steak dinner was served to all employees—"two-shift launch appreciation dinner."

KYRON OF CANADA (B)*

Jeffrey Gandz and Eileen D. Watson

Union chairman, Ed Trowbridge, talked about his work at Kyron of Canada, and his involvement in the Participation Program:

I really like my job as union chairman. I've been with Kyron for 30 years, and involved with the union for more than 26. It gives me a lot of opportunities to travel — mostly to the U.S., to visit various Kyron locals there, and to attend meetings of the national Kyron bargaining council, besides working for the members at the plant. I'm proud to say that I know almost all of the people I represent. The workers in the Trillium plant have no idea of all the responsibility I carry, and how many activities I'm involved in. There are plenty of problems in my own life related to my being away from home a lot, and often my job as a union chairman in this plant is very frustrating — but I've learned to live with it. People who substitute for me when I'm on holidays — I had seven weeks last summer — get all choked up when they're not getting results. Whereas I've learned to keep trying, hang in there, keep banging away. Our grievance procedure takes too long, though. I'd rather get things settled on the plant floor immediately.

All we want is for our workers to be treated with dignity — but you can't trust management. I just heard that one of our people wanted to leave work early yesterday to take his wife to the doctor, and his supervisor said he couldn't go! And they refuse to get rid of time clocks, which are being phased out in the U.S. And would you believe it, they expect us to be grateful for cleaning up the plant — well, we're not! They should have taken care of fixing up the plant years ago.

I've attended many sets of negotiations, and the story is always the same. Kyron Motor Company is notoriously difficult to deal with. Even when profits are excellent they won't share with the workers. I have sat in negotiations with intelligent people across the table from me, lying. I know they're lying; they know they're lying. I get good information from all over the continent. Someone picks up the hot-line phone and tells the Trillium plant workers what's happening — what's *really* happening — in the States. And I can always phone anybody in the States, or I can phone Solidarity House for the truth about what's really going on.

---

*Some details have been slightly altered, and all names have been disguised.

The end result of any of our negotiations always hinges on the dollars. Kyron has a bad strike record — I remember in 1953 and 1954 we were out for three months. We wanted everything... improved wages, working conditions, the works. Now the company gives us nothing but excuses. They're telling us that Japanese competition and other countries' imports are supposed to be keeping our profits down. Well, I got a trip to Japan last year. It was a good trip, and it was great spending some time with the plant manager, Fairley — but I knew in advance that there's no way the Canadian lifestyle can adapt to the lifestyle of the Japanese autoworkers. Their lives are based on working for the factory, but life is more than that for us Canadians. Besides, we had the same system as the Japanese in Nova Scotia years ago, when the coal mines ran their own show. The workers got deeply in debt, and the people were terribly poor and hungry, almost slaves to the company. So the Japanese system didn't work over here. And we've got better technology than they have — in fact, they borrowed our technology in the first place! We've got the technology and knowledge to build better than the Japanese, and if this company weren't so greedy for profits we could do it.

Some Kyron management decisions make no sense. We lost our Queensway line to the U.S. — the best quality car we've ever produced. Why management decided that, I'll never know. We were close to 100 percent perfect quality. Funny — rumors about losing that car were all over the plant long before the Trillium management heard officially — or if they heard officially they weren't telling us. We told them we were going to lose that car — the official announcement came days later.

Participation Programs are the big thing in the U.S., being pushed by headquarters. We're trying at Trillium, but it's not working here. We had high hopes when it first began, although we had doubts that the company would live up to its part of the bargain. I think the basic problem is that it has been kept very secret what is really happening. They elected people within their own zones to sit on each zone committee, but what's happening is that they took away the elected steward's function in the zone. Our fear is that the zone committees will start getting things out of the company, where stewards have not been successful in the past. Like, the union steward in the final assembly department tried and tried to get a fan and a drinking fountain in a certain place. Management sat back and argued and argued, and nothing was done. Then all of a sudden these little Participation Program groups got together. The chairman of the P.P. group said, "We need a drinking fountain," and they got it right away. How come P.P. can do it when the union can't? And they aren't reporting to the membership. Everything is in the dark.

But how effective are these Participation Program committees really? In the old days people used to bring their radios in to work, and listened to the news or music or whatever, but the company put a stop to that. Then in the material handling department, one of the first wants that their committee talked about was music, and guess what? They started piping in music to that area! And they brought in new enclosed offices for the foremen to work out of, fancy shirts for them to wear, and we just laughed. Our union office has been an inadequate facility for years. We asked and asked the company to build us new union offices, and they told us, "No way."[1]

---

[1] The union offices were upgraded by the end of November, 1983.

The company sent me with other union members to a U.S. plant to sit in on P.P. meetings there, to see what happens. Their meetings are no different from what I do on a day-to-day basis. I meet with the workers in lots of committees, and one-to-one, too. At the Trillium plant we got the union steward to attend the meetings of the zone committee to police them — we firmly believe that the ultimate purpose of the Participation Program idea is to get the union out of the plant. We feel that Kyron is determined to get the union out, even though it might take 20 years using that P.P. approach. Of course, this will never happen.

I'm telling you, the company is interested only in making money — a lot of money. We have just come through the hardest negotiating situation that we've ever had. We lost millions for our members. The company put it to us that they needed us to back down; cars weren't selling, Trillium was on a one-shift operation, layoffs all over the plant. We gave up many benefits, including some of our paid holidays. We didn't get the 3 percent bonus we normally get. We went to a benefit plan that is not as good as the one we had before. Drug prescriptions are not covered now. But we knew the auto industry was in trouble, and we didn't push. Now we see all the auto companies making a big profit. We're going to be a lot tougher in negotiations next time.

Basically, company policy is the same today as it was after the first president retired. At one time the union had no problems dealing with management because the big boss was a very easy person to approach. He could resolve problems easily. You'd just walk in, tell him about it, and he would do something. However, an executive board runs the corporation now, and all they know is how to make a dollar. They leave the people stuff up to plant managers, and just keep applying all kinds of pressure to get 60 cars per hour off the assembly line. How the plant manager gets to 60 cars an hour, they couldn't care less.

There's a ton of red tape required for day-to-day procedures. For instance, in dealing with management the supervisor has no authority about pay claims. The general foreman may say, "Yes, we've made a mistake in this worker's pay claim," and write a ticket saying, "Can we pay this employee?" But suppose I'm working on the seven o'clock shift. My supervisor comes in at ten or noon, and there's a vacuum. I think we should give certain general foremen the responsibility and authority to resolve problems...because now, where the supervisor has to go is to the general supervisor, who goes to the superintendent, who goes to the manager to get the pay claims signed. Passing the buck is the name of the game until you get to someone who has real authority to resolve problems. Of course, the superintendent can always go to labor relations...

We're having problems with some of the supervisors. The supervisor is supposed to know everybody's job, and won't let people work at their own trade, which they really know better than the supervisor. They won't allow journeymen to work as proper tradespeople. The supervisor should allow the tradespeople more freedom. They should ask how something should be done, instead of telling them and telling them wrong. For instance, we've got an electrical foreman supervising motor mechanics. He doesn't know anything about forklift trucks, and yet he's telling the motor mechanics what to do! He should tell them what job is required, and ask them how to do it best. Then Kyron would get an honest day's work out of them, even though there are some bad apples in the bunch. And that would be better than any old Participation Program.

WARNER-LAMBERT'S CORPORATE CREED (A)

Jeffrey Gandz and Nadine Hayes

Wayne Britt, vice president of Human Resources at Warner-Lambert Canada (W-L) had just returned from a senior management meeting in Miami Lakes, Florida. He and other senior executives from Warner-Lambert's global operations had been discussing the newly developed corporate creed and he had to decide how to introduce it to the Canadian operation and ensure that it resulted in improved organizational effectiveness.

Company Background

Warner-Lambert Canada Inc. (W-L), a wholly-owned subsidiary of Warner-Lambert Company of New Jersey, marketed and manufactured health care products through its Parke Davis division, and confectionery products through its Adams Brands division. W-L employed 1500 employees in manufacturing locations in Ontario, five regional distribution centers, and a research institute. It had sales of over $200 million and was considered one of the global company's most successful affiliates.

The Parke Davis division manufactured and marketed ethical pharmaceutical products such as Ponstan and LoEstrin, which were detailed to doctors and distributed through drug wholesalers and pharmacists, as well as over the counter products such as Sinutab and Listerine, which were advertised to the general public and distributed through wholesalers, drug and food stores. The Adams Brands division marketed and manufactured brands such as Certs, Clorets, Chiclets and Trident through wholesalers and drug, food and variety stores. The two divisions were served by centralized corporate human resources, finance, research and development, and manufacturing groups, but each had its own sales and marketing functions. An organization chart, showing the number of people in each department and division, is shown in Exhibit 1.

W-L Canada had a reputation as a fair and equitable employer. The management personnel attracted by Frank Cleary, W-L's first board chairman and a patriarch figure in the organization, were of the highest quality. He had demanded a positive attitude, an emphasis on meeting and talking with people, and the desire to work within a family-type atmosphere. This orientation had been maintained throughout the company's 60-year existence and W-L had recently been recognized by The Financial Post as one of the 100 best companies to work for in Canada. The citation mentioned the company's above average efforts in employee communications, career development, affirmative action and job security.

Communication at W-L had always been open, with regular staff meetings instituted in the early 1960s. These were expanded and developed into all-employee orientation/information meetings that continued to be held twice each year. Two key tools of communication were the in-house publications: a quarterly newspaper, *By-Line*, and a monthly newsletter, *UpDater*. Annual opinion surveys were given to different employee groups and the results were published in the *By-Line*.

Personal development was greatly encouraged at W-L. As well as in-house seminars and courses, the annual performance appraisal system allowed employees to identify their career aspirations and pinpoint their needs. The employee's goals and performance would then be analyzed by senior managers and relevant feedback would be given to each employee. An annual human resources organization audit also occurred each year involving the president, each division head and Wayne Britt. The major objective of this audit was to review a career dialogue form completed by each member of the supervisory management group. This dialogue form, prepared by the employee, outlined the current performance level and the potential development capacity of that employee, and it then served as the basis for career planning for the individual and succession planning for the company.

Job security at W-L was considered a high priority and a management objective. The program that was in place dealt with situations such as service recognition, career and financial counselling, and out-placement.

Wayne Britt described the culture at W-L as a "partnership" and stated:

> Our W-L culture reflects an informality and a spirit akin to family. It encourages teamwork and participation; it discourages approaches to problems which are less than open and candid. Our culture is less easy to describe than it is to observe. It's also far easier to lose it than to build it.

CREED Background

The senior executive team at Warner-Lambert's global headquarters in Morris Plains, N.J. were concerned with "how to make Warner-Lambert an even better company — one more fully able to reach its potential, and also more productive." They felt that Warner-Lambert had no well-documented principles, code or creed against which to measure its own performance — or against which others could measure its performance. It was felt that an explicit pronouncement of the company's goals, values and principles of management would move it towards becoming an excellent company. These ideas were strongly supported by the literature of the time, such as Peters' and Waterman's *In Search of Excellence*, and several highly publicized incidents such as Johnson and Johnson's handling of the Tylenol crisis.

The 287-word document which they developed was the result of many management sessions, task force recommendations and extensive discussions (see Exhibit 2). After it was adopted by W-L executives in New Jersey, they decided to introduce it to senior managers from the world-wide affiliates and to start a process whereby these companies would buy into the CREED and turn the statement into concrete actions to benefit the business.

Eighty senior managers from all Warner-Lambert's domestic and international operations were called to a meeting at Miami Lakes, Florida. They were introduced to the new CREED and given the objective of developing plans for implementing it. In groups of ten they looked at what W-L did well, what it did not do well, and what could be done better with respect to the five publics outlined in the CREED. The eight groups then selected the five best recommendations they had developed for each public, resulting in a total of 40 recommendations for each public.

The managers were then organized into five groups, each assigned to one of the publics. These groups derived the five best recommendations from their initial 40 recommendations. These five were presented to the president and chairman of Warner-Lambert Company of N.J. The total outcome was 25 recommendations — five for each public. Examples of these recommendations were:

• Build employee awareness of "customer" importance:
  — top-down leadership to stress significance of customers
  — make subject a PMS[1] standard
  — define the customers and communicate the definitions by division
  — institute corporate-wide program to train/educate employees on customers' importance — use appropriate media
  — encourage employees to give feedback on customer reactions from their personal experiences
  — use motto to reinforce customer importance (N.B. we could use a corporate motto)
• Improve recognition and reward systems for all employees to foster innovation and increase productivity
  — survey all locations and find out what reward/recognition systems are in place and obtain suggestions
  — communicate findings to all human resource managers
  — create task force to review systems and come up with five/ten recommendations that could be applied worldwide
• Demonstrate senior management's commitment to innovations and creativity
  — establish innovation fund in 1986 financial plan

---

[1]PMS is the Warner-Lambert acronym for Performance Management System.

- change from a follower to a leader in regard to employee benefits (e.g. cafeteria benefit program)
- decrease bureaucracy and centralization and move toward self-contained profit centers

- Encourage employees to participate in community affairs
  - contribute staff time for community affairs: teach, loan executives, speakers' bureau, plant tours
  - reflect in PMS standards

The 20 senior human resource executives in attendance were then challenged to go back to their respective affiliates and to develop a process for ensuring that recommendations consistent with the CREED were developed and implemented within these affiliates.

Spreading The Word

The Miami Lakes meeting had been inspiring, and Britt was eager to begin telling people in W-L Canada of the discussion. However, he was unsure of the best way to approach this challenge. Initially there was the question of who to tell and involve in the process. He had to determine the best way to eventually inform all employees. He could begin some form of introduction at the top levels of the organization and work downward, hoping for excitement to be generated by example. Conversely, he could begin at the bottom and attempt to push the excitement upwards, hoping for a greater commitment from the lower levels because of this increased involvement.

Then there was the question of format. The three day session at Miami Lakes was informative, gruelling and inspirational. Would the same format be appropriate for Canada, or should it be shaped to reflect the increased focus the recommendations would be taking? Would it make sense to run this format for plant and lower-level clerical workers or just for management?

The focus was an issue in itself. The recommendations from Miami Lakes, although meaningful and understandable, were global and conceptual. Wayne felt that they needed to be clarified to be more meaningful to the Canadian operation. The question was how best to do this so that it would not be perceived as a management directive. Also, he was unsure of what he should expect in the form of recommendations from the employees, and if he should give them some direction before they began.

Another issue was the time-frame he should be looking at for an implementation period. Even though there was no direction or expectation from the parent company, Wayne felt it would be appropriate to establish a tentative schedule.

With all these variables having a potential impact on the CREED operationalization, Wayne was uncertain as to how to communicate the excitement he felt in Miami Lakes and maintain it throughout an implementation process.

EXHIBIT 1

WARNER-LAMBERT CANADA

Organizational Chart

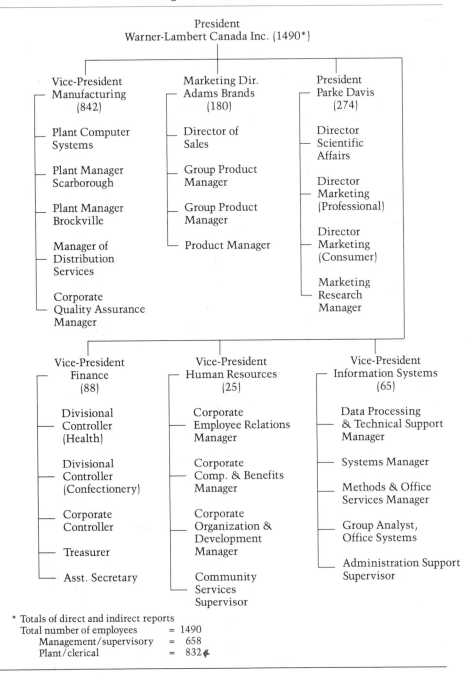

President
Warner-Lambert Canada Inc. (1490*)

596

Vice-President
Manufacturing
(842)

Plant Computer
Systems

Plant Manager
Scarborough

Plant Manager
Brockville

Manager of
Distribution
Services

Corporate
Quality Assurance
Manager

Marketing Dir.
Adams Brands
(180)

Director of
Sales

Group Product
Manager

Group Product
Manager

Product Manager

President
Parke Davis
(274)

Director
Scientific
Affairs

Director
Marketing
(Professional)

Director
Marketing
(Consumer)

Marketing
Research
Manager

Vice-President
Finance
(88)

Divisional
Controller
(Health)

Divisional
Controller
(Confectionery)

Corporate
Controller

Treasurer

Asst. Secretary

Vice-President
Human Resources
(25)

Corporate
Employee Relations
Manager

Corporate
Comp. & Benefits
Manager

Corporate
Organization &
Development
Manager

Community
Services
Supervisor

Vice-President
Information Systems
(65)

Data Processing
& Technical Support
Manager

Systems Manager

Methods & Office
Services Manager

Group Analyst,
Office Systems

Administration Support
Supervisor

* Totals of direct and indirect reports
Total number of employees   = 1490
    Management/supervisory   = 658
    Plant/clerical   = 832

EXHIBIT 2
WARNER-LAMBERT'S CORPORATE CREED

WARNER-LAMBERT CREED

597

OUR MISSION is to achieve leadership in advancing the health and well-being of people throughout the world. We believe this mission can best be accomplished by recognizing and meeting our fundamental responsibilities to our customers, employees, shareholders, suppliers and society.

To Our Customers

WE ARE COMMITTED to providing high-quality health care and consumer products of real value that meet customer needs. We are committed to continued investment in the discovery of safe and effective products to enhance people's lives.

To Our Employees

WE ARE COMMITTED to attracting and retaining capable people, providing them with challenging work in an open and participatory environment, marked by equal opportunity for personal growth. Performance will be evaluated on the basis of fair and objective standards. Creativity and innovation will be encouraged. Employees will be treated with dignity and respect. They will be actively encouraged to make suggestions for improving the effectiveness of the enterprise and the quality of work life.

To Our Shareholders

WE ARE COMMITTED to providing a fair and attractive economic return to our shareholders, and we are prepared to take prudent risks to achieve sustainable long-term corporate growth.

To Our Suppliers

WE ARE COMMITTED to dealing with our suppliers and all our business partners in a fair and equitable manner, recognizing our mutual interests.

To Society

WE ARE COMMITTED to being good corporate citizens, actively initiating and supporting efforts concerned with the health of society, particularly the vitality of the worldwide communities in which we operate.

ABOVE ALL, our dealings with these constituencies will be conducted with the utmost integrity, adhering to the highest standards of ethical and just conduct.

WARNER LAMBERT

WARNER-LAMBERT PROJECT SPENCER

David C. Shaw and Mary Anne Beauchamp

In March, 1984 Victor McDonough, vice president of finance at Warner-Lambert Canada Inc. (W-L) was evaluating Project Spencer's financial feasibility. The target date to present his final analysis and recommendation on this proposal was April 1984.

Project Spencer was a proposal to rationalize Warner-Lambert's production facilities. The code name "Spencer" was derived from the early 1983 executive session at Spencer Hall, the management center at the University of Western Ontario in London, Ontario. That was where a proposed evaluation of the company's manufacturing facilities was initially considered and it was agreed to proceed with a study by Cunningham-Limp Consulting Engineers.

In February 1984 Ken Belch, vice president of manufacturing, received a report from Cunningham-Limp on the utilization of production facilities for the Health Care Division. The report confirmed that the Health Care Division had two under utilized manufacturing facilities. The company's strategic plan for this division called for a maintenance of production levels in the next five years at current levels involving a slight decline in line utilization at both plants.

The proposal called for a consolidation of the two health care plant operations in one location and a relocation of the distribution center. Because this rationalization plan would affect many employees if implemented, maintaining confidentiality at this stage was critical. Robert Campbell, the plant manager at 2200 Eglinton Avenue in Scarborough, Ontario was assigned as project leader.

Company Background

Warner-Lambert Canada Inc. was an international affiliate of Warner-Lambert Company, with head offices in New Jersey, U.S.A. The Canadian company developed, manufactured, marketed, and distributed a wide range of consumer and professional products in the confectionery and health care areas, "for the enjoyment, well-being and comfort of Canadians across the country." Health care products were manufactured at the Warner-Lambert plant at 2200 Eglinton Avenue, Scarborough, Ontario (Metropolitan Toronto), and at the wholly owned subsidiary Parke-Davis Canada Inc. in Brockville, Ontario, about 300 kilometres east of Toronto. Confectionery goods were produced at the wholly owned subsidiary Adams Brands Limited at 40 Bertrand Avenue, Scarborough, Ontario. The major products produced at the three facilities are listed in Exhibit 1. The Canadian company also operated a research center in Mississauga, Ontario. Warner-Lambert maintained distribution centers across the country. The company employed 45 000 people worldwide, including 1600 in Canada. International sales in 1983 were about $3 billion, of which the Canadian affiliate contributed in excess of $200 million.

Consolidation Plan

On the strength of the Cunningham-Limp Consulting Engineers report, Warner Lambert management decided that the production operations at 2200 Eglinton could be moved to the Brockville operation. The study confirmed that sufficient space was available in Brockville to accommodate this manufacturing consolidation plan, provided that the Brockville distribution facility was relocated to the 2200 Eglinton facility. The alternative of moving the Brockville production lines to the 2200 Eglinton facility was rejected because sufficient space was not available and the cost of expanding the 2200 Eglinton facility exceeded that of consolidation in Brockville.

The proposal which emerged for the Brockville consolidation of the production operations maintained the basic configuration of the current Brockville facility except it would:

- relocate Brockville distribution to Toronto to make space available for manufacturing and material warehousing;
- relocate suppository manufacturing and packaging in the current dry packaging area;
- relocate material storage to the current distribution warehouse to relieve space to relocate liquid filling lines;
- install the toothpaste manufacturing facility in the dry packaging area;
- install mouthwash manufacturing in the current raw material storage area;
- expand and relocate the liquid packaging to the current raw and packaging materials storage area;
- clean up the piping and ceiling area in liquid manufacturing; and
- create a bulk storage area outside the cafeteria and rear of the building for alcohol, mineral oil, glycerin, etc.

Bromo Seltzer manufacturing and packaging would remain at 2200 Eglinton, while the packaging of Rolaid bottles and Listerine lozenges would relocate to 40 Bertrand, where these products were currently manufactured. All other 2200 plant operations manufacturing and packaging facilities would be relocated to Brockville, and the Brockville distribution operation would be transferred to the 2200 Eglinton facility.

A breakdown of the costs and savings associated with this proposed rationalization appears in Exhibit 2. The space vacated by the consolidation would be 50 950 square feet (15 530 square metres) at 2200 Eglinton. The distribution relocation from Brockville would fill 8300 square feet. Management considered moving the operations of Deseret Canada Inc., a wholly owned subsidiary of Warner-Lambert, which currently occupies leased space, to 2200 Eglinton, if the consolidation project was implemented. The Deseret operations would fill 18 000 square feet. Filling of the remaining vacated space at 2200 Eglinton was under investigation (see Exhibit 3).

Inventory Buildup

To implement these changes a ten week inventory build-up was required in early 1985 to provide coverage during the production disruption and the transfer and retraining of employees. Inventory requirements had to be forecast with accuracy in order to reduce the risks of stockouts, which would result in lost sales. The estimated value of this additional finished goods inventory was $2 500 000. Inventory levels were expected to return to normal levels by the end of 1985.

The marketing group expressed concerns as to whether the proposed inventory levels were satisfactory. Many health care products were sold on the basis of special promotions to the stores, and Warner-Lambert could be vulnerable if competitors initiated major selling promotions during this period when it could not counter with its own promotions because of constrained supply.

Scheduling

A tentative schedule for the rationalization appears in Exhibit 4. The plan was to inform employees in September 1984 of the pending employee moves and potential for layoff to take effect in 1985. The company at that time committed to seek all possible alternatives to relocate affected employees within other operations in the company.

In order to optimize efficiency and minimize cost, the construction would occur in April to June of 1985, and the transfer of operations to Brockville would occur mainly during Warner-Lambert's annual three week shutdown in

July, 1985. This would involve relocating, installing, and testing the equipment, and getting back into production within a compressed amount of time.

A major key to the construction and move schedule was the inventory build schedule. Warner-Lambert had to obtain materials and supplies, and have sufficient line hours with sufficient trained people to build the required inventory to last during the equipment downtime. This posed a difficult problem, because at this time many trained people would be transferring to other positions within the company, or opting for the severance package and terminating.

Human Resource Concerns

Project Spencer involved displacing about 120 employees, including both transferring people and eliminating positions (see Exhibit 5).

The major costs of Project Spencer were a) capital equipment costs and b) human resource expenses. The major benefits were savings achieved through the elimination of 40 employment positions and transportation savings due to the consolidation of the Brockville distribution warehouse with the Toronto warehouse.

The company estimated there would be 89 positions transferred from Toronto to Brockville, and 23 Brockville distribution positions to Toronto. The company was concerned that many employees who were well established in Metropolitan Toronto would be reluctant to transfer to a much smaller and quieter town of 20 000 people. It was assumed that only eight employees would readily transfer from Toronto to Brockville, and 28 Brockville distribution employees would transfer to Brockville manufacturing, leaving a total of 53 unfilled positions in Brockville. Warner-Lambert determined that this would mean there were 83 redundant employees in Toronto, comprised of 43 workers not willing to transfer and 40 workers holding the positions that would be eliminated. Details are presented in Exhibit 5.

A layoff of workers conflicted with Warner-Lambert's "Meaningful People Management Philosophy" which the company viewed as a key element of its success. This philosophy emphasized that motivated employees were hired and retained with encouragement to achieve excellence.

Wayne Britt, vice president of human resources, was concerned about the effects of the 83 employee separations. The four major risks identified by Britt's evaluation were:

- the negative effect of eliminating positions on the company's reputation — in the eyes of its employees, to the consumers of Warner-Lambert's products, and for investors in the company;
- the possibility of unionization attempts at the 2200 Eglinton or the 40

Bertrand plants in Toronto, and especially at the Brockville facility which had a history of such attempts;

- the possibility of severe work slowdowns, product quality problems, or even sabotaging of machinery or materials, especially since the move would require inventory buildups by those employees whose jobs would be affected by Project Spencer; and

- the possibility of employees filing lawsuits against the company for unlawful dismissal or inadequate severance pay.

The human resource department submitted to Campbell's Project Spencer team a prognosis of the employee relations climate that may exist after the announcement of the elimination of 40 positions and the termination of redundant employees not willing to transfer to Brockville. It was as follows:

> This announcement will be the most devastating one ever made since this building was occupied by us in 1967. The reaction from those directly impacted will be hostility...not simply disappointment. The reaction from others in the building will be one of shock followed by a "can this be the same company who has had such a high regard for its people, etc. etc."

> The 40 Bertrand staff will be relieved it hasn't affected them heavily...but they'll be far less confident of their future security. "Will we be next?"

> Confidence and trust will be replaced by suspicion and doubt for a period of time.

The human resource department proposed that, if the company adopted the relocation plan, it try to find employment for as many of the 120 employees affected as possible by creating vacancies within the company through such techniques as offering an early retirement package to all workers aged 60 to 65. The department proposed offering transfers and retraining in Brockville, the Toronto distribution center, and the 40 Bertrand plant for otherwise terminated employees to fill positions which became vacant due to early retirement or were created because of the expansion of the distribution center. The possibilities that the human resources group considered were as follows:

- some employees would take advantage of the offer of a fully subsidized transfer to Brockville;
- some employees would relocate to the new positions moving to 40 Bertrand;
- some employees would transfer to the expanded Toronto distribution area;
- some employees would be provided with existing positions at 2200 Eglinton that were being filled by temporary employees;
- some employees would assume positions which became available over the next year through normal attrition;
- some employees in the 60–65 age category would avail themselves of a very attractive special early retirement provision;
- some employees would elect to leave the company; and

• some employees would be laid off if sufficient openings had not been created and transfers to Brockville were not taken.

The human resources group proposed that every displaced employee would be involved in individual counselling and offered either a transfer, early retirement, or severance pay. The severance package suggested was very fair compared to that required by law and that generally offered by other companies in a similar situation.

The solution offered by the human resource department would be costly and time consuming, but would reduce the tension for employees and their families who had the potential of being displaced by the consolidation project.

The Financial Factors

W-L's head office in the U.S. had set the hurdle rate for the Canadian operation to use in evaluating projects at 20 percent.

The period of benefit was estimated at 10 years. The depreciation allowed for tax purposes in Canada (Capital Cost Allowance — CCA rate) on the equipment required was 25 percent in year one, 50 percent in year two, and 25 percent in the following year, all on the original cost. The CCA rate on buildings was 2.5 percent in year one, and 5 percent for the future years on a declining balance basis. Warner-Lambert's book depreciation policy on equipment was a life of 15 years, depreciated on a straight-line basis, and for buildings the life was 40 years, also depreciated using a straight-line method.

During a discussion with McDonough about the financial aspects of the project, Campbell argued that the company hurdle rate of 20 percent was inappropriate because the cost savings on this project were virtually certain. He argued that the 20 percent hurdle rate was intended to be used to evaluate new products, and the plant and equipment to produce them, which involved the uncertainties of product acceptance, market share, production techniques and costs, and all of the other business risks. In this case the costs and the savings were known.

McDonough was concerned about the negative response to the proposal taken by the human resource group. While he understood Campbell's argument that the savings were virtually guaranteed, he was not sure that the project was risk-free. Certainly this was not a typical capital expenditure proposal. He had his staff accumulate financial information which he may want to use in analyzing the proposal. These data are presented in Exhibit 6.

EXHIBIT 1
WARNER-LAMBERT PROJECT SPENCER

The Major Products Produced by Warner-Lambert

HEALTH CARE DIVISION

Warner-Lambert Canada Inc., 2200 Eglinton Avenue, Scarborough, Ontario produces and/or packages:
- Personal health care products (mouthwashes, Bromo, Efferdent)
- Professional health care products (Anusol, Beben)
- Schick safety razor products
- Deseret masks and surgical scrubs
- Rolaids bottle filling
- Plastic bottle production

Parke-Davis Canada Inc., Brockville, Ontario (Wholly owned subsidiary) produces and/or packages:
- Consumer health care products (Benylin, Sterisol, Agarol, Sinutab, Gelusil)
- Professional health care products (Dilantin, Choledyl, Mylanta, Ponstan, Elase)
- Personal health care products (Compoz, Bantron)

CONFECTIONERY DIVISION

Adams Brands Limited, 40 Bertrand Avenue, Scarborough, Ontario (Wholly owned subsidiary) produces and/or packages:
- Chewing gum (Trident, Dentyne, Chiclets, Bubblicious, Freshen-Up, Clorets)
- Breath mints (Clorets, Certs, Trident)
- Other (Rolaids, Halls Mentholyptus, Strepsils)
- Specialty candy

EXHIBIT 2
WARNER-LAMBERT PROJECT SPENCER

Costs and Savings of the Consolidation Proposal

COSTS

	(in Thousands)
Capital costs	$2440
Moving & other non-capital costs	582
Human resources costs	1871
(to provide severance, relocation, counselling and training for the 83 employees who will become redundant in the Toronto operation)	
Total project cost	$4893

EXHIBIT 2 (continued)

WARNER-LAMBERT PROJECT SPENCER

ANNUAL SAVINGS

	(in Thousands)
Elimination of duplicate management & service staff (40 eliminated positions)	$1859
Reduced operating expenses (ie. systems terminals, travel, stationery)	153
Transportation of plastic bottles savings from Toronto to Brockville	31
Direct labor productivity improvement (through better utilization of equipment and people)	179
1986 – 1% ($31)	
1987 – 4% ($130)	
1988 – 5% ($167)	
Occupancy cost savings (by moving the Deseret (scrubs & masks) operations to fill 18 000 sq. ft. of the vacated space at 2200 Eglinton)	189
Reduced freight costs (on shipping pharmaceutical products through the consolidation of customer orders)	122
Total project annual savings	$2 533

605

Computation of human resource costs

	No. of employees	Completed yrs. service	# Weeks pay	Average weighted rate/week incl. benefits 1984 rates	Total Cdn. $
					(in Thousands)
Supervisory management	23	12	20	895	411.7
Office clerical	4	8	16	493	31.6
Hourly indirect	23	14	22	594	300.6
Hourly direct	33	14	22	464	336.9
	83				1080.8
		Less 20%			216.2
		Total probable severance			864.2
		Adjustment for 1985 rates (+6.5%)			56.2
		Total severance			920.8
		Relocation cost			250.0
		Employee counselling			100.0
		Retraining			150.0
		Provision for early retirement			450.0
		Total costs			1870.8

EXHIBIT 3
WARNER-LAMBERT PROJECT SPENCER

Space created at 2200 Eglinton

The relocation of the Manufacturing facilities to Brockville would free up space in 2200 as follow:

	Square Feet
Liquid manufacturing	3 651
Packaging room	19 159
Misc. manufacturing/pkging/office	4 600
Plastics manufacturing	8 300
Plastic bottle storage	13 200
Set-up area	780
Weigh room	1 260
Total	50 950

Usage:

	Square Feet
Distribution	8 300
Relocate Deseret operations	18 000

Other possible usage:

New computer room	)
New training center	) 13 200
Available for R&D	11 500
Total	51 000

EXHIBIT 4
WARNER-LAMBERT PROJECT SPENCER

Preliminary construction and move schedule

Area/Line	Construction	Move 1985
1. Home perm		* May
Deseret masks		* May
2. Rolaids bottles**		* May
Listerine lozenges**		* May
3. Trigon process	April	May
4. Schick packaging	April	May
5. Anusol suppository manufacturing	May	June
Anusol suppository packaging		June
6. Liquid manufacturing	Apr/May/June	July
Liquid packaging	Apr/May/June	July
7. Distribution	June	July
8. Toothpaste	June/July	August
9. Deseret scrubs		August
10. Efferdent	May/June/July	Sept
11. Plastics	July/Aug/Sept	October

*Can be moved at anytime—no construction required
**Relocated to 40 Bertrand Avenue Plant

EXHIBIT 5
WARNER-LAMBERT PROJECT SPENCER

Savings Through Positions Eliminated

	2200 Plant	2200 Q.A.*	Brockville Dist'n	Total
Authorized positions	124	17	28	169
Positions retained at 2200 Eglinton	(9)	(2)	—	(11)
Positions transferred to 40 Bertrand	(9)	—	—	(9)
Positions transferred to Brockville	(81)	(8)	—	(89)
Positions transferred to Toronto Distribution	—	—	(23)	(23)
Positions eliminated (2200/Q.A./Distribution)	25	7	5	37
Other positions eliminated (Cost & MIS)	3	—	—	3
Total positions eliminated	28	7	5	40

*Quality Assurance (Q.A.) is currently located in the 2200 plant

Potential Unfilled Positions in Brockville Manufacturing

Positions transferred from 2200	89
Brockville Distribution employees relocated into Manufacturing	(28)
Estimated employees that will transfer from Toronto	(8)
Total potential unfilled positions	53

Redundant Employees

	2200 Plant	2200 Q.A.	Total
Authorized number of employees	124	17	141
Current unfilled positions	(10)	—	(10)
Actual number of employees	114	17	131
Employees retained at 2200	(9)	(2)	(11)
Employees transferred to 40 Bertrand	(9)	—	(9)
Probable employee transfers to Brockville	(8)	—	(8)
Employees transferred to T.O. Dist'n	(23)	—	(23)
Redundant employees	65	15	80
Other redundant employees (Cost & MIS)	3	—	3
Total redundant employees	68	15	83

EXHIBIT 6
WARNER-LAMBERT PROJECT SPENCER

Financial Data — March 1984

Interest rates

Government of Canada

Treasury Bills — 90 days	10.53
Bonds — 1 to 3 Years	11.50
— 3 to 5 Years	11.87
— 5 to 10 Years	12.58
— Over 10 Years	13.06
Corporate long term bond yields	13.80
Bank prime rates	11.50
Beta — Warner Lambert Company (U.S. percent)	1.00

Parent company shares are listed on NYSE.

NOTE: The Canadian corporation does not produce separate financial statements for the public. The parent company has a ratio of debt to total financing of 40 percent which is considered normal for the entire operation.

BEHIND THAT "WE MAKE IT ... SO CAN YOU" SPIRIT

WARNER-LAMBERT CANADA...
"PROUD OF ITS PAST...OPTIMISTIC ABOUT ITS
FUTURE... COMMITTED TO EXCELLENCE...A
COMPANY GUIDED BY DEMANDING PERFORMANCE
OBJECTIVES AND REINFORCED THROUGH A
MEANINGFUL PEOPLE MANAGEMENT APPROACH".

DEMANDING PERFORMANCE OBJECTIVES

WARNER-LAMBERT CANADA is a results-oriented company. This characteristic is
evidenced by each of our management programs and processes. Our key corporate
objectives and the steps we have taken to meet them include:

◆ ACHIEVING OUTSTANDING FINANCIAL SUCCESS THROUGH STEADY AND
RELIABLE GROWTH.
We are constantly reviewing and raising our growth targets. The Canadian
affiliate intends to be the best developed business within our world-wide
organization. The consistent achievement of aggressive but reasonable
profit targets affords us the opportunity to pursue objectives in both
'people development' and 'social responsibility' areas, while operating as an
autonomous affiliate of the world-wide corporation.

◆ ESTABLISHING A STRONG MARKET POSITION IN ALL OF OUR BUSINESSES.
WE have the goal of becoming a major market factor in each industry where we
compete. Today, as a result of unique strategies, we lead in the Chewing
Gums, Portable Breath Fresheners, Cough Drops, Throat Lozenges, Cough
Syrups, Sinus Remedies, Upset Stomach Remedies and Oral Antiseptics markets.
We have strong and meaningful brand positioning in many other markets.

◆ INVESTING AND INNOVATING TO ASSURE FUTURE GROWTH IN PROFITABILITY
AND PRODUCTIVITY.
Substantial reinvestment of earnings in the business, especially in marketing and
research and development programs, is a major key to our continued success.
Each year, we invest heavily in the development and launching of new products.
In addition, each division has a strategic business plan to improve the
productivity of its manpower and physical assets.

◆ PROVIDING QUALITY PRODUCTS AND SERVICES TO OUR CUSTOMERS.
Our products must fill real needs and provide lasting value for the consumer and
health professionals. Thus, we research consumer needs and clinically test our
products against stringent quality assurance standards.

◆ EXERCISING OUR RESPONSIBILITY AS CITIZENS
We actively pursue public policies that encourage free enterprise and foster the
development of healthy conditions for our business. Our corporate contributions
program reflects this commitment to improving the environment in which we
operate.

A MEANINGFUL PEOPLE MANAGEMENT PHILOSOPHY

WARNER-LAMBERT CANADA'S ambitious business objectives require the hiring of
talented people and encouraging them to achieve excellence. Our meaningful
people management philosophy is a key element of our success. Wholly supported
by our executives, this philosophy permits us to recruit and retain motivated
people. The main elements of our people management philosophy include:

♦ RELATIVELY AUTONOMOUS DIVISIONS; SUPPORTED BY A LEAN, INVOLVED MANAGEMENT TEAM.

♦ ORGANIZATION STRUCTURE WITH OPEN COMMUNICATION LINES, where decision-making is prompt, participative and progressive.

♦ AN INFORMAL ATMOSPHERE AND A BROAD RANGE OF MANAGEMENT STYLES that encourages employees to express their points of view while being considerate of the views of others.

♦ THE DEVELOPMENT OF SUPERVISORS AND MANAGERS. Whenever possible, we fill vacancies by promoting from within. Besides ensuring continuity of management, this is one of the important ways we honour our commitment to foster a climate of personal growth.

♦ A REMUNERATION PACKAGE which is equal to or better than good competitive averages for comparable work done within progressive organizations in our industries and areas.

♦ ENTREPRENEURSHIP. We encourage risk-taking in strategy, programs, and people decisions.

♦ A HIGH CONCERN FOR THE INDIVIDUAL AND DIGNITY OF EACH EMPLOYEE. We encourage their development by providing in-house training programs and reimburse the cost of relevant external programs. As well, each employee is assigned a specific business area for which he/she is responsible and accountable.

♦ AN ATMOSPHERE OF PHYSICAL AND MENTAL WELL-BEING that equates safety with quality products. We are leaders in the development and implementation of programs and practices to achieve this objective.

♦ EQUAL OPPORTUNITY FOR ALL EMPLOYEES without regard for race, physical handicap, colour, religion, national origin, conviction of an offense when a pardon has been granted, nationality, ancestry, political belief, sex or age. Thus, such factors are not considered to be appropriate in hiring or job-related decisions.

♦ STANDARDS OF PERFORMANCE. We strive for excellence and expect no less than a 'fully satisfactory' rating from each employee through our performance appraisal and management by objectives system.

"TRY AS WE DO...WE ARE FAR FROM PERFECT"

We are aware of the continuing need to adjust our performance objectives and people management philosophy so that we can continue to deal effectively with the opportunities that come with internal change and the increasingly challenging external environment. The foregoing is our target, rather than our reality.

While our aim is to have work objectives for all employees, this sometimes does not occur. Not all managers are effective. Sometimes people are left out of decisions which affect them. Not all managers are free of prejudice. Some employees do not know what is expected of them, nor how their performance is assessed.

Despite these shortcomings, we adhere to our beliefs as stated earlier in this document. We are constantly striving to improve the selection and training of managers. We continue to implement procedures which encourage participation within our management by objectives system.

Every employee of WARNER-LAMBERT CANADA has a right to be treated according to the philosophy set out in this document. If apparently treated unfairly, we encourage employees to make their views known. Simply stated, our intent is to bring philosophy and reality even closer together.

REDWATER (A):
THE REDWATER SHUFFLE

Joseph J. DiStefano and Eileen D. Watson

"So what's going on in Redwater, Anne? The petroleum industry grapevine tells me great things are happening — but I want to hear the story from you!"

Former MBA classmates Anne Bennett and Cathy Parker grinned at one another across the restaurant table. It was a cool but sunny October afternoon. Cathy had just arrived in Edmonton to visit her friend Anne. This was their first reunion since graduation and the two were still catching up on a 15-month news backlog. Anne replied:

> I'm not surprised to hear that people are talking, Cathy. On the positive side, some really exciting and innovative human resource management approaches are going on! Of course, there are lots of problems at Redwater these days, all related to larger issues facing Imperial Oil Limited (IOL) and Esso Chemical and the entire industry. In the past two years, Esso's agricultural chemicals group has slipped from a highly profitable position to a huge loss last year.
>
> Our Redwater ag-chem operation constitutes a major part of Esso Chemical; so, needless to say, we are under great pressure to reverse this trend. We're looking for solutions. I believe improved management of the plant's human resources holds a key to our turnaround. Although nothing's written down, the HR principles on which the complex was founded could be identified and made fully operational, with excellent results... but let me tell you what we've done already.

Agricultural Chemicals Complex (ACC) and Imperial

Anne Bennett had been hired as human resources employee relations analyst at the Esso Agricultural Chemicals Complex in Redwater, Alberta, 60 kilometres northeast of Edmonton. A leading producer of chemical fertilizers (Engro brand), the company was operated by the Esso Chemical Canada division of Imperial Oil Limited, Canada's largest energy company and an affiliate of Exxon Corporation. Besides the Chemical division, IOL managed two other major operating segments: Esso Resources Canada Limited, which produced crude oil, natural gas and coal, and explored for base metals and other minerals; and Esso Petroleum Canada, which operated five refineries and marketed a wide variety of petroleum products.

The Redwater ACC began operations in 1969, when grain farmers began to turn to chemical fertilizers to replenish basic plant nutrients — nitrogen, phosphorus and potassium. Over the years the capacity of the complex grew tremendously through equipment changes, unit modifications, and expansion. The previous year a major expansion in the Phosphatic Department was completed, and plans were underway for a $450 million expansion in the Nitrogenous Department for the next year.

The complex covered 370 hectares and, with the planned expansion, would be capable of producing approximately 1.6 million tonnes annually. As many as 300 trucks a day passed through the complex, and railroad shipments filled approximately 11 000 cars a year.

More than 500 people were employed at the Redwater site (see Exhibit 1 for a partial organization chart).

History of Human Resource Management at Redwater

While waiting for lunch to be served, Anne began describing her experiences in human resource management at Redwater:

First, let me give you some background on our situation, Cathy. Back in the late 1960s when the complex was under construction, the far-sighted management team initiated what came to be known as the Redwater System — a pretty unique way of running the people part of a company like ours. They started by developing a cooperative team concept — both the hands-on workers and the engineers would talk over any problems and work out solutions together. It was a very effective process. Yet back in 1967 labor-management relations concepts elsewhere were more confrontational than cooperative...so the team concept was seen as a radically different way to run a company, and very forward-thinking. There was no union or industrial council saying we couldn't do this. The employees themselves were in tune with the principles behind management's actions, and were pleased to be considered an important part of the total Redwater picture.

So we learned from our successes with the system, and when the plant moved from the construction phase to the operating stage we just carried on the same way. The whole plant was organized on the Redwater System philosophy, translated into management behavior and actions. Everyone was considered equal — operations, maintenance, management. Everybody was on salary. There were no time clocks, and everyone worked a 40-hour week. Nobody was a blue collar worker; everyone's title was "technician." Instead of negotiating communications between employee and employer, everyone met together regularly in works meetings, as they were called, (incidentally, we still have works meetings), where the management or superintendent of that plant would meet with each crew and talk about what was going on around the plant. That was really critical, because so many people wanted to know exactly what was happening. They had been totally involved previously, so how could that stop? So a lot of talking went on regularly about day-to-day happenings, people's ideas, problems — really open communication.

The other integral part of that Redwater System was the cross-training component. This was the first example in North America at that time where a plant operator could also work in maintenance. A certain proportion of an operator's shift schedule was spent building maintenance skills. You can imagine how much more flexibility that provided. The idea of having everybody multi-skilled was great for productivity for the plant, particularly since it was running 24 hours a day — if some problem arose on your shift, you didn't have to call a maintenance technician away from home, you could do something yourself.

It was a good thing that Redwater's first management team gave such strong leadership. They were ahead of their time. I'm told the HR manager kept insisting that people management is not HR's responsibility, it's a line responsibility. He thought the role of the HR manager should be a thought-provoking and challenging one, but implementation of good HR practices was up to the line manager. And when he left, the focus shifted away from the HR manager to other managers carrying on their own versions of the Redwater System.

Anne Bennett's Experiences at Redwater

So I arrived in Redwater last summer. As you know, my education prior to getting my MBA was mathematics and computer science; and my first full-time job was in computer design on a financial analysis team with Bell Canada.

On graduation I wanted a real challenge — and what could be more challenging than working as an employee relations analyst in an agricultural chemicals complex in a rural setting one hour's drive north-east of Edmonton! The size and scope of the complex are awesome — I was tremendously impressed when I first saw it. The huge site houses two major production systems — a nitrogenous plant and a phosphorus plant. One group of employees produces ammonia from natural gas — this system is clean, computer controlled and run by technicians working in a sheltered, comfortable environment. The phosphorus group's environment is dirty, noisy, sometimes unpleasant — the process involves grinding phosphate rock and using sulphuric acid to extract phosphorus from the residue. A third group, the materials handling and storage (MHS) group, looks after the acquisition and movement of raw materials and finished products. Each group has its own manager, maintenance and operations supervisors and foremen, technical support engineers and staff, and other support staff.

Redwater is a unique place. It's a farming community miles away from other industrial areas. A lot of the workers own farms still — they'll go home after shift and plow their fields! Families are important. People are used to working together in family groups . . . and in fact, an employee at our plant might have a father, son, daughter, daughter-in-law, son-in-law, all working there. Outsiders might see that as inbreeding, but we don't. We see it as added people power if one member of the family is happy and recommends another. But we have no qualms about getting rid of poor performers, even if they are family members, and our people respect that.

Esso Chemical in general, and the Redwater Ag-Chem Complex in particular, saw a lot of growth through the early and mid-1970s. Chemical fertilizers were in high demand to increase crop yields, and we were doing really well. We were living off the boom of Alberta...and then came 1978 and 1979, and things started to fall through just a little. A slight slide escalated into a disastrous downturn two years ago...but I'll tell you some good news, first. Gordon Zelt arrived at Redwater as plant manager just prior to the downturn.

Gord is a chemical engineer with years of experience in a broad range of functions in the petroleum industry. He has successfully tackled production, economics, and operations, and loves manufacturing above all. He came to Redwater to maintain the existing plant and to manage the construction of expansion projects as well. Gord is a plant manager with a vision and high principles and a management style that reflects those principles. From the beginning he practised a real "walk-around-meet-the-people" style. Really friendly, very family oriented...he's been a great supporter of our social club, always on the spot at social events, flipping hamburgers for the kids!

Heavy Pressures and Response

The economy started to falter and the ag-chem business fell along with it. Senior executives started blaming Redwater's problems on manufacturing; and when I arrived on the scene last summer it was as if the business was just dropping out from underneath us. There was a lot of speculation that they were going to sell the plant, or close it down, or simply close down sections of the plant. A lot of uncertainty — constant questions like, "How are we going to get out of this mess?" "What's going to happen to us?"

The way I see it, there were probably three or four key factors causing the business downturn. First of all, we were linked in with the whole petroleum side from the standpoint that 75 percent of our costs are natural gas costs. With the National Energy Policy changes, our costs started to rise — our products were costing us a lot more. We perceived we did not have control over those costs. We perceived ourselves as a manufacturing unit without control over marketing or over our supply side.

Another factor was the depressed economy. Farmers just couldn't afford to pay for fertilizer, an inventory cost. The farmers who had traditionally bought fertilizer in the fall but weren't going to get paybacks until the next fall couldn't financially manage that any more. Which meant that we had a real shift — we sold half the product we could have normally sold in the fall. Quite a variance in the cyclical nature of our sales occurred, caused by a shift to spring sales just before planting.

Other factors entered in. Optimistic projections indicated the continuance of a booming economy, so we produced what turned out to be an oversupply of fertilizer. At the same time, there were trends away from chemical fertilizers — the impact of environmentalists and conservationists. And we began to notice increasingly high supply costs for other raw materials besides natural gas. Our phosphate rock came from a Florida mine through the Panama Canal to Vancouver, then was shipped to us in empty grain cars — and it was escalating in cost. We needed to monitor our costs from the time phosphate rock was mined and put on the boat in Florida, to delivery in Redwater — we needed to better manage that aspect of our business.

And my own perception is that probably one of the biggest factors in our predicament is that we've been abusing the Redwater system. It has never been written down anywhere, and people have put their own interpretations on it — especially new people who have arrived in the past few years. Yes, economics and environment are major concerns, but if your people aren't determined to make a difference in a bad situation and "go for it," you're lost. And because so many new people have come into the plant — we've been hiring for the planned expansion[1] — the system has become watered down, and has all but disappeared.

At any rate, Imperial has just taken action to modify its chemical investment program, including a decision to withdraw from the Petalta project, our $650-million joint project with the Alberta Energy Company already underway. They will maintain other planned investments in projects with the potential for high future earnings growth, like the Redwater expansion projects; but they are really pushing for more efficient operations right now.

So we've had some shocks here at Redwater — closing down Petalta, delaying our sulphuric acid plant start-up, rumors about closing the phosphate plant entirely, or maybe even the total complex — morale is deteriorating. I've seen the expression on the plant manager's face, and the other managers...we have some great managers, and a few ball-and-chain style managers — if they want something done, they whap you with an iron ball! But they're all affected by the uncertainty and the worry.

I should mention that head office personnel people began to take more notice of Redwater in the late 1970s. For instance, an official memo came down from corporate headquarters that office workers, engineers and corporate staff were to work 35 hours a week, like in Calgary and in Toronto. We stood fast and said "No way! At Redwater, we're all equal. We all work 40 hours." So they compromised on $37\frac{1}{2}$, something like that. I get so frustrated when corporate policies come through where we've had no input! Their interfering began when the downturn started to occur in the business — prior to that our system seemed to be working, so they didn't try to fix it. And also, in the late 1970s there was a lot more interest in HR policies, and movement towards increased HR awareness throughout the corporation. HR policies were established at headquarters; but instead of giving us the intent or the principle, they gave us the rule. So the trend was toward an HR manager becoming a rule administrator, rather than a people person.

But fortunately, an especially dynamic HR manager came to this site in 1980 — Norm Draper. The combination of a plant manager who was a real people person — Gord Zelt — with an action-oriented, creative, visionary HR field person really clicked! Gord and Norm started looking at the Redwater System, how good it had been, and started bringing in some real positive changes. Cross-training had slowed to the point of being almost non-existent, so Norm started to get people talking about it again. He organized a whole new training department in HR, 90 percent oriented to plant operations training, not management training. He helped people realize that technologies were changing — people had to be really flexible, and needed additional skills.

I arrived in the summer of 1981, just after Norm had left. I felt quite alone, living

---

[1] Expansion plans at Redwater included a $450-million world-class plant to produce nitrogen fertilizers and a $50-million expansion to the phosphate-fertilizer plant.

in a small town — other management personnel commuted daily from Edmonton — trying to build credibility. I was uncertain about how to proceed, so I spent time at first getting to know people all over the complex by asking, 'Who's been your best HR person?' Everybody said, "Norm Draper," "Norm Draper." I asked, "Why? What are some of his characteristics? How can I emulate him?" And they told many stories about his warmth, his caring, his listening skills. An example of his style is, Norm rarely used the interoffice mail system. If he had something to deliver, he'd deliver it by hand. He was always walking around, seeing lots of people "accidentally." They never thought he was wandering about with nothing to do — he had a purpose.

People told me stories about an exciting project, completed just after I arrived, called the Materials Management QWL Study. Prior to 1980 the storehouse and purchasing groups had a 25 percent annual turnover rate, due to many factors — dirty, isolated work environments, no training provided for the job, constant negative feedback about inefficiencies. With the assistance of an HR rep and many meetings with the entire team of 22 MM people, many changes were made. Instead of isolated locations, with buying clerks purchasing commodities separately for each department, the entire group was brought together in a new building located in the centre of the complex, no more than a couple of minutes' walking distance from all maintenance centers.

The group reorganized all their procedures. With centralized commodity buying, significant savings were realized. Each member of the purchasing group became a specialist in some area — one rep bought all the pipeline for the plants, for example, which gave us quite a negotiating edge with our suppliers. Both the purchasing and storehouse members redesigned their jobs. As well, a training progression system was set up in the storehouse, with four skill areas to be learned — tool crib, shipping and receiving, counter, and inventory control. They'll all become technicians, with cross-training to follow. Some have already earned trade tickets in materials management. More training opportunities are coming, for instance the option to learn buying and purchasing and become an expediter.

Although consultants were called in to make recommendations on job design, training programs, layout and inventory systems for the new building, management decided to go with the recommendations of the MM team instead. And the team sparked the design of a computerized system to give better inventory control. It took a long time to work this through, but it was worth it — a million dollar savings was made the first year! And storehouse and purchasing turnover has been nil since this project started.

The Redwater Shuffle

Cathy, let me tell you what happened in Human Resources last summer. As you know, the ANC plant[2] under construction is scheduled for start-up next spring. In anticipation, we hired extra young engineers, thinking they'd get experience here

---

[2]The Alberta Nitrogen Complex, or ANC, consisted of a world-scale ammonia unit and world-scale urea unit plus associated utilities and shipping facilities.

and then go on to the Petalta project, get experience there, then move on to another project. Well, as I mentioned before, all development plans were cancelled, and only the ANC plant was going to continue — so many young engineers would find themselves without projects to keep them busy, after the start-up. Layoffs were not the answer — one of Gord's principles is, you'd better plan your manpower so you never have to have a layoff. The whole plant knows about his concern for people. He often says that if even one person has to be laid off, we'll all be laid off — that's quite a commitment!

Then an exciting thing happened! Gord had observed my work with the off-the-job safety committee. We had real success using group decision-making processes — and I guess that's partly why he walked into my office one day last June and said, "Here's my proposal. I want to put together a task force, a committee that represents both operations people and engineers, and I want your group to deal with this problem — it affects every single person in this plant. I think we can keep these new engineers within IOL, if we just find some way to keep them involved and challenged for six months to a year. But how can we do this to everyone's satisfaction? Would you like to attempt a solution?"

I was really pleased. They gave me a committee — two foremen, one each from Nitrogenous and Phosphatic; two operators, again one from each plant; a young engineer and a young technologist, both with only about a year's service; and an engineer who had about three years' service — he had been involved in recruiting engineers the year before, so he was sensitive to the needs of new engineers, both from a personal perspective and from knowing them during the hiring process.

Because I was the coordinator and chairman, I had a dream of what I wanted . . . but likewise, I had to appreciate that every other person came to that committee with dreams, too. They all did. Everybody came with what they thought would be the ideal solution, and so we merged our eight viewpoints. And the eight were almost identical. By the way, the members were chosen not simply to look after their own interests, but to represent their peers and the total group. So realizing how strong the vision was in me, and then seeing the others' similar ideas . . . I just knew — we all knew! — that the whole plant had to be thinking this way too.

We sure had time constraints! Our committee got together in mid-July and our idea, if it went over with the employees, had to be implemented by mid-September. We soon narrowed the proposed placement function for the engineers to Operations. We needed to hire 10 to 15 new operators for the start-up, a period of six months to a year beginning in mid-September. But we didn't want to hire operators now and lay them off next year. If 10 to 15 engineers would volunteer to fill those operator openings, our idea would prove successful.

Our committee became known, fondly, as the "Redwater Shuffle," because we were looking for a complete switch — engineers' roles with operators'. We also did a lot of shuffling around the entire complex, trying to speak to every single individual who worked there! We tried to get people's ideas and input through the works meetings, where 10 to 12 employees met with their supervisor or manager. If we couldn't meet with them in groups, we found a way to meet them individually coming off the night shift or any other way.

So we'd go to the works meetings — I went to about three-quarters of the meetings personally — and in effect, we'd say, "We have a potentially serious problem involving our new engineers. At Redwater we've always pulled together as a family — we don't want to hire people and then let them go. We don't know what will happen in the future, but we have a suggestion: that we temporarily put some new engineers to work on a voluntary basis alongside regular operations personnel for a period of six months to a year. By that time we can most likely place them elsewhere within ECC and IOL." And I volunteered right away to give up my job and work in Operations myself for a year. In fact, two others on the committee also volunteered — the young technologist and a young engineer.

We got new ideas at every meeting, and approval of our basic idea at every stage. We put out several memos during the project, telling everyone what we were doing and what changes were being made. It was like a mass group process — 500 people working through group decision making! We discussed everything — where the engineers could be placed after the spring start-up, specifically which engineering projects could be delayed in order to release engineers into Operations, how the operators could best train their new colleagues, and so on. We discussed issues of personal concern too — for instance, a young engineer wanted to know what experience he'd gain in Operations, and how that would be accredited towards his professional status. And an operator said, "Well, I've got to stay on one post, I can't be wandering around looking after theirs. They've got to do the real work of an operator."

And so we went back to the original theory in the Redwater System that everybody's equal. The whole salary scale was discussed and it's all compatible. We got accreditation from the Alberta Professional Engineering Association — they said this would be a valuable credit. I worked long hours with the engineering superintendent, itemizing the engineering positions we could free up by delaying certain capital projects. Next year, when the volunteer engineers come off operations, there will be jobs for them to go to as the delayed projects come on stream again. We in Human Resources would have found more time — four to six months' time — within which to start placing these people throughout the rest of Imperial Oil and Exxon.

During the process, I met with Gord nearly every day and told him what was going on, and he'd ask, "Do you really think this is going to work?" I'd say, "Yep, it's going to work. Trust me, it's going to work!" And he'd say, "Shouldn't we do this?" I'd answer, "No, let it happen! You have a lot of ideas and they're super, but they're your ideas — let the people develop their own ideas." It would have been easy for us to give a ready-made solution, but letting them develop the program and then volunteer for it should pay off in the end.

I warned, "It's going to take a lot of intensive time." And Gord said, "We only have till September 15." I said, "I'm certain we're going to do it." I had faith. By that time I had been at Redwater exactly one year, and felt completely at home. I loved the people there. I believed in the people, and I had faith in what they could do. That's all I needed...I just kept on going, saying, "This is going to work!" Our task force thought of every detail, involved every person in the plant...we had every aspect covered.

Fifteen engineers (plus myself) volunteered for the 10 positions. So 10 engineers actually started working in Operations on September 13. The success of that project made people realize that by having everybody involved, everybody communicated with, the voluntary aspect emphasized, and a goal and a direction, the Redwater System worked! Our task force group was proud of its accomplishment. (See Exhibit 2 for the article "*Job Shuffle Offers Unique Solution*.")

Since the Shuffle, we've had another success which also has its roots in the

Redwater System. The manager from Materials Handling and Shipping approached us with a request: "Can you help us? We're spending too much on overtime, and we want to be more efficient. A shift change might be the answer. How do we go about it?" The department was operating on a five-day week, with two teams on the day shift and one each on evenings and nights. However, this did not take into account the need for 24-hour delivery seven days a week during the spring and fall when product demand was highest. Weekend work, involving overtime, was often essential. Also, contract shippers who were brought in to supply additional labor as needed had a different foreman every three weeks; we couldn't count on good continuous leadership.

That project was literally worked through in a week. We put together a committee — each crew picked a rep, plus their foremen picked a rep. We started on a Tuesday, and spelled out all possible options, with pros and cons. We put together a shift change package Thursday noon to send home with every MHS employee, so that his or her family could look over the package on the weekend. This is another Redwater trait...families need to know what's going on at the plant.

The committee recommended that the MHS department operate twelve-hour shifts, seven days a week, with a day shift only on Saturdays and Sundays. Each team member would work 12 shifts of 12 hours duration, five on nights and seven on days. There would also be two eight-hour days available for communication meetings and safety or related training sessions. Contract shippers, instead of rotating, would stay with the shipping team they were assigned to, follow the same schedule, and thus stay with the same foreman. They also started going to works meetings, becoming part of the Redwater team.

The following Tuesday we had a vote, because in Alberta you have to have a formal vote with a minimum of 75 percent support in order to change a shift schedule. The vote was 96 percent to go with this change. And the committee also recommended three or four major changes involving teamwork and group efficiency — organization of job assignments, effectiveness of works meetings, and so on. We expect to save a half million dollars next year on the shift change alone; but the efficiency ideas coming out of this group's work are super, with potentially great lasting impact on profitability.[3]

Now I'm telling Gord that we've got to do more. We can't focus only on current construction — what happens when it ends? I think we should institutionalize the gains we've made. I believe that the Redwater System could be made a familiar and permanent part of everybody's work environment at this plant...but I wonder how to go about accomplishing that. What do you think, Cathy?

---

[3]Savings in 1983 were considerable. The MHS department manager reported "...overtime has been reduced, and total manpower per tonne shipped is down 26 percent from 1982...and we've had fewer serious injuries." (See Exhibit 3 for the article _Savings on Shipping Costs at Redwater._)

EXHIBIT 1

REDWATER (A): THE REDWATER SHUFFLE

Redwater ACC Partial Table of Organization, 1982

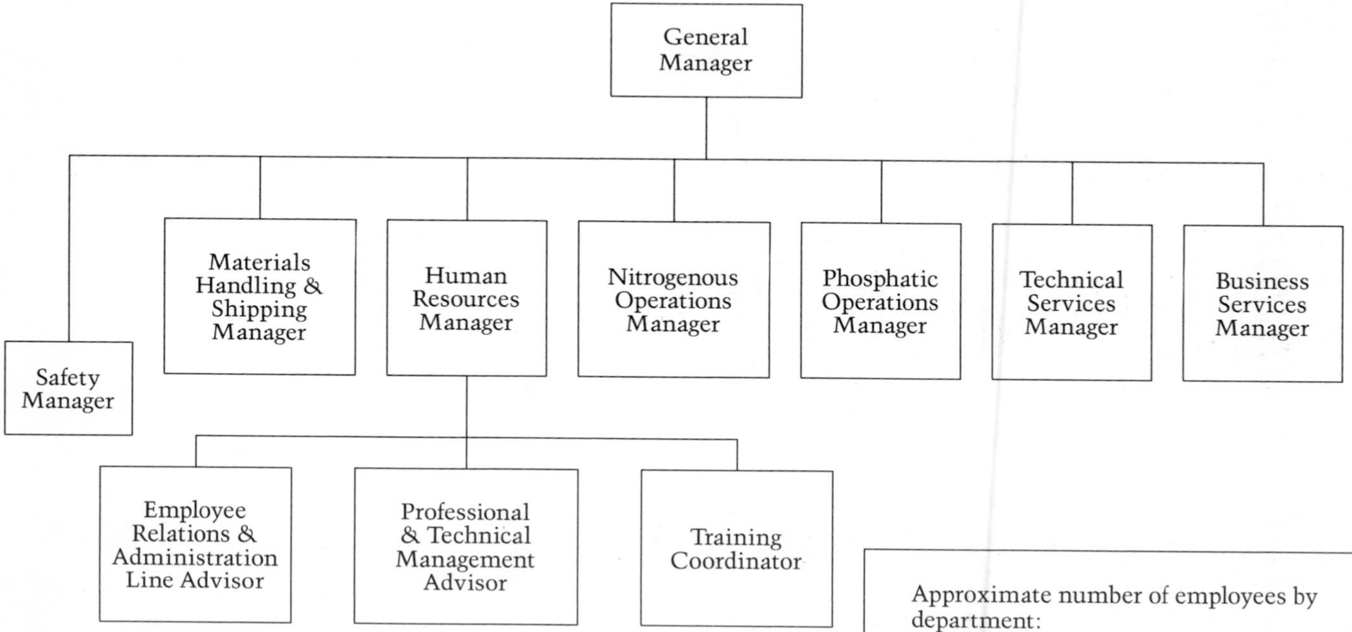

Organization chart:

General Manager

- Materials Handling & Shipping Manager
- Human Resources Manager
- Nitrogenous Operations Manager
- Phosphatic Operations Manager
- Technical Services Manager
- Business Services Manager

Under Human Resources Manager:
- Professional & Technical Management Advisor
- Training Coordinator
- Employee Relations & Administration Line Advisor
- Safety Manager

Approximate number of employees by department:

Department	
Safety	4
Materials Handling & Shipping	50
Human Resources	13
Nitrogenous	150
Phosphatic	145
Technical Services	60
Business Services	75

EXHIBIT 2
REDWATER (A): THE REDWATER SHUFFLE*

Job shuffle offers unique solution

Ten junior engineers and technologists at the agricultural chemicals complex at Redwater, Alta., are working as process operators in the nitrogenous operating units as a unique solution to a temporary staff imbalance.

It's called the "Redwater Shuffle" and everyone's benefiting from it.

The 10 engineers and technologists who volunteered to shuffle jobs are getting hands-on experience in a work area that most of their counterparts only deal with conceptually. And plant management was able to match up onsite skills with staffing requirements.

The plan was conceived by Gordon Zelt, manager of the complex, and implemented last summer by a committee of two operations foremen, two operators, two engineers, a technologist and Anne Bennett, a human resources adviser at the complex. "We were looking ahead to the summer of 1983 when there was a good possibility that we would have more engineers and technologists on staff than we would need," says Bennett. "At the same time, the start-up of an addition to the nitrogenous operation last September was going to mean hiring 20 new operators, 10 of whom might be needed only until September, 1983. We realized that the two situations could provide mutual solutions."

The committee's proposal was unique to the company's operations anywhere: put off some of the delayable technical projects at Redwater to allow 10 engineers and technologists to transfer to process operator positions.

The plan went into effect last fall and 10 employees committed to a one-year reassignment as process operators. At the end of that time, they will be assigned to a technical project at Redwater or elsewhere in the company.

One of the participants, Tony Nutting, a 23-year-old project engineer, claims the experience he's getting as an operator is invaluable.

"It really shows you what an engineer can do to improve things from several points of view," he says. "At the design stage you can save people frustration. You can make their work safer — by placing a valve so that an operator doesn't have to use a ladder to get to it, for instance."

Nutting and technologist Dave Dix, 22, another volunteer for the Redwater Shuffle, both say they are enjoying the experience of getting a practical overview of a project they formerly saw only in bits and isolated pieces.

The operations staff at the complex is also pleased with the results of the program. Several of them have commented that the engineers and technologists fit in as operators and are part of the operations team.

*From the IOL employee publication *The Reporter*, February 1983 edition.

EXHIBIT 3
REDWATER (A): THE REDWATER SHUFFLE

Newspaper clipping, *The Reporter*, October 1983

This month The Reporter salutes...

Saving on shipping costs at Redwater*

Materials handling and shipping employees at Esso Chemical's Redwater fertilizer complex have devised a system that is saving the company $200 000 a year and is resulting in higher productivity.

Late last year, a review of the department's operations identified several potential opportunities to increase productivity and efficiency. Management believed employees should be directly involved so discussions were held with each of four shipping teams and a special committee was struck.

Each team elected one representative. Joe Fedoruk, Denis Rondeau, Ken Nixon and Barry Zdrill, all shipping technicians, were joined by foreman Ernie Osbust and Anne Bennett, a human resources adviser. They identified several areas in which change could be beneficial. The materials handling and shipping department had been operating on a five-day week, with two teams on the day shift and one each on evenings and nights. However, this did not take into account the need for 24-hour delivery seven days a week during the spring and fall when product demand is highest. Weekend work, involving overtime, was often essential, particularly in unloading phosphate rock deliveries from railroad hoppers when the hoppers were needed elsewhere.

In addition, contract shippers, who supplied additional labor as needed, had a different foreman every three weeks. The result was inconsistent leadership and lack of continuity.

The committee recommended proceeding with significant changes in coverage, shift length and contract shippers' schedules. A 28-day cycle of work was agreed upon, during which each team member works 12 shifts of 12 hours duration, five on nights and seven on days. There are also two eight-hour days that are often used for communication meetings and safety or related training sessions.

The department now operates seven days a week, with a day shift only on Saturdays and Sundays. Employees receive a minimum of 48 hours off when they change shifts and in every 28-day cycle there is a break of five-and-a-half consecutive days off. The total number of days worked is 14 out of every 28. Contract shippers, instead of rotating, now stay with the shipping team they are assigned to, follow the same schedule and thus stay with the same foreman.

Mike Chorlton, manager of the materials handling and shipping department, notes that overtime has been reduced and that total manpower per tonne shipped is down 26 percent from 1982. "Also, so far this year we have had fewer serious injuries."

Bill McEwen, a unit superintendent, worked closely with the committee as did Ray Zuk, the operations supervisor. Says McEwen: "We have achieved or exceeded all our objectives for this year. The only problem we have encountered is scheduling of holidays and we are asking the teams to help resolve that." Zuk believes that because the original proposals received 95-percent support everyone wants to make the system work "and now that we've tried it, I don't think any of the employees would go back to the old system."

Barry Zdrill agrees: "Even though I lost about half of what I earned last year in overtime, I'd never want to go back to the eight-hour shifts."

Among the advantages Zdrill sees are the extended periods of time off and the feeling of being able to achieve a lot of work on each shift. "You're not just getting started and it's time to quit, as it was on an eight-hour rotation. So we do more and we're more efficient. And that's the name of the game today."

---

*From the October 1983 edition.

PHOTOTYPESET FOR QUALITY